The Director's Handbook

Pg 78

The Director's Handbook

Edited by

George Bull

 McGRAW-HILL · LONDON

New York · Toronto · Sydney · Johannesburg · Mexico · Panama

Published by

McGraw-Hill Publishing Company Limited
MAIDENHEAD · BERKSHIRE · ENGLAND

94209

PRINTED AND BOUND IN GREAT BRITAIN

Preface

Sir Paul Chambers

This comprehensive handbook for directors, which contains contributions from distinguished men and women, all of whom have some contact, direct or indirect, with companies of one kind or another, is much to be welcomed. There is nothing else of its kind in existence.

The success of the relatively small handbook issued by the Institute of Directors, entitled *Standard Boardroom Practice*, is an indication of the directors' growing need for authoritative guidance in their many duties.

Scientists, classical scholars, engineers, lawyers, accountants, and men from many other professions or vocations are found in boardrooms, and arguments as to which of them make the best directors are rather pointless. However good a man may be at his own profession he will not be a good director unless he recognizes that he needs to know a good deal about matters outside that profession. In the higher management and direction of medium or large companies there is much to be learned that does not fall within the boundaries of any one profession.

I do not believe there is any such person as a good professional director who has no background of an intellectual or professional character; invariably a man with all the qualities and breadth of view of a good director has nearly always been good at something else first. When such a person becomes a director it would be useless for him to attempt a comprehensive study of law, accountancy, engineering, or other profession or discipline that will (or may) have a bearing on decisions he has to reach—alone or with others. He does, however, need to get acquainted with those aspects of these professions and disciplines that are relevant to the issues to be decided in the Boardroom.

It is here that this handbook will be invaluable; it is tailor-made for the director. It covers a wide spectrum of duties, from those of a legal or philosophical character to those concerned with such important matters as taxation, capital raising, mergers, recruitment, health, marketing, and general management organization and efficiency.

The responsibilities of directors, whether their companies are large international enterprises or relatively small family businesses, require the capacity to consider problems and reach decisions where a whole range of different factors is involved. The factors may include highly technical problems related to the erection of a modern plant, marketing—both in Britain or overseas—and legal and ethical questions involving the conduct of a director in relation to his company's affairs and to the interests of his shareholders. A good director need not be a lawyer, but he ought to have a good general understanding of company law; he need not be an economist, but he needs to understand the broad economic factors that will have a bearing on the success of the company's business; he need not be an expert in all the technical aspects of the manufacturing operations in which his company may be engaged, but he needs to understand the nature of the technological problems and to appreciate what is involved. His function as a co-ordinator and, with his colleagues, as the final judge of policy and of action requires the capacity to look at any one major problem from a detached point of view, that of a co-ordinator who takes all factors into account, and not from the point of view of a technical expert of one kind or another.

It is for this reason that the gulf between good directors and poor directors is so wide. The good director needs qualities of intellect and character that are difficult to describe or define but are so easily recognized by his colleagues if they are themselves competent and experienced directors.

This handbook should be read and then kept for reference by every director who is anxious to do his job competently and who has the long-term interests of his company at heart.

Introduction

**George Bull
(Editor)**

The rising output of professional boardroom literature in the United Kingdom, the expansion at several levels of specialist business education, and the improvement in quality of British management in general, have secured for the United Kingdom a stock of expertise and knowledge, sometimes even in advance of that of the United States. The information and the original thinking exist. Coupled with the pace of change forced on some boardrooms and eagerly embraced by many others, they are transforming British business. Many directors, however, find that the guidance and information are not always easily accessible, or not available in a form readily assimilated by those who are not experts, or not adapted to their own practical requirements. This *Handbook* is meant to help fill the gaps.

In doing so it endeavours to achieve two objectives. First, it is a work of reference for the busy executive, as up to date as possible and covering as wide an area as is practicable. The key is the Index, by means of which the reader can check, for example, the meaning and application of a certain management technique, the role of a particular business organization, or the services provided by a specific research organization, financial institution or government department. Contributors to the *Handbook* have been concerned chiefly to give factual information, and to supplement this with useful sources and addresses.

The *Handbook* is also intended to help executives extend their knowledge by providing stimulating discussion by experts on a wide range of subjects. Many articles are deliberately aimed at helping towards the solution of management problems. All of them aim to give a concise and readable account, in clear language, of the recent developments and skills in particular fields. Managers, and directors as well (even though the legal function of the latter remains distinct) are compelled by the increasing complexity of business both to specialize more than ever in the past and yet to keep reasonably abreast of developments in areas other than their own. For those anxious to extend their understanding outside their own immediate fields, the *Handbook* offers either a serious course of study, touching on the art as well as the skills of management, or a book in which to browse profitably.

As any chairman or managing director will admit, a man can forge ahead in business—perhaps in big business especially—with surprising gaps in his knowledge, conscious that there seems always too little time to fill them, no matter how assiduous his reading of the business Press or attendance at management courses. At the top, the director must know where to go for specialist knowledge; the *Handbook* will put a great deal of it at his finger-tips, and point to other sources of information.

Despite the quickening trend towards mergers, there are still a great many more small and medium-sized firms in Britain than big companies, and for this reason there is considerable emphasis throughout the *Handbook* on information of use to the directors and managers of these firms. They, also, are the executives who have to do more than one job within the company and who will find different chapters invaluable, as they put on their different hats. All the same, the executive rising through the ranks of a major organization will find that many of the chapters deepen his understanding, and even stretch his mind.

The scheme of the *Handbook* was drawn up with the above objectives in mind, and in consultation with men immersed in business activities. The key chapter is the first—the Company in the 1970s—which is intended to give the broad background to boardroom responsibilities and company law at the present time, looking towards the future, and exploring the highly topical problem of the functions of the company director within his company and in the wide social and economic context. Thereafter, the chapters have been grouped and dovetailed to deal logically with related areas of business interest, such as tax and finance, management functions and techniques, general employee relations, and public relations in its widest sense.

The chapter on management techniques will be for many readers the most difficult, but also the most rewarding, in the book, introduced by a special survey of company functions and completed with a glossary of techniques for quick appraisal. By use of the Index, the information it gives can be supplemented by reference to other generally less technical articles in the *Handbook*.

The *Handbook* was also motivated by the desire to provide lively material by authors with informed, keen, and even controversial views on their subjects. In general, the brief given to the ninety contributors—drawn from financial and in-

viii

dustrial journalism, from the academic and trade union worlds, and from business itself—was to inform, stimulate, and even to provoke. They would all agree that if what they have written acts as a stimulus to further enquiry as well as providing helpful information, they will have been successful.

Few people can be unaware of the pressures to which businessmen are increasingly subject, especially in a democratic country whose well-being is so dependent on the efficiency of its companies as is the United Kingdom. The scheme of the *Handbook* itself illustrates the growing demands being made on business executives; this is brought out especially by two chapters, neither of which might have been thought necessary in a business handbook, say, twenty years ago: the chapter on 'Key Techniques for Management' and that on 'Business and Government'. These illustrate the increasing intellectual sophistication nowadays demanded of the successful executive and the growth of unprecedented demands on his energies and intelligence from society and the State. For this reason, several chapters of the *Handbook*, which is meant to assist principally directors, managers and new entrants into the exciting world of business, should also interest those seriously concerned with the problems of contemporary society, some of which are created by business endeavours and attitudes and all of which are influenced by them. The *Handbook* summarizes much of the contemporary orthodoxy—and, some would say, a few of the flourishing heresies—of business thinking on the threshold of the 1970s.

Like any successful company, the *Handbook* is a result of teamwork, in this case on the part of the business books staff of McGraw-Hill Publishing Company and many of the Editor's friends and colleagues in business and journalism. Thanks are due to the Institute of Directors; especially the Director-General, Sir Richard Powell, the Editor-in-Chief of *The Director*, Mr E. D. Foster, and Mr P. D. Bunyan, the Librarian, who has acted in an advisory capacity on the many reading lists; to the authors themselves; and to those with whom many of them have discussed their contributions.

Appreciation is also extended to Mr William Clarke, Economic Adviser to *The Director* and director of National and Grindlays Bank, Mr Gerald Spier; Mr Ronald Clark; Mr William Norris, and Mr Richard Bailey.

Acknowledgements are due to McGraw-Hill Inc. for permission to reproduce illustrations from *New Product Decisions* by Edgar A. Pessemier; to Booz, Allen & Hamilton for permission to reproduce the chart, 'Life Cycle of a Hypothetical Product'; and to *The Daily Telegraph* for permission to reproduce the article 'Businessman's Guide to Whitehall'.

Contents

xii

xiv

List of Contributors

Max K. Adler

Director of studies, College of Marketing, London. Author of *Modern Market Research, Lectures in Market Research, A Short Guide to Market Research in Europe*, and *Marketing and Market Research*.

Derek Allen

Lecturer, University of Nottingham, engaged in research in the field of Technological Forecasting and Decision Theory. Author of papers on the selection and evaluation of projects. Originator of EMIP (Equivalent Means Investment Period).

J. C. Anderson

Professor of Electrical Materials, Imperial College, London. At one time Deputy Director of College Studies, E.M.I. Institutes Ltd., he has since held a number of academic and research posts, and has been a research engineer with R.C.A. Ltd. He holds a number of industrial consultancies.

Ian Andrew

Fellow of the Institute of Chartered Accountants in England and Wales.

D. J. Ashton-Jones

Joint Managing Director, Harris & Hunter Ltd. Frequent contributor to business and marketing publications.

Richard Bailey

Partner, Gibb–Ewbank Industrial Consultants. For ten years he was Director of the independent research institute, Political and Economic Planning. From 1964 to 1966 he served as a special adviser to the National Economic Development Council.

John Bittleston

Marketing adviser to the Ranks Hovis McDougall Group. Fellow of the Institute of Practitioners in Advertising. Formerly Assistant Managing Director of S. H. Benson Ltd., and secretary to the Education Committee of the Market Research Society.

Balint Bodroghy

Director, Peter Ward Associates (Interplan) Ltd., and Interplan Research Ltd. Formerly senior consultant and corporate planner, L'Air Liquide Canada Ltd. Contributor to *Engineering* and to *The Director*. Visiting lecturer, British Institute of Management and Regent Street Polytechnic School of Management Studies.

David Boyd

Manager, Industry Research. Regular contributor to *The Director* and other publications, with a special interest in the structure of industrial organizations.

C. R. E. Brooke

A member of the Industrial Reorganization Corporation staff since its inception in 1966. Formerly a member of H.M. Diplomatic Service. Commercial attaché in Israel, 1964–1966.

D. A. Brown

Technical Director, AGB Research Ltd. Formerly, General Sales Manager, Black and Decker Ltd. Vice-Chairman of the Market Research Society. Regular contributor to management and marketing publications.

George Bull (Editor)

Editor of *The Director*. Read history at Oxford and has since worked as a journalist on the staff of *The Financial Times*, and the McGraw-Hill World News Bureau. His books include *Bid for Power* (with Anthony Vice), *Vatican Politics*, and several translations including '*The Prince*' of *Niccolò Machiavelli*.

Elizabeth Burney

Staff writer, *The Economist*. Author of *Housing on Trial*, and contributor to *The Director* and other journals, and to sound and television broadcasting.

Patrick Keith Cameron

Director of Interlang Ltd., language training consultants and publishers. Formerly head of studies, Institute of Directors Languages Centre. Directing editor of the series *Languages for the Businessman*.

Michael Carroll

Director, National Marketing Council. Assistant to the Marketing Director, Allied Breweries Ltd. Director, Grants of St James's (Holdings) Ltd.

H. F. R. Catherwood

Director General, National Economic Development Office, and member, National Economic Development Council. Member, British National Export Council. Formerly chief industrial adviser, Department of Economic Affairs, and managing director, British Aluminium Co. Ltd. Author of *The Christian in Industrial Society*, and *Britain with the Brakes Off*.

Sir Fife Clark, CBE

Director General of the Central Office of Information since 1954. Formerly Adviser on Public

Relations to the Prime Minister, and Adviser on Government Public Relations. First President of the International Public Relations Association. Founder member, Past President and Fellow of the British Institute of Public Relations.

Ronald Clark

Author. Science correspondent of *The Director*. Has written extensively on the application of science to modern life. His books include *Tizard, The Birth of the Bomb, The Huxleys, The Rise of the Boffins*, and *J. B. S. Haldane*.

Patrick Coldstream

Business development officer, Morgan Grenfell & Co. Ltd. Formerly Commercial Editor, the *Financial Times* and author of the 'World of Management' column. Regular contributor to *Management Today*, *New Society*, and other publications. Member of the National Economic Development Council's committee on Management Education, Training and Development.

Robert Collin

Assistant editor, *Financial Times*. Regular contributor to *The Director* and other publications.

Leslie Coulthard

Director, P.A. Management Consultants Ltd. Formerly with Blackwood Hodge Ltd., and Procter and Gamble Ltd. Regular contributor to *Management Today*, *The Director*, and other publications. Contributor to *Handbook of Management Technology*. Visiting lecturer, British Institute of Management, and several universities.

C. A. Curthoys

Chief Information Officer and Head of Publications, British Productivity Council. Industrial writer (productivity techniques) and journalist. Formerly editorial executive on national newspapers.

John Davies, MBE

Director General of the Confederation of British Industry. Member of the National Economic Development Council, the Council of Industrial Design, the National Joint Advisory Committee to the Department of Employment and Productivity, the Public Schools Commission, and the Council of the University of Sussex. He is a Fellow of the Royal Society of Arts, and a Governor of the National Institute of Economic and Social Research. Formerly Vice-Chairman and Managing Director, Shell Mex and BP Ltd.

Basil Z. de Ferranti

Director, International Computers Ltd. Member of Parliament for Morecambe and Lonsdale, 1958–64. Parliamentary Secretary, Ministry of Aviation, 1962, resigning to avoid conflict of interest. Member of the Council of the Institute of Electrical Engineers, 1962–65.

Basil W. Denning

Senior Lecturer in Business Policy and Organization at the London Graduate School of Business Studies. Vice-Chairman of the Long Range Planning Society. Visiting Lecturer at the Graduate Business School, University of Cape Town. Contributor to business publications.

James Derriman

Joint Managing Director, Charles Barker & Sons Ltd. Barrister-at-Law. Member of the Professional Practices Committee and Education Committee at the Institute of Public Relations. Lecturer on law to I.P.R. final course.

Arthur F. Earle

Principal, London Graduate School of Business Studies. Director, British Aluminium Company Ltd., and Hoover Ltd. Member of various NEDO committees.

C. E. Escritt

Secretary, Oxford University Appointments Committee. Professorial Fellow, Keble College, Oxford. Formerly Group Assistant Sales Manager and Group Training Officer, Tootal Broadhurst Lee Company Ltd.

Christopher Fildes

Formerly, Business Editor, *The Spectator*, and now on the staff of the *Daily Mail*. Regular contributor to *The Director* and other business publications.

Lord Fiske, CBE

Chairman, Decimal Currency Board. Began his career in the Bank of England, and remained there until 1935. Became a member of the London County Council in 1946 and was chairman of the Town Planning Committee and chairman of the Housing Committee. Leader of the Greater London Council until April 1967. Vice-Chairman of the Governors of the Centre for Environmental Studies, and a Trustee of the Civic Trust.

Kenneth Fleet

City Editor of the *Daily Telegraph*. Previously City Editor of the *Sunday Telegraph*. Writer of 'The City' column in *The Director*.

Allan Fletcher

Controller, Internal Consultants, Rank-Xerox Ltd. Previously head of Industrial Marketing, Honeywell Computers Ltd. Author of *Management and Mathematics* (with Geoffrey Clarke), and *Computer Science and Management*. Frequent contributor to management publications.

Norman J. Freeman, CBE

General Manager (Insurance and Investments) Imperial Chemical Industries Ltd. Managing Director, Imperial Chemicals Insurance Ltd. Chairman, British Shippers' Council. Member of Economic Development Committee for the Movement of Exports, and Export Council for Europe Chairman of the E.D.C. report 'Through Transport to Europe'.

David Galloway

Head of UK research in a London stockbroking firm. Formerly deputy City Editor, *Sunday Telegraph*, member of the *Daily Mail* City staff, and deputy Editor, Beaverbrook's *Investors Guide*. Regular contributor to *The Director*.

John Garnett

Director, The Industrial Society. While with Imperial Chemical Industries (1947–1962) was Personnel Manager, Plastics Division and, from 1955–62, Head of Communications Section to the company as a whole. Author of *The Manager's Responsibility for Communication*.

John Gaselee

Formerly Insurance Correspondent of *The Financial Times* and now a broadcaster and writer on insurance, pension, and allied topics for a wide range of publications in Britain and overseas. Author of *Insurance*.

David E. Gibbs

Member, London Stock Exchange. Came to the City in 1951 as an insurance broker. Moved to stockbroking in 1957 and became a member in 1963. Since then has made a special study of Containerization, and is the author of two booklets on the subject.

Herbert W. Grace

Fellow, Chartered Institute of Patent Agents. Patents Controller of National Research Development Corporation, and Patents Manager, Hovercraft Development Ltd. Formerly with the Patents Branch, Ministry of Supply. Lecturer, Comparative Administration Trust.

John Hamway

A practising solicitor. Director of, and consultant to, a number of property and land development companies.

Nige! Hawkes

News Editor of *Nature*.

W. J. Heygate

Joint Deputy Director General, British National Export Council. Joined the Export Council for Europe in 1961, and was appointed Chief Executive in 1964.

Peter Hobday

Associate Editor, *The Director*, and regular contributor to a number of business publications, including *British Industry*, *Scotland Magazine*, and *Business Management*. London correspondent of *Burroughs Clearing House*, a monthly American banking journal.

Simon Hodgson

A consultant with Industrial Market Research Ltd., responsible for co-ordinating studies in a wide variety of industries in this country, Europe, and the USA.

Royden Hodson

Regions Editor, *The Financial Times*. Regular broadcaster on industrial and economic affairs.

Sir John Hunter, CBE

Chairman, Central Training Council, 1964–68. Chairman and Managing Director, Swan Hunter Group Ltd. Chairman, Swan Hunter & Tyne Shipbuilders Ltd., Swan Hunter (Dry Docks) Ltd., Brims and Company Ltd., Wallsend Slipway and Engineering Company Ltd., Barclay Curle & Company Ltd., M. N. Swinburne and Sons Ltd.

H. Ingham

Director, Centre for Interfirm Comparison Ltd., an independent organization established in 1959 by the British Institute of Management in association with the British Productivity Council. Joint author of *Interfirm Comparison for Management*, he has written a number of papers on productivity measurement and interfirm comparison.

H. B. Jackson

Chief Executive and Manager, Barclays Export Finance Company Ltd. Chairman of the Institute of Export. Lecturer on Foreign Trade for the Institute of Bankers. Has been engaged for the past fifteen years in assisting exporters with their problems, and has led three selling missions to Europe.

The Rt. Hon. Aubrey Jones

Chairman, National Board for Prices and Incomes. Minister of Fuel and Power, 1955–57. Minister of Supply, 1957–59. Governor, National Institute for Economic and Social Research. Member of Parliament (Birmingham, Hall Green) 1950–65.

Colin Joynson

Managing Director, G. W. Joynson & Co. Ltd., members of the United Kingdom Commodity Exchanges., Chairman, Slann & Davies Ltd., Chairman, Thompson, Kraay & Co. Ltd., Chairman, Cookson Oilcakes & Oilseeds Co. Ltd., Director, London Commodity Exchange.

J. T. Kendall, FRSE

Head of Process Research and Development, National Cash Register Company, Dayton, Ohio. Formerly Managing Director, Edwards High Vacuum Ltd., and General Manager (Technical), Texas Instruments Ltd., Bedford. Graduate of Cambridge University and Leverhulme Research Fellow at Imperial College, London.

J. Leicester

Chairman, Committee of Directors of Research Associations. Director of Research, British Launderers' Research Association. Formerly with the Royal Naval Scientific Service. Member, UK Atomic Energy Desalination R & D Committee, Advisory Committee on Scientific and Technical Information to the Minister for Education and Science, Research Control Committee of the British Scientific Instrument Research Association.

Elizabeth Mack

Head of Information and Library Services, ASLIB. Formerly Information Officer at ASLIB and in industry, following public library service, and teaching. Occasional lecturer on information topics.

John Marsh, CBE

Director General, British Institute of Management. Formerly Director of the Institute of Personnel Management, and Director, the Industrial Welfare Society. Author of *People at Work*, *Partners in Work Relations*, and *Work and Leisure Digest*. Holds a number of honorary appointments in management and education fields, and lectures extensively abroad on behalf of H.M. Government.

Reginald May

At the time of writing was management adviser, Unilever Ltd. and is now Supervisory Consultant with Industrial Administration Ltd. He has worked on Product Forecasting and Planning assignments in Britain and overseas. One of the contributors to *Business Economics*, and to various business publications including *The Director*.

M. John Mills

Executive Assistant to Consumer Goods Director, Brown & Polson Ltd. Formerly Divisional Executive, Decca Radio & Television, Marketing Director, Morphy-Richards (Cray) Ltd., Associate Director, Spottiswood Advertising Ltd. Member of the teaching faculty of the Institute of Marketing.

G. E. Milward

The businessman who, in 1943, was appointed to H.M. Treasury to start training in O & M for the Civil Service. On retirement in 1957 he was invited to take charge of similar research and training in industry. Author of several standard textbooks on the subject of O & M.

James Morrell

Chairman, James Morrell & Associates Ltd., economic consultants. Economic adviser to the Charterhouse Group. Economic editor, *Management Today*. Frequent lecturer on forecasting and investment subjects, and author of various papers in these fields.

Denys Munby

Reader in the Economics and Organization of Transport, Oxford University, and Fellow of Nuffield College, Oxford. Assistant Director, Department of Economic Affairs, 1964–66. Author of articles on transport, regional planning, housing, the nationalized industries, etc. Joint editor of the *Journal of Transport Economics and Policy*.

W. G. Norris

Industrial Consultant to *The Director*. Managing Director, Uplands Press Ltd. Formerly Managing Director, Leonard Hill Publications, where he first became responsible for organizing exhibitions. Regular contributor to *The Director* and other management publications.

Alan Parker

A Chartered Accountant, and member of the staff of *The Economist*.

Hugh Parker

Managing Director, McKinsey & Company (UK). Director, McKinsey Foundation for Management Research. Director, American Chamber of Commerce in the UK. Member, Council of the Management Centre at University of Bradford. Member, Council of Management, Oxford Centre for Management Studies. Member, Editorial Board, *Management Decision*, and frequent speaker on management subjects to business schools, management training centres, etc.

James Pilditch

Chairman, Allied International Designers Ltd. He formed his own design company in 1959 after spending several years in North America. Author of *The Silent Salesman*, and *The Business of Product Design*, he has also written many articles on design, marketing and related subjects.

Sir Richard Powell, MC

Director-General of the Institute of Directors since 1954. Director, Bovis Holdings Ltd.

J. R. H. Pringle

Associate Editor, *The Banker*. On the staff of *The Economist*, London. London Editor, *The Bankers Magazine*, Boston, Massachusetts. Regular contributor to *The Guardian* and several other newspapers and periodicals.

George Pulay

City Editor, *The Times* until August 1968; now Managing Director, Charles Barker City Ltd. A financial journalist since 1951, he previously worked on the *Daily Telegraph* and the *News Chronicle*. He broadcasts frequently and contributes to numerous publications.

Robinson P. Rigg

Audiovisual consultant. Managing Director, Robin Publications Ltd., and European Editor, *Business Screen*. Formerly Industrial Films correspondent to *The Financial Times*. Chairman, Industrial Film Correspondents' Group. Author of *Audiovisual Aids and Techniques*, and regular contributor to *The Times*, *The Director*, and other publications.

The Rt. Hon. Lord Robens

Chairman, National Coal Board. Past President of the Advertising Association. Director of the Bank of England. Director, Times Newspapers Ltd. Minister of Labour and National Service, 1951. Member, National Economic Development Council, Royal Commission on Trade Unions, and Employers' Associations.

Jean and Andrew Robertson

Jean Robertson is Travel Editor of the *Sunday Times*. Andrew Robertson is Senior Research

Fellow at Sussex University in the Science Policy Research Unit. Together they contribute a weekly column, 'Value Judgement', on consumer affairs, in the *New Statesman*.

T. G. P. Rogers

Director of Personnel, IBM United Kingdom Ltd. Previously, Personnel Director, Hardy Spicer Ltd., Chief Personnel Officer, Mars Ltd., and Factory Personnel Manager, Procter & Gamble Ltd. Contributor to *The Times*, *Management Today*, and various management periodicals.

H. Samuels, OBE

Barrister-at-Law, Middle Temple. Author. General Editor, *Knight's Industrial Reports*, and contributor (Labour Laws) to the *Encyclopedia Brittanica*, and *Encyclopedia of Court Forms and Precedents*.

J. M. Samuels

Senior Lecturer in Finance and Accounting, Graduate Centre for Management Studies, Birmingham. Formerly Visiting Associate Professor of Industrial Administration, Purdue University, USA, and Lecturer in Business Finance, University of Birmingham. Author of numerous articles on Investment Decision Making, Profitability and Growth in Companies, and Transfer Pricing in Decentralized Organizations, in professional and academic journals.

G. W. Scarlett

Area Manager (London and South East England) of Industrial and Commercial Finance Corporation Ltd.

Andreas Whittam Smith

Deputy City Editor, the *Daily Telegraph*

Gerald L. E. Spier

Head of Economic Analysis Department, National Research Development Corporation. Commercial Manager, Tracked Hovercraft Ltd. Member of the Industrial Marketing Research Association. Author and lecturer on financial appraisal and marketing.

Nicholas A. H. Stacey

Executive Director, Chesham Amalgamations & Investments Ltd. Formerly Economic and Marketing Adviser, General Electric Company Ltd. Visiting Scholar, Graduate Business School, Columbia University, New York. Delivered 'Economics' Address, Annual Meeting, British Association for the Advancement of Science. Author, lecturer, and broadcaster.

Ronald Stevens

Public Relations Adviser to the Electricity Council. Formerly Labour Correspondent of the *Financial Times*. Industrial Correspondent of the *Daily Telegraph*, regular contributor to management publications, and occasional broadcaster on labour relations subjects.

E. J. Sturgess, CBE

Chairman, Location of Offices Bureau. Formerly Chief Engineer for Shell, and then head of Shell's management training centre near London. Previously technical adviser to the British Government on NATO pipelines. Vice-President, Institute of Petroleum 1955–58. Chairman, Institute of Petroleum Engineering Committee, 1948–59

Alfred Tack

Chairman and Managing Director, Tack Industries Ltd., Tack Tuition Ltd., Tack Management Consultants Ltd., and associated companies. Author of *How to Train Yourself to Succeed in Selling, Marketing: The Sales Manager's Role*, and six other books on selling and sales management.

P. F. D. Tennant, OBE

Director General, British National Export Council. Press Attaché, Stockholm, 1939–45, and Paris 1945–50. Deputy Commandant, British Sector, Berlin, 1950–52. Overseas Director and Deputy Director General, Federation of British Industries, 1952–65.

C. Gordon Tether

Writer of the *Financial Times* daily 'Lombard Column' on world financial and economic affairs. Regular contributor to the *Bankers Magazine* and other journals, and to BBC home and overseas radio programmes. Lecturer on national and international economic subjects to a wide variety of organizations in the United Kingdom and overseas.

A. G. Touche

Fellow of the Institute of Chartered Accountants in England and Wales. He is primarily concerned with the management of investment trust companies.

Tim Traverse-Healy

Immediate past President, Institute of Public Relations. Partner Traverse-Healy & Lyons. Previously, Chairman and European Director of Infoplan Ltd. Honorary Public Relations Adviser to the Advertising Association; member of the Westminster Commission on Mass Media; member of the Communications Advisory Committee of the British National Export Council.

K. Trickett

Technical Director, P-E Consulting Group Ltd. Head of technical division, specializing in the study of distribution problems and design of warehouses for industrial and commercial clients. Member of the UK Committee ICHCA. Author of papers on mechanical handling, warehousing design and factory layout for the Institute of Directors, Institute of Production Engineers, the Supermarkets Association, and others.

John Tyzack, CBE

Founder and chairman, John Tyzack & Partners Ltd., management consultants. His working life has been in agriculture, public service, the RAF, in public industry (as Director, BEA) and in private industry as a director of engineering companies. He was appointed a CBE (Mil.) in 1944 for his work on the planning of the operation 'Overlord'.

C. E. Waller

Editor of the *Purchasing Journal, Purchasing Bulletin*, and the *Institute of Purchasing and Supply Educational Review*. He has had a wide experience in industrial and technical publishing, is the author of four books on travel subjects, and a contributor to many business publications.

F. R. L. Wentworth

Distribution Director, Schweppes (Home) Ltd. A Cambridge MA in Law and Economics, and a Member of the Institute of Transport Association, he is the author of several articles on distribution in such publications as *The Director* and the *Financial Times*. Leader of the British Institute of Management's first seminars on distribution, and chairman of BIM's distribution forums.

J. B. Whelan

Chairman, Cowan Investment Company Ltd. Formerly taxation correspondent of *The Director*, *The Law Times*, *Financial Times*, and other publications. Member of the Institute of Directors' Taxation Committee.

R. F. M. (Martin) Wilkinson

Chairman, the London Stock Exchange, and Chairman of the Federation of Stock Exchanges in Great Britain and Ireland.

The Rt. Hon. George Woodcock, CBE

General Secretary of the Trades Union Congress since 1960. Member of the Royal Commission on Trade Unions and Employers' Organisations. Vice-Chairman of the National Savings Committee, a vice-president of the International Confederation of Free Trade Unions, and a member of the National Economic Development Council. In 1963 he was awarded the CBE, and in June 1967 was appointed to the Privy Council.

H. Beric Wright

Director, Institute of Directors' Medical Centre. After service overseas for an international oil company as surgical and industrial medical officer, joined the I. of D. in 1958 and has built up their medical activities concerned with the health problems of business men. Author and editor of numerous articles and publications in this field, and contributor to medical and scientific journals.

1. The Company in the 1970s

1.1 The Company

George Pulay

The company is the backbone of the industrial society. Whether private or public, large or small, the company is right at the heart of business life. Without it industry and commerce could not function. There are over 527,000 registered companies in Britain today, the vast majority of which are private companies—some 511,962 at the last official count. The number of public companies was 15,298, and those with a share capital numbered 10,678 with a combined issue capital of £12,388 million.

A new Companies Act received the Royal Assent in the summer of 1967. This was the first major piece of company legislation since the 1948 Companies Act, itself born out of the Cohen Committee's report. Although hailed at the time as an enlightened piece of legislation, this act was soon found to have many loopholes. A series of major company scandals in the late 1950s brought matters to a head and led to the appointment of the Jenkins Committee, which by 1962 had put forward a whole set of new proposals. It took another five years, a host of amendments, and a Labour Government anxious to seek disclosure of political contributions by companies, and, not least, several insurance scandals, to get the 1967 Act passed. But this was only the first bite. A second instalment to this Act was promised. (The effects of the new Act, especially the removal of the private exempt company, will be discussed later in this chapter.)

History

To get some perspective on the evolution of the company it is worth bearing in mind that English joint stock companies go back over three centuries. Probably the most famous of all the early 'chartered' companies was the East India Company, formed in 1600. Seventy years later came the Hudson's Bay Company, and in 1694 the Bank of England. In those days companies were incorporated by special acts of Parliament or Royal Charter, although other bodies, which would now be called companies, were already carrying on business. Rapid industrial expansion in the nineteenth century led to the need for a new approach, and in 1844 the vast majority of companies were enabled to obtain incorporation without charter or special act. The same year, incidentally, saw the first provisions for the winding up of companies. It took another eleven years before the emergence of the limited liability company, the basis of the modern joint stock company. Under Acts of 1855 and 1856, all companies could obtain certificates of incorporation with limited liability. The first of a whole series of company legislation providing for incorporation and setting out a code of regulations came in 1862. Although there followed a wholesale series of amendments over the next forty odd years, the major pieces of legislation were the Companies (Consolidation) Act of 1908, the Companies Act 1929, and the Companies Act 1948.

As the pace of industry has continued to quicken over the past century, so has the growth of joint stock companies. Without the advent of the limited liability principle, i.e., that each shareholder's liability is limited to the amount of shares he owns, industry would not have been able to obtain the finance necessary to expand its capacity. The principle has remained the same ever since, even though technical and, particularly, tax considerations have tended to change points of emphasis; for the availability of adequate financial resources, whether for the one-man business or the giant corporation, is the key to commercial and industrial development. And even in this age of bigness, the natural evolution of business from the individual to partnership, to limited liability company and, possibly, to public status has continued as before (certainly until the 1965 Finance Act). The man with drive, with talent and/or with an inventive mind will create his business. Soon, if at all successful, it will get too big for him to run it alone. First, he may look around for a suitable partner; next, he may need some outside finance to expand his workshop, buy additional plant or whatever. This will be the time when incorporation as a company is likely. The availability of a company's books for inspection may well prove helpful in securing outside finance, be it from the bank, or friendly and trusted individuals. Indeed, it becomes essential on the eventual path towards raising public funds. In a partnership, which under the more recent tax legislation has regained considerable attractions, outside assessment of its financial status is far less straightforward, but there are compensatory factors as will be shown.

Recent legislation

Two major pieces of recent legislation are already affecting and will continue to affect

4

the pattern of Britain's company structure. The 1965 Finance Act brought into being the 'close' company, which is a company controlled by five or fewer persons, though an entire family is looked upon as a person in this context. The restrictions imposed on these companies are such as to reduce the advantages of forming a small company altogether.

As a follow-on from there, the new Companies Act of 1967 abolished the exempt private company. These are companies that were exempt from filing accounts annually at the Board of Trade's Companies House. They were companies with less than fifty shareholders, and they were not able to seek money from the public. The great majority of all registered companies in Britain was in this category. Although there are (or were) still a few large private concerns—Pilkington Glass and the Sainsbury grocery chain come to mind—most of the private companies are small. Many of them were companies of convenience; companies incorporated for good tax reasons, for until the 1965 Finance Act there were many advantages for small businesses and even individuals to form private companies. They enabled the proprietors to take out liberal expenses, and the directors-shareholders could pay themselves salaries taxed as income at lower rate before having to meet profits tax and income tax on unearned profits taken out.

All these advantages have now disappeared, and there is little doubt that under the new Company law the near automatic incorporation of small private limited companies will cease.

What is a close company?

The close company came into being under the 1965 Finance Act, the most controversial piece of financial legislation since the Second World War, and is defined in detail in the Eighteenth Schedule to the Act. The main criteria as set out by the Taxation Committee of the Association of Certified and Corporate Accountants are as follows:

1. a company under the control of five or fewer participators or of directors who are themselves participators even if their number is more than five; or
2. a company in which more than half of the amount of its income could be apportioned among five or fewer participators or among directors who are participators. For the purpose of this definition, the income is that which could be apportioned and sub-apportioned for surtax purposes if the company itself and all companies through which sub-apportionments could be made were close companies.

Close companies have some features in common with companies that were previously subject to surtax directions under the Income Tax Acts, and some with companies that were formerly director-controlled for profits tax purposes. The key disadvantage from a tax point of view is that income tax and surtax must be paid if their dividend payments and other distributions fall below a required standard. Other disadvantages, as cited by the Association of Certified and Corporate Accountants, are:

(a) the amount of directors' remuneration that can be deducted in computing profits for corporation tax purposes is restricted;
(b) certain loans are treated as distributions for income tax purposes;
(c) certain payments of interest and certain other payments are treated as distributions in close companies although they would not be so treated in other companies. In consequence, a company is prohibited from deducting such payment in computing profits for corporation tax purposes, even though they would otherwise qualify for deductions.

Company or partnership?

The advent of the close company, coupled, as it happens, with the relaxation of the partnership rule, poses the question for the small and even medium-sized 'private' business: should it be a limited company or partnership? Although the decision will naturally depend on many individual considerations, it is probably fair to say that the rush towards the private limited company, which has gathered momentum in the past twenty years, is likely to be reversed; that the smaller businesses will have to assess most carefully where the balance of advantage lies.

Leaving aside, for a moment, the question of taxation, there is still a basic difference between company and partnership. With the limited liability company, each shareholder, and in the case of the private company, usually each director, is personally liable only to the extent of his investment in the company. In a partnership, every partner is fully liable. On the face of it, therefore, a partnership should, to the outside world, inspire more confidence than a limited company. This was so in the beginning, in the latter part of the last century, when 'limited liability' was a new creature. It is still so in the eyes of many discerning bankers or accountants. For if one has any faith or trust in the management—and this is surely one of the fundamental tenets when it comes to raising finance—there is a great deal to be said in favour of a business in which each partner or owner is fully liable in the event of disaster. And yet, in recent times, a kind of psychological barrier seems to have been built up and has tended to lead to a better image for a company than a partnership in trade and industry. (In certain professions, such as the law, accountancy, medicine, and the Stock Exchange, partnerships are, of course, the rule.)

Another factor favouring the company is the question of outside finance. Only a company can, in fact, seek funds from the public, and probably as a result of this ruling and because its books are open to inspection, companies appear to have enjoyed a better credit standing in the eyes of the general public. They have, one might say, enjoyed a certain cachet, though not necessarily for the right reasons.

6

The question of choice thus affects only the private business that has no plans for the time being to go to the public for funds or seek a market quotation. And here the balance of advantage will in the first place depend on size, more specifically on size of profits. For a business with small profits, say, in the £6,000–£8,000 bracket, a limited company may still prove the best answer, even under the new tax arrangements; for a company is allowed pay up to £4,000 in fees for a single director and up to £7,000 for two directors. These advantages disappear as profits move higher, and for the normal private business making annual profits of, say, £20,000 to £50,000 a partnership would prove more advantageous.

In tax terms the position is broadly this: a company's total profits are liable to corporation tax; in addition, that part of the profits which is distributed bears income tax and, if applicable, surtax in the hands of the recipient. Undistributed profits bear no further liability but they will usually increase the gain subject to capital gains tax when a shareholder disposes of his shares. In a partnership, each partner's share of profits is subject to income tax and surtax in his hands, but there is no corporation tax and there is greater flexibility in determining what a profit is.

There are other considerations too. English law does not recognize a partnership apart from its members. A limited company, on the other hand, is a separate legal person in law whether controlled absolutely by one or more directors. Dissolution of a partnership and even the retirement of one of the partners, especially one with a big stake in the firm, causes special problems. There is also the question of carrying forward trading losses. All in all, the decision will very much depend on each individual case, on the future plans of the business and the question of succession. It is scarcely surprising that tax lawyers and accountants have been busier these past few years than ever before.

Forming a company

The actual mechanics of forming a company are easy and straightforward. If it is a question of transferring an existing business into a private company, and no outside financial injection is needed, the business can be transferred for an agreed sum representing the value of the property being fed into the new company. Nor is it necessary to transfer all the assets of the business to the company.

Again, on the assumption that the introduction of fresh capital is not necessary, the vendor of the business simply parts with his interest in exchange for shares in the company. If the business is owned by more than one person and the company is to be under similar control, shares will be allotted to the proprietors in proportion to their respective interests.

There are quite a number of different companies that could be formed, e.g., a company with its liability limited by guarantee and not having a share capital, or a company with unlimited liability and having a share capital; but these are the exceptions rather than the rule. We are talking about the ordinary private company, now no longer exempt, with its liability limited by shares.

Every such company formed must produce the following documents on incorporation:

Memorandum of Association

Articles of Association (printed)

Statement of Nominal Capital

Declaration of compliance with the requirements of the Companies Act, 1967. (This declaration may be made either by a solicitor involved in the formation of the company or by a person named in the Articles of Association as a director or secretary.)

Notice of the situation of the Registered Office must be lodged with the Registrar of Companies within fourteen days of the date of incorporation. Particulars of the directors and secretary must also be lodged with the Registrar within fourteen days from the appointment of the first director.

Documents must be signed and dated, and the Memorandum of Articles of Association of a private company must be signed by at least two subscribers. The number of shares subscribed by each member must be filled in and various other details supplied. The documents are examined by the Registrar and if no queries arise they are provisionally accepted on payment of duty and fees.

Usually, a few days later, after another official scrutiny, a Certificate of Incorporation will be issued. A private company may start operating as such immediately after incorporation.

Board objectives

The Memorandum and Articles are the most important documents. The first is effectively the company's charter; the second largely regulates its internal affairs. The Memorandum of Association must contain the following five points:

1. the name of the company (with Limited as the last word)
2. the situation of the registered office—whether England or Scotland;
3. the objects of the company;
4. that liability of the members is limited;
5. the amount of share capital and the division of it into shares of fixed amount.

Finding a suitable name for the company is clearly of great importance (although a company's name may be changed after passing the requisite special resolution). The area of choice is large but not unlimited. The Board of Trade has the power to reject any name it considers unsuitable or misleading. Notes of guidance on the choice of names have been issued by the Registrar of Companies (C 186).

A name will be refused if it is too like that of an existing company; if it is held to be misleading; if it includes a surname which is not the surname of a director, except when there are valid reasons; and it must not include the words Co-operative or 'Building Society'.

A name suggesting any connection with the Crown will not ordinarily be allowed; similarly, the word 'British' will not ordinarily be allowed unless the undertaking is British controlled and is also of substantial size and importance in its particular field of business. 'Imperial', 'Commonwealth', 'National', 'International', and 'Corporation' are also labels very carefully vetted. Names including 'Bank', 'Banking', 'Investment Trust' or simply 'Trust' will be allowed only when circumstances justify. (Though here, it is fair to comment that some undesirable companies have slipped through the net.)

No less important is the choice of a company's objects. As only business that is expressly authorized or at least implied in the Memorandum may be carried on, the clause requires particular attention. It should give the directors scope not merely to carry on the business for which the company has been formed. Maximum freedom and flexibility to broaden its base seems desirable. Legal terminology has come to grips with this problem.

The principle of limited liability is self-explanatory. It may be worth noting that when a member has paid the entire nominal amount of the shares held, his liability ceases. If shares are transferred before they are fully paid up the liability devolves on the transferee. Should the company go into liquidation within a year and the transferee fail to discharge his liability, the transferor will be held liable to the extent of the unpaid amount on the shares.

The share capital may be divided into different classes, and the shares into which the capital is divided may be of any amount and in different classes of different amounts. Details of the various classes of shares and the rights attaching to them should be spelled out in the Articles of Association.

Articles of Association

Every company must have this kind of internal rule book. Good specimens are available, and company lawyers and accountants are as familiar with these as with other aspects of company formation. The Articles, then, should define the classes of shares, their voting power and all rights attaching to them; and give appropriate details on restrictions of the transfer of shares.

The Articles normally appoint the first directors and chairman, and prescribe the order of their retirement and re-election. Particularly in relation to the appointment of directors for a given term of office it should be borne in mind that Articles of Association are subject to alteration at any time by special resolution. A safer form of contract to achieve this end is an agreement between a director and the company.

Although the powers of the directors should be given there is no need to spell

9

them out in detail. General provisions can cover this point. More important is the insertion of a clause authorizing the directors to appoint a managing director or manager, to delegate to him appropriate powers, and to determine his remuneration. If this is not specifically stated, sanction of the company in general meeting must be obtained to such an appointment. For the small company this may not be so important; but at a later stage it might. Directors' remunerations and borrowing powers will also be laid down in this section.

Duties and fees

Stamp duty payable on registration of limited companies with share capital is determined by the amount of nominal capital. Duty is paid at the rate of 10s. per £100 of capital. The Memorandum of Association must carry a fee stamp the amount of which is determined on a sliding scale from a minimum of £20, covering up to £2,000 capital, to a maximum of £58 for capital of £525,000 or above. Deed stamps of 10s. each are payable on the Memorandum and Articles of Association and fee stamps of 5s. each on the Articles, Notice of Situation of Registered Office, Particulars of Directors and Secretary, and Declaration of Compliance—together another £2.

To give three examples: the total duties and fees payable for a company with £100 nominal capital will be £4 10s.; for £1,000 capital, £9; for £10,000, £58 5s.; for £100,000, £530 15s., and for £1,000,000, £5,052.

If the new company acquires property or a business, and part of the purchase price is satisfied by the allotment of fully or partly paid shares, the Agreement for Sale must be lodged with the Registrar in addition to the Return of Allotments. This agreement must be stamped with *ad valorem* conveyance duty for the transfer of assets such as fixed plant and machinery, book debts, cash on deposit, goodwill, and benefit of contracts, etc. For the purpose of stamp duty the liabilities assumed by the company have to be added to the purchase price payable in cash or in shares or debentures, both of which are calculated at their par value. A fixed duty of 10s. or 6d., depending on whether the document is under seal or hand, must also be paid.

The rate of duty is on a sliding scale: it is nil up to a consideration of £5,500; 10s. per £100 where the total does not exceed £7,000, and £1 per £100 on any amount above £7,000.

The actual forms that have to be filled in on the formation of a company are available from the Companies Registration Office of the Board of Trade either free or at nominal rates.

Outside finance

Having established a business as a private company, this may run happily along its course for quite some time; but sooner or later, if the company is to grow and expand, the question of outside finance is likely to arise. There are basically two kinds of finance required by private companies: new money for the business and cash for the proprietors. When the two needs are combined and the private company is sufficiently well established, its advisers may well suggest going public, seeking an official quotation. But this is not essential at this stage. Private companies can, and do, attract outside finance without going public. One might say it is the first step towards it.

But let us stay with the private company a little longer. Taking a typical family business, the present level of taxation, and especially estate duty, is likely to make it imperative for the proprietors to realize at least part of their interest in the business. Equally, a company's progress can easily be held back unless the proprietors are prepared to part with some of their interest or equity and thus enable the company to obtain outside finance. There are quite a number of organizations specializing in helping private companies in this way. An Institute of Directors' publication, *Finance Problems of the Smaller Company*, is a good guide to such companies. All these specialized financial institutions can be considered as company nurseries: helping the smaller companies first to get outside finance and qualified financial advice and, later, using their expertise in grooming the companies for a possible public flotation in due course.

The process of vetting a private company for outside help is fairly similar in both cases, though with a private company there will be no need to comply with full prospectus requirements. The process will usually start with an accountant's report. This will form the basis for proprietors and their advisers to make an assessment of the future potential.

The cost of an independent accountant's report will, of course, depend on the size of the business, but, say, for a company earning between £25,000 and £100,000 this will be somewhere in the region of £400 to £500. It is, of course, the earnings capacity which will determine the value put on a company by an outside investor. Fixed assets and the strength of the balance sheets are essential features. In the end, however, it is the earnings capacity on the assets employed that will decide the terms on which a new investor is brought in; not to forget the quality of existing management and plans for management succession which are an ever more important consideration in rating a company. It is not surprising either that an outside investor in a private, unquoted company, will seek better returns than are available in comparable businesses quoted on the Stock Exchange.

Until the 1967 Companies Act, the exempt private company—the majority of private companies were in this category—was exempt from filing its annual accounts with the Registrar. It was therefore impossible for a competitor to go along to Companies House and study the financial position of such a company. Now that every company with very few exceptions must file its accounts, a climate may gradually be created that will make it far easier for the smaller business to attract outside capital if it so desires.

At the same time, the creation of the Close company, with its tax disadvantages under the corporation tax system, is expected to lead to the introduction of more outside capital into private concerns and may well accentuate the movement for 'going public'; for companies whose ordinary shares are quoted on the Stock Exchange, and of which shares carrying not less than 35 per cent of the voting power are held by the public, avoid close company status.

Going public

Several of the key reasons for a company deciding to go public, to seek an introduction or quotation of its shares on a stock exchange, are similar to those of a private company looking for outside finance: the owners may wish to turn part of their shares into cash; to provide for retirement and estate duty; or simply to avoid having too many assets locked away in one company; or to rid itself of close company status.

Additional finance that can be raised through family or friends is usually limited. If it is to be raised from the public, it is most easily effected if the company's shares are quoted, because it is only then that the company will attract the attention of the institutional investors, the insurance companies, investment trusts, pension funds, etc.

There are, however, two other incentives for directors deciding to go public, one readily definable, the other less so. A company with a stock exchange quotation can use its shares to acquire other companies. This has become a potent factor in recent years. Amalgamations and mergers by share exchange have become one of the classic ways of expansion and diversification. Especially in times of inflationary pressures— and most of the post-war period has seen a steady erosion of the currency—paper is more attractive than cash. It is also, mostly, more readily available!

Finally, there is the question of status or image. And there is no doubt that, generally speaking, a stock exchange quotation will enhance a company's standing. The mere fact that the SE authorities have let it through the turnstiles is a kind of testimonial.

Four methods

There are four methods of going public, of floating a company: an offer for sale; an issue by prospectus; a share placing; or a share introduction. All will give the company 'public' status; enable the shares to be dealt in on a recognized stock exchange; and will enable that company to tap the public for more funds at some future date.

Broadly, a private company will have to satisfy the authorities on a progressive profit record and on solid and continuing management. If the company has recently suffered an earnings setback, or if management or boardroom changes are about to take place, it would clearly be more prudent to delay the marketing unless there are very special circumstances.

Once the decision has been taken, the company will seek the services of a stockbroker or issuing house, or both. The company's banker or auditors will probably have made the necessary suggestions and arrangements by then. Normally, small issues tend to be handled by stockbrokers and larger ones by merchant bank-issuing houses; but there is no firm rule. A company can, and does, choose its flotation sponsor, and this is a highly competitive sector of the City.

Preparation of a ten-year profit record; a careful survey of the company's articles; probably several changes in the articles and a likely recasting of the company's capital structure are the usual main steps before actual flotation.

Requirements for going public are:
1. A company must have a minimum market value of £250,000.
2. There must be a minimum market value of £100,000 for any one security for which quotation is being sought.
3. At least 35 per cent of the issued equity capital, or securities convertible into equity capital, for which quotation is sought, must be in the hands of the public. In very large issues, the Council may be prepared to allow the distribution of a lower percentage.
4. At least 30 per cent of any class of issued fixed income capital (e.g., preference shares or loan stock) for which quotation is sought must be in the hands of the public.

It is difficult to be dogmatic about how big a company should be before going public, as the type of trade and state of the market are important factors to be taken into account. It is the profit record of a company that really matters, although naturally its assets are also taken into consideration. For a London quotation, net profits before taxation of £100,000 p.a. should have been achieved, but in a provincial Stock Exchange a lesser figure would be acceptable.

Investors will be looking for growth and yield as well as certainty of dividend and security of capital. The yardstick of growth will be the record of profits over recent years and so far as dividend is concerned, adequate 'cover' will certainly be looked for, i.e., the number of times the dividend is covered by available profits.

Offer for sale

In an offer for sale, and in an issue by prospectus, there is a general invitation to the public to apply for shares. This is done by advertising the issue (prospectus) together with an application form in at least two newspapers. Further application forms will be available at the company's bankers, brokers and/or issuing house.

With an offer for sale, the issuing house will subscribe for or purchase from the vendors the shares to be marketed and then offer them as principal to the public. With an issue by prospectus, the company invites applications direct with the issuing house underwriting the issue. Whereas under an offer for sale the issuing house can sell old and new shares, the company can invite subscription only for new shares.

This is certainly the most popular method as far as the Stock Exchange is concerned, and it also tends to attract the widest public interest. It is favoured as an issuing method because it ensures that the public can get the shares at the issue price. The shares are going to be widely spread which, in turn, will make for a broadly based and, hence, realistic market. But it is an expensive way of coming to the market. For a medium-sized issue, say, raising £200,000, the cost of an offer for sale could be just over 10 per cent. As the issue gets larger, so the relative cost goes down. A table of comparative costs between offers for sale and a placing recently compiled by Charterhouse Japhet & Thomasson is given below.

Amount being raised	Method	Possible cost	% cost
£200,000	placing	£13,500	6·7
£200,000	offer for sale	£21,500	10·7
£500,000	offer for sale	£33,000	6·6
£1,000,000	offer for sale	£48,000	4·8

Placing of shares

A share placing is an appropriate way of marketing if the value of shares being marketed is small and if the sponsors are content to forgo the publicity an offer for sale usually provides. There are few placings of equity involving more than £250,000 though there are far bigger amounts frequently placed in the fixed interest market.

In contrast to a public offer, there is no general invitation to the public, but again, at least 35 per cent of the company's ordinary capital must be subject of the placing and at least 25 per cent must be made available to the public through the Stock Exchange. The reason for restricting equity placings to smaller amounts is that the Stock Exchange is anxious that the public should have a fair chance of acquiring shares at the issue price and that an active market should develop in the shares.

Introduction of shares

As the term applies, an introduction is the method for seeking a quotation without raising money. It cannot be used if the company wishes to raise funds by an issue of shares or when the existing shareholders wish to dispose of a large block. To make any market at all, existing shareholders will make some shares available. The Stock Exchange authorities vet any application for an introduction carefully to ensure that there will be a realistic market. They will pass an introduction if the shares are already fairly well spread and when control is not too concentrated. No more than 65 per cent of the capital should be held by less than five people.

For an introduction, no prospectus is required, but the Stock Exchange requires the same sort of information that is widely circulated and advertised in the press. It is, however, still by far the cheapest method of going public.

With a placing, advertisements must be published in two newspapers. If it is a London Stock Exchange quotation, both newspapers must be nationals; if it is a provincial quotation, one of the newspapers can be local. This is clearly more expensive than an introduction, but it does not involve underwriting and the handling of applications from the public, which can run into many thousands of pounds. On the other hand, if the company's name is well known, a more advantagous price can often be obtained for the company by a public issue. A good example recently was Ladbroke's, the well known bookmaking group, whose shares were marketed in the autumn of 1967 and attracted 61,013 applications for 121,670,000 shares. As there were only 1,350,000 shares on offer, the issue was just about a hundred times oversubscribed. The shares were offered at 10s. 0d. When dealing began, they raced ahead to 13s. 3d. on the first day.

Choosing an issuing house

The choice of the issuing house, whether broker or merchant bank, is important. It is quite usual for smaller issues to be handled by stockbroking firms alone. In a larger company the chances are that it will have worked with a merchant bank for some time, in which event the merchant bank would probably act as the issuing house, bringing in a stockbroker as well. Another advantage of having a merchant bank is that it has the practice and expertise of advising companies on the best financial structure.

There is also the question of prestige. The choice of a well-known issuing house of first-class repute will help the company. Moreover, sponsorship is not just a matter of form. Should the company fail to live up to early expectations any discredit would automatically rub off on the issuing house.

Once chosen, the issuing house will prepare everything in connection with the issue, all the necessary documents, and, not least, will determine the timetable. Timing of an issue is all important. Many a good issue has gone sour because the terms were fixed but the market had turned by the time the crucial day arrived. Nor are the issuing house's duties over when the issue has been made. Although procedure will follow a well-trodden pattern, the responsible issuing house will always be there to guide the company and advise it on how to handle its profit statements, possibly even on how to conduct its relations with its new public.

The Stock Exchange itself has laid down a certain code of behaviour for public companies. This gives details of how the profit statements should be put out, their frequency and timing. Half-yearly statements are strongly recommended and will become fully acceptable before long. Even quarterly statements are becoming more frequent. Resistance here, for seasonal or other reasons, is being broken down. Once a seasonal pattern has been established, it is argued among the progressives, this should not be a stumbling block. And there is no doubt that the trend towards more and more disclosure is likely to continue for some time.

The Stock Exchange, as an institution, has to see that a fair and efficient market is provided for securities. Where fairness is concerned, this can be achieved only if there is—in the words of a joint chairman of the Quotations Committee—'equal opportunity for all to possess the information necessary to make a balanced investment judgement. The more certain the public feels that it will be told all necessary facts the less attention it will pay to rumour. Once the Stock Exchange has seen that information is available it is not its function to pass judgement on the merits or value of a security.'

To guide companies aspiring to obtain a market quotation the Stock Exchange Council has published its own rule book.* This sets out in detail not only the various methods and documents required for going public, but also the kind of information a public company is required to give and how to give it.

There are good reasons why the Stock Exchange Council should take maximum care in vetting new companies and in making sure that existing ones live up to the code laid down. In the first place, many smaller companies have tended to come forward in recent years as a result of the death duty and other tax problems. Secondly, there has been mounting activity on the merger front, with occasionally hard fought battles between two or more companies. In several cases, during these take-over tussles, information that has changed the investment status of a given company has come to light; information which, it can be argued, should have been in the possession of the shareholders—the proprietors—of the company earlier. Finally, there have been too many company scandals. True, in relation to the near 10,000 securities listed on the London Stock Exchange, the number of company frauds has been relatively small, but it is in the interest of the Stock Exchange itself, and the country as a whole, to ensure that everything possible is done to prevent the public investor from being defrauded. The US has a special Government watchdog body known as the Securities and Exchange Commission (SEC), which has tremendous powers for investigating doubtful prospectuses and dealings on the exchanges. The London Stock Exchange has always felt that it could carry out its own policing methods best, basing its case largely on the argument that official interference does not make for efficiency. The recent insurance company fiascos (in which the Stock Exchange had, of course, no part whatsoever) revived public debate on whether a body on the lines of the SEC would not be beneficial in Britain too. Indeed, the City now has its own

* *See* Reading list at end of section.

takeover panel, the Watchdog Committee under the direction of Sir Humphrey Mynors, which has already intervened in some takeover struggles.

For the time being, the Board of Trade has assumed greater powers and has closed some of the more gaping loopholes. Again, the new Companies Act should prove helpful in this direction, for the greater the official demand for information the more difficult it will be for undesirable companies to slip through the net. And it is in the area of new disclosures that the 1967 Companies Act has gone a long way. Nor are the new disclosure rules of interest only to shareholders. Several are of more general interest to the community as a whole, which is in line with modern thinking. More information and more disclosure has been the tendency since the Second World War. The mystique surrounding so many activities of the City, the heart of the financial community, were finally blown sky high in the British Aluminium affair and the Bank Rate Tribunal in the 1950s. These were milestones in British financial history and led to a much franker and, therefore, usually better informed public debate on financial affairs.

It is now eight years since the Jenkins Committee was first appointed to report on the state of British company law. It produced its monumental findings in 1962. Some of its recommendations found their way into the 1965 Companies Bill, which was delayed by the 1966 election. In the end, it was the insurance scandals that provided sufficient urgency for the new Companies Act to become law in 1967.

Key points on the disclosure front are: that subsidiary companies and their country of incorporation must be revealed each year, subject to Board of Trade relaxation in individual cases; all trade investments amounting to more than 10 per cent of a company's capital must be disclosed.

Directors have to make available more information on their fees and salaries, and those of senior executives. Under the old act, only total sums paid to the board as fees and salaries had to be given. Now the chairman's pay must be given and the number of directors whose pay falls within rising bands of £2,500 each. Independent companies, where all the directors receive less than £7,500 together, are exempt from this disclosure rule.

Companies must also state how many employees, who are not necessarily directors, earn over £10,000, also in steps of £2,500. On the trading side, too, companies must give more information. Any significant changes in the activities of a company must be notified, as should major changes in fixed assets. Turnover and profits should be broken down for the various major classes of business, if more than one. As before, banks, insurance, and shipping companies have special dispensation. Export turnover details are asked for, as are details of contributions to political or charitable purposes. (This was one reason for the Labour Government's revision of company law.) Details of directors' share dealings are required, and service contracts for more than one year are open to inspection by members. Directors are also no longer able to deal in options in the shares of their companies.

2*

The list is long, and much of the additional information should prove to the general good. Much of it, too, is long overdue, not least the additional powers bestowed on the Board of Trade to investigate suspect companies. No piece of legislation will ever prevent the occasional crook from defrauding the shareholder or the public. All that can be done is to make it as difficult as possible for him without overloading the bureaucratic machine and stifling private enterprise, and without driving businessmen and (especially company secretaries) to distraction by the sheer volume of form filling.

On a more positive note, though, there is everything to be said for making public companies as public spirited and as forthcoming with information as their name implies. For industry and commerce to be able to thrive and expand, the market place must be allowed to function as smoothly as possible, and it will be able to do so only if it has the public's, the investor's, fullest confidence.

Reading list

BOOKS

Standard Boardroom Practice (Institute of Directors, 1968)
Buckley on the Companies Acts (Butterworth, 1964)
Handbook on the Formation, Management and Winding up of Joint Stock Companies, Sir Francis Gore-Brown (Jordan and Sons, 41st Edition)
Report of the Company Law Committee, Command Paper 1749, (H.M.S.O. 1962)
Close Companies, N. E. Mustoe (Butterworth, 1967)
How to Form a Private Company, D. St. Clair Morgan and Gordon E. Morris (Jordan and Sons, 27th Edition, 1968)
Going Public, Anthony Vice (Thomas de la Rue)
Admission to Securities to Quotation (From offices of the Council of the London Stock Exchange or other Federated Exchanges)
What to Include in Company Accounts Now, A. G. Touche (Butterworth, 1967)
The Companies Act 1967: An Introduction (Oyez Publications)
Finance Problems of the Smaller Company: An Institute of Directors Guide to the City (Institute of Directors, 1967)
Sources of Capital (Associated of Certified and Corporate Accountants, 1965)

JOURNALS

The Journal of Business Law, edited by Clive M. Schmilthoff (Published quarterly by Stevens and Sons)

Useful Addresses

Association of Certified and Corporate Accountants, 22 Bedford Square, London WC 1
Board of Trade Headquarters, 1 Victoria Street, London SW 1
Federation of Stock Exchanges in Great Britain and Ireland, c/o The Stock Exchange, Throgmorton Street, London EC 2
Institute of Chartered Accountants in England and Wales, 56 Goswell Road, London EC 1

1.2 The Company Director

The Legal Correspondent, *The Director*

Functions of the director

The function of a director is to give a sense of direction to the activities of his company. For this, he must always have in his mind the primary purpose of his company, and use it as a standard by which to judge the future plans and day-to-day decisions of the board and those under him.

In the old days a company director could define the objects of his company quite simply: 'We sell furniture'. If asked what was planned for next year he would say, 'We shall continue to sell furniture'. Nowadays, he must keep his outlook broad: plans for the next year may include the formation of a finance company subsidiary; the purchase of an interest in a small company of furniture manufacturers; the opening of new branches in three towns some distance from the Head Office, with quite different tastes in furniture; an experiment in stocking linens and a wider range of electrical fittings; and the raising of additional finance by debenture loan and the sale and lease back of some freeholds.

It is at boardroom level that all such matters are first seriously discussed, and at which the final decisions are taken. The economists and the students of business law will point out that the directors are the servants of the company, and the company is in the ownership of the shareholders who may, if they wish, convene a meeting and dismiss the whole board without notice. In fact, no board that does its job well is dismissed. The directors may be asked to explain their new policy; there may be grumbles at heavy appropriations of profits for future projects; and additional capital may be subscribed slowly and unwillingly; but the decisions of the board will to all intents be final if they are good decisions and are well carried out.

Again, the company lawyers will point out that the activities of a company are set out in its Memorandum of Association, and that these are exceeded only under peril of having commercial contracts set aside as *ultra vires*. The answer to this is that, if the Board decide that expansion along certain lines is in the interests of the company, the proper step is to have the Memorandum amended, and it is the business of the company lawyer to point the way.

More recently, the social reformers and the politicians have emphasized that modern companies have obligations to the community: the board should take account of the impact upon society of the activities of their company, and should admit the employees to a share in the ownership and management. One answer is that the board have had no training in social work and are content to leave this to those who are qualified; they have (collectively) no political ambitions, and are generally content to leave the government of the country to competent politicians; and they have not yet, any more than anyone else, found a useful function in the boardroom for the fitter straight from a day's work at the factory bench.

In short, work in the boardroom is a specialized job for which comparatively few are fitted. No man is qualified to make boardroom decisions unless he is prepared to accept the consequences of failure.

Legal responsibilities of the board

When all this has been said, it still remains true that the board must act within the prescribed legal framework. The Memorandum, until it is altered, leaves open only certain trading or commercial activities to their company; the Articles, until amended, severely restrict the borrowing powers of the directors, and perhaps their powers to commit the company to new ventures as well. They have a paramount duty to the company, and the shareholders as proprietors, which will prevent them from using the company resources for a number of purposes that may appeal to them personally, while the law generally, and the two present Companies Acts in particular (those of 1948 and 1967) will compel them to a number of courses, and forbid them a number of actions, all of which in their personal capacities they may find disagreeable.

The overall duty of directors is said to be, first and foremost, as agents and trustees for the company in all aspects of their work, so that, for instance, no director might compete in a private capacity with any of the activities of the company, nor even use knowledge acquired by him in the course of his work for the company to make a private profit for himself. The extreme in this direction was the case of the directors of a mining company who took up rights in Canada which their company had resolved not to pursue, and were later held accountable to the company for the profit made.

In another direction, there is an overall trust to use the resources of the company strictly for the objects of the company. The best example of this trust and, regrettably, its occasional unpunished abuse, is when a board, with the best intentions in the world, attempts to put out of the reach of the company and a bidder some property the board believes is attracting the bidder, the object being to discourage the bid altogether. This manoeuvre might be for the ultimate good of the company, its staff, its business goodwill, and the shareholders, but it is vitiated by the inevitable fact that a secondary effect of the manoeuvre is to prolong the sitting board in office. There is, thus, a plain benefit to the board from the disposal of the company property, so that the whole transaction is voidable at the instance of the company.

A third example of the same strict trust has often been illustrated in the courts in the challenge to the preferential allocation of shares to certain classes of shareholders. The extreme example of this, perhaps, occurred when it was resolved by the board of one company to issue bonus shares of 'one-for-one', which was interpreted in practice as meaning one voting share for the holder of one voting share, and one non-voting share for the holder of one non-voting share. The courts held this wrong, for the terms of issue of the original non-voting shares were that they should be equal in all respects with the voting shares except only in the absence of their vote.

'Insider dealing'

In contrast, there was no duty on a director, until 1967, to refrain from dealing in the shares of his company with a view to making a personal profit on the strength of his knowledge of the company affairs as director. Under the 1967 Companies Act, however, dealing in options of his group is now forbidden, and all dealings in shares must be disclosed to shareholders. Even so, there is no duty to account either to the company or the shareholders for profits made, but it is obviously hoped by those sponsoring these clauses in the 1967 Act that if profits are, in fact, made by the use of confidential knowledge (and it is difficult enough to stop it), then these will be shamed into modesty.

The director as employer

Strictly speaking, the company director is not the employer of any of the persons who work under him. Normally, the director is an employee of the company, and so are all those who work under him in the service of the company. It was vividly illustrated in the Boulting Brothers' case (when two company directors were faced with a demand by a trade union for back payments of union dues on the footing that they were still members of the union), that a man may be both employer and employee at the same time. A school headmaster is a good example of this, and so, for most practical purposes, is the foreman of a gang. Further than this, the line between employer and employee is by no means clearly drawn, even after allowing for the fact that a man may sit on both sides of the line without any great practical discomfort.

In the limited company, however, the basic fact is that all subordinate employees of the company are appointed (and if necessary sacked as well) by the board, or those given authority to do so by the board. Those responsibilities of the employer which fall upon the company are, in practice, discharged by the board, or the subordinates to whom they delegate their authority, and if the board fail in their duties, direct or indirect, they will suffer, even though it is the company that is initially summoned before the court or sued for damages by an employee.

The duties are most clearly illustrated in the liability for accidents. There is a duty imposed upon every 'occupier' of a factory under the Factories Acts to comply with certain positive duties, such as the fencing of all dangerous machinery. If the machinery is not fenced, then the occupier of the premises is liable to a fine should the Factories Inspector call in and spot the offence. In the case of a limited company occupier, the fine is imposed upon the company.

If there is an accident at a machine, and this is due to the failure to fence, then the employee sues the company employer; anything that is to be said in defence may be urged by the director or, more likely, by the foreman on the factory floor. Damages are given against the company employer, but reduced if the injured man was also, in part, responsible for the accident.

Common Law duties

Similarly, there is a number of rather more vague duties owed by every employer to the men he employs. They used to be listed broadly as four in number: to provide safe premises; to devise and ensure that a safe system of work was operated; to pay the agreed remuneration; and to indemnify the employee from any consequences of obeying the employer's instructions.

If every employer were to fulfil those four basic, and largely commonsense requirements, the accident rate in industry would be dramatically lowered. (It would not, however, disappear altogether, because of the foolishness of many employees who contribute, often enough, the greater part of the carelessness that causes an accident.)

Building Regulations, Shops Offices and Railway Premises Acts, and a large number of other general duties, connected for the most part with accident prevention, health, and welfare, also impose onerous duties upon the employer. In all these the director himself bears the ultimate responsibility for breach and infringement of the law. In the larger companies, of course, there are safety officers, welfare officers, and personnel training officers who have made these branches of the law their own special study. If they fail in their duties, however, it is still the company employer that pays, and the director who takes the primary responsibility: duties imposed upon the employer by law cannot usually be delegated to a specialist in order to relieve the employer from liability in the courts.

It follows from this that the director must bear primary responsibility for a number of matters in safety, health, and welfare, whether he has been trained in them or not, as soon as he is appointed to his position in the company, and even if there are specialists working under him on these matters, he must still familiarize himself with at least some of the duties of the office of these men, for he bears responsibility for their mistakes.

As a start, how many directors know the necessary contents of a first-aid box and whether it is required in a room in which only one shorthand typist works? In what circumstances is a thermometer required to be exhibited in a room where people are employed, and is any temperature prescribed for such a room? What is the employer required to do by law if one person in the room complains that the temperature is, say, only 42°F?

(Organizations exist to help employers tackle such questions as these. The Industrial Welfare Society is one.)

Hire and fire

Most of the other aspects of employment are fairly plain sailing. Most people get to know, while still working below boardroom level, what the proper notice is to give to a clerk, a typist, or a factory general manager. Pay during sickness is often a rather tricky matter, for an employee is entitled to full pay while sick for any length of absence until he is dismissed from his job—a step few employers take during illness. The alternative is to insert a term in the contract of engagement that full pay will be given for a limited period only, followed by half pay for a certain period, after which, in default of a return to work within that period, the employment is regarded as terminated. Anything less specific leaves the way open for serious misunderstandings and bitterness, however much to blame the employee may have been in his conduct.

Pension rights and welfare schemes will, of course, be worked out in co-operation with professional advice, and if there are misunderstandings here, the responsibility will not normally be that of the director; nor will his company be left to sort out the misunderstanding alone.

Employees abroad

There are two classes of employees overseas: those appointed in the home country and sent out, with or without families, for limited periods; and those appointed abroad in the name of the employing organization in this country. (Those resident abroad who are employed locally by the agent in his own name, or by a locally formed subsidiary company, are not normally the responsibility of the Head Office at all.)

23

There is no particular legal difficulty over the employment contracts of those engaged in this country and sent abroad, for their contracts continue to be governed by English law. If there are difficulties in their method of payment, these can usually be sorted out quite effectively by the simple method of making pay available in this country for savings, tax, and the use of families, leaving the employee to draw abroad what he requires for his own use in local currency. (If he is lent to an associated organization abroad there may be difficulties in the remittance of his pay for certain purposes, and these should be worked out in advance before the arrangement for the loan is concluded.)

The engagement of employees and the appointment of agents abroad is, in contrast, becoming a problem of increasing rather than of diminishing complexity. The contract is almost necessarily subject to the law of the place where the employee is engaged. It would hardly be fair to him to expect otherwise, and in any event the law of his country might override any other provisions in the contract. Other countries have their own health and welfare schemes, and this means that there may be compulsory deductions from pay, and compulsory benefits for the employee, which may greatly increase the budgeted cost of his employment.

Local law may, once again, demand certain amenities in the office or other place of work, although it is unlikely to go so far as a thermometer under the constant view of the staff. There may well be generous holiday requirements, however, as well as the usual highly inconvenient local festivals and public holidays. Whether office parties will be expected of an English employer is a minor question, but there will certainly be different ideas on hours of work and punctuality, from the hour earlier start expected of the manager in Germany, to the half-an-hour late start which is the matter-of-course opening of the working day in the summer in Madrid.

Most important of all, perhaps, is the requirement of long notice to terminate an engagement, whether of employee or agent, in some continental countries; and stranger still to English ears at present, the possibility of appeal against dismissal which some employees abroad are able to urge in the local tribunals or courts.

No one opening a small office abroad expects to plough through a manual of commercial law in the idiom of the legal system of the country chosen for expansion. Nor will it necessarily pay to consult a local lawyer, either at length before opening an office, or as each fresh problem in staff relations arises. Some prudent enquiries on local law and customs ought to be made, however, whether from a trade delegation or legation in this country, or of a local organization in the place where the office is intended to be established. Half the battle in a conflict of laws is to know where the problems are likely to arise.

The directors as officers

The Chairman is, in practice, normally the most important member of the board of directors, elected by the other board members to an office which bears primary responsibility for all the major decisions of the board of the company. He is paid a salary accordingly. In law, in contrast, there is little to note on his personal position as a permanent official, beyond the separate treatment for disclosure of his salary required by the 1967 Act. Instead, most of the law on the company chairman is concerned with his function at meetings from which the office and his name derive.

Every meeting requires a chairman, because it is desirable that there should be someone, and only one person, to thump the table when things look like getting out of hand. The duties of the chairman of a meeting are, in fact, a little wider than this, though they can be stated quite shortly: it is his duty to see that the meeting works through the agenda; that proceedings are conducted in an orderly fashion; and that the sense and sentiments of the persons present is allowed expression by speech and vote.

The company or the board usually elect a chairman as a permanent officer, and it is he who takes the chair at a meeting of the board or the members, but if he is not present, then all the powers of chairman at any particular meeting devolve upon that person who takes the chair at that particular meeting. If no member of the board, for instance, is present at a company meeting, then the shareholders may elect one of their number to take the chair, and he will exercise all the functions of chairman—except, of course, any exercisable, in accordance with the company Articles, by one particular paid official only.

Conduct of meetings

The conduct of the chairman may vary as widely as his character and the reasons for which he has been chosen for that office. In an expanding company, built up from small beginnings by one man with drive, it will normally be that one man who himself assumes, or is elected to the chair. He will, by his own presence alone, virtually make meetings of the board or even the company, deriving support from his colleagues by the force of his character or the voting control he ultimately exercises.

At the other extreme, the diplomatist will be elected to the larger company, in which a number of outside directors working part-time on the board will respect only a chairman of absolute integrity and good manners.

Not many chairmen are closely acquainted with all the nice points of law and procedure that may possibly arise at a company meeting, preferring usually to rely upon the secretary with his little book. There is one important point of law, however, with which all must be familiar, and that is their own right to vote.

The casting vote

Many chairmen, imitating the best example of the great debating chambers, prefer not to vote with others on any issue, but to abide by the decisions of the meeting whether they seem wise or not. When the votes are equally divided, then those present look to the chairman to exercise his vote, as a casting vote, and, by convention, the chairman is expected to vote in the way that preserves the state of affairs as it is, or in other words to vote against change.

Not every chairman is content to assume this role. What is more, it is strictly an incorrect use of the vote. The chairman is a member of the meeting, and if he is to vote at all, he should vote when everyone else votes. Then, if there is equality of votes, this produces a deadlock, and the motion is not decided. In order to avoid this situation, the chairman is given, by the rules of some companies and some meetings, a casting vote, which is, in fact, a second vote. It is this vote he is expected to cast against change.

At the same time, two votes for one man, and this one the man who is supposed to ensure fairness and impartiality in his conduct of the meeting, hardly accords with good sense or good manners, and there is much to be said for the deferment of his own vote by the chairman so that he, in effect, uses only one vote to ensure the carrying or defeat of a motion, which is cast on the express or implied invitation of those who cannot otherwise decide the point.

In small companies, the vote can become of critical importance where there are differences between members with large shareholdings. In one company, where two associates held 50 per cent of the shares each, both being on the board, one of the two passed a small shareholding to a third person. In the absence of the 50 per cent shareholder, the two elected the larger shareholder to the chairmanship, so that on his return the 50 per cent shareholder found himself outvoted on every issue. His 50 per cent shareholding was equalled by the combined votes of the other two, and the chairman carried the day every time with his casting vote, as permitted by the Articles. Even on appeal to the courts there was little that could be done.

The managing director

The managing director's position in a company may vary between that of a driving force at the top (for he may be chairman as well) and, at the other extreme, a promoted executive who has managed to work his way into the boardroom from humble beginnings by sheer hard work and brilliance. It depends very much upon his own character and abilities, as well as upon the terms of his appointment and the size of the company, whether he makes of himself the dominant authority, or a working manager slightly out of his depth in matters of long-term policy.

He may be the liaison officer between the gentleman at the top and the executives in the offices and on the factory floor, but he may still become the leader of both sets of his colleagues even if he did not start that way as the founder and boss of his own business. There is no law on what a managing director should do or should be: he is, in law, merely a servant and an officer of the company—another member of the board.

Dual capacity

What is rather interesting about his position in law is that he has strictly two capacities and two different sets of rights at the same time. As manager of the company he is directly under the control of his colleagues on the board: to ensure the efficient conduct of the business of the company they must be able to remove him without notice, on paying the usual damages. Occasions justifying this extreme step might, for instance, be serious misconduct likely to harm the interests of the company (when damages might not be payable to him at all); or serious disagreement with the board such as to bring deadlock in the company business. If the board cannot dismiss the manager either by the terms of his appointment or by reliance upon their ordinary right as employers to bar a man summarily from the business premises, then the company cannot be managed efficiently, or come to that, cannot be directed from the board at all.

On the other hand, members of the board cannot dismiss each other. They may be dismissed without notice, in effect, by an ordinary general meeting of the company, in which case they may claim salary or damages for breach of contract, but there is no power in a majority of members of the board to dismiss a fellow-member, however obstructive he may be or however badly he may be damaging the interests of the company.

There is, thus, always the theoretical possibility with a managing director that he may be dismissed from his position as manager, and yet by virtue of a separate appointment to the board (which is frequently made explicitly in his contract of engagement) he may insist on remaining as a director, and attending board meetings to the embarrassment of his colleagues. The situation seems, at first sight, a little far-fetched, but it did in fact once occur, and led to an application in the courts. The point is raised here not so much for the probability that it may arise again, but in order that the terms of appointment of managing directors may be considered in the light of this dual capacity.

In the larger company, obviously, resignation is the more dignified course when there are disagreements (subject to any considerations of damages for breach of contract if the director prefers dismissal). In the smaller companies, however, the quarrel is often between persons rather than over the management and direction of the company; and the stakes are livelihoods and comparatively large shareholdings, rather than policies and prestige.

The part-time director

Part-time directors are usually appointed for the special skills, knowledge, or connections they have that, it is thought, may be useful to the company. A manufacturing company might well take on to its board: a person acquainted with political and economic problems in its country of supply; a banker, an economist, and a marketing expert in its country of production; and a member of an exporting concern familiar with conditions in areas in which it hoped to expand sales overseas. Their presence at a board meeting only once or twice a year might prove invaluable.

The real worth of such members of the board lies, therefore, not in their direct assistance at a board meeting by voting on an internal company matter, but rather in the information they feel able to give, and the advice that flows from their special interests and knowledge in one limited sphere. For them, the constant problem, therefore, is how far they may use the knowledge acquired in the discharge of another office, usually an office of trust and confidence, to assist in the problems of the company.

Information gained by a director from one office, if confidential, should neither be communicated nor even used in any other office. On the other hand, any information that is not acquired in confidence, but arises from general decisions taken at meetings for the future policy of a company, may be used in a general sense.

A director who knows that his company will be switching to synthetic rubber instead of the natural product, because of some new advantages discovered in the use of synthetic rubber, or because of the discovery that some new substance may be added to give synthetic rubber a novel advantage, may well warn a company producing natural rubber that the market might be shrinking in the future, because that warning could be based on any one of a number of reasons; but he could not, of course, warn the board of a rival producer of synthetic rubber that it was about to lose markets to an improved synthetic product. The differences are subtle, and depend upon the type of information, the sense in which it is divulged, the purpose for which it is given or acquired, and the interests of those to whom it is given and those whom the information concerns.

In the courts, it has been made fairly clear that information given in strict confidence may not be divulged merely because it could be obtained without breach of confidence from another source. The only safe test appears to be one of conscience: if those from whom the information was acquired were present in the meeting at which it might be divulged, would they regard the person imparting the information as abusing his trust?

Financial interests

A director may have a financial interest in the company in three different ways: as an employee, taking a salary, and perhaps commission as well, dependent upon profits, plus, probably, certain collateral advantages, generally referred to collectively as perquisites. Next, the director may have a stake in his company or group as an

28

investor, or at any rate as a holder of shares. Third, the director may have contractual arrangements with his company, as for example when he owns land which the company occupies for its business purposes, or when he is a member of a partnership that renders professional services to his company, or a director or even only a shareholder of another company that has trading contracts or financing arrangements.

A director is expected to take a stake in the company through qualification shares, but he is the subject of adverse comment if he increases that stake in anticipation of good times, and decreases it as bad times approach, as any prudent investor would normally try to do. Again, while he must, as an officer of the company, do his best to obtain supplies on the best terms available for the company business, he is at once brought under suspicion if he, personally, forms another company to make sure that supplies will be available. The explanation lies, of course, in that much can be done in an underhand way in such double situations. The director will, therefore, normally be above suspicion if he merely discloses to his colleagues, or shareholders, what he has done and what he is doing.

Two further duties are imposed upon him by statute. In addition to disclosure, he must refrain from voting on matters in which he has an interest. In another direction, as shareholder, (or in this case speculator) he must refrain from dealing in options for the shares of his company or group (Section 25 of the Companies Act 1967). Option and share dealings are the easiest subject and may be treated first.

Option and share dealings

No director may deal in options of the shares or debentures of his company or group. This prohibition does not extend to allotment letters or convertible debentures. The prohibition covers the wives, and children under twenty-one, as well as nominees of directors, so that for the whole effect of the prohibition Sections 25 and 30 of the Act must be read together. There appears to be no relief in the Act for those directors who have no control over the actions of their wives or children.

Dealings in shares are covered by Sections 27, 28, and 29 of the same Act, the Companies Act 1967. Under these sections there is a duty on a director to notify the company not only of his holdings of shares, but of the holdings of his wife, and children under twenty-one, and of his entering into a contract to buy or sell shares (which covers dealings on the Stock Exchange, which are not recorded in the books of the company because they are cancelled in the same account).

All such holdings and contracts with the shares of the company or its holding company or subsidiary must be notified to the company within fourteen days, and must then be recorded in a register kept by the company at the registered office, open to inspection without charge to members, and to other persons at a shilling a time. The section also covers the rights of directors to subscribe for shares of the companies.

Interests in trust and joint holdings are not excused.

Interests under service contracts

More public attention has been given to the disadvantages to a company from long-term contracts than to collateral advantages, although the question of outsize commission has hit the headlines of the press on occasions. The emphasis on the Companies Act is therefore upon disclosure of service contracts for fixed periods, without means of premature termination, rather than upon the exact terms. It is, therefore, only those service contracts that cannot be terminated within a year that must be disclosed to members. Copies must be kept available at (normally) the registered office.

Apart from this, there is the additional safeguard, as far as investors and the public are concerned, against undisclosed high salaries in the requirement that salaries should be disclosed in the accounts in groups of £2,500 and upwards, with the Chairman's, or the highest paid officer's, set out separately. This does not apply to unquoted companies. In practice, the requirement of disclosure of service contracts to members of the company has ensured press publicity for the individual salaries of the top men of many large public companies.

Retirement and removal

Directors do not just go on and on. At one time they did, and there are some who think that they still should, but the Companies Act has prescribed an age limit, subject to re-election, and the modern pace of events means that the position of most members of the board is brought up forcibly for reconsideration very much more often than formerly.

There are exceptions. A private company which had recently 'gone public' was found to have two directors on its books with contracts intended to last the working life of the two men—a fixed term contract at a certain salary, in short, without provision for earlier termination, until the age of sixty-five.

Even from the point of view of the director, such security of employment is by no means an unmixed blessing. The man who negotiates such a contract, as a result, sees himself ensconced in the position he has built up for himself in his business through half a lifetime of struggle: if anyone should try to dismiss him, for good reason or bad, the cost for them will be a number of years' salary.

He might reflect, however, that a long-term promise of service may also prove a tie to him. Conditions change rapidly, and whether or not control passes to others, it is a burdensome obligation to bind oneself to work, through good times and bad, in the same material interest, forsaking all others. If he really is sure of his competence to manage the business he has built up, is it not likely that he would be competent to manage another and greater enterprise, for which the rewards would be correspondingly larger?

The courts will not, because they cannot, oblige a man to honour a contract of personal services, and they have seldom been asked to give damages against any employee, from office boy to director, who has refused to carry out his duties at work. Nevertheless, to break an engagement for a specified number of years leaving a rudderless (or should it be pilotless?) company to shift for itself, would leave the director open to a very large claim for lost profits from the company employer, if those who took over thought it in their interests to go to court.

Again, it is unlikely that a man who leaves one position in breach of contract to start work in another will find himself engaged to the best of new employers. Quite incidentally, he will also leave the new employer open to a claim at law for 'inducing breach of contract' if the new employer knew of the life-long engagement and knowingly offered more tempting terms to the director. In present conditions of company disclosure no new employer could, with much conviction, plead ignorance of the terms of a director's contract.

Position of the company

From the point of view of a company employer, the life-long engagement of a director, for whatever historical reasons, will generally carry more decided disadvantages than advantages. Continuity of service at board level is, certainly, assured, at a salary level that will not be subject to undue pressure in times of inflation or greatly increased profits. Additionally, continuity of employment can be guaranteed to many other employees, because the long-term engagement of one director, with the prospect of heavy compensation for dismissal, makes the company a less attractive proposition for a bidder who has eyes on its assets. At the same time, the discouragement to a bidder is often strongly to the disadvantage of shareholders.

In bad times, a high salary for the board, irrespective of company ability to afford it, is bad for company, shareholders, and employees, and even in good times, it is not always wise to have a board of managers on fixed salaries, with little interest in taking or making more business as opportunity offers.

This reasoning may or may not have been behind those who secured the provisions for disclosure of directors' service contracts which now appear in Section 26 of the Companies Act 1967, but it may well have softened some of the opposition to the clause.

A significant omission from Section 26, which required the disclosure of contracts, is that of contracts that have less than twelve months to run or, to put it more precisely, can be terminated within twelve months without compensation. Subject to one small academic point, which is unlikely to be tested in the courts, this exception covers probably a fair majority of all serving directors.

Indefinite contracts

Service contracts for fixed periods are usually made with an eye to possible changed conditions, for comparatively short periods. This makes provision for earlier determination, at the option of one or both sides, unnecessary. Our peculiar tax system, which decrees that any payment made for earlier determination of such a contract shall be subject to income tax if specified in the original contract, operates against the inclusion of such clauses. A boardroom row followed by a dismissal in breach of contract leads to a settlement or award of damages by the court. These payments, in contrast to sums previously agreed in the contract, are deductible for tax purposes from the profits for of the company employer, but are normally received tax-free by the dismissed director.

In contrast, service contracts that are not for fixed periods are always subject to the condition, implied by law, that they may be terminated on either side by the giving of reasonable notice; otherwise, they would be necessarily contracts for life, and the law does not like life contracts.

What is reasonable notice is, as the lawyers say, a question of fact. It is not, however, an easy fact to ascertain. Six months would be regarded as the minimum for any director. Twenty or thirty years ago the cases were in favour of much longer notice for those in more important positions: a bank clerk was always entitled to three months, while the editor of a newspaper, who once claimed in the courts, was awarded twelve months' salary.

The length of notice accepted by others is evidence, but not always compelling evidence, of what is reasonable: for a man may be prepared to settle for much less than he is entitled to at law rather than attract the publicity of a court case in claiming against his employing company, since his chances of obtaining a new position after such publicity would be very low. Few cases are, in fact, taken to court, which means that any change under present conditions towards the acceptance of shorter notice has not been reflected in decided cases. Conversely, the pool of unemployed persons in the late 'forties and 'fifties is an argument for giving a man longer, rather than shorter, notice in which to seek an alternative position.

Dismissal

To sum up what has been implied if not expressed in the preceding pages, a director may be removed from his position by giving notice in accordance with the terms of his contract. If there is no provision for giving notice, then reasonable notice is implied, which will probably be not less than six nor more than twelve months.

No man has a right to 'work out his notice', as is sometimes said—and this means that any employer has the right to require a man to leave his position immediately, for good or bad reasons, provided only that he pays the salary that would have been earned during a period of notice. This sum must include any commission that might probably have been earned in the period, as well as compensation for loss of, for instance, private use of a company car or flat. It will, however, be reduced by the amount of income tax the dismissed person would have paid. The employer does not pay this notional tax deduction over to the Revenue, because it is not tax deducted from salary.

A full-time director may be dismissed by the company in general meeting by a simple majority vote of the shareholders. He is then entitled to compensation provided that he is actually 'dismissed' by a positive vote. If he should be so provoked by criticism that he tenders his resignation, and this is accepted, then he has voluntarily surrendered his rights to compensation. The dilemma of a director in this situation is the same as that for any other employee: the advantage of saying later, when applying for a new position, that a man has resigned, has to be set against the alternative very real benefits of a salary upon dismissal. Salary will perhaps keep a man and his family going immediately, but it may make for more difficulties in the long run.

Bid and board

There is one aspect of the retirement or removal of a director from his position that deserves special mention because of its particular delicacy and difficulty, and that is the question of continuity in employment of the board after a bid. Naturally, when a bidder has acquired control of a company, it is entirely up to him whether he retains the services of the board or terminates their contracts either by giving due notice or by paying compensation in lieu.

Modern bids have not, however, followed the former straight pattern of offer and acceptance from one outside source, the bidder making something of a guess at the assets of the company he is proposing to acquire from what information is made public in the normal course of the company accounts. Shareholders and boards have demanded a closer price for a bid acceptance, and it is now not uncommon for something like a bid auction to take place before control passes.

In these circumstances it is common practice either for a board to make estimates and give valuations of the worth of their own company, should the bid come without previous warning, or for some previous consultation to take place, possibly with a view to an uncontested merger, before the bidder changes his mind and makes an outright offer to all shareholders.

The ethics of such bids and auctions have been much discussed, and attempts to lay down a code have been only partially successful because of the considerable practical difficulty of attacking a *fait accompli* which itself sets a precedent. Again, new methods of bidding and conducting market transactions simultaneously are introduced with each large power struggle, and as fast as the tactics on one occasion are examined and deprecated, new bidders with new ideas appear on the scene.

The path is fairly clear, however, on one important point for directors. If they have had prior discussions with a potential bidder, then they may be expected to have raised the question of their own personal future. If the bidder indicates that he will in the new circumstances be making changes, then the present board are likely to be accused of concealing an interest if they know that the success of a bid will mean a fair amount of lump sum compensation for them upon the termination of their appointments. Conversely, if they have been assured of continuity in their appointments after the bid, they are again likely to be accused of concealing an interest in its success if they do not allow this fact to be known to the shareholders.

The third possibility, that their appointments may be terminated without compensation if the bid is successful, may be thought to be influencing their conduct if they are not able to recommend acceptance to other shareholders. There is still a fourth possibility, that they may lose their positions without compensation and yet still feel that the bid should be recommended, in which case it is only too obvious that they might gain more ready acceptance of their recommendation if they were to disclose the circumstances.

From all of which it becomes obvious that if the board knew, or can guess at, their own probable future after a successful bid, it is in some cases their duty to disclose what they know, and in all cases strongly advisable.

Reading list

BOOKS

The Company Director: His Functions, Powers & Duties, Alfred Read (Jordan & Sons, 1968)
The Director Looks at his Job, C. C. Brown and E. E. Smith (Columbia University Press, 1957)
The Board of Directors and Effective Management, H. Koontz (McGraw-Hill, 1967)
The Efficient Executive, Peter F. Drucker (Heinemann, 1967)
Management Principles: A Primer for Directors & Potential Directors, Walter Puckey (Hutchinson, 1962)
Managers and their Jobs, Rosemary Stewart (Macmillan, 1967)
The Great Organizers, Ernest Dale (McGraw-Hill, 1960)
The Professional Manager, D. McGregor (McGraw-Hill, 1967)

JOURNALS

'The Money-Spinners in the Boardroom', H. Stuart-Taylor (*The Director*, October 1967)
'Managers at the Top', Robert Heller and Geoffrey Foster (*Management Today*, January 1968)
'Characteristics of British Company Directors', Roger Betts (*Journal of Management Studies*, February 1967)

1.3 Key Functions of the Board

Hugh Parker

In no area of management are there wider variations in practice between companies than in the way different boards interpret and carry out their managerial, as distinct from their legal, role. The legal responsibilities of directors, both as individuals and collectively as boards, are on the whole clearly defined and well understood. But the functions of directors and boards as part of the management organization responsible for doing the things necessary to maintain the competitive strength and profitability of their company are on the whole much less clearly understood.

As a result, many boards fail either to recognize or to fulfil their managerial responsibilities. Many directors indeed seem to be concerned only with broad 'policy' matters, and feel little or no personal liability for the way the company is actually being managed. When the results of poor management inevitably appear, they are too often attributed by the board to unfavourable trading conditions or to the effects of Government action or to any number of other 'uncontrollable' factors.

The board of directors is legally accountable to its shareholders for the profitable management of their capital, but in many cases this accountability is not translated into effective pressure on the company's executive management to produce results. The failure by many boards to consider themselves directly responsible for how profitably their companies are being managed thus appears to be a root cause of the inadequate profit returns achieved by many companies under conditions of severe competition and pressure on profits.

It is the purpose of this section to examine this proposition more closely, to identify the reasons for it, and to discuss its implications both for the individual director and for the total board.

Evolution of the role and composition of boards*

The typical UK industrial company of today has been in existence for generations—often for more than a century—and has evolved from a small one-man or one-family business into a medium-sized or even quite large public company. In this process of growth the company will typically have experienced periods of great prosperity, interspersed by occasional periods of hard times and low profits. But taken over their whole history, the average record of the majority of companies surviving today has been one of profitable growth.

At some stage, the typical company will have gone public; the original family owners will, for one reason or another, have sold all or part of their equity to outside shareholders. By this action, of course, the board becomes accountable to a new and different group of owners who almost certainly will have different expectations from the company's management than the original owners may have had. This, in turn, implies a different role and set of responsibilities for the directors. But often these changed conditions appear to have been neither recognized nor acted on by the boards. The question is, why not?

Considering again the history of this hypothetical 'typical company' one finds that the original board, when the company was still a small private company, consisted of the founding father, some sons and other members of the family, and perhaps a trusted family solicitor, banker or friend or two. In successive generations the composition of the original family board may have been expanded to include a few more outsiders, but even these will have been unquestioningly loyal to the owners of the business who admitted them to the family club.

In the course of time a 'seat on the board' became recognized as the ultimate reward for a loyal employee for long and faithful service to the company. The emphasis was on the man's proven loyalty to the firm and to its owner-proprietors (the Germans even have a word for it—'Firmentreue'), which was the main reason for his election in the first place and the main guideline for his subsequent conduct as a director. Many boards finally consisted predominantly of men promoted from within the company, many of them also retaining executive or managerial positions within the company. This is the situation in so many public UK companies today that it is still probably more 'typical' than not.

One result of this evolutionary process in the composition of boardrooms is that many boards today are almost incapable of fulfilling their basic legal function to guard the shareholders' and the company's long-term interest, and to take prompt

* This specifically refers to the boards of public industrial companies in the United Kingdom.

steps to correct unsatisfactory management performance when this leads to unacceptable profit results.

The reason for this is obvious: if all or a majority of its directors are also the acting managers of a company, it is unrealistic to expect them to be objectively critical of the company's profit performance, which is, after all, a direct reflection of their own personal performance as managers. And it is even more unrealistic to expect a board consisting largely of executive managers to take the tough remedial action that may be necessary to correct bad performance, especially if this should involve the replacement of one or more key managers, i.e., themselves.

It is often said that executive directors have only to recognize that they 'wear two hats' and to act independently in each role. Many conscientious directors do indeed try to act correctly in each of their dual capacities, and a few succeed; but many more do not. Their dilemma is highlighted in the following passage:

> 'It is for managers to manage and for directors to direct. A director should never forget that he is put on the board by the shareholders to see that the company's business is operated at its maximum efficiency and yields an adequate return for the shareholders. The directors engage the managers—and the managers engage the workers—for the same end.'

But if all or most of the directors are also the managers, '*quis custodiet custodes ipsos?*'. The resolution of this dilemma hinges, first, on the issue of what managerial functions should properly be assumed by the board, both collectively and as individual directors, and second, on how boards should be constituted so that they can properly perform these functions.

Managerial functions of the board

There are essentially five managerial functions that a board must perform in fulfilling its broad legal responsibility to safeguard the shareholders' and company's long-term interests. As will be clear, some of these fall partly or entirely under the rather vague heading of 'policy making'. But all impinge directly on and are directly involved in some degree with the day-to-day functions of executive management. These five basic board functions are:

1. To establish the longer term objectives of the company, and the basic strategies by which these are to be attained.
2. To define the specific policies (in respect of such things as finance, personnel, marketing and the like) that are to be followed in implementing the company's strategies.
3. To decide the organizational structure of the company's management, and to make appointments of individuals to fill key positions in it.

4. To develop management planning, information, and control systems appropriate to the organizational structure of the company, and to use these systems effectively to ensure control by the board at all times over the results produced by the executive management.
5. To take decisions on such matters that the Articles of Association may reserve to the board (e.g., payment of dividends, disposal of corporate assets, appointments to the board), or that the board in its own discretion decides not to delegate (e.g., capital projects above a certain amount, diversification into a new business).

These are the five key functions of every board, although few can claim to perform all of them well. (It would, however, be easy to draw up a long list of things that are done by many boards which they should never do at all.) But let us consider these functions of the board more closely.

Setting corporate objectives and strategies
In the highly competitive world conditions of today it is essential for every company to have clearly defined objectives for its longer term growth and return on capital, and clear strategies for achieving them. And it is a basic responsibility of the board, which it cannot delegate or abdicate, to decide what these corporate objectives and strategies should be.

There are two main reasons why such objectives are essential. First, to provide an agreed frame of reference within which the board itself can make sound decisions. And second, to provide a basis for organizing the management structure of the company and for developing an appropriate management planning and control system, including the setting of standards of performance for executive managers down the line.

While there is a good deal of talk currently about 'management by objectives' there is no precise definition of what is meant by 'long-range corporate objectives'. They can be stated very specifically, e.g., 'to double company sales in five years with increasing earnings per share', or, in very broad terms, e.g., 'to become a world leader in the international chemicals industry'. Experience tends to show that the more specific and quantifiable the board's statement of objective is, the more purposeful and effective will be the management planning and control processes that are based on them.

There is also considerable debate about how such corporate objectives should be set. The two main schools of thought on this question are, on the one hand, that corporate objectives should be set by the board or by the chairman, arbitrarily if necessary, and, on the other hand, that they are merely the summation of the objectives set by divisional or subsidiary company managers down the line. Here again, experience suggests that the former approach produces more demanding targets that really 'stretch' the capabilities of down-the-line managers, and thus is more likely to get the maximum profit return on the company's total assets.

38

Because the financial, human, and other resources of any company are always limited, it is essential that they be deployed to optimum effect. There is always more than one way to achieve an objective, and the board must evaluate all reasonable alternatives in deciding the best strategy in any given set of circumstances. This is the meaning of 'strategy' in this context.

For example, a growth objective of 15 per cent per year (i.e., doubling in five years) can be achieved by several different strategies: by internal growth, by acquisition, by merger, or by some combination of all of these. Again, a company can adopt a strategy of growth in its own industry, or of growth through diversification. But which of these will be the most advantageous for the company is a vital board decision, and will, of course, depend on a wide range of factors.

The key point is that unless the board systematically examines all the possible alternatives, and unless it collects and analyses all the relevant facts before reaching a decision, the company will drift into whichever course seems to be the most expedient at the time. And this course will not necessarily ensure the most profitable use of the company's limited resources.

Defining corporate policies

This second function of the board, to define the company's basic policies, is probably one that most boards think they do fairly well. One reason for this feeling may be the rather vague definition of what is meant by 'policy making'. In its loosest sense, *any* board decision can be represented as a 'policy' decision. But in its stricter sense a policy decision on a particular issue is, or should be, a disciplined board process that results in a general guideline that can be applied to other similar issues in the future. In this sense, a policy is a statement of general principles and specific rules to be used as guidelines for, and constraints on, future decisions and actions of management at all levels of the organization.

By this definition, most board policy decisions tend to be one-off rulings on specific issues. When similar issues arise in the future, the board will have to consider and decide on each issue again and again. This *ad hoc* way of making policy decisions has a number of serious disadvantages, which moreover increase dramatically as the company grows larger.

First, this method obviously wastes a lot of the board's time. It is a more efficient use of its time if the board considers current issues not only on their own merits but also as precedents or guidelines for the future. Having made a policy decision once, similar issues can in future often be decided by line managers without further reference to the board, since a known precedent exists as a guideline.

Second, and even more important, the absence of clearly defined policy guidelines makes delegation of responsibility and authority virtually impossible, especially in large companies. In small organizations, daily contact and communication between board members and line management is usually quite close. Therefore, little formal definition of company policy is necessary since it is generally understood. But as companies get larger this no longer applies. In such companies, if the board wish to adopt the organizational concepts of delegation and 'management by exception' they must codify and promulgate more formally the basic policies that line managers are expected to know and follow in day-to-day decisions.

Maintaining the management organization

From time to time, boards realize that the organizational structures of their companies are no longer suited to their present or future needs. This often leads to a thorough reorganization which, in a large company, can be a major undertaking that may divert the attention of management for months or even years.

One reason why such complete reorganizations are often necessary is the failure of boards to review the organizations of their companies regularly. Most industries and companies are today in an almost constant state of change. One of the first responsibilities of the board is to ensure that the company is responsive to the changes in its competitive environment, and that its long-term strategy and annual plans reflect these changes. To do this effectively, however, adjustments must often be made to the management organization of the company. These adjustments are broadly of two kinds: in terms of structure, and in terms of people.

Structural changes have to do with the re-assignment of responsibilities and authorities, and the re-alignment of working relationships. In other words, these are the kinds of changes that are reflected in changed organization charts and position descriptions, and are usually fairly straightforward—although they can also be quite meaningless if they are confined to changes on paper only.

Changes in the assignments of people are a different matter. Because they affect the status and remuneration of individuals within the company structure, they are usually difficult to make and can have adverse effects on morale. For these reasons such decisions are sometimes avoided or delayed by boards until the cumulative defects of the organization become so glaring that drastic action is finally precipitated by some crisis in the affairs of the company.

To avoid such major reorganizations, both in structural and people terms, boards should have the management organization under more or less constant review. Comparatively minor re-alignments to the structure and re-assignments of people as a normal and continuing process of change are less disruptive to the enterprise than a major upheaval every five or ten years.

Another extremely important function of the board in the organizational context is to ensure that promising younger managers of high potential are identified early enough in their careers so that they are promoted and rewarded on their merits. Competent managers are the scarcest resource of all, and probably more companies are held back by this constraint than by any other. No board, therefore, can risk frustrating, and so perhaps losing, their best young men through lack of timely recognition.

Maintaining effective planning information and control systems

A common deficiency in many large companies today is the lack of an effective system of management planning, information, and control. As a result of this, many boards simply do not know enough about the present and past actions of their executive managements—let alone about their future intentions—to have effective control over their companies' results. Considering the legal liabilities of boards, this is an extremely serious deficiency.

This is not to say, of course, that boards have no information or control at all. Often they get great quantities of information, but too often it is the wrong kind of information presented in the wrong form, and at the wrong time, i.e., too late to be useful for control.

The key to effective control lies in the word 'planning'—one of the most misused and misunderstood words in current management usage. This is not the place for a detailed discussion of what planning is and how it is done. But in its essence, 'planning' in the management sense consists of four main parts.

First, a quantified statement of an objective or set of objectives to be achieved by a company, a subsidiary, a division, a department, or whatever organizational unit is involved. Second, a fact-based statement of all feasible alternative ways of achieving the stated objective, the pros and cons of each, and the specific course finally selected. Third, a statement of all the action steps necessary to implement the selected course, with clear assignments of individual responsibility for carrying out, and target dates for completion of, each step. And fourth, a statement of the financial implications of the whole action programme, i.e., a budget to show the expected revenue, capital, cash flow, and profit results of the whole plan.

These are the four main elements that constitute a basic 'management plan'. Typically, however, boards seldom get to see and review their company's management plan in any detail, and quite often they do not see one at all, for the simple reason that none exists. What they commonly do get to see, and approve, are budgets in one form or another, but unless these budgets are supported by all the other elements of a plan, they can be almost meaningless as a basis for effective control.

Effective control, by the board, of a company's results thus depends on three factors: (1) adequate knowledge in advance and in specific terms of what management proposes to do, i.e., its plan, and an opportunity to review and challenge this plan in detail before it is put into effect; (2) timely and accurate information on management's progress in carrying out its plan, and the actual results that are being achieved compared with planned results; and (3) the will and ability to challenge deviations from the plan, to find out what action management proposes to get the

3

plan back on course and, if necessary, to intervene if management does not seem capable of doing so.

This is an abbreviated and simplified description of what is meant by an 'effective management planning, information and control system'. Some companies have parts of such a system (i.e., sales and capital budgets) but very few have fully developed such an integrated system as summarized here. One of the most important functions of the board is therefore to ensure that such a system is developed and put into effect, and thereafter that it is used as an instrument of effective control.

Making major decisions

The fifth function of the board involves making decisions that they either cannot legally, or do not wish, to delegate. On the whole, this function is better understood and more consistently performed than the preceding four, probably because the decision-making authorities of the boards have been pretty well established through many years of practice. This does not mean, however, that even this decision-making role is necessarily always well performed. Many boards fall short of good practice in two specific ways.

First, even though a board may intend to delegate certain operating decisions to executives and managers down the line, they often do not do so in practice. Many boards are in the habit of interesting and involving themselves in things that are the proper concern of their subordinate managers—with bad effects on the performance of both. The main reasons for this are, usually, lack of definition of organizational limits of authority, lack of an effective information and control system to permit the board to practise 'delegation without abdication', and lack of confidence in the senior line managers.

A second major weakness in the decision-making performance of many boards is a tendency to make important decisions on totally inadequate information, again for several reasons. First, because no clearly thought-through company objectives, strategies, plans or policies exist to provide a framework within which informed decisions can be made. Second, because adequate staff is lacking to do the research and analysis that is essential for reaching sound decisions. Finally, many boards are, by their make-up, so operations-oriented that they do not have the time or the inclination to keep themselves abreast of the technological, economic, political, and other external factors that today have such an important bearing on virtually all major corporate decisions.

To improve their decision-making performance many boards thus need to define more clearly just which decisions they should take themselves and which to delegate, and then discipline themselves to act accordingly. And, finally, they should take steps to improve the quality of data on which these board-level decisions will be based.

42

Board structure and composition

Let us now consider how boards themselves should be organized to ensure that they are capable of fulfilling their basic managerial functions. Here it must be said that there is little agreement or consistency of practice among companies on what constitutes the 'optimum' boardroom structure. One reason for this is undoubtedly the wide variations in the traditions, business philosophies, and competitive environments of different companies. Major differences in each of these factors exist between, say, a bank, a manufacturing company, and an insurance company; and significant differences will even be found between companies in the same category.

There are, basically, four questions that need to be asked concerning the structure of a board:

1. How large should it be in its total number of members?
2. What ratio of directors should be inside (or executive) members, and how many should be outside (or non-executive) members?
3. What should be the relationships between individual directors and the line managers of the company?
4. What specific responsibilities should be assigned to individual directors?

Size of the board

Clearly, the board must be big enough to do its job. But this, in turn, depends on so many variables—the size and complexity of the company, its competitive environment, the capacity of individual board members, and so on—that no fixed number can be laid down.

On the other hand, some guidelines have evolved from the practical experience of companies in a wide variety of industries and businesses. There is, of course, some correlation between the size of the organization and the size of the board. Analysis of a random sample of 100 UK manufacturing companies showed that more than 90 per cent of these companies fell within the following ranges of board size:

	Total Board Members		
	Min	Max	Avge
Small (less than £10 million total assets)	3	10	6
Medium (£10 to £100 million)	7	14	11
Large (more than £100 million)	10	22	15

Balance of the board

Even more important than the question of absolute board size, though related to it, is the question of balance in board membership, which must be considered under several different kinds of balance: between executive and non-executive directors; by age and tenure; by special knowledge or areas of interest; between full-time and part-time members; and so forth.

Here again, variations in need and practice between different companies and between different kinds of business are so wide as to make any formula for establishing the best balance quite unrealistic. In addition, there are the practical limitations of availability; few companies can expect to attract as directors all the candidates they might ideally like.

One significant trend that has been going on for some years in the USA, and now increasingly seen in the UK, especially in larger companies, is toward a higher ratio of outside non-executive directors. Among these companies there also seems to be a tendency to appoint outside directors with specially relevant experience or qualifications, rather than on the strength of titles, family connections, or social distinction.

In my opinion it is virtually essential for a board to have a substantial proportion of non-executive members, that is, of the order of one-third to one-half, and in some circumstances even more, if it is to perform effectively its basic function of objectively guiding the affairs of the company in the best interests of its shareholders. A board that consists entirely of executive members, i.e., of men who bear full-time executive responsibilities within the company, is strictly speaking not a board at all, but really a management committee.

The one clear point that can be made on this matter of board balance is that it is an important factor for all boards to keep in mind, and that it should ultimately be related to the specific needs of each company.

Relationship between directors and managers

In virtually all American companies it is common practice for the board to delegate responsibility and authority for implementing its will to a chief executive officer—typically bearing the title of President or Executive Vice President. This is indeed accepted as standard practice to such an extent that in one recent American book on the subject of boards it is assumed, as a matter of course, that there is a single chief executive officer to whom and through whom the board can delegate substantial executive authority to the line management organization.

Where such a single chief executive officer exists, the basic relationship between the board as a whole and the line management is fairly straightforward. The chief executive officer (in the UK he would typically have the title of Managing Director) is accountable to the board, through the Chairman, for carrying out the responsibilities delegated to him, i.e., for implementing corporate plans, policies, and programmes approved by the board, and for achieving agreed profit and growth results.

In many UK companies, however, there is no single chief executive. This function may be divided among several individuals (e.g., two or more deputy chairmen or joint managing directors); it may be combined with the role of, and per-

44

formed by the same individual as, the chairman; or it may be divided among all the executive directors who, thus, collectively act as a so-called 'multiple chief executive'.

In all such companies where the direct line of command between the board and its line management is divided and unclear, serious problems are bound to arise sooner or later, usually when the company is under competitive pressure or in a profit squeeze. (When times are easy and things are going well, almost any form of organization will work.)

The main problem arising in such companies is the anomaly of several individuals of equal status (directors), each responsible for some part of the business, being collectively responsible for the total corporate results and accountable for these results to a group (the whole board) of which they are themselves members. This situation is almost guaranteed to make effective delegation and control a practical impossibility.

Where the position of a single managing director does exist, relationships between him and the board as a whole, and between individual line managers and individual directors, can be quite easily defined. The basic principle here is that all the line managers subordinate to the managing director are directly accountable to him, and he, in turn, is wholly accountable to his chairman and board for the total results achieved by his management team.

This clear-cut line relationship does not, of course, rule out advisory or functional relationships between individual directors and down-the-line managers, so long as these do not erode the line authority of the managing director.

Specific responsibilities of individual directors

By definition, an executive director is responsible for some corporate function (e.g., finance or personnel) or operating unit (e.g., a subsidiary or division). The question of what specific responsibilities should be assigned to directors therefore really arises only in connection with non-executive directors.

In many companies the question is answered, or side-stepped, by not making any formal assignments of responsibility to non-executive directors. But usually in such cases it is tacitly understood that individual directors will interest themselves in, and offer their views on, matters that fall within their own personal experience or sphere of competence. Thus, a banker will be recognized as the board's main authority on financial matters, an accountant on accounting matters, a scientist on research, and so on.

There is, however, an increasing trend, as company affairs become more international and complex, to assign to both executive and non-executive directors more formal responsibility for one or more 'spheres of special interest' that may be of special profit importance to the company. Thus, for example, an oil company depending heavily on the Middle East for its supply of crude oil may well assign to one director the formal responsibility of keeping himself thoroughly informed on the political, social, and economic developments that may affect the company's interests in that area.

Or as another example, a company's profits may be especially sensitive to the cost of a basic raw material (e.g., cocoa or iron ore), or to maintaining a strong position in a particularly profitable market (e.g., the US market for whisky). In such companies it is now increasingly common practice for one director (usually non-executive) to take a close interest in, and to become the board's recognized authority on, the particular profit factor in question.

The obvious difficulty that arises from this practice is, of course, the potential conflict of interest or authority that it may create between a non-executive director and an executive director or line manager. If one director or manager has executive responsibility for the purchasing function, and is accountable for this function to the managing director, the same responsibility and authority clearly cannot be assigned to another director as well.

This potential conflict can, however, be avoided, given a clear distinction between the line responsibility of the executive director or manager, on the one hand, and the 'sphere of special interest' of the non-executive director, on the other. And above all, of course, this arrangement depends on the good will and understanding between the individuals concerned.

In this section the basic functions of the board have to some extent been over-simplified for the sake of clarity and brevity, and also for the sake of emphasizing certain points. In real life, of course, things are never simple and straightforward where human organizations and relationships are concerned.

This is particularly true of the way different boards interpret and perform their duties, where there are, in practice, almost infinite variations. And in practice almost any of these variations can work well provided that all the basic *functions* of the board are understood, and that the basic board *structure* is such as to make it possible for them to be carried out.

The following quotation from Harold Koontz's recent book *The Board of Directors and Effective Management* provides a pertinent comment in conclusion:

'There has unquestionably been a failure to recognize the contributions that a board can make to a company. Through its pressure on the chief executive and, through him, on the other company executives, the effective board can force establishment of clear and better goals and more logical policies and plans to assure their attainment. Through deliberation, it can greatly contribute to adequate consideration of major problems and the subtle strategic variables involved. It can, moreover, be a source of great strength and assistance to the top executive group of a company. Much of the weakness of boards stems from sheer unawareness, on the part of top company executives, of the potential of a capable board.'

46

Reading list

BOOKS

The Will To Manage, Marvin Bower (McGraw-Hill, 1967)
Standard Boardroom Practice (Institute of Directors, 1968)
Corporate Strategy, Igor Ansoff (McGraw-Hill, 1965)
The Concept of the Corporation, Peter F. Drucker (New English Library, 1964)
Management and Machiavelli, Anthony Jay (Hodder and Stoughton, 1967)
Organization in Business Management, A Guide for Managers and Potential Managers, Walter Puckey (Hutchinson, 1963)
Higher Control in Management, T. G. Rose (Pitman, Seventh Edition, 1964)
The Principles and Practice of Management, E. F. L. Brech (Longmans Green, Second Edition, 1963)

Useful addresses

American Management Association, 1515 Broadway, Times Square, New York City, N.Y.
McKinsey Foundation for Management Research, 245 Park Avenue, New York City, N.Y.
National Industrial Conference Board, 845 Third Avenue, New York City, N.Y.

1.4 Top Management and Long-range Planning

Basil W. Denning

Elsewhere in this chapter (section 1.3), Mr Hugh Parker has focused attention on the managerial functions of the board of directors. In brief he has listed these as being:

1. To establish long-term objectives and basic methods of attainment.
2. To define specific policies to be followed.
3. To decide the organizational structure.
4. To develop planning, information, and control systems.
5. To decide certain legal matters reserved to the Board.

He subsequently expands on the first four of these activities. This section will use these major responsibilities as a point of departure for a discussion of long-range planning on the assumption that it is essentially concerned with determining and achieving a proper future for the business, and that this is, and must remain, a key function of the board of directors.

Since 1964, there has been much discussion about long-range planning and the greater need for it in national, educational, industrial, and commercial activities. This upsurge of interest has produced two major misconceptions. One of these is that long-range planning is a totally new activity. Yet, in practice, it is clear that various types of long-range planning have always been carried out by most sizeable organizations. Oil refineries have been built to last for fifteen or twenty years, forests that will produce mature wood fifty years hence have been planted, sophisticated research

48

and development work has been undertaken in areas such as colour television and the development of nuclear energy to produce usable products or services seven, ten or fifteen years later, and individual companies have carefully exploited certain competitive advantages without immediate return over periods of years before achieving their pay-off. In the armed services, long-range planning of officer structures has been practised and the level of officer entry determined on this basis for decades.

The second misconception seems to assume that long-range planning involves the application of a series of new management techniques but that these techniques have marginal relevance to the real problems of running a business organization. It is suggested that both these sets of ideas badly misrepresent the aims of and the needs for corporate long-range planning.

An alternative view, which has more direct relevance to the board function, stems from the increasingly difficult challenge facing the top manager in carrying out the key elements in his managerial task. Most companies today are required to deal with an accelerating rate of technological change, a rapid rate of social and market change, increasing capital intensity, and increasing international competition. Managerial responses to these factors have varied, but among them have been:

1. An increasing tendency to concentrate into a small number of dominating large units in each industry.
2. The resulting development of more complicated organizational structures.
3. An increasing need to employ more sophisticated analytical approaches to the long-term problems of the company.

These responses have, in turn, created their complications for top management and, in conjunction with the factors that brought them about, have greatly increased the risks attached to poor top management decisions. Thus, many companies have in the past few years introduced 'long-range planning' as a separate specific activity. Thus, the aspect of 'long-range planning' that appears to be new is the development of formal long-range planning systems for the company as a whole, designed:

(a) To ensure that top management's task is aided as much as possible by careful analysis and consideration of alternative courses of action and, perhaps more important, to ensure that corporate objectives and strategy are regularly and systematically reappraised.

(b) To ensure that the most careful evaluation is made of projects (broadly defined to include building a new plant, acquiring another company, developing a new product or entering a new market) most of which now require the commitment of large capital sums for long periods of time.

(c) To develop an organizational process that co-ordinates the future activities of different units in large diverse organizations and increases top management's ability to control these activities.

It may be of interest here to indicate the rate of growth of long-range planning systems. In research carried out by questionnaire, in 1967, to the 'Top 300' companies in *The Times* list, 65 companies were carrying out systematic long-range planning over three years or more. Of these 65 companies, 22 had introduced long-range planning of this type between 1964 and 1967. Furthermore, out of 136 companies who replied but did not complete the questionnaire, 27 stated that they were in the process of introducing systematic long-range planning.

What sort of formal long-range planning systems have been introduced and how have they been organized? As with all organizational processes it is not possible to set out general rules that should always be followed. Nevertheless, it is possible to develop an approach to the creation of a long-range planning system for application in particular situations, and the remainder of this section will concentrate on describing this approach.

The elements of a long-range planning process

A long-range planning process should be designed to organize three separate types of planning into one coherent pattern. These types of planning are:

(a) Strategic Planning. The function of strategic planning is to determine the future posture of the business in relation to its changing environment.
(b) Project Planning. The function of project planning is to assess new projects, to integrate new projects into the firm and to execute the projects efficiently.
(c) Operational Planning. The function of operational planning is to translate strategic plans into action, to co-ordinate diverse activities and to allow top management consideration of future operations in specific terms.

A properly organized long-range planning process will ensure that all these planning activities are integrated in such a way that top management can

(a) Make strategic and project decisions after proper analysis of the best information available.
(b) Approve projects which conform to the strategic plan and are economically attractive.
(c) View the business as a whole in terms of size, market share, profitability, managerial strength, etc., at a point of time three, five, or seven years hence.
(d) Approve the proposed activities of operational units in specific terms.
(e) Compare the actual results of operational activities and new projects against planned results, thus exercising more effective control.

The activities involved in the long-range planning process

A diagram of a long-range planning process is given in Fig 1.1. The diagram has

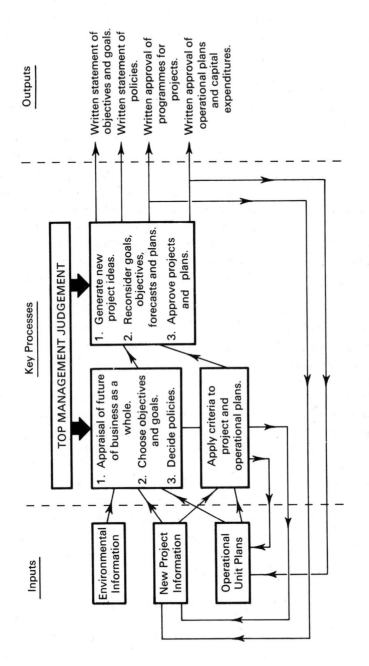

Fig. 1.1. Simple flow diagram of a long range planning process

deliberately been kept simple, and would need substantial amplification if it was intended to be used by any one organization, but it does draw attention to the key aspects of the planning process, and it can be viewed as a simple system defined by inputs, processes, and outputs.

A. *Inputs*

There are three basic inputs into the planning process: environmental information, new project information, and operational plans and forecasts.

Environmental information is needed on a systematic basis about the long-term economic position; developments in the technology appropriate to the business and any other technology likely to produce products that may replace the present product line; changes in the educational and social system with forecasts of the resulting changes in skills, abilities, and expectations of future personnel; political changes and influences, and the probabilities of new Government regulations and taxation; actual and possible developments by competition, including changes in the structure of an industry. Increasingly, with the rapid development of large international companies this information needs to be collected systematically on a global basis.

New project information is required about all types of major new projects, a project being broadly defined. During the course of a year many projects may be under consideration, such as research and development for new products, plans to enter new markets, the licensing of new products, the development of new manufacturing facilities, or examination of companies for acquisition. In practice, project ideas will tend to be generated in many parts of the organization and, normally, some criteria are required to decide which projects must be evaluated and decided centrally. These criteria normally include a minimum size in terms of finance and company rules about projects that can be regarded as having strategic importance.

The last major series of inputs arise from the forward projection of the operating units of the business. Within a company that is planning forward on a regular basis, it will be normal for every unit, division, or subsidiary annually to prepare plans for three, five, or seven years ahead. The bringing together of these plans at the organization's centre enables a detailed examination to be made of the key measures of the business, turnover, product line, profitability, number of employees, strength of management structure, at a future point of time.

B. *Corporate planning processes involving top management*

The various informational inputs noted above enable top management to carry out its principal planning tasks. These can briefly be described as follows:

(a) *Appraisal of the future of the company as a whole.* By drawing together the operational projections, plus those new projects appraised centrally, a picture of the whole company at a future point in time can be established and the question raised as to whether this is a satisfactory picture. Strengths and weaknesses can be analysed with respect to current business and possible extensions of activity.

(b) *Determination of objectives and goals.* During this appraisal, an assessment should be made in quantitative terms of the future market standing (e.g., market shares, total turnover, and growth), the product range, innovation, productivity, the financial and physical resources, and profitability. Judgements can also be made qualitatively about the required performance and development of managers or the need for outside recruitment, the need for changes in the relationship with the labour force and the implications for certain key relationships outside the firm, such as central or local government relations. If examination of proposed achievements in each of these dimensions meets the expectations of the Board, then plans can be approved and corporate goals can be enunciated. If they do not meet the Board's expectations, then, re-examination along each of these lines can be made, and different goals set.

(c) *Determination of Policies.* With objectives and goals defined, top management is in a position to develop its policies. In the limited sense of long-range planning these can be regarded as being of two types: the setting of criteria for selection and choice of projects, and the development of standards for overall performance by subsidiary units. Policies are most realistically viewed as long-term decisions to guide action by others, and in this sense, the establishment of selection criteria and standards of performance are important policy decisions.

(d) *Application of Criteria.* Final judgement may now be reached by top management on the proposals submitted by operational and functional units, project teams, or other special staff units. In practice, few of the final decisions can ever be made by the mechanistic application of strict criteria, but decision-making is eased by agreed understanding of the criteria that will be used by the board.

At this stage, the planning process is likely to involve a further cycle, with project and operational proposals being sent back for re-appraisal and re-examination before going through the same cycle a second or third time.

C. *Outputs*
The identifiable outputs of a corporate planning process are fourfold:

1. A written statement of objectives and goals.
2. A written statement of planning criteria.
3. Written approval of programmes for new projects.
4. Written approval of operational plans and delegated capital expenditures.

The last two of these are important, not only because they give final top management approval for action but also because they provide the basic standards against which subsequent action and performance can be measured. Some of the final plans will be in budgetary form, and in this sense, the planning cycle can be regarded as a lengthening out of a normal budgeting cycle. Long-range plans should not, however, be confined merely to financial figures, and should include the other dimensions of required action against which progress can subsequently be measured.

The time span of planning

Different companies plan out to different time horizons for many reasons. There is a general tendency to choose five years as a reasonable compromise between the need for an adequate time perspective and the costs of planning in detail to time periods when, because of so many unknowns, the exercise would be unrealistic.

Whereas there are few prescriptive rules about the length of time over which planning should be carried out, there are some guides on how to reach a decision on this point. They are:

(a) The planning cycle should be long enough to include the full time for bringing new large capital projects into existence, including the time required for negotiating the necessary outside finance.
(b) The planning cycle should be long enough to allow reasoned consideration of major technological changes.
(c) The planning cycle should be longer than any cyclical patterns that may exist in the economy if the product sold is affected by cyclical swings.
(d) Special planning cycles and processes may be necessary to deal with projects of especial length such as forest plantations, development of shipping fleets, life insurance, or oil-field exploration and research.
(e) Long-range planning should be a continuous process. This means that while three, five, or seven years may be selected as the time period over which planning takes place, the forward planning for this time period should be carried out every year. In other words, the concept of a rolling plan should be adopted.

There are few sizeable companies that can afford not to indulge in systematic planning over less than three years.

The organization of long-range planning

The organization of long-range planning is carried out in a wide variety of different ways in different companies. There are few general statements of value about what is, of necessity, an intensely individual corporate process, but there are one or two factors that should always be borne in mind.

(a) No effective long-range planning process is likely to be maintained in the face of operational pressures unless one man at a senior level is appointed to ensure that planning is effectively carried out.
(b) There is no record of long-range planning being carried out effectively unless the activity has had the active support of the Chief Executive.
(c) The introduction of systematic long-range planning will have an impact on the

real power-structure of the company and may cause concern to managers of decentralized units. For this reason, it is a mistake to use long-range planning as a method of reorganization, and wiser to introduce it after any needed organizational changes have been made.

(d) The responsibility for the detailed work involved in long-range planning may be carried out centrally or be decentralized to operating units. The question as to who should take responsibility for the different aspects of long-range planning involves organizational decisions similar to those required for any systematic process such as management development or cost control. It will usually be necessary, however, to create a small central staff to assist the executive in charge of planning. Companies with experience of long-range planning have usually provided a small central staff with expertise in economic assessment, the relevant technology operations research, market research, and finance.

(e) Whereas the initial thrust for long-range planning tends to arise from the finance department, American experience suggests that corporate planning is best if it is not headed by the chief accountant or controller. The reason for this lies in the attitudes needed in the two jobs. One is guardian of the company's assets. The other is the explorer of new areas of activity, and this calls for imagination, flexibility, and risk taking. Increasingly, the tendency is to appoint a man of general managerial capability who commands the respect of other senior executives in the company, and to provide the necessary technical expertise through specialist subordinates.

(f) In a decentralized organizational structure it will be necessary to appoint to groups or divisions the equivalent of a long-range planning manager to assist group or divisional chief executives with their planning. It may not be necessary for this to be a full-time job, but the responsibility should be clearly defined.

(g) Systematic long-range planning can be built only on a basis of efficient budgeting and control systems and a thorough understanding of the financial and economic aspects of operations. Where this underpinning is missing or is unrealistic, the quality of long-range plans will be poor.

(h) The introduction of systematic long-range planning rarely produces immediate results since it is a difficult managerial exercise, frequently requires changes in the time-horizons over which operating managers think, involving an attitudinal change, and is rarely carried out effectively in the first cycle.

(i) The aim should be to have longer range planning regarded as a normal part of the overall process of managing the company rather than a special separate exercise. This is likely to be achieved only after several cycles have been completed.

Techniques for long-range planning

Comparatively few techniques can specifically be regarded as being applicable to long-term planning only. Within each functional area there are specific techniques of forecasting for short, medium, and long-range purposes. Increasingly, mathematical models are being used for many types of forecast, but these models require substantial and crucial top management judgements if they are to give helpful results.

Certain forms of analysis and helpful structured approaches to these problems can be found in the literature quoted at the end of this section, but long-range planning should draw widely on any relevant managerial technique. The major problems in this area are conceptual, organizational, and judgemental.

Summary

Directors carry specific managerial responsibilities in addition to their legal responsibilities. In the increasingly complex industrial and commercial world, the fulfilling of these responsibilities requires special assistance. An important form of help large companies are increasingly adopting is the development of systematic long-range planning processes that incorporate strategic, project, and operational planning. Properly used and organized, these processes can assist top management in their key tasks of setting objectives and goals, formulating policy, deciding on major projects, and co-ordinating and controlling large organizations.

Reading list

BOOKS

Long Range Planning in American Industry, Brian W. Scott (American Management Association—Bailey Brothers and Swinfen, London, 1965)
Corporate Strategy, H. I. Ansoff (McGraw-Hill, 1966)
Long Range Planning: The Executive Viewpoint, E. Kirby Warren (Prentice-Hall, 1966)
Planning for Company Growth: The Executive's Guide to Effective Long-Range Planning, Bruce Payne (McGraw-Hill, 1963)
Long Range Planning for Management, Ed. D. W. Ewing (Harper and Row, revised edition 1963)
Managerial Long Range Planning, Ed. G. A. Steiner (McGraw-Hill, 1963)
Multi-National Corporate Planning, G. A. Steiner and Cannon (Macmillan, 1966)
Long Range Planning, Ernest Dale (British Institute of Management, 1967)

JOURNALS

'Budgetary Control and Long Range Planning', Ian Hay Davison (*Management Accounting*, October 1967)
'Long Range Corporate Planning', Hugh P. Buckner, New Management Techniques No. 7 (*The Director*, April 1967)
'Do you Plan for Years Ahead?', Bruce Payne (*International Management*, December 1963)
'How to Assure Poor Long-Range Planning for your Company', George A. Steiner (*California Management Review*, Summer 1965)

'Corporate Planning for British Industry', Ian Clark (*Enterprise*, Vol. I, 1966)
'Long-Range Formal Planning in Perspective', Brian J. Loasley (*Journal of Management Studies*, October 1967)

Useful addresses

Society for Long Range Planning, 131/132 Terminal House, Grosvenor Gardens, London SW 1

1.5 The Changing Company Environment

John Tyzack

Every director is conscious of how, during recent years, the pressures from society have grown, and companies have increasingly come to be regarded as accountable to interests far wider than the shareholders. The State demands that companies should be efficient, and may actively intervene if industries or firms are seen to be falling short. Inevitably, pressures on the larger companies are transmitted to small concerns. The young director in a big organization is the one chiefly affected by the changing nature of his responsibilities and his role, but even in the small private company, directors are aware of being under pressure (and even attack) from many quarters, and are far from sure of what their function should be in a modern industrial society. If the director can become clearer about his role, or at least more aware of the forces that are changing the functions of the boardroom and the company in the context of society as a whole, the chances are that he will perform more efficiently and be less surprised by political and social developments as they affect his business life: indeed, he may be ready to take advantage of them.

Ideas about the role and responsibilities of the board and the director are changing rapidly under the influence of swift industrial and social change in the country as a whole. The young manager (partly because the title 'director' is the one prestige label in British industry) is still inclined to see the boardroom as presenting the final door to successful business achievement. But once he has become a director, he usually expects, above all, to demonstrate what a professional manager can do. In

58

fact, although today's professional manager is invariably anxious to join the board, when he thinks about the duties and responsibilities of a director it is almost always in terms of a continuing managerial role. I very much doubt whether a 'directing role' as distinct from a 'managing role' has any real meaning for him. If he is forced to think about it, he is liable to slip back to the past and relate the former to ownership.

This managerial attitude of the young director towards the role of the board, and the uncertainties among many older men about their functions as directors, reflect pressures arising from the fast pace of technological change and its wide-ranging, social consequences. Directors are having to adjust to unprecedented demands arising from a rapidly changing environment. Only in very small companies can they still try to avoid looking outwards and relating their own role to those of the other groups—social, political, trade union, consumer—that make up the community in which they work. It often seems that sound business decisions today must take greater account of all the external factors than of those present inside the business.

Do directors understand the underlying reasons for change, and is it possible for them to foresee the direction it is likely to take? Can they continuously adapt themselves, and can they evolve a philosophy capable of guiding them in a period of exceptionally rapid change? What is to be the characteristic function of the board-room, as opposed to management, in the future? These questions are made more difficult by the fact that boards themselves are the critical controlling and directing element of a large group within society—industry. Because boards have the broad duty of directing industry, and must organize themselves to do this effectively, we must look at two questions: the position industry occupies in the community, and the position the board occupies in relation to the community as a whole and to industry of which it forms a part.

In considering industry, do we include the nationalized industries? I am convinced that we should. Must we also look at the workers and the trade unions, or the consumers? If we do, shall we not find that they pull in such different directions that industry really has no identity at all?

If we examine a company engaged on an actual project such as building a factory, we find that the people deployed consist of three main groups: workers, management, and contract services (the purchasing company could make a fourth). There will be argument, possibly wrangling between the groups, perhaps strikes, and to that extent all can pull in different directions. When the building is finally completed, however, it has been a corporate achievement depending for its success on co-operation between all the groups. The company is shown to have identity because it has done something and created something. Industry has an identity because it makes and sells things or organizes and sells services.

We are a highly industrialized society, but the community still remains something distinct from industry. The history of a community is the story of the interplay of its power groupings. A company is a microcosm of a community. Industry, with its varied official and unofficial groupings, is a larger, more diffuse microcosm. But the company and its board are subject to a much more precise definition. Part of this definition lies within the Companies Acts but, basically, the company and its board exist to meet some quite simple needs.

A group of people come together with the purpose of establishing a business enterprise. This is done within the customs and legal requirements of the society in which we live, which is broadly that of all western industrial society. The owners or shareholders provide the money and set out the terms of reference within which the enterprise shall operate. But a large number of individuals cannot themselves set up the business, organize it, manage it, and work in it. Therefore, they do what is accepted and natural within our social structure, they elect a committee to act on their behalf and to be answerable to them.

There really is no magic in this, and it is important that this should be understood. There is nothing in the concept of a board of directors that is contrary to practices that have very deep roots in our social structure. The elected committee is the system by which we run nearly all our activities, from central government to the local cricket club. Moreover, over the years, a set of rules and practice that determine how a committee shall work have developed, and these vary little between one committee and another. Probably the most important difference between a board of directors and, say, the committee of a scientific society or a social club, is that boardroom practice has been largely codified in the laws enshrined in the various Companies Acts.

There is, however, one particular aspect of the board as a committee that is rarely appreciated. Any committee in any situation produces power problems. Because it is a small group of people at the very centre of control, individual relationships and relative power positions can become critical. There can be nothing so ruthless and so uninhibited as a battle within the board: an important factor in assessing the actual role it plays.

Most of us usually visualize a normal business career pattern as a single unbroken line rising, one hopes, to a peak as company director. This is too simple a picture, and can be misleading. In larger enterprises at least, there can be two breaks in that line. The first, a small one, is when a man is appointed to a subsidiary company board. The second, which is a real gap, is when he is appointed to the main group board. At this point a manager moves into a very different environment, where individual personalities and their conflicts, the workings of power politics, domination by an individual, can be most acute and most dangerous. By far the majority of the personal disasters at top board level come about because the manager has not understood that he has jumped across a deep gap from a managerial environment into something that is different in character.

The board exercises control and direction over the enterprise and is accountable to the shareholders at annual general meeting. Since the shareholders' object in putting up the money was to get a return on it, the board's achievement is measured in financial terms, and we have yet to devise any satisfactory alternative measurement.

There is nothing in the concept of a board of directors that runs contrary to the social structure that has evolved over the centuries, but like that social structure it will come under challenge and criticism, sometimes even violent attack, if it does not appear to be moving in line with changing social needs. Because social/industrial demands of today are very different indeed from what they were only thirty years ago, we are forced to look critically at top direction in industry, just as in the political context we are looking critically at the very structure of government.

Rapid technological change is bringing about rapid changes in society between various groups. Unless boardroom organization responds to these changes, in turn, it will come under increasing criticism and attack and fail to perform efficiently. On the whole, (unlike the industrial revolution, which threw up autocratic leaders such as Ford, Rockefeller, Carnegie, who have been compared to the mediaeval 'robber barons') the technological revolution of today is encouraging more 'democratic' group relations and attitudes throughout industry. But at the same time, as companies are expected to respond more sensitively to the demands of consumers and employees, because of their own growing size and economic strength they are inviting growing interference on the part of government.

Given that industry must grow larger and that the community as a whole will increasingly demand that industry should demonstrate a wide social consciousness, directors would be foolish, I believe, if they did not expect, and even plan for, far greater public contol of industry. This means that there will be increasing restrictions on the freedom of action of the entrepreneur, and renewed attempts, despite the failures of the recent past, to fit business enterprises into some form of national planning. I very much doubt whether this means more nationalization: government is more sophisticated than it was twenty years ago, and considerable control can be exercised without ownership.

What do these pressures from outside mean for the structure of the board in the future, and the role of the director as distinct from the manager? We may certainly expect changes in the law. Legal change is invariably preceded by changes in community attitudes; a more considerate attitude to workers in industry, for example, developed long before employers' obligations were carefully spelled out in law. Today, consumers are far more alive to their own interests and are starting to organize themselves, as workers did a century ago. Before long, therefore, boards may have to treat consumer representatives with at least as much consideration as they treat worker representatives now. Shall we see in the not too distant future these developing forces reflected in a new board structure? In Germany, worker participation on boards is already obligatory. It may only be a question of time before we go in the same direction, with possibly consumer participation as well. Directors would be on the board to look after the interests of the groups they represent.

Shall we see also a government-appointed director with the role of looking after the public interest? The idea may be very unwelcome to many or most directors who have grown up accustomed to the present board structure; and certainly powerful arguments can be deployed against it. But we must expect to see it increasingly urged that worker, consumer, and even government representation on the board could work to the company's advantage as well as to that of the community.

One of the board's primary duties could be defined as that of keeping the company related to developments outside itself, particularly in the community as a whole. This is a constantly changing situation with which the working director, and particularly the manager, may be out of touch. It is possible that this wider representation might be able to guide a board and a company to more rapid and effective adaptation to the changing world outside. If the community demands that boardroom practice and law should move in this direction, then we could see the evolution of a two-tier structure—a controlling and directing board, and a board of management. The former might consist of chairman, non-executive directors, representatives of other interests, and the managing director. The board of management, under the chairmanship of the managing director, would be composed of the top managers charged with putting the directing board's policies into effect. Already, trends in both Germany and the United States seem to point in this direction.

The possibility that boardroom structure will evolve in the way I have suggested above, however contested the suggestion may be, serves at least to emphasize that there is no reason to assume that the boardroom is immune to change, any more than the company or society at large. I have discussed, in very broad terms, the changes in society that are likely to impinge increasingly on directors in future years, and of which they should be at least aware. The young post-war generation now climbing higher in British management will, quite clearly, have to deal with a far faster pace of change than any previous generation. But already, the swiftness of technological and social change has affected the age at which men are elected to British boardrooms —it has been falling rapidly now for two decades. It is no longer unusual for men under forty to become chief executives or board directors.

The young director will want to continue in a position of power and in control of affairs for as long as he can. Is he able to prolong his adaptability beyond the age at which most men have lost it? The time to prepare for this is in youth, when it is relatively easy to establish a wide range of contacts and interests. The man who has not done this while he is young, will find business life increasingly hard as he grows older. The competent and effective director need not be a specialist, indeed should not remain a specialist even if he began as one; but he must cultivate an understanding of the world at large in which industry has to operate and with which it has to come to terms.

Because this is an age of technological revolution, the director should be aware of developments in technology and of the potentialities these can put within his grasp. But even more important, he must understand human nature—how men reacted to change in the past, and how they can be expected to react now. More and more information businessmen need is processed to a degree and with a speed that was inconceivable only twenty years ago. It is natural to assume that the area of intuitive decision is rapidly being reduced. But an understanding of people, and therefore of history, is as necessary as figures, and I believe that for the top managers and directors the growth of information storage and retrieval pushes the frontier of intuitive decision only further ahead, and its importance still remains the same.

The ideal director would combine the innovation and adaptability of youth with the wisdom and experience of age. Understanding this, the advanced company today tries to give its most promising young men as much experience as they can cram in in the shortest space of time. Thereby they can join the board while they are still young and, given adaptability, they may hope to remain effective to a reasonable age of retirement.

For the future, directors may expect to see their powers shorn, their status made less exclusive, and their period of office reduced. If they do not like this, is there anything they can do to stop it? I very much doubt it, as I suspect that these changes are inexorable. When the community starts moving in a particular direction it is generally irreversible. Journalists say they can sometimes hasten a trend, but never halt or reverse it, and manufacturers are usually of the same opinion.

However, those who move with the trend and adapt to it, instead of fighting against it, usually come out more or less unscathed. The French and Russian aristocracies failed to move with the democratic trends of their time, and mostly paid for it with their lives. The more agile English aristocracy came through with power and wealth, which have not altogether vanished even now. Marxist historians say that no class has ever assisted in its own liquidation. The answer to that is that no class that is sufficiently aware, sufficiently intelligent, sufficiently adaptable, and understands the nature of power, has ever had to.

The community as a whole is entitled, as it has done, to establish a control over boards, both legally through a sequence of Companies Acts, as well as by establishing in many different ways a code of practice. In the ultimate, the people are master. But it has always seemed to me that society seeks to keep a balance of power and to prevent total power getting into the hands of an individual or very small group. In this sense, a board is certainly a desirable control on management. The changing environment will profoundly change the attitudes of directors over future years and also, even if not in the ways I have suggested, industry's boardroom structure. But the job of director will grow rather than diminish in importance.

Reading list

BOOKS

New Concepts in Management (British Institute of Management, 1962)

63

Towards a Sociology of Management, Sir Geoffrey Vickers (Chapman & Hall, 1967)

The Companies Act, 1967, S. W. Magnus and M. Estrin (Butterworth & Co., 1967)

Report of the Company Law Committee, Command Paper 1749 (H.M.S.O. June 1962)

Conceptual Foundations of Business; an outline of the major ideas sustaining business enterprise in the Western world, by Richard Eells and Clarence Walton (Richard D. Irwin, 1961)

The Genesis of Modern Management; a study of the industrial revolution in Great Britain, by Sidney Pollard (Edward Arnold, 1965)

JOURNALS

The Director (monthly) (Institute of Directors)

Journal of Management Studies (Quarterly) (Basil Blackwell, Oxford)

Harvard Business Review (Bi-monthly) (Agents: McGraw-Hill American Circulation Department, Maidenhead)

2. Tax, Finance and Growth

2.1 Raising Capital

James Morrell

Business generates most of its capital requirements from its own savings. However, it will be seen from Table 2.1 that a sizeable proportion of the total funds available to the company sector is financed by new capital issues.

Table 2.1

Financing of investment
UK industrial and commercial companies
aggregates for 1963-1965
(Source: *Financial Statistics*)

	£ million	%		£ million	%
Gross fixed capital formation	8,708	55·1	Undistributed Income	11,473	72·6
Increase in stocks	2,166	13·7	Net proceeds of capital issues	1,703	10·8
Available to other sectors etc.	4,928	31·2	Loans, Mortgages etc.	2,626	16·6
	15,802	100·0		15,802	100·0

The change in the tax system and the introduction of a corporation tax that tends to favour retention of profits has provided an incentive to business to reduce its dependence on outside capital. Nevertheless, the national aggregates mask a vast range of different experiences, and although capital raised outside the firm may appear to be a minor factor when viewed in the context of the national totals, it will be of critical importance to the growth of the important dynamic sectors of the economy.

The pattern of financing varies from industry to industry and firm to firm, and different types of business find it advisable to use different combinations of credit and capital resources, depending upon the degree of risk and scale.

The scope of the capital market

The capital and money markets are best viewed as a whole. In seeking sources of capital, it is as well to remember that there is a vast unified market that spans from the provision of day-to-day short-term credit at one end, to permanent risk capital at the other. For example, a firm may be able to meet its cash requirements for the purchase of machinery with the help of a bank advance. Although the bank advance is a temporary form of finance, it will be seen that it provides an alternative source of capital to shareholders' funds. It is in this sense that the capital market must be viewed in the round, for the actions of savers and investors, borrowers and lenders, all influence the determination of interest rates in the markets.

We therefore have to think of the capital and money market being linked through a thread of interest rates. Although the rate of interest charged for a loan is of a very different magnitude from the rate earned on capital employed in industry, these two prices are related through the workings of the market.

Savings

In assessing the available sources of capital, we must keep in mind the way in which the flow of savings becomes available for investment. As we have seen, the company sector generates a vast amount of savings out of profits. This is the largest single item of savings. The government and public authorities also generate savings through the tax system and, in addition, the nationalized industries create savings (mostly in the form of depreciation provisions) which are available to finance a large part of their own investment programmes.

Personal savings have risen from a very low level after the Second World War to a magnitude of considerable importance in the 1960s. The largest part of personal savings is generated through contractual obligations. A growing part of the population saves through life assurance and pension schemes. Funds generated in this way have a natural tendency to rise as incomes rise. The resulting savings are invested

68

primarily through the stock market, and find their way into government securities, industrial fixed income stocks, equity shares, and into real estate. In addition, a growing volume of personal savings is devoted to house purchase through mortgages provided by the building societies and insurance companies.

The more volatile elements in personal savings are channelled into national savings, the building society movement, and into deposits with the banks and hire-purchase companies. These forms of savings are frequently undertaken to provide for short-term eventualities, and it is notable that part of national savings is used as a short-term repository for such things as holidays and Christmas spending.

Whether or not these various forms of savings are available in the open capital market, it should be borne in mind that each component exercises an influence on the supply of capital in the economy at large. Thus, where companies finance all their investment programmes out of their own savings, both the savings and the invest-ment aspect of their actions must still be regarded as of consequence for the capital market. Directors will have had in mind the respective rates of interest bearing on decisions, and they will have been influenced by the general level of interest rates in the economy.

The United Kingdom probably has the most highly developed capital market in the world. The ease with which huge amounts of money change hands in the gilt-edged market is not paralleled in any other centre. In addition, the money markets are highly specialized and developed, and *as a general rule there is no shortage of capital for any class of borrower. Provided the borrower is credit-worthy, and has a sound project in view, he can have every confidence, in today's markets, of finding the resources he needs.*

We propose to examine the sources of capital available to the borrower, starting from the provision of short-term finance for the smaller business, and concluding with the provision of long-term capital from the open market.

Short-term finance

Bank credit
The first source of short-term capital to which firms will turn will be bank credit. Traditionally, the banks concentrate on providing credit for short-term require-ments. These are generally met by advances, and arrangements are usually negotiated in such a way that the borrower can rely on receiving facilities for a period of up to a year. In most cases, renewal of the loan presents no difficulties, but as a general rule, bank advances are suitable for self-liquidating transactions over a relatively short period.

Seasonal demands, for example, are coverable by bank credit, and farmers are able to anticipate sales of annual crops. Similarly, finance can be obtained against specific contracts, and short-term loans can be negotiated for 'bridging' finance. In these cases, loans are made for a short period against the expectation of arranging long-term finance. Stocks can also be financed by bank overdrafts, and in these, the goods themselves are available as security against the bank advance.

In some instances, banks will arrange for longer-term finance, but this is more likely to be for special assistance to house purchasers than to business in general.

Rates of interest on bank advances are linked to Bank Rate. A first-class industrial borrower may pay no more than one per cent over Bank Rate, and as a rule the rates charged will vary between one and two per cent over Bank Rate, and subject to a minimum level.

Trade credit

Businesses will also be able to use trade credit as a means of supplementing working capital. In some cases, trade credit is a larger item in a firm's balance sheet than bank credit. Many small firms are highly dependent upon the credit terms they get from their suppliers, and in times of credit restriction, find themselves vulnerable to the pressures exerted at all levels of business to retrench on the supply of credit.

Bill finance

Foreign trade is largely financed by use of the Bill of Exchange. When goods are shipped from one country to another, the supplier will be unlikely to receive payment until his goods have arrived at their destination. In the nineteenth century, the period of transit could be lengthy, and a convenient means of financing this trade was devised by the introduction of the Bill of Exchange. By this means, a supplier is able to get cash immediately for the goods in question, subject to discount at the ruling rate of interest.

The same principle is applied in the provision of credit on other forms of bills. Widely used in the nineteenth century, this means of credit finance largely disappeared in the twentieth century, but has been revived more recently. Domestic trade can be financed in this way, and payment for goods can be secured immediately after despatch.

Invoice discounting

A variation of this procedure is obtainable through invoice discounting. As with bill finance, the period of credit is restricted to the short-term. There are a number of companies specializing in this form of finance, and facilities are normally only granted to business with a turnover in excess of £100,000. The rate of interest charged on this kind of operation is, however, greater than that involved in bill finance.

Medium-term finance

Hire-purchase finance

In recent years there has been a growing use of hire-purchase finance as a means of acquiring capital equipment by business. Many small firms have found it convenient to acquire equipment through the hire-purchase system. Periods of repayment are generally for between three and five years, and finance of this kind is attractive where investment in plant and machinery can be made to produce immediate returns at a high yield.

Equipment leasing

A development of the same idea has led to the provision of finance for equipment leasing. There are several advantages of this form of finance, particularly in fields where there are rapid changes in technology. Thus, where office equipment, such as the computer, is subject to rapid model developments over the life of a piece of equipment, there are advantages in leasing rather than buying. Equipment is available immediately, the rentals are fully allowable against tax, and the leasing system does not impinge upon the availability of other forms of credit. Most forms of durable equipment can now be rented for long periods. The cost may be lower than hire-purchase finance, and there is a growing number of firms who provide this kind of facility.

Government grants

A wide range of institutions offer special facilities for different kinds of business. Since the First World War, government has intervened increasingly in industry, and has established numbers of schemes designed to help particular industries; for example, grants are available to agriculture and horticulture, for fishing, for film making, for research, and for regional development. There is now a system of investment grants to provide incentives for the location of industry in areas where unemployment tends to be above the national average, and these grants are in addition to investment grants applicable to industry in general.

Special schemes

In addition to government grants, a number of bodies provide capital for special purposes. The Ship Mortgage Finance Company was established to assist British ship-owners in financing work in British shipyards with capital subscribed by leading insurance companies and financial institutions. Its loans are secured as first mortgages.

The Agricultural Mortgage Corporation also provides long-term loans secured by first mortgages on land and buildings. The capital was, in this case, subscribed by the banks, and most of its funds are raised by the issue of debentures.

Another institution has facilities to aid technical development. The inventor who may find difficulty in raising funds for the development of a new project can now turn to Technical Development Capital Limited, a company formed in 1962 and financed by leading financial institutions. This scheme is administered by ICFC (*see* below).

Finally, some reference must be made to the Industrial Reorganisation Corporation (IRC) (*see* section 15.6) formed by the Government with the object of promoting rationalization in industry. Although the IRC will probably be the originator of schemes of rationalization and will provide capital to make such schemes possible, it may be that, in future, the Corporation will be able to receive approaches from industry for assistance.

Long-term capital

A particularly worrying problem in the inter-war period was the apparent lack of availability of capital for the smaller business. Whereas most new businesses are built up from private savings and family resources, there comes a point in the growth of such firms when capital requirements may be in excess of the credit available from bank finance and other short-term sources.

Industrial and Commercial Finance Corporation

To meet this situation, the Industrial and Commercial Finance Corporation was established in 1945. Its aim was to assist small concerns needing long-term capital, and finance is provided either through loans, or ordinary shares, or combinations of the various forms of security. The majority of loans are secured, and some capital has been made available in the form of redeemable and non-redeemable preference shares. ICFC has a large block of capital available for assistance of smaller businesses, and it also operates a plant purchase scheme.

Estate Duties Investment Trust

The ICFC also manages the Estate Duties Investment Trust. The burden of death duties falling on family businesses has been a considerable problem, and a sudden liability for death duties could involve the winding-up of a sound family business. The Estate Duties Investment Trust was designed to relieve the problem of finding the finance for estate duty in such a way as to facilitate the continuation of the company concerned as a separate business. A number of other private institutions provide similar facilities.

Finance Corporation for Industry

The Finance Corporation for Industry was also set up in 1945 to provide finance for the purposes of rehabilitation and development if it could be considered to be in the national interest. Funds are provided only in cases where the requirements are in excess of £250,000, and where the borrower can show that the finance cannot be obtained elsewhere

Charterhouse Industrial Development

Capital for private companies is also available from Charterhouse Industrial Development Company, a subsidiary of the Charterhouse Group. CID, which first entered this field in 1934, specializes in small and medium sized expanding companies and its facilities are available in the form of both loan and equity capital.

New issues

Apart from the special requirements catered for by the institutions referred to above, long-term capital is raised principally through the new issues market. As we saw at the outset, new issues account for approximately 10 per cent of industry's financing. The pattern of financing is shown in Table 2.2.

Table 2.2

New Issues in the UK
by UK quoted public companies

(Source: *Financial Statistics*)

	Ordinary Shares % of Total	Fixed Interest Stocks % of Total	Total £ million
1961	76	24	583
1962	59	41	439
1963	43	57	445
1964	42	58	520
1965	19	81	446
1966	23	77	701
1967	15	85	478

Although the majority of new issues have been for fixed interest stocks, this proportion is increasing under the impact of the corporation tax, and there is already a noticeable change in the pattern of financing.

New issues are arranged by members of the Issuing Houses Association (over fifty in number) (*see* section 4.7) who are, in the main, the merchant banks. The issuing house will advise on the type of issue, size, and terms that may be most suitable. It will also advise on timing and will handle all the technical and legal requirements involved.

New issues are required to be covered by a prospectus and advertisement in at least two leading newspapers. In consequence, a new issue is a costly business, and the expenses are proportionately high for a small issue. As a result, the new issue

4

is much more of an economic proposition for the larger corporation than the small. In addition a company will find it possible to make a new issue on acceptable terms only if it has a satisfactory profit record and sound future prospects.

Equity capital

Equity capital is provided either by rights issues to existing shareholders, by public issue of new shares, or by private placings.

Rights issues are made to existing shareholders in proportion to their existing holdings in the company, notification of the issue being made to shareholders by circular letter. The advantage of this method of raising permanent capital to the quoted company is that the shareholder can exercise the option not to take up his entitlement of new shares by selling his rights in the market. The price of shares to be issued in this way is invariably pitched below the market price of existing shares. In this way, rights will command a premium and a market value provided nothing intervenes (such as an international crisis) to depress the share price below the issue price of the rights.

New public issues of equities may arise on a company seeking a public quotation for its shares (going public) or as the outcome of merger, acquisition, or reorganization.

Private placings are a suitable means of acquiring capital for the smaller firm. The firm may be able to do this itself or it may use the services of an issuing house. The issuing house will arrange the placing with its clients and institutional friends. If the securities in question have a quotation, then it will be possible to place the shares through members of a stock exchange.

Issues by tender

Considerable attention has been focused in recent years on the method of issuing shares to the public. In theory, the most efficient way of determining a price for shares is to use the market mechanism to the full. Issue by tender meets this requirement. Although used extensively in the nineteenth century, this method of issue dropped into disuse and has been revived in the 1960s on a limited scale only. However, in view of increasing study and discussion of the methods and costs of issuing, it may be that issues by tender will again become more frequent.

Fixed interest issues

Permanent capital is also raised by means of preference shares. In view of the disadvantages placed on this kind of issue by the change in the tax system, the preference share is likely to be of less significance in the future.

More reliance, as we have noted, will be placed upon mortgage and loan finance. Debentures are secured by a charge over a company's assets and are generally

74

repayable over a specified period. Companies having an official Stock Exchange quotation will, as a rule, be able to raise debenture finance, though only the medium and large-sized public companies will be in a position to acquire substantial amounts in this way. New issues of loan stock and debentures still require to be covered by prospectus and advertised in the same way as issues of shares.

The subscribers to new issues

It is as well to keep in mind the sources of long-term capital. Most new money channelled into Stock Exchange securities comes from insurance companies and the pension funds. The investment trusts handle a body of funds that has grown with the market rather than through injections of new money. The Unit Trust movement is relatively new, and so far small, and its funds derived from new money will be channelled into quoted securities. Thus, the investment and Unit Trust movements cannot be counted as major sources of new capital for industry, although investment trusts are sometimes prepared to take an interest in smaller companies and to hold a considerable quantity of unquoted securities.

The insurance companies, however, by virtue of their size and the steadiness of their flow of new money are the main support of the new issue market. Thus, the companies have been able to provide capital for the special institutions already referred to. They can be approached directly for various forms of financing, such as purchase and the lease back of property. Offices, shops, and factory premises can be financed in this way. They will also make mortgage loans of a sizeable amount, but it must be remembered that with most capital facilities the company provides it will expect to handle the insurance business of the borrower.

Pension funds do not have this flexibility, but by virtue of their rapidly growing size and strength they must be reckoned an important factor in the support of the new issue market.

Building societies are able to assist business with mortgage loans only to a limited extent. Solicitors and mortgage brokers are also sources of mortgage finance but in all cases facilities will be provided against a sound, saleable property only. In this respect, a debenture issue is a more flexible instrument for the quoted company, for the terms of the debenture can be arranged according to the requirements of the lenders.

Advice

Most firms will need to seek advice as to the most suitable means of raising capital. The small firms will be able to turn to their bankers for advice on all aspects of short-term financing, and as the firm grows and its capital requirements become more complex, the bank will be able to suggest further sources of capital.

The merchant banks are available to advise and help with all forms of financing, and if a firm has no connection with a merchant bank it will be possible to seek advice and introductions through a leading firm of stockbrokers.

Finally, we repeat the view that there is no shortage of capital in the UK for any sound, credit-worthy firm with a good project.

Reading list

BOOKS

Investment Proposals and Decisions, B. R. Williams and W. P. Scott (Allen & Unwin, 1965)
Business Finance: Theory and Management, Archer D'Ambrosio (Macmillan, 1966)
Financing Your Business (Engineering Industries Association, 1966)
Business Finance, F. W. Paish (Pitman 3rd Edition, 1965)
The Financing of Small Business, James Bates (Sweet and Maxwell, 1964)
The City in the World Economy, W. M. Clarke (Institute of Economic Affairs, 1965)
Finance Problems of the Smaller Company: An Institute of Directors Guide to the City (Institute of Directors, 1967)
Admission of Securities to Quotation: Memoranda of Guidance and Requirements of the Federation of Stock Exchanges (Council of the London Stock Exchange, 1966)

Useful addresses

Finance Corporation for Industry, 4 Bread Street, London EC 2
Industrial and Commercial Finance Corporation, Piercy House, 7 Copthall Avenue, London EC 2
Industrial Reorganisation Corporation, 46 Pall Mall, London SW 1

2.2 Company Taxation

J. B. Whelan

No director in his senses would dream of computing his company's tax liability in these days of unparalleled complexity in Revenue law. That is a task which even his skilled advisers, the accountants and the lawyers, find difficult and, often, perilous.

Nevertheless, the fact remains that no director can afford to ignore the vital subject of taxation. Ignorance can be as dangerous as well-intentioned amateur meddling; for example, an innocent transfer of shares or even the appointment of someone to the Board, can have an effect on the taxation of the company. And the damage cannot always be put right with the same ease.

In fact, there is a minimum of tax law and principles that every executive should know, no matter how well he may be equipped with advisers. Even these, whether employed within or without the company, will perform their tasks more efficiently if their client—or boss—can speak the same language. Further, their advice will be all the more intelligible and valuable.

In this discussion, therefore, I am making an attempt to set out simply, by question and answer, what every director ought to know or, certainly, know about. This is not intended to be comprehensive, but it *is* basic; some directors may know much more and in greater detail; the vast majority may know just as much; some few may not.

Without bringing in the examination room atmosphere, most directors could well treat the material as a test paper. If, on reading it through, they find that they pretty well know it all, then the conscience of each is clear. If anyone does not know the answers, his conscience may be clear if, like the good lawyer, he knows where to find them.

Corporation Tax

At the date of writing it is fortunate that we can omit any reference to the complicated transitional provisions that were inevitable when we changed over from profits tax and income tax to corporation tax. It is now admitted by most accountants that it was these transitional provisions rather than the new principles that caused so many headaches during the unfortunate years of 1965 and 1966.

Outline

In the past, income tax was essentially interwoven between the company and its shareholders. However much the courts changed their minds on the subject, the idea was that a company paid income tax on its profits and that income tax was 'passed on' to its shareholders in the sense that, when a dividend was paid, income tax was deemed to have been paid on it. In its short and unfortunate history, profits tax was not dealt with in the same way; it was a tax apart. Now, both income tax and profits tax have gone and we are left with an entirely new concept known as Corporation Tax.

The basic principle underlying Corporation Tax is the separation of a company from its shareholders. No matter what your Memorandum and Articles may say about incorporating individuals into a company, so far as Revenue law is concerned, once a company is established it is a being on its own. There is, in fact, no connection between it and its shareholders, apart from the obvious fact that the shareholders own shares in it. The fact that it is taxed bears no relationship whatsoever to its shareholding.

It does not matter that this could be described as legalized daylight robbery. The fact remains that after a company has been taxed and has paid its share of its profits to the Inland Revenue, any distribution it makes of the balance of its profits to its shareholders is an entirely separate matter. Each dividend has to be taxed as part of the liability, not of the company but of the shareholder. Tax is certainly deducted by the company, but merely as a part of the machinery of collection. The tax is the shareholder's, and his liability is defined under a new Schedule known as Schedule F.

It will be seen, therefore, that the introduction of the Corporation Tax together with the new Capital Gains Tax has far-reaching effects. The State—or the Inland Revenue—has a built-in interest not only in the profits of the company, not only in income tax on its distributions, but also in any capital appreciation the company may enjoy. The State will get its share of those either through Capital Gains Tax during the shareholder's lifetime, or through Capital Gains Tax plus Estate Duty after his death. This silent encroachment is absolute, and there is very little, if any, possibility of its removal in our lifetime or thereafter. In other words, we may as well learn to live with it.

Assessment

Q. Corporation Tax is being assessed on the current year basis. Is this a new idea?

A. There is nothing particularly novel about the current year basis. We are already well familiar with the process in Profits Tax. The point now, is that all company taxation is assessed on the actual year and not by reference to any other period.

Q. Does this mean that the previous artificial concept of the previous year's profits has now gone?

A. Yes.

Q. Does this mean that at any time in a company's commercial year the accountants can draw interim accounts and let the directors know precisely how much profit has been made and the tax payable?

A. Unfortunately, no. Corporation Tax is payable in arrears. That is to say, on Budget Day of each year the Chancellor of the Exchequer will announce the rate of Corporation Tax payable on profits made to the 31 March just ended.

Q. This may be convenient enough for those companies whose accounting date is the 31 March in any one year. What, however, is the position of those companies whose accounting date goes to 30 June, 30 September, 31 December or, in fact, any other date between the 1 April in one year and the 31 March in the next?

A. The accounts will have to be split. Assume, for example, that your company's accounts are taken to the 31 December. For the purposes of Corporation Tax the profits of three months to 31 March will be taxed at the rate applicable for that particular year and the profits for the remaining nine months will be taxed at the rate applicable to the next year.

Q. This may be bad enough for a company whose accounts have to be taken to the 31 December, but what is the position of a company whose accounts go, say, to the 30 September in any year? The rate of tax on half the company's profits to 31 March previously are known, but the rate to 30 September is not known. Does this mean that the company must guess the rate of, or hold up, its accounts until the 31 March?

A. Yes. It must either wait, which will be extremely inconvenient for the company and its shareholders, or it can make a guess as to what the rate of tax is going to be between 1 April and 30 September.

Q. Why cannot the rate of tax for any year be announced in advance? For example, why cannot the Chancellor of the Exchequer announce at the next Budget Day what the rate of tax will be for the year ended 31 March 1970?

A. The reason is that a Chancellor must have some idea of the profits available before he can tax them. In other words, he budgets for the coming year. This is, of course, ridiculous, and it would make very little difference in practice if the Chancellor announced the rates in advance. He did so with income tax in 1964.

Close companies

Q. Can it be said that a close company is, for practical purposes, the same as a private company for surtax purposes under the previous legislation?

A. No. The definition is much wider and much more intricate. However, some attempt has been made to clear up some of the anomalies applicable to surtax companies.

Q. What, shortly, are the main disadvantages suffered by a close company?

A. The disadvantages, which will be dealt with separately later, can be classified under five headings:

1. The remuneration of some of the directors is restricted;
2. There is a liability in respect of the amount to which the company does not distribute its profits, i.e., a shortfall. This is similar to the old surtax direction but it now applies to income tax as well because a company does not now pay income tax;
3. There is a surtax direction but not quite so harsh as the previous surtax direction;
4. Any interest on loans made by directors or 'participators' is treated as a distribution or a dividend and is not allowed as a deduction for computing Corporation Tax;
5. Any loan to a participator or to an 'associate' is regarded as a distribution.

Q. How do you define a close company?

A. A close company is either:
1. a company under the control of five or fewer participators; or
2. a company under the control of participators who are directors.

Q. This seems a much simpler definition than the previous one for surtax purposes. Is it really as simple as that?

A. Unfortunately, no. We not only have to find out what constitutes a director, a participator, and an associate, but there are also other complications.

Q. A participator is defined very clearly by paragraph 4 (1) of Schedule 18 of the Finance Act 1965 as a 'person having a share or interest in the capital or income of the company'. These words have a familiar ring, and it is difficult to know how they can be regarded as complex.

A. The meaning of 'participator' is extended by Corporation Tax legislation to a degree that almost baffles the imagination. It includes:

(a) any person who possesses or is entitled to acquire share capital or voting rights in the company;
(b) any person who is a loan creditor of the company;
(c) any person who possesses or is entitled to acquire a right to receive or participate in distributions of a company.

Q. Take the first definition. When looking at a person who possesses or is entitled to acquire share capital or voting rights in the company, does this really mean the present tense?

A. No. It means either presently or in the future, and it also includes a person who has an option to take up shares.

Q. Is there any complication in the expression 'loan creditor'?

A. This is immensely complicated. One can only advise anyone who wants to get to the bottom of it to read Beattie's *Corporation Tax*, p. 130, which sets out this definition in detail.

Q. Are there any complications with regard to 'any person who possesses or is entitled to acquire a right'?

A. It has already been suggested that the definition of participator is already so wide that this particular definition does not add anything to it. However, case histories in the courts will eventually show whether this assumption is correct or not.

Q. Does this cover the lot?

A. No. There is a further provision that refers to any person who is 'entitled to secure' income or assets, whether present or future, of the company that would be applied directly or indirectly for his benefit. These apparently meaningless words should be treated with the greatest respect, especially where a company is connected with a settlement.

Q. Having defined a participator, does this clear the field when it comes to considering what amounts to control?

A. No. When you are considering what is a participator, you must also include in relation to each participator his 'associates' and, also, companies of which he and his associates have control.

Q. What is an associate of a participator?

A. The basic idea is that any relation whether husband or wife, child or parent, brother or sister, partner of the participator may be a party to some scheme by which less tax is paid. Therefore, such a person is treated as an associate and, therefore, as the same person as the participator himself.

Q. What about trustees of settlements and executors of estates of deceased persons?

A. These people are included.

4*

Directors

Q. How does the definition of a director differ from the old legislation?

A. It is not dissimilar. The word 'director' includes not only a person who is actually a director but any person occupying the position of a director by whatever name called.

Q. What percentage of the capital of a company must a non-director hold before he is caught under this definition?

A. The definition includes a manager or a person otherwise concerned in the management of the company's trade or business if he is remunerated out of the funds of that business and is able directly or indirectly to control 20 per cent or more of the ordinary share capital of the company.

Q. Does this include beneficial ownership of shares?

A. Yes. And it does not matter by what medium beneficial ownership is maintained.

Q. How can one, at short notice, get down to the job of ascertaining the beneficial ownership or its control through shareholdings?

A. Quite frankly, it is better not to do this quickly but to ask the company's accountants to look at any particular situation, either factual or envisaged. However, if the job must be done quickly one should refer to Examples 45, 46, 47, and 48 in Beattie's *Corporation Tax*. A close examination of these examples will show how many obstructions there are to overcome before a company can clear itself of the stigma of a close company.

Q. What are the exemptions from the rules that define a close company?

A. There are, in fact, four, but it will be seen that only one is of practical importance. The four are:

1. A non-resident company. (Note that this test on examination will be found to be different from the case of a company for which exemption was sought for surtax purposes);

2. a company controlled by the Crown;

3. a company the control of which is, by reason of the beneficial ownership of its shares, in the hands of one or more non-close companies. This definition has given false hope to many. It is possible, in theory, to give many examples of how a company may be regarded as controlled or not controlled as the case may be. The lesson of experience, however, is to look at your own company, to take a sheet of paper, and write down the controlling interest and then to examine the persons who actually own these controlling interests. Only by close examination of the interests of each individual shareholder, whether he is an individual or a company, can it be ascertained whether the test is fulfilled;

4. a quoted company. This must represent at least 95 per cent of the exempted companies. It is a company whose shares carry not less than 35 per cent of the voting power and are beneficially held by the public.

Q. Are there any particular conditions attached to this type of share?

A. Yes. Four points stand out immediately. These are:

(a) the shares must, in fact, have the right to participate in profits;

(b) such shares are not considered to be held by the public if they are held by any director or an associate of a director or any company that is under the control of such a director;

(c) the shares must have been allotted unconditionally to, or acquired unconditionally by, the public. Note here again, for the purpose of research, the difference between 'allotted' and 'acquired';

(d) the shares must have been quoted in the official list of a recognized stock exchange and been the subject of dealings within the twelve months preceding the time in which the company claims to be exempt from treatment as a close company. Plus a few extra restrictions contained in Schedule 11 of the Finance Act 1967.

Q. What is the object of all these restrictions?

A. The idea is to frustrate those who try to dress up a company as a public company while nevertheless retaining its essential private character.

Q. But supposing one has no intention of tax avoidance but nevertheless wishes to have a public company that has a good deal of private investment?

A. The fact must be accepted that the legislation is so widely drawn that it is possible, quite innocently, to fall within its net unless great care is taken.

Restrictions

Q. Before dealing with the restrictions set out in the legislation, what is the position of a company whose shares are held by a settlement? One hears gruesome stories of pitfalls in existence for an unwary and completely innocent settlor, who might also be a director of a private company.

A. The textbooks are almost silent on this subject, but the stories heard are quite as gruesome as they have been suggested. They are in the *Law Reports*. Anyone who is a settlor of a settlement, and that settlement comprises shares either in a company or in a company that is a member of a group that are close companies should study section 408 of The Income Tax Act 1952 in detail. It will be seen that the most innocent transactions have involved settlors in many thousands of pounds of surtax liability simply through a lack of know-how.

Q. I understand that section 408 operates only where a settlor receives a capital payment from a company concerned. Why should this worry the average settlor?

A. Again, study section 408. From this you will see that if you take a loan from such a company or even if you are repaid a loan you have made to such a company, the loan or the repayment as the case may be is regarded as a capital payment.

83

Q. What is the limit of the liability?

A. The amount of the loan you receive or the repayment you receive is regarded as a kind of net dividend, and you are liable to surtax on its gross equivalent.

Q. Is there any limitation on the amount of this liability?

A. Yes, but it is illusory. You may pay income tax only on the amount of income undistributed by the settlement each year. In practice this can be a crippling sum.

Q. Supposing I receive a loan from such a company and repay it—does that get rid of the difficulty?

A. No. The difficulty remains until your sins are paid in full, i.e., when you have paid the full amount of surtax.

Q. Has this anything to do with the existing penalties on loans to participators from private companies?

A. No. It is simply an additional burden.

Remuneration

Q. What is the point of restricting a director's remuneration when he has, in any event, paid full income tax and surtax on that remuneration?

A. Do not forget that this restriction on remuneration is a hang-over from Profits Tax days. The idea in Profits Tax days, when all profits tax was regarded as an expense for income tax, was that one could just swamp a company's liabilities simply by paying large remuneration. Nowadays, although there is no need for this restriction, it is maintained for no other reason than to make a close company pay more tax.

Q. What kind of director is involved in the running of a close company?

A. There are four types of director:

  1. the whole time service director who is a man who works full time and does not own or control more than 5 per cent of the ordinary share capital of the company. (Remember that this restriction also applies to his wife and children. If they have a share holding and the aggregate amounts to more than 5 per cent, then he loses his immunity.) Apart from that, this director is not subject to any restrictions.

  2. Now comes the full-time working director. This is the person who although he owns more than 5 per cent of the ordinary share capital nevertheless works full time in the business;

  3. Then there is the director proper. For Corporation Tax purposes this includes the person who may be a manager, secretary, or person working in some such capacity who either alone or with associates owns not less than 20 per cent of the share capital;

  4. Then there is the professional director, often a solicitor or accountant who should be able to look after his own position quite adequately.

Q. What are the restrictions on remuneration?

A. It is best to answer this by stating what remuneration is allowed. Putting aside the whole-time service director and the professional director the lowest following is the remuneration allowed:

1. 15 per cent of the profits of the year;
2. 15 per cent of the average profits of the preceding three years;
3. £4,000 for one director, £7,000 for two directors, £10,000 for three directors, and £13,000 for four directors. The top limit is £4,000 for any individual, but where any one director gets less, his deficiency can be set off against the excess of another. Note that a deficiency works from the highest paid downwards.

Shortfalls

Q. What is the idea behind the new doctrine of shortfalls?

A. The basic object of the Corporation Tax is to encourage companies to retain their profits and not to distribute them to their shareholders. In close companies, however, there is a suspicion that profits will be unnecessarily retained thus avoiding income tax and surtax.

Q. How does this reconcile with the surtax direction?

A. It is something entirely new. It is, in fact, an income tax direction.

Q. If a company holding is subject to Capital Gains Tax when it is sold and to Estate Duty when the owner dies, what object is there from the tax point of view in having such a shortfall?

A. There is no logic about it. The shortfall enables the tax to be collected more quickly. The Revenue will then be in a position to gather income tax, surtax and, in due course, Capital Gains Tax and Death Duty.

Q. What is the distribution that a company must make?

A. The maximum distribution should be the whole of the company's investment income plus 60 per cent of its trading income.

Q. Does this mean then that a company should pay 40 per cent Corporation Tax *and* income tax on its profits?

A. No. The 60 per cent is calculated on the amount of the profits of the company that is left after paying Corporation Tax. At present rates, this amounts to 36 per cent.

Q. Is this distribution mandatory?

A. No, if the company can show that the required standard of distribution could not be maintained, having regard to the circumstances of the company. (The onus of proof is on the company.)

Q. What kind of circumstances justify the need to plough back profits?

A. It is really a question of liquidity. Other circumstances would be the need to plough back profits for new plant and machinery, credit, development, and expansion.

Q. Are there any exemptions for small companies?

A. Where the net trading income (after Corporation Tax) is less than £1,500 there is complete exemption. This is the equivalent of £2,500 profits before tax.

Q. Are there any abatements?

A. Yes, but so trivial these days that they are hardly worth mentioning. If the trading income does not exceed £9,000, then there is a small liability based on a formula.

Q. Is there any investment income relief?

A. Yes, but again a very trivial affair. This is 10 per cent of any estate or trading income with a maximum deduction of £200. This really applies to small companies that have a small amount of investment income, e.g., dividends on trade investments, required for the purpose of the actual trading.

Q. How is the shortfall charged?

A. It is charged to income tax at the standard rate.

Q. Are there any reliefs?

A. Yes. The income tax can be offset by:

1. any excess of franked investment income (see below) over dividends paid for the year concerned;
2. any surplus franked investment income brought forward;
3. any excess remuneration of directors that was disallowed.

Q. Assuming that tax has been paid on a shortfall, what is the position when a dividend is subsequently paid?

A. In this case the tax is available as a credit against the income tax to be accounted for on any subsequent dividends paid in excess of the required standard for that particular year.

Q. When tax has been paid on an income tax shortfall, does this mean that the company is free from further assessment?

A. No. As indicated previously, there is always the surtax direction. In this case the surtax direction will be almost automatic.

Q. Does this mean that an actual surtax direction covers the total income without any regard to the requirements of the company?

A. No. The same figure will be used but it will be seen that this is less than 100 per cent. The position is still oppressive, of course, but not quite so bad as it used to be.

Q. When there is an assessment in respect of a shortfall, who has to pay?

A. This will be a liability to surtax in the hands of the individual member.

Loans to participators

Q. Does the new legislation relate to loans to participators only?

A. No. It also covers a loan to an associate of a participator.

Q. But supposing a participator or his associate is paying a commercial interest on the loan, does this make any difference?

A. No. The idea behind the legislation is that the loan is being paid instead of salary or a dividend. The loan is therefore regarded as a distribution that has to be grossed up and income tax paid on the gross amount.

Q. Who has to pay the income tax?

A. The assessment is made on the company under the new Schedule F.

Q. Can the position be put right?

A. Yes. When a loan is repaid, then relief is granted.

Q. Does this apply to part of a loan?

A. Yes.

Loan interest

Q. In what cases is loan interest payable by a close company regarded as a distribution and not as an expense?

A. Strictly speaking, any loan interest paid to a director, an annuity or other annual payment to a participator or rent or other outgoings in excess of a reasonable commercial consideration will not be allowed as a deduction in the case of a close company.

Q. What is the effect of this?

A. Not only will tax be payable but it will also greatly increase the cost of borrowing.

Q. What is the idea behind this?

A. It is felt that a director or his associate is lending the money instead of investing and that the two things amount to the same.

Q. But is this not ridiculous in a company that may require short loans for short and varying periods?

A. It is.

Q. But does this not mean that there is, in fact, no difference between funding a loan from an outside source at 10 per cent and a loan from yourself at 6 per cent.

A. It does.

Payment of tax

Q. What is meant by the expression 'franked investment income'?

A. This means income received by way of distribution of profit from another body corporate that is subject to Corporation Tax. Broadly speaking, this represents dividends from United Kingdom companies.

Q. Does the recipient company have to pay Corporation Tax again?

A. No. As Corporation Tax has already been levied it would amount to double taxation if it were once more to be subject to this charge.

Q. Does income tax have to be levied?

A. Yes, income tax must be deducted at source and accounted for by the paying company under Schedule F.

Q. What is the income tax position?

A. The income tax will not be repayable, but it may be set off against income tax, which the company has to account for on its *own* payment of dividends.

Q. What happens where there is an excess? For example, supposing a company receives more by way of investment income than it actually pays out?

A. The excess will be available for carry forward in respect of future distributions.

Q. How long can the company claim credit or off-set for this excess?

A. Indefinitely.

Q. What is the position with groups of companies?

A. In such, there may be an election to pay dividends gross.

Q. What kind of companies can use this election?

A. Subsidiaries and consortiums.

Q. What is a consortium?

A. A company 75 per cent of whose ordinary share capital is owned by five or fewer companies each owning not less than 5 per cent.

Distributions

Q. Apart from loans and interest on loans made by participators, what payments by a company are now regarded as distributions?

A. Apart from the two benefits referred to later, there are various types of distribution. The most important are:

1. an income dividend or a capital dividend;
2. any other distributions including a distribution in specie;
3. a bonus issue of redeemable shares or securities.

Q. Does this cover a repayment or return of capital?

A. No. Neither does it cover any amount for which any new consideration is given. If any question like this arises it is well to look into the matter further in detail before the operation is started.

Q. What kind of benefits are included as distributions?

A. In close companies, any rent, royalties, or, in fact, anything that represents more than a reasonable commercial consideration and, also, the usual expenses or benefits in kind.

Q. What is the actual charge to tax on a distribution?

A. The charge would be on the grossed up equivalent of the actual amount of cash paid out.

Q. Does this mean globally or individually?

A. It means to the person concerned.

Q. Who has to account for the tax?

A. The position is similar to that in PAYE. The company will be required to account for the tax on a monthly basis.

Q. Although we have covered this subject partly under the payment of Corporation Tax, what is the position so far as an ordinary or preference dividend received from another United Kingdom company?

A. As tax will have been suffered by deduction, this tax will be available as an off-set against the tax the company must itself account on its own distributions.

Q. Can any excess income tax suffered be carried forward?

A. Yes.

Q. Again, at the risk of repetition, is it a fact that in the case of inter-company dividends these can be paid gross if an election is made?

A. Yes.

Q. What is the position in the case of non-franked income, i.e., income which, although income tax has been deducted, has not already been subjected to Corporation Tax?

A. In such a case the income tax (not the income) can be off-set against Corporation Tax and, if this exceeds the Corporation Tax liability, a claim for repayment can be made.

Q. What types of non-franked income are chiefly envisaged here?

A. These can be interest on debentures from United Kingdom companies and dividends from overseas companies (paid through a paying agent) and interest on certain government securities.

Q. What is the present position relating to payments of interest and other annual payments?

A. Previously a company, or indeed anybody, who paid interest or annual interest, was able to deduct income tax at source. If the company had sufficient income that had suffered income tax, then it was able to retain that income tax to off-set its own tax liabilities. It must be remembered that this is not to be confused with an expense. Income was simply paid out, tax was deducted, and this was regarded as a proper retention. Under the new system, tax will still be deducted from annual payments made but it cannot be regarded as having been paid out of income brought into charge for income tax purposes. What it really amounts to is that you deduct tax and account for it to the Inland Revenue.

Q. What is the position with regard to charges between one company and another?

A. Assuming that both companies are liable to Corporation Tax and that one of them is the subsidiary of the other, or the consortium position arises, then the charge may be paid gross.

Q. What benefit is this when income tax has to be paid eventually?

A. It does enable the money represented by the tax to be used by way of capital in the meantime.

Q. Let us for the moment go back to income tax payable in respect of a shortfall. Supposing there is an excess of franked investment income either in the present or previous years, can this excess be regarded as covering the amount of the deficiency in the distribution?

A. Yes.

Q. What happens in the case of excess remuneration to a director?

A. The same principles apply.

Q. Although it cannot be strictly regarded as a distribution, what is the position relating to annual payments made under a seven-year covenant in respect of a charity?

A. These are deductible for Corporation Tax although they might not have been for income tax purposes. In point of fact, many such payments were made by companies that could not claim they were for the purposes of the trade, but as tax was deducted the question became academic.

Inter-company relief

Q. In what way does the new relief given under section 20 of the Finance Act 1967 differ from the subvention payments scheme that has been in operation since 1953?

A. Apart from cutting out a number of irritating anomalies, the new scheme is tidier than the subvention payments scheme but it can hardly be called revolutionary.

Q. Basically, what is the new scheme?

A. Where a company in a group suffers a loss and another company in the group has a profit, then the loss of one company can be set off against the profits of the other.

Q. Does any cash have to pass between the profit-making company and the loss-making company?

A. No. The basis of the old subvention scheme was that cash had to pass between one company and the other. In fact, this was farcical as it amounted to nothing more than taking money from one pocket and putting it into another. Further, owing to the curious drafting of section 20 of the Finance Act 1953 there were certain difficulties of a technical nature, and the Inland Revenue actually took one company to the House of Lords.

Q. Obviously this is a reference to the recent case of *Davies, Jenkins & Co. Ltd.* v. *Davies*. What was the technical difficulty in that case which is now avoided by the new legislation?

A. In the case of *Davies, Jenkins & Co., Ltd. v. Davies* the Revenue tried to disallow a payment between a profit-making company and a loss-making company in the same group on grounds that are now seen to be purely technical. At one point, the companies fell within the definition set out in section 20, namely, that they were both members of a group, one had made a loss, and the other a profit, in corresponding accounting periods. However, before the payment was made by the profit-making company to the loss-making company, the loss-making company had ceased to trade. The Revenue contended that the company should still be trading when the payment was made. Although the company was eventually successful it had to fight all the way to the House of Lords before establishing a simple point.

Q. It is said that there is difference between the wording of the original Bill and that contained in the Finance Act. What kind of company is now affected by the new legislation?

A. The new relief known as 'group relief' is available to:

(a) companies that are members of the same group;
(b) members of a consortium.

Q. Before looking at the definitions of companies, let us look at one apparent difficulty in the wording of the Act. In section 20 it is noted that relief may be surrendered by a 'surrendering company' and claimed by a 'claimant company'. In paragraph 1 of schedule 10 it is enacted that if 'the one company' had incurred a loss, the amount of the loss may be set off against the total profits of 'the other company'. Is there any difference here between the types of company referred to in section 20 and in paragraph 1?

A. No. Paragraph 1 is really repeating the strange wording of section 20.

Q. What types of company are covered by this new relief?

A. The new relief applies only to bodies corporate resident in the United Kingdom.

Q. When do the new provisions relating to group relief come into force?

A. They came into force on the passing of the Finance Act 1967, which received the Royal Assent on the 21 July 1967.

Q. Does this mean that accounts have to be split?

A. The new provisions and the cessation of the subvention payments apply to accounting periods ending *after* the commencement of the Act.

Q. What constitutes a subsidiary company for the purposes of group relief?

A. The word 'subsidiary' has the meaning assigned to it for profits tax purposes by the Finance Act 1938, namely, three-quarters ownership of the ordinary voting share capital, with the usual provisions relating to a chain of ownership through two or more companies.

Q. What were the amendments relating to a company that is a member of the consortium, which were introduced during the passing of the Finance Bill?

A. Section 20 (2) shows the extent of the amendment and admitted an important type of company to relief. These are:

1. a surrendering company that is a trading company owned by a consortium and *not* a subsidiary of any company, and a claimant company that is a member of a consortium;

2. (a) where the surrendering company is a 90 per cent subsidiary of a holding company owned by a consortium *and*

   (b) is *not* a subsidiary of a company other than the holding company, *and* the claimant company is a member of the consortium;

3. where the surrendering company is a holding company owned by a consortium and which is not a subsidiary of any company *and* the claimant company is a member of a consortium.

Q. Does this apply to shares of companies held by finance companies?

A. No. No claim can be made if a profit on the sale of the share capital of a surrendering or holding company that member owns would be treated as a trading receipt by that member.

Q. What happens when there are two or more claimant companies in respect of the same surrendering company?

A. Provided it relates to the same accounting period these companies can make a claim.

Q. How is group membership defined?

A. The Act puts it simply, namely, 'two companies shall be deemed to be members of a group of companies if one is a subsidiary of the other or both are subsidiaries of a third company'.

Q. What is meant by a 'holding company'?

A. Here, again, the Act is fairly clear and defines a holding company as 'a company the business of which consists wholly or mainly in the holding of shares or securities of companies which are its 90 per cent subsidiaries and which are trading companies'.

Q. Supposing, after relief has been given, one company makes a payment to the other, what effect does it have for Corporation Tax purposes?

A. It is ignored when computing the profits or losses of either company and, further, is not regarded as a distribution or a charge on income.

Q. Does this 'payment for group relief' mean that any payment can be made?

A. No. It must not exceed the amount surrendered by way of group relief.

Q. What is the position relating to capital allowances?

A. Paragraph 2 of schedule 10 is worthy of careful study. The effect is that capital allowances which cannot be covered by the relevant income of one company can be set off by the profits of another for its corresponding accounting period.

Q. What is the position relating to charges on income?

A. Where the charges payable on income exceed the profits of one company they may be set off for Corporation Tax purposes against the total profits of the other company. (*See* paragraph 4).

Q. What is the relationship between group relief and other relief?

A. Paragraph 5 should be studied. This states that group relief for an accounting period shall be allowed as a deduction . . . for the period 'before reduction by any relief derived from a subsequent accounting period but as reduced by any other relief from tax'.

Q. Paragraph 6 refers to corresponding accounting periods. Does this mean that accounting periods that overlap each other must be regarded as corresponding?

A. Unfortunately no. Paragraph 6 sets out in detail a method by which the amount of a loss that may be set off against the total profits of the profit-making company is dealt with on a fractional basis.

Q. What are the conditions for relief so far as time is concerned?

A. The two companies must be members of the same group throughout the whole of the corresponding periods, but this must be read subject to very important amendments made to the tenth schedule while the Bill was in progress through Parliament. These are contained in Paragraph 8 and are far too lengthy and tortuous to be dealt with shortly.

Q. When must a claim be made under the new section?

A. It must be made within two years from the end of the surrendering company's accounting period to which the claim relates.

Q. Must the claim be for the full amount available?

A. No.

Q. Going back to the old subvention payment provisions, it will be remembered that a great deal of difficulty related to the 'agreement' that had to be made between the companies concerned. Is this difficulty continued?

A. No. A claim shall require the consent of the surrendering company notified, 'to the Inspector in such form as the Board may require'.

The betterment levy (*see also* section 12.3)

Q. What is the object of the Betterment Levy?

A. The idea is that the State should share in the profit that accrues to the individual owner of land where he either is permitted to develop his land or which sometimes merely accrues in hope or expectation that he will be given permission.

Q. When is the levy imposed?

A. This capital levy becomes payable whenever the development value is realized by a landowner.

Q. What does 'development value' mean?

A. It is not precisely defined in the Act but it is described as any additional element of value that is realized from land over and above the value for its current use and that is attributable to the possibilities of putting the land or some other land to another and more profitable use.

Q. Does this not really mean an increase in the value of the land?

A. No. The levy is charged only on the development value and not on increases in what the Act calls 'current use value'.

Q. Is this a temporary tax?

A. Yes, in the sense that once development value is paid for it is not chargeable again.

Q. Is the levy a charge on the property so as to amount to a 'clog'?

A. No. The levy is payable by the person who actually realizes the development value.

Q. How can a person carry out development?

A. In two ways. He can either carry out the development himself or he can dispose of the land to someone else who intends to develop it.

Q. Does this mean, therefore, that the levy is not imposed until either the landowner has taken the decision to develop or has converted the development value into cash?

A. Yes.

Q. How is the development value calculated?

A. There are some very complicated valuation provisions, but essentially it amounts to a comparison between the value of the land in its undeveloped state, assuming that no material development is possible, and the value in the open market taking into account the development potential. The levy is charged on the difference.

Q. Does not this, in fact, amount to the difference between what the land was bought for and what it was sold for?

A. In some cases yes, but more frequently the lower figure is a matter of valuation and will almost usually differ from the price paid for the land. The levy is not an automatic percentage.

Q. But may not a landowner hesitate to improve his land on the grounds that he is simply increasing the development potential?

A. No, such expenditure is a deductible expense from the development value before the levy is charged.

Q. What happens if the calculation shows a deficit?

A. This adverse balance is treated as a credit that can be used by the landowner to reduce further charges to levy, and can be used in connection with future dealings for the same land.

Q. What are the chances of an unfair double charge for levy, estate duty or capital gains tax?

A. A number of provisions have been made to avoid this, and the Finance Act 1967 (section 33 and 34) and schedule 14 removes the possibility of a simultaneous charge to both Betterment Levy and Capital Gains Tax or Corporation Tax.

Selective employment tax

Q. What employees are covered by the new tax?

A. The tax covers all employees for whom National Insurance contributions are made and is payable by the employer only.

Q. What provisions are there for repayment of the tax and for 'premiums'?

A. The Employment Payments Act 1966 provides for repayment of the tax and premiums in varying degrees and in certain defined classes. These are broadly:

Manufacturing and other named industries
Agriculture and associated industries
Charities
Private individuals.

Q. How does an employer know whether he is in one of these exempted or semi-exempted classes?

A. He should seek registration, and he does this by asking for an application form SEP 1 from his local Employment Exchange, and send the completed form to that office.

Q. What happens then?

A. The employer will receive a letter from the Employment Exchange saying either that the establishment has been registered as one which qualifies for premium or refund or that it fails to qualify for either.

Q. What happens when the employer is notified that his establishment has been registered as qualifying for (a) payment of premium, or (b) refund—how does he make his claim?

A. The local Employment Exchange will send him the appropriate forms. There are separate forms for a claim for a premium and claim for refund.

Q. How will the claim be paid?

A. Payment will be made by the Department of Employment and Productivity by credit transfer to the account nominated by the employer on his claim form. At the same time, a note that the credit transfer has been made will be sent to the employer and a new claim form will be sent for the next period.

Q. What are the reliefs given under the Finance Act 1967?

A. There are two types, the first relating to an employee who works less than twenty-one hours a week and the other relating to employees employed outside the United Kingdom and that curious area defined under the Continental Shelf Act 1964.

Q. When does the new relief start?

A. It is in respect of any contribution week beginning on or after 4 September 1967.

Q. Does this refer to all employees?

A. No—there is quite a number of exceptions, one of them relates to an employed person who was treated for the purpose of the tax as a boy or girl under the age of 18.

Q. What is the amount of the relief?

A. It is one half of the tax paid.

Q. Is there any difference of treatment between people who work at an hourly rate and those who are in other types of employment?

A. Yes. Where an employee is employed at an hourly rate, then these hours—and these hours only—are taken into consideration. In the case of any other employment, then any intervals allowed for meals and rest must be taken into consideration.

Q. What happens where a person is employed by different employers who are associated companies?

A. In that case, 'except as the Minister may in any particular case or class of cases otherwise direct', the employee is treated as employed in any particular week in both or all of those employments by the actual employer by whom the tax was paid.

Q. What is the concession given in respect of this 'overseas' employee?

A. Here the Act provides that relief will be given to a person employed for a continuous period of more than thirteen contribution weeks wholly outside this country.

Q. What is the amount of the payment?

A. It amounts to the whole payment.

Q. Are there any restrictions on this new relief?

A. Yes, there are numerous restrictions and they are set out in schedule 12 of the Act.

Q. How is the repayment obtained?

A. The payment will be made on the production by the employer of such records as the Department may specify.

Reading list

Corporation Tax, Percy F. Hughes (Taxation Publishing, 1966 (with supplements))

Corporation Tax, C. N. Beattie (Butterworth, Second edition 1967 (with supplements))

The Development of Firms (special reference to the economic effects of taxation), A. S. MacKintosh (Cambridge University Press, 1963)

Capital Gains Tax, and *Corporation Tax* (both with supplements), Board of Inland Revenue (H.M.S.O., 1966)

Selective Employment Payments Act : a Guide for Employers, Ministry of Labour (H.M.S.O., 1966)

Useful addresses

Institute of Taxation, 15 Cliffords Inn, London EC 4
Commissioners of Inland Revenue, Surtax Office (Companies Division), 31 The Broadway,
    London SW 19
Institute of Chartered Accountants in England and Wales, 56 Goswell Road, London EC 1
Institute of Chartered Accountants in Scotland, 27 Queen Street, Edinburgh 2
Institute of Chartered Accountants in Ireland, 7 Fitzwilliam Place, Dublin 2

2.3 Company Reports and Accounts

A. G. Touche

Annual report and accounts

A company's annual report and accounts are a record of the stewardship of the directors as reported to the shareholders. The directors are appointed by the shareholders to direct the company and must account to the shareholders, who are the proprietors.

In smaller companies, the shareholders and the directors may well be the same people, and knowledge of the affairs of the company will be available to them in their day-to-day executive capacities or at the regular board meetings. In large companies, however, the shareholders are normally not in close contact with the day-to-day affairs of the company and rely on annual reports and accounts issued by the directors, and on any interim reports that may be issued half-yearly or quarterly.

Over the years, financial reporting has greatly improved and shareholders have been provided with an increasing amount of information about their companies. There is, however, often a tendency for directors to give only the information that they are obliged to give, either by legislation or the Stock Exchange requirements for quotations. There is the fear that additional information will be useful to competitors and, therefore, detrimental to the company.

The main contents of the annual report and accounts are:

1. The balance sheet
This shows the position of the company as at the date of the balance sheet. It is a

financial photograph at a particular moment in time. It shows the current assets such as cash, the liabilities, the fixed assets such as plant and machinery, and the source of the funds employed in the business such as the shareholders' capital and the reserves.

2. The profit and loss account

This gives information about the income and expenses and the balance of profit or loss on the company's trading for the period under review, which is normally one year. It also shows how the year's profit is being divided between dividends and reserves.

3. The directors' report

Information additional to that required in the balance sheet and profit and loss account must be disclosed here, such as the principal activities of the company during its financial year.

4. The chairman's statement

Unlike the balance sheet, the profit and loss account, and the directors' report, the chairman's statement is not a statutory requirement. It is the speech he makes at the annual general meeting. Formerly, the first that was heard of the speech was when it was delivered at the annual general meeting and then advertised in the press. Now the speech is usually circulated before the meeting with the annual accounts, and possibly supplemented by additional remarks at the meeting. It contains more chatty information than the drier statutory requirements; indeed some chairmen use their statements as an occasion to air many diverse views, some of which may have little relevance to the company concerned. It is particularly useful for the statement to comment on progress since the end of the company's financial year, and to give an indication of the future outlook.

The evolution of the legislation governing company accounts has been through a series of companies acts. These acts inevitably tend to follow events rather than to anticipate them. However, the amount of information now available to the shareholder as a result of the Companies Act 1967 makes the requirements of the Companies Act 1929, for example, look threadbare indeed.

There is one popular misconception about balance sheets that needs to be corrected. It is sometimes thought that a balance sheet shows the value of a business. This is by no means so, and two examples will illustrate why.

A company might have no figure of goodwill in its balance sheet, yet, if it manufactures a nationally known proprietary product, the value of the goodwill might be very great indeed.

Fixed assets such as buildings and machinery are normally entered in balance sheets at their historical cost less depreciation, the balance representing that part of the historical cost that has not yet been used up in the course of time. For example, if a piece of machinery has a life of ten years, normally depreciation of 1/10th will be written off it each year, the residual cost remaining in the balance sheet. At a time of rising prices, however, the actual value of fixed assets can often be very much greater than the residual figure of the historical costs. Land and buildings are an even better example of assets that can appreciate.

Broadly speaking, a subsidiary company is one over which the holding, or parent, company has voting control. Where a company has one or more subsidiary companies, it is normal for accounts to be issued combining the results of the subsidiaries with the results of the holding company. Such accounts are called consolidated accounts. Where consolidated accounts are not issued for a group of companies, some other form of group accounts must be issued, such as the separate accounts of each company.

Where consolidated accounts are issued, the holding company's own profit and loss account need not be issued; a consolidated profit and loss account is issued which incorporates the income, expenses, and profit or loss of the group of companies, and shows how much of the profit is attributable to minority interests.

A consolidated balance sheet, however, does not excuse the holding company from issuing its own balance sheet in addition. Therefore, the accounts of a company with subsidiary companies normally consist of the holding company's balance sheet, together with the group's consolidated balance sheet, and the group's consolidated profit and loss account.

Although there is no statutory requirement, many companies issue, with their annual report and accounts, a statistical table showing information about the company's (or the groups) position and results for a number of years, possibly ten. The table might show profit before tax, tax, profit earned for ordinary shareholders, dividends, profit retained in the business, total shareholders' funds (i.e., capital and reserves), long-term loans invested in the business, total capital employed (i.e., shareholders' funds plus loan capital), and profit before tax as a percentage of capital employed. The possible variations in statistical tables are many, and the information most useful depends on the circumstances of each company. Included, sometimes, is a statement showing the source and application of funds, which is a summary of the causes of changes in the position shown by this year's and last year's balance sheets.

The information given in the statistical table of the profit before tax expressed as a percentage of the capital employed in the business is a very important statistic, which analysts like to obtain from accounts. This shows how fruitfully the directors are using the funds in their care, and the trend upwards or downwards in the percentage shows whether a company is prospering or declining. A very low percentage (e.g. 5 per cent) shows that the company is not doing well and could be worth more to shareholders dead than alive. If the company is a quoted company, it might be vulnerable to a take-over bid by somebody who thinks he can get a better return on the capital employed. A very high percentage (e.g. 30 per cent) can also be treated with some scepticism, because it might suggest that there is room for more competition; new entrants into the trade might make profits harder to earn.

Unfortunately, the percentage must be taken with a large pinch of salt, chiefly because the present value of fixed assets may be much more than the balance sheet figures; the percentage earned on the real capital employed is then much less than the apparent percentage obtained from analysing the accounts. Indeed, it is possible for a company to be showing a profit in accounts based on historical cost, whereas in reality the company is making a loss, which would be revealed if accounts could be prepared on the basis of current values. If fixed assets were included in the balance sheet at current values the charge for depreciation in the profit and loss account could well be significantly larger, and thus tip a balance of profit into a balance of loss.

The company secretary

The Companies Acts provide that every company shall have a secretary, but they do not clearly define his duties. The secretary may be an individual, a firm, or another company. He is usually appointed by the directors without reference to the shareholders and is responsible for ensuring that the company complies with the provisions both of its own Articles and of the Companies Acts.

While the secretary need not be professionally qualified, there are specialist professional bodies for company secretaries, whose members must take examinations before they can join. The specialist bodies are The Chartered Institute of Secretaries and the Corporation of Secretaries. Lawyers and members of the main accountancy bodies are also recognized as being fitted by their training to act as company secretaries.

In the largest companies, the secretary may have a department to help him with his numerous responsibilities. They include dealing with the requirements of the Companies Acts, attending and minuting board meetings and shareholders' meetings, and ensuring that the regulations governing the company under the Companies Acts and the company's Memorandum and Articles are complied with. The secretary of a quoted company must also ensure that the Stock Exchange regulations are complied with, these regulations being additional to the requirements of the Companies Acts.

He usually has many duties additional to those of a company secretary pure and simple. His close knowledge of the company's affairs often leads him to give advice on them, and he may also be responsible for insurance, personnel work, pension funds, property management, and many other administrative duties, including sometimes the company's accounts.

Although the ultimate responsibility for complying with the provisions of the Companies Acts rests with the directors, they look to the company secretary to ensure that the statutes are observed. It is he who ensures that minutes of meetings, registers of shareholders and debenture holders, of directors and secretaries, of mortgages, of directors' shareholdings and service contracts, and so on are kept. He keeps the company's seal, and issues share certificates and debenture certificates when there is no registrar for this duty. Failure to comply with the requirements can involve the directors 'and any officer' in fines and even imprisonment.

The chief accountant

In the smaller company, the secretary may act also as accountant. Large companies, however, usually have a chief accountant, who is responsible for maintenance of the accounting records, preparation of financial information including the annual accounts, and for the day-to-day financial operations of the company. Whereas the secretary is a statutory officer of the company, and all companies must have a secretary, the chief accountant is not. He is an employee of the company, and no company is obliged to have a chief accountant.

As with the secretary, so there is no necessity for the chief accountant to be professionally qualified. Very often, however, he is a member of one of the leading professional accountancy bodies, which are: The Institute of Chartered Accountants in England and Wales, The Institute of Chartered Accountants of Scotland, The Institute of Chartered Accountants in Ireland, and The Association of Certified and Corporate Accountants.

The auditors

Companies are required by the Companies Acts to have an independent auditor, who reports to the shareholders on the annual accounts. The Companies Acts disqualify certain people, such as directors, from being auditors, and lay down the qualifications required. The auditor is, therefore, the only person connected with companies who must have a professional qualification, or at least Board of Trade authorization. Usually, auditors are firms of practising accountants, so from now on reference is made to 'the auditors' instead of to 'the auditor'.

Auditors are normally members of one of the leading professional accountancy bodies, mentioned above, which have rigorous admission and ethical standards.

Auditors are normally appointed by the shareholders at the annual general meeting. They hold their office from the date of their appointment until the conclusion of the next annual general meeting. However, they are automatically reappointed unless no longer qualified to act, or they have given notice that they are unwilling to continue, or a resolution is passed appointing someone else.

The auditors must report on every balance sheet, profit and loss account, and group accounts presented to shareholders. Group accounts usually take the form of consolidated accounts, which consolidate the figures of the holding company, sometimes called the parent company, with those of subsidiary companies. If the auditors are not satisfied that the accounts reflect a true and fair view of the company's affairs, or that proper books have been kept, or if they have not received all the information and explanations they require, they must say so in their report to the shareholders, which must be issued with the accounts.

To satisfy themselves that proper books have been kept and that the accounts show a true and fair view of the company's affairs, the auditors will inspect books, accounts, and vouchers, and seek explanations from the company's officers for this purpose. While they must exercise reasonable skill and care they are not expected to act as financial detectives. One Judge defined their duties as those of a watchdog rather than a bloodhound.

One of the most difficult tasks of the auditors is to satisfy themselves as to the valuation in the balance sheet of stock and work-in-progress. Changes in this valuation alter the year's profit by a corresponding amount, so its importance can readily be seen.

The auditors' report must be read at general meetings, and the auditors must receive notice of, and may attend, general meetings of the company. They may also be heard at meetings on any matters that concern them as auditors.

In practice, it is the directors who choose the auditors, their choice being confirmed by the shareholders. The choice of auditors should depend on the requirements of the company. Often a company, particularly a small company, will rely on the auditors to prepare the annual accounts and even to write up the books of account. Where work of this nature is needed it is often easier for a local firm to provide staff for this purpose. On the other hand, companies with complex requirements may find that they need the experience and facilities of the larger firms, particularly where work is needed in connection with overseas subsidiaries.

The fees charged by the firm of auditors are usually based on the time taken. It is therefore difficult for them to give a firm quotation in advance, before they can be fully aware of all the work that must be done.

The auditors have no legal responsibility for the preparation of accounts or for their content; their duty is to report on them to shareholders. They are, however, normally consulted on the form of the accounts. If they think that the accounts are not properly prepared and do not comply with the Companies Acts, they will request the directors to alter the accounts. If the directors refuse, the auditors' remedy is then to qualify their report on the accounts and say in what way they are not satisfied.

Ideally, the auditors should receive the accounts and supporting information and schedules at the beginning of the audit, the company having prepared the accounts and the auditors having played no part in their preparation. But very often, particularly where smaller companies are concerned, the auditors play a big part in the actual preparation of the accounts. Where they virtually prepare the accounts they are really acting as consulting accountants, a function that is distinct from their function as auditors reporting to shareholders.

Because of their close knowledge of the company and their wide experience, the accountancy firms that act as auditors are frequently asked to do other work for the company. They often advise on accounting systems, taxation matters, and so on. Some accountancy firms have set up management consulting departments to assist their clients with the introduction of new accounting systems, accounting machines, computers, costing systems, budgetary control, and similar matters.

These professional services are in no way the responsibility of the auditors as such, but their close knowledge of a company over a number of years often gives them a wealth of background information that enables them to carry out such work efficiently and economically.

Reading list

Accounting Requirements of the Companies Act, A. G. Touche (Butterworth, 1967)
How to Read a Balance Sheet (International Labour Office, Geneva, 1966)
A Simple Guide to Shareholding and Company Accounts, John Wood (Putnam, 1955)
Understanding Accounts, Robert S. Waldrun (Nelson, 1965)
Secretarial Practice, 7th edition, Chartered Institute of Secretaries (Heffer & Sons, Cambridge)
The Elusive Art of Accounting, H. I. Ross (Ronalds Press, 1966)
A Guide to Company Balance Sheets and Profit & Loss Accounts, F. H. Jones, Sixth edition 1964, and supplement (Heffer & Sons, Cambridge)
Manual of Auditing, V. R. V. Cooper (Gee & Co., 1966)
Report of the Company Law Committee (H.M.S.O. 1962)
Financial & Management Accounting Practice in the United Steel Companies (United Steel Companies Ltd., Sheffield)

Useful addresses

Institute of Chartered Accountants in England and Wales, 56 Goswell Road, London EC 1
Institute of Chartered Accountants of Scotland, 27 Queen Street, Edinburgh 2
Institute of Chartered Accountants in Ireland, 7 Fitzwilliam Place, Dublin 2
Association of Certified and Corporate Accountants, 22 Bedford Square, London WC 1
Chartered Institute of Secretaries, 16 Park Crescent, London W 1
Corporation of Secretaries, 13 Devonshire Street, London W 1

2.4 Preparing for Decimal Currency

Lord Fiske

On 14 July 1967 the Decimal Currency Bill received Royal Assent and became the Decimal Currency Act 1967. This event marked the end of a controversy that has exercised Parliament periodically for over 150 years. Two questions have been the cause of this protracted debate: first, 'Should we decimalize our currency?', and second, 'If so, what decimal system should we adopt?' The two questions have always been closely bound up together. Indeed it is the difficulty of answering the second question that has been largely responsible for the considerable delay in answering the first one. Controversy over choice of system has been largely responsible for denying us the benefits of a decimal system for many years. It is this that explains why 120 years have elapsed since the florin was introduced, in 1849, as one-tenth of a pound and with the specific intention that it should be the first step to a full decimal system.

The 1967 Act put an end at last to this controversy, and brought us to the much less discussed stage of deciding how the chosen system was to be introduced.

During 1967–68 the Board concentrated on marking out more clearly the guidelines laid down in the Act, and the pattern of the changeover is now clear. Progress up to the end of March 1968 was set out in the first Annual Report. The date for the introduction of decimal currency has been fixed for 15 February 1971—'D Day'—and the Republic of Ireland, the Channel Islands, and the Isle of Man have decided to change to the same system on the same day. We shall retain the £

as the basic unit, but it will be divided into 100 'new pence' (written '*p*'). There will be a $\frac{1}{2}p$ to give the necessary flexibility. Six coins will circulate, the first two of which you will probably already have been given in your change. These are the 5*p* and 10*p*, 'silver' coins of exactly the same dimensions, weight, and value as the shilling and two shilling pieces. The third silver—actually cupro-nickel—coin is the 50*p*, worth 10*s*, which will be introduced in October 1969. In size, it is between the florin and half-crown and has seven curved sides. We believe this 'equilateral curve heptagon' to be unique in coinage. The bronze $\frac{1}{2}p$, 1*p*, and 2*p*, which are of the same alloy as our present coppers and roughly equivalent in size to the silver threepenny bit, the farthing, and the halfpenny, have no £*sd* equivalents and will not be legal tender until D Day. They will be in wide use before D Day for training and similar purposes.

Apart from the 10*s* note, which will be gradually replaced by the 50*p*, we shall lose two of our present units before D Day. The halfpenny will be demonetized on 1 August 1969 and the halfcrown on 1 January 1970. The banks are introducing separate bags for the two coins and will cease to issue them, except by request, as the date of demonetization approaches. After that date, they will not be legal tender, and cannot be used as money.

All the coins except the 50*p* are available already in souvenir sets. The 50*p* was not included because its design had not been finalized.

Some decisions have still to be made, most of them relating to the changeover period. For example, it must be determined how £*sd* references in legislation, contracts, and the like should be converted into decimal currency; how £*sd* debts should be settled in decimal; and what legal tender arrangements should be made. Official conversion tables will have to be worked out for £*sd* amounts which do not convert exactly to decimal and for some purposes will have the force of law. New legislation will settle these questions fairly soon.

The broad changeover pattern

One of the key facts about the changeover to decimal currency is that it cannot be achieved overnight. Several countries have now gone decimal from £*sd* systems similar to our own, and the general changeover pattern is clear. We, in this country, are fortunate to be able to draw on the experience of countries such as South Africa, which went decimal in February 1961, Australia, which decimalized in February 1966, and New Zealand, which decimalized in 1967. All three countries adopted a broadly similar changeover pattern and all three had Decimal Currency Boards like ours.

D Day

On D Day the decimal currency will become our official currency. The banks will switch completely to decimal working so that all cheques and other bank documents will be drawn in decimal. So that they have time to make the changeover—to clear cheques in the pipeline, to balance and then convert their ledger accounts—the banks will close from Thursday to Saturday, 11–13 February, before D Day. Most government departments, the Post Office, and a substantial section of industry, commerce, and the retail trade will also change over on D Day. Decimal bronze coins will appear and a large proportion of our everyday cash transactions will be in decimal. To help shoppers, price labels in shops may well quote both the new decimal price and the old £sd one, and people will be provided with pocket conversion tables.

But not all shops and other organizations will switch to decimals immediately. This is because it is impossible to convert or replace, overnight, all the monetary machines which now record £sd—machines such as cash registers, adding and accounting machines, price-computing scales, and postage franking machines. Organizations will gradually switch to decimals as their machines are converted or replaced, and thus both old and new currencies must for a period circulate together. In a given street some shops may be £sd and some may be decimal. The buses may be £sd and the trains decimal. People will, in fact, for a time have to think and do business in both currencies.

The changeover period will be a difficult one both for the public and for industry and commerce. The banks, too, are affected because they must continue to supply pennies and threepenny pieces for organizations that have not changed. Problems will arise, particularly in shops, about the extent to which the two bronze coinages can be regarded as interchangeable, and special legal tender provisions will have to apply. It is clearly in the interests of us all that the changeover period should be kept to the bare minimum, and one of the Decimal Currency Board's chief tasks is to examine, with the machine industry and others, ways and means of keeping it short. The auguries are good. Australia thought she would need two years and completed the operation in less than one and a half years. New Zealand originally thought in terms of eighteen months . . . and in the event shortened it to ten and a half months.

We are planning a maximum period of eighteen months. Of course, most of us—both individuals and organizations—will be decimalized long before then, and if possible the changeover period will be shortened. It will certainly not be lengthened. The end of the changeover period will be marked by the final demonetization of the penny, threepenny bit, and sixpence.

Changeover problems

We can roughly divide the work of the changeover into five categories:

First, coinage work. About 5–6,000 million decimal coins will be needed, and the immense task of producing them will fall on the Royal Mint. A new factory is being built in South Wales. Distributing the new coins and withdrawing the old ones will also place a heavy burden on the banks.

Second, machine work. Probably, about five million machines will be affected by the changeover in this country, half of them business machines such as cash registers, and half of them coin-operated machines. This is roughly ten times the size of the machine problem in Australia. The conversion and replacement programme will place a heavy burden on the machine industry.

Third, there is a heavy load of non-machine conversion work—alteration of price and stationery, devising of dual-price labels, drawing up of conversion tables; all kinds of dual-accounting problems.

Fourth, there are cash handling problems, particularly during the period of dual-currency working, which fall mainly on the retail trade, transport interests, the Post Office, and others who deal with the public in everyday money matters.

Fifth, there is a great deal of work to be done on public education and training— the revision of school textbooks and teaching and examination syllabuses, the preparation of publicity material, the mounting of publicity and training schemes both for the general public and for specific groups with special interests such as shop assistants, bus conductors, the old, and so on.

The need for early planning

The foregoing gives only the broadest description of the work involved in the switch to decimals. The work and the problems differ from organization to organization. Most organizations have problems, however, because all of them deal with money in one way or another, and in the interests of a smooth and efficient changeover it is essential that they should identify these problems as soon as possible. It is over two years to D Day, and there may still be the temptation to conclude that nothing needs to be done yet, or perhaps to assume that things can, for the time being, be left to the Decimal Currency Board. This is not so. It is true that the introduction of decimal currency into an organization does not call for many top-level policy decisions. Many of the problems are problems of detail. But it does call for concentrated and detailed attention at responsible middle-management levels.

It is certainly not too early for the directors of large organizations outside Government to follow the practice of Government departments and appoint a fairly senior member of staff to be 'decimalization officer'. The task of the decimalization officer, who might well be full-time as D Day draws nearer, would be to identify the problems that decimalization will bring throughout the whole organization, to investigate ways and means of solving them quickly and economically, to liaise with decimalization officers in similar organizations, and perhaps with the appropriate trade association or even the Decimal Currency Board. He would also obviously need to consult, as soon as possible, with the manufacturer of the business machines used by his organization to determine what programme of replacement or conversion is appropriate. And the decimalization officer would need to bear in mind the effect on stationery and printing requirements. Decimalization may well place a heavy burden on the printing industry, and those who place their orders late may be disappointed.

Two examples of many ways in which a keen decimalization officer might be able to benefit his organization are: First, decimalization obviously calls for changes in a company's accounting system. It would probably be a pity if these changes were confined to the minimum and introduced at the last moment. Decimalization should provide an opportunity for a fresh 'organization and methods'-type approach to an accounting system and it may be that a more searching reappraisal would show the possibility of benefits not immediately obvious—perhaps a simplification of procedures, or the introduction of new types of machines. One possibility that many boardrooms may wish to examine is that of introducing a decimal system for internal accounting purposes well before the changeover date. One virtue of the £ system is that it makes this kind of early internal decimalization possible.

A second possibility to be borne in mind during the preparatory period is that of so adjusting prices when changes are under discussion that they will decimalize easily when 1971 arrives. Any £sd amount that is a multiple of sixpence has an exact decimal equivalent. No rounding is involved and no cash handling difficulties arise during the transition. I do not for one moment suggest that the advent of decimalization should be used as an excuse for price increases. But experience elsewhere shows how easy the decimalization of these easily convertible amounts can be achieved.

Exactly what is the Board's role in the conversion to a decimal currency system? Our job, quite simply, is to do all we can to facilitate the changeover. But alone we can do nothing. Decimalization calls for team work and effort from all of us. Manufacturers know their business better than we can hope to know it. And, of course, they know their customers and their requirements better than we do. Machine problems, particularly those of individual users, must essentially be thrashed out between suppliers and users. We have appointed a Machine Committee, consisting of three professional engineers on the Board, to advise us on machine problems, and they are supported by highly qualified engineers on the staff. Our aim, working mainly through the industry and its representative bodies, is to keep ourselves informed of the plans the companies are making, to co-ordinate and guide where co-ordination and guidance seem called for, to consider general representations made to us by the industry and by users, and, perhaps, to make recommendations to the Government on them, to stimulate activity where it might seem to us from our central position that things are lagging behind.

One task that falls to the Board is that of considering representations concerning compensation for the costs incurred in the changeover—mainly, of course, machine costs. On this there has been some misunderstanding and some clarification is needed.

The Board cannot, for example, recommend a general scheme of compensation for machine users. The Government have decided there will be no such scheme. What we must do is to examine representatives from those who regard themselves as special cases that justify an exception being made to the Government's declared general policy. The Decimal Currency Board has carefully considered the representations made to it, and criteria have emerged which 'special cases' will have to satisfy. These criteria are tough, as they have to be if a general scheme of compensation is excluded, and no organization so far has satisfied them. For the vast majority of firms, it is safe to assume that there will be no compensation although the Board will continue to consider any representations submitted to it.

I have explained something of the background in the changeover to decimal currency, the history, and the changeover period. I have also mentioned the Board's role in this exciting task. I must, however, emphasize that the Board came into existence as a statutory body only in mid-1967. We do not claim to know all the answers or even all the questions; our programme is still being developed, and it is clear that we shall continue to be faced with many changing situations as we approach D Day. A number of our preliminary views might need to be amended as circumstances change, and some of the contents of this article may be superseded by recent developments.

I have said a lot about problems and about the hard work ahead. But I do not want to give the impression that decimalization means only difficulties and hard work. It is an opportunity as well as a challenge. D Day, in 1971, will not be a day of national crisis and universal confusion. It will mark another step towards a more modern, forward-looking, and efficient Britain. And it will be an enjoyable experience. The changeover in New Zealand was marked by a great sense of enthusiasm and team-spirit. Directors enjoyed training themselves and their staffs for the changeover; they enjoyed solving their problems. If we all approach our various decimalization problems with the same vigour, imagination, and foresight that much of the office machine industry is showing, I am confident that in 1971 we shall achieve not only the biggest changeover but the smoothest, the most enjoyable, and the most beneficial.

Reading list

Changing to the Metric System: Conversion Factors, Symbols, and Definitions, Anderton and Begg (H.M.S.O. 1966)
Metrication in the United Kingdom (Institute of Production Engineers, 1967)
Decimal Money—A Preliminary Survey (Published by Bank Education Service, 1967)
Report of Committee on Inquiry on Decimal Currency (Cmnd 2145), (H.M.S.O. 1963)
Decimal Currency in the United Kingdom (Cmnd 3164), (H.M.S.O. 1966)
Decimal Currency Act 1967 (H.M.S.O.)
Decimal Currency: Expression of amounts in printing, writing and in speech (H.M.S.O. 1968) Code No. 70-973

Decimal Currency: Three years to go. Facts and forecasts (H.M.S.O. 1968) Code No. 70-983
First Annual Report of the Decimal Currency Board (H.M.S.O. 1968) House of Commons
    Paper No. 303

Useful addresses

Decimal Currency Board, Standard House, 27 Northumberland Avenue, London WC 2
Bank Education Service, 10 Lombard Street, London EC 3

2.5 Common Sense on Company Mergers

Nicholas A. H. Stacey

Mergers between, and acquisition of, companies are as old as business; the main reason for their rising importance can be attributed to the rigours of competition, to the need to restructure industry, and to changes of attitude. Businessmen are nowadays looking at company 'get togethers' in a different light, having perceived their dynamic role in respect of their own firms and, also, of their competitors and customers. The next few years will witness still more and still larger mergers, which will quicken the transformation of the structure of industry.

Industrialists are often adventurous in the development of new technologies or products, in the application of novel production methods, and in adopting unorthodox modes of distribution, but they are traditionally less adventurous, because they are less informed, when it comes to opportunities to change the corporate status of their firms. However, the recent rate of company marriages indicates that many businessmen are more aware of mergers than before, and a growing number participate in bringing them about.

It has become apparent that the merger game is not the exclusive preserve of giants. Owners of medium-sized companies are just as prone to acquire firms as big concerns, and successive acquisitions by comparatively small firms to create larger units have also become commonplace.

In the 1930s, difficult economic circumstances forced mergers on many of the basic industries; rationalization seemed invariably to entail the closure of firms, and unemployment. In fact, the mergers of those days saved numerous companies from extinction and countless people from unemployment. This was not always and everywhere evident. And the emotional overtones still apparent today—in which the critics of mergers luxuriate—are a legacy of nearly forty years ago.

Recently, business sentiment has swung sharply in favour of mergers. However, more than just a change in emotional attitudes has been necessary to bring about a revolution in boardroom attitudes to corporate weddings. The impetus has come from changing economic, industrial, and international conditions. One of the most important springs of action has been the growth of competition for British business, both domestic and foreign. Competition narrows margins and reduces profits. To counter the reduction in profitability, the businessman must increase his trade. This means that output must be larger and costs must be kept in check. So larger units are needed to take advantage of mass production and mass distribution. And these larger units are gradually emerging.

The role of government has also been important. Apart from deliberate acts by Whitehall to encourage concentration by merger, the alternating years of famine and plenty in the British economy—the 'stop-go' policies of governments—have made it less easy for many firms to survive or to remain prosperous. This is one of the mainsprings for concentration in an economy where, in any case, too many firms are making too many consumer and industrial products in too small a quantity. There are still too many firms in Britain whose continuing ability to eke out a precarious living brings no benefit to consumers and nothing but anxiety to their owners and employees. Their profitability and contribution to the general good are pitifully small. The two are invariably linked.

No wonder that since the mid-'fifties successive governments have been anxious to merge firms into larger units. This endeavour has been less difficult in sectors where the government is a principal purchaser, such as aircraft and shipbuilding. As for the rest, in an industrial democracy the government may have powers of persuasion and can offer blandishments, but coercion is impracticable. Governments can provide the framework in which business operates, but only business can take the steps to adjust a complex economy to new circumstances. Nonetheless, the introduction of a new government agency in 1966—the Industrial Reorganisation Corporation (*see* section 15.6)—and a codification of the merger and acquisition rules, in the Mergers and Amalgamations Act 1965, mark the end of an era and the beginning of a new one. The act of merging has been officially twice blessed.

The rise of international companies and the sharpening of international competition and the vast sums needed for research and development are probably the factors that have weighed most with governments. There are, of course, many British companies that are large by European and even world standards, but by no means in all sectors. For instance, in electrical manufacturing, the size of the large companies in Western Germany or in Holland has been two or three times that of their British counterparts. Compared with their counterparts in the United States, many 'giant' British companies are still pygmies. All this is not to say that only large companies can survive; for most manufacturing activities, British companies have not reached the 'optimum' size for effective and profitable competitive operations.

Who should merge?

The chances of a reasonably-sized company acquiring or being acquired in British business today are one in sixty. Thus, it is reasonable to assume that during the next decade or two a great many businessmen will have some experience either of selling or buying a business. For this reason alone, businessmen ought to have some understanding of the mechanism of mergers, if for no better reason than to be less timid about them. But this does not imply that directors of companies should explore merger opportunities 'by going alone'. It is one kind of skill to sell electrical transformers successfully, manufacture some of the best hydraulics machinery, or to have built up a highly successful company in some type of proprietary, fast-selling, consumer product; it is an entirely different thing to negotiate businesses, to find the right firm to buy or to find the right home for one's own company. This is the realm of the specialist. Mergers and acquisitions are not a prizegiving or a garden party. They affect the whole existence and survival of the firm.

Businessmen owning or managing medium-sized companies are often remarkably uninformed on the vexed question of company marriages. In large enterprises, the board is supported by permanently employed internal advisers, and there may well be a small section under the chairman or managing director scrutinizing industries or technologies in which to expand. In the case of most small companies, the issue of mergers or acquisitions does not loom very large. A small manufacturing business—say up to eighty people employed—is not readily acquirable as such. The owner is invariably the managing director, the chief purchasing officer, the star salesman, the chief engineer, and, at times, the best packer in the organization. There is, therefore, no delegation of major responsibilities. If one buys a small firm, one really buys the man. Exceptions apart, small businesses as a rule should grow in size before they become a worthwhile proposition for their owners to sell or for another company to buy. And in this context, companies earning less than £30,000 a year net before tax should be classed as small firms.

Many small businesses will always remain small, notwithstanding the fact that their owners will make a splendid living by running them. Many businessmen wish to stay comparatively small; they own the 'two Rolls-Royce' firms, are satisfied with their rewards, and are reluctant to risk further expansion. But, if such a company proves to be extremely profitable and the owners are thinking of negotiating, it will be easiest of all to sell to another company exactly in the same field. Moreover, among today's small firms is the potential for exciting future growth. The 'high flyers' are managed by dynamic businessmen who realize that, for the solidly based firm, building up a management team and delegating responsibilities are the best ways of rapid expansion. What is so interesting about the so-called 'little men' today is the possibility that, say, ten to fifteen years after establishment, the small firm can become very large indeed. The examples of Tesco, Broadmead, Viyella, amply testify to this effect.

This rapid build-up is a new phenomenon. At the turn of the century certainly, and before the Second World War probably, it would have taken three times as long as it takes today to build up a small firm into something very substantial. That is why so many small and medium-sized firms remained family firms for so long. It took, perhaps, two generations of a family to lift a business to any size. But dynastic succession is no longer necessary.

The problem of growth for the larger firm is comparatively simple, and for the small firm comparatively difficult. This leaves the middle-size firm as the most dynamic corporate device for growth. Where the small firm ceases and the medium-size firm begins is open to argument. However, medium-sized firms may be considered as beginning at the point where they earn in excess of £50/60,000 per annum net before tax and their net assets are over £100,000. This is a wide financial yardstick, especially if we add the suggestion that the big company comes into being at a net asset figure of £500,000 and annual profits of £200,000. But it will hold good for the 1960s and early 1970s at least. All medium-sized firms have one characteristic in common; they possess at least the rudiments of a management structure, and many of them are poised for some kind of corporate deal.

In this scheme of things, it is the medium-sized company—private or public— which has the dual opportunity of becoming either a large company by internal or external growth, or of being acquired by a large company, or merging with a company of its own size. The owners and managers of such enterprises must be aware of the elementary 'whys and wherefores' of corporate marriages in order to arrive at the right decisions or recognize the right suggestions, in respect of their firms. Yet it is the businessman with the medium-size company who is frequently on the horns of a dilemma about mergers and acquisitions. Whereas in the small company merger opportunities do not loom very large, and, let it be said, are not specially important, and in the large company there are specialists to steer a proposition, say, a corporate policy section, in the medium-size firms the businessman has rarely had time to inform himself of the pros and cons of the corporate marriage game. Nor are his customary outside advisers always specially knowledgeable about mergers, and there is no reason why they should be!

The importance of finding the right home for the medium-size company or acquiring for it the right type of smaller company is greater than is generally realized. It is the medium-sized company that is most frequently the really dynamic sector in an industry, capable of further growth under the right kind of guidance. For this reason the medium-size firm, properly handled, can become a good engine of progress; it can also fritter away its own advantages.

Public or private?

The important question for a medium-size firm is whether or not to go public, i.e., obtain a stock exchange quotation, and this is relevant to the question of growth through mergers. In some businessmen's eyes, going public is the inevitable goal in the corporate game. However, on reflection, the act of going public or arranging a placing for a proportion of the shares should be examined meticulously because these may not be at all times in the company's or in its owners' fundamental interest. The most telling reasons for a private company to go public are, first, to allow the owners to get some money for their past hard work and, second, to have a vehicle ready for expansion with which to buy other companies.

In order to get some money for the owners, going public does not always gain them more money than simply negotiating the company for a suitable acquisition. Of course, if the owners wish to retain control, through a public issue or by a placing, they would get relatively more money than by selling a minority stake to a banking corporation or to another firm. One difficulty remains if the owners retain a large parcel of shares—say, 60 per cent to 65 per cent. There being a small market in the shares, prices can be artifically high and the sale of even a small parcel can depress the price. This is a special problem when one of the major shareholders dies, since his shares cannot be liquidated through the market easily or quickly, except at a sizeable discount.

Pricing—illusion and reality

Whatever the disposition of the owners—whether they want to obtain a public quotation for their company, wish to acquire other companies, or merge with a company—the value of the firm must be ascertained. To assess the value of a company for a flotation, the financial considerations, such as the profit record and the asset position, naturally loom large, in addition to considerations such as whether or not the company is in an expanding sector of industry, is well poised for further expansion, and happens to be in a fashionable sector of industry. In assessing a company's value for acquisition there is an all-important further consideration, namely, what are the integration advantages for the buyer. For, unless there are integration advantages—that is, unless in a merger between companies, two and two make five or six and not four—there is little sense in effecting a corporate get together.

Sellers and buyers of companies must be well aware of the approximate rule-of-thumb value of a company. The added value of a company, which accrues to the owners as a result of integrating skills and resources, can materialize only if the basic commercial values are right and are properly computed. In this respect, too often heavy weather is made by the seller of companies about valuation, and for a number of reasons. It must be admitted that in arriving at a proper price, orthodox views on value can be misleading. The cause of confusion often centres on the asset position. There are too many firms with over-large assets that are not fully earning their keep, if at all. The illusion that assets are valuable in themselves, even if they fail to earn commensurate returns, is difficult to dispel. Perhaps the high rate of company taxation in Britain has given an unintended fillip to this theory. Since profits are heavily taxed, businessmen will tend to overspend on assets—in machine building and in building extensions—arguing that if this can be accomplished by employing direct labour then all these additions are paid for by pre-tax profits. The weight and range of taxation puts a premium on avoidance. While a good asset position is necessary, building up in the company too heavy an asset position, not justified by profitability, will not greatly enhance its value. This is why, in numerous instances, when profits are below a certain level, companies are purchased on a discounted asset basis. Naturally, any unneeded cash in the assets equation is exempt from this criticism, since the buyer usually buys the cash element not required in the company for cash. There is a long way to go until the asset position is relegated to a secondary role in the mind of the businessman. Some professional advisers have much to answer for in emphasizing the undue importance of assets.

If one wanted a rule about the ratio of asset value to the purchase price of a company based on profits, then it might be argued, as an example, that the value of the assets should account for between two-thirds and four-fifths of the price. This applies to firms in manufacturing; in the service trades, and in retailing and wholesaling, assets may well comprise less than two-thirds of the purchase price. Thus, while assets are not an unimportant factor in valuations, they take second place to profits. Putting this in another way, the balance sheet plays second fiddle to the profit and loss account. This is accounted for by the fact that the value of a company is basically determined by the company's profitability. If its profitability is erratic or declining, the chances of a public flotation are slender, and the value of the company, in general, is less.

Here another difficulty is encountered. Assuming that the average of x-years' profits is taken as the basis of valuation, then, in the case of a company with declining profits, the average will come out higher and, in the case of a progressive company with rising profits, the average will come out lower than recent earnings. Hence, under the average profitability rule, old-established declining firms may well be valued higher than the younger, thrusting enterprises. In recent years, in the manufacturing industries, the value of a company could vary from a three to seven times pre-tax profit multiplier. In many of the service trades, the multiplier was at the lower end. In specially efficient and well-managed firms, and in circumstances of a high degree of integration possibilities, a higher coefficient of profits has been paid. This coefficient has varied and has been partly determined by the fashions of the time and the length of purse of the buyer. Electronics companies were tinted with glamour in the mid-1950s, building and civil engineering in the early 1960s. Buyers of such companies at high prices may well have regretted the investment.

Assuming, as an illustration, a four to five times multiplier valuation for a firm and, also, assuming that the relevant pre-tax profits are £75,000, the capitalized value of such a private company to the buyer may vary between £300,000 and £375,000. In this corporate example the value of assets, excluding unwanted cash, in relation to the total price can be assumed not to exceed £300,000. The buyer of a company may well be prepared to pay an additional sum if the integration of his company with the firm to be acquired could bring significant advantages. However, the buyer cannot be expected to pay much more for the acquired company just because he can put that company's assets to better use than the previous owners. The bonus is largely the buyer's. One does not send in a company doctor and pay a premium in advance.

In some companies profits have risen exceptionally fast, mostly thanks to the labours of the owner. If the owner, for various reasons, wishes to capitalize on his years of hard work at the end of a period of fast profits expansion, the question may well be asked is he trying to 'get out' in his peak earnings year? Provided the owner has confidence in the continued progress of his enterprise, he may well be amenable to offer the firm wishing to acquire him certain safeguards. The simplest method in such circumstances is to evolve a reward formula. One such example may be the acquisition of, say, 51 per cent of a company on a profit multiplier to be agreed. The balancing 49 per cent would then be acquired in subsequent years—usually in two or three years—using the same multiplier, but based on the higher profits if they are earned. Naturally, if the profits decline, the remaining shares would be purchased at a lower profits multiplier. Hence, the owner runs the risk of getting less. This formula provides for rewards and penalties.

Businessmen either buy or sell companies. In each instance, different considerations apply and different criteria obtain.

Buying a company

The profitable employment of surplus cash is not a good enough reason by itself for the acquisition of companies. Too many businessmen have bought too many companies on these grounds, and the investment has rarely been successful. Nor should industrialists wish to add to their stock of companies just because at certain times it is all the rage to buy. It has been said, with some irony, that three features may put a corporation in the 'sophisticated class': buying a computer; buying a Harvard Business School graduate; or buying a company. The last expedient is the most risky!

The purpose of the purchase must be carefully examined. Is horizontal or vertical expansion the motivating force? Does the firm want to become a holding company? Are there geographical considerations at home or abroad? Or, and this is less frequent, is the merger being effected for a reverse takeover, so that a public quotation is obtained for a successful private company by the back door?

Only when these objectives have been analysed can the businessman progress a stage further and deliberate on the expenditure he is prepared to incur. Irrespective of whether the company to be acquired is private or public, a conscious decision must be made about the maximum price the buyer is prepared to pay. The buyer should not be tempted to pay excessively, lest another bidder may loom on the horizon. The best acquisition is not necessarily that where the company was bought by the highest bidder. Some of the prices currently paid for companies are so high that it will take the buyers many years to make their investments worthwhile. Overbidding sometimes deters other firms from buying similar companies because prices have hardened unduly. Builders merchanting is a good example, where prices paid over the recent past were too high to integrate one of the most fragmented industries into substantial groups.

Selling a company

As a rule, the buyers of businesses are either public companies or, less frequently, substantial private companies. In the case of sellers the opposite prevails—the number of private companies acquired exceeds the number of public companies acquired by a ratio of ten to one. The seller is usually a businessman who sells the company he built up himself or a family who may have owned the company for several generations.

There are many reasons for selling a company. The lack of proper financial resources for expansion, the need to introduce professional management, the opportunity to expand faster in tandem with another firm, or the special facilities in marketing, manufacture, or research that may be available in the chosen partner. But, in addition to corporate reasons, there may well be pressing personal reasons for the owner of a firm wishing to negotiate part or whole of his equity: provisions for death duties, encashing on his life's work, desire to retire, or the need to find a partner capable of taking over, in the absence of family succession. What must be emphasized is that, for the greater part, companies acquired are profitable firms. The delusion persists, particularly in the mind of the smaller businessman, that companies merge mainly because they want to get out of a mess. This is nonsense!

Finding a partner

Let there be no misunderstanding about this: merger negotiations are the most delicate part of company business. Therefore, any intentions to arrange for a corporate wedding must be implemented with the utmost care and in a confidential manner. In the past, and even today, numerous businessmen did their own casting around for companies, approaching likely prospects direct. At the buying end, the acquiring company's chief executive has often taken upon himself the task of finding, approaching, and negotiating the purchase of an 'apparently' suitable company. It is interesting to reflect that, even in today's complicated economic, industrial, and political conditions, some company chairmen go off alone to land the right prospect. Such attempts are usually characteristic of first-generation entrepreneurs with a flourishing business, who fervently believe in the nineteenth-century romantic German concept of the 'strong man'. Such men pursue their acquisition campaign without the risk of obtaining professional help—so essential in modern business.

It is quite remarkable that businessmen who manufacture equipment of the highest precision and utmost sophistication, and who would insist on employing only skilled technicians and scientists and use only the best, up-to-date testing gear, are prepared to buy companies on hunch. Happily, in most substantial firms, while the best features of entrepreneurial thrust are properly canalized, management has also been professionalized. And professionally well-qualified management is aware that negotiating for the acquisition of companies requires skills they rarely possess and, if they do, rarely or never use. The most successful firms in the acquisition game examine many aspects of the vendor company's business before a decision is reached. No single man is able to do that.

The opportunities are always there, even for the owner of the vendor firm, to 'play at big business' and find his own partner. Just because the owner of the firm is aware of his competitors or suppliers, he may mistakenly believe that these are his best or only chances for being acquired. Yet how can he judge that the one or two firms he knows well enough to approach their directors with a suggested offer are his best bets? How can he exercise the value judgement that he is selling to a partner as near 'optimum' as possible in the industrial sense, and at as good a price as he may expect? Clearly, he cannot. He does not know who wants to buy what and when. He is restricting his market.

Role of the merger broker

The first rule is that one should not, initially, try to negotiate with the other party face to face—any direct approach weakens the approacher's hand. An approach should preferably be conducted by an intermediary. By having an intermediary both the buyers and sellers of businesses have room for manoeuvre. With direct confrontation at the initial stages, the facility to negotiate without loss of face is dissipated —on both sides.

The second rule is to utilize the confidential services of professionals, in this case that of a merger broker—a professional broker, a banker, or other qualified person. No merger broker worth his salt will look at the financial aspects of a deal until he has first ascertained and satisfied himself about the industrial compatability of the proposed corporate marriage. What this means is that money becomes the second, and not the first, consideration in his initial discussions. Problems of production, distribution, patents, research, development of new products, market shares, exports and imports, the plans and position of directors, the employment of executives and staff, grafting on new activities, transforming others: all these need first to be examined before an intelligent offer can be formulated for any company. The lamentable conditions arising from many mergers can be attributed to talking money first, clinching the deal second, and leaving rational thinking about co-ordination to the last.

In the large international company, the area of potential acquisition errors is narrowed, since a corporate planning unit of some kind, whose task is to carry out feasibility studies on the likely direction of expansion, will have been set up. But the search for the appropriate company and the effort of locating likely acquisitions is rarely accomplished from the inside of giant companies. The larger and the more professional an enterprise, the more frequently it employs outside professional services, if for no other reasons than to monitor the findings of its own people.

The medium-sized and smaller public company embarking upon a programme of acquisition has even less experience in this sphere, as a rule, than the large. These companies need the services of the professional broker not only to find acquisitions for them but also to obtain advice about the direction they should travel. Here, the merger broker can perform his most creative role by working up possible combinations for a get-together based on his knowledge of industry.

Envisaging possible corporate deals is not a mechanical task; it is not sufficient to have the nimblest fingers for flicking through large wads of Exchange Telegraph cards, however useful they may be at a much more advanced state of negotiations, and then only for quoted companies. A well-established merger broker will have detailed knowledge of the expansion intentions of his clients, in terms of technologies, products, geographical areas and money availabilities. All these have to be matched when dreaming up a merger or seeking an acquisition.

When the merger broker goes 'out in the field' to find the right firm for acquisition, he also has a corporate profile to which he works. Suitable corporate brides are far from being commonplace; they have to be found. And even when found, the courtship will probably be of long duration. It is nothing exceptional to witness courtships of two to three years duration before the bans can be announced.

Naturally, professional intermediaries charge a fee, and professional merger brokers have their fixed scale of charges. Most of them work on a brokerage basis which is due only on the successful conclusion of a deal they have introduced and helped to negotiate. Usually, the acquiring party—the firm buying a company—pays the fees. The owner of the vendor company incurs no charges. The larger the total consideration involved in a deal, including cash, shares, etc., the relatively smaller the percentage upon which the brokerage fee is based. This sliding-scale is based on the readily graspable principle that the problems of negotiating are not reduced proportionately in smaller transactions. The larger the firm to be bought, the more professional its management and, therefore, the easier to discuss industrial commercial and financial details, although the negotiations may well be rather lengthy and involved.*

Business brokers have grown in importance on their record of bringing about many successful deals, avoiding acrimonious arguments, public badinage or loss of face, and by insisting that 'bargains' are bad business. In any bargain, one party to the deal must be disappointed, which is not the ideal arrangement for the future well-being of the combined firms. A merger broker puts his 'good housekeeping seal' on a deal negotiated by him. The time may even come when chairmen of public companies will make a point in announcing in their annual reports that an acquisition is endorsed by a merger broker of good standing.

Conclusion

Mergers and acquisitions are here to stay; their number and the value of the transactions will continue to grow. Small, medium, and large companies will continue to merge, and, as a result, the average size of companies in British industry will increase. This will bring immense benefit to British business by changing the structure of industry, thereby making it more resilient and competitive. Its accomplishment cannot be left to chance, a little science as well as sensibility must be included in the effort.

* On the subject of fees it should not be left unsaid that an immense amount of work goes into the research effort of finding a suitable vendor or merger partner, in having the information processed by specialists, and in spending time negotiating between the parties with an understanding of all the factors involved. And if, after months of negotiations, nothing comes of the proposed deal, the business broker must still pay his costs without getting a fee. A specialist merger broker lives on acquisitions and mergers alone. If a deal is worthwhile, it must be worthwhile including the business broker's fee, which usually amounts to 3 per cent on a deal of half a million £, and 2 per cent on a million £ deal.

Reading list

BOOKS

The City Code on Take-overs and Mergers (Issuing Houses Association, 1968)
Balance-sheet for Take-overs, Anthony Vice (Barrie and Rockliff for the Institute of Economic Affairs, 1960)

Who Owns Whom: A Directory of Parent, Associate and Subsidiary Companies in Industry and Commerce (Roskill, 1967)

Take-overs and Amalgamations, M. A. Weinberg (Sweet and Maxwell, Second Edition, 1967)

Finance Problems of the Smaller Company (Institute of Directors, 1967)

Mergers in Modern Business, Nicholas A. H. Stacey (Hutchinson, 1966)

The Corporation in Modern Society, Edited by Edward S. Mason (Harvard University Press, 1961)

Management Problems of Corporate Acquisitions, Myles L. Mace and George G. Montgomery Jr. (Harvard University Press, 1962)

Bid for Power, George Bull and Anthony Vice (Elek Books, Third Edition, 1961)

Management of Mergers, Nicholas A. H. Stacey (Pergamon Press, 1967)

Mergers: Volume I—*Past and Present* (1963) Volume II—*The Impact on Managers* (1963) Volume III—*The Impact on the Shopfloor* (1966) (Published by the Acton Society Trust, London)

JOURNALS

'Check List for Mergers' (*Financial Times*, 23 and 27 February 1968)

'Mergers and Management', Nicholas A. H. Stacey (*Management Accounting*, February 1967)

Useful addresses

The Board of Trade, Industries and Manufacturers Department, 1 Victoria Street, London SW 1

Industrial Reorganisation Corporation, 46 Pall Mall, London SW 1

Monopolies Commission, 8 Cornwall Terrace, Regents Park, London NW 1

Issuing Houses Association, St Albans House, Goldsmith Street, London EC 2

3. Key Techniques for Management

3.1 A Survey of Management Functions

Gerald L. E. Spier

A Board of Directors may consist of just one man and his wife, with the former (or the latter) supplying the entire labour force as well as taking all decisions. It may, equally, consist of a larger number of independent professionals, none of them involved in any departmental or executive responsibility in the firm. Although it is usual to have a managing director, it is not necessary, as the chief executive can easily make his report to the board without being a member of it.

It is evident, therefore, that a board may not, in fact, engage in any but the remotest management functions itself. However, the proper execution and control of these functions is a matter of prime concern. The smaller the firm, the more likely it is that some functions will be overlooked because of pressure of work, or simply through disinclination. The larger organization may, on the other hand, lose sight of the interrelation of management problems occurring in different departments. These are the reasons for this section. The description of individual techniques, in the sections that follow, should show which decisions can be made as a result of rigorous analysis, and which are purely a matter of good judgement; what sort of information can or should be available, and how it may be used.

Admitting, then, that management problems are only necessarily of board concern at one remove, it is still important to identify them. Popularly, management means handling people: leading them and motivating them. Many books on the subject deal with nothing else. Certainly this is a most important aspect of managerial responsibility, and the main one in some departments, but it cannot be the only one, for that would leave out of account entirely the concept as it applies to 'managing a *business*'. An agent can do this without any personnel at all. There is an entrepreneurial risk-bearing side to management that becomes increasingly important in the higher echelons. In order not to lose sight of these, management will be dealt with under three headings: operational, organizational, strategic. The actual meaning of each of these will become obvious as functions are described, but briefly, the strategic is concerned with what to do, the organizational with who does what and how to control them and the process; the operational with actual *doing*.

The content of each of these will vary with departments. Nine major divisions of the firm will be examined: production, sales, finance, marketing, planning, accounts, personnel, research, chief executive's office. It must be emphasized that this division applies equally to the firm run by one man (who is, in fact, merely filling a number of quite different posts at one and the same time).

The exception is production. Many firms do very well without manufacturing anything. Some firms might do better if they were more critical of the demands of this department. Business in the United Kingdom, however, largely grew out of this side of the firm, and there is a feeling, still current, that all other activities are somehow parasitic. Out of deference to history, this subject will be taken first.

Production

(a) *Strategy*. The main strategic problem is concerned with the process. Any given quantity of any given article can be manufacturered in a number of different ways with varying mixes of labour and capital. The production strategist is aware of all of these, with their relevant advantages and drawbacks. Some of them may require too much capital; some of them may use machinery which, while momentarily advantageous, will soon be obsolete; some may require a highly specialized, rare type of labour; some may need an expensive material as a forming rather than user requirement. There are very many further alternatives with further implications for flexibility, lead time, and type of capital employed.

(b) *Organization*. This division will be concerned with three separate problems: things, records, and men. By 'things' are meant such matters as work flow, critical path studies, machine loading, maintenance policy, stocking and ordering procedures. Many of these are susceptible to operational research study in so far as there is a large mathematical content in their solution. It is suggested, however, that the OR facility itself be situated in the chief executive's office. This is both because it is also required by other departments, and because relatively junior personnel will be supplying solutions which bind high-level management. Production should, however, provide its own liaison either with this group or, if there is no justification for within-the-firm capacity, with an outside agency.

Records are kept, to a large extent, to meet requirements originating outside the department; in accounts, for instance, finance, or marketing. There must be clearly defined internal procedures and responsibilities for these. In addition, the strategic side may wish to make use of such an internal facility for the preparation of its own presentations. Routine stocking and ordering procedures will also depend on internal records and reporting. Here there will be a general impact of the Organization and Methods departments similar to that of the Operational Research department; from the same location and for the same reasons.

Men are fundamental to the production side of the firm in a special kind of way. This is, unfortunately, recognized largely in deference to trade union demands. It is more logically and humanly based on a special relationship between workmen and the firm. There is a greater identity of interest between them than in the case, say, of an accountant or a salesman, who have career prospects and ambitions that may well be independent of their present employment. Good information and consultation procedures, and special qualities of leadership, are therefore essential. Problems need to be solved on wage differentials, methods of payment, and chains of command. Above all, there is the question of trust; easy to write about, difficult to achieve.

(c) *Operations.* This is where the hard contact between management and labour occurs. It is one thing to have a carefully drawn up work flow diagram; it is quite another to push the work through. Those who cannot do it often refer to the managers responsible for this side as 'glorified progress-chasers'.

Because of the close relationship between men and management, which has been mentioned, responsibilities for time-setting and inspection naturally lie in this department. This closes the loop, for these skills provide feed-back for strategy, especially from the point of view of Value Engineering.

Sales

(a) *Strategy.* The problem for this division is how to sell: the identification of unique selling points, if this is to be the method; discounts, and whether they are to be for quantity or position in the trade; promotions; the general sales approach. Other matters of concern are the size and type of sales force, and the devising of its training programme. Because of the customer contact involved, servicing may also be run by the sales division, as may those aspects of customer relations that do not directly lead to sales: public relations of a certain kind, contact-men in general, and the whole apparatus of trouble-shooting and apologizing, which becomes necessary at some time or other.

(b) *Organization.* This sub-divides in the same way as for production. 'Things', here, mean the goods that the firm produces—the progressing of salesmen's orders, and all promotional materials, leaflets, and samples. Physical distribution may be run by the sales division, but can also be an organizational or operational problem of the production division. The advantage of siting it in sales is in the control this gives on distribution costs, especially if there are full-load problems, or if order-taking can be phased to give cost advantages. For this reason also, the export side of distribution—shipping—is usually closely connected with the sales function.

Records again fulfil two purposes: the meeting of the external requirements of departments such as accounts and marketing, and the internal requirements connected with promotion campaign planning and control, and salesmen remuneration. The external requirements are especially important for order progressing and credit control; the internal, for devising and reviewing payment methods.

Men, here, mean *salesmen*. The good ones are highly mobile between jobs, and the problem in this case is to create an identity of interest between men and the firm. The identity will communicate itself in the pay packet. The matter is complicated by such factors as the firm wanting to hold back on sales, or insisting on time being spent on good-will calls, or giving the best men a difficult area. To cover these strategic requirements, alternative systems to straight commission payments can be devised: varying basic salaries; points systems which take account of anything from personal appearance through the number of calls to the quantity of new business introduced; and bonuses for all kinds of targets. An important factor, best left to the field manager, is how best to 'sell' these arrangements to the salesman himself.

Great assistance can be provided in all three categories by Operational Research (OR) and Organization and Methods (O & M).

(c) *Operations*. This requires another 'progress-chaser', sitting on the sales-man's back and making him get the orders. Where he is a purely indoor man, he must expect his field man to earn more than he does. Where he is himself a superior salesman, a different relationship exists, and the pattern of this organization comes under the 'strategy' heading. In either case, the sales manager must have a close interest in the support provided to his men in the form, for instance, of sales advertising and discretionary discounts. This leads back to the strategic side again, and also to marketing. It is as well to remember that the connection of the salesman is with the buyer, not necessarily the consumer. He will have a highly specialized, and by no means disinterested, view of the market and its exploitation. This is the most useful when it is most fully appreciated.

Finance

(a) *Strategy*. There are all kinds of different types of money at different prices. There are continuous opportunities for changing one kind for another. Ordinary shares or debentures, bank overdrafts or deferred preference shares. The choice is wide and the mix capable of considerable variety. Financial strategy, however, does not consist only in choosing between these sources at a given moment of time, but also of planning the timing of profits, and the general financial structure of the company, to create opportunities. The department does not look only to lenders, or investors, for its funds. Credit policy, cash discounts, the holding of debts from exports in different ways; all these are important in the financial field, as are strategic buying and the stocking policy.

A special concern is that of risk: what the firm can afford to lose for what chance of what reward.

(b) *Organization*. Although the accounts department is sometimes considered the organization arm of finance, the two departments will be discussed separately. The accounts department provides the figures finance requires: profit forecasts, management ratios, and so on. The finance personnel will specify their requirements and use them for information or public relations work, or feed them to the operation side. They will also have charge of certain notional reserves such as those required to replace existing machinery. They will create the material that shows the difference, say, between these and what is being provided by straightforward amortization. They will also be interested in the financial aspects of any budgets that may be prepared, especially in their cash flow implications. They may do their own cash flow forecasting, or have it done elsewhere in the firm.

(c) *Operations*. This entails finding the money; a highly personal assignment, with little room for delegation. Here, status is necessary, and it may be essential for for the job to carry a directorship. In any case the person whose responsibility it is will have considerable influence on the strategic side since what is planned is directly affected by what he can achieve. Choice of financial strategy may be dictated, at least in certain respects, by his own personality and who his friends are.

Marketing

(a) *Strategy*. Marketing is concerned with selling the 'best' configuration of the firm's products at a profit. Strategy has to solve the problem presented by the interaction of price, quality, and selling costs. A lower price may sell more goods; the overall profit may nonetheless be reduced.

Although ideas may often originate in the sales department, they still need a professional investigation they are unlikely to receive outside the marketing section. While a salesman may suggest that sales would increase if packaging were changed, it is not his job to sit and think of such things.

Advertising budgets and their implications are calculated in this division, and various methods of spending them are considered. Pricing policy is a special responsibility, and there is a strong interest in the real cost of any production programmes and the true effect of changes in quantity or quality on the firm.

(b) *Organization*. The department is semi-professional and its organization problems are confined largely to office management and salary policy. It does have a special information and liaison problem, in that it has to provide feed-back from accounts, production, and sales to its own strategy group, and perhaps be in a position to perform operations that will criticize the output of these departments, whether on the side of value engineering, costing, or sales 'explanations'. Another special problem may be set by the periodic need to engage temporary survey staff.

(c) *Operations*. This side forages for the facts that provide the quantitive basis for the strategist. There may be capacity for this within the company, or it may be done through agents. The responsibilities are the same: the correctness of the facts, their relevance, their interpretation. Market research, media research, economic analysis, forecasts, and competition and technology surveys, are among the outputs. Analysis may require co-operation from OR, so there is need for a link. The department itself may be used for forecasts, commercial and technological, required by the planning department.

Planning

(a) *Strategy*. The planning department crystallizes the objectives of the firm: profits, profit growth, or physical growth, and is concerned with such basic questions as whether the firm is in the right business, or indeed what business it is really in. Is the aircraft manufacturing company selling aeroplanes, or a transport system? If the latter, should it not also be interested in buses and trains, as competition or as a complement; to be fought against, or acquired?

The planning department must look a long way ahead: five or ten years. Its personnel have the advantage that they may never be confronted with their mistakes; they are spared the crises of ordinary business. Everyone else in the firm knows this, and so there is a necessity for the heads of this section to convey a feeling of urgency and importance, not only to their own staff but also, especially, to the other sections with which they work, and to the managing director. A vital function, if anything is to be achieved by planning, is to sell the concept as well as the plan.

(b) *Organization*. As with marketing, good interdepartmental information procedures are necessary. In this case, however, one is looking for signs in what is presented, rather than asking for the answers to specific questions. O & M must ensure that there is the greatest opportunity for fruitful interchange.

Pay presents a difficult problem. A good planner is not a man who produces plans well, but who produces good plans. Despite the remoteness of the work there is a strong entrepreneurial content that is difficult to reward or make explicit. The latter can be done by giving the planner the responsibility for executing his plan. In any case it is not a bad idea to make planners live with that thought.

The question of reward normally depends, in the first instance, on the accord between planner and chief executive. This is not necessarily advisable and can turn the department into a means of justifying the latter's preconceptions.

(c) *Operations.* These come under various headings. There is the quantification of what one is planning for. The gap must be closed between objectives and the extrapolation of current business, and the identification of the means to fill this gap. There is the preparation of a plan to encompass these means.

Additionally, the department may be charged with obtaining the material for short-range planning. This means collecting and collating departmental forecasts so that, for instance, sales do not gear themselves to dispose of more than production can produce. At the other extreme, it may deal with technological forecasting. As has already been mentioned, both these functions can be performed in the marketing department.

Accounts

(a) *Strategy.* This is closely allied to finance. A distinction is best made by allowing financial considerations to dictate how and when surpluses are earned; accounting to dictate when and how they are shown. This is largely taxation and risk strategy, and the accountant, as an expert on this, can give great help to the financial manager.

The other aspect of accounts strategy is ensuring that the correct presentation is used for each information or legal aspect.

(b) *Organization.* First-class control is required to ensure that only *necessary* paperwork is produced, that it is produced in the best form, and that it is made available throughout the firm.

This expertise can help other departments and even lead to the establishment of an information centre, although this will depend on the requirements of the individual firm, as interpreted by its O & M department.

Accounts is the most professionalized department, and work management is consequently easier here than in most others. The choice of mechanical aids is considerable—from adding machines to computers—and making the correct choice depends on a deep understanding of all the aspects of the work.

(c) *Operations.* In addition to the collection, storage, and presentation of data for various purposes, it is necessary to ensure that certain legal requirements are fulfilled. This means close co-operation between accountants and auditors as well as a special link with the board. This may be through the office of the company secretary, who has prime internal responsibility for the legality of the enterprise.

Personnel

(a) *Strategy.* People are one of the main assets of a company, and their suitability and loyalty can have a tremendous effect on every aspect of its work. This department must lay down the programmes of recruitment and training, standards of pay and promotion, and methods of man management control that will allow the firm to make the best use of what it has got and to get the best it can afford. This must take into account not only present requirements but future needs, and there will, accordingly, be close co-operation with the planning department.

(b) *Organization*. A great deal of paperwork can be generated here, too: applications for jobs, personal histories of employees, tables of comparative earnings, superannuation and insurance documents. As well as maintaining all these records there is the creation and maintenance of the delicate relationship between the department, which has the overall personnel responsibility, and individual managers, who should have a strong feeling of personal responsibility for their staff.

(c) *Operations*. The most obvious are those concerned with hiring and firing, especially as far as ensuring that managers give proper interviews. Equally important is job measurement, including the assessment of, and giving of due value to, the discretionary element in all work at every level.

There is an advantage in handling union matters here, because of the greater professionalism, detachment, and consequent impartiality as compared with the production department. There can be circumstances, however, where these can be equally *dis*advantageous, and there is no single ideal method.

Negotiation of pension schemes and personal insurances is logically done in the personnel department but, because of the nature of the considerations involved in making a choice, this is often sub-contracted into the accounts department.

Research and development

(a) *Strategy*. The first problem is what to research into; the second, the establishment of priorities; the third, who is to do it. The research problems will be concerned with improvements both in processes and in the final article, as well as with new products and ideas.

The degree to which it is necessary to establish priorities will depend on the allocation the manager can get; the extent to which he can sell his services to the chief executive or to the board. This is more difficult than, say, in marketing, where a relationship between business risks and the amount of money spent can be established at least notionally. Expenditure on R & D may, on the other hand, be completely abortive over quite a lengthy period.

(b) *Organization*. The personnel is diverse and, therefore, not susceptible to standardized treatment. There may be learned scientists and engineers who like working on their own without disturbance. There will almost certainly be a small workshop with many of the characteristics of an ordinary factory. The R & D manager must deal with each man according to his kind, but without letting go all idea of work measurement simply because the work involved is research. He is quite as likely to need critical path analysis as his factory counterpart, and will need to work closely with marketing and finance to produce useful forecasts of commercial viability.

Changes in R & D targets, inevitable in any programme, need careful monitoring and must be fed back to the sales and cost projections.

Careful watch must be kept over industrial property rights in sub-contracted research, and patent aspects require attention from the defensive and active development sides.

(c) *Operations*. These are similar to production except for the differences that arise out of the smaller size and, hence, closer personal relationships. Also, the workers are remote from the commercial results of what they are doing, and in the higher grades are often more attached to a research project than to the firm for which they are undertaking it. Any changes in direction of programmes require very special handling to obtain full co-operation and to maintain loyalty.

Chief Executive's office

(a) *Strategy*. The chief executive may be compared to the conductor of an orchestra. If he is managing director he has considerable influence on the choice of music. In any case he is responsible for the way it is played. He has, at the strategic level, to choose between various good reasons for doing different things, or the same things differently, put to him by various departmental heads. He then has to ensure that dissidents go along with his choice.

From a more negative viewpoint, because he is chief executive he must forget his previous job and not give preference to production, or sales, or wherever he came from himself. This requires a special kind of self-effacement as well as a special sort of self-assertion.

(b) *Organization*. As mentioned previously, both O & M and OR stand in a special relationship to the chief executive. They are not only a service imposed upon the rest of the firm, but also his method of ensuring that procedures are followed and that he gets the best possible presentation for purposes of decision making.

He may use the company secretary, an assistant managing director, a personal assistant, or a special manager with any of a number of titles, to undertake the responsibility for this part of his role, and thereby relieve him of all organizational work.

(c) *Operations*. The extent of these depends on the chief executive's relationship with the board as a whole and with the chairman. At the least, he will have to represent the company to the outside world. He will have to report to the board all that the company has done, is doing, and intends to do, and convince them of the excellence of his trusteeship. Above all, he is responsible for the selection and retention of his own top management. Not a few companies have been successful due to the chief executive's skill in this one sphere.

These management jobs, involving responsibility for what is done as well as for doing it, are not an exhaustive list. The selection of techniques in the following sections of this chapter is even less complete. Their presentation should, however, help to illustrate both the complexity of business and the range of methods for dealing with this complexity. An additional aid to good management is the understanding by one department of the problems of the others; as important for a one-man firm as for multi-divisional organizations.

Reading list

BOOKS

The Principles and Practices of Management, E. F. L. Brech (Longmans, Green, 1965)
Management: its Nature and Significance, E. F. L. Brech (Pitman, 4th Edition, 1967)
Management: a Book of Readings, Koontz & O'Donnell (McGraw-Hill, 1964)
Management: Theory and Practice, Ernest Dale (McGraw-Hill, 1965)
Structure in Management: a study of different forms and their effectiveness, Isabel Blain (National Institute of Industrial Psychology, 1964)
The Great Organizers, Ernest Dale (McGraw-Hill, 1960)
Management Survey, Sir Frederic Hooper (Pitman, 2nd edition 1961)
The Making of Scientific Management, Vol. II: Management in British Industry, L. Urwick and E. F. L. Brech (Management Publications Trust, 1946)

JOURNALS

'What is Scientific Management?', H. F. R. Catherwood (*Journal of Management Studies*, May 1966)

3.2 Costing

Ian Andrew

One of the most natural questions that management can ask of the accountant is 'what does it cost to produce this or provide that?' The necessary, but irritating, reply, 'what do you want the figures for?' emphasizes that costing (that is, the techniques and processes of ascertaining costs) is not an exact science capable of producing a 'true' cost with universal application, but rather the art of applying certain conventions according to the facts of the case and the uses to which the figures are to be put.

A knowledge of these conventions and when and how they can be applied is essential, therefore, to those calculating the cost figures. An understanding of these conventions and their limitations is also essential to those using the figures because cost data should be interpreted in the light of the bases on which they were calculated, and because cost data calculated for one purpose can be dangerously misleading if used unthinkingly for another purpose.

Use of cost data

Management requires information about the costs of the products or services that it produces or provides for a number of different purposes, the most important of which are:

(a) *Planning*: in order to determine the financial implications of the various alternative courses of action that could be followed, for example, whether to produce or provide the output or service itself or whether to acquire it from outside ('make-or-buy' decisions), whether to start or continue manufacturing a certain product in view of the market price obtainable, whether to accept a large order at terms below the normal selling price;

(b) *Control*: in order to exercise control over the costs of producing or providing the output or service by comparing the actual cost incurred with some kind of 'yardstick' cost, either as a special exercise or as a part of a budgetary control system;

(c) *Pricing*: where the price to be charged is determined mainly by the cost of producing the product or service, it is necessary to calculate that cost, either in advance (in the majority of cases) or in retrospect (for cost-plus contracts);

(d) *Accounting*: in order to value for accounting purposes, for example, work-in-progress and stocks of components and finished goods.

Composition of costs

All costing methods usually recognize three major elements of cost, namely, materials, labour, and other expenses. The procedures used for ascertaining the usage and cost of each of these elements in producing or providing any one product or service vary between themselves and from case to case. The procedural techniques available are numerous and are discussed in any standard textbook on costing.

The basic distinction between these main elements of cost illustrates the need to identify how the cost data is to be used (and, by implication, the user) before being able to calculate any useful figures. For example, the answer to the question, 'What do the materials in this book cost?' depends on whether the enquiry comes from the printer, the publisher, or the bookseller. To the printer, the material cost is that of the paper, the ink, the binding, and the jacket. To the publisher, it is the printer's price, consisting of the printer's materials, labour, other expenses, and profits. To the bookseller, the materials cost is the publisher's price, including the cost of the book from the printer, the publisher's profit, and the distribution costs.

In addition to classifying costs by the main elements of labour, materials and other expenses it is frequently desirable to analyse the costs further. For example, a fairly typical analysis would:

(a) classify the costs first by main activity. For example, the activities could be:
    production;
    distribution;
    selling;
    administration.
(b) classify each of the main elements of cost into meaningful components within each activity, for example:

138

    (i) materials could be analysed into:
       steel rod;
       nuts and bolts;
       packing material;
   (ii) labour could be analysed into:
       turners;
       fitters;
       cleaners;
       supervisors;
  (iii) other expenses could be analysed into:
       depreciation;
       power;
       rent and rates.

It is the purpose of an organization and expense code (accounts code) to provide an unambiguous and consistent analysis of costs in the detail required by management. The degree of detail required will depend upon the uses to which the cost data is to be put.

Methods of costing

The type of business and purposes for which cost data is required will determine the method of costing that should be employed; the main methods available provide the choice of:

(a) the basis on which the costs will be calculated, that is, by the two basic methods of job costing or departmental costing or a combination of these, *and*
(b) whether the costs will be calculated after or before the event being costed, that is, as historic or standard costs, *and*
(c) what costs will be included in the figures, that is, whether marginal, direct or full (absorption) costing will be used.

Job or departmental costing

Job costing involves charging materials, labour and other expenses to individual jobs, a 'job' being defined as:

(a) one or all of the operations involved in the production of a product or part of a product;
(b) a part or the whole of a project or contract.

In this sense of 'job' there is no real distinction between the traditional 'job', 'batch' or 'contract' costing systems, the only difference being that a 'job' usually refs to the production of single or 'one-off' items, whereas a 'batch' usually refers to a discrete group of identical items produced together. Contract costing is essentially job costing applied to specific jobs or contracts lasting over a relatively long period of time, for example, contracts of a civil engineering nature.

Departmental costing involves charging materials, labour and other expenses to the department incurring the expenditure. This information can then be used to express the cost of the following, depending upon the definition of the 'department' and the purpose of the costing exercise:

(a) the department itself;
(b) the service the department provides, either in total or as a cost per unit of the service. This latter figure is calculated by dividing the total cost by the quantum of service provided;
(c) the process the department undertakes. A process is essentially the operation of plant either producing output continuously or in non-discrete units or so that costs cannot be identified to individual jobs. A crude distillation unit in an oil refinery, a coke oven and a heat treatment plant are examples of processes in this context. In such circumstances, it is then possible to express the cost per unit of output by dividing the total cost of the process (that is, the department) by the output achieved.

The cost of a particular product can then be calculated by either:

(a) pure job (contract, batch) costing, *or*
(b) pure departmental (process) costing, *or*
(c) a combination of job and departmental costing. For example, a product may go through an assembly stage and then a plating process. The assembly costs could be ascertained by the job costing method whereas the plating costs could be calculated by the departmental (process) method.

Historic or standard costs

Historic costing involves ascertaining the actual costs of the materials, labour, and other expenses used after they have been incurred. This method is applicable to any of the foregoing costing bases. While the method has to be used for certain purposes, for example, for 'cost-plus' pricing, and has the virtue of apparent simplicity, it has considerable disadvantages; these include:

(a) a lack of objectivity for control purposes. This is probably the most serious disadvantage, as the comparison of the actual costs incurred with any previous historic costs (last period, last year) proves nothing other than that they are different. No indication is given as to whether it is the previous or current actual costs, or both, that are good or bad;

(b) a lack of consistency, that is, the cost of either a job or a unit of output will appear to vary from period to period although the underlying factors have not changed. For example, the cost of a unit of output calculated on a historical actual cost basis will vary with the volume of output if the total costs do not vary directly in proportion to the volume of output.

Standard costing involves the use of 'standards of performance' that are used as the basis for calculating standard, or predetermined, costs. Standard costs define, as scientifically as possible, what the costs should be, under stated conditions of efficiency and level of activity, to produce a certain amount of output. Standard costing is, of essence, a 'before the event' exercise, and its adoption forces management to think ahead and to consider what costs ought to be incurred in producing this product or that service. In the process, management can consider alternative methods of production and operating and the effect on costs of each such method. Furthermore, these standards can be based on target prices, efficiencies, production methods, mixes, and outputs so that an objective comparison with the actual events (and costs) can be made and meaningful differences (variances) ascertained. In addition, the adoption of standard costing can often result in a saving of clerical effort and the production of cost data more quickly than by using historical costing methods.

Standards can be applied to the materials, labour and other expenses incurred in the production or provision of a product or a service, to the yield and to the sales. For example, standards can be defined for:

(a) materials—in respect of price, mix, scrap, and yield;
(b) labour—in respect of rate of pay, productive time, and efficiency;
(c) other expenses—in respect of price and usage;
(d) output—in respect of the quantity of good and bad output over a given period of time or for a given quantity of input;
(e) sales—in respect of price, mix, and volume.

The application of standard costing to job costs implies the ascertainment of the standard quantum of materials, labour, and other expenses required and their evaluation at standard prices. The application of standard costing to departmental costing, in order to calculate the standard cost of the unit of output, involves defining the level of activity at which the department will operate and the standard costs of achieving that output. Where the output of a department is either a mix of products or services, or is an otherwise unmeasured service that will be used by other departments or for other job costs, it is sometimes convenient to convert the output into a homogeneous unit, such as the 'standard hour'. A standard hour is a hypothetical hour that measures the amount of work that should be performed or provided in one hour. It is then possible to express the departmental costs in terms of a standard cost per standard hour. The usage of that service by jobs or other departments can then be defined in standard hours, from which the cost of the service can then be calculated.

The standard cost of a product can be calculated from the standard job costs, or the standard usage of departmental processes, or services, or a combination of the two methods by aggregating the standard job costs and the standard usage (expressed, if necessary, in standard hours) of the process or service at a standard cost. By analysing the actual costs to correspond with the manner in which the standard costs were built up, the total difference between total standard and actual costs can be analysed (variance analysis) to provide information on the causes of the departures from the plan. This analysis can guide management to the reasons for the variances and, thus, to the action that should be taken either to eliminate the causes of unfavourable variances, to exploit favourable variances or to revise its plans (standards) if those have been proved invalid. Finally, the existence of standards provides a basis for estimating the costs of new products or services through the aggregation of the standard costs of component products or services.

Marginal, direct, and full costing

Management is frequently concerned with decisions that hinge upon how costs vary with changes in other factors, such as the level of output. Costs that tend to vary in direct proportion to variations in the volume of output are known as variable costs. Costs that tend to be unaffected by variations in the volume of output are known as fixed costs. Costs that are partly fixed and partly variable are known as semi-variable costs.

Marginal costing

A knowledge of this variability of costs enables the marginal cost of a product or service to be calculated, the marginal cost of a product or service being the amount at any given volume of output by which aggregate costs are changed if the volume of output is increased or decreased by one unit. However, the terms variable and fixed are relative to the time scale involved and to the size of the change in the volume of production considered. Over a long enough period, nearly all costs are variable, and for large changes in the volume of production, certain fixed costs are bound to change even in the short term. It is essential, therefore, to define both the time scale and the magnitude of the change envisaged before defining whether a cost is variable or fixed and before calculating a marginal cost. It is important, therefore, to ensure that a marginal cost calculated for one purpose is not applied to another problem without first making sure that the data is valid for the second use.

A knowledge of the variability of costs enables a break-even chart (Fig 3.1) to be compiled, which shows the level of variable, semi-variable, fixed and total costs to be plotted against different levels of output. On the same graph, the sales revenue earned can be plotted against output. The intersection of the total revenue and total

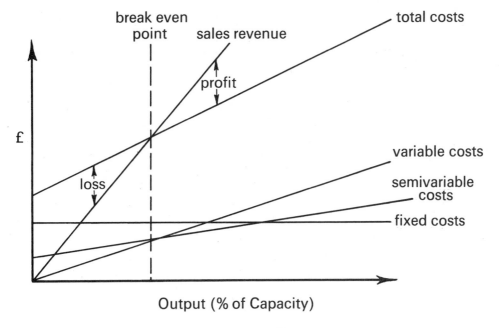

Fig. 3.1. A Breakeven Chart

cost lines indicates the break-even output where revenue just equals total costs. Output in excess of the break-even point will yield a profit; output below the break-even point will result in a loss.

Marginal cost data is invaluable for making a number of planning and pricing decisions, such as whether or not to accept a large contract at a reduced price, although considerable dangers exist if marginal costing is employed generally for pricing purposes. Make-or-buy decisions can also be made on marginal cost data. A knowledge of the variability of costs also allows budgets to be 'flexed' to show what total costs should have been to produce the output actually achieved.

Direct costing

Costs that can be specifically identified with a particular product or service are said to be specific to that product or service. Costs that cannot be identified specifically with a product or service are said to be joint costs. Variable costs and the variable part of semi-variable costs must, by definition, be specific. Fixed costs can be either specific or joint.

Direct costing is concerned with ascertaining the costs directly incurred in the production of the product or service being costed. The direct cost of a product or service will consist, therefore, of the variable costs and specific fixed costs incurred in the production. Again, the distinction between joint and specific costs is a relative one only, and large changes in output can affect the classification of an item of cost.

A knowledge of the direct costs are of indispensable value for planning purposes; for example, in deciding whether to start or discontinue production of a particular product. Direct costs differ from marginal costs by the inclusion of specific fixed costs. Where the unit direct cost is derived by calculating the total direct costs and dividing by the output achieved (for example in 'batch' or 'departmental' (process) costing), then, because the fixed costs do not vary with output, the unit direct cost will depend upon the actual volume of output achieved or planned. The application of standard costing overcomes this problem by nominating a standard (or target) output, calculating the standard costs of producing that output and, from these figures, the unit standard cost of the product or service.

Full costing

Full costing (absorption costing) is concerned with the ascertainment of the total cost of a product or service, including an appropriate share of the joint fixed costs. This apportionment of joint fixed costs is not a matter of cost analysis, as there can be no 'correct' basis for dividing these. Their apportionment can be a matter of judgement or policy only.

In a standard costing system, both the specific and the joint fixed costs are normally apportioned on a basis of a predetermined level of output so that, at that output, all the fixed costs would be absorbed by the output. Any under-absorption of the fixed costs is a measure of the cost of providing capacity in excess of that required by the actual production.

Relationship between the financial and cost accounts

Cost accounts can be kept outside the normal books of account on a memorandum basis. Such an arrangement is liable to produce inaccurate, incomplete, and mis-leading data unless the cost records are reconciled frequently with the financial accounts to ensure the former's accuracy. Such reconciliations are tedious and time-consuming.

The integration of the financial and cost accounts obviates these problems. If, in addition, budgetary control and standard costing techniques are employed, the foundation for an invaluable, well-controlled management information system is created.

Reading list

The Case for Marginal Costing, S. Dixon (Institute of Chartered Accountants in England & Wales, 1967)
Direct Standard Costs for Decision Making and Control, W. Wright (McGraw-Hill, 1962)
Standard Costing, J. Batty (Macdonald & Evans, 1960)

Cost Accounting: a Managerial Approach, M. Backer and L. E. Jacobsen (McGraw-Hill, 1964)
Cost Reduction, (Institute of Cost & Works Accountants, 1959)
Notes on Financial and Costing Statements: A Course of Studies Paper (Administrative Staff College, Henley, 1963)
Cost Control, E. C. D. Evans (Macdonald & Co., 1964)
Cost Reduction in Industry (O.E.E.C. (now O.E.C.D.), Paris, 1961)

Useful addresses

Association of Certified and Corporate Accountants, 22 Bedford Square, London WC 1
Institute of Cost and Works Accountants, 63 Portland Place, London W 1
Institute of Chartered Accountants in England and Wales, 56 Goswell Road, London EC 1
Institute of Chartered Accountants in Ireland, 7 Fitzwilliam Place, Dublin 2
Institute of Chartered Accountants of Scotland, 27 Queen Street, Edinburgh 2

3.3 Budgets and Budgetary Control

Ian Andrew

Objectives

Every business or organization has objectives it is seeking to achieve. Sometimes these objectives are laid down in a clearly expressed policy statement, while on other occasions, they are contained in vague, verbal statements. However, regardless of the manner in which the objectives are expressed, management must make a plan and take some action if they are to be achieved. This means, whether aware of it or not, that management has to formulate some plan of action. This plan may vary from a few thoughts jotted down on the back of an envelope to a complex model developed on a computer, but if the business is to continue, somewhere there must be a plan.

In some businesses, these objectives can be achieved by a simple plan; in others, intricate and integrated plans will be required. Such would be the case, for example, where one of the objectives was to introduce a new product on to the market. In these circumstances separate plans would need to be drawn up for all the main activities such as market research, product research, and development, capital expenditure on new plant, and the recruitment and training of labour. However, all these plans would be interacting. For example, a modification to the plan for expenditure on plant whereby more specialized equipment would be purchased, would almost certainly affect the plan for the recruitment and training of labour to operate the plant.

Whatever the nature of the objectives and the subsequent plans needed to achieve them, these plans need to be expressed in financial terms before a final decision can be made on their suitability. It is this financial evaluation of agreed plans, and the subsequent monitoring of actual performance against these plans, that is referred to as budgeting or budgetary control.

Objectives and scope of budgetary control

The principal objectives of budgetary control are to plan and control the financial results of the business and to provide better cost control and improved information on the profitability of the products and/or services supplied. The creation of budgets is the planning aspect of the technique, and the periodic comparison between actual and budgeted results in order to highlight important differences between them is the control aspect.

If management is to obtain the greatest benefits from using budgetary control, it is essential for all aspects of the business to be covered in sufficient detail. For example, it is not enough to prepare budgets for sales and costs only. While these are obviously important sections of the budget, they, in turn, affect the level of, for example, creditors, stocks, and debtors. Similarly, the relationship between production, finished stocks, sales, and debtors directly affects the amount of cash available for purchasing raw materials and paying wages and for investment in capital expenditure projects. So budgets must be prepared for all aspects of the business, that is: income or sales; the cost of production and providing services; capital expenditure; the purchase of necessary raw materials, bought out parts and services; man power; stocks and work-in-progress; debtors and creditors; cash flow.

While the items listed above cover the principal headings under which budgets should be prepared, there would be little point, for example, in preparing sales and production cost budgets in total only. Little control would be achieved, except in the smallest organization, without some analysis of sales by markets and products, and of production costs by the various departments, and the elements of cost involved. Similarly, budgets for capital expenditure would need to be analysed, for example, by projects or by expenditure authority levels. The precise form of analysis must suit the particular organization, and the budgets and actual results should be expressed in sufficient detail so that the causes of fluctuations (variances) between them can be readily identified. For example, if labour costs can be affected by changes in basic pay, bonus and overtime working, it may be desirable to prepare separate budgets under each of the three headings.

Budgeting can, if properly used, be one of the most useful tools available to management for assisting them in both planning and controlling their business. Improperly used, it can be merely a waste of time and money. For example, sometimes it involves just taking last year's total figures for sales and the main cost elements (such as wages, materials and the main overheads), and adding or subtracting any likely changes to arrive at this year's figures. These budgets are then compared during the year with the actual expenditure, the main objective often being merely to ensure that every penny of the budget is spent rather than the greatest economy is achieved. At the end of the year, management meets, and everyone pats everyone else on the back and says, 'What a good boy am I; we have met our budget'.

In this form, budgeting is nothing more than the preparation of control totals used to ensure that no more than a predetermined total sum is spent. In many other instances, it is just a complicated exercise in arithmetic that satisfies the tidy minds of bureaucrats and accountants but is of little help to executives and managers. Budgeting, if properly used, is a simple but effective means of planning and controlling; simple, that is, to understand, but not always as simple to use efficiently.

Essential features of budgetary control

A system of budgetary control is unlikely to be successful, unless it has top level support and is based on some overall quantitative plan, and unless managers are made individually accountable.

Top level support
A decision to prepare budgets and introduce a system of budgetary control must be seen to have the backing of the most senior level of management. This is absolutely vital and cannot be overemphasized. All too often this whole-hearted support is lacking and, as a result, the preparation of budgets degenerates into a tedious exercise rather than a positive and imaginative part of management planning.

Overall quantitative plan
Before budgetary control can be used efficiently as either a planning or control tool, top management must take two steps. Firstly, they must prepare an overall quantitative plan for the whole business. In other words, they must define their objectives. For example, one of the objectives of a local authority could be either to build 1,000 houses of a certain standard at the minimum cost or to build the maximum number of houses with a total cost of £3 million. Secondly, having decided what the objectives are, and defined a plan, they must decide whether the existing organization and resources are adequate to achieve these and, if so, which managers will be responsible for each part of the organization.

Individual accountability
It is important that specific managers should be held responsible for the income and costs they can control. Indeed, it is essential that each manager should prepare

148

the budget of the income and/or costs for which he is to be held responsible. It is naïve to think that a manager will work conscientiously to a budget that has been prepared by someone else. However, if he is allowed to put forward his own budget and justify his own proposals, there is no reason why he should not accept personal responsibility for the actual results.

Budget committee

It is clear that individual managers are unlikely to have the necessary overall understanding and appreciation of the objectives of the business to enable them to put forward a budget that is compatible with the budgets prepared by other managers. There is need, therefore, for someone who, or, in a large organization, some committee, which can be held responsible for the co-ordination, review, and approval of the various budgets. One method of dealing with this is to form a budget committee. This committee should consist of senior managers who have a sufficiently broad appreciation of the company's objectives to enable them to carry out their function effectively. However, it is essential that the Chairman of this committee should be a sufficiently senior member of the organization to enable him to take decisions, and in most cases where this has proved to be most successful, the Chairman has been the Managing Director or General Manager himself.

Budget review

The budget committee should be responsible for carrying out a critical review of budgets before putting forward a comprehensive and co-ordinated financial budget for the entire business to the Board of Directors. In carrying out this review they should be considering, for example, what should or could happen if alternative courses of action were followed; whether the best use is going to be made of the resources available. During this review stage, the committee might have to refer back some of the budgets to the managers concerned, either because they were considered to be unduly optimistic or pessimistic or because they were not compatible with the objectives of the business. Furthermore, this reference back to the managers concerned is important if the principle of individual accountability is to be maintained and the imposition of arbitrary alterations to the budget is to be avoided.

Budget period

It is not possible to lay down any hard and fast rule regarding the period of time for which budgets should be prepared. This is because a number of factors have to be taken into account before a final choice can be made, and these factors are important to varying degrees in different industries. There is no doubt, however, that one year is the usual period covered by a budget, but businesses do prepare budgets for longer or shorter periods. For example, during a period when extensive new production facilities are being provided in a company it may be desirable to prepare a new budget every few months because of the significantly different levels of production, labour costs, and sales expected at various stages in the installation of the new facilities.

In addition to short-term budgets the need for long-term forecasts of financial results covering, say, five to ten years ahead is increasing as the impact of increased competition and technological changes are felt. This long-term aspect is, however, outside the scope of this section and is referred to elsewhere (*see* section 1.4).

Control through budgets

In addition to helping the management of a business to plan the future of an organization, budgets are used as a control tool. When they are used for this purpose, as they usually are, the original annual budget is generally broken down three ways, namely, by period (monthly or quarterly), by responsibility (to reflect the manager responsible), and by type of expense (wages, materials, fuel, etc.). The actual income and expenditure is then recorded in the same way and is compared with the original budget.

Used in this way, the comparison of, for example, the actual and budgeted cost reveals where there has been an over- or underspending compared with the original budget. However, it does not indicate why the over- or underspending took place; nor does it of itself prevent the over- or underspending taking place.

A number of techniques can be used to improve the use of budgetary control as a control tool; two of these, budget revisions and flexible budgets, are dealt with below. A third and most valuable technique, standard costing, is dealt with in section 3.2 (*see* p. 140).

Budget revisions
From time to time circumstances change and make the most carefully prepared budgets no longer entirely appropriate. This happens, for example, where there has been a national wages award since the budgets were prepared. In these circumstances, the original budget can be revised; comparison can then be made between the original and revised budget and actual cost so that the effect of the wages award can be separately identified. This helps to separate out that part of the difference that is under the control of the manager and for which he can be held responsible, and that part he cannot control and for which he cannot be held responsible. This technique is useful in that it can be used to identify all minor changes or errors in the original budget that are not the responsibility of managers; any major changes will usually mean the preparation of a new budget.

Flexible budgets

Flexible budgets depend on the ability to differentiate between costs that tend to vary with changes in output or with other factors and those that do not. If this distinction between 'variable' and 'fixed' costs is made, the original budget for a variable cost item (which would be based on a specified output) can be adjusted to show the cost that should have been incurred for the output actually achieved. This clearly gives a much more realistic figure for comparison with actual results. Indeed, without this facility, actual results can be compared with the original budget to show an apparent underspending, although, in the light of the actual output achieved, the costs incurred could be higher than they should have been. Flexible budgets accordingly enable costs to be controlled more effectively by providing information that enables decisions to be made as to what should be done to adjust resources in the light of changing circumstances.

This analysis of costs into variable and fixed, also enables assessments to be made of the likely outcome of pursuing alternative courses of action. For example, a series of cost budgets for different assumed levels of output could be prepared in conjunction with the appropriate sales budgets to show the expected profitability of each one.

Advantages of budgetary control

Budgetary control has a number of important advantages, which are outlined below.

Review of the financial effect of plans

It has already been explained that it should be the responsibility of the budget committee to review the budgets before they are finally approved. An important aspect of this review is to ensure that the expected financial effect of the plans on which the budgets are based are acceptable. While the broad objectives of the business will have been laid down before the preparation of the various budgets was started, it does not necessarily follow that, once the individual budgets are put together into one comprehensive and co-ordinated budget for the entire business, the objectives will be fully met. It is clearly an advantage, if this is the case, that it should be highlighted before the business puts all its plans into operation. In these circumstances, some of the plans will have to be reconsidered to ensure that the required financial results will be achieved.

Monitoring actual results

Another advantage of budgetary control is that actual results can be compared with the budgets at regular intervals (for example, monthly, quarterly) to indicate the extent to which the latter are being achieved. These comparisons will be improved by showing not only the results for the period under review but also the cumulative results for the year to date, or moving annual totals. The importance of using flexible budgets and budget revisions to ensure that these comparisons are realistic has already been mentioned, and it is usually desirable that such comparisons are made in the same detail as the budgets were prepared.

Management by exception
The monitoring of actual results enables the extent of differences or variances from the budget to be ascertained. The significance of any variance can then be determined so that selected information can be presented to management. This ability to report only those variances that are significantly different from the budget enables management to concentrate on the exceptions from the expected results rather than spend valuable time examining all the results.

Variance analysis
The usefulness of the variances is improved if they are analysed to indicate the principal reasons for them. For example, an overspending compared with budget could be caused by either using too much labour to do a particular job or because the labour has been paid more than expected. The total difference would normally be described as an expense variance, but if standards of performance are laid down for the amount of labour to be used on a particular job separately from the wage rates to be paid, then the expense variance can itself be analysed into a labour efficiency variance and a wage rate variance. This more detailed analysis can usually be provided only when the sort of standards of performance referred to in section 3.2, on 'costing' (p. 137) have been laid down.

Variance analysis also highlights for management the areas where further investigation is required before a final decision is made on the appropriate action to be taken to correct any adverse results or to perpetuate any favourable trends.

Basis for product costs and standard costs
The existence of budgets makes it possible to analyse the budgeted costs over the products and services to be provided where an assessment can be made of the work to be done on each product and service in each department. Even if such an assessment is only approximate, it can provide useful information on the likely costs of products and services. However, where a system of budgetary control is used in conjunction with standards of performance for such factors as material usage and labour efficiency, then the expected costs of products and services can be calculated.

Conclusion

Budgets and budgetary control are increasingly assisting managers to plan and control their businesses better, and their application is equally suitable in both manufacturing and service industries. To summarize, the essential elements of budgetary control are to:

(a) decide what the objectives of the business are;
(b) determine the plans needed to achieve the objectives;
(c) evaluate the various plans in financial terms so that budgets for sales, costs, capital expenditure, and the financial position of the business can be established;
(d) co-ordinate, review, and approve the agreed plans and budgets;
(e) make regular comparisons between the budgeted and actual results;
(f) use the information in (e) to highlight areas for further investigation so that appropriate action can be taken to ensure that the budgeted results are achieved or improved upon.

Reading list

BOOKS

Business Budgets and Accounts, 3rd Edition, H. C. Edey (Hutchinson, 1966)
Business Planning and Control, S. V. Bishop (Institute of Chartered Accountants, 1966)
Flexible Budgetary Control and Standard Costs, D. F. Evans-Hemming (Macdonald and Evans, 1952)
Budgetary Control, H. P. Court (Sweet and Maxwell, 1951)
Budgetary Control and Standard Costs: The Practice of Accountancy as an aid to Management, J. A. Scott (Pitman, 5th Edition 1963)
Budgetary Control: An Effective Tool for the Management of Small and Medium Sized Enterprises (O.E.C.D., Paris, 2nd Edition 1960)
Increasing Profits in the Smaller Business: A Guide to Management Control (British Institute of Management, 1960)
Period Planning & Budgetary Control, E. C. D. Evans (Macdonald and Co., 1964)
Budgeting: Key to Planning & Control, R. L. Jones and H. G. Trentin (American Management Association, 1967)
Management Accounting for Profit Control, T. W. Keller and W. L. Ferrara (McGraw-Hill, 2nd Edition, 1966)

JOURNALS

'Capital Budgeting in the Corporation Tax Regime', G. H. Lawson and D. W. Windle (*Journal of Management Studies*, May 1967)

3.4 Financial Planning: Methods of Finance

G. W. Scarlett

One of the responsibilities of management lies in the attainment of the maximum long-term return on the equity shareholders' funds locked up in their company. Equity share capital means, in this context, that part of the issued share capital which has the right to participate beyond a specified amount in a distribution either as respects dividends or as respects capital. The term 'equity capital' is, therefore, normally synonymous with ordinary share capital. The equity shareholders' funds consist not only of the amount of the issued ordinary share capital but also of the premium (if any) paid on issue of ordinary shares, reserves (e.g., surpluses arising from revaluation of fixed assets), and undistributed profits, which belong to the equity shareholders but have not been distributed to them either because it would be illegal to do so or because management has decided that a part of the profits earned must be retained in the business. It is worth recording that between 50 and 60 per cent of total investment in most developed countries is provided from undistributed profits plus provisions for depreciation of fixed assets.

It will be recognized that management also has a responsibility, when planning its finances, to consider with a reasonable degree of prudence the interests both of those who have lent their company money on a fixed interest basis and of their suppliers who have sold goods or services on credit.

Gearing

Management has, therefore, in determining the appropriate method of finance to balance the need to obtain the maximum return on the equity capital against the risk of imprudent or excessive borrowings that may endanger the very existence of their company. Two of the ratios used to guide management in striking this balance are, first, the gearing ratio (or leverage ratio), and secondly, the borrowing ratio. Gearing may be defined as the use of fixed interest capital to provide additional earnings for the equity, and the gearing ratio is the relationship between fixed interest capital (monies borrowed and preference capital) and the equity fund, i.e., issued ordinary share capital, reserves, and undistributed profits. The borrowing ratio is the relationship between monies borrowed and the total issued share capital, including preference capital, plus the reserves and undistributed profits.

Figures 3.2 and 3.3 may help to illustrate the importance of adequate gearing.

Company A

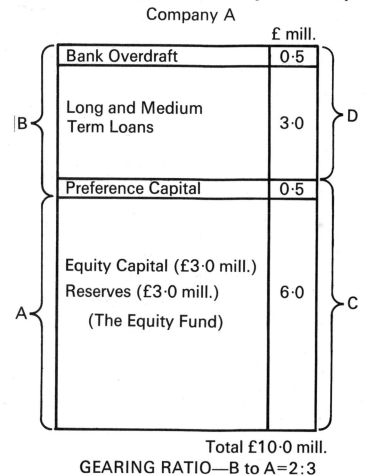

£ mill.

Bank Overdraft	0·5
Long and Medium Term Loans	3·0
Preference Capital	0·5
Equity Capital (£3·0 mill.) Reserves (£3·0 mill.) (The Equity Fund)	6·0

Total £10·0 mill.

GEARING RATIO—B to A=2:3

BORROWING RATIO—D to C=7:13

Fig. 3.2. Capital Structure of Company 'A'

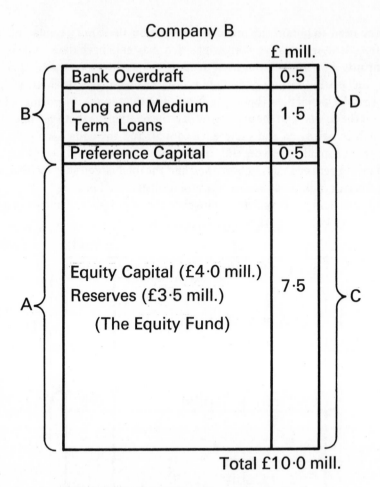

Company B

£ mill.

Bank Overdraft	0·5	
Long and Medium Term Loans	1·5	
Preference Capital	0·5	
Equity Capital (£4·0 mill.) Reserves (£3·5 mill.) (The Equity Fund)	7·5	

Total £10·0 mill.

GEARING RATIO—B to A=1:3

BORROWING RATIO—D to C=1:4

Fig. 3.3. Capital Structure of Company 'B'

The two companies are of equal size and, if it is assumed that they are in comparable trades and are both earning similar trading profits, say £2 million before interest and tax, it is evident, without going into detailed calculations, that the rate of return on earnings on the equity fund of Company *A* is higher than that on Company *B*. This reflects the fact that Company *A* has a gearing ratio of 2:3 as against Company *B*'s ratio of 1:3.

The above illustrations and comments demonstrate that the management of Company *A* has, *prima facie*, done a better job for its equity shareholders than the management of Company *B*, without in any way acting imprudently by resorting to excessive borrowings in relation to the equity fund. It is not possible to lay down hard and fast rules as to the correct gearing ratio, as this must to a large extent depend on the nature of the business, the degree of risk inherent in its operations and the view taken of its growth prospects, which may be bound up with the general economic situation. Wise management will keep something in reserve for contingencies; if a manufacturing business is working to a full gearing, say a ratio of fixed interest capital to the equity fund of $4:5$, it would be prudent to have a contingency plan in the event of the company becoming short of funds. Management should not put itself into the position of losing its power of manoeuvre, and in determining its gearing ratio this must be borne in mind.

It is worth recording that, according to a Board of Trade survey in respect of quoted public companies (excluding banks and finance houses), the gearing ratio in 1964 was in the region of $1:3$; this is less than the figure for 1948, and a substantially lower gearing ratio than existed pre-war. There is, however, evidence from later statistics that this ratio has probably been increasing to something nearer $2:5$ in 1966, mainly as a result of the introduction of Corporation Tax.

Planning for growth requires financial planning, and skill is required in balancing the rate of a company's expansion against the required rate of injection of outside money and in deciding what form this outside money should take. The purpose of the remainder of this section is to consider briefly some of the various forms of outside finance available. The paragraphs dealing with the different methods of borrowing are divided, for convenience, into long, medium and short term, but it should be emphasized that these are not terms of precise definition and there is often an overlap from one to the other. This is particularly evident when considering, for example, leasing and credit facilities available to exporters.

Share capital

The rights attaching to the shares of a company are normally set out in the Articles of Association, and it must be emphasized that there are many permutations of these rights, and a particular class of share is not always what it appears to be from its title. With this reservation it can be said that there are two main classes of share capital equity shares, bearing in mind the definition in the first paragraph of this section, and preference shares.

Preference shares, as their title indicates, normally carry preferential rights as to repayment of capital on a winding up and as to dividend in priority to equity shares. These shares may be redeemable, usually at fixed dates, or irredeemable. Under the Companies Act 1948 redeemable preference shares may be redeemed only out of profits otherwise available for dividend or out of the proceeds of a fresh issue of shares made for the purposes of the redemption. A holder of irredeemable preference shares can, in normal circumstances, realize his investment while the company is a going concern, only by selling his shares if he can find a buyer.

If reference is made to Figs 3.2 and 3.3, it will be noted that in calculating the borrowing ratio the preference capital was coupled with the equity fund and, thus, formed part of the borrowing base. In calculating the gearing ratio the preference capital is included as part of the fixed interest capital. Preference shares thus fulfil two most useful functions. Firstly, their issue increases a company's ability to borrow without the equity shareholders having to find further finance, and secondly, the gearing is increased, i.e., fixed interest capital is being used to provide additional earnings for the equity. The introduction of Corporation Tax in the Finance Act of 1965 has, however, seriously detracted from the advantages of preference shares. The fixed interest capital of a company (both loan and preference capital) should be at the lowest possible rate of interest. Under the provisions relating to Corporation Tax (up to and including the Finance Act 1968) interest on loan capital is, in normal circumstances (there are exceptions to this), an allowable charge in calculating liability to Corporation Tax, whereas dividends on preference capital are not, and are treated as distributions. It thus follows that with Corporation Tax at $42\frac{1}{2}$ per cent, a preference share carrying a fixed dividend of $7\frac{1}{2}$ per cent is equivalent, in terms of cost to a company earning taxable profits, to a loan carrying interest at 13 per cent. The issue of preference shares can now be considered desirable only in exceptional circumstances, usually dictated by special tax considerations (including the provisions relating to distributions by what are known as 'close companies'), but sometimes is still necessary as a means of increasing the base for supporting borrowed monies.

Long-term capital

'Long-term' usually denotes monies borrowed at an agreed rate of interest for periods ranging from five to twenty-five years, and sometimes thirty years. The repayment of the borrowed money can be by periodical instalments, by operation of a sinking fund, or by a lump sum repayment at the end of the loan, or by a combination of these methods.

A long-term loan may be secured or unsecured, and the degree of security that has to be provided will, in part, depend upon the financial strength of the company. The loan may be secured in a variety of ways, ranging from a fixed charge on specified assets, e.g., a mortgage on specified property, to a general charge on all the assets of a company. The latter may take the form of a fixed charge on the property and a floating charge on all the other assets of a company. The main distinction between a fixed and floating charge lies in the fact that with the fixed charge the underlying specified asset(s) constituting the security for the advance cannot, in practice, be disposed of without the consent of the lender. As a fixed charge has to specify the assets so charged, it is clearly only appropriate where the assets are (a) of material value, (b) easy to identify, and (c) not likely to be disposed of or replaced from time to time in the ordinary course of running a business.

Since the introduction of Corporation Tax in 1965 there has been an increase in the issue of what are known as subordinated loans, but in this context the term 'subordinated' usually means that the lender's claims are subordinated to those of other unsecured creditors, i.e., in the event of a winding up of the company the holders of subordinated loan stock will not be repaid in part or in full until all the other unsecured creditors have received 20s. in the £. The terms for repayment are usually conditional upon the tangible assets of the company exceeding its liabilities at the date of repayment. Interest on the loan is normally an allowable charge for Corporation Tax, hence its attraction compared with preference shares. In view of the subordination factor, loans of this type should, in theory, form part of the base for supporting borrowed monies, but it has to be borne in mind that whereas preference shares can only be redeemed subject to the fulfilment of conditions laid down in the Companies Act, this is not so in the case of subordinated loans, when repayment can be made subject to the fulfilment of whatever conditions are laid down in the document setting out the terms of the loan.

The device of selling premises and leasing them back on agreed terms is broadly comparable to long-term finance. This is an appropriate method of raising finance in those cases where the value of premises occupied represents a large proportion of a company's total assets, and when the capital represented by the asset can be more profitably employed elsewhere in the business. The disadvantages are that future increases in the value of the property are usually lost unless the terms of the deal provide for repurchase, the cost is often high (the rent payable in relation to the sale price expressed as a rate of interest) and the sale may give rise to a liability for Capital Gains Tax.

Medium-term credit

The expression 'medium-term' cannot be exactly defined, but is usually taken as covering loans from one or two to five years, and will, therefore, cover term loans from the banks, including finance for exports where credit has to be granted to the customers, hire purchase for the acquisition of plant and equipment, and hire purchase for the financing of retail sales. It is not the purpose of this section to detail the exact mechanism or advantages and disadvantages of each particular method of finance, but it should be recorded that the essence of the use of medium-term credit is that the transaction for which the credit was obtained provides the money to enable repayment to be made. This is so in the case of finance obtained to cover, say, three years' credit given to an export customer, and should be broadly so in the case of hire–purchase finance, i.e., the equipment or plant purchased should itself generate a cash flow sufficient to meet the instalments as they fall due. If hire-purchase finance is used indiscriminately, without bearing the above in mind, a company may find itself in difficulties and be short of cash to meet the instalments when due.

Equipment leasing is effectively another means of obtaining medium-term credit or, in some cases, long-term credit, to enable plant and equipment to be acquired. The plant or equipment remains in the ownership of the lessor and is rented or leased to the user who thus has the use of the equipment without the initial outlay of its cost. Future instalments due under the terms of the lease entered into do not appear as a liability in a company's balance sheet, and leasing is sometimes resorted to when authorized capital budgets are exhausted and when borrowing limits have been reached. Management should not, however, forget that rents due under the terms of a lease are cash outgoings, and in this respect do not differ from instalments due under hire purchase or deferred payment agreements.

It is not within the scope of this section to debate the advantages and disadvantages of leasing as compared with hire-purchase, as these are, at times, complex, and the choice of method will be influenced by the availability of investment grants and tax considerations. The comparison of the true cost of hire-purchase as against leasing is best calculated by using Discounted Cash Flow techniques.

It would be inappropriate to close this paragraph without reference to medium-term credit facilities available for exporters. These are now considerable, and are usually linked with the ability of the exporter to obtain insurance cover from the Export Credits Guarantee Department (ECGD) of the Board of Trade (*see also* section 10.5(b)). Detailed information on finance for exports—long, medium and short term—can be found in Board of Trade Export Handbook No. 1 (Services for British Exporters, including a chapter on Finance) and Board of Trade Export Handbook No. 2 (ECGD Credit Insurance and Financial Support Services). Both these handbooks can be obtained free of charge on application to the Information Bureau, Board of Trade.

Short-term credit

The bank overdraft is far and away the largest source of short-term finance and, with minor exceptions, the cheapest. The rate of interest on an overdraft, which is payable only on the amount actually overdrawn from day to day, is likely to be about 1 or $1\frac{1}{2}$ per cent, or sometimes 2 per cent, over Bank Rate, with an agreed minimum. It is usual for overdraft limits to be agreed for periods ranging up to twelve months but, in fact, amounts borrowed are nearly always repayable on demand, and it follows, therefore, that bank finance is, in the main, devoted to acquisition of assets that are reasonably quickly turned into cash, i.e., raw materials, work-in-progress, finished stocks, and debtors. Bankers will, however, at times provide finance for acquisition of fixed assets and on a term basis with an agreed repayment programme.

Management will be wise to make proper use of overdraft facilities, but must bear in mind that in times of 'credit squeezes' the banks, under pressure from Government policy, may seek a reduction in overdraft limits.

The Bill of Exchange is a time-honoured method for financing trade throughout the world. The seller, in effect, receives, instead of cash for his goods, a piece of paper—a Bill of Exchange—on which the purchaser undertakes to pay for his goods in x days' time. With this piece of paper the seller may be able to go to his bank and exchange it for cash, i.e., discount the bill. There will, of course, be a charge for this, the rate of interest depending on the status of the seller and the purchaser, i.e., the parties to the Bill of Exchange. If the transaction relates to goods exported, and such transaction is insured with ECGD, the rate of interest charged for discounting will clearly be reduced.

A refinement of the Bill of Exchange is the use of an Acceptance Credit, which involves using the credit of a merchant bank to obtain a finer rate of interest. In its simplest form, the use of an Acceptance Credit involves an agreement between merchant bank and trader whereby the former agrees to put his name on Bills of Exchange (as acceptor of the Bills) up to agreed amounts and for agreed periods. There should be underlying commercial transactions which are self-liquidating, such as the purchase of raw materials or the sale of goods.

There is a most helpful explanation of the mechanism of Bills of Exchange and Acceptance Credits in *Financing your Business*, issued by the Engineering Industries Association.

Factoring of book debts is not, perhaps, strictly speaking, borrowing, but it is certainly a means of obtaining additional finance. The factor provides two services: first, he takes over the clerical functions relating to sales accounting, and he takes over credit control and debt collection; secondly, he buys the company's debts on agreed terms, often guaranteeing the accounts of approved customers. The factor will, of course, be remunerated for his services, charging in the range $\frac{3}{4}$ to 2 per cent on value of debts purchased, and will also charge interest linked to Bank Rate to the extent that he puts his client in funds before he receives payment for the debtors he has purchased. This may be done on a formula basis by agreement of an average maturity date for the clients' invoices.

Management has to assess the cost of the accounting service in relation to likely savings arising in its own departments, and to compare the amount and the cost of the finance that will be made available from the financial service provided by the factor, with other and more traditional methods.

Invoice discounting is not to be confused with the services provided by factors, briefly described in the preceding paragraph. Invoice discounting is solely a financial arrangement for converting a proportion of book debts into cash. The finance company specializing in this type of transaction, in effect, advances cash against debtors; the documentation of the transaction can be done in a variety of ways. There is nearly always recourse to the company, and its financial standing is, therefore, of importance to the finance company. The cost should be carefully compared with other available methods of short-term credit.

Conclusion

This section is not intended to be an exhaustive catalogue of all the different methods of finance, nor has space permitted a more detailed study of the advantages and disadvantages of each particular type of finance. Much depends on the circumstances of each case, but common to all is the need for a financial plan in the light of a company's basic objectives and its view of the overall business environment, and to prepare this plan properly it is essential to have a knowledge of the financial weapons available.

Reading list

BOOKS

The Management of Business Finance, P. G. Hastings (Van Nostrand, 1966)
Capital Budgeting and Company Finance, Merrett and Sykes (Longmans, Green, 1967)
Finance for Management, Page and Canaway (Heinemann, 1966)
The Management Problems of Expansion, Frank Broadway (Business Publications, 1966)
Capital Investment Decisions (Industrial and Commercial Finance Corp. Ltd., 1967)
Financing your Business (Engineering Industries Association, 1967)
Sources of Capital (Association of Certified and Corporate Accountants, revised edition, 1965)

Useful addresses

Board of Trade Information Bureau, 1 Victoria Street, London SW 1
Industrial and Commercial Finance Corporation Ltd., 7 Copthall Avenue, London EC 2
Finance Corporation for Industry, 4 Bread Street, London EC 2

3.5 Decision Theory

Derek Allen

In the management of any organization, complex decisions are made by balancing a variety of contributing factors. The skill and experience needed are 'business judgement'. In exercising this, a knowledge of the elements of Decision Theory can be of practical assistance. Although it may not be possible to assign numbers to all the factors entering a decision, the mental processes involved in decision-making can be simplified by quantifying as much as possible. The analysis of the quantified problem indicates the appropriate decision, which may then be modified by considering any intangible factors outside the quantified problem.

Decisions are concerned with selecting a particular course of action from possible alternatives. There are three steps in making the selection. First, the possible outcomes of each action are predicted; secondly, each action is evaluated in terms of the desirability of the resulting outcome; and thirdly, a criterion of desirability is applied to select the preferred action.

Often, the outcome of a particular action is uncertain, in other words there is more than one possible outcome. These alternative outcomes can have different desirabilities which must be considered in evaluating the desirability of the action. To do this the relative chances or probabilities that each outcome will occur are needed. The probability of an outcome is a number between 0 (meaning it will definitely not occur) and 1 (meaning it is certain to occur). The probabilities of all the alternative outcomes of an action must add up to one, since one of them is bound to occur.

Considerable attention is being given to value systems for measuring desirabilities. The most common one is the straightforward economic system of gains and losses. Sometimes a system based on the concept of Utility would be better. The utility system diverges from the economic system, especially when large sums of money are involved. The properties of the economic system are widely recognized and accepted, but there is no similar agreement on utility.

When desirabilities are measured in economic terms, the decision criterion is also economic. Where there is only one possible outcome for each action, the criterion is to select the action that maximizes net gains (or minimizes losses). Where actions have multiple uncertain outcomes, the criterion must also take account of risks. The way this can be done will be discussed later.

Decision-making is based on information, much of which is in the form of predictions which are themselves based on past experience or are made intuitively. The information needed for a decision-making procedure consists of a list of alternative actions, a list of alternative outcomes for each action, the probability and desirability of each outcome, and the appropriate decision criterion to apply. Given these, the preferred action can be selected with no further guesswork.

The technique can be illustrated by a simplified example of a decision whether or not to invest in a new manufacturing project. There are two possible actions; 'invest' or 'not invest'. We shall assume, at first, that there is only one possible outcome for each action. The project will achieve a specified profitability if the 'invest' action is selected, otherwise the capital will remain invested elsewhere. Desirabilities are measured in terms of the DCF return over ten years and for the project this is predicted to be 25 per cent. Invested elsewhere the capital will produce a return of 8 per cent. The position is set out in Table 3.1. The decision criterion used is to maximize return, and so it is obvious that the preferred action is 'invest'.

Table 3.1

Straightforward decision

Action (DCF return %)	
Invest in project	Do not invest
25	8

Now suppose it is known that a competitor may also be considering entering the same field. If he does, it will reduce the return for the project to 5 per cent. The new position is given in Table 3.2. A chance event, such as the state of competition, over which the decision-maker has no control, is known as a State of Nature. With no competition the preferred action is 'invest'. With competition, 'not invest' is preferable.

Table 3.2

Decision with alternative outcomes

State of Nature	Action (DCF return %)	
	Invest in project	Do not invest
No competition	25	8
Competition	5	8

To go further we need to know the probabilities of the possible states and the corresponding outcomes. The probability of competition is estimated as 0·25. The probability of the other state (no competition) must be 0·75 (i.e., 1·00—0·25). Put another way, the odds against competition are 3 to 1. One decision criterion would be to consider only the most probable outcomes for each action in maximizing the return. Since 'no competition' has the higher probability the preferred action on this basis is 'invest' (25 per cent return compared with 8 per cent).

Another criterion is to use Expectation in maximizing the return. The 'expected' return is the average of the individual returns for each alternative outcome weighted according to their probabilities. For this example the calculation of the expectations is shown in Table 3.3. For 'invest' it is 20 per cent and for 'not invest' 8 per cent. With this criterion the preferred action is therefore 'invest'.

Table 3.3

Decision using expectation

State of Nature	Probability	Action (DCF return %)	
		Invest in project	Do not invest
No competition	0·75 (A)	25 (Y)	8 (Y)
Competition	0·25 (B)	5 (Z)	8 (Z)
Expectation = $(A \times Y) + (B \times Z)$		20	8

If the probabilities were 0·1 for 'no competition' and 0·9 for 'competition' the expectations would be 7·0 per cent for 'invest' and 8 per cent for 'not invest', and the opposite action, 'not invest' would be preferable.

In using expectation we are looking at the average effect of repeating the same decision several times. On separate occasions any one of the possible outcomes can occur. The relative frequencies with which they do, depend on their probabilities, so that the average effect is given by expectation. If this is only one project among many, an organization may be prepared to gain on the swings what it loses on the rounda-bouts. As long as the group of projects as a whole shows an attractive return, in the long run the failure of any individual project may be an acceptable risk. In this situation expectation is a reasonable decision criterion to use.

If, however, a project will absorb a major part of an organization's resources, the management may not be willing to risk the prospect, however remote, of not obtain-ing an adequate return. In this case a suitable decision criterion is to select the action that minimizes the maximum possible loss that could be incurred. This is the Minimax criterion. In the example, this criterion leads to the action 'not invest', since the lowest possible return for this is 8 per cent compared with 5 per cent for 'invest'. The minimax criterion ensures that the worst outcome is avoided, and represents the policy of playing safe. This security is usually obtained by giving up the chance of a high return. In the example, by not investing and thus ensuring a return of 8 per cent, the risk of obtaining only 5 per cent is avoided, but at the same time the chance of obtaining 25 per cent is forfeited.

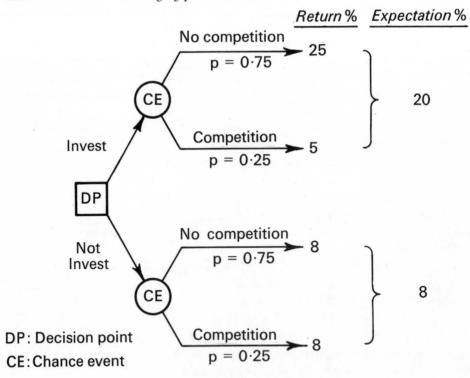

Fig. 3.4. Decision network of investment problem

Some decision problems are dealt with more easily by representing them as decision networks or trees rather than as matrices in the way just described. The investment problem is shown as a decision network in Fig 3.4. It starts at a decision point from which two arrows indicate the alternative actions. The arrows end at chance event points, and new arrows from these indicate the alternative outcomes, which are labelled with their probabilities. At the end of each outcome arrow is a statement of the associated economic measure. A decision network can easily accommodate any number of alternative outcomes, and problems involving two or more decision points in sequence can be dealt with.

The use of decision networks is further illustrated by the following problem. A process can possibly be improved by means of research. If a research programme is successful, and the results are implemented, a saving will be achieved on the process operating costs. If it is unsuccessful, a second research programme can be carried out and this could also result in a saving. The detailed situation is shown in the decision network of Fig 3.5. At decision point 1 there are two alternative actions: carry out research programme I at a cost of £8,000, or use the existing process at no additional cost and with no subsequent saving. If programme I is carried out it has a 0·8 probability of success and 0·2 of failure. If it is successful, the next decision is whether to apply the results at a cost of £15,000 to produce a saving of £75,000, or whether to use the existing process. If programme I is unsuccessful, the decision then is whether to use the existing process or whether to carry out research programme II at a cost of £4,000. If programme II is carried out it has a 0·1 probability of success and 0·9 of failure. If it is successful, the next decision is whether to apply the results at a cost of £10,000 to produce a savings of £30,000 or whether to still use the existing process. If it is unsuccessful, the decision must be to use the existing process.

There is only one decision to be made immediately, that at decision point 1. The remaining decisions need be made only as and when they arise. However, later decisions follow as consequences of earlier decisions, and this is taken into account by a 'roll-back' analysis starting with the later decisions and working back to the initial decision. At each decision point the expectations for the alternative actions are calculated, and the most attractive one is selected as the Position Value of that decision point.

The analysis is shown in Table 3.4 The economic measure used is the net cash value. The position value of decision point 5 is zero, and that of point 4 is £20,000, corresponding to the action to apply the results. The position value of point 3 is zero, corresponding to using the existing process, since the expectation for research programme II is negative (a loss of £2,000). In finding the position values of an earlier decision point the position values of the following ones are used in the calculation. Continuing in this way, the position value of decision point 1 works out at £40,000, corresponding to carrying out research programme I. The immediate

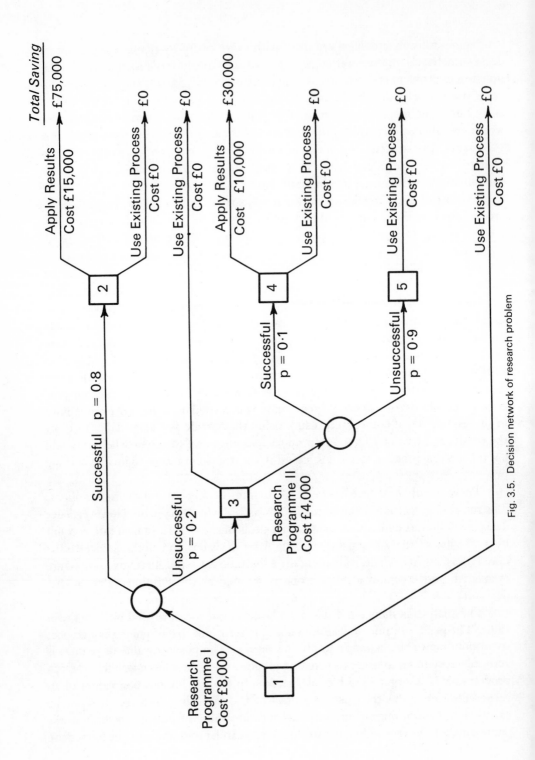

Fig. 3.5. Decision network of research problem

action, therefore, should be to carry out programme I, as this has an expectation £40,000 higher than the alternative. If it is unsuccessful, the existing process should be used rather than carry out research programme II, unless, of course, the predictions are modified in the meantime.

Decision Theory can be applied to a much wider range of problems than is indicated by these examples. It is particularly useful for repetitive routine decisions at a lower management level, such as quality control, where the actions, outcomes, and probabilities are well defined and are based on reliable information from past experience. Once such a decision system has been set up and tested it can be operated according to a set of rules and requires a minimum of judgement to be exercised in individual cases.

Table 3.4
Analysis of research problem network

Decision point		Expectation for each action £	Position value, k
5		0	0
4	(1)	30,000 − 10,000 = 20,000	20,000
	(2)	0	
3	(1)	0	0
	(2)	$(20,000 \times 0 \cdot 1) + (0 \times 0 \cdot 9) - 4,000 = -2,000$	
2	(1)	75,000 − 15,000 = 60,000	60,000
	(2)	0	
1	(1)	$(60,000 \times 0 \cdot 8) + (0 \times 0 \cdot 2) - 8,000 = 40,000$	40,000
	(2)	0	

At a higher management level each decision tends to have new features, and so each should be considered afresh for the alternative actions open, the basis for the predictions of outcomes and probabilities, and the type of economic measure and decision criterion that is appropriate. It is not always possible for the decision-maker himself to sift the information on which predictions are made and he has of necessity to rely on the judgement of others. The decision-maker must ensure that he receives exactly the data he needs, otherwise there is a danger that a bias may be built into predictions by those who are not fully aware of their purpose and implications. This could distort the picture for the decision-maker and even prejudge aspects of the decision.

In some decision problems where the situation is entirely novel it may not be possible to assign probabilities with any confidence. All that can be said is whether an outcome is credible or not. This idea of Credibility is being put on a quantitative basis and promises to be of more use than probability in such cases. Unlike probability, the credibilities of alternative outcomes are not interdependent—any number of outcomes may be credible at the same time without affecting one another. With no knowledge, uncertainty is high and the range of credible outcomes is very wide. As knowledge increases, uncertainty is reduced, some outcomes are eliminated, and the range of credible outcomes is reduced, until, with complete knowledge, only one credible outcome remains.

In the space available it has been possible to indicate only very briefly some techniques of decision-making based on Decision Theory. The use of these systematic approaches enables many aspects of a complex decision problem to be clarified by evaluating the consequences of alternative actions using a few carefully thought-out predictions.

Reading list

BOOKS

Elementary Decision Theory, H. Chernoff and L. E. Moses (Wiley, 1960)
Design for Decision, I. D. J. Bross (Macmillan, 1961)
The New Science of Management Decision, Herbert A. Simon (Harper and Brothers, New York, 1960)
New Thinking in Management: A Guide for Managers, F. de P. Hanika, An Administrative Staff College Publication (Hutchinson, 1965)
The Management of Innovation, Tom Burns and G. M. Stelker (Tavistock Publications, 1961)

JOURNALS

'Decision Trees for Decision-Making', J. F. Magee (*Harvard Business Review*, July/August 1964)
'Decision Trees in Capital Investment', J. F. Magee (*Harvard Business Review*, September/October 1964)
'Credibility Forecasts and their Applications to the Economic Assessment of Novel Research and Development Projects', D. H. Allen (*Operational Research Quarterly*, Volume 19 No. 1, March 1968)

3.6 Operational Research

Allan Fletcher

The history of effective operational research goes back to the early days of the Second World War. Then, it was referred to as operational analysis. The approach to problems had been carried out on a spasmodic basis earlier, but it was the necessity of conditions in those early months that caused a cohesion into a discipline.

A definition of OR is: 'Operational Research is a scientific method of providing executive departments with a quantitative basis for decisions regarding the operations under their control'.

The birth of OR in the military environment led to a number of successes, particularly search theory in studies such as merchant vessel sinking and the pattern of a mortar bombardment strategy. At the end of the war, in the Imperial forces, there were approximately 1,000 OR workers. With the end of hostilities, a great number of these scientists returned to their original discipline. However, a few decided to sell their new-found skills to industry, and groups started to be formed. In particular, steel, coal, and railways founded groups.

In the early days, the interdiscipline approach was more general. However, because of industrial or commercial security, it was necessary to mask case studies in the generalizations of mathematical symbolism, and because of this, and the rigour of this discipline, more and more emphasis is now placed on mathematics as a qualification for OR.

Procedure

The procedure by which an operational research worker approaches a problem may be analysed into six phases:

1. Formulating the problem

The formulation requires not only a definition of the area of decision-making to be studied, but also an agreed measure of the effectiveness of the study. It is important that the criteria for judging the work be agreed at this early stage, for on too many occasions when this is not done, the scientist and management disagree over the results of the study because each has used different criteria of judgement.

Other adjacent areas of responsibility that may be affected by the study should also be defined. An organization cannot have its mode of operation changed without the change having repercussions throughout the organization. Their possible repercussions should be noted at the start of the study.

2. Construction of the model

The model of the system under review may be physical, e.g., a wind tunnel analogue, or a mathematical one. Usually, the models are mathematical, but not necessarily. Why have a model? Well, this is the operational research worker's test-tube. It is here that he manipulates the distilled version of the system under consideration.

It is unlikely that management would allow anyone to experiment with the actual system; it would be far too costly. However, if the Operational Research worker can explain the complex shop floor situation in a set of equations he may then manipulate these in any way he wishes, without disastrous results to the profits.

3. Deriving a solution to the model

This is probably the easiest part of the exercise. Often OR workers are called 'boffins' or 'backroom boys'. However, it is only this stage of any project that provides an excuse for the scientist to retreat to his ivory tower.

A solution may be obtained in three ways:

(a) *Iterative*. Here the mathematical expressions are such that they have no analytical solution. Numerical approximations are made to the solution until one is selected in which the approximations are acceptable.
(b) *Analytical*. Analytical solutions are obtained in the abstract, using such mathematical tools as matrix, algebra, and calculus.
(c) *Simulation*. This is used on occasions when the problem defies either the analytical or iterative approach; but this method will be discussed at length later.

4. Testing the model

In the construction of a model, assumptions have been made. Data may have been transformed. It is essential to ascertain that these assumptions and generalizations have not made the solution impractical. Too often the scientist goes to management with a solution to a problem that has been so distorted in the model stage that the solution has little to do with the original problem. To be successful in this area there must be constant feed-back. If possible, it is useful for a member of the operating department to be seconded to the OR team.

5. Establish control

We operate in a dynamic environment. A system designed at one moment in time will not meet the circumstances occurring in some time period later. This is simply because the problem area itself has changed. It is necessary then, when designing a system or solution, to ascertain the critical parameters and the range of values of these parameters for which the solution is optimal. In the jargon of the OR world, this is sometimes referred to as 'sensitivity analysis' or the 'robustness of the solution'.

6. Implementation

There is little to be said about this stage, or, on the other hand, there are books to be written on the subject. It is the most important phase of the project. If a company does not implement the findings of the OR group, it is wasting its resources. It should not employ such a group. Failure to implement could be due to many reasons both in management and in the OR group. In the author's view, implementation is the prime responsibility of the manager of the OR team.

Reasons for failure to implement are:

(a) Bad analysis. This is often caused by the failure to test the system thoroughly before implementation.
(b) Poor summarization with management. Management require to follow the thought process behind the solution and be convinced of the feasibility.
(c) Uneconomic solutions. It should always be remembered that the company has to make a profit. It is futile to suggest solutions that involve large computer or clerical effort without consequent relative benefits. These benefits may not always be quantifiable in terms of sterling.
(d) Poor communications with workers or clerks on the shop floor. Unless the co-operation of staff at all levels is obtained, a revised method of working is almost impossible to implement.

Briefly then, these are the steps in an operational research project and some of the pitfalls. Now, let us examine a few of the techniques in the OR worker's 'tool bag'.

Linear Programming

Probably the most well known OR technique is that of linear programming. The technique was developed by George Dantzig in 1948, and the first application was the calculation of minimum cost diets. In the last sentence is the essential element of linear programming. It is an optimizing technique. It will either minimize or maximize mathematical linear functions, subject to a number of constraints.

This sounds very technical, but let us pause for a moment to understand fully the implication of this sentence. Recalling first-year algebra it may be remembered that to solve simultaneous equations an equation is required for each variable: e.g.,

$$2x+3y = 7 \tag{1}$$
$$x+5y = 7 \tag{2}$$

Multiplying eq. (1) by 1, and eq. (2) by 2 (i.e., the co-efficient of x) we get:

$$2x+3y = 7 \tag{3}$$
$$2x+10y = 14 \tag{4}$$

Now, subtracting eq. (3) from eq. (4) we get:

$$0+7y = 7$$
$$y = 1$$

Substituting this value for y in eq. (1), we find $x = 2$.

However, we want to go a little further than this. We will see in Fig 3.6 that

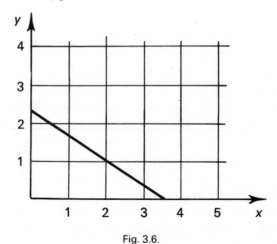

Fig. 3.6.

all points on the line satisfy eq. (1). Now, let us consider an inequality, i.e., instead of stating an expression is equal to an amount, we say that it is less than or equal to this amount, which may be written

$$2x+3y \le 7 \tag{5}$$
$$2x+3y \ge 7 \tag{6}$$

174

Expression (6) states that $2x+3y$ is greater than or equal to 7. The shaded areas in Figs 3.7 and 3.8 show the area that meets the requirements of statements (5) and (6) respectively. These shaded areas are feasible solutions to the statements, e.g., $x=1$, $y=1$ is a feasible solution for statement (5), and $x=3$, $y=3$ is a feasible solution to statement (6). Now, linear programming requires the problem to be

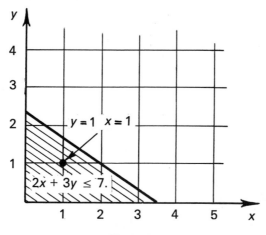

Fig. 3.7.

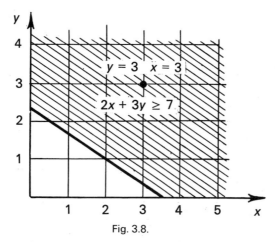

Fig. 3.8.

formulated into a number of equations and inequalities, and, as there is not an exact solution, an objective is formulated. The greatest or smallest value of this objective is then found, subject to the equations or constraints as they are called.

It is not intended to show how the computational procedure is carried out, for any practical problem is too large for hand computation. The computer manufacturers all have a suite of programs that handle this type of problem. A problem of 1,000 variables with 800 equations took twenty-one minutes on an IBM 360/50.

However, if we are not going to discuss computation, it is intended to discuss formulation and applications. As already stated, it has been used for diet problems, and now almost all cattle feed compounders use the technique to get the recipe for the various mixes of cattle feed. This ensures that the mix meets the stated protein, starch, and amino-acid requirements, and these requirements are met at least cost.

However, a growing application of this technique is in production planning, and it is this application we will use as an illustration. It will be stylized to a large extent because these problems tend to be very large indeed.

Consider two products on two machines in a factory. The amount produced has to be equal or greater than the forecast of demand.

	Machine 1	Machine 2
Product 1	x_1	x_3
Product 2	x_2	x_4
Forecast for Product 1	y_1	
Forecast for Product 2	y_2	

Two machines are constrained by labour.

Labour content	Machine 1	Machine 2
x_1	7 hr	3 hr
x_2	4 hr	8 hr

There are two operators who work a 42-hour week. These can now be expressed as the following

$$
\begin{aligned}
7x_1 + 4x_2 &\le 42 \\
3x_3 + 8x_4 &\le 42 \\
x_1 + x_3 &\ge y_1 \\
x_2 + x_4 &\ge y_2
\end{aligned}
$$

We now have to decide what is the objective. We might decide that this would be to minimize the cost of production, and so associate with each variable the marginal costs of production. It is important that we consider only the marginal costs, i.e., those costs that vary with one more unit of production on that machine, and say these costs are:

$$\text{min:} \quad c_1 x_1 + c_2 x_2 + c_3 x_3 + c_4 x_4 = Z$$

In practice, it is possible to consider stocking strategies, procurement of new materials allowing for lead times, labour fluctuations, capital availability, and market constraint, and there are now a number of companies using the techniques to assist in their medium-term planning.

One of the great advantages of linear programming is that it gives an indication of the possibility of increasing capacity or the opportunity of alternative investment strategy. It is this type of information that has been found the most useful contribution to decision-making. For example, a company may have decided upon a production strategy. However, forecasts received at a later date indicate a deviation from this strategy. The linear programme gives data on the amount involved in short fall of production and the alternative marketing strategy costs.

Uses of linear programming have been:

Cattle feed mix
Allocation of resources of a farm
Production planning
Budget planning
Transportation problems
Blending: Oil
         Tobacco
Utilization of resources between divisions.

This, then, is a typical OR model. The manipulation of the matrix or array is the task of the scientist, and he does this until he produces an array that acts in the same manner as the system under study. It is then that he goes to his managers with his results.

Controlling stocks

In the area of stock control, the OR scientists have made a major contribution to the economy, and have produced a number of mathematical models of the situation. It is not intended to go through the analysis here, but to discuss the general philosophy of the OR approach.

The costs involved in developing a stocking strategy are:

(a) stock-holding costs
(b) procurement costs
(c) cost of being out-of-stock

These should be the marginal costs of holding one more unit of stock. In the case of stock-holding, this may, in certain circumstances, omit labour, light, heat, and rent. The costs would be insurance, interest, and risk of obsolescence.

The approach to stock control is to consider that the stock is a reservoir with a controlled input and a random output. Now, by manipulating the input, the OR scientist can show to what extent the demand may be met for various levels of stock. He would, in fact, present to management a chart (Fig 3.9) that would show how investment in stock will give an improvement in customer service. It can be seen in the example, that to move the customer service level from 75 to 80 per cent involves relatively small investment in capital. However, to improve customer service from 93 to 95 per cent requires a relatively large investment in stock. Given this data, management can make the appropriate decisions on a more quantified basis.

Fig. 3.9.

The importance of this approach to stocking problems becomes even more important when the business is involved with a manufacturing process. Here, the uncoupling of manufacture from demand is further complicated by the need for the coupling processes within the manufacturing area.

Simulation techniques

We have so far discussed models that have unique solutions, and the manipulation or solution of the model derives this unique solution. However, there are some problems that defy mathematical analysis and further, there are problems where a measure of sensitivity of the answer is required rather than the unique solution. For both these purposes, the ideal type of model is a simulation model.

A simulation model, as the name implies, is a reproduction of the actual situation in a model that can be made to react in a similar manner as the original system. This is done by sampling from frequency distribution. Simulation models have been constructed for the study of harbour facilities, for an examination into stocking strategies, and for the study of advertising effectiveness. A frequency distribution is given in Table 3.5.

Table 3.5

Event	Occurrence (or frequency)	Cumulative frequency
0	70	70
1	30	100
2	20	120
3	10	130
4	5	135
5	0	135

The events in the table may well be anything, but let us imagine they are the arrival of orders in the post. The table states that on 70 occasions no order arrived; on 30 occasions one order arrived, and so on. Now, if we wished to simulate this state of affairs, we could sample from random number tables, and if the number lay between 1 and 70, we would say that no order arrived on that day. If the random number lay between 71–100, we would attribute one order to that day. If the number lay between 101–120, two orders had arrived. This particular method is wasteful in random numbers, and in fact, we would convert the cumulative column to percentages.

In a practical model, many such frequency distributions would be constructed, and one decision would be moved to the next. In the harbour problem, we could look up the tide table and decide whether for the time period being sampled, the boat could enter; then decide from a frequency distribution, how long the boat is going to occupy a berth. Then, from another table, we could decide the number of dockers that would be required. By logging the times it would be possible to estimate the waiting times of ships to obtain berths.

Simulation has been used for machine scheduling, control of personnel, bus scheduling, stock control, market simulation, and all problems involving queuing.

Conclusion

In this brief resumé of operational research, it has been possible to discuss only three types of models. There are other models, Critical Path (PERT), Dynamic Programming, Queuing Theory etc. The important aspect to remember is that OR is concerned with the resolution of conflict. The compromise of objectives and costs. To resolve the conflict the OR worker constructs a model, and experiments with this model.

The quality control of the OR worker is mainly concerned with ensuring that the model used is not too far from reality. Further, it is one of communication. All too often excellent results of long research programmes are lost because of bad communication of ideas. It is therefore important that between personnel in an OR group, the quality of communications is good.

It has been shown in the past that a company that had a thriving group had a change of leadership. The new leader was a brilliant technician but inadequate in communicating the ideas of the group; in time, the group stagnated and the leader had to be replaced. This point should not be overlooked in the staffing of the group.

The usual management controls of budget and management by objectives can be used effectively to control an OR group. It is said, on occasions, that it is impossible to estimate the time and effort required to do an OR project. This is not true. Any project can be broken down, and an initial survey undertaken with a time limit. Then another part of the problem can be tackled on a time basis, and so on. This approach stops problems or projects continuing to produce results without management review. An OR team which does not produce results that can be implemented in practice, is a wasted investment of the company. The extent of implementation must be the criteria of judgement.

Reading list

BOOKS

Production Planning and Inventory Control, John F. Magee and David M. Boodman (McGraw-Hill, New York, 2nd Edition, 1967)
Decision and Control, Stafford Beer (John Wiley, 1966)
Linear Programming, Robert O. Ferguson and Lauren F. Sargent (McGraw-Hill, 1958)
Operational Research for Management, M. J. Sargeant (Heinemann, 1965)
The Compleat Strategyst, John D. Williams (McGraw-Hill, 1965)
Operations Research for Management Vol I, Edited by Joseph F. McCloskey and Florence N. Trefethen (John Hopkins/Oxford University Press, 1954)
Operations Research for Management Vol II, Case histories, methods, information handling, Edited by Joseph F. McCloskey and John M. Coppinger (John Hopkins/Oxford University Press, 1956)
Management and Mathematics: The Practical Techniques Available, Allan Fletcher and Geoffrey Clark (Business Publications, 1964)
Introduction to Operations Research, C. W. Churchman, R. L. Ackoff and E. L. Arnoff (John Wiley, 1957)
Science and the Manager, R. W. Revans (MacDonald, 1965)

JOURNALS

'What is Operational Research?', B. H. P. Rivett (*Journal of Management Studies*, May 1967)
The Production Engineer, Special issue on Operational Research under guest editorship of Professor S. Elion, February 1967 (Institution of Production Engineers)

Useful addresses

OR Society, 62 Cannon Street, London EC 4

3.7 New Project Analysis

Gerald L. E. Spier

New projects are here defined as the assumption of risks and seizures of opportunities outside the normal activity of a firm. Thus, the four seasonal shows of a fashion house are not new projects in the same sense that a decision by the same firm to go into the 'ready-made' or men's wear markets would be. The position of firms in a technologically changing environment will be examined, especially to the extent that it appears to fall between the two categories.

Problems associated with new project analysis fall into two groups. First, there is the recognition both of the extent to which new projects will be necessary for the continuance of the business and of the type of new project that should be sought. This is the sphere of long-range planning, identifying the background into which new projects should fit. Second, there is the assessment of the individual opportunities identified or created, and their control.

Long-range planning

To plan effectively, the first requisite is to state the objectives. Even if these are merely to continue at the present rate of profit or use of capacity (and in many cases this itself may be no mean achievement), it must be clearly recognized which of these possibly competing requirements is the most desired, and why. Once this sort of question is settled, forecasts of up to five, ten, or more years must be made for the business as it is at the present. The discrepancy between this forecast and the goal is noted (the planning gap) and the job of overcoming it begins.

The procedure can be highly sophisticated and keep a whole department busy. The principles, however, are simple. A gap may exist for three reasons:

(1) the resources of the firm or its effort are too small;
(2) the balance of resources is changing;
(3) the business or product line is changing.

The first is really outside the scope of this section, although it is common enough and one of the reasons for mergers. An important strategy decision is whether to be a predator or a prey, for it is not always necessarily better to be the former.

The second poses the question of whether to correct the balance or utilize the imbalance. Thus, an 'own product' firm which sees over-capacity developing in its factories (because, for instance, of improved efficiency) may start looking for jobbing work as an alternative to increasing its product range and taking on new salesmen. Similarly, a cash surplus can be utilized not only for straightforward expansion but also for acquisitions or diversification.

The third covers the most fundamental problems. For example, with the growing use of plastics for the transport of liquids, should a firm remain in cooperage? If not, should it recognize itself as being in the liquids-handling business and go over to plastics, or should it decide that its work is carpentry and try to, say, devise a new form of collapsible crate?

There is another category, which falls between (2) and (3) above, which has already been hinted at, and to which parts of what follows will be equally relevant. This is the technologically-based industry in an environment of rapid change. Electronics immediately spring to mind as an example, but there are many others. Here, technology, not fashion, dictates the rate of new product introduction. Technological forecasting can give some idea of the rate, and this is essential for solving the basic problems of such an industry. The balance between research effort, and production and sales effort has often changed by such an order of magnitude that the firm itself is not aware whether it is in a research-based or production-based situation. In many instances it is in the former category and the firm must create a structure in which it can live off its researchers as the couturier lives off his designers: factory and cutting room are geared to this, be it for one of the great names who originate for the top end of the market, or for the mass-producers who copy for the lower end. The fashion trade has been able to create some degree of stability by recognizing this range and the commercial logic of any particular position within it. There are factors that make it more difficult in the technological sphere, but the principle is none the less the same.

Project appraisal

There are four main headings for appraisal. The order given here is for literary convenience only. As a lot of work can be involved it is best, in practice, to use methods that will give progressive reductions in the numbers to be studied.

Fit

This covers the relationship of the project to the present business of the firm and to its long-range plan. It should be examined from the points of view of the quality *and* the quantity of the resources. A by-no-means exhaustive check-list would contain these questions:

Is factory space adequate?
Is the sales force adequate?
Are the financial resources adequate?
Are the customers the same?
Is the type of labour the same?
Is the type of machinery the same?
How does seasonal or cyclical variation in demand complement current patterns?
Will the bulk or specific value of the article alter current physical handling and
    distribution methods?
Are new types of quality control, inspection, etc., necessary, and can these run in
    parallel with existing methods?
If new labour or salesmen are required, can they and their special work be integrated
    into the existing organization?

One concept that should be studied at the same time, although it is not really an element of 'fit', is that of 'threshold of investment'. In considering the resource position it must be remembered that some projects require a basic minimum of investment without which either completion or exploitation are inconceivable. Computers and prime movers immediately spring to mind on the development and the production sides, detergents in the world of marketing. It may be possible in a special case to go against the general trend, but any attempt to do so other than consciously, with explicit reasons for expecting success and that take full account of the basis of the normal position, are doomed to failure.

Time

What may be worth producing today may not be worth considering if it cannot be marketed until the day after tomorrow. It is essential to know how long it would take from the decision to proceed to completion ('lead time'). The useful technique for coping with this problem is critical path analysis. This simply consists of noting all the activities required for completion, and reporting them in the form of a network, showing which activities can be conducted in parallel, and which must be carried out sequentially. The actual method can be studied from a number of excellent books of varying complexity. The result is an indication of the shortest possible time to finish the project for a certain level of resources and a certain level of risk. It also shows where additional resources can be applied most effectively to reduce this time, exactly what risks are implicit in the network as drawn, and what further risks could be accepted.

This risk aspect is special to new project networks and is the result of the project logic and risk logic differing. Thus, for a new vehicle design, motor, body, and suspensions can all be developed in parallel and brought together at the end of the project. The best design for each of these three makes certain assumptions about the nature of the other two, so that there is a certain logic in undertaking the work sequentially, especially if there is any doubt concerning the possibility of one of the elements functioning at all. There is conflict, and this can be resolved only by judgement, aided by clear presentation. A well-designed critical path study should supply this.

Critical path analysis can get fairly complicated—often necessarily so—and it is important to keep a sense of proportion. Obviously, if the preparation of the study is going to affect significantly the overall lead time, this may well be intolerable. The answer is to sacrifice detail, rather than abandon the exercise, unless one engages in business as an alternative to horse-racing.

Profit
This takes us one step further into the realm of conjecture and, however unwilling one may be, no one can doubt that the subject is important. It is a budgeting exercise involving forecasts of costs, price, and turnover. Each element is critical, and each may be wrongly forecast. The objective here is not so much actual accuracy, as to determine the consistency of expectations in the three fields : to see whether even the best is good enough. Such forecasting also provides an information base for the control of the project, its acceleration or abandonment as reality diverges from expectation for better or for worse.

This part of the analysis may show, for instance, that higher turnovers than those originally anticipated are necessary. This simply may mean increased production, or higher price coupled with higher quality. Whatever the solution, it may entail re-assessment under all the other headings. The process would be subjected to rigorous iteration until the best balance emerged. In fact, it will be necessary for a decision to be taken before much more than one circle can be completed. The effect of the decision must be studied under each heading to ensure that its implications are fully understood.

The reporting of profit is as difficult as the budget exercise that precedes it. Undoubtedly, net present value (or its obverse : internal rate of return) represents the best form. However, at whatever stage profit is taken, decisions about stocks, specific capital, and so on, are problems for the accountants. The actual method is less important than that it should be consistent, and that management should be fully aware of the assumptions. There is a world of difference between taking the project to the stage where all capital is written off at the 'normal' rate, or taking it to its cash break-even point and writing stocks and residual capital to 'profit' at either book or resale value.

Risk

Profit analysis may have shown that the return at present value represents a 100 per cent increase. However, if the risks are three to one against, is a two to one pay-off acceptable? This raises three subsidiary questions:

Who says the odds are three to one against?
What other opportunities are there?
How much of the firm's resources are committed?

The actual determination of the odds is not only difficult—it can never be checked. It is for this reason that it may be valid, despite such advanced concepts as net present value, to consider break-even time as a measure of risk, if not reward. A more sophisticated way of doing the same thing is to calculate the equivalent maximum investment period, which takes note not only of break-even time but also of the shape of the cash flow curve up to that point.

The analysis is complicated if there is a number of competing, mutually exclusive opportunities. This is a special case arising mainly in the larger organizations and then, generally, not in the same department. Usually, one is confronted with a situation in which there is not a number of horses on which to bet, but rather just one horse that may or not finish the course, depending not only on the horse but also on whether someone moves the winning post.

Where choice exists it must be made. It cannot be organized to resolve itself. The decision-maker must be given every assistance. He cannot justifiably be precommitted. In the last resort, high risks and poor return may be acceptable if the project contributes to some other long-range boardroom objective.

Where the resource commitment is high, the pay-off will need to be correspondingly even higher. A firm can afford small failures where it cannot afford large ones, however favourable the notional odds. It is readier to accept risky propositions at the bottom end of the scale. So we come full circle and have to study the risk in relation to available resources and fit. This does not mean that a 'make or break' decision is always unjustified. Circumstances, as revealed by the study for the long range plan, may dictate it. The essential is once again full consciousness of the implications of the choice. Entrepreneurial skill alone can ensure that the correct one is made. The case for the semi-scientific approach outlined above lies entirely in the assumption that the good entrepreneur functions best in an environment of knowledge and consistent presentation.

Reading list

BOOKS

New Product Decisions: An Analytical Approach, E. A. Pessemier (McGraw-Hill, New York, 1966)

How to Launch a New Product, Robert Leduc, translated from the French by Richard F. Maycock and John Wardle (Crosby Lockwood, 1966)

Product Management in Action, Edited by R. H. Offord (Business Publications, 1967)

Critical-Path Method, L. R. Shaffer, J. B. Ritter, and W. L. Meyer (McGraw-Hill, New York, 1965)

JOURNALS

'New Products: How to Avoid Joining the Failures', M. John Mills (*The Director*, August 1966)

'Project Assessment', Gerald L. E. Spier (*The Director*, October 1966)

3.8 Pricing

Gerald L. E. Spier

An effective pricing policy for either goods or services (with jobbing manufacture coming more under the second than the first category) must take note of five analytical concepts. Of these, three are external to the firm: elasticity of the market, value in use, and appraised cost; two are internal: resource loading, and planning.

Elasticity of the market

This concept is borrowed from the economist. In terms of price it considers the proportionate change in demand that results from a proportionate change in price. For example, if it is expected that doubling the price will halve the sales, then the elasticity is one (unity). If the price is halved and sales thereby doubled, the elasticity is again unity. If on halving the price, sales more than double, then elasticity is greater than unity and the market is considered elastic. If, on the other hand, large changes in price have little effect on sales, then the market is inelastic.

It must be noted, first, that this elasticity of the market is a relationship between changes in demand and changes in price. It does not describe changes in the average or overall profit. In pricing, therefore, two things which may conflict have to be considered: the elasticity of quantity, and elasticity of profitability. If a price decrease of 5 per cent is followed by a sales increase of 10 per cent, turnover will be up by 4·5 per cent. Profits, however, must be down, as the increase in turnover is itself insufficient to cover the 5 per cent reduction even if the direct cost of the extra goods produced was zero.

Secondly, the application of the concept must not be confined to price alone. Every selling feature of a commodity can be analysed the same way: advertising, packaging, durability, service, bonus offers, discounts, commissions. Where years of statistics and introspection makes this possible, there is an obvious use for model-building (*see* section 3.6, p. 172). In general, however, one has to rely on 'hunch', but only after all these factors have at least been considered. If expectations and reality are constantly recorded and compared, these hunches can be improved by conscious experience. It is always well to document these areas of intuition as if mathematical systems were to be applied later—for discipline, information, and perhaps even a subsequent system installation.

Value in use

This is such a powerful contributing factor to responsiveness to changes in price, advertising, etc., that it is worth studying on its own. It is the answer to the questions: what is it worth to any customer or group of customers, firstly to have a product or service at all, secondly to have it from me? There are some who might pay vastly more than production costs, however defined, so vital is it to their requirements. These may also pay a premium for faster delivery (an economist will recognize that jam today is a different commodity from jam tomorrow), or the differential advantages accruing to the owner of a scarce commodity. It is doubtful whether all those who bought ballpoint pens for £2 really needed them for writing under water, but at the time they conveyed status. Similarly, firms may invest in uneconomic but novel plant for the sake of their own image.

Consideration of value in use enables a firm to choose its market and to design effectively for it. If it looks as if the restricted, high price market will be the best, small improvements in reliability may make a vast difference to the chances and degree of success. If it is a lower priced mass market that is attractive, then it may be best to ignore the special requirements of a few users for the sake of increased overall profits. There is an obvious connection between this marketing approach and value engineering (*see* section 3.11, p. 207).

Appraised cost

Most articles 'look' a certain price. Departures from this in either direction need explanation: upwards, perhaps in terms of research or invisible qualities; downwards, in terms of scale of production or modern methods.

This tendency to 'look a price' can also have effects on design. The most important feature, however, is its possible effect on goodwill. Firms introducing a new product are often tempted to 'cream the market' or 'slide down the demand curve'. To start with, when only a pilot plant is in operation, one sells at a very high price to those for whom the equipment is the greatest value in use. Gradually, as quantity increases, prices are lowered until they come down to 'normal'. There should be a minimum loss of goodwill if the extra price of the first units is justified for the purchaser by the extra time during which he enjoys its use, although it may take some 'selling' to make him appreciate this.

A price too far above appraised cost may also attract competition. In all this it should be remembered that appraised cost has nothing to do with the actual cost of production of the individual firm, although it may, and should, act as a critique of both this actual cost and the costing system. Thus, greater efficiency may enable a firm to make special profits which should not, except under the influence of planning and finance requirements, influence its pricing policy.

Resource loading

The objective of pricing is not just to maximize the profits on one article. It is rather to make the largest contribution to overall profitability over a period. Alternative uses of plant, equipment, space, salesmen, and other services have therefore to be considered, and this includes excess capacity, or the cost of not using available resources. The only way to cope with this may be the study of alternative overall budgets for the firm as a whole. Comparisons between standard costs and receipts may disguise more than they clarify. This is a sphere, moreover, in which operational research can be of great value in providing rigorously calculated solutions.

Planning

The question must be studied not only in the context of the present situation of the firm, but also of the planned future. The effect of the latter can best be illustrated by reference to a firm that feels price stability to be an advantage, and that is planning mass production but wants to start selling on a basis of rather less ambitious methods. It will fix its price on the assumption that mass production has been installed. It is obvious that in the normal sales plan associated with such production it would over-sell at that price. It can, however, cause demand to be diminished by less advertising, inferior packaging, inferior materials, or just bad delivery, until the new plant is installed. The firm must weigh carefully the disadvantages of all these forms of rationing against each other. Too much success in the early stages can lead to failure later. Unsatisfied demand is as great a spur to competition as a price too far above 'appraised cost'.

A firm may also want to introduce a new product at a very low price in order to establish itself in a market into which it intends to introduce other goods later. Here, the product acts as a sort of loss-leader with long-range strategy of much more importance than immediate profit on the article.

On the other hand, where expansion is planned, pricing must also take into account how that expansion is to be funded. While price stability or the use of a loss-leader may be either good for one's image or a good way to get into a new market, it may be necessary to make high profits simply in order to attract the capital required for subsequent full market penetration.

All this is a far cry from 'cost plus'. It is obvious that an effective policy depends on the use of many techniques described elsewhere: market research, budgeting of various kinds, forecasting, to mention only a few. This is to be expected since pricing decisions are among the most important for the success of any business. The number and nature of the variables may mean that there is no one optimum solution. On the other hand, good solutions are most likely to come from an awareness of the rival claims one is trying to satisfy, and the knowledge of the types of effect any particular decision is likely to have.

Organization

Pricing decisions are traditionally the province of the chief executive. He will seek advice from the following departments:

Marketing—all questions of elasticity, value in use, appraised cost

Operational research (which may also be located in the accounts or production sections)—all questions regarding product-mix strategy

Planning

Finance

Feed-back information to correct or confirm these decisions will originate in the following departments:

Sales—through records and reporting forms

Marketing—through follow-up research and intelligence

Production—actual resource utilization, and stock reports

Accounts—actual profitability

Reading list

BOOKS

Pricing for Higher Profit, S. A. Tucker (McGraw-Hill, 1966)

Product Analysis Pricing, W. Brown and E. Jaques (Heinemann, 1964)

New Developments in Pricing Strategy (Bradford University Management Centre, Seminar Manual, 1967)

Price Policies and Marketing Management, R. A. Lynn (Richard D. Irwin Inc., 1967)

Marketing Industrial Goods (Chapter 3 Part 1) J. Denning (Editor), (Business Publications, 1968)

JOURNALS

'The Accountant's Contribution to the Pricing Decision', John Sizer (*Journal of Management Studies*, May 1966)

Useful addresses

Market Research Society, 39 Hertford Street, London W 1

3.9 Business Forecasting

Reginald May

Forecasting is a vital business activity, since in any form of company planning it is necessary to determine some picture of the future. In the language of the business economist, there are two primary types of forecasting; forecasting the national or international economy is called 'macro-economic' forecasting, and that concerned with an industry or a company is termed 'micro-economic' forecasting. In business, greater attention is given to micro-economic forecasting, which is generally known as company forecasting. Macro-economic forecasting is not ignored, however, since all company planning must take note of it, particularly if the demand for a company's products is directly correlated with some macro-economic factor or factors.

Forecasting within a company can be termed as either long-term (or range) forecasting (*see* section 1.4) or short-term forecasting, depending on the objective of the forecast.

Since forecasting is related to planning and is an essential part of the planning process, it would be as well to start with a brief description of the different levels of business planning.

There are two levels of planning commonly found in business; long-range and operations planning.

Long-range planning is concerned with the examination of a company's potential market in order to evaluate the risk involved in committing the company's assets to the same market in the future, and with determining what additional innovation and investment will be required to realize the potential of the market or for entering new markets.

Operations planning deals with the planning aspects of managing the company's current operations with the view to maximizing short-term market opportunities, and optimizing the employment of the company's assets. Operations planning is often divided into annual and shorter term planning.

An outline of these two levels of planning, showing the different forecasts required, is shown in Fig 3.10.

The way in which business forecasting is carried out and the information required for these different levels of planning, is dependent upon the type of products manufactured and/or marketed. In the capital equipment industries a study of replacement policies, the life of its own and comparable products, and an assessment of the investment policies, and the economic expectations of its customers is the usual way in which forecasts are made.

In the consumer product field, studies of customer purchasing power and customer preferences, forecasts of raw material availability and prices, assessment of production constraints, and an analysis of past sales, and competitor behaviour are the important considerations. The type and details of the information required are dependent upon the forecast horizon. For long-range forecasts a greater range of information but with less precision is required, compared with the information required for the formulation of short-term sales plans. The approach to forecasting will depend upon the objectives it is meant to attain.

The degree to which a company will forecast the effect and interaction of general economic forces will depend upon its resources, even though it is quite clear that every business will be affected in one form or another by the state, and rate of growth, of the economy.

Forecasting for long-range plans
Long-range forecasting in a consumer product company is probably more concerned with general economic forces than are annual and short-term forecasting. The rate of growth of the domestic budget would be important, as would forecasts of essential raw materials; the growth of other products which compete both for the company's markets and for its materials would also be important.

Sociological studies may also be used to attempt to determine the future behaviour of consumers.

In addition to economic factors in long-range planning, forecasts of essential services and facilities will also be made, for example manpower forecasts. From these forecasts plans can be formulated for the expansion of capacity, product development, and diversification.

Long-range planning is often carried out at board level, assisted by reports from economists. It is probably true that long-range planning has not been given the

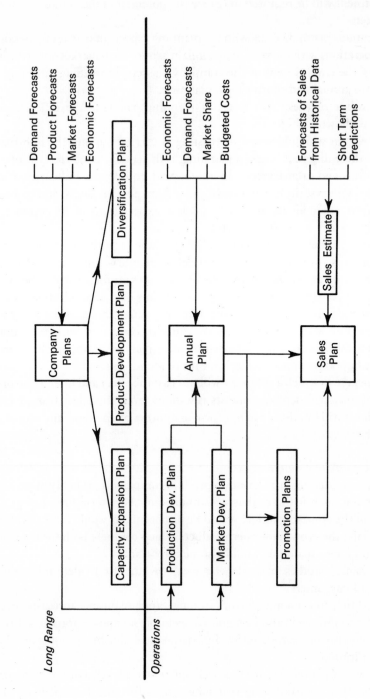

Fig. 3.10. Forecasts required for different planning levels

194

importance it deserves by British industry at large. It is indicative but encouraging that a Society for Long Range Planning has been formed in the UK in recognition of the need for planners to exchange experience and techniques, both on a national and international basis.

Forecasting for annual plans

The way in which annual plans are formulated depends very much upon the type of industry a company is in. The starting point in most companies, however, is to prepare forecasts of the demand for its products, although in some industries forecasts of the availability of the supply of raw materials are equally important. In the consumer product field, the forecast of demand for annual plans is often carried out brand by brand, and each brand manager may be responsible for presenting estimates for the brand or group of brands for which he is responsible. The brand manager will usually have available to him the services of his company's economists, planners, accountants, and market researchers; in addition, he may have the services of outside advisers and agencies.

In preparing his estimate he typically draws upon economic reports, historical sales data, market research reports, and estimates of manufacturing costs for different levels of production. From this information he is able to prepare an estimate of sales for his brand or brands based upon certain specified conditions. The conditions usually specified cover levels of advertising, promotional plans, price and selling effort, etc. The estimates for each brand may then be brought together by a senior brand executive who formulates the annual marketing plan; it is often at this stage that the company objectives in terms of profit and growth targets are considered, the validity of the estimates are investigated, and the views of other executives and managers are solicited. The resultant marketing plan is then evaluated in terms of costs and profits and in terms of production capacities. The marketing plan then becomes the proposed annual plan. The board of directors may either adopt or amend the annual plan. The finalized annual plan provides the basis for the selling, production, revenue, cost and profit targets for the forthcoming year.

Action can also be taken to provide the necessary facilities for attaining these targets.

Forecasting for short-term plans

Forecast of sales for the formulation of the sales plan in many companies is usually the responsibility of a sales planner or a central planning unit. The information used in constructing these forecasts may include short-term economic factors, past sales data, availability of raw materials, and targets set out in the annual plan.

Economic factors, short-term predicted events, and the information obtained by market research investigators are extremely important and relevant for short-term forecasting, but in most businesses it has been found that the analysis and projection of historical sales data often provides the best guide to future sales.

Techniques used in forecasting

No forecasts can be exactly accurate since they are formed from imperfect and incomplete information, under conditions of uncertainty; what is important, however, is the degree of inaccuracy in the forecast. Statistical methods assist in deriving useful information from past sales, which can be used to forecast future sales and to enable the probability and size of errors to be estimated.

The approach to business statistical forecasting is concerned not only with finding the most appropriate statistical method to provide the best estimate of future demand, but also with determining what is the most suitable data for analysis. In some businesses, orders booked or received may be the best guide to future sales; in others, factory or depot despatches may be a better guide.

In general, consumer product companies supply their customers from stocks that may be held in a number of depots located in different parts of the country. Therefore, the objective of short-term forecasting for such companies is to forecast demand in order to set stocks to provide a high level of customer service (customer service in this sense being defined as the ability to supply a customer on demand), and to place orders on their factories in sufficient size and frequency for economical manufacture and production stability, while minimizing their capital tied up in stocks.

The statistical methods used in short-term forecasting described here assist in determining the demand characteristic(s) from the analysis of past demand data. The demand characteristic(s) of a product may be an underlying trend, or a recurring pattern (for instance seasonal), or it may be random. A single product may be found to have one or other of these characteristics, or it may even have all of them.

Once the demand characteristics of a product are known, forecasts can be made that will enable stock levels to be set to meet estimated demand (with an added safety level to meet a probable higher demand), orders of the right size and frequency can be placed on the factory, and goods can be delivered to the depots in economical loads.

These methods can greatly assist in understanding the behaviour of demand and in making business forecasts.

Moving averages
The moving average method is probably the most simple and most common of all the statistical methods used in forecasting. It is based on the assumption that although irregular fluctuations in sales are a poor guide to future sales, the underlying trend is important. By averaging the trend and the irregular fluctuation in sales together, the effects of fluctuations are smoothed and are added to the trend.

The method of calculation is to take the total sales for a number of consecutive periods and to divide this total of sales by the number of periods whose sales are included in the total.

The disadvantage of the method is that the moving average always lags behind the current demand, and still further behind the future level of sales. This is most serious in times of a steady rise or fall in demand; how serious will depend upon the extent of the rise or fall and the number of periods included in the averaging. If the business is seasonal, and the number of periods included in the average overlap seasons, then the seasonal effect will be lost in the average.

However, the moving average can be adjusted for the trend effect during the period of lag and for seasonal variations.

The moving average method is simple to operate, but it is necessary to keep records of sales for each of the periods included in the average.

Exponential smoothing

The technique of exponential smoothing evolved from research, during the Second World War, to discover ways of tracking and predicting the future position of enemy aircraft while in flight, for use on gunnery ranges.

This technique, popularized by R. G. Brown, which is now being widely used in the area of inventory control, is a weighted moving average with special features. In using moving averages the oldest information is dropped when new information is added, whereas with exponential smoothing, in theory, the old information is never dropped but greater weight is given to the new information. However, with exponential smoothing, only one figure of past demand has to be retained, which is the last computed average. This means that exponential smoothing is not only a more sensitive technique than simple moving averages since it gives a greater weight to new information without entirely discarding the influence of the old, but it is also more economical since it does not require records of past demand to be kept.

The type of exponential formula (or model) to be used will depend upon the demand characteristic(s) of the product. All the models, however, have two principal components, the weight to be given to past demand, and the weight to be given to the most recent information. The factor chosen as the weight given to the most recent information is called the 'smoothing constant' or 'alpha'. Variations can be covered either by double smoothing, which attempts to follow the trend, or triple smoothing, which is appropriate to more rapid changes. The effect of double and treble smoothing is to modify the single smoothed value.

Simulation techniques are used to determine the most suitable model for forecasting the demand for any given product.

Forecast error analysis

In business, the accuracy of demand forecasting is critical to the efficient operation of the business. If the forecast of demand is too low, stocks will not be available to supply customers, resulting in loss of profit and custom, or urgent orders have to be placed on the factory, resulting in higher production costs. If the forecast is too high, unnecessary capital will be tied up in stocks, and production may have to be adjusted downwards, resulting in instability.

Therefore, an important aspect of statistical methods used in demand forecasting is concerned with the range of expected inaccuracy of the forecast. Using control chart techniques, similar to those used by quality engineers, limits can be established based on past experience. These limits can be used to set the levels of safety stock. Tracking signals are also used to ensure that the forecast is controlled.

Simulation

In many business forecasts, account must be taken of the interaction of the variation in demand levels, and the decision rules used at the separate units that make up the business system, since the effect of the interaction in demand levels and some decision rules is to magnify the extent of the separate variations.

One analysis of conditions that may arise in a business system undertaken at MIT by Jay Forrester has shown that a small variation in demand at the retail shop is buffered by the retail stock. This higher demand at the retail level subsequently leads to a higher demand on the wholesalers, where, once again, stocks initially buffer the higher demand. Finally, the wholesaler demand is passed on to the factory, but by this time the small variation has grown considerably, since the retailers and wholesalers wish to replenish their stocks and to be able to meet the new higher level of demand. The converse is true with a fall off in demand. These upsurges and falls come in cycles, and the pattern and frequency of the cycle varies according to the type of market. This cyclical behaviour of demand brings about production and distribution instability.

The cause of this problem is that static rules are used in each stage of the chain, whereas the forces acting upon the rules are dynamic.

In his work, Forrester has given these dynamic forces mathematical expression, and a programme called dynamo, which accompanies the work, is a powerful tool for analysing the behaviour of different stages in the chain from market demand to production.

This approach to business problems that often do not have exact analytical solutions because of the large number and behaviour of factors entering the problems, is called simulation.

Simulation is a procedure that is concerned with building a representational model of a business activity in mathematical form. The first step is to study and understand the behaviour of the activity, in order to build a model that can be experimented with.

By experimenting with models, and by using different decision rules and past or synthetic data of demand, it is possible to produce better forecasts in situations where, previously, forecasting was considered to be impossible or impractical. A further advantage of simulation is that the experimenting with models does not disrupt the running of the business.

With the capability of computers now available, it is possible to build large-scale models of business systems.

However, building and experimenting with simulations is expensive, and whereas the techniques have been used to determine the solutions to small and medium-size problems, very little has been done to build large-scale models in the business field.

These statistical techniques assist in determining the best forecast of future demand from the characteristic(s) of past demand. However, forecasting literally means throwing the past ahead, and very few companies do just this. Normally, the forecast is amended to take predicted events into account before it is adopted as an estimate of future demand for planning purposes.

However, disciplines should be introduced to ensure that a good forecast does not become a poor estimate because unnecessary weight is given to personal views.

Reading list

BOOKS

An Introduction to Business Forecasting (Institute of Cost and Works Accountants, 1960)
Risk, Uncertainty and Profit, Frank H. Knight (Harper & Row, 1965)
Business Economics (chapter 3), Reginald May (Macmillan, 1968)
Short-term Forecasting, G. A. Coutie *et al.* (I.C.I. Monograph No. 2) (Oliver & Boyd, 1964)
Business Growth, R. S. Edwards and H. Townsend (Macmillan, 1966)
Statistical Forecasting for Inventory Control, R. G. Brown (McGraw-Hill, 1959)
The Finance and Analysis of Capital Projects, A. J. Merrett and A. Sykes (Longmans, Green, 1963)
Planning Production Inventories and Work Force, Holt, Modigliani & Simon (Prentice, Hall, 1960)

3.10 Profit Forecasting

J. M. Samuels

Over recent years, a large volume of literature has appeared on the subject of evaluating the profitability of capital investment. The problem the company faces is whether or not to commit resources that have value, to a project whose benefits will be spread over several time periods. Techniques that were once widely used as a criteria for such decision-making have been shown to be misleading and, possibly, to give incorrect results. The by now familiar 'discounted cash flow' approach, has received widespread acceptance.

Present techniques emphasize the timing of the returns from the particular investment: the resulting cash flow. It is the present value of the future returns that is one of the most important factors in the investment decision, and the returns to be earned in the future are not usually worth that full amount today, when the decision is being made. If somebody promises a company £1,000 in ten years time, today the offer is only worth, say, £700 to that company, for it could invest the £700 in a bank, earn a rate of interest on it, and so have the £1,000 available in ten years time.

This concept of present value is a realization of the opportunity cost of money; it is significant whether or not inflation exists. If the value of money is changing due to inflation in the economic system, then this should be allowed for in the investment decision, in addition to the normal discounting process.

Ignoring the time value of money would overrate the importance of a proposed capital investment that gave high returns a number of years into the future. The time factor has become of increasing importance with the growing government interference in business investment decisions, through possible high investment allowances in early years, and taxation policies with regard to depreciation in later years. The after-tax cash flow can look very different from the pre-tax cash flow, and, of course, being the one the company actually faces, it should be the one it uses in its investment calculations.

This section deals only with one type of investment the company is faced with: the purchase of an asset from the use of which the company expects to earn returns. The first step in measuring the profitability of the prospective investment is then to forecast the cash flows; the initial outflow of funds, and then the returns coming in over the project's life, with a possible scrap value at the end, allowance being made for any tax allowance and for future tax payments.

There are many factors, of course, that need to be considered, such as technological change, activities of competitors, availability of management and labour, and possible changes in government policy. These are reflected in the forecasts of cash flow, but all introduce elements of uncertainty into the expected figure. All affect the risk attached to an investment. Inflation should be taken into account, as this may affect the present value of the capital expenditures if they have to be incurred over more than one time period. It is not so significant, as may be thought, in estimating the cash inflow over time, for if the value of money is falling, it is likely the company will be increasing its prices and wages, and so the relative position of future inflation on the estimates of the present value may not be significant. The danger of the falling real value of the revenue is overcome by rising prices. Whereas much of the emphasis in the literature on the subject is on using the correct criteria, it should not be forgotten that however sophisticated the criteria used, the importance that can be attached to the results will depend on the accuracy of the forecast of cash flows.

Having made the forecast, the next step is to decide on the criteria by which the investments will be judged. With a normal type of investment decision, if a choice has to be made on the allocation of funds the projects should be chosen that will maximize the profits of the company, subject to the level of risk. It is the duty of management to earn the highest returns possible on the equity capital it controls. If it does not do this, the company runs the risk of being taken over by another management offering the shareholders higher returns. The problem is to decide what is the real expected profitability of an investment.

The two main capital budgeting criteria that do not involve discounting are the cash payback method and the return on investment. The cash payback does not really involve a forecast of profit; it is merely concerned with the length of time a particular project will take before the recovery of the initial investment. If an investment cost £5,000 and earns £2,500 in each of the first two years of its life, then the payback period is obviously two years. This method is not concerned with what happens after this repayment, and so is not profit maximizing criteria. Projects are ranked in order of their payback period, the ones with the shorter period being considered the more desirable. This is a safety first criteria, investing in projects that will show the earliest return. It is obviously a limited technique, but reflects one of the factors that management often likes to consider in an investment decision.

The second method, the return on the investment, is the average income to be earned in each year of the project's life, divided by the average value of the investment. The average value of the investment is its initial cost plus the salvage value, if any, divided by two. This is allowing for straight-line depreciation over the asset's life. There are several variations on this later method; instead of looking at the average return to average investment, it might be decided to look at the returns on the investment in the first year, or on the return for any other representative year in the asset's life.

The failing of both these methods is that they do not allow for the timing of the returns over the different years of the asset's life. The returns in the earlier years are more valuable than returns in later years. This is obvious when reinvestment possibilities are considered. It might be thought that to some extent the payback period with its emphasis only on the returns up to the break-even time allows for this, but all it is in fact doing is giving all the returns in the first few years a weighting of one, and the returns after payoff a zero weighting.

There are two main present value techniques or discounting techniques, both of which are unfortunately known by a number of names. One is the internal rate of return, sometimes known as the yield method or the trial-and-error method; the other, the net present value or the net gain method. The former is in no way a new technique, being the same measure as the economic concept of the 'marginal efficiency of capital', defined by Keynes as, 'the rate of discount which would make the present value of . . . the returns expected from the capital asset during its life, just equal to its supply price'. The equation that, when solved, will give this rate is:

$$C = \frac{S_1}{(1+r)} + \frac{S_2}{(1+r)^2} + \cdots \frac{S_n}{(1+r)^n}$$

Where C = cost of asset,
  S_1 = net cash flow expected from the asset in the first year of its life,
  S_n = net cash flow expected from the asset in the nth year of its life,
  r = the internal rate of return, or the marginal efficiency of the asset.

As can be seen from the equation, the estimate of the profitability of the project, which is the rate of return earned from investing in the asset, depends upon the estimates of the cost, and upon the estimates of the returns in each year of the project's life. These estimates having been made, a rate of return, r, is found that will solve the equation. In practice this means trying a number of different r's until one is found that makes both sides of the equation equal; hence, one of the names of the techniques, the trial-and-error method.

If a choice has to be made between a number of different projects, under this criteria the one is chosen (other factors such as risk and life of project being equal) that shows the highest internal rate of return. If the choice that has to be made is a simple accept or reject decision, then the internal rate of return is compared with the cost of capital. If the cost of the capital is greater than the returns from investing the capital in the project, the investment is not worth while.

The internal rate is purely a solving rate; the higher the estimated net cash flow each year, the higher the rate needed to equate them with the cost. One of the criticisms that can be made of this method is that it does not involve a discount rate representing the companies' relative evaluation of current and postponed returns. All time periods are treated on a par, and if interest rates are expected to change in future, returns in some years being more valuable than in others, this cannot be allowed for in this criteria. Another criticism of the technique is that there is not always a unique rate of return for a project. There may be two rates, both of which solve the equation. This may happen if there is a change in the sign of the flow of net cash returns over the project's life, there being a mathematical rule that in such a problem the number of positive solutions is at the most equal to the number of reversals in the sign in the flow of returns. A unique rate of return can often be found as a result of certain assumptions and adjustments, but it is, nevertheless, a problem with this investment criteria.

Apparently many businessmen like to use this criteria in preference to the alternative net present value, as it gives a percentage rate of return with which they are used to working. The resulting solution to the alternative criteria is just a sum of money, which is the difference between the discounted costs and the discounted returns.

$$\text{NPV} = \frac{S_1}{(1+i)} + \frac{S_2}{(1+i)^2} + \cdots \frac{S_n}{(1+i)^n} - \frac{C_1}{(1+i)} - \frac{C_n}{(1+i)^n}$$

where i = cost of capital.

If the resulting net present value is positive, the project is worth while. If a choice has to be made between projects, the one with the highest present value, other things again being equal, is the most profitable.

It may be noted that the above equation allows for the cost of the project to cover more than one year, which is also permissible in the equation for the internal rate criteria. It means that, if the project is going to take more than one year to complete, £1,000 that has to be spent next year, is now, when the decision is being made, only equivalent to say an outlay of £950, allowing for the possible interest on the capital outlay in the one year.

The obvious difficulty with this method is in deciding what interest rate to use for discounting. It is now necessary to decide on a rate before the calculations are made, so it is a crucial point in determining the present value. With the internal rate criteria, the cost of capital had to be considered only after the internal rate of return had been found. An explicit decision did not have to be made at such an early stage of the profitability calculations.

A point that has to be considered when deciding between two projects using either of the criteria is that the comparison should be made for the two projects over the same time horizon. If one project has a shorter life than the other, and they are required to perform the same task, then adjustments must be made to the shorter period project to allow for further investment after this date.

The two criteria will always give the same answer to the question of whether a particular project is profitable or not, an accept or reject decision. If, however, a choice has to be made between a number of mutually exclusive investments, or, within the limits of an overall budget, a number of investments are to be selected, then the two criteria can give a different order of ranking, or preference, for the investments. Theoretical discussions usually come to the conclusion that the present value criteria is the more correct in the vast majority of cases. However, as previously stated, many businessmen prefer the internal rate of return, because the yield is an easier concept to work with than the lump sum of money from the present value criteria.

There is a temptation to compare the discounted net present value with the cost of the project, so obtaining an index. This should not be done, as it can lead to wrong decisions.

In a capital rationing situation, when a company, rather than accepting all projects that increase the present value of the firm must choose the optimal batch, a different selection procedure is needed. It is not sufficient to rank all the projects in order of profitability and then select the most profitable. Not all the capital might be used in this method, and it may be advantageous to delay some of the projects until later periods. A technique that can, in certain circumstances, deal with this type of decision-making situation can be found in mathematical programming.

Perhaps mention should be made here of what is known as the MAPI Formula, developed by, and named after, the research branch of the Machinery and Allied Products Institute (USA). Projects are ranked by what is called an 'Urgency Rating'. The higher the rating, the more desirable the project. The rating is a type of yield on investment and, in many cases, it will give a ranking of projects equal to the internal rate of return method. The failings of this later method will also apply to the results of the formula.

Even though a company may be using the theoretically best investment criteria, this overcomes only one of the difficulties in the way of profit forecasting. All investment criteria are sensitive to errors in forecasts. For example, a project costing £3,000 is expected to give a cash inflow of £1,000 per annum for five years. The estimated internal rate of return is 20 per cent. If the actual cash inflow for each of the five years turns out to be £900, the actual internal rate of return is 15 per cent. A 10 per cent error in the forecast has led to a 25 per cent change in the rate of return. This degree of inaccuracy in the forecast is not large by normal standards, but it has led to a large change in the internal rate of return. Similar fluctuations occur in all the other criteria in response to errors in forecast.

Before too much emphasis is placed on the profit forecast, and before a project is accepted, if the internal rate is, say, 20 per cent, whereas it would have been rejected if the calculations had shown a rate of 16 per cent, it would be as well to discover how sensitive the acceptance criteria is to errors in forecast. Some estimate of probability might well be attached to the forecasted returns.

This leads to another difficulty with the normal mechanical estimates of profitability. It has been assumed in the criteria that a company would prefer a project with a 20 per cent rate of return rather than one with, say, a 10 per cent rate. But what would be the choice if the 10 per cent return for the one project was a certainty, whereas the 20 per cent project had large risks attached to it? Some projects can give very high returns but also have some chance of low returns, depending on circumstances outside the firm's control. The criteria as described above make no allowances for the different levels of risk attached to different projects.

There are several different approaches to the problem of risk, but it is not possible to go into them all in detail here. One is to adjust the discounting rate in the present value criteria, and the cut-off point in the internal rate method. If a project is very risky, use a higher rate as a requirement before acceptance. This is a reasonable approach, because if the company were forced to go to the capital market for each individual project, the cost of capital would be higher on a risky project. The problem in using a variable rate for discounting is that subjective factors now enter the calculation in the decision on the particular rate to use for a project.

Another way of taking account of risk in the calculations is, where possible, to construct a probability distribution of expected returns, and then calculate not just the mean expected return each year but also the possible variance about the mean. The riskier projects will have the bigger variances. Then, when the expected returns of the different projects are considered, the possible variance about this can also be allowed for. It is likely, however, that a firm finding it difficult to estimate one figure for the returns expected in a year, will find it even harder to estimate a range of possible returns with the probability attached to each value. One way round this problem is to attach one figure, a confidence level, to the estimated cash flow for each year, finishing with some overall confidence level attached to the project's expected return.

The result of all these possible adjustments to the stream of cash flows is to show, as near as possible, the true opportunities of an investment for a company. The decision depends, in the end, on the preferences of the decision maker, his estimate of the profitability, the attitude of the company towards risk, and the time preference of the business.

The principal objective of the decision-maker should be to maximize the present value of the equity of the current owners. The only way this can be achieved, allowing for the time value of money, is through the principle of discounting, and through the concept of the cost of capital. It is admittedly very difficult for a company to determine this cost with any great accuracy, and it is often not just one rate that has to be determined but a schedule of rates depending on the amounts to be supplied. However, it is only through these concepts that the real profitability of an investment for a company can be determined. Without some knowledge of the cost of the capital going into the investment, it is not possible to determine the extent of its profitability.

Reading list

Discounted Cash Flow, M. G. Wright (McGraw-Hill, 1967)
The Capital Budgeting Decision, H. Bierman and S. Smidt (Macmillan, 1960)
The Finance and Analysis of Capital Projects, A. J. Merret and A. Sykes (Longmans, Green, 1963)
The Profitable Use of Capital in Industry (Institute of Cost and Works Accountants, 1965)
Investment Decision in Industry, R. Wright (Chapman and Hall, 1964)
Appraisal of Investment Projects by Discounted Cash Flow: Principles and Some Short Cut Techniques, A. M. Alfred and J. B. Evans (Chapman and Hall, 1967)
An Industrial Accountant's Experience in Capital Appraisal (Conference Paper) D. G. Cochrane (Graduate Centre for Management Studies, Birmingham: February 1967)
Business Ratios (3 issues yearly, Dun and Bradstreet Ltd.)

3.11 Value Engineering

C. A. Curthoys

Value Engineering (or Value Analysis) is one of the many cost-cutting techniques open to any management, at any time. As cost-consciousness has grown, so has the application of Value Engineering, a happening that is more than a happy coincidence.

Properly applied, there is no more rewarding exercise in cost reduction than Value Engineering and none, perhaps, that gives more satisfaction to those involved in it. Its origin, in 1947, is generally attributed to the General Electric Company of America, one of whose design engineers had been working on cost reduction of several of the company's products. He was, however, dissatisfied to the extent that he was convinced that much more would be achieved if there could be a wider understanding *by everybody* of value in a product; this to concern any product whether in production or still to be launched. The aim was to provide a product that would incorporate *necessary* quality and reliability, able to function as, and for as long as, it was required to do, at the lowest cost consistent with these targets.

The more usual methods of cost reduction were focused on minimizing the labour and materials content in the manufacture of a component or part. The difference of emphasis, now, was to examine the functions of the product first. Once these could be identified in detail, then the parts performing those functions could be scrutinized.

So successful were these principles when applied by General Electric that, three years later, training in the new technique was provided for supplier firms. By 1954, many US companies were applying it.

Within two years, the technique was an established management procedure in a large number of manufacturing firms. The sellers' market which followed the Second World War had finally disappeared; competition for the buyers' favours was fierce and likely to grow fiercer. In the battle for business, the weapons of value and price needed to be constantly re-examined and overhauled with the most effective aids. Nowhere was this more urgent than in the United Kingdom.

Value Engineering was the answer. Of the many excellent and essential aids to management, none concentrates on materials so much as Value Engineering. Indeed, most of the other techniques look, first, to saving direct labour costs which are only fractionally involved in total production cost. So, while labour costs will be constantly under review, it is only too easy to continue to ignore, or rather not realize, the savings that can be made in materials and components *without*, in any way, reducing the quality and reliability of the product, or its function. Any change in production method which, while cutting costs, adversely affects any of these must, obviously, be rejected as too dangerous and short-sighted. The effective appeal of Value Engineering is that it provides its own safeguards against such happenings.

It is an organized system that sets out to provide a product at the lowest possible cost, relative to its specified performance and function. This means that it can, and does, eliminate unnecessary cost in an existing product, or of a new one, because it demands the answers to some vital questions:

Is the production method, employed or projected, the best possible? Is there not a 'better way'?

When an existing product was first launched, was any process, or part of a process, introduced to meet a circumstance that no longer obtains? If so, has it ever been modified?

Are the cost data as detailed and as accurate as they are believed to be?

Are the requirements laid down in the specification essential? Can limits be relaxed to simplify manufacture, or allow another method? Would direct labour costs be cut by such a modified method, i.e., by eliminating any operation?

Have the materials, or components, employed become technological anachronisms because of advances made in providing cheaper, but just as effective, substitutes? For example, can nylon or plastics efficiently replace metal with consequent cost-saving?

These are not the only questions to be answered but they may be taken as the main ones. Yet even the right answers to these questions cannot be regarded as reasons for complacency. The rate of progress, these days, is jet-propelled. Today's best way will be second-best by tomorrow and the search for efficient production must be continuous. 'There's Always a Better Way': this, the philosophy of the

British Productivity Council, is no easy-sounding, meaningless slogan. It sums up, exactly, the situation facing management in the industrial situation of today and tomorrow.

Certainly, the first requirement of any 'Better Way' must be to cut production costs while safeguarding the product. Equally certain is it that merely to contain costs, albeit in the face of increasingly expensive materials, components, labour costs, etc., is not enough. All directors recognize only too well that costs must be held and that unless they are so limited their firms' futures are in jeopardy. It is not sufficient that costs should be contained in a measure that just ensures survival. *They must be reduced.*

It has been emphasized that the functioning of the product should not, in any way, be impaired. Reference has been made, too, to the *value* of a product. It may, therefore, be useful at this point to reiterate that when all cost elements that can be proved to be unnecessary have been eliminated, then, what is left is the lowest cost at which the product can be made to function with the required reliability.

So, value is relative to cost and function; to satisfying the customer at a minimum expenditure of materials, machinery, and manpower. And, as the design engineer of General Electric discovered, it is highly important that *everybody* involved in the design and manufacture of a product should understand this. In fact, the chain is incomplete unless those responsible for marketing and distribution do not, similarly, appreciate the position. For example, unnecessary handling will add to the cost and reduce the product value.

Thus, Value Engineering is a *team effort* and if one member of the team fails to play his part, then savings and improvements made in other directions may well be reduced or negatived altogether.

It is a paramount requirement that management should impress on personnel, at every level, the essential need to remove all unjustified production cost. From the Board, once it has made the decision to apply Value Engineering, must come complete support and backing, as necessary, for the Value Engineering team as it goes about its tasks.

But, first, it is necessary to establish the membership of the team. This, of course, will vary not only from industry to industry but, often, from firm to firm in like industries. A typical team will consist of senior representatives of: production engineering; design, cost accounting or estimating; technical buying and sales.

The team leader (and chairman) should be a full-time value engineer; a secretary to keep notes of subjects discussed and to prepare agendas for meetings completes the basic team, which can be augmented by specialists as occasion demands.

The value engineer, appointed by the Board, will report to the directors, hence decision-making and action on those decisions need not suffer delay.

Before going on to consider how the team goes into action, it should be remarked that lack of a full-time value engineer—as, for example, in a small firm with a comparatively small range of products—is no bar to the application of the technique. A VE committee can be formed on the same basis as a team and with a director as chairman.

Many firms, at present lacking a VE team or committee, will have a 'brainstorming' group composed of senior representatives of production, design, buying, and sales. The group will look at a product, or products, carefully examining the make-up and function of each to suggest improvements and ways to cut costs. One idea leads to another . . . and another. There is seldom any lack of ideas at such meetings. All are noted, sifted, and assessed, and those that pass scrutiny as being desirable and practicable are passed on to departments for further examination. Eventually, and usually it *is* eventually and not 'immediately', proposals emerge and are submitted to the departmental head whose approval must be given before the changes can be put into operation.

There are drawbacks to this method of approach, the most serious being that it is not an organized activity, that it lacks a leader and a system. The remedy is to formalize the brainstorming activity by having a chairman and secretary (as with a value engineer-led team).

The importance of a director-chairman lies in his knowledge of company policy and, also, that his presence signifies boardroom support. He will have also the status to restrain forceful personalities whose enthusiasm or just plain aggressiveness may well slow down the flow of ideas from those whose keenness is there but not so evident.

As with 'brainstorming', a VE committee's ideas have to be passed back to various departments, uncoordinated by any one person. With a VE *team*, however, led by a value engineer, there is not only a technically-qualified leader but one who is empowered to report directly to the Board.

So what is a technically-qualified value engineer? Can a firm produce its own man or must he be imported? A lucid answer to this was given at the conference of the European Organization for Quality Control, in London, in June, 1967, by Mr J. F. A. Gibson, VE consultant to AEI Ltd. 'Training in value techniques', he said then, 'can be obtained by reading, by attendance at seminars, by employing consultants either to train only or to conduct a first exercise which will also provide initial training. In the event, practice or 'learning by doing' is the greatest teacher which can be most usefully supported by attendance at seminars, after some experience has been gained.'

Mr Gibson makes one important condition for the choice of candidate for training as value engineer: 'He must be a man of personality and tact, combined with tenacity'. This recognizes that, human nature being what it is, and none of us without blemish, some senior people may tend to regard projected savings as reflecting on themselves or their departments. Good personal relations, therefore, are a 'must', and it is a happy fact that the very form and nature of the activities of a

VE team, or of a VE committee, are conducive to harmonious working because they bring departments closer together. Each gets a better idea—if, indeed, there was much idea at all before—of the other's problems; departments appreciate more convincingly that they are working for the same organization and have the same aims in view. Not 'Whose side are you on?', not 'Are you for me or against me?', but 'We're *with* you'. This is not merely a philosophical supposition; it is the very real experience of those firms that practise VE, and there is plenty of case history material to substantiate the claim.

People, personal relationships, matter greatly, whatever the techniques, however large or small the changes to be proposed. Without integrated effort by personnel who understand 'what it is all about' and what the other chaps are up to, neither VE nor any similar procedure can promise full success.

Now, having set up the team, or committee, the next step is to choose the product for the initial analysis. This will, or should, entail consideration of the product range, product costs, volume of production, etc. How often the team goes into session will depend on what emerges from these considerations. In any event, too-frequent meetings that take the part-time members away from their other responsibilities are not recommended by those with experience.

One product—probably one that is a good seller—having been selected for attention, a sample of the assembled product and another dissembled are required; in the latter case, the components and examples of the raw materials used need to be identified and displayed for ease of examination. (And, of course, any samples of rival firms' products should be similarly 'broken down' for comparison.)

Drawings, specifications, costings, overheads, ordering procedures and quantities, details of manufacturing, processing and assembly of the product are among other required information. It is possible, often likely, that much of this information will not be readily available at the start, hence, in making correct preparation for the value analysis exercise there is a bonus in the form of additional facts and figures not previously sought in such detail or, in fact, not known at all. This prompts the question: How many managements, for instance, know with certainty what their scrap costs are for a particular product? Of course, *somebody* knows, but if the product is showing a reasonable profit who wants to improve on it? The VE team will.

Some interesting figures can be quoted on average savings effected by VE. In America, one consultancy service claims to have saved clients £12 million in four years; however relative that sum may be to the capital employed it is still an impressive amount.

A booklet of case histories, published by the BPC illustrates savings by British firms. These include an engineering firm that has been saving at least £150,000 a year, and another which replaced a machined steel rod with a moulded, plastic one effecting an 85 per cent saving.

An office-machine manufacturing firm saved £9,000 in a year by value engineering a number of small projects. These economies came after management had sent three men to a seminar in Manchester. They reported, unanimously, that VE should be introduced. It was not long before projects put in hand showed potential savings of £50,000 a year. The interesting aspect of this case history is that the management was moved by a *supplier* who suggested that a slight modification in the specification for rubber feet fitted to various models would cut costs. It did, by £2,000 a year.

These few instances of the effectiveness of VE could be multiplied by thousands, if necessary. They typify what is being achieved by firms in different fields and of different sizes; they demonstrate, too, that the aggregate of savings on small components can be substantial.

Two points should be noted: the supplier is able, often, to assist in discussions with the customer, and the customer who knows what he wants can be of practical help to the manufacturer; so they should consult whenever practicable. Frequently, it will be possible (as in the case of the rubber foot-rests for office machines) to save on materials and simplify manufacture by talks between maker and buyer. Limits previously considered rigid, materials or components regarded as 'musts', will be found to be flexible and replaceable without affecting the product—except to lower its production cost.

Cost is the arbiter in determining profit and it can be expressed in telling figures. Beyond any assessment in £ s. d., however, are the 'intangibles' such as closer co-operation within the firm and with the customer and supplier, and the revitalized thinking that comes from a value engineering exercise competently carried out.

Reading list

BOOKS

Techniques of Value Analysis and Engineering, Lawrence D. Miles (McGraw-Hill, New York, 1961)
Value Analysis, William L. Gage (McGraw-Hill, London, 1967)
Value Analysis, Sixteen case Studies (British Productivity Council, 1964)

JOURNALS

'How to get Value from Analysis', Arthur Garratt (*Management Today*, May 1967)
'The Value Concept: Its Effect on Profit and Organization', P. Fatharly (*The Director*, January 1966)
'Marketing-Oriented Value Analysis' (*Sales Management*, Vol. 88, June 15th, 1962)
'Value Analysis and the Accountant', H. L. C. Leslie (*N.A.A. Bulletin*, Vol. 43, October 1961)
'A Practical Approach to Value Analysis', D. Fram (*Product Engineering*, Vol. 33, No. 3, 5th February, 1962)
Value Engineering (Pergamon Press)

Useful addresses

British Productivity Council, Vintry House, Queen Street Place, London EC 4
European Organization for Quality Control, Weena 700, Rotterdam, Holland
Management Consultants' Register, British Institute of Management, Management House, Parker Street, Kingsway, London WC 2
Management Consultants Association Ltd., 23 Cromwell Place, London SW 7

3.12 O and M Control

G. E. Milward

Most directors have so many different and pressing subjects to consider that the organization of the company itself seldom receives much time and thought unless and until its creakings become too obvious to be ignored. By this time the organization is sick, and staff are at cross-purposes, or looking for another job. A consultant may now be called in, some functions will be altered, and staff numbers reduced.

The business of reorganization would not be foreign to any executive director. He must know the policy changes that are coming and must design and test the framework within which the company may easily and economically carry out those policies. To do this, he must know the alternative groupings of functions used by other companies and why these work better in one than another. He must also know at first hand the technical considerations that affect groupings, the Board's own requirements for financial and executive control, together with the limitations and the potential of the existing management. Three broad considerations emerge—those of policy, organization, and staff. The experienced outside consultant should know possible groupings from having seen them in action elsewhere, but he will only know what he is allowed to find out about future policies and staff. The inside director should know the first and third from daily contact with the business, but he is unlikely to know very much about alternative groupings at first hand, unless he has served with a number of other companies. If he can gain a knowledge of the alternatives of organization, he will be a much better man to carry out a reorganization than an outsider, provided he can step back and get into true perspective the organization in which he has served for some time, and can overcome the difficulties of displacing friends and colleagues who no longer adapt themselves to new work.

Unfortunately, but for a good reason, few companies welcome critical discussion of their own organization, and the interchange of the real technical and policy constraints that govern reorganization is seldom possible, except when a small number of companies agree to expose to one another the real facts of their respective organizations. This has been done, but not more than seven companies in such a group seem able to avoid the generalizations that usually obscure the issues. Confidence is vital, for rumours about reorganization have resulted in valuable men leaving to go to competitors.

The man responsible for reorganization must have an open mind; he must find out why an existing grouping was previously adopted; he must decide what purposes the present organization should serve; he must study the technical, financial, and historical constraints that stand, or appear to stand in the way of change; and he must have the courage and tenacity to steer a course between those constraints. If he has a suitable O & M manager, some of this work may be shared. If he cannot find out the alternative forms of organization with their limitations and advantages in real life, the company must support him with consultants who have suitable experience to offer, and a first-class man to allocate to them, but such men are rare and much depends on their abilities.

Reorganization is too often preoccupied with the overall shape of the company without sufficient attention being given to the methods by which policy is translated into profit. The director, consultant, or manager must understand the causes of faulty management, as well as the reasons for another man's apparent ability to manage another unit successfully. Although some of the considerations that govern a company's main organization are different from those affecting middle organization, which again differ from those that operate in the works, the sales force or the office, each level affects those above and below.

To the three considerations enumerated earlier, those of policy, organization and staff, a knowledge of the methods at present used, and of those about to be used, is essential, and here the practical O & M manager can be of great value. His job, in the context of this section of the chapter, is to advise on office methods and to study the effect that new methods should have on the company's organization. In some companies, O & M has been involved in the factory, the stores, maintenance, transport, purchasing, production scheduling etc.; and the same manager will have a wider detailed knowledge of methods generally, with a correspondingly greater value to his company.

The study of methods, as of organization, should employ the engineering approach, of writing a specification of what is required without prejudging the issue by guessing at methods. In factories and in offices, much of the work that is done, and the information that is collected, is unnecessary, and some of it is not used. The streamlining of work is the simplification of procedure, which in itself is seldom easy. In an existing office procedure, some twenty or more extractions, copyings, summarizings etc., may be made, often involving the sorting or re-sorting of the originals and their copies. The trained man will have to study each step in the existing procedure and establish its purpose, if any. To do this he must possess a considerable knowledge of what the management wants and needs, and must find out what information a modern auditor must have. He will then build up a specification for the system and verify with management that this will meet their needs before permitting himself to guess the answer, the method. Already he will find that much of the existing procedure is out of date and can be dispensed with.

With this specification in writing he must next think about the processes involved, for each process—recording, selecting, copying, computation—has its own very considerable field of alternative machines that will carry out the specification in whole or in part, economically or extravagantly. There may be as many as sixteen possible solutions to what looks a simple job, and some will cost up to ten times as much as another. These differences in cost may become enormous. Sixpence saved on each invoice, when nine thousand invoices a day are involved, mounts up to a large sum. In nationalized industry an office may issue over a million statements a quarter, and every unnecessary expense per item becomes highly significant financially.

Cost is not the only measure of effectiveness. Time may be very important. The ability to issue statements of account fourteen days earlier than previously has resulted in a faster turnover of payment of account so that a more expensive but much faster process was amply justified by getting in the money ten days earlier. Similarly, companies have reduced their inventory and lowered re-order quantities while speeding up the re-order process by going electronic.

A complete knowledge of all the different and rapidly developing machinery is unlikely to be possessed by one man. Companies, except for the very largest, need to keep in touch with others to pool experience of as many machines as possible, before buying a particular one. Even large companies can learn from one another's mistakes and successes.

Something has now been said about an organization survey and a methods assignment, and the reading list at the end will cover most of the latter. O & M as a control is a different subject, although closely allied to what has already been written. If a director is held responsible, among other duties, for reorganization, he will need to make a plan to cover the phased survey of the company, with such reorganization as may be necessary, and leave this plan sufficiently flexible to permit quick action when a new activity is taken on or an existing subsidiary or department gets into difficulties. ('Organization Planning' at departmental level was popular in America for some time but here we are concerned with the responsibilities of a director rather than those of a manager.) The idea of O & M and/or Management Services has been based upon an advisory service to be provided for the company, its directors, and managers. In some companies, a director has been charged either with seeing that good advice is not lightly disregarded, or with direct responsibility for methods and for some organization. In these cases considerable success and some large savings have been achieved. Without support from the Board little can be done unless an outstanding manager is put in charge. Such a man gets asked for help in speeding up work and reducing cost, and this serves as an excellent control through which the management keeps itself up to date.

What perhaps needs to be emphasized is that each director and manager is responsible not only for particular activities but for seeing that those activities cost no more than they should. The first responsibility of a line manager often obscures the second, partly because he hasn't the time for both. Hence, the O & M service, which, to succeed, must be sponsored by a director.

Reading list

BOOKS

Organization and Methods, Edited by G. E. Milward (Macmillan, 4th Edition, 1967)
Application of O & M, Edited by G. E. Milward (Macdonald and Evans, 1964)
Further Applications of O & M, G. E. Milward and P. H. S. Wroe (Macdonald and Evans, 1966)
Office Economy and O & M, G. E. Milward and P. H. S. Wroe (Macmillan, 1964)
How to Cut Office Costs, H. H. Longman (Anbar Publications, 1967)
Work Study, R. M. Currie (Pitman, 1960)
The Practice of O & M, compiled by the Management Services Division of HM Treasury, (H.M.S.O.)
The Purpose and Practice of Motion Study, Anne G. Shaw (Columbine Press, 2nd Edition, 1960)
Office Organization and Method, Geoffrey Mills and Oliver Standingford (Pitman, 4th Edition, 1968)

3.13 Interfirm Comparison

H. Ingham

The end product of Interfirm Comparison (IFC)

The end product of an interfirm comparison (IFC) is not a statistical survey but the flash of insight in the mind of the managing director of a firm that has taken part in such an exercise. The results of this give him an instant and vivid picture of how his firm's profitability, its costs, its stock turnover, the utilization of its plant, machinery, and other fixed resources compare with those of other firms in his industry.

The way in which the results of the IFC are presented to him makes him see at once:

where his business is weaker than its competitors;
what weaknesses call for his personal attention;
in what directions improvements are indicated.

A motor car distributor found, for instance, that his profit on capital was comparatively low, mainly because while his competitors could recondition and sell used cars within about two months after they had purchased them, his firm sold them only after three months or more. Why? Because he operates in the centre of a large town where he cannot expand workshop facilities. Should he then rent additional workshop space in the suburbs? Should he reduce his second-hand car purchases and direct his efforts into other more profitable activities (e.g., sales of new vehicles)?

These are policy questions whose importance, but for its participation in an IFC, the management of the firm might not have recognized.

Top management and IFC

It cannot be emphasized too strongly that the content of an IFC should appeal to those at top management level in the firms concerned because:

(a) A stimulus to self-criticism at top level will have the strongest impact on the development of the firm concerned.
(b) Top management is in the best position to decide on remedial action, and to see to its implementation.
(c) Top management is in the best position to decide whether the firm concerned should take part in an IFC.

This means that an IFC will have the greatest impact if it deals with matters of concern to the man at the top, i.e., the man who is not primarily concerned with any one major function or department of the business, but who is responsible for ensuring that through proper co-ordination of the manufacturing, marketing, and other major operations of the business, sales are balanced with total capacity in such a way that a satisfactory profit is earned on the capital employed in the operations of the business.

Management ratios

This concern determines the choice of the data—management ratios—to be covered in an IFC for the Managing Director; i.e., they will take as a starting point the ratio of

$$\frac{\text{operating profit}}{\text{operating assets}}$$

which reflects the earning power of the operations of a business, and shows whether profitable use has been made of its assets. This is the 'primary ratio' in an IFC for the Managing Director. The other ratios of the IFC must show *why* the primary ratio differs between firms.

Table 3.6 shows a set of such 'management ratios'* for a particular company (company D). This, a medium-sized engineering company, offers in its catalogue a wide range of certain light engineering products. Last year (column 1) the newly appointed managing director was rather shocked to find that the company's return on operating assets (ratio 1) was only 2·6 per cent. To get a first answer to the question of why this was so low, the managing director has to take account of two relation-

* The way in which these ratios are related to each other is illustrated in the pyramid diagram, Fig 3.11, p. 230. The pyramid method was devised by H. Ingham and L. Taylor Harrington, and first described in an article by them in 1956, as a basis for interfirm comparison of particular relevance to top management.

Table 3.6

Centre for *INTERFIRM COMPARISON Ltd.*

The Management Ratios of Company D

Ratio	Last year	This year
Return on assets		
1. Operating profit/Operating assets (%)	2·6	3·5
Profit margin on sales and turnover of assets		
2. Operating profit/Sales (%)	2·9	3·6
3. Sales/Operating assets (times per year)	0·90	0·98
Departmental costs (as a percentage of sales)		
4. Production cost of sales	76·0	73·9
5. Distribution and marketing costs	6·7	8·1
6. General and administrative costs	14·4	14·4
Production costs (as a percentage of sales value of production)		
7. Materials costs	30·9	30·8
8. Works labour costs	25·0	23·2
9. Other production costs	20·1	19·9
General asset utilization (£s per £1,000 of sales)		
3a. Operating assets	1,111	1,016
10. Current assets	419	411
11. Fixed assets	692	605
Current asset utilization (£s per £1,000 of sales)		
12. Material stocks	91	87
13. Work in progress	54	50
14. Finished stocks	57	69
15. Debtors	217	205
Fixed asset utilization (£s per £1,000 of sales)		
16. Land and buildings	295	289
17. Plant, machinery and works equipment	389	309
18. Vehicles	8	7

ships (ratios), namely that between the firm's operating profit and its sales (ratio 2), and that between its sales and its operating assets (ratio 3). Ratio 2 shows *what* profit margin has been earned on sales, while ratio 3 shows *how often* the margin has been earned on assets in the year. The relation between these two ratios and their joint impact on ratio 1 becomes clear when it is realized that ratio 2 multiplied by ratio 3 equals ratio 1; i.e.

$$\frac{\text{operating profit}}{\text{sales}} \times \frac{\text{sales}}{\text{operating assets}} = \frac{\text{operating profit}}{\text{operating assets}}$$

Ratio 3, in Table 3.6, shows how many times assets have been turned over in a year. Ratio 3a indicates the assets used per £1,000 of sales. Thus, the return on operating assets of a firm depends on the relationship between its ratios 2 and 3 (and 3a), but each of these depends on other important relationships, i.e., ratio 2 on those between a firm's sales and profits (and, therefore, its costs—ratios 4 to 9), while ratios 3 and 3a are determined by the relationships between the firm's sales and assets (ratios 3a to 18).

In other words, a firm's return on operating assets (ratio 1) is determined by a combination of the sales/cost and sales/asset ratios 2 to 18 of Table 3.6, and, therefore, by the relationships between sales and operations that result from the co-ordination activities of higher management. Each of these ratios relates sales (or sales value of production) to a major cost or asset item and, therefore, reflects a specific facet of overall co-ordination; but it is higher management's responsibility to create that overall balance between these specific relationships that will cause the combination of ratios 2 to 18 to give rise to a satisfactory return on operating assets.

Ratios 2 to 18 have, in fact, the double function of determining a firm's return on operating assets and of indicating that overall balance between a firm's sales and its operations through which it has earned its particular return on operating assets.

The discussion of Table 3.7 will show that there is, of course, more than one combination or pattern of ratios—each associated with a particular sales/production policy—that can result in a satisfactory return on operating assets.

The position of company D.

Reverting to company D's position (Table 3.6), the managing director established that most of the orders received by the company in the past had been small and in respect of different, technically unrelated products. These had to be made in small batches or even on a one-off basis: larger orders, which would have enabled the firm to manufacture in longer and more economic runs, were the exception rather than the rule; but hardly any effort had been made in the past to identify those products in the company's wide range which could be made as standard products for stock in economic runs without undue risk of accumulations of unsaleable stocks.

On the basis of an analysis of past sales and an assessment of future demand, the managing director decided that a number of standard products were to be made for stock in economic runs. He expected that sales of these items would represent about 40 per cent of total sales; this would help him to achieve a more satisfactory rate of utilization of labour and machine hours, and to reduce the risk of accumulations of work in progress.

Even though, in the course of the year, actual sales of stock produced items fell

Table 3.7

Centre for INTERFIRM COMPARISON Ltd

IFC of Management Ratios

Ratio	A	B	C	D	E	Median*
Return on assets						
1. Operating profit/Operating assets (%)	12·1	9·1	7·5	3·5	2·0	7·5
Profit margin on sales and turnover of assets						
2. Operating profit/Sales (%)	11·2	8·6	7·6	3·6	2·2	7·6
3. Sales/Operating assets (times per year)	1·08	1·06	0·99	0·98	0·92	0·99
Departmental costs (as a percentage of sales)						
4. Production cost of sales	65·8	66·4	70·2	73·9	77·4	70·2
5. Distribution and marketing costs	10·2	12·5	7·6	8·1	7·3	8·1
6. General and administrative costs	12·8	12·5	14·6	14·4	13·1	13·1
Production costs (as a percentage of sales value of production)						
7. Materials costs	33·6	32·8	30·7	30·8	30·5	30·8
8. Works labour costs	20·4	21·3	22·4	23·2	25·3	22·4
9. Other production costs	11·8	12·3	17·1	19·9	21·6	17·1
General asset utilization (£s per £1,000 of sales)						
3a. Operating assets	922	943	1,003	1,016	1,081	1,003
10. Current assets	432	421	442	411	399	421
11. Fixed assets	490	522	561	605	682	561
Current asset utilization (£s per £1,000 of sales)						
12. Material stocks	104	73	149	87	96	96
13. Work in progress	39	40	44	50	55	44
14. Finished stocks	72	90	25	69	13	69
15. Debtors	217	218	224	205	235	217
Fixed asset utilization (£s per £1,000 of sales)						
16. Land and buildings	282	274	284	289	321	284
17. Plant, machinery and works equipment	197	239	267	309	352	267
18. Vehicles	11	9	10	7	9	9

* The median provides an indication of the middle performance in the range. It is preferred to the arithmetic average since it is not so much affected by extremes. The median is calculated by listing, for each ratio, the figures of firms in order of size (i.e., size of ratio) from the highest to the lowest. The median is the figure half way down the list.

short of his expectation (representing only 25 per cent of total sales) the firm's ratios for 'this year' (*see* Table 3.6) show already some considerable improvements: return on operating assets (ratio 1) has gone up from 2·6 per cent to 3·6 per cent because both the firm's profit on sales and turnover of assets have improved. Profits on sales (ratio 2) have risen because the firm's production cost ratio (ratio 4) has gone down;

this, in turn, is due to better utilization of resources, as indicated by reductions in the works labour cost and production overhead ratios 8 and 9.

The firm's new stock production policy, which made production in longer runs possible, is also reflected in the improved work in progress and plant investment utilization ratios 13 and 17; i.e., with less production in small batches, production orders could be carried out more speedily and there were fewer jobs that were only partly completed. The rise in the firm's finished stock investment ratio 14 reflects, of course, the planned stock build-up; this, in turn, made it necessary to strengthen the marketing side of the business, hence the higher ratio 5.

Comparing the ratios reflecting his new policy with those of the previous period, the managing director feels rather happy about the firm's progress; but he feels less happy when he receives the results of an IFC in which his firm (D) has taken part (*see* Table 3.7).

The management ratios of other firms—an example of IFC

The other companies whose ratios are shown in Table 3.7* offer in their catalogue a wide range of products of the kind made by firm D; their size is also similar to that of firm D. The five firms differ mainly† in respect of their overall marketing and production policy, i.e., each firm adopts a different approach to the question of whether the financial risk of building up stocks of standard items, and the intensive marketing effort needed to sell them are justified by the cost advantages of making standard products in long production runs.

In arriving at the figures from which the ratios were calculated, the firms have used the same definitions of accounting terms and the same valuation principles. With the help of a price index provided to them by the organization conducting the IFC all firms have, for instance, expressed the values of their plant and machinery in terms of current replacement values, not in terms of historical cost. It is, of course, essential that the ratios of firms taking part in an IFC are based on comparable accounting data (*see* 'Questions arising', below). If this were not so, differences between the ratios of firms would rightly be suspected of being due to differences in the accounting bases used, and could not be put down to differences in policy or performance.

Interpreting the results of an IFC to participating firms

The following comments addressed to the management of *firm D* will illustrate how

---

* This is, of course, a much abbreviated example. In the actual IFC from which these ratios (slightly changed to avoid identification of the industry concerned) were taken, 44 firms took part; furthermore, the actual IFC provided many additional ratios on detailed aspects of performance.

† For the treatment of differences between firms and their figures in an IFC see the paragraph 'Questions arising', below.

differences between the ratios of firms can be interpreted to participants, partly with the help of background information provided by them. The confidential report the managing director of *firm D* has received with the comparative table is too detailed and long to be reproduced here. However, this report* would refer to the relatively unfavourable ratios 1 to 3 of *firm D* and state that its ratio 2 is relatively low, mainly because of its relatively high production cost ratio 4. Comments on the firm's distribution and marketing cost ratio 5 would probably be as follows:

'Your relatively low distribution and marketing cost ratio 5, lower than those of *firms A and B*, is not an indication of strength on your part. These two firms, after some market research and analysis of past sales, decided to make several products in their range for stock in order to obtain economic production runs and to be able to offer quick deliveries. The higher ratios of *firms A and B* reflect their more intensive marketing effort, which is necessitated by their decision to make standard products for stock, whose sales are expected to represent 50 per cent and 70 per cent of total sales respectively, while you planned sales of such products to represent only 40 per cent of your sales.

'Even though the actual percentages achieved by these firms did not quite reach their original targets, the fact that they had set their sights higher than you in this respect, helped them to plan for longer runs and thus to obtain greater production economies than you. The success of their sales/production policy helped these firms to earn a higher return on operating assets than you; hence the above comment that your low ratio 5 is not a sign of strength in your case. Ratios 5 of *firms C and E* are relatively low because these firms make only a few end products for stock and, therefore, need not make an intensive product-orientated selling effort. *Firm E* is primarily concerned with manufacture to customers' orders and has not taken steps to identify either the end products or the components that could be made for stock in economic runs, but *firm C* obtains economic production runs by making for stock those standard components and parts that are common to many of its end products.'

These comments would be followed by references to the causes of *firm D*'s relatively high ratios 8 and 9, i.e., its high incidence of 'specials', which is partly due to its failure to meet the original target of 40 per cent standard product sales, and partly to the fact that the firm's plans envisage ex. stock sales which represent only 40 per cent of turnover (*see* comments on ratio 5 above).

As to *firm E*, the report would point out that its high ratios 8 and 9 are due to an order mix which did not favour economic production planning, and to the absence of any attempt to identify and make standard products. The more favourable ratios 8 and 9 of *firm C* would be explained as being due to that firm's policy of standardizing and making for stock in economic runs those parts and components common to the

---

* Individual confidential reports commenting on differences between their ratios and those of others are provided to all firms taking part in an interfirm comparison.

end products of its range (a policy which, incidentally, is also applied by *firm A*). Thus, *firm C* can meet orders for a variety of end products in its range without encountering the production planning problems of *firm E*.

Firm D will be told that this policy also accounts for the relatively high materials stock investment ratios (ratio 12) of *firms A and C* (since in this IFC stock produced components are shown under this heading). *Firm D* will also be told that its work in progress ratio 13 and finished stock investment ratio 14 are relatively high because orders for standard products fell short of the 40 per cent target figure, and because this target is itself lower than those of *firms A and B*. *Firm E*'s high ratio 13 and low ratio reflect that firm's policy of dealing with each order as it comes. *Firm C*'s ratio 14 is low because the firm concentrates on production of common components for stock.

There would, of course, also be comments on differences between the fixed asset investment utilization ratios, e.g., that the high ratio 16 (land and buildings) of *firm E* is not only due to under-utilization of this asset item, but also to the use of land and buildings of relatively high value. The low ratio 17 (plant and machinery) of *firm A* would be explained by reference to the firm's favourable rate of plant capacity utilization (resulting from its stock production policy) and its relatively high percentage of bought out finished parts; this, on the one hand, reduces the need for certain machines, but, on the other, causes the firm's ratio of materials costs/sales value of production (ratio 7) to be relatively high, since the firm has to pay suppliers' total costs and profits in respect of a relatively large percentage of the components used by it.

The report would conclude that *firm D* should consider changing its present policy in four ways, i.e., the firm should:

(a) try to identify a larger percentage than before of products that might be made for stock;
(b) try to improve its marketing performance so as to ensure that sales targets for stock produced standard products can be met more effectively;
(c) try to identify components which, since they are common to its range of products, can be made for stock in economic runs;
(d) try to obtain prices for 'specials' which compensate it for the higher cost of making them.

Questions arising

The above example shows:

(i) that a firm can be unduly self-satisfied if it judges its performance on the basis of its own ratios only;

(ii) that a properly presented and interpreted IFC helps management to see whether the profitability of its business stands up to competitive performance, and, should this not be so, in what directions improvements are indicated.

However, the example will also give rise to a number of questions:

(a) Confidentiality

First of all, how do IFC data become available? Clearly their availability depends on the willingness of firms in an industry to contribute their figures to an outsider, the organization conducting the IFC; but are firms not afraid that this will do them harm?

There are already several thousand firms in more than sixty British industries and trades which have contributed their figures in the course of an IFC. They did not suffer any harm, because the following steps are usually taken to ensure their anonymity and the confidentiality of their data: participating firms contribute their figures anonymously, i.e., under code numbers given to them by the organization conducting the IFC. This organization uses the figures of firms to calculate ratios or percentages which are then shown, under code numbers, on tables like Table 3.7. This presentation, in the form of ratios, reduces the possibility of identification.

Furthermore, it should be noted that these ratios are unlikely to be the same as those that might be calculated from published accounts, because most of the information on which the ratios are based is not given in published accounts, and because, for the purpose of the comparison, such key items as the figures of profit and assets (both fixed and current) are defined in a special way.

(b) Accounting comparability

This leads us to the next question, already touched on in the previous paragraph: are the figures of participating firms comparable? Will not the fact that firms may use different bases for, e.g., the valuation and depreciation of assets, the definitions of 'sales' and items of cost, destroy the comparability of their figures?

The answer to this question is that, in a properly conducted IFC, all participants will calculate their figures on the same uniform bases prepared for them and in consultation with them by the organization conducting the exercise; that the figures contributed by individual firms are carefully checked; and that any query arising is fully discussed with the firm concerned.

For instance, a definition of 'production cost' must include a statement of the point at which 'production' is deemed to end and 'distribution' begins, as well as a definition of the constituent items of cost to be included and the method of arriving at them. A comparison of production labour costs as a separate ratio will involve settling a number of points if the figures are to be comparable, e.g., is direct labour only, or are both direct and indirect labour to be included? If 'direct labour' only, how is it to be defined? What categories of activity does it include? What treatment is

226

to be given to items such as overtime, shift, and holiday pay? To national insurance and pension contributions? This example shows that published accounts of individual firms cannot be used as a basis for an IFC, partly because these would not provide the minimum of data needed for a set of management ratios (e.g., no details of costs and stocks), and partly because one could not assume that different firms had used the same definitions and valuation methods in arriving at their sales, cost, profit, and asset figures.

In this connection, it is amusing to read about the firm that has demonstrated that, by using eight different bases in defining and valuing the component parts of the ratio of 'profit/capital employed', it could show for the same accounting period nine different ratios of return on capital, ranging from 39·5 per cent to 8·3 per cent. In calculating the high ratio, the firm had stated 'capital employed' as 'net assets', and fixed assets at book value; it had calculated assets on the basis of annual averages, and had not decreased profits by additional depreciation. In calculating the low ratio, capital employed was stated as 'gross assets', fixed assets were shown at new replacement value, individual asset items were calculated on the basis of monthly averages, and profits were decreased by additional depreciation.

This case shows that it is essential to lay down uniform rules and definitions, and to ensure that these are adhered to, if the figures of individual firms are to be comparable. The case also suggests that because the underlying figures are taken from published accounts, league tables and published industry ratio averages of return on capital should not be used as yardsticks by individual firms.

(c) Similarity of firms
But even if successful arrangements can be made regarding the accounting comparability of firms taking part in an IFC, will the firms themselves not be different in respect of, say, their size, stock policy, degree of mechanization, marketing methods? We know that the five firms in Table 3.7 are of similar size and make similar products. We have found, however, that they are different in major respects, i.e., in their overall marketing and production policy.

Would the fact that there are such differences between these firms rule out IFC? There are people who say: 'Like should be compared with like; no two firms are really alike; therefore IFCs are useless'. Is this true? Are IFCs ruled out unless the firms are all of the same size, make the same products in the same way, operate in the same locality, employ the same kind of plant, use the same methods of distribution, etc?

The answer is that the object of IFC is not to compare 'firms' as such, but to reveal what effect certain differences in their features and practices have on their performance. In fact, if there were no differences between the firms taking part they could learn nothing from the comparison.

Some major dissimilarities between firms (e.g., size) can be dealt with by means of grouping, i.e., by tabulating together the ratios of firms that have a major characteristic in common, but there are practical limits to such grouping if more than one or two dissimilarities have to be taken into account. These are best treated by way of individual interpretation of ratio differences on the basis of background information as shown in the example of Table 3.7.

Conclusion

IFC helps higher management to diagnose weaknesses and set targets of performance, but it can do this only if the firms of an industry are willing to join forces in a properly organized co-operative effort. It speaks for the soundness of British management that thousands of firms have already taken part in IFC. Most of these are conducted by specialist organizations under the auspices of a trade association. After all, a trade association exists to provide a basis for co-operation in matters where the prosperity of member firms is advanced more effectively by joint action than by independent action on the part of individual firms. A trade association, therefore, provides the obvious focal point for an IFC.

Recently, the efforts of trade associations have been reinforced by the activities of the 'little Neddies'; some of these have greatly assisted the development of IFC by providing financial support that made it possible for all interested firms in the industries concerned to take part in the schemes provided for them.

This support is given because IFC stimulates and enables managements to keep business policies and operations under constant critical review, and to take the appropriate decisions. The aggregate of these decisions taken at the level of individual firms is bound to have a favourable impact on national economic development.

Reading list

BOOKS

Interfirm Comparison for Management, H. Ingham and L. Taylor Harrington (British Institute of Management, 1958)

Interfirm Comparison: A New Instrument of Self-Diagnosis, Sir Robert A. Maclean (Centre for Interfirm Comparison, 1967)

Interfirm Comparison: A New Instrument of Management Self-Diagnosis, Dr A. W. Clark (Centre for Interfirm Comparison, 1967)

The Companies Act 1967 and its Implications for Interfirm Comparison, C. A. Westwick (Centre for Interfirm Comparison, 1967)

Interfirm Comparison in Depth (Centre for Interfirm Comparison, 1967)

Interfirm Comparison—Concepts and Misconceptions (Centre for Interfirm Comparison, 1967)

Published Accounts—Your Yardstick of Performance? (Centre for Interfirm Comparison, 1967)

Efficiency Comparison within Large Organizations (Centre for Interfirm Comparison, 1962)

Interfirm Comparison: An Incentive to Productivity, Project No. 379 (The European Productivity Agency of O.E.E.C.—now O.E.C.D.—Paris, 1956)

The Use of Ratios in the Study of Business Fluctuations and Trends, Management Information No. 4, K. W. Bevan, (The General Educational Trust of the Institute of Chartered Accountants in England and Wales, 1966)

JOURNALS

Business Ratios (three times a year) (Dun and Bradstreet Ltd., London, in association with Moodies Services Ltd.)

Useful addresses

Centre for Interfirm Comparison Ltd., Management House, Parker Street, London WC 2

This is an example of ratios used in comparisons for light/engineering companies, e.g., manufacturers offering a wide range of electric switches.

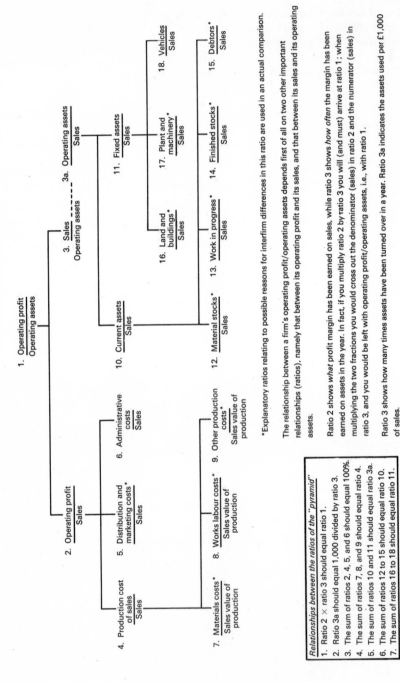

*Explanatory ratios relating to possible reasons for interfirm differences in this ratio are used in an actual comparison.

The relationship between a firm's operating profit/operating assets depends first of all on two other important relationships (ratios), namely that between its operating profit and its sales, and that between its sales and its operating assets.

Ratio 2 shows *what* profit margin has been earned on sales, while ratio 3 shows *how often* the margin has been earned on assets in the year. In fact, if you multiply ratio 2 by ratio 3 you will (and must) arrive at ratio 1 : when multiplying the two fractions you would cross out the denominator (sales) in ratio 2 and the numerator (sales) in ratio 3, and you would be left with operating profit/operating assets, i.e., with ratio 1.

Ratio 3 shows how many times assets have been turned over in a year. Ratio 3a indicates the assets used per £1,000 of sales.

Thus, the return on operating assets of a firm depends on the relationship between its ratios 2 and 3, and this, in turn, depends on the relationships between its sales and its profits (and, therefore, its costs), and between its sales and its assets.

Relationships between the ratios of the "pyramid"
1. Ratio 2 × ratio 3 should equal ratio 1.
2. Ratio 3a should equal 1,000 divided by ratio 3.
3. The sum of ratios 2, 4, 5, and 6 should equal 100%.
4. The sum of ratios 7, 8, and 9 should equal ratio 4.
5. The sum of ratios 10 and 11 should equal ratio 3a.
6. The sum of ratios 12 to 15 should equal ratio 10.
7. The sum of ratios 16 to 18 should equal ratio 11.

Fig. 3.11. 'Pyramid' of Ratios

3.14 A Summary of Techniques

Balint Bodroghy

Problems, if they occur often enough, will lead to the establishment of techniques for solving them. Once developed, the techniques find wider application than originally intended and the one-to-one correspondence of technique and problem disappears. It is thus easy to forget that management techniques are not subjects in a curriculum but parts of an organic hierarchy of skills, overlapping, redundant, and inseparable. At the highest level of the hierarchy one would expect to find simply 'good management'. Reduced to bare essentials it consists of information handling and decision-making. Each is dependent on the other, and both are supported by a variety of techniques.

The tangled relationship of management problems and techniques is shown in Fig 3.12. The usefulness of a technique and its position in the hierarchy depends on the nature of the problem. A brief description of the techniques listed is given in the following pages, and an attempt is made to establish the context of their application. The list is by no means complete, and the selection is somewhat arbitrary since there is no clear distinction between management and other techniques used in business. A technique, when new, is of concern to management, but once established, it becomes the routine of accounting, production, or marketing personnel. Thus, value analysis and management accounting are included, but production engineering and book-keeping are not, and may the omission be forgiven.

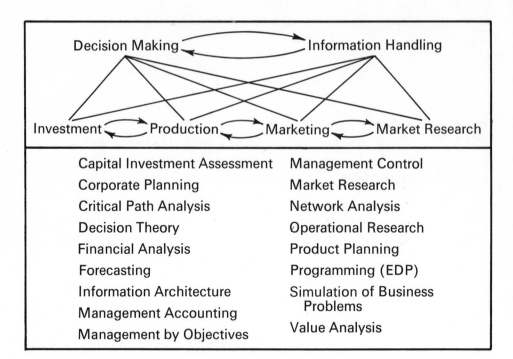

Fig. 3.12.

Capital investment assessment

Decisions on capital investment, invariably involving a choice between similar or dissimilar alternatives, require the support of analytical work. Under the general term capital investment assessment come a number of techniques of varying sophistication, starting with payback calculations and reaching into simulation. The choice of technique is often more difficult than its application.

With the exception of trivial or short-term projects, the assessment needs to be based on a time-dependent valuation of money. This is not a question of inflation, but of recognition that cash, suitably invested, can earn a return that is a function of time. The rate of return depends on the economic conditions in general and the investor's attitude to risk, and it will be subject to fluctuations.

A second important problem is the choice of an accounting system. The cash flow basis, where only real cash movements across an imaginary boundary drawn around the project are considered (thus neglecting book-keeping entries such as depreciation or stock write-off) has some merit, and leads to the discounted cash flow method. Marginal accounting, when the project boundary is drawn to include the entire company, and the effect of variations in the proposed investment on the whole is evaluated, could give a much clearer understanding of the problem but will lead to considerable accounting complexity. This may introduce systematic errors that invalidate the results.

In general, the sophistication of the technique should suit the complexity of the problem and the reliability of available information.

Corporate planning

More art than technique, corporate planning is essentially the process of bringing into harmony a corporation's scope, assets and objectives over a period of time. Such planning is essential for corporations suffering from financial inertia. An investment company, by switching funds from one area of business to another can react to new situations as quickly as its decision-process permits. A manufacturing or merchandizing company, with highly differentiated assets and skills, is slow to react, and some form of long-range corporate plan is required to anticipate future needs and, thus, to permit continuous adaptation.

The starting point of planning could be the definition of objectives (what should the balance sheet of the future look like), in which case scope and assets must be brought into harmony. It could start with an analysis of the company's assets and skills (what are we really good at, or what do we like to do), in which case a wide examination of the scope in related and unrelated fields covering the time-span of the plan will lead to a forecast of performance. Or it could start with scope (what business are we in) to define realistic objectives and the assets needed for their attainment. In any case, corporate planning is a reiterative process in which a circular solution is repeated until a true harmony between scope, assets, and objectives is reached.

Critical path analysis

The determination of the particular series of acts and events in a network (the critical series) which determines the length of time required to accomplish a task is critical path analysis. It is an extension of network analysis, required whenever the task is complex and unfamiliar so that the critical path is not self evident or known from experience. Determination of the critical path and the 'float' (i.e., surplus time) available for each action that is not on the critical path permits the optimum deployment of resources and may lead to significant economies or the shortening of the time needed to complete the task.

The time required for each act or event making up a network is estimated and the path of longest total time (the critical path) is found by trial. Parallel paths will require less time and, consequently, may be assigned a float. Computer programmes are available to find the critical path and float for projects of extreme complexity such as the construction of a chemical plant or ship, or the launching of a new product.

Decision theory

The rational examination of a series of linked decisions and outcomes, where the outcomes are subject to uncertainty, involves the application of decision theory in one of its many forms. The technique, largely in its infancy, can be a valuable aid to the businessman's own highly refined sense for judging the balance between risk and return in essentially unpredictable situations.

In its simplest form the theory involves the construction of a decision tree, representing all foreseeable decisions in a chain (alternative as well as sequential), and all possible outcomes. The problem can then be analysed by separately considering the likelihood (the probability of a particular outcome) and the decision-maker's preference for the outcome at each stage of the problem. The former is an objective probability, the latter a subjective preference strongly influenced by the decision-maker's situation at the time of the decision.

In general, a complex problem can only be solved backwards by dealing with the furthest decisions first and the immediate choice last. Each step may be solved by replacing the values of uncertain outcomes by their 'certainty equivalent', that is, the certain value that would just induce the decision-maker to forego his right to participate in the gamble.

Financial analysis

Interpretation of company financial statements in the light of technical, commercial, and economic developments affecting its business and the measures taken by management as a consequence, is financial analysis.

Originally this was the approach of institutional investors such as trust funds, mutual funds (unit trusts), or insurance companies to portfolio selection. Increasingly, it is found that an understanding of financial analysis is helpful also in take-over situations, (on either side of the battle) and the preparation of statements and annual reports for companies sensitive to investor goodwill.

The two main elements are historic and projective, and both involve a synthesis of views on the company and its environment. In the historic review, an attempt is made to relate the company's past financial performance to known indicators of market behaviour and to the performance of competitors, noting the main internal events (such as changes in management, gearing, or productive assets) that have a bearing on performance. A forecast is then derived from projections of market indicators, an assessment of the company's scope for action, and a judgement of the management's ability to exploit it.

The strategies for bid or defence in a take-over will emerge from the opposing analysts' views on performance under different managements.

Forecasting

Decisions concern the future, and a forecast is implicit in each. Forecasting is therefore a constant preoccupation of management.

All forecasts (outside the realm of clairvoyance) are based on extrapolation of one form or another. Extrapolation is the assumption that an observed trend will continue in the future. This may concern a relationship such as *per capita* consumption of sweets, or a behaviour, such as government attitude to social services or the marketing policies of a competitor.

In its simplest (and most dangerous) form, extrapolation consists simply of extending a trend line on a graph of historic data into the future. On this basis one would forecast that there will be no room to stand in India in a few decades time. A more intelligent approach is to extrapolate several related trends and to derive from these a complex extrapolation. In the case of India's population this would consist of separate extrapolations of birth-rate and death-rate, and the birth-rate itself would be forecast from an extrapolation of the progress of education, the growth of the professional classes, the accumulation of private and national wealth, and the attitude of government towards population stability.

To combine the trends it is useful first to express each as a time-dependent mathematical function, using various curve-fitting and smoothing techniques (regression analysis, de-seasonalization etc.). These can be superimposed and combined to produce a forecast.

The uncertainties inherent in forecasting may be handled by probabilistic methods or the establishment of limits of confidence.

Management accounting

The presentation of financial data as part of the information task of management decisions and control is management accounting.

The need for management accounting arises from: (1) the competitive pressure on management to increase its speed of response to change; (2) the reduced margin for error in the response; (3) the conservatism and slowness of conventional accounting and auditing procedures; and (4) the distortions introduced into accounting by the artefacts of taxation, particularly depreciation and depletion allowances and grants.

Management accounts reduce the mass of business information originating in the company to a digestible form. A variety of simple techniques is used to aid interpretation. Examples are break-even charts showing the relationship between sales and profit graphically; variance curves or tables, indicating the deviations from expected and budgeted performance to enable the manager to recognize exceptions;

235

and the charting of performance ratios (backlog to deliveries, output per machine-hour, reject per unit run, etc.) to serve as early indicators of changes that may require action.

The design of management accounting systems is one part of the problem of information architecture.

Management by objectives

Performance of key executives in an organization depends on motivation as well as ability. Among various motivating forces such as recognition, competition, and reward, the setting of self-imposed targets is the most subtle, providing a powerful method for exploiting a manager's native abilities to the full. Management by objectives is the systematic framework for doing so.

To implement such a programme the executive's functions, responsibilities, and tasks are discussed with his superior. The aim of the discussion is to bring to light quantitative measures of performance, and to establish a ranking of value to the company. The outcome of the discussion is a programme for attaining specific targets in a given time. Ideally, the programme should be proposed by the executive himself, but in any case he should agree to it and accept its feasibility.

The impact of management by objectives will be felt most strongly in administrative and service functions where measures of performance are not readily available. In some organizations it is considered an aid to executive development, and it is hoped that a useful residue of self-discipline will remain when the novelty of the programme has worn off.

Management control

Decisions require implementation. Since in most business situations this is delegated, management must exercise control. In many respects the control of a business is analogous to the control of a chemical process, and much of the theory of process control is directly applicable. Control involves measurement, comparison, and action. Measurement implies the existence of standards, and comparison requires the establishment of targets. In a feed-back control system the results achieved are compared with targets, and action is taken to bring these into line. It is suitable for the day-to-day control of line responsibilities.

More appropriate to general management is feed-forward control, where changes in conditions (the market, the economy, or in technology) are anticipated, and adjustments are made in controllable variables (manpower, stock levels, gearing) to optimize the company's structure in the new situation.

Elements of management control are accounting, budgeting, market, and

236

economic research, and forecasting, and these are brought together through the appropriate choice of information architecture.

Market research

There is a need to re-establish contact between market and management, now separated by intermediaries inside and outside the company. Market research can accomplish this, and uses some interesting new techniques in the process. (*See also* section 9.2.)

The purpose of market research may be to find out who buys a given product, to measure market potential or market share, or to obtain historical information for the purpose of forecasting. The techniques used differ accordingly.

Random sampling (interviewing a representative fraction of the market population) was originally the basis of research and continues to play an important part. Stratified sampling is used when the purchasing power of buyers is unevenly distributed (as in the case of most industrial products) making it difficult to produce a truly representative sample of conveniently small size. Since a great deal of market information is available from published sources, desk research is now of even greater importance. The use of indicators (such as petrol consumption per automobile) can save much time and improve accuracy by focusing on the problem a number of independent information sources available on different products, periods, or countries. These must be adjusted for economic and technical change, and tested for statistical significance before use.

Network analysis

The study of the sequence and interrelation of acts and events involved in the accomplishment of a complex task is network analysis. It is useful whenever tasks involving a multiplicity of discrete steps, such as the construction of a plant, or the introduction of a new system of office administration is to be accomplished smoothly within a given time. The technique is limited to tasks involving familiar acts and events that can be predicted with a degree of certainty.

The network, similar in appearance to a series-parallel electrical circuit diagram, is prepared by representing each discrete act or event by means of a line (say *AB*) of arbitrary length. The line *AB* is joined on to all other lines that represent acts or events that must, by the nature of the task, immediately precede *AB*. Similarly, lines representing acts or events that must follow immediately upon the completion of *AB*, are joined to the end of line *AB*.

Junctions between two or more lines (i.e. nodes *A* and *B*) represent points in time. All acts or events pointing to a node must be complete by the date represented by the node, thus providing a comprehensive map for planning and co-ordinating a project.

237

Operational research

Operational research is not a technique but a state of mind: the belief that engineering solutions can be found to non-engineering (i.e. business, public, government or military) problems using scientific methods. Where the belief is justified, the results can be spectacular, but there is a tendency sometimes to underestimate complexity and to overestimate the ability to simplify without destroying the relevance of the solution.

A simple test of a problem's suitability for OR treatment is to compare it with bridge or poker. If it is like bridge, OR will probably help; if it is like poker, it is best left alone.

Since simplification and approximation is inherent in the OR treatment of business problems, the sensitivity of the solution to each simplifying assumption must be tested before allowing it. Similarly, the range over which an approximation is acceptable must be established, and corresponding limitations imposed on the solution. Finally, the accuracy of the information available has a strong bearing on the use to which the results can be put (which is different and independent from the usefulness of results).

Properly applied, operational research is an important management aid— otherwise, it is a compulsive hobby.

Information architecture

Management decisions, at all levels, are based on information. The design of systems for gathering, processing, and displaying information is information architecture.

The increasing complexity and competitiveness of business (which leaves a shrinking margin for error), coupled with the enormous processing capability of computers, makes the architectural approach (from the ground up) to information processing essential.

The design of information systems to suit the requirements of a particular business involves more than organization and methods study in the office and the programming of computers. Since information is expensive, the minimum needed for a given level of decisions should be displayed at each point of the organization. But since the possession of key information can produce commercial benefits totally out of proportion to its cost, the designer of the system must use his judgement, coupled with an intimate understanding of the business, to decide on a delicate and important balance.

Product planning

It is slightly confusing that the term product planning is used to denote two quite distinct activities: the planning of an individual product (such as next year's dish-

238

washer) and the planning of a company's or division's product range in a changing economic and technical context. The former is a problem of line management; the latter of general management.

Product planning (line) is a complex decision problem embracing technical, commercial, and psychological elements coupled with uncertainty, and, as a consequence, risk. The management techniques involved may include market research, test marketing, network analysis, decision theory and others, in addition to industrial design and production planning.

Product planning (general) is a part of corporate planning (the existence of such a plan is assumed) with the task of optimizing the utilization of a company's (or division's) skills and assets. As a consequence, the starting point is an audit of the company's assets, followed by the definition of product areas to give new projections to existing skills. The project ends with the search for new products fitting into a coherent long-term strategy.

Programming (EDP)

In its vulgar form, programming is simply the conversion of a proposed solution to a problem into a form suitable for electronic data processing. But problem solving and programming are inseparable in all but routine applications, since to make effective use of EDP, its capabilities and limitations must be considered in formulating the solution.

When electronic data processing is applied to continuing administrative, accounting or process control tasks, the program is merely a set of instructions specifying where and how to store information, what to do with it (generally involving simple arithmetic), and how to present it.

When EDP is used to solve a unique scientific or business problem, programming also involves its reduction to a mathematical form suitable for solution by computer. A linear or quadratic programme uses a set of linear or quadratic equations. A dynamic program contains instructions to solve a problem involving a series of decisions; a Simplex program is used for optimization; and an integer program excludes fractional solutions (i.e., buy $1\frac{3}{4}$ machine tools).

A mathematical model of a company, process, or economy is built up from such elements, and only the complexity and method of use by repeated interrogation differ from the problem of a unique solution described above.

Simulation of business problems

Simulation is an attempt to study management problems under laboratory, that is controlled and accelerated, conditions. It permits the recreation of complex business situations and the exploration of different courses of action without incurring the penalties of failure. The principal limitation is the inability to represent the full complexity of a real business problem in a model that can be manipulated meaningfully. This is true in spite of the information handling capacity of computers.

The mathematical expression of the relationship between changes in price and the corresponding change in demand for a product (price-elasticity of demand) is a simple form of simulation. But many other such relationships must be added to describe the behaviour of a market. The reaction of competitors, presence of substitute products, the effects of advertising, changes in the economic climate, consumer psychology, and others, must be accounted for. The scope is limited only by the student's ability to foresee, quantify, and manipulate the results.

For practical purposes, considerable simplification of the problem is inevitable. But it is important to test the sensitivity of the system described before omitting any factor from the model.

Value analysis

The systematic substitution in a product of designs, components or materials of lower cost but giving the minimum performance demanded, is the purpose of value analysis. The need for value analysis arose from shortcomings in the training of engineers and designers who were not sufficiently cost-conscious, or who did not devote sufficient attention to detail, or who were unfamiliar with production techniques. Ideally, it should be part of the discipline of design and not a form of postoperative care as so often happens.

Value analysis must start with the functional specifications of the product. This includes life, reliability, and the complete range of service conditions as well as the circumstances of production. The full force of product design, material science, tool design, and production engineering is then brought to bear systematically on every feature, subassembly, or component in the product to achieve the minimum cost compatible with the specifications.

The cost reductions can be spectacular. These are mainly achieved through changes in materials, the realization that wider tolerances can be accepted if certain changes are made in design, the elimination of individual components, and improvements in tooling.

Reading list

BOOKS

Glossary of Management Techniques, J. Argenti and C. Rope (British Institute of Management booklet, 1967)
Glossary of Management Techniques, H.M. Treasury booklet (H.M.S.O. 1967)
Performance and Profitability, M. J. Clay and B. H. Walley (Longmans, Green, 1965)

2,001 Business Terms and What They Mean, Alexander Hamilton Institute (Doubleday, 1962)

Annual Review of Management Techniques, special supplement to *Management Today*

JOURNALS

'The Application of Management Techniques', J. R. Potts (*Management Accounting*, February 1968)

'New Management Techniques' (a series of articles periodically in *The Director*)

'Management Terms Needn't be Gobbledygook', E. Benge (*Factory*, March 1961)

'There's No Management Technique Like Commonsense', Thomas McAuliffe (*The Director*, July 1967)

4. The City of London

4.1 Services of the City

Robert Collin

The ordinary businessman is not to be blamed if he regards the City of London as uncomprehending and incomprehensible. The City may be a wonderful piece of machinery to those who are familiar with it; to people in other parts of the country it must often seem a remote place where attitudes that have long died out elsewhere linger on—the guild tradition, in particular, that specialized trades should be respected as mysteries. Yet the popular picture of the City as an aloof society, held together by its own close ties of history, geography, and common interest is obsolescent. Most of the commuters who swarm in each morning to work in one or other section of it have only a rough-and-ready idea of what their fellow-travellers do for a living. Their sense of community springs largely from the belief that outsiders exist who have no idea of it at all, and the number of these complete outsiders is being rapidly reduced by the diffusion of financial knowledge.

London has traditionally looked abroad for trade. Its merchants, who later became its merchant bankers, have always believed in the value of keeping in close touch with business conditions here, there and everywhere abroad. The City not merely accounted for a large part of total world trade in Britain's heyday but shipped, insured and financed an even larger part; it was London bankers, too, who raised the capital for spreading industrialization over the globe. The recollection of those great days has not dried up. A worldwide network of shipping, merchanting, and insurance facilities centred in the City still earns the country a large amount of foreign exchange. The traditional overseas lending business of banks has been badly hampered by exchange control on transactions outside the sterling area, but they, too, have developed new methods of financing international trade and raising capital for foreign borrowers, and their links with financial institutions in other countries have become more varied and complex than ever before. The international market expertise of London is still unrivalled, even by New York; many City institutions can still afford to take a broader and more confident view of their place in the world than is usual in contemporary Britain.

Tradition has disadvantages. The youngest partners of some City firms would have found it difficult, even a few years ago, to rouse interest, when their elders and betters were reminiscing about the making and breaking of Latin American governments, in the difficulties of an engineering firm in the Midlands. But this particular form of nostalgia has now disappeared almost completely: for two generations past, and especially since the end of the last war, the City has been turning more and more for its business towards domestic industry. The Bank of England was forced in the nineteen-thirties to take a lead in bringing about rationalization of the country's heavy industries. It was then that the Macmillan Committee underlined the lack of facilities tailored to the special needs of small industrial companies. It was then, too, that new varieties of financial enterprise—hire purchase companies, for example— first began to flourish.

The seeds planted in the 'thirties began to sprout vigorously twenty years later in peaceful prosperity. New merchant banks, handicapped in competing with the establishment on traditional ground, broke out of it by offering to provide large industrial firms with financial advice—advice, in particular, about the promotion and repulsion of take-over bids—they had come to need badly. A proliferation of industrial holding companies helped to familiarize many family-controlled firms with the advantages of a Stock Exchange quotation. New issues luxuriated. Private institutions began to compete harder with the publicly-sponsored Industrial and Commercial Finance Corporation in searching out promising private companies to back. Hire purchase finance firms, exempted from official restrictions that applied to the lending powers of the banks, extended rapidly the size and the scope of their business. Some fingers were burnt, some scandals erupted into the headlines, but a good deal of fruitful development took place.

All the leading City institutions had learnt by the beginning of the nineteen-sixties to swim with the tide. The stuffiest merchant banks now take a close interest in the affairs of domestic industry, not only passively through their investment departments but through an active search for new industrial clients to advise on the whole range of financial problems they are likely to encounter. The commercial banks, whose influence in the City has long been much less than the size of their resources would have supported, have simultaneously begun to branch out into new territory: first into hire purchase finance, for example, and more recently into the underwriting and floating of industrial issues. Miscegenation, too, is under way, with the commercial banks buying their way into the special expertise and self-confidence of the merchants. Old habits are dying fast; young men are being given their heads; the City is now looking for industrial business at home more vigorously than ever before.

This change of attitude has not yet altered the fact that many businessmen are uncertain about what the City has to offer them and are chary of seeking its advice. Those who need the services of the Baltic, or Lloyds, or the various commodity markets will find their own way to them sooner or later. Finance is the great stumbling-block, and a great gulf seems to be set between the sympathetic local bank manager and the remote City expert. But this is a gulf that has to be jumped by every successful firm that outgrows its local boots and needs to raise more permanent capital; and the real need of such firms, whether or not their directors realize it, is the service of a professional adviser familiar with the tax and legal aspects of their problem, conversant with the wide range of facilities available to meet their shortage of working and fixed capital, and able to recommend them, with a word over the telephone, to this or that powerful source of cash.

The City is not entirely to blame for a reputation of aloofness: many family-controlled firms are reluctant to seek fresh capital or even good advice if it has to be bought at the price of a more searching inquiry into their business than the bank manager has ever demanded. But permanent capital is hard to come by, and those who live on expertise and personal contacts take different risks from institutions that lend money only against good security. The ideal City adviser is like the ideal GP, treating the particular symptoms of which the patient complains as an opportunity for analysing his whole state and agreeing, only when he accepts the analysis, to put him in touch with specialists. This rigorous approach, which serves to keep off the incompetent, may sometimes repel firms that are competent but shy; these should comfort themselves with the thought that the City never makes any pretence of understanding the technical details of anybody's business. If it is a good business, held off from further success only by a shortage of capital, the shortage can probably be made good at the price of an inquisition. Once the need to pay this price is accepted, doors open; it becomes a continuing advantage, in most cases, to have on tap the advice of a City firm familiar both with the particular circumstances of its client and with the abstract world of finance.

It is advice and introductions, above all, that the City has to offer. Every firm has financial advice available to it from its bank, its solicitor, and its accountant; every firm can consult the nearest HP finance house, factor, export agent, or stockbroker and get new ideas from them. The advantage of the City is simply that it can take a broad view of all these partial services in relation to individual circumstances and put its clients in immediate touch with those that will best help them. It is an 'old-boy' racket of a sort—though the phrase betrays incomprehension of the way in which financial business must inevitably work. It is a racket, however, that is constantly looking for new recruits: London's stockbrokers are only now beginning to stretch their old rules and invade the provinces; merchant banks—see the list of provincial branches in the Institute of Directors' useful guide to the financial problems of small companies—have been on the hunt for years past.

The larger and more famous merchant banks, certainly, live on famous reputations: none of them is likely to take on as client a small firm making gas jets, say, in Cumberland, unless it is likely to become much larger very rapidly with the bank's assistance. But they are all advertising for industrial business nowadays, and the worst rebuff that the chairman of the Cumberland firm need expect is the recommendation of another, more suitable name to approach. The probability is that he will be recommended to the Industrial and Commercial Finance Corporation, which has branches in fourteen cities and exists to provide advice and capital for small firms; or to rivals like the Charterhouse Industrial Development Group and the subsidiaries of United Dominions Trust. But he can be sure, nowadays, of being passed on to someone who can meet his difficulties, provided only that they are soluble in financial terms. The City is actively out for his business.

Reading list

BOOKS

Committee on the Working of the Monetary System, Command Paper 827 (H.M.S.O. 1959)
How the City Works, Oscar R. Hobson (Dickens Press, 1966)
The City in the World Economy, William M. Clarke (Institute of Economic Affairs, 1966)
Britain's Invisible Earnings, The Report of the Committee on Invisible Exports, Director of the Study William M. Clarke (British National Export Council, 1967)

Useful addresses

Industrial and Commercial Finance Corporation, Piercy House, 7 Copthall Avenue, London EC 2
Banking Information Service, 10 Lombard Street, London EC 3
British Insurance Association, Aldermary House, Queen Street, London EC 4

4.2 The Stock Exchange

R. F. M. (Martin) Wilkinson

The London Stock Exchange was not created, but has developed slowly over a period of nearly three hundred years. The need for a market in stocks and shares arose in the seventeenth century when the government and trading concerns wanted to raise money for their enterprises. Stocks and shares thereafter were issued and bought and sold on an ever-increasing scale, and people began to make a living by bringing together buyers and sellers. Dealers carried on their business in the coffee houses around Change Alley and, later, a meeting place was found in the old Royal Exchange building. As a reminder of the old coffee-house days, the attendants of the Stock Exchange today are still known as waiters, and shares of several of the early companies such as the Hudson's Bay Company are still traded.

In 1773, the stockbrokers decided to take over a building at the corner of Threadneedle Street and Sweetings Alley and the title 'The Stock Exchange' was placed above the door. In 1801, the Stock Exchange moved to the Capel Court site, in the 1850s the premises were reconstructed, and in the 1880s they were enlarged again. At present the Stock Exchange is once again being rebuilt and this reconstruction will, it is hoped, be completed by 1972.

There are approximately 3,300 members of the London Stock Exchange and they are divided into brokers and jobbers; there are about 200 firms of brokers and 40 firms of jobbers. The broker is the agent of the public and receives commission from the public for the transactions he arranges. The jobber is a principal, and deals only with a broker who is buying and selling. The jobber quotes two prices to the broker, the lower being the one at which he will buy, and the higher the one at which he will sell, and the difference between these two prices is known as the 'jobber's turn'.

The Stock Exchange is governed by a council consisting of thirty-six members who are stockbrokers and jobbers elected by their fellow members. The Government Broker is an *ex officio* member of the council, and is himself a stockbroker, who is also the liaison officer between the Stock Exchange and the Bank of England and the Government.

Stockbroking has not been immune from the vast changes in conditions that have marked the post-war years. There have always been close ties between the London and other stock exchanges, but it was realized in 1962 that such general developments as the speeding up of communications, the trend towards larger units, and the increasing use of machines for all aspects of business made it more than ever desirable that there should be much closer co-ordination of the activities of the twenty-four stock exchanges in Great Britain and Ireland, so a Committee was formed whose task it was to prepare a scheme that would produce this closer co-ordination.

By 1965 this Committee had completed its work and, on 1 July of that year, Federation was formed, 'to promote co-ordination of the activities of stock exchanges in Great Britain and Ireland, to promote good service to and safeguards for the investing public, to promote facilities for companies having or seeking quotation and to promote the interests of the Federated Exchanges and their Members'. Admission to the Federation was conditional upon exchanges accepting regulations on compensation to members of the public, the grant of quotation, branch offices and rules no less stringent than the rules laid down by the Federation on such matters as requirements, dealing arrangements, etc., and provision was made for other matters to be brought under the Federation as and when conditions seemed appropriate.

The period since Federation's inception has seen an acceleration in the rate of change in conditions. The development that has had most bearing on the operation of Federation has been the continued regionalization of exchanges outside London. This has reduced the number of stock exchanges in Great Britain and Ireland to eight (London, Midlands and Western, Northern, Scottish, Belfast, Cork, Dublin and the Provincial Brokers Stock Exchange). Of similar importance has been the trend towards larger stockbroking units, which has generated a desire and an ability to extend their field of operation, and the advance of electronics both in member firms' offices and in the exchange themselves, all taking place against a background of a greatly reduced turnover in securities.

With the exception of a relatively small amount of purely local issues with their main market on a provincial exchange, most government, nationalized industries, local authority, and foreign loans and securities of public companies are quoted in London.

Obtaining a stock exchange quotation is no easy or nominal matter, particularly for company securities. In the latter cases, especially with complete newcomers, the information requested on profits, finances, management, type of business, future prospects, methods of valuing stock-in-trade, reasons for raising new capital or asking for a quotation and other key matters goes well beyond the present Companies Act. The future is also looked after by the 'General Undertaking' which must be given when an application is made for a quotation in any new securities.

Boards of directors have to agree, among other things, to issue half-yearly reports, to publish, promptly, details of dividends or other distributions (or the passing of dividends or interest payments) and the acquisition or realization of major assets; to include in annual reports descriptions of the operations of the company and its subsidiaries together with sectional or geographical analyses of turnover and profits, to provide details of interests in and the nature of investments in associated concerns; and, a newer feature, to set out the names and holdings of any large shareholders and of each director.

New securities come to the Stock Exchange in different ways. These are: offers to the public by or on behalf of a company or borrower at fixed prices (a prospectus issue); offers to the public by or on behalf of a third party also at a fixed price (an offer for sale); a public offer by tender; placings of securities of existing companies; introductions of securities that are fairly widely held but in which there is no official market; rights offers to holders of existing securities; capitalization issues to holders of existing securities; open offers to holders of existing securities; share or loan capital issued in consideration for new assets acquired; exchanges for or conversion of existing securities; and the exercise of options.

Turnover in London is large. For example, during the year to 31 March 1968, the daily average of purchases and sales exceeded £147 million, of which the gilt-edged group accounted for no less than £109 million. Various steps are being taken to improve facilities. London has started a rebuilding scheme that will make it the most up-to-date stock market in the world. The various provincial exchanges are grouping themselves geographically into single trading floors with a view to increased efficiency. Continuous efforts are being made to improve services to the investing public and to give the maximum protection against abuses of market facilities. And lastly, investors are protected against loss through the default of members by large compensation funds.

Reading list

BOOKS

The Stock Exchange, H. D. Berman (Pitman, 1966)
The Stock Exchange: Its History and Functions, E. Victor Morgan (Elek Books, 1962)
Stockbroking Today, J. Dundas Hamilton (Macmillan, 1968)

Understanding the Financial Section of Your Newspaper, G. Rawcliffe (Edward Arnold, 1967)
The Stock Exchange Year Book (2 volumes) (published annually by Thomas Skinner & Co.)
Admission of Securities to Quotation, issued by authority of the Committee of the Federation
of Stock Exchanges in Gt. Britain and Ireland, and available from Stock Exchanges

JOURNAL

The Stock Exchange Journal (published quarterly on behalf of the Council of the Stock
Exchange by The Times Newspapers Ltd.)

Useful addresses

The London Stock Exchange, 54-61 Threadneedle Street, London EC 2
The Society of Investment Analysts, 21 Godliman Street, London EC 4
Wider Share Ownership Council, 4 Angel Court, London EC 2

4.3 The Bank of England and the Clearing Banks

Kenneth Fleet

The Bank of England is the central bank of the United Kingdom. As such, it has a unique place and authority in the monetary system.

The Bank is an agent of and adviser to the Government. As the Government's agent, the Bank in the final analysis has no choice other than to carry out the Government's instruction. The Bank of England Act of 1946 gave the Treasury power to issue to the Bank any direction it thinks necessary in the national interest. No direction of this kind has yet had to be given. As the Government's adviser in economic and monetary matters, the Bank is free to say what it will. Frequently, in public, the Bank expresses its thoughts and offers advice. The degree to which that advice is taken is a measure of the Bank's influence with the Government.

At certain periods the Bank's influence is strong. The ultimate exercise in Bank influence was the return to the gold standard in 1925—the high-water mark in the Governorship of Montagu Norman and a low-water mark in the development of Winston Churchill, who was then Chancellor of Exchequer.

The Bank is a practised hand with instruments of monetary policy—Bank Rate and credit control. If the Government of the day follows an active monetary policy, the Bank's influence is enhanced. The 1945–51 Labour Governments eshewed monetary policy; succeeding Conservative Governments relied on it heavily.

The Bank's influence is in the descendant; for two main reasons. The fundamental concern of all central bankers is with sound money. They believe, not without cause, that the persistent erosion of the value of money and savings is dangerous economically, morally and, in the end, politically. The Bank of England has operated in a country where for twenty-five years inflation has not been counted the major evil.

The Bank's influence is also waning because its mystique is evaporating. In his biography of Montagu Norman, Andrew Boyle describes Winston Churchill, in 1925, as, 'distinctly at a loss. What could he do but float on the underground stream of informed opinion, blindly believing in something esoteric which he could not grasp at all, and hoping that he would not in the end be confounded.'

The underground stream has now come into the open; the opinions of the Bank are freely scrutinized and analysed. The mysteries of central banking are no longer mysteries: central bankers are not blindly believed.

The scales having gone from the eyes of Treasury officials (and others), the relationship between Bank and Treasury has tilted. The Treasury now looks down at the Bank.

The Bank of England was established on 27th July 1694, specifically to provide £1·2 million for the war against France (1689-97) in return for a Royal Charter of Incorporation and an annuity of £100,000. The first bank in England capitalized by public subscription, it engaged from the beginning in normal banking business and it issued banknotes.

The Bank Charter Act of 1844 required the Bank to publish a weekly statement (the Bank Return, made up as of Wednesday night) in which the assets and liabilities of the Issue Department are stated separately from the assets and liabilities of the Banking Department. The organization of the Bank does not correspond with this division in the Bank return.

The statutory authority for the Bank is now the Bank of England Act of 1946, one of the first post-war Labour Government's nationalization measures. The capital subscribed by the Bank's stockholders (£14,553,000) was acquired by the Government and is held on the Government's behalf by the Treasury solicitor. The Bank's legal status is that of a chartered corporation with perpetual succession, a new charter having come into force simultaneously with the passing of the 1946 Act.

The Bank is managed by a Court of Directors consisting of the Governor (at present Sir Leslie O'Brien), Deputy Governor (Sir Maurice Parsons) and sixteen directors. All are appointed by the Crown, the Governor and his deputy for five years, the other directors for four. All are eligible for reappointment. The Court is barred to aliens, Ministers of the Crown, paid employees of government departments, and members of the House of Commons.

Up to four directors, in addition to the Governor and Deputy Governor, may be full-time executives. Non-executive directors are drawn from various industries and the financial community. Conventionally, there is one trade unionist, and no one who is a director of a large clearing bank. The customary retiring age is seventy.

The Court meets at least once a week, usually on Thursdays when the Bank Rate decision is posted. There are eight standing committees, of which the Committee of Treasury (nothing formally to do with Her Majesty's Treasury), as the policy and supervising committee, is the most important. The Committee of Treasury, which also meets normally once a week, consists of the Governor, his deputy, one other executive director, and four part-time directors.

The Bank is organized in departments, each sub-divided into offices dealing with different aspects of a department's work. The departments are: (1) Cashier's Department (2) Accountant's Department (3) Central Banking Information Department (4) Establishment Department (5) Secretary's Department (6) Audit Department. There is also a small number of advisers to the Governors who are not within any department.

The Chief Cashier, whose signature appears on all banknotes (printed at the Bank's own printing works in Debden, Essex), is the Bank's chief executive officer. His department is concerned with the note issue, exchange control, managing the Exchange Equalization Account (wherein lies the sterling area's gold and foreign currency reserves), and the Bank's banking operations. The Bank maintains accounts for the Government, for other banks, including banks overseas, for discount houses, for a small number of private customers (no new private accounts are opened), and for Bank Staff.

Also within the Chief Cashier's Department are:

The Discount Office, which deals with and supervises the London discount market and keeps itself informed about the financial standing of banks and other businesses;

The Loans Office, which is concerned with issuing Government loans and Treasury bills and the payment of interest to holders of government debt;

The Dealing and Accounts Office, which is responsible for operations in gold and foreign exchange;

The Exchange Control Office, which administers the control and transfer of funds and securities between residents and non-residents;

The Commodities Office, which maintains contact with the commodity markets.

The Central Banking Information Department collects and interprets current financial and economic information and is occupied with relations with the International Monetary Fund, the International Bank for Reconstruction and Development, the Bank for International Settlements, and other international organizations. The same department is responsible for the Bank's annual report (the accounting year ends on February 28/29) and the *Quarterly Bulletin*, a vehicle, part statistical, for the Bank's account of the economic and financial situation, the discussion of monetary policy, and expert articles on the Bank's and the City of London's specialized activities.

The Royal Charter of 1694 defined the Bank's object as to promote, 'the public Good and Benefit of our People'. This it endeavours to do from the head office in Threadneedle Street, London (with an overspill in a large post-war block near St Paul's Cathedral) and eight branches: in Fleet Street, London (the Law Courts branch), Birmingham, Bristol, Leeds, Liverpool, Manchester, Newcastle and Southampton. The Bank also has an office in Glasgow to help administer the Exchange Control Act in Scotland and Northern Ireland.

The Bank of England does not formally control the clearing banks but it does have sharp practical weapons to hand if its informal requests to do 'this', or refrain from doing 'that', are not met. The Bank as the traditional link with the banking community is the channel for the Government's views and requirements. The Bank of England Act authorizes the Bank to, 'request information from and make recommendations to bankers', and if the Treasury so decides, to, 'issue directions to any banker for the purpose of securing that effect is given to any such request or recommendation'.

Four-fifths of Britain's banking business is done by the eleven London clearing banks: Barclays, Midland, Lloyds, National Provincial, Westminster, Martins, District (owned by National Provincial), Williams Deacon's, Glyn Mills, (both owned by the Royal Bank of Scotland), National (predominantly an Irish Bank) and Coutts (owned by National Provincial).

In 1968, National Provincial and Westminster merged to form National Westminster, and Barclays acquired Martins.

There are five clearing banks in Scotland, of which only the Bank of Scotland is not owned or partly owned by English banks or is without English bank connections.

The two most important representative bodies are the Committee of London Bankers and the British Bankers' Association.

The primary business of the clearing, or joint stock banks is to receive, transfer and cash deposits from the public. Deposits take two main forms: current account deposits, on which no interest is paid; and deposit accounts, on which banks pay interest generally at a rate 2 per cent below Bank Rate.

Banks' deposit liabilities are matched by various kinds of asset. These fall into three broad categories:

1. liquid assets (conventionally at least 28 per cent of gross deposits): cash, loans to the London money market that are repayable at call, Treasury and other bills.
2. investments: mainly British Government and government guaranteed securities with lives of less than ten years.
3. advances to customers by way of overdraft or loan.

Advances are the banks' chief money-making asset. Traditionally, British banks prefer to advance money for short-term, self-liquidating transactions—stock in trade, property bridging operations, temporary financing of capital developments. Increasingly they are providing longer term finance, notably for export contracts and the construction of ships.

Bank advances cost most customers one or two per cent above Bank Rate. Nationalized industries borrow at Bank Rate, and exceptionally creditworthy companies half per cent over. Several banks specialize in lending to farmers.

Other services include: executor and trustee work, income tax returns and claims, investment services, remittance of money abroad, security facilities (safe deposits, night safes), and travel.

The banks' overseas services are equally comprehensive—bills of exchange, documentary credits and other methods of financing foreign trade, foreign exchange. Most leading banks have become major sources of information on overseas business in all its aspects. None is farther away than the nearest branch.

Reading list

BOOKS

Montagu Norman, Andrew Boyle (Cassell, 1967)
Committee on the Working of the Monetary System (*The Radcliffe Committee*), Command Paper 827 (H.M.S.O., 1959)
The British Banking Mechanism, W. Manning Dacey (Hutchinson, 1962)
History of the Bank of England, A. Andreades (Frank Cass, 1966)
The British Banking System—Central Office of Information, Ref. pamphlet 65 (H.M.S.O. 1968)
The Report of the Bank Rate Tribunal, Command Paper 350 (H.M.S.O. 1958)
Lord Norman, Sir Henry Clay (Macmillan, 1957)
Eight European Central Banks, the Bank for International Settlements (Allen and Unwin, 1963)

JOURNALS

Bank of England Quarterly Bulletin (issued by the Economic Intelligence Department of the Bank of England)

Useful addresses

The British Bankers' Association, 10 Lombard Street, London EC 3
The Committee of London Clearing Bankers, 10 Lombard Street, London EC 3
Banking Information Service, 10 Lombard Street, London EC 3

4.4 The Merchant Banks

Patrick Coldstream

The public seems always to have wanted to give merchant banks a special glamour not attached to other business organizations. In 1967, probably for the first time, they were described in a long television programme and seemed to emerge as a cross between kings of a financial jungle and high priests of a strikingly obscure cult. It may be exciting to believe in a fantasy world of High Finance peopled with financial figures a little larger than life, but it is unhelpful both to the merchant banks and the businessman who are, or could be, their customers. Real life is more pedestrian, and while merchant bankers aim to inspire confidence they do not want or deserve to inspire awe.

This is particularly true since the most important service the merchant banks offer is to interpret the needs of industry and the City to each other and to act as a bridge between the two. The City is a technical place, where most firms specialize in a quite narrow field; most industrial companies that want to tap the City's financial resources need some guidance in identifying precisely what their own needs are and how they might best (and especially most cheaply) be provided for. This guidance is what merchant banks provide: they act as go-between for those who want to borrow and those who want to lend, try to make City complexities plainer to those in industry whose main business is elsewhere, and to ease the path of their customers through the City by sponsoring them, underwriting their credit, and sharing some of their risks. It follows that, if merchant banks are wrongly felt to be remote from the everyday world, then they are the victims of their own romantic reputation.

The best reason for visiting a merchant bank is, in fact, to ask just what it and the City at large has to offer. No company can expect to make the best of its financial management unless it knows about the full range of choices open to it. It needs to decide, for example, whether to finance its short-term commitments by the familiar means of a bank overdraft and credit from its suppliers, or whether it might do better to cover some of them by means of an 'acceptance credit', which is less well known. A very efficient short-term money market is operated in the City by the Discount houses who regularly buy and sell, at very fine rates, bills of exchange. In order to command the finest rate the bill must bear on its face the 'acceptance', by a recognized bank, of the obligation to meet the bill at maturity. Merchant banks who provide this service are known as 'accepting houses', and once they have 'accepted' the credit risk on a bill (usually at three or six months maturity) it can then be sold at a discount on its face-value for immediate cash. The rate of discount is generally lower than the bank overdraft rate, but the accepting house charges a commission (1 per cent or a little more) for taking the risk.

This is a field where the merchant bank is not putting up its own capital (although it has a liability) but is sponsoring and accepting the credit risk. But it will also advise its clients on whether an acceptance credit is or is not, in the circumstances, the best way of meeting a need. Acceptance credits are almost always linked to the movement of goods—the credit on exports, for example, or finance for imports or the purchase of raw materials. Sometimes their total cost is below the customer's overdraft rate; sometimes slightly above it. If an accepting house thinks overdraft rates are likely to rise, it may point out the advantages to a company of arranging a credit for some months ahead at the currently going rate. It may well offer (this is common practice) a continuing acceptance facility within a certain limit.

The term of credit that British exporters need to offer their customers has been steadily lengthening. Foreign buyers of capital goods often judge competing suppliers on the deferred payment terms they are able to offer. Such arrangements often involve syndicates of both commercial banks and insurance companies. The merchant banks have built up considerable experience in organizing this type of scheme, linking buyers, sellers, and lenders together with the Export Credits Guarantee Department, and ensuring that lenders are repaid when the time comes. The merchant banks sometimes provide some of such credit themselves but, typically, their main service is in knowing where it can be found.

But the service that brings merchant banks into closest touch with industry's underlying needs and problems is that of raising long-term capital. They charge a commission on money raised, but in return for this they offer a comprehensive service: advising on the type and amount of securities to be issued, organizing those who are involved, finding the lenders, suggesting the yield to be offered, and finally relieving the company of risk by agreeing to take-up stock that is not taken elsewhere.

Thus, and again typically, a good merchant bank acts on a company's behalf as adviser, sponsor, go-between, and risk-taker; it is not itself a major provider of capital.

Merchant banks have at least as much to offer to the smaller and growing companies as they have to the very big ones. Some private companies with forward-looking managements have thought it worth while to consult a merchant bank well before they were ready to offer shares to the public, and have formed a close relationship that has been valuable to both sides. Some banks have symbolized this relationship by taking an equity stake in the company and, perhaps, lending it some money as well. Others prefer to let their smaller clients remain financially independent of them. It is for the company itself to decide what sort of connection it prefers.

The company whose shares are already quoted on the Stock Exchange has nevertheless to make the continuing series of decisions on how to ensure that it will have the supply of capital it needs in the years immediately ahead. Often, the right answer is to raise additional permanent funds in the market, and that in itself may not be a very difficult decision to make. But it raises a string of ancillary decisions that can be less straightforward but (sometimes unexpectedly to the company) can make a marked difference to its future. Loan capital is usually cheaper to service than equity, but since it is necessary to preserve a reasonable relationship between the amount of share capital and reserves and the total amount of borrowing, any debt incurred now may restrict the scope for borrowing in the future. The higher the burden of interest a company incurs, the more violently will profits for equity shareholders fluctuate with the fortunes of the company (the phenomenon of 'gearing').

What then is the best possible distribution of risk and probable earnings between the company's owners and its creditors? In their capacity as 'issuing houses' merchant banks specialize in helping companies to make up their minds on this sort of thing; in doing so they draw on everyday contact with the major investing institutions, the insurance companies and pension funds. They also suggest to their clients a range of less general and more technical questions a company ought to answer before committing itself to the market. Indeed, the quality of a bank's financial advice can be partly judged on the number of awkward questions it raises with its customers. Is it better, for example, for a company to mortgage its assets to lenders or to keep them free but accept more or less stringent limits on its borrowing thereafter? All borrowers accept some restriction on their freedom of action to assure lenders that their position will be securely maintained, but it is all too easy for a badly advised company to find its future scope inhibited to a degree it had not foreseen.

Finding answers to these questions is partly a matter of technical knowledge, partly of experience, and partly of judgement. A merchant bank adviser can generally add something to the skills a company already possesses within its own financial department. Moreover, the issuing house is obliged to take the risks of its own judgements. It must choose a price for a stock that is as cheap as possible for its customers' sake, yet attractive enough in the market to attract subscribers among the investors. Once the final agreement on the issue is signed up, the company is sure of getting its money at the agreed cost; if investors prove not to want the stock it is the issuing house that takes it up. And with the risks, issuing houses also take a good deal of the drudgery of an issue off a company's shoulders: issuing securities involves prolonged meetings with lawyers, accountants, and trustees for loan or debenture stockholders, drafting documents, and correcting proofs of small print.

It is through issuing and the giving of general financial advice that merchant banks have moved naturally into handling mergers and take-over bids. For every 'bid' situation that hits the headlines, there are many more mergers and amalgamations that are handled without fuss or much publicity by the merchant banks on a mutually agreed basis. But bids are often occasions when a company wants a financial adviser suddenly and for the first time. Merchant banks welcome the business, when it comes, and are happy to work in a hurry at short notice, but the fact remains that the quality of their advice varies with the amount of information they are given, and the financial adviser is likely to give the best guidance to a company he has had regular dealings with and knows quite well. Indeed, it can often happen that the victim of an unwanted bid could have forestalled the bid altogether if it had ordered its financial affairs better in the past.

The truth is that some companies get more than others from their professional advisers, and this is particularly true of merchant banks. Those who get the best service are not by any means always the biggest customers, but simply those who ask for it. Financial advisers expect to give advice on financial planning, in diversification policy, and acquisitions, on negotiations with Government departments and public financial bodies like the Industrial Reorganization Corporation. They can sometimes suggest take-over possibilities, or opportunities for joint ventures. Their own connections abroad can be useful to their clients.

It is a considerable step for a company to take another organization fully into its confidence, and it is one that both sides would want to take slowly. (The banker, after all, must be assured of the soundness of a company that may want to use its name.) But there can be no doubt that this is the way for a client to make the best of a merchant bank, particularly since most are prepared to give a great deal of everyday advice without charging special fees and to recompense themselves by charging a commission only if and when some major transaction takes place.

The company finance director who decides to talk to a merchant banker for the first time will find that most of them have a diverse range of other sorts of service to offer. Some have built-up research departments to back a service of portfolio management, and are taking on the management of a growing proportion of company pension funds on behalf of their clients. Some banks have special knowledge of particular parts of the world, one of Scandinavia, for example, and several of Latin America. Others have major leasing departments for those who need capital equipment but prefer to pay for the use of it by instalments as it earns its return in the business. Others, again, deal in commodities: timber, gold, insurance, or shipping.

However keen to market the services of his own organization, any merchant banker would agree that different banks suit different customers. The banks are not at all the same in the way they work, their particular strengths, their connections and special interests. Any company that is thinking of going to one of them for the first time may well find it useful, and even interesting, to talk to two or three. Accountants and company lawyers should be able to make some recommendations; other companies with City connections may be able to talk from experience. But it is an individual choice for each company. And if a merchant bank is well-organized, its directors will have time for extended discussion across the whole range of a company's financial situation. There is everything to be said against choosing financial advisers in a hurry.

Reading list

BOOKS

Merchant Banking—Practice and Prospects, George Young (Weidenfeld and Nicolson, 1966)
The Merchant Banking Arena: with Case Studies, Richard Kellett (Macmillan, 1967)
Equity Issues and the London Capital Market, A. J. Merrett, M. Howe, and G. D. Newbould (Longmans, Green, 1967)
The Role of the Merchant Banks Today, Edward Reid (Institute of Bankers, 1963)
Committee on the Working of the Monetary System (*The Radcliffe Report*), Command Paper 827 (H.M.S.O., August, 1959)

JOURNALS

'The Role of the Merchant Banker', G. Thompson (*Journal of the Royal Society of Arts*, August 1966)

Useful addresses

The Institute of Bankers, 10 Lombard Street, London EC 3
The Accepting Houses Committee, St Albans House, Goldsmith Street, London EC 2

4.5 The Insurance Market

Alan Parker

Businessmen usually think of insurance as something like electricity: something that enters into cost calculations because it is something everybody has to have but is, otherwise, simply grumbled about and paid for. Like electricity, it is commonly assumed to be a homogeneous product, sold at a fixed and inflexible price. The consumer merely chooses how much he buys, within fairly narrow limits. Insurance is something that is bought but cannot itself be seen or touched.

Nevertheless, insurance is far from being a homogeneous commodity. It is as diverse as the range of risks to which businesses and human beings are exposed in modern life. The range of insurance products is limitless. The number of suppliers is enormous. Very often the price is open to negotiation. In theory, the price of insurance is largely determined by the market, and it reflects the nature of the risk concerned. In practice, the market is not perfect. The lazy director—whose interest in his insurance is only aroused once a year when the time comes to pay his bill—is probably not buying the cover that exactly matches his needs. And he is probably paying too much.

The British insurance market consists of two interlocking parts: Lloyd's and the companies. They interlock in the sense that an insurance broker can place his client's business either with a company or with a Lloyd's underwriter, if the broker is himself a member of Lloyd's. If he is not, he would still consider the two markets, but to approach the Lloyd's underwriter he would need to go through a Lloyd's broker.

Of the two markets, Lloyd's is the older. In fact, it dates back further than the Bank of England itself. Lloyd's developed naturally out of the commercial life of London in the seventeenth and eighteenth centuries, and to a striking degree the principles underlying its operation still retain much of the flavour of that time.

Thus, Lloyd's is not a company; there is no limited liability. The main job of the committee of the Corporation of Lloyd's is to make the ground rules, to ensure that members are running their underwriting prudently and without jeopardizing the name of Lloyd's. Apart from this minimum of supervision, the underwriting members themselves accept or reject the risks. Each underwriter is accountable only to the syndicate for which he is working, the members of which share the syndicate's profits, and meet its losses. All the members of the syndicate would be members of Lloyd's, but often only in name, and they are generally known as 'names' for this reason. They consist of underwriters and brokers, who usually like to have cuts in several underwriting syndicates, and of wealthy individuals who do not actually work at Lloyd's.

All 'names' are liable for the losses of their syndicates to the full extent of their fortunes. And if a syndicate cannot meet its claims, theoretically other Lloyd's members would have to chip in. But because of the Corporation's arrangements for trust funds and deposits, the chances of such a levy are comfortably remote. In any case, to become a 'name', an outsider needs to pass a wealth test, in which he demonstrates that his fortune is at least £75,000. But despite this reliance on personal riches for its risk capital, Lloyd's still refuses to allow women ever to become 'names'. Well known 'names' include Sir Isaac Wolfson, Mr Reginald Maudling, Mr Ernest Marples, and Sir William Lyons.

Each syndicate sticks to one class of insurance. Lloyd's has traditionally been the home of marine insurance. Indeed, even today, the insurance companies, which have hogged a fair slice of all marine insurance, still have their marine underwriters operating from back rooms in the Lloyd's building. More recently it has established a strong position in the fast growing market for aviation insurance. It also covers fire, motor and general risks, and even short-term life insurance, but not long-term.

Access to the Lloyd's underwriter is through the Lloyd's broker. The broker's job is to do the best he can for his client. He will hawk the risk around the underwriters to get the cheapest rate. Normally, the risk would be split between several underwriters, with each taking a 'line'. The broker would normally try to get one of the most authoritative underwriters in that class of risk to take the first line as a 'lead'; others, and insurance company underwriters, would then be more easily persuaded to take other lines at the same rate. With a Lloyd's policy, therefore, the risk is, in fact, carved up between a number of syndicates.

This is less true when risks are underwritten by an insurance company. Since an insurance company is itself bigger than the typical underwriting syndicate, it can afford to take a larger slice of any given risk. Also, because of Lloyd's rules, Lloyd's underwriters are less free than are companies to reinsure part of their risks with other underwriters. This factor is a further limitation on the proportion of a risk the Lloyd's underwriter can take. Even if a risk is to be insured entirely with a single company, this does not dispense with the need for the broker. Not only do premium rates vary from company to company for many categories of business, but companies also vary in the way they deal with claims, in the sorts of conditions and extensions they like to attach to the cover they provide, and in the types of business in which they specialize, even while offering a comprehensive service as well. There are also many companies specializing in particular types of business—especially marine insurance—whose names would not be known to the ordinary businessman who is taking his insurances seriously.

Indeed, of the galaxy of insurance companies clustered in Britain's two insurance centres (London and Liverpool), there are a great many whose names even the broker would not need to know. These are the companies that handle only reinsurance. Nearly all insurance companies handle a certain amount of reinsurance, which is essentially risk-spreading between insurers, as distinct from within the 'portfolio' of risks of an individual company (or underwriter).

Insurance is basically a process whereby risks are spread between the insured, with each paying a share of the total estimated losses, regardless of whose ship (for example) sinks. Reinsurance is carrying the process a stage further: the insurers spread their risks among themselves. An insurer who is covering one ship worth £1 million is far more exposed to risk himself than another insurer who is insuring two ships each worth £500,000, even though the premium might be exactly the same. The first of these underwriters might, therefore, reinsure half the risk with some other insurer. In return, he might be able to persuade this other insurer to reinsure some of his risks with him. Very often, reinsurance is exchanged in this way under long-term agreements between companies. In the main, each company would be aiming to get the maximum variety of risks into its portfolio: between different types of insurance (fire, accident, etc.), different types of property insurance (houses, factories, shops, valuables, etc.), between different countries, between different types of countries (industrialized, agricultural) and so on. Reinsurance business is even exchanged across the Iron Curtain. The Soviet state insurance organization reinsures several of its risks in the London market, and likes to take a slice of British and world-wide insurance reinsured with itself in return. Thus, when a drought in Mongolia a few years ago caused the death of great numbers of sheep, Lloyd's underwriters had to cough up their portion of the loss.

In addition, there are more involved types of reinsurance, such as 'first loss', where a company reinsures for all claims of up to a certain amount, or proportion of the sum assured, keeping only the 'catastrophes' for itself, and its converse, 'stop loss', where the company reinsures for claims of more than a certain amount, but agrees to pay out claims of up to this amount. There are endless possibilities. The Jumbo Jets, now coming into service, cause a particular problem. Air insurance is a problem, anyway, because such a high proportion of the claims are 'total losses'. But the loss of a Jumbo Jet could cost insurers £20 to £30 million in one lump. And troubles seldom come singly: in 1967 for example there were three major airline disasters in a single week. To make risks of this size bearable to the industry at all, will require reinsurance on a massive scale to spread them right round the entire market, not just in London, but all over the world, on both sides of the Iron Curtain.

These complexities, fortunately for him, do not directly concern the director when he is arranging his insurances. His contact with the company would be either direct, or through an insurance broker, or through a part-time agent. Theoretically, the premium payable would be exactly the same in all three cases: the agent or broker would be remunerated by the company on a commission basis. But it is not always so simple in practice. Because of the considerable bargaining power of the large customer, it can deal direct with the insurance company, and can insist on being treated simultaneously as agent and customer.

This is known as an 'own case' agency, and means that the customer gets for himself the commission that would otherwise have been paid to the agent. So, by having an 'own case' agency, a businessman can effectively get his insurance at 10 per cent or 15 per cent off, as compared with going to an ordinary agent or broker.

The advantage of going to an agent is, usually, convenience. The agent might, for example, be the businessman's accountant, whom he would see regularly anyway and who might be more knowledgeable about insurance than the businessman himself could be bothered to be.

As with the part-time agent, the businessman does not get his commission if he deals through a broker. The advantage of the broker is the service he provides. Thus, when choosing a broker it is important to make sure that this service really will be forthcoming; the safest way is to choose a member of one of the recognized associations, or a Lloyd's broker. The broker ought to know the market thoroughly for all the types of insurance, together with all the complications of each. This is partly a matter of knowing the best terms for which a particular sort of cover can be bought, and where most cheaply; it is also a matter of knowing the best underwriter to go to for a particularly tricky risk. It is usually common knowledge in the market that such and such an underwriter (either at Lloyd's or with a particular company) has specialized in so and so and is therefore most likely to give the cover on conditions most suited to a particular customer's needs.

The broker ought, also, to be familiar himself with the ins and outs of some of the newer types of business insurance. Loss of profits insurance for example—insurance against the loss of profits that would have been earned in the year or two after a fire has destroyed the factory—is an immensely complex subject, yet there has been an enormous growth in demand for it from businessmen in the last few years.

The director needs expert advice, not only on where his cover can best be bought, but on exactly what type of cover he needs.

Another example is product insurance: the insurance against liability for claims for loss or injury arising from the malfunctioning or defectiveness of one of one's products. Obviously vulnerable are manufacturers of instruments for aircraft, and manufacturers of drugs. The general pattern is that new risks are usually pioneered on Lloyd's. As demand grows, the companies start writing the risk too, and eventually one or more of them may make a speciality of it, perhaps to a greater extent than any Lloyd's underwriter.

The broker is also supposed to keep his client's insurances under review, reminding him periodically of any obvious gaps, and when, owing to inflation, the sums assured have become out of date and insufficient. He ought also to be equipped to give detailed advice when, say, a new factory is being built. This is not just a matter of complying with the fire regulations. Often, quite small alterations in design can result in a significant saving in insurance premiums, not just once, but annually throughout the life of the factory. The large firm of brokers would probably have an expert in sprinkler installations on its staff. The broker ought also to handle the businessman's claims for him, when they occur, advising him whether the treatment he is getting from the insurer is reasonable, acting as his client's advocate if not, and, in the extreme case, advising whether legal proceedings would be worth the candle.

Finally, there is the point that the broker's goodwill is more important to the insurer than the goodwill of one individual business firm: this can be important both in getting cover and when making claims.

Even a Lloyd's underwriter will privately admit that he often has to 'support' a particular broker—to accept a risk, not on its own merits, but in the prospect of getting better risks from that broker later, in sections where competition on premium rates is less fierce.

Thus, the business firm ought to get both service and expertise from a firm of brokers. True, it would not get commission on its own insurances, as if it were its own agent, but brokers claim they can often save as much as this by shopping around the market on the businessman's behalf. Certainly, if the businessman has a serious claim, having the broker on tap, with his advice and his advocacy, ought to save him time, and possibly money as well.

For the medium-sized business, the only sensible alternative to using a broker is to establish the company's own insurance department, staffed by experienced insurance men. For most run-of-the-mill risks they might become as expert as a firm of brokers, and the business would also have the advantages of dealing with insurance companies directly, and (if it is big) using its own bargaining power to get better terms. But it would still need to go through a Lloyd's broker in order to place business with a Lloyd's underwriter. Either way the businessman needs insurance expertise, either on his own payroll, or in his broker's office. It has never been good policy to rely on the manager of the local insurance company whose duty is to his own top managers and shareholders. It will be even worse policy in future, now that insurance companies are getting increasingly professional in their whole approach to underwriting, cutting out risks that do not pay, getting others properly rated, making more use of statistics and computers. Nowadays, the businessman, as the buyer of insurance, must become equally professional.

Reading list

BOOKS

Elements of Insurance, W. A. Dinsdale (Pitman, 1958)
A Handbook to Marine Insurance, V. Dover (Witherby, 1962)
Planned Life Assurance, Martin Paterson (Business Publications, 1966)
Principles and Practice of Accident Insurance, W. A. Dinsdale (Buckley, 1960)
Insurance of Exports, H. A. Turner and V. R. Robertson (Pitman, 1966)
Consequential Loss Insurance and Claims, D. Riley (Sweet and Maxwell, 1959)
Insurance, John Gaselee (Collins Nutshell Books)
Lloyd's of London, D. E. W. Gibb (Macmillan, 1957) O.P.

Useful addresses

The Association of Insurance Brokers, 3 Hyde Park Place, London W 2
British Insurance Association, Aldemary House, Queen Street, London EC 4
The Corporation of Insurance Brokers, 15 St Helen's Place, London EC 3
Institute of London Underwriters, 40 Lime Street, London EC 3
Liverpool Underwriters Association, Derby House, Exchange Buildings, Liverpool 2
Lloyd's Insurance Brokers Association of London, London EC 3

4.6 The Commodity Markets

Colin Joynson

Of all the functions of the City of London, trading in commodities is certainly the most long-established and traditional. London was a great trading port long before it became a major financial centre, and it was in the early centuries that the City was really established as a centre of commerce. The leading London commodity traders became experts in the handling of produce for home use and export, and also participated to a large extent in re-export, or entrepot, trade between the major industrialized consumption centres and the widely-scattered primary producers. Thus, London has a centuries-old tradition in commodities trading which, indeed, has stimulated many of the other financial activities, such as insurance and banking, of the City.

Despite this honoured past, as exemplified in the history-steeped streets around Mincing Lane, which first became dominant in commodities around the end of the tenth century, the many benefits of the London Commodity Exchanges are by no means well known. And this is on the face of it surprising, especially when one considers that stock exchange dealing, which is considerably more complicated and abstract than trade in vital raw materials, is widely practised and understood.

The City of London provides facilities for dealing in almost every conceivable commodity; for example, tea, coffee, cocoa, diamonds, furs, spices, hides, skins, fishmeal, metals and metal ores can all be traded with the minimum of fuss. In some cases, the markets are highly organized, particularly the terminal markets (discussed below). In other cases, trading is a simple matter of ringing up the principal dealers in the markets concerned, or, perhaps, attending the appropriate auctions. Generally, we shall assume that those who require supplies of relatively rare items, say, spices, are already fully aware of the organization of their own particular market, so there would be very little point in going into these markets in detail. Most of the lesser markets simply consist of various middlemen, between producers and consumers, who are prepared to buy or sell the commodity in question at modest commission rates; and dealing is accomplished informally rather than via a trading floor. Bristles, for example, are auctioned at regular intervals in the City, and both brokers and consumers replenish their supplies at these public auctions according to their requirements. Sometimes the middlemen deal as principals, i.e., they actually buy for their own account and on-sell at a small profit margin, and sometimes they act as brokers, charging a commission for their expertise in finding the cheapest producer or the most generous consumer. The vast financial network of the City, covering as it does shipping, insurance, freight, warehousing, export and import financing, etc., is a necessary adjunct to the operation of these markets.

The physical process of marketing is often more informal than public. In other words, actual trading 'floors' exist only in a few cases (for example, rubber), and, even where the floors do exist, business in physicals is usually conducted side by side with terminal business. In fact, the majority of physicals are traded informally between the offices of the firms concerned, and there is no necessity to employ the trading floor, if it exists. These firms usually belong to the appropriate commodity organization that provides services such as a standard delivery contract and arbitration services.

In recent years, the trend away from organized physical markets seems to be continuing because of the relative lack of business compared with past years. This, in turn, has been caused by the following factors.

First, a considerable volume of direct trading between producers and consumers now takes place, inspired by the increased size of the modern production complexes; this, of course, causes a decline in the relative importance of a public market. Second, increasing Government intervention in commodity schemes, both on the marketing and production side, has the same effect. Third, the increasing financial capabilities of centres other than London have caused a shift in the pattern of marketing. For example, the City used to finance all the Eastern rubber trade; now, however, finance can be found from local sources, so the centre of the market has shifted to Singapore.

So far, we have considered only 'physical' markets, namely, markets where dealings take place in the actual physical commodity for a delivery date either now or in the near future. But the backbone of London commodity markets is the terminal or future markets, where commodities are traded for delivery on some future date, which may be many months ahead. At present such markets exist for wool tops, soyabean oil, sunflower seed oil, copper, lead, tin, zinc, silver, coffee, sugar, cocoa, rubber, cotton, and grains.

Futures markets carry out two main functions of price-fixing and risk-bearing, (and the problem of which came first is rather like the hen and the egg). However, in the UK at least, risk-bearing seems to have been the more important. Historically, most contracts for physical delivery were drawn up on c.i.f. terms; that is, the charges for freight and insurance to the delivery point were included in the price. Furthermore, these contracts were usually entered into before the goods were shipped, and thus the UK dealers were often 'at risk' for some months until the goods could be sold on arrival to customers. This applied particularly to the UK merchants, because of their large entrepot trade with other countries. Consequently, any market on which these risks could be insured—by selling forward—would be extremely useful. And this is precisely what a futures market provides. In addition, it aids the speculator to perform his price-fixing function without incurring delivery problems; and it provides hedging facilities to both producers and consumers.

At this stage, then, we can define a futures contract as an agreement to buy or sell a specified quantity of a specified commodity at a specified delivery date. Broadly, agreements cover those commodities that can be accurately graded, and are relatively stable in both supply and demand. Apart from price fixing, the aim of these markets is to provide an insurance against future risk. This is known as 'hedging'. The operation is still a mysterious business to many people, but in essence the principle of hedging, vital to many businesses, is extremely simple.

All that must be remembered is that the purpose of hedging is to avoid loss rather than make profits. The commodity markets are employed as price insuring mechanisms, and hedging is a procedure designed to minimize commodity marketing and processing losses that could occur if the market moved adversely. Hedges come in two varieties, the short and the long. The former implies the sale of futures contracts to offset the possible price decline in a physical commodity which, for one reason or another, has to be held by the merchant or the producer for some time. The long hedge involves a purchase of futures to offset a possible price rise in a physical commodity that has been budgeted for at a set price, but not yet purchased. In both cases, therefore, the price of the commitment is effectively 'fixed' on the futures market, and it does not matter what happens to the physical price. This assumption, while not precisely correct, is sufficiently realistic in most circumstances.

It follows that hedges are useful to a variety of people. First, any merchant or manufacturer holding stocks can insure against price declines; second a producer can similarly insure his imminent crop; third, an importer or manfacturer who has forward commitments can cover his requirements. And, furthermore, it is always simpler to obtain financing if the goods are hedged. Taking the operations of a producer as an example, what happens is that he sells futures to the extent of his impending crop; then, when he is ready to sell the actual produce, he will do so and buy back his futures contracts in order to close his position. Any loss on his crop price should be precisely reflected in his profit on the futures sales contracts. Note that he does not actually deliver against his futures sales commitments. This he can do, if his commodity is of 'tenderable' quality, and, indeed, a moment's reflection shows that the option of delivery is essential to futures markets, for otherwise they become divorced from reality. But it will usually be more convenient for him to sell to his actual outlets, thus avoiding possible shipping, storage, and grading costs, and, in consequence, obtaining his cash more rapidly. (This does lead to accusations that commodity markets are gargantuan casinos, since so few of the actual contracts entered into are consummated by physical delivery. But, as we have seen, this is unjust, since the nature of the hedge does not demand delivery on the futures markets.)

Speculation does of course exist, and indeed, is necessary. The aim of the speculator is to predict future price movements in commodities correctly, and he is willing to bear the risk of loss in the hope of making profits. Thus, he adds to the general volume of trading; and the broader the market, the more efficient it becomes. In other words, the larger the number of speculative transactions, the greater the hedging possibilities; and, ultimately, hedging is not possible at all unless a class of trader exists who is prepared to accept the risks that the hedger wishes to dispose of.

The mechanics of trading

There is nothing mysterious about commodity trading. Commodity markets, or exchanges, are organized markets on the lines of stock markets, and anyone can trade who makes the necessary arrangements with member broker firms. In the UK most commodity markets are situated in London, with certain ancillary markets in other important centres of commerce.

Generally, each commodity has its own market organization responsible for establishing the various rules and regulations governing trading, membership, etc. Most members are businessmen, engaged in producing, marketing, or processing commodities, and brokers, whose principal activity is to execute orders for their clients. Trading is normally carried out between brokers by open outcry in a convenient centre.

The actual market organization is run by a committee of (unpaid) members who are prominent in the trade, while, in addition, certain paid staff are appointed to handle administration. Further, some commodity exchange associations operate in conjunction with a clearing house that operates in a manner similar to a bank clearing house. Thus, wool tops, soyabean oil, sunflower seed oil, coffee, cocoa, and sugar are under the London Produce Clearing House, while rubber, grains, and cotton have their own organizations.

Every trading member of the exchange, who must be a member of the clearing house, must put up original deposits with the clearing house and maintain them in the event of adverse price fluctuations. At the close of the day, instead of making cash settlements with each other, brokers settle with the clearing house; and thus, in this way, brokers are protected from financial upsets in other brokerage houses, since the broker deals only with the clearing house on one side and with his client on the other. In addition, clearing houses handle all the problems involved with contracts where the holder gives notice of his intention to deliver against the contract (i.e., 'tender').

As already pointed out, the futures contract on each particular market is precisely defined as to grade; and trading is carried out for certain specified months, in a certain specified quantity or 'lot' of a convenient size. Trading is carried out by the brokers who are members of the relevant market.

Unlike their stock exchange counterparts, not all brokers deal in every commodity; some tend to specialize in one or two major commodities. Of course, even if the broker selected does not deal directly in the required commodity, he can no doubt deal with another broker who is a member. But, in the first instance, it is worth while finding a broker who deals in the selected commodity. If the client is in the trade, he can select an old-established specialist in his commodity; alternatively, however, particularly if he is a speculator, he might prefer the all-round broker who handles all commodities, can deal in all markets, and is aware of the interactions between various commodities.

For those who have no knowledge of the firms in the trade, the secretary of the market organization in the relevant commodity will be happy to provide a list of members. As mentioned above, each commodity has a separate governing group, so it is not possible, as in the case of the Stock Exchange, to contact a central authority. On the other hand, those who wish to investigate commodities further should have little difficulty in contacting the appropriate organization. Furthermore, they will find a constant stream of information regarding prices, markets, turnover, and economic and statistical information in the pages of the national press.

Having contacted the most appropriate broker, and decided upon the investment or 'hedge' to be made, the client must consider the problem of cash. And here there is a basic difference between the commodity markets and the stock market. In the latter, full cash payment for the investment is required; in the former, only a deposit, or percentage of the total commitment, is demanded. The usual figure is between 10 and 20 per cent, depending upon the commodity. Thus, for example, a purchase of the minimum contract of sugar—50 tons—at £20 per ton will involve an initial outlay of £100, not £1,000. Of course, the broker reserves the right to call for additional margin at any time if prices are moving adversely; but, as we have seen, this does not invalidate the hedge, it merely makes the financing more expensive.

Having accomplished the deal, the broker will send a contract to the client detailing what has been done, and advising the price, etc. Most commodity authorities have established minimum commission rates that members must charge non-members, but, in fact, the rate is low, seldom exceeding 1 per cent for buying and selling. Moreover, the client pays no interest charge on the difference between his margin and the full value of the quantity of the commodity represented by the futures contract. Charges can be reduced further if the client, considering that he is likely to do a large volume of business, decides to become an associate member of the relevant market. He pays a subscription for this privilege, and he must still deal through a full 'floor' member; but his commission rates are approximately halved.

If the client, having obtained his futures contract, does nothing until the delivery date, he runs the risk of having to pay full value against a warehouse receipt. Liquidation of the contract is simple. He merely sells through his broker the equivalent quantity for the same delivery date at the going price, thus offsetting his original contract. This can be done at any time within trading hours on any day, and the client will obviously know when it is appropriate. His profit, against which he may have to set off the loss on his physicals, if he is hedging, is simply the difference between his buying and selling price adjusted for fees (brokerage, and clearing house fees).

It will be apparent that commodity futures markets are fairly flexible in operation, and, moreover, that costs and the general level of statistical information compare favourably with some stock exchanges. Indeed, there is very little that cannot be accomplished in the way of trades. Selling short, for example, is often routine in hedging, and is no more difficult than opening a long position. Furthermore, since futures quotations usually run to about a year ahead, short sales can be held open for some time—an attraction to 'bearish' speculators. Apart from short sales, option dealing is common, as are arbitrage operations, not only between different centres but also between different delivery dates. Put Call and Double options operate in much the same manner as on the stock exchange, except that the costs, averaging 10 per cent p.a. of the current price, are considerably less, while the time period can run up to twelve months, or more. Spreads, or straddles, are extremely useful, not only from an arbitrage point of view but also for various other important applications such as the postponement of capital gains tax (or indeed, its reduction) and currency hedging. In addition, spreads between allied products can be extremely useful as, for example, in the US, where the major soyabean crushers often buy soyabean futures and sell futures of the two main products—oil and meal—in order to protect their profit margins. Much the same principle can be employed in wool and other markets.

Physical markets have been declining in importance in recent years, so we have devoted much of our attention to the benefits of risk-bearing provided by the highly organized terminal markets. Indeed, the latter appear to be booming at present, with new markets opened in 1967/68 covering soyabean oil and sunflower seed oil—the first new ventures since 1958—while the more traditional futures markets such as cocoa and sugar show continuous expansion, despite the increasing efforts of governments to regulate free markets. In the background, the futures markets continue to provide their essential price-fixing function, supplying free-market yardsticks to producers, consumers, merchants, and governments throughout the world.

Reading list

BOOKS

How The City Works, Oscar R. Hobson (Dickens Press, 1966)

Britain's Invisible Earnings (Chapter VI), Report of the Committee on Invisible Exports (British National Export Council, 1967)

The London Commodity Exchange (London Commodity Exchange, Plantation House, Mincing Lane, London EC 3)

Joynsons Futures Handbook & Commodity Guides (G. W. Joynson & Co. Ltd., 52 Cornhill, London EC 3)

Useful addresses

London Commodity Exchange, Plantation House, Mincing Lane, London EC 3

The London Commodity Exchanges:

London Metal Exchange, 1 Metal Exchange Buildings, Whittington Avenue, London EC 3

Corn Exchange, Mark Lane, London EC 3

The United Terminal Sugar Market Association, Plantation House, Mincing Lane, London EC 3

London Cocoa Terminal Market Association, Dunster House, Mincing Lane, London EC 3

London Copra Association, Audrey House, 5-7 Houndsditch, London EC 3

The General Produce Brokers' Association of London, Plantation House, Mincing Lane, London EC 3

The Coffee Terminal Market Association of London, Plantation House, Mincing Lane, London EC 3

The London Jute Association, 69 Cannon Street, London EC 4

The Rubber Growers' Trade Association of London, Plantation House, Mincing Lane, London EC 3

The London Shellac Trade Association, Plantation House, Mincing Lane, London EC 3

London Vegetable Oil Terminal Market Association, Dunster House, Mincing Lane, London EC 3

London Wool Terminal Market Association, Plantation House, Mincing Lane, London EC 3

4.7 The City Associations

C. Gordon Tether

The Finance Houses Association is the most important of the bodies representing financial institutions engaged primarily in instalment credit activity, and such modern variations of it as industrial leasing. It was founded in its original form shortly after the Second World War to provide the dozen or so largest hire purchase finance houses with a forum for discussion of matters of common interest. With the subsequent rapid growth of the hire purchase activity, it began to assume wider responsibilities. From the late 1950s these included the supervision—in the interests of preserving the industry's good name—of interest rates charged by members to the public, and commissions paid to motor vehicle dealers for introducing business, until such discipline was deemed to be against the public interest by the Restrictive Practices Court.

In 1965 the association was merged with the Industrial Bankers Association, a body that had been formed in 1957 to assist the advancement of medium-sized hire purchase finance houses. The necessary change in entry rules and the withdrawal, a little earlier, of the behaviour rules, brought in finance houses that had previously been outside both associations, and membership rose sharply. By the beginning of 1968 it comprised some 40 groups controlling about 110 companies.

Under the revised rules the association will normally consider granting membership to companies with a minimum of £200,000 of paid-up share capital and reserves; a lower figure will be accepted only in special circumstances. Since the association is concerned with the maintenance of high standards of conduct among finance houses, companies applying for membership are subject to a careful examination embracing balance-sheet structure, business record, and management experience.

The main role of the association is to protect finance houses engaged in instalment financing, including hire purchase, credit sales, and industrial leasing. The measure of the responsibility it shoulders on this account and the power it wields may be gauged from the fact that its members transacted some five-sixths of all instalment credit business handled by finance houses in 1967, and, roughly, a half of all such activity, most of the balance being arranged by department stores and retailers out of their own resources or with money obtained outside the FHA.

In its protective role, the association is primarily concerned with providing the finance houses section of the instalment credit industry with collective representation in negotiations with the authorities on all aspects of government policy affecting its interests. This relates not only to the methods the authorities employ to influence the behaviour of the volume of instalment credit business, but also to all legislation proposals that would materially affect such activity. The association may submit proposals for new legislation when existing arrangements are considered to be inadequate. To assist it with this side of its work, the association maintains close links with official and other bodies most closely concerned with instalment credit, notably the Board of Trade and the Bank of England. Close contact is also maintained with the Lord Chancellor's Department on such matters as the smooth working of Court procedure in relation to instalment credit cases.

The association's second principal function is to see that members are kept informed about new legislation and legal decisions that affect their interests, and to provide them with guidance where appropriate. Such overall guidance does not now extend to policies to be followed in dealings with the public, but it does cover such other matters as education, staff training, credit information, and money transfer. In addition, the association is ready to assist members on an individual basis with their legal, financial, and other problems. As part of this service, the association maintains a credit register wherein details of credit made available to large customers are recorded as well as a register of retailers to whom advances have been made for stocking purposes, the purposes of both mechanisms being to prevent members being exposed to bad debts through excessive growth of multiple indebtedness.

The association also keeps the public informed about the industry through the press and broadcast service, and in other ways.

Meetings of all members of the association are held twice a year but control resides in the hands of a management committee consisting of sixteen persons elected by members and presided over by a chairman who holds office for two years. Day-to-day administration is in the hands of a Director-Secretary. Much of the work of the association is carried out by specialist sub-committees.

Since it was reconstituted and its base broadened, the Association has come to be recognized as competent to represent the finance houses section of the hire purchase instalment credit industry by the authorities and the business world. Its public image has at the same time been greatly improved by evidence that it is adopting a more enlightened attitude to hire purchase problems than it did up to the beginning of the 1960s.

Hire Purchase Trade Association

The Hire Purchase Trade Association's work overlaps that of the Finance Houses Association but it is to a large extent a complementary organization. Membership is much wider, all concerns operating in the instalment credit field, down to the smallest retailer, being eligible. The Association covers the same ground as the FHA in that it both makes representations to the authorities on legislation and similar matters bearing on instalment credit activity and keeps members informed about the implications of new legislation or similar developments for their business. It is complementary to that of FHA in that it acts as a supplier of contract forms and other specialized stationery needed by members, and runs, in conjunction with other organizations, registers covering the instalment credit activities of the general public for the purpose of limiting access to members facilities by customers with bad credit records.

The Association is supervised by a council presided over by a chairman and vice-chairman. The day-to-day conduct of its affairs is in the hands of the secretary and his staff.

Accepting Houses Committee

The Accepting Houses Committee is one of the oldest associations on the British financial scene. It is also among the most conservative, there having been little change either in its membership or in its basic form since it was set up in 1914.

Its purpose today is still primarily what it was when it was established: to provide a mechanism for the exchange of information and other forms of collaboration between merchant banks of substance who have a major interest in international financing activities that hinge on the use of acceptance credit (the facility that enables traders to finance their activities more easily and cheaply by getting their paper endorsed by a banking house of standing). The number of members at the beginning of 1968, sixteen, was close to the original figure, and comprised, with only a few exceptions, the founders.

As this implies, the privilege of membership is jealously guarded. Only those houses whose paper is considered eligible for re-discount at the Bank of England may belong, and, as the Bank is prepared to grant this facility only to companies that can demonstrate they are of the highest standing, this hurdle is not easily surmounted.

278

Moreover, it is not the only one that confronts would-be members. Thus, some merchant banks that have developed an active business in international acceptance credit in the half-century since the Committee came into being have been denied membership (even though their paper had qualified for re-discounting at the Bank of England) for such apparent reasons as lack of size and inability to show a sufficient emphasis on acceptance credit business in their activities viewed as a whole.

The Committee's executive is composed of one senior director drawn from each of the member companies. In earlier times, each of the houses provided the chairman on a rotation basis for a period of two years, but Sir Edward Reid had served as chairman for some twenty years before he retired at the end of 1966.

The Committee's collaboration function falls into two parts. One relates to the exchange of information and views on matters affecting international financial business in a general way, such as the credit-worthiness of other countries and their financial institutions, dual taxation systems and so on. The second part is concerned with acting as a negotiating body for members in matters touching their collective interests. These may involve company law, monetary policy, exchange control, capital issue restrictions and may often involve the association in discussions with government departments, the Bank of England, and other financial bodies.

Despite its insistence on jealously guarding its good name, the Committee does not attempt to influence the behaviour of houses already in the club. The exception to this rule arises in respect of the commissions charged for accepting customers' paper, all members being required to conform to agreed minimum figures.

The continuing growth of London's importance as an international financial centre during the 1960s, despite the £'s proneness to crisis, has added to the importance of the Committee's role. So has the increasing tendency for the authorities to rely on directives issued through the Bank of England for achieving suitable control over credit-creation by London banking houses. In considering, however, the Committee's significance, it has to be noted that some of the merchant banks now prominent in the international financial field are not members of the Committee and yet have an importance far outweighing that of a number of its less weighty members.

Issuing Houses Association

Just as the Accepting Houses Committee provides a collaboration machinery for merchant banks with a particularly strong interest in short-term international finance, so does the Issuing Houses Association for merchant banks, and similar institutions, specializing in capital market activities of a longer-term character. It is, however, a younger body, dating only from 1946, and a far less closely-knit organization.

At the beginning of 1968 it had close to five dozen members, all domiciled in Britain (though in some cases having overseas offshoots located mostly in the

Commonwealth). Many of the members engage in such other business as banking, accepting house activity, and investment trust management but the Association is concerned with their activities only in their capacity as issuing houses. All institutions engaged in capital issue business are eligible for membership provided they can show they would be worthy of the Association's badge, which means, in practice, that the Association has nothing of the exclusiveness associated with the Accepting Houses Committee. It is governed by an executive committee of ten, elected by members with the broad intention of ensuring that the interests of houses of varying size are taken care of. The chairman of the committee is appointed from among the members and normally serves for a two-year term. The Committee has a small staff handling day-to-day affairs under the supervision of its secretary.

The Association's main function is to serve as a negotiating body for the capital issue industry in matters affecting its interests. This in the main entails dealing with government departments, the Bank of England, and the Stock Exchange, the subjects with which it is usually most concerned being the repercussions on new issue activity of Budgetary developments, monetary policy and exchange control, and Stock Exchange procedures in relation to commissions on security transactions and similar matters.

Under its rules, the Association cannot 'fetter, prescribe, or regulate' the manner in which members carry on their businesses. But the friction generated in recent years in the City by take-over battles between major industrial and commercial firms and in which issuing houses, acting in their capacity of advisers on capital reorganization to the firms concerned, have been found on opposing sides, has resulted in the Association being driven to play an important part in evolving a code of behaviour for members engaged in such activities. To this end, it took steps, in 1967, to work out a suitable code, and arranged for the Bank of England to take the lead in establishing the necessary policing arrangements by creating a special panel with supervisory powers.

Though reluctantly taken, the Association's decision to accept certain responsibilities in relation to the conduct of its members has added materially to the importance of its roles. Working in the same direction has been the considerable increase in recent years in the amount of business moving to issuing houses as a result of the expansion, consolidation, and reorganization of British industry, and from the growth of international financial traffic through London on account of the City's extensive participation in the development of the market in Euro-currency loans. So, too, has been the wider official use for promoting economic policy of restrictions on capital exports and the directive form of control over domestic financing activity.

Instalment Credit Industry

This is a section of the British financial system that has come to play a much more important part in the financing of domestic activity in the post-war period, its total lendings having been equivalent, in the 1960s to about a quarter of those of the commercial banks. The main concern of the industry is with meeting the increasing demand from the general public for deferred payments facilities for backing purchases of motor vehicles and other consumer durables. But it has, of late, also participated to a growing extent in the work of financing the capital development of industrial and commercial companies.

In earlier times, almost half the industry's business was in the hands of department stores and other retail trading concerns. But more recently it has come to be dominated by specialist finance houses, which were responsible for some two-thirds of all activity in the 1966–67 period. These institutions were for the most part wholly independent until the late 1950s. About 1957, however, the banking system, taking the view that competition for lending business stemming from industry's rapid growth could be most effectively tackled by securing a substantial stake in its ownership, partly or wholly acquired houses that accounted for, roughly, half its annual turnover. However, the banks almost invariably insisted on keeping their new interests functioning as separate entities, and the suggestion, in the 1967 report on banking, by the Prices and Incomes Board, that they would do better to integrate such activities, met with strong resistance.

The banking invasion was initially followed by a period of unusually rapid expansion. But excessive competition for dealer custom brought about a steep rise in the incidence of bad debts. The restraining effect on growth of the ensuing reorganization was underlined by the tendency for official disinflationary measures to fall with particular force on lending for financing consumer goods purchases. So, though the loans total continued to grow during much of the 1960s, it represented a materially smaller percentage of bank lending in the second half of the 1960s than it did in the first half. Although American experience suggests that there is still considerable room for further growth in the long-term, the short-term outlook is uncertain in 1967–68, at least in view of the emphasis being placed on consumer credit restraint by the Government's thinking on economic rehabilitation.

Much of the industry's business still takes the traditional form of hire purchase. But the wider interest it is taking in lending to business concerns, and the accompanying search for ways of overcoming official policy deterrents to consumer credit creation, have in recent years brought a marked switch to other forms of lending, such as equipment leasing and personal loans. So far as the mobilization of lending resources is concerned, the emphasis is still on borrowing from the banks. But much more use is being made of other methods, including that of borrowing short-term foreign balances in the money market.

Many of the bigger finance houses have in recent years forged links with companies engaged in similar business in other advanced countries. They, and most of the medium-sized concerns, are members of the Finance Houses Association, while most

281

finance houses of substance, and retail trading establishments providing consumer credit facilities, belong to the Hire Purchase Trade Association.

Reading list

BOOKS

Hire Purchase in a Free Society, Harris, Naylor and Seldon (Hutchinson for The Institute of Economic Affairs, Third Revised Edition, 1961)
British Issuing Houses (Issuing House Association, 1965)
Background to Service (a booklet on the history of the Hire Purchase Association), (Hire Purchase Trade Association)

JOURNALS

'Credit', Quarterly Review of the Finance Houses Association
'What the Merchant Bank Does', The Accountant's Magazine (Journal of the Institute of Chartered Accountants of Scotland), December 1967

Useful addresses

Accepting Houses Committee, St Albans House, Goldsmith Street, London EC 2
Finance Houses Association, 14 Queen Anne's Gate, London SW 1
Hire Purchase Trade Association, 3 Berners Street, London W 1
Industrial Bankers Association (incorporated with Finance Houses Association), 14 Queen Anne's Gate, London SW 1
Issuing Houses Association, St Albans House, Goldsmith Street, London EC 2

4.8 Factoring

Peter Hobday

Factoring came across the Atlantic to Britain about ten years ago, and in that short time several misconceptions have arisen about its role in industry. Directors have been worried about losing control of their businesses, or that their bank managers would reduce their overdrafts if they used the service. Some believe that factoring is another word for debt collecting, and if used openly could frighten customers away. It has also been said that factoring is an expensive way of increasing a firm's available cash. Some companies would say that they are too big for factors; the majority would say they are too small. Many have never heard of it. But factoring is here to stay. Already, there are some impressive case histories of its success.

Factoring is a very simple concept. A factor assumes all responsibility for collecting money, for 100 per cent of the credit risk, and, as an added service, takes over the whole complicated business of book-keeping. By and large, the fee for all this is between $\frac{3}{4}$ and 2 per cent of turnover, and in addition, of course, there is a charge of up to 2 per cent over Bank Rate for funds generated through the initial payment made to the client in advance of settlement to the factor by the client's customers. This is calculated on a day-to-day basis, much like overdraft facilities. In short, the factor buys a company's book debts and finally collects payment from a buyer without recourse to the seller. That, as far as the majority is concerned, is 'true' factoring. There is a minority view, namely, that a factor can have recourse to a seller if a debt goes sour on him. This division between 'recourse' and 'non-recourse' factoring has

283

been one of the talking points of the industry until recently. In some ways, this has been a hindrance to factoring companies in getting their message across to board-rooms. Nowadays this is less of a division, and often the final form of a factoring agreement will depend on what seems best suited to each individual case.

All this underlines the fact that any company considering factoring should 'shop around' before deciding. This is a young service industry, and it has not as yet evolved specialized fields of operation, although this is coming. Already, some factors are known for the service they provide; others for the industries to which they have limited their sphere of operations. But as each begins to build up what might be called a 'personality' of its own, there is much room for manoeuvre, and intending clients may be surprised at the flexibility of most factors in accommodating the particular problems of their customers.

All factors claim that one of the immediate results of using their services is that a firm achieves a quicker flow of cash and, therefore, a higher rate of turnover. No director needs to be reminded that the reluctance of some firms to pay their bills is a hindrance to growth, particularly for a small to medium-sized concern. The factors can argue persuasively on this point. A steady flow of cash into a firm rather than a build-up of book debts improves the firm's liquidity position, thus providing more available capital for growth. In short, book debts have been turned into cash, without borrowing.

Some directors may see dangers in this. What, they will wonder, will be the reaction of their usual sources of finance, principally their bank manager? Will he ask for the overdraft to be reduced immediately? In the early days, this could have been a problem, but the banks nowadays understand more clearly the need for factoring. In 1968, two of the big five, the National Provincial and Lloyds took con-trolling interests, via subsidiaries, in two of the leading factoring firms. The banks, like the factors, would now argue that their services are complementary. They have a mutual interest in seeing a good firm grow.

Another worry is whether by selling one's sales ledger debts to a factor, a firm loses control over its marketing operation. The factors contend, again with some justification, that as long as a company's clients are creditworthy there is no inter-ference. If they are not creditworthy, then the firm should not be selling to them in the first place.

It is when one gets into this side of factoring that the service aspect, as opposed to the purely financial aspect, becomes attractive. For a fixed and agreed cost, the factors will take over much of the accounting function and, in the long run, save their clients time, worry, and money on book-keeping, legal fees, and other out-of-pocket expenses such as annual credit insurance premiums, bad debt losses, and the costs of the services of credit agencies.

The factors also claim that they can be of immense help on the export front. Factors have been spreading the gospel of factoring throughout Europe. The advantage here, apart, once again, from the purely financial aspect, is the credit check on a customer whom one might never have met. The local factoring firm, in the export market, will know or be able to find out the financial standing of a company. This information will be relayed back to the office whence the export is being made. It is all part of the service, say the factors, and when it comes to foreign markets a very comforting one, it would seem.

Despite some early setbacks, factoring has been growing slowly but steadily over the past few years in Britain. At present, turnover is about £100 million a year, which is still only a small amount in the total credit and financial structure of the country. Four hundred companies at most are being factored today. However, the factors are confidently predicting a growth in turnover of at least £500 million by 1972. Yet, even if they are right in their prediction, this will still be less than a quarter of the current annual turnover of factoring carried out in the United States. In 1967 it reached £3,500 million, and it is expected to grow even further. Of course, the sheer size of the American market accounts for much of this. Selling goods across the United States is like selling all over Europe, and one of the main attractions of factoring for Americans is that credit rating over such distances is a hazardous and costly operation. Apart from this, constant growth is the first rule of business to the average American so that he has been quicker to see the potentialities of factoring.

Factoring must not be confused with debt collecting or invoice discounting, both well-established and vital ingredients in the financial structure of the country. It claims to provide much more than either of these, and indeed it does. To any objective observer it would seem to be a service at least worth considering by any growing concern that finds itself short of capital. Equity in the firm can be sold to raise the money, but, in the process, this means some weakening of control. One of the factoring companies has worked out a fictional example of how they, as factors, could help in this context.

The directors of a small company with a turnover of £100,000 a year want to expand to a turnover of £200,000 over, say, two years. For the purpose of the example, it is assumed that further permanent or semi-permanent facilities are not available from its bankers. The company's profit is £10,000. At this size, it is probably a private company and will therefore be worth about three times its net profit before tax, i.e., £30,000. To achieve this required expansion, the directors compute that it will require a capital inflow of £15,000. If this were raised through a sale of the equity, shareholders may have to relinquish 50 per cent of their holdings, and, therefore, 50 per cent of the net profits.

Factoring could allow the company to realize up to 80 per cent of the value of its book debts, which are likely to be of the order of £20,000 in a company with a turnover of £100,000. Thus, the necessary £15,000 could be had without control of the company changing hands and with a subsequent increase in profit distribution to original shareholders.

The cost of the operation would, at first, be about £3,000, and by the time the company had achieved its target of doubling turnover, this would be about £4,500—in the long run a cheap price to pay for keeping control of the company and enjoying the fruits of its success.

Factoring should never be considered as a last resort of financing. Factors, like consultants of any sort, should be brought in early on, and the association allowed to grow as the company grows. Factors can keep a firm's financial position healthy; they cannot come up with a miracle cure if the patient is really ill.

As yet, there is no association of factoring companies from whom independent advice can be obtained, nor a list of names from which to choose. This may yet come, as the factoring business grows and multiplies.

Reading list

JOURNALS

'Who's Who in Factoring', Victoria Brittain (*Times Review of Industry*, July 1967)
'Seven Fat Years for the Factors?', Peter Hobday (*The Director*, May 1967)
'Factoring', A. G. Stoke (*The Chartered Secretary*, August/September 1967)
'Factoring—a Tonic for Tired Capital', Dennis A. Young (*Westminster Review*, October 1967)
'Is a Factor in Your Favour?', Nigel Farrow (*Business Management*, July 1967)

5. Recruitment and Training

5.1 Recruiting and Training Executives

Leslie Coulthard

Every director has 'people problems'

In an age of increasing specialization, it is inevitable that the majority of directors in British industry and commerce will have arrived in the boardroom via one or other of the specialist functions.

Trained and developed as an accountant, a production man or a marketing expert, the specialist on his way to the top has to convert into a 'generalist'. Exceptions to this, of course, are the *entrepreneurs*—the Jack Cohens of the supermarket world and the Joe Hymans of the textile industry—who start off doing everything themselves and develop as generalists from square one. For the rest of us, however, the problem remains: how to gain the necessary experience in other management fields to operate successfully at board level?

As individuals, we rarely sit down to work out exactly how we spend our time, but it is a salutary exercise. A recent analysis of the way some of my friends at the top of major companies spend their working week proved of very great interest to them and to me. It emerged that between one third and one half of the time they spend running their businesses is concerned with what we could collectively call 'people problems'.

Many chief executives and directors do not realize how much time they devote to the personnel function and, therefore, do not study it as much as they need to do, whereas others do not give it enough time at all, with dire results.

Having determined the company's objectives, the board's first executive task is to recruit people for all levels within an effective organization structure designed to achieve such objectives. This involves:

(a) The selection of people with adequate skills and calibre, their training, development and deployment.
(b) Influencing the morale and tone of the company by good human relations and industrial relations, the creation of sound communications, and suitable conditions in which people are encouraged to work effectively.
(c) Blending together an effective team to manage the company successfully today, and to ensure its management in the future.

From the smallest private business to the largest multi-product corporation, these are vital problems occupying time at the top level. As organizations grow, such problems assume greater importance. Lord Robens who, as Chairman of the National Coal Board with 500,000 people on his payroll, is one of Britain's biggest employers, agrees that 'people problems' occupy the major part of his time. People, he maintains, are the real attraction of his job. Since he could certainly double or quadruple his earnings by moving into private business, we must accept his word for this motivation.

The larger the organization, the greater the need for specialists to handle financial, production, personnel, marketing, and technical problems and the more the chief executive needs to delegate, organize, and co-ordinate. Delegation presupposes that the team is composed of men of adequate calibre and ability, doing jobs they understand, for which they have received suitable training and development. It requires them to be organized effectively and motivated successfully to optimize effort as a cohesive team capable of achieving the company's objectives. Given that directors, and particularly managing directors, have the prime function of policy-makers, it is apparent that the subsequent decisions flow more readily in a company that is well organized, adequately manned, and suitably motivated.

Recruitment of executives and directors

There are two obvious approaches to a company's recruitment policy—the 'grow your own' and 'recruit the ready-made' policies. Some organizations stick rigidly to one or the other, but most tend to have a policy that is a mixture of the two.

The first approach involves finding the right raw material and 'growing your own' management for future needs. Such a policy is followed by Shell, ICI, Unilever, and Procter and Gamble, among the largest and most successful companies in the UK. It is rare indeed to find any of these big four resorting to the alternative of recruiting ready-made executives.

Some firms are simply not large enough to run their own management development schemes, whereas others simply prefer to let other firms do so, and then buy their management 'ready-made'.

The existence of expensive management training programmes, together with first-class personnel policies, are sometimes necessary attractions to good-quality raw material in the first place. Having attracted this material, companies go out of their way to retain it by policies of 'promotion from within', superior side benefits, and sophisticated salary policies.

Firms buying their management ready made, gain by introducing new blood and new ideas, but usually need to offer higher-than-average salaries, and they are faced with high pension premiums. The major risks, of course, are that the man who is successful in one environment may not succeed in another team with the peculiarities of its organization and overall policies. External recruitment to fill senior vacancies can also be bad for morale and lead to the departure of up-and-coming junior managers.

Before embarking on any recruitment exercise, it is wise to look closely at both current needs and available people within the company. It is also desirable to project the company's organization forward and to look to see whether the requisite skills will be available to cope with future needs one, five, and ten years ahead.

Expansion plans, diversification exercises, changing technologies, new products, different markets: all will influence the type of managerial skills that will be required in the short and long term. An audit of the present skills, abilities and potential of your existing staff must be superimposed on such short- and long-term organization structures. Only in this way is it possible to assess the real needs—current, short and long term—in terms of manpower, managerial, staff, and operatives.

Given that a thorough review of the company's available managerial potential reveals the need to recruit, it may be timely to look at the company's existing selection methods and your own interviewing technique. Before doing so, however, let us put this exercise into perspective by looking at the costs of failure in selection.

Failure is expensive, whether you pick the wrong man who turns out to be incompetent, or your choice is a good man who turns out to be incompatible. Either way, whether you subsequently have to fire him or he resigns, bad selection is expensive.

How much does it cost to have a change of executive resulting from a termination or a resignation? Given an idea of this cost, real and hidden, we might find good reasons for tightening up our selection procedures. An ineffective marketing director, whose contribution declines for twelve months before you finally decide to fire him, may cost you tens of thousands of pounds. Remember, it is not simply the three months or six months salary in lieu of notice, but many other items that are involved: an advertising appropriation badly spent,
increased labour turnover in the sales force,

territories unmanned or badly covered,

drop in sales volume,

rise in costs,

competition taking advantage of your weaknesses.

Depending on the speed with which you stop the rot, we may be talking in terms of £50,000 or even £250,000 in many medium-sized companies before remedial action is taken. Putting the matter right is not inexpensive either. Apart from the costs of advertising for his replacement and the managing director's time in interviewing candidates, it may be several months before the newcomer can really achieve full effectiveness in the job.

Bad selection costs money and before you embark on another similar exercise, some careful re-examination is advisable.

Company selection procedures

Few employers would ever regard themselves as bad employers, and yet reputations vary enormously in this respect. What is your company's reputation as an employer? Ask yourself this question, but, also, ask some of your friends outside. Your reputation has many facets. Naturally, the more successful and the more profitable your operation, the better. But people seeking a new job and a new career are looking for other things as well. Are you well known for your good personnel and industrial relations policies? Are you looked upon as a 'hire and fire outfit'? Or an unhappy ship? Is it well known that your training schemes and development programmes are well conceived and effective? Are your pay policies, pensions, and fringe benefits comparable with those of your competitors, locally and nationally? Are working conditions good?

A company's image is of vital importance in attracting people of the right calibre. Walk into your offices one day with your eyes wide open. Assume you have never set foot in the place before and look at your company through the eyes of a prospective recruit. What do you see? I suspect many of you will be shattered. The dingy reception area; the cigarette-smoking receptionist; the surly commissionaire; the filthy waiting room with ashtrays piled high. Is this the impression you like to give to your prospective recruit?

Remember that *selection is a two-way process*. You are out to pick the best employee. The applicant, for his part, is looking for the best company that can offer him the right career. First impressions count. I have heard of many excellent candidates turning away without waiting to be interviewed, on the assumption that if the firm is slipshod in superficial things, the organization is probably not for them.

Every company has its own method of dealing with the selection of management, depending on the status of the Personnel Department. Sometimes, preliminary sifting occurs here, and suitable candidates are then passed on to departmental executives.

In many companies, however, divisional and departmental managers or directors carry out their own interviewing from scratch and only need to obtain Board approval for certain key appointments.

Other organizations select second and third-line management by carrying out panel interviews, where a committee of directors and senior management see candidates together. The proponents of this method claim certain advantages—that everyone involved in the final decision sees the candidate in the same circumstances, hears his answers, and watches his reactions to the same series of questions—but the system leaves much to be desired.

My own view is that at the initial selection stage at any rate, interviews should be carried out individually, with those involved in the decision taking part in a carefully planned programme. The programme should set out to avoid repeating the same questions, each interviewer undertaking to probe in depth one or more specific areas of the man's background, training, and experience. In this way, considerably more ground can be covered and in greater overall depth, than in the panel interview. A post-mortem meeting follows at which each member of the interviewing team, in order of seniority, offers his view of the man and gives his assessment. (The team should report in ascending order of seniority . . . for obvious reasons!) Such team post-mortems usually end with a vote as to whether the man should be hired or not, or seen again. Remember that the manager, to whom the newcomer will be responsible, needs to convince himself that he is getting a good recruit. He should never be able to turn round in the future and say, 'I was not in favour of hiring him in the first place'.

The more senior and crucial the appointment, the less often are we able to take a decision on the strength of one interview or series of interviews on a single day. Frequently, both the company and the man need to give the matter further thought, and a second or even a third session may be necessary.

Selection methods for directors

Often, the most crucial appointments within your company are those immediately below the Board or, occasionally, direct into the boardroom. In such cases, the chief executive himself may need to carry out all the preliminary work personally since it is often impossible to delegate the preliminary work to the personnel manager or boardroom colleagues.

Finding a first-class man is like looking for a needle in a haystack: before we start, it is useful to know what we need the needle for, and we should be able to recognize the needle when we find it.

Before looking for the right man, be sure you know enough about the job you want him to tackle. Get agreement from all concerned on the definition of the task to be given to the newcomer. In only 10 per cent of British companies can one find the job descriptions that simplify enormously the job of recruitment, as well as improving management organization. If your company does not have such descriptions, may I suggest that on the occasion of the next senior post recruitment, the exercise should begin by drawing up a full job description. This will include such details as:

To whom the job is responsible; and for what?
How many staff in what organization structure are responsible to the man?
What are the limits of his responsibility and authority—for finance, people, assets, and functions?
Is the situation likely to change in the immediate future, and call for a redistribution of responsibilities?

These questions will give rise to many others, and at the end of such a preliminary exercise, the size, shape and scope of the task, both now and in the immediate future, will be better understood.

Next, let us attempt to specify the ideal man to fill this appointment. What is the *ideal age bracket* to fit into the existing company structure and into the future management succession plan? It is naturally undesirable to recruit a No. 2 aged sixty to work under a No. 1 aged sixty-four, unless we are planning to develop the No. 3 within the next few years as the ultimate replacement for the No. 1.

Next examine the *educational, professional, and technical education and training* that are desirable in the new recruit. Here, one must warn that when specifying minimum requirements, it is essential to avoid over-egging the specification. Far too often companies employ a PhD, say, on work that is well below his capability; as a result, they soon lose a perfectly good man because he is underemployed.

The next step is to decide on the type and depth of *experience* to be called for in the candidate. What does he need to know? Does he need particular expertise and experience in your industry? in a particular product area? in certain management techniques?

Having sketched the ideal man, the next most important question is: Where is he now? What sort of firm is he in? What job is he holding? This is going a long way in the right direction towards the man you want. If you can establish where such timber grows, where you will find such people, you are well on the way to establishing:

(a) How to set about attracting him by your advertisement or other means of making contact?
(b) How much you need to pay to attract him?

Assuming that your old-boy net does not provide the answer, and you wish to carry out the recruitment yourself, advertising is the next step. Before dashing off a few words of copy to the local newspaper, more thought will pay dividends; perusal of the appointments columns will confirm that many employers fail to understand the purpose of their advertisement. Far too many fail to establish their basic requirements in the announcement; even more just do not understand that the prime reason for advertising is to attract suitable candidates with whom they can begin to negotiate.

To attract the right man, your advertisement must be based on an awareness of *what he wants to know*. The right man is not necessarily unemployed or about to be fired and scrambling for a job to keep his bank manager happy. The chances are that he is seeking a logical extension of his career pattern and may need to be persuaded, even at this early stage, that your proposition is worth investigating. Thus, tell him what the job is, the scope, and the future. Where you need to remain anonymous, give enough clues about location, industry, size and scope of both the company and the job to spark off his imagination. Above all, indicate the size and responsibility involved by quoting the terms and conditions of employment. It will save you time and energy to indicate these items more precisely than by using ambiguous terms like: 'General Manager required—four figure salary'.

Assume, however, that your advertising or other sources of candidates have provided you with an interviewing programme. By meticulously prompt correspondence and personally worded invitations you have persuaded the right, or possibly right, candidates to come along. Unfortunately, the pack is well shuffled and the few possibles will be mixed up with many less acceptable people. What next?

The interview

Having witnessed many interviews over the years, I make no apology for repeating the maxim '*Selection is a Two-way Process*'. Remember that, although we hope that the right man is on your interviewing programme, he is not immediately recognizable, and that he is looking and listening as carefully as you are. He is trying to decide whether he wants to join you and whether the job you are offering is, in all respects, in line with his career plan. The interview then has two aims:

1. to decide which is the right man, and
2. to ensure that he agrees that the job is right for him.

Everything must be geared to these two targets simultaneously. Every candidate must be treated as if he may be the right man. Each interview must, therefore, follow a similar pattern.

The whole aim of the interview from the interviewer's standpoint is to obtain enough evidence, enough facts on which the selection decision can be taken. In a nutshell, this means obtaining enough information about the man's past and current performance to judge:

(a) whether or not he will fit into your organization.
(b) whether he has the necessary ability and potential to carry out the task you have in mind, and
(c) whether he will go on developing to fill future needs.

We need to extract facts first, to establish the outline of the man, and then subsequently clothe those facts with opinions about his strengths, weaknesses, and motivation. In seeking evidence of motivation, the most important word in the interviewer's vocabulary is '*why?*'.

'Why did you join the RAF rather than the Army?'
'Why did you fail that examination?'
'Why did you move on to the A. B. C. Company?'
'Why are you interested in joining us?'
'Why do you want to leave your present company?'
'Why do you feel you are now ready for a bigger job?'
and so on.

In the course of your interview you are seeking facts about the total man. These will include, if you are thorough, the details of his family background, his education, academic attainments, career history, what companies he has been employed by, what tasks he carried out, what training and experience he gained. From this outline you should obtain a good deal of evidence of his achievement.

The son of a refuse collector who takes A levels and obtains a commission in the Navy has achieved greater things than the son of a brigadier who ended up as a first-lieutenant in the Army. To measure achievement, we need to know the take-off point.

Family background and academic achievement are far from unimportant, but once you are happy on these two points by far the most vital stage of the interview will be that concerning the candidate's knowledge, experience, and skills applicable to the task for which he is an applicant. In discussing the various jobs held, ask for the full picture. You must extract details about the company concerned: the structure of its management and where he fitted; to whom he was responsible and for what. Get him to draw the organization structure as an exercise in controlled explanation. Ask him to define his job and to fix the parameters of his authority. What decisions did he take, and which were referred to his superior? What type of men and staff did he control? How did he control them? How did he develop them? What managerial techniques were installed in the company? How did his role fit into the total pattern? What impact had he made on the job he had held? What problems had he met? What solutions had he devised and implemented, with what success? What were his contacts internally and externally? How did he get on with his subordinates and superiors? How would he have improved the company's organization or his division's organization if he had had a free hand? Were any of his suggestions accepted? Which were turned down? Why?

All these questions underline the fact that the interviewer must not be satisfied with the preliminary outline given by the candidate. Never accept a job title as a satisfactory description of its functions. Titles vary from one company to another. In one, the sales director may have a staff of one, his secretary. In another, a sales director may control every aspect of marketing and have a staff of three hundred.

Older textbooks on interviewing insisted that the interviewer should make the candidate do all the talking: 'Use encouraging noises.' 'You only learn when he is talking.'

This is true enough, and a valuable rule at the outset, when you want to build up the candidate's confidence and, thus, warm him up. But make sure that he is telling you what you want to know, not what he feels he would like you to know.

Word your questions carefully to elicit facts that are important in making your decision. Avoid leading questions by asking for opinions related to facts. But remember you can also learn from his questions. Give him the opportunity to ask questions either at intervals in the course of the conversation, or at the end of your own interrogation. The nature of these questions, the importance he attaches to them by the priority in which they are posed, are sound indicators of the man's intellect, business acumen, tact, his sense of values, and his priorities.

Every interview merits some preparation by candidate and interviewer alike. You, the interviewer, should know, in advance, what you want to find out, and to have your pattern of interrogation laid out. The right man will have given some thought about your company and the job you are offering. The right man will have gone to some lengths to brief himself about you as soon as he knows your company's identity, which may have been revealed only by your letter of invitation.

The better candidate has done his homework, looked up your company's history and accounts, knows something about your products or service and your markets and can, therefore, ask a series of probing questions. The quality of his interrogation often reveals the quality of the candidate. Beware of the individual who has no questions to ask, because he is 'sure that you are the right company'. The chances are that he is already unemployed or has a strong feeling that his present employer is about to fire him.

The candidate's decision to join you is an important business decision for him personally. If he is capable of making such decisions on minimal evidence when his own career is at stake, would he be equally slipshod in taking decisions on your account?

No man is perfect, few companies are perfect. Expect, therefore, that the right man will probe a few delicate areas. Why is the job vacant? Why was the last incumbent fired? Why do you not have a suitable replacement internally? What are the snags of the job? If you have not already outlined the snags, please do not withhold them from him. Every company, like every family, has a skeleton in the cupboard. Don't hide yours—at any rate, don't hide it when an appointment decision is approaching. You need not reveal all your secrets and inadequacies to every candidate, but when you feel you have the right man asking the questions, be honest with him.

If the sales director is incompetent or an alcoholic, don't send him on leave during the interviewing programme. If you are having a bad year, with sales down and competition hardening, don't paint the lily and give the impression that everything is fine. He will find out after he joins you and, if you have withheld key information of this kind, he will not readily forgive and certainly not be prepared to trust you until you have won his respect again. Give him the unvarnished facts. I have known good candidates turn down offers of excellent jobs because they did not feel the managing director was telling them everything.

Apart from being honest, it is a rewarding exercise to tell the candidate about the snags and difficulties that lie ahead, since you want to know how he reacts to such situations.

Finalizing the appointment

The more senior the job, the more important that the appointment should not be rushed (but remember that good men often receive several offers at once). Make sure you know all that is to be known about your man. Equally, make sure that he has all the facts on which he can make the right decision. Some employers still feel it is unnecessary for the candidate to see the job location. Before an appointment is made, the candidate must see the plant, the offices, and meet all other directors, his future colleagues, and subordinates.

What are the remaining snags? There are a few more hurdles to jump:

(a) the negotiation of satisfactory terms and conditions of employment;
(b) the confirmation of facts on which you have based your decision by as many checks as are feasible and by taking up references;
(c) where necessary (and I suggest it is necessary more often than not at board level) seeing the candidate's wife.

(a) *Terms and Conditions.* At the start of your exercise in determining where your ideal candidate might be, you will have examined the market situation. What is such a man earning now? What additional side benefits is he likely to have? How do you make the new proposition attractive to him? Your researches at the outset will have roughly established the formula to be offered. When the final negotiations begin, however, it is important that these questions are reconsidered.

In his letter of application, your preferred candidate will have probably set out the conditions applicable to his present job. This is obviously the starting point. Check these to ensure that the figures are as stated; that the bonus figure he earned last year is the actual figure, not the one that he could have earned had the budget been achieved.

Assess with great care the formula that you are prepared to offer if he accepts the appointment. Companies that get involved in external recruitment only occasionally, often find that such exercises indicate that their existing salary levels are below market rates.

'If we take him we shall have to raise everybody's salary in the management team!' If this remark leads to a decision to take a second-rater, the company soon finds that it has made a mistake. It would, of course, be equally wrong impetuously to raise everybody's salary on the strength of this situation, and yet this single piece of evidence should certainly not go unheeded. The financial negotiations with the selected candidate are, however, crucial in that any 'take it or leave it' attitude on the part of the company can be fatal.

The candidate may withdraw, and the exercise may need to be repeated at enormous cost in executive time, advertising, and so on. Such costs may be two or three times the sum separating the offer that is rejected, and the offer that would be acceptable. It is in this delicate financial negotiation stage that an outsider, the company's accountant or consultant, can be a valuable professional go-between.

(b) *References—the importance of checking the facts.* The short list interviews have been carried out, and by this time you may have had two or three sessions with the better candidates. You are on the point of making an appointment, but let us not forget the final and vital stage of checking the facts.

The whole aim of interviewing is, to repeat, to elicit enough facts on which to make a forecast about the candidate's future performance. Interviews will have ranged over the man's whole career, beginning with his education or family background, and working through his commercial or industrial experience. The good interviewer is checking what his man knows or claims to know and what he has done or claims to have done.

By careful check and countercheck during the course of a single discussion or a series of interviews, many important points will have been established—pieces in a jig-saw puzzle the interviewer sets out to piece together. There remains the problem, however, of confirming the veracity of some of the vital claims made by the candidate. These can only be done by taking up references, or by substantiating in other ways the facts on which we make our forecast.

All directors have at some time or another been in the interview situation on the other side of the desk—'selling' themselves to a prospective employer. We all know that in such a situation we present the facts we feel the prospective employer wants to know, and we present them as favourably as possible. The majority of us do not set out to tell lies, but by careful omissions we can often present a better picture than the plain unvarnished facts, in their full detail, would give.

Minor omissions or even white lies may, in some situations, be completely harmless. In others, they may amount to complete misrepresentation. Scores of people when discussing their education will say 'And I took my finals in 1965', implying that they passed the examination or took their degree. A further question would prompt the reply that while they sat the examination, they failed. All too often the second question goes unasked.

It is common practice to drop the tiny word 'to' when a candidate is describing the job he has held. The man who describes himself as Assistant General Manager when, in fact, he is Assistant to the General Manager, is obviously setting out to mislead.

Another common failing is to inflate the salaries and total value of previous jobs. In my estimation, 10 per cent of people applying for jobs are inclined to exaggerate their earnings by 10 to 15 per cent. This often takes the form of quoting the top of the bracket for the job they have just left rather than the actual figure on their pay-slip. When challenged, the answer usually is, 'Oh, that is what I could expect to have earned if I remained there!' Another trick is to quote the maximum bonus earnable in a particular job rather than that which was actually earned. Service in Her Majesty's Forces is another point subject to imaginative embroidery. So many candidates seem to feel it is necessary to have been commissioned to be regarded as successful, that a small yet significant number of people feel they must claim a commission they never held.

As we all know, men with brilliant war records often turned out to be flops in civilian life, while the record book is full of Army privates who became millionaire businessmen. In the same way, men with brilliant academic records often turn out to be useless in a commercial setting. Mr Joe Hyman, chairman of Viyella Ltd, is on record as complaining that the more education a man has, the less commercial he often turns out to be. Many misguided candidates cling to the view, however, that a good academic record and a first-class war record are essential to impress prospective employers.

Some paper qualifications can be checked quite easily by asking for a sight of the degree or diploma. Professional qualifications can be verified by the use of the appropriate reference books. If you have any doubt about a man's claim that he was commissioned, the appropriate Army, Royal Air Force, or Navy list will give the answer.

Basic facts can be checked, and frankly they should be checked more frequently.

Of greater importance, however, are the checks on a man's past employment and the nature of the jobs he has held. Here we come to the subject of references. It is said that on the night that justice caught up with Al Capone in Chicago, his wallet contained a wad of letters testifying to his honesty, integrity, and social conscience! The story makes the point that most references are not worth the paper they are written on. Testimonials, as such, are a flash-back to a bygone age when the chamber-maid was required to provide proof of her honesty and cleanliness. In my experience, written references handed over at interview are as useless as those carried by Al Capone. Few people are inclined to carry testimony to their weaknesses, and yet, of course, this is the whole point of taking up references.

Nearly as bad as the reference handed over at an interview is the reference directors may seek, in all good faith, by writing to past employers. It is true that this is one way of verifying basic data: that a man was employed by the ABC Company between 5 June 1960 and 10 September 1966, that he held the post of sales manager and that he was paid £3,000 per annum. Beyond the bare facts, however, it is rarely that a written reference gives much more that is of value. The clever author can occasionally prompt a prospective employer to think again by 'damning with faint praise' and raising doubt or even suspicion. Unfortunately, however, the British libel laws deter many people from commiting their opinions in writing to a third party. Although there are few enough cases of libel action resulting from a written reference of this kind, one can understand the caution adopted by the reference giver. The answer is to find alternative methods of obtaining the additional information and verification required.

The two satisfactory ways of checking on a man required for a key post are to telephone his previous employers or, if the job really warrants it, to call on them. Although this involves some time, remember that the man you appoint to a key position can create havoc if he is the wrong man. The procedure recommended is relatively simple and merely requires a methodical approach. Having obtained the candidate's permission to take up references, write to each employer in turn. Tell him that you are contemplating Mr X as a prospective employee and say that you will be telephoning him on a specific day in the near future at a particular time. This will enable him to look up the records of the man in question and to be forearmed with some of the information you may require.

When you make your call, take time to build rapport, tell him about the post you are dealing with, and ask initially for the basic detail—dates, job titles, salaries, and so on—about your candidate. Your real need is to confirm that the jobs your candidate held had the responsibilities and authority he claimed. You want to know whether his success was as claimed. Perhaps your one query is regarding the way in which the man operated within the management team in his previous job. Get your informant to talk as freely as possible by avoiding the leading question. Talk around your doubts:

'We have a number of tricky individuals in our management here, and I am wondering how well he will get on with us . . .'

'We are running through a very difficult patch at the moment with our labour—I am not sure whether he is tactful enough in handling union situations . . .'

Perhaps the best question to ask is: 'Would you take him back on to your staff?' If the referee pauses, you want to know the reasons for his hesitation!

Although the telephone reference is far more revealing than its typed counterpart, a word of caution is needed. Beware of the gushing referee who is full of unqualified praise: there must have been *something* not quite right in your man. Also, beware when your telephone informant is over-critical. Probe his criticisms. 'Please explain, Mr X'. 'Can you give me an example?' Remember that the employer who has lost, or thinks he is about to lose, a good man may not be activated by the highest motives. I have met one or two cases where an employer has given a bad reference in order to hold on to his man.

(c) *His Wife*. In the course of your various meetings with the selected applicant, you will have learned whether or not his personality is compatible with the rest of the team. If things work out well, he will be staying with you for several years.

In suggesting that personality, temperament, and background should be compatible, I am not for one moment advocating that you should look for people of the same tastes and background as the rest of the team. Often, of course, the most creative team environment is where people of different temperaments and tastes are intermingled.

Let us assume you like the candidate and he is acceptable under all headings. Should you see his wife? It is, of course, the man you are hiring, the man you will need to work with; but nobody should underrate the importance of the wife of a senior executive or director. There are many reasons why a meeting with her—not an interview—is desirable.

If you are asking him (and her) to move house or to live in another country, it is vital that you should be certain that she approves the project and is happy at the prospect of uprooting herself and her children. If she accepts the move grudgingly, and is unhappy in her new environment, you can be certain that this will rub off on your new executive's performance. Invite them both to spend some time, at your expense, in the locality to examine housing, educational facilities, and the general social amenities. Don't take the candidate's word for it that his wife will settle down. There are numerous cases on record of appointments that have ended prematurely because wives could not settle down, find a suitable house, or be satisfied that local educational facilities were acceptable.

If your company is one where directors meet regularly for social occasions, it may not be essential, but perhaps desirable, that the wife would fit into your social group. Unhappily there are all too many instances where the man himself fits perfectly but, for one reason or another, his wife is incompatible. Many jobs call for a great deal of entertaining, both of senior people within the company or of customers and clients. The wife who finds this a bore or totally unacceptable may prove to be a distinct drawback.

If in doubt, therefore, invite his wife along to make sure that they are both happy with the proposition, happy to make the move, and understand the full implications of the new job.

If it involves travel, put it to her that this is in his interests and hers also, since it will further his career. The wife who finds out too late that the job involves extended travel at home or abroad may prove to be your enemy rather than your ally.

Motivating management

There are four major factors involved in management motivation. They can be summed up as the total company environment, job satisfaction, status, and remuneration.

1. The total environment

Most people want to work for respectable companies involved in respectable businesses. Inside any company, we all tend to work better when the climate is right. The firm that relies on 'hire and fire' methods, that takes decisions that ignore the reactions of its employees, that resorts to unethical or near-the-bone business methods, tends to find difficulty in attracting and keeping good people.

For the most part, executives are attracted to the successful company, although inevitably a tougher minority are more interested in finding the ailing firm that provides the stimulating challenge, with high rewards for success.

2. Job satisfaction

Most intelligent people are in search of an outlet for all their talents: one that will stretch them to the full and, in so doing, extend their total capability. Companies are well advised to seek such individuals rather than those who are satisfied by a job they can 'do on their heads'.

Senior jobs should not be tied inflexibly to out-of-date job descriptions, but be tailor-made to provide outlets for each individual as he develops. Job descriptions can then be redrafted in line with the company's revised objectives to give the individual maximum scope. Regular review of the organization structure is, however, desirable to avoid the overlap of responsibilities that tends to cause personal animosity and inhibits good team work. The individual achieves complete job satisfaction when he knows how to judge his own performance and, more important, how he is judged by his superior.

Efforts to show how each individual's efforts fit into the team's success will usually pay rewards. One of the major side benefits of the current system of 'management by objectives' is the psychological benefit afforded when the individual achieves objectives he and his superior have planned. Involvement in the company's success creates high morale.

3. Status

To many, status is sometimes more important than cash. We all know how important the carpet and the hat-stand can be in the career progression of our middle-ranking civil servants. The key to the executive wash-room is another sought-after landmark. Rank, as established by title, is perhaps the most important. The title 'director' is cherished by many and sought after by more.

In the advertising world, the initiative may come from the client who wants to feel that he is dealing with the man at the top. To appease the client and to reward the up-and-coming executive, many an agency has created more 'directors' than it has room for around the boardroom table, and the term 'associate director' is widely used.

When industrial companies are taken over by larger corporations in which, eventually, there is only one main board, and subsidiaries become operating divisions, it can create a real problem. Subsidiary boards are perpetuated or, in some cases, created in order to give key individuals the title they are seeking or the directorship they are unwilling to forgo.

It is a rare man indeed who, having been a director in his previous company, is prepared to lose the title on making a move to another, even when the new post carries a higher salary. Perhaps it is personal pride; perhaps he doesn't want to have his wife explain to her friends that he is no longer a director.

4. Remuneration

Every time a company hires a new person it is applying a salary policy. There is ample evidence that many companies apply a different policy on each occasion, leading to anomalies and, inevitably, to serious problems for the future. A number of points need to be carefully watched to ensure a sound and balanced remuneration approach. The key points are:

(a) *The Job.* Before a fair value can be placed on the individual job, its content must be analysed. A job description is invaluable both at the recruitment stage, and also when evaluation is attempted. What are the parameters of responsibility and authority? What contribution does the job make to the overall effectiveness and success of the team's operation? Systems of job evaluation analyse, under various headings, the job's overall importance, and make possible comparisons with jobs inside and outside the company.

(b) *Man Specification.* This sets out to describe the ideal man, his education, experience, skills, ability, and potential, and must be looked at closely, along with the demands of the post.

(c) *Supply and Demand.* There is a market for talent, just as there is for any other commodity. The forces of supply and demand are involved, forcing up the value of those people who are in short supply, as witness the extraordinary salaries paid to computer personnel in the computer age.

No salary scheme can remain satisfactory for long without periodic reference to the market. What is the price (salary, bonus, and fringe benefits, etc.) paid for similar jobs carried out in similar conditions in other companies? Such comparisons are not easy to arrive at, since there are no universally adopted titles that indicate identical levels of responsibility. In one company, the company secretary may be restricted to the firm's legal requirements and to handling the pension fund, insurances, etc. In another, the company secretary may fulfil the complete financial, secretarial, and accounting role with functions similar to those of a financial controller elsewhere. Such problems underline the need to carry out a job evaluation exercise that should cover all typical tasks to establish their constituent responsibilities and make it possible to compare 'apples with apples'.

(d) *Internal Comparability*. Having achieved some balance with the market, a company then must take care to ensure a high degree of internal comparability. High morale is related not merely to the absolute figure paid to an individual, but also to his relative worth within the team. Everybody wants to feel that his contribution to the company's success is indicated by the fairness of the salary scales.

It is not too difficult to estimate the relative contributions of the sales representative, field sales manager, and sales manager respectively, but there is obviously a major problem to be overcome in comparing the contributions of the sales manager and the chief accountant.

This can best be achieved after analysis of their respective responsibilities and contributions by careful job evaluation. Failure to achieve some form of balance will inevitably lead to internal jealousy, lack of co-operation and, in some cases, the frustration that leads to the loss of a key man.

(e) *Specialization*. Although a relatively minor factor, specialization should not be ignored. The company that requires only one biochemist or research physicist may find that it has locked away in him such a great deal of confidential information and experience that they cannot afford to release him. Apart from the risk of losing this know-how to a competitor, they themselves would find it impossible to operate without his peculiar knowledge and skills. As the years go by, such a man's value to his company increases faster than is sometimes recognized. The news of his impending departure could lead to situations approaching near panic. Don't lose sight of him at salary review time.

(f) *Security*. There are companies at the two extremes of the job-security scale. In a few industrial giants, the staff feel that unless they are 'caught with their hands in the till' they have a job for life. At the other end of the scale, there are executives who cannot guarantee that their jobs will still be there at the end of next week.

The student of 'boardroom changes' cannot fail to see that, in certain organizations, security of tenure is by no means high. In boardrooms and bars, the movements of friends and acquaintances are regularly topics of conversation, and the company with high executive turnover is earmarked as one to be avoided.

When, as is inevitable, such a firm advertises vacancies, it needs to pay a premium—a 'hire and fire' premium—to attract people who are prepared to risk the inevitability of a further change within a relatively short time. Security is directly reflected in pay scales. Larger, somewhat bureaucratic companies, with security on the same level as the civil service, tend to be able to move slightly behind the market.

(g) *Side Benefits*. American salary figures tend to be two-, three-, or four-times greater than for similar jobs in Britain. In many respects, however, American side benefits are usually less favourable. On average, for instance, pensions rarely exceed

11*

25 to 30 per cent as opposed to the $66\frac{2}{3}$ per cent maximum allowable by British law. Relatively few American executives and directors are provided with cars.

These facts seem to reflect the American philosophy, which says, 'let us pay the man what he is worth and let him spend it the way that he prefers'.

A further major influence, of course, is the British personal taxation system which has prompted employers to move towards a remuneration pattern offering the greatest benefit to their staff. With no sign of relaxation in the direct taxation area, there is a growing movement towards providing 'Top Hat' pension funds. It has been estimated that 30 to 40 per cent of British executives earning over £5,000 per annum are now covered by full Top Hat schemes.

In the US and many continental countries, executives and directors are able to create reasonable capital sums during their careers. Our British tax levels prohibit any substantial capital formation and, as a result, companies are becoming more interested in pension plans that allow commutation.

Under such schemes, a man having a salary of £9,000 with full Top Hat pension rights would receive a pension of £6,000, of which he could commute £1,500 to give a capital sum of £15,000 plus a pension salary of £4,500, for the rest of his life. Commutation rights, which are by no means universal, are one explanation of the relatively high gross salaries payable by certain companies.

(h) *Incentives*. American productivity is considerably higher in conditions where shop-floor operatives and senior management alike are motivated by high incentive payments, stock options, shares of profit, etc., and are allowed to keep more of their earnings by a less stringent taxation level.

Bonus incentives geared closely to sales and marketing objectives are equally potent at sales representative, field sales management, sales manager, and sales director level. (This has been proved conclusively by Procter and Gamble, the soap and detergent giant, which has applied such strong motivation for many decades.) Bonus incentives in some form are equally effective in other areas of management, provided the aims of the finance director, production director, marketing director, and chief executive are closely geared into the company's overall objectives.

We all accept that the man in business on his own account seems prepared to work harder, to work longer hours, and to work more diligently, and we accept that this is, in part, prompted by the promise of higher rewards. Many people who, in previous generations, might have been entrepreneurs are now salaried employees, in the huge public companies of today.

Why should not these people react in the same way as the entrepeneur by working harder to achieve company prosperity in which they have a direct share? By relating managers' and directors' earnings to company profits, you can pay the maximum that can be afforded with safety and, thus, attract and retain the best available talent.

In *My Years with General Motors*, Alfred Sloan refers to two important concepts—decentralization and financial incentives for management—as being 'the cornerstones of General Motors' organization policy'. Decentralization in General Motors allowed the delegation to key divisional management of quantifiable authority and responsibility to which managerial rewards could be related. Although we have Sloan's high faith in the effectiveness of these two interrelated concepts, he admits that there is no mathematically demonstrable proof of the effectiveness of the General Motors bonus plan which has now run for forty years and covers 14,000 managers.

One can but quote Sloan's opinion echoed in the words of his life-long associate Walter Carpenter:

'. . . we do have, to support our assurance in its effectiveness, the record of General Motors' success over a long period of years, we have evidence of its contribution towards the assembling and retention of an organization of outstanding men . . .'

No proof—only the creation of the world's largest industrial company and the architect's faith that financial incentives were partly responsible for its astounding growth. Before dismissing as pointless any financial incentive plan on the basis that little would be left after decimation by surtax, chairmen should first look at all items that must be included in what the Americans would call the 'compensation plan'.

A company may well find, for instance, that it is not providing the best pension arrangements, i.e., up to the two-thirds of final salary already mentioned. The additional premium to bring the existing pension plan up to the maximum allowed by the Inland Revenue may not in fact be high. Since this is not subject to tax, it provides a valuable way of augmenting the real value of the job. Needless to say, the facility for commutation, mentioned earlier, provides an additional attractive benefit at a time when the prospects of capital formation during a working career are distinctly limited.

The development of managers

'The be-all and end-all of corporate existence is profit.' This statement was recently made by Mr Harold S. Geneen, chairman and president of the International Telephone and Telegraph Corporation, one of the world's largest multi-product businesses. This may be an over-simplification (although it is one likely to appeal enormously to ITT's shareholders.)

All too frequently, none the less, management development schemes are devised that ignore the fact that, whatever else they achieve, the programmes must be a continuous process of building better managers to enable the company to earn profits and go on earning profits in the future. Managers should be developed to run businesses. Businesses should not be run to develop managers.

How can you combine more effective day-to-day management with more effective growth of both individual managers and the management team?

Performance planning, a version of the technique called 'management by objectives', may be the answer. It is a programme of closely integrated procedures, designed to improve current management performance, which also speeds the development of individuals and leads to better co-ordination of the entire management effort. The process is not instant management. It needs time, a good deal of thought, and a high calibre executive to act as full-time co-ordinator.

It is based on several well-tried principles:

1. Managers accomplish tasks more effectively and more readily when they understand how and where they fit into the total pattern, and where responsibilities are clearly defined.
2. Greater efficiency is achieved and more individual development results when goals and/or targets are set for each managerial job.
3. Even greater improvement results if the individual concerned is involved in setting the targets for himself.
4. Key people are retained, and individual development occurs more readily, when the company provides the maximum information about its overall objectives and organization structure, the definition of jobs, the criteria used to select men for promotion and the company's remuneration policies.
5. The development of his subordinates is an essential function of every manager.
6. What is good for a man's personal development is usually good for the company.

There are five major steps in the cycle, which is usually repetitive:

Step 1—Personal data
Each manager regularly brings himself up-to-date on each subordinate's education, background knowledge, training, experience, interests and ambitions. (Regrettably, personnel records in many companies leave a good deal to be desired.)

How can a manager manage without knowing all the basic facts about his team?

Step 2—Job description and objectives
Each man writes a complete Job Description for his own job in a standard format providing broad guide-lines. Job descriptions concentrate on aims and objectives of the job, rather than the duties associated with it. These are then discussed with a man's superior, who often finds points of divergence, overlap or 'no man's land' between two of his subordinate's jobs, which need to be sorted out.

Step 3—Job criteria
Having agreed with his superior on the real aims and objectives of his post, the man

sets down the quantitative and qualitative criteria on which he feels that his performance should be judged. This phase will be considerably simplified where companies employ management accounting techniques that throw up costing data, and budgets of volume, expenditure, revenue, profit, etc. The criteria step may thus include:

Sales volume to reach x thousand by a particular date.
Costs to be reduced by y pence per unit.
Scrap to be halved by a particular date.
Labour turnover to be reduced by 5 per cent.

Where quantitative objectives are impractical, qualitative improvement may be specified, e.g., a deliberate attempt to improve internal communication.

Job objectives and criteria form the subject of the main meeting between manager and subordinate. Where the manager finds that his view of the post varies enormously, he may need to demonstrate how the job should be done, and raise the sights of the job holder. At the end of this session, however, both should better understand the scope of the job. The man himself will know the criteria on which he can form his own judgements and, also, how his superior will judge his performance.

Target setting may appear to be difficult, if not impossible, for certain jobs, and the opponents of the management by objectives technique tend to regard this as a serious drawback. Given serious thought, however, there are few jobs for which neither quantitative or qualitative targets can be set.

Step 4—Plan to achieve objectives

Naturally, where a plan requires a better than previous performance, the manager may need to set up a programme of training for the individual concerned, or give him personal on-the-job coaching.

Step 5—Measurement of achievements

The length of the individual programme will vary, depending on the individual's needs and the status of the post, but at the end of each 'objective period' there must be a post-mortem on the results achieved before a new cycle starts.

Throughout the exercise the accent is on personal involvement. The man draws up his own job description, sets his own targets, plans their achievement, and measures his performance, always under the close supervision of his boss.

The manager helps, counsels and advises—in other words, he manages! He does not abdicate any responsibility, although he will inevitably find himself delegating more and more as subordinate performance improves.

Performance Planning concentrates on management development by on-the-job training. It vastly improves the annual reporting procedures or merit-rating adopted by the more sophisticated firms by providing specific criteria as the basis of objective judgement of staff. Given this approach, the use of internal and external training courses, seminars, and post-graduate business schools falls readily into place, with substantial all-round benefits.

A major benefit is that all members of the staff are covered, with all-round improvement in company efficiency, rather than the company's whole effort being concentrated on the few crown princes, or on the graduate intake that is often the target of envy and suspicion of the rest.

Selecting men for the board

When selecting candidates for election to the board, it is clearly useful to start by defining the job. Obviously, the job definition will vary, depending on whether we are seeking outside directors or full-time executive directors.

It might be useful to add a few more points for consideration before appointments are made.

Outside directors

An examination of the qualifications, combined knowledge, and experience of all existing board members may well throw up gaps that could be filled to advantage from outside. Desirable expertise could perhaps be special knowledge of taxation or company law, broader knowledge of markets with similar problems to the company's own markets, experience of selecting high quality management, knowledge of developing management techniques, which could be of future assistance.

In general, however, the outside director's role should be to balance the inbred internal thinking of the executive directors. He is there to question decisions, to prompt further investigation where he is unconvinced, and to suggest alternatives as a means of ensuring that the board's policy is thoroughly hammered out. This demands a man of substantial business experience, absolute integrity, and trained judgement.

Executive directors

The choice of executive directors, and the need to ensure their adequate development before promotion to the board, provides even greater problems. More and more firms are adopting the sensible policy of promoting from within. Regrettably, some companies are still beset by the age-old problem of the director who does not want to hire a capable subordinate, regarding such a man as a threat to his security. We all condemn this as a short-sighted policy, and yet we all know that it happens. It can only be changed when the company adopts the principle that it is every man's basic responsibility to find, train, and develop his own successor, preferably from within.

The individuals who rise to the top among available internal staff will have developed in a specialist function. It is important, in planning a company's management succession, that steps should be taken to broaden each individual to take a wider view of the company's operating problems before arriving in the boardroom. This inevitably means that men need to be spotted well in advance of the need to promote them. Consultants are repeatedly surprised at the lack of management succession planning, even in relatively sophisticated organizations. In one case, I found, on examining the top management of a large organization employing 4,000 people, that of the seven board members only two had adequate successors within the company, and five of the existing incumbents were due to retire within two years. This situation is typical of many in which a group of directors all around the same age level have been elected together. They have grown old together, and nobody has noticed that retirement is approaching fast.

All chief executives should jot down the ages and the retirement dates of the various members of their boards. Ask each individual director to nominate his successor:

(a) when he actually retires, and
(b) if, for any reason including sudden death, the seat were to fall vacant in the meantime.

Given effective management succession plans, and allowing an adequate period of grooming, it should be possible, by simple job rotation, to move the high-flyer through one, two, or even a series of posts, which will give him a broader view of the company's total problems. When he arrives at board level, therefore, he should be able to look upon the company situation as a director rather than as the head of a specialist function. All too many boardroom problems stem from the narrow-minded view taken by individuals who cannot see anyone's problems other than those applicable to their own departments.

The excuse that a man cannot be spared for this type of rotation is, of course, nonsense, Obviously, he will need to be spared in due course, and every opportunity must be taken to give further experience to his own subordinate who will, ultimately, be promoted in his place.

Such training plans may appear expensive, but the alternative is often more dangerous. Leave such planning too long and the company faces an emergency decision: whether to risk a man who is patently unprepared for the bigger job or to recruit a ready-made director. Having missed the promotion, the talented man you have failed to develop looks for his opportunity elsewhere.

How can a management consultant help?

The outside management consultant can provide a useful service in the area discussed already, i.e., selection, training, motivation, and payment of executives and directors.

Selection

The selection of managers and executives is usually a function in which the company's personnel manager can help a great deal, but when the posts concerned are on a par with, or senior to his own, the task may be transferred to a director, the managing director or the chairman himself. In these circumstances, the director concerned faces a number of problems. The task of replacing the chief accountant, for example, may occur only once in a decade, and so the director involved in the selection will be relatively inexperienced in looking at suitable applicants. The management consultant, on the other hand, in recent months may well have interviewed scores or hundreds of accountants employed in similar posts elsewhere. The average exercise involves a consultant in vetting one to two hundred applications, interviewing twenty or thirty candidates, and submitting three or four men on the short list. If similar exercises are repeated—and half a dozen chief accountant vacancies inside as many months may not be uncommon—it is apparent that the consultant can make his comparisons against a background of scores of interviews. In assessing men from numerous companies, with varied industrial experience, he has a broader base against which to measure each individual. The managing director seeking the right man in such circumstances lacks this extensive knowledge and experience of the type of man he is seeking.

Before the exercise begins, the consultant can advise on the important question of terms and conditions to be offered to the new incumbent. Where market prices have been changed—and most of them have quite rapidly in recent years—the terms to be offered to the new man may be radically different from those that applied to his predecessor. The consultant often finds that a client who has already carried out an abortive exercise has failed to apply the correct salary and other conditions. The result has been either that suitable men were not attracted to reply in the first place, or turned the job down when they found the company's ideas were not in line with their own. Again, the consultant can be more objective in drawing up the necessary job definition and specification, which precedes the advertising and interviewing programmes.

As an example, the chances are that in the next five to ten years the job of chief accountant will be totally different from that actually carried out by the previous holder of the job. Whereas in the past the chief accountant role has often been filled quite successfully by the professional man with the historical approach to accountancy, with the extension of forward planning, budgeting, and an added emphasis on costs, the chief accountant role will probably be changed into that now normally associated with the title of financial controller. Such a job calls for an entirely different background and experience—and, often, a totally different type of individual whose temperament is geared to participating in the forward planning of the business rather than keeping the record of where the business has been.

The management consultant has, therefore, much to offer even in this preliminary stage to ensure that your company takes advantage of each job vacancy, not only to review its requirements, but to seek out people equipped to maintain the company's competitiveness.

Far too often, jobs are filled on subjective judgements. In the case of private companies, the son of, say, the managing director may be put into a job for which he is neither completely satisfactory nor necessarily the best man available inside the company. Where personal interests or internal politics may influence a decision, the third party consultant can introduce an objective line of thought which, when accompanied by suitable, tactful, explanation, may avoid an otherwise inevitable calamity.

One of the earliest advantages to be noted by consultant firms' clients was the fact that as a third party professional, the consultant could attract applications from better quality candidates than the company itself. The reasons are obvious. Many companies do not wish to announce to the world that they are seeking a particular type of individual. In some cases, where the present incumbent is less than effective, they may not wish to inform him in advance that his replacement is being sought. It has been proved conclusively that the better known firms of management consultants can attract a broader cross-section of candidates of demonstrably higher calibre than companies advertising on their own account. This is particularly true when the company resorts to the box number, since few people holding senior appointments are prepared to send an application into the blue. The obvious deterrent is the possibility that the advertiser may be someone known personally to the candidate. It is not unknown for a man to answer an advertisement placed by his own company! The consultant normally undertakes to reveal the identity of the client. The British consultant conceals the candidate's identity until he knows to whom it is to be revealed. American consultants operating in an entirely different business climate often reveal the identities of candidates to the client before revealing the client's name to the candidate. (American executives must be more trusting than British in this respect.)

British consultants have built up a reputation among candidates for establishing complete facts about a job, its snags as well as its advantages, and they rarely wittingly get involved with a client who is untrustworthy. This is because at initial briefing sessions with the client, a consultant, again because of his third party status, probes much more deeply and effectively than most candidates can.

In my own company, it is the practice to spend a good deal of time outlining the company's history, present position, and future potential as well as drawing the organization structure and explaining in great detail the ramifications of the post.

When he meets this type of approach, the candidate feels equally uninhibited in setting forward his own case. He reveals far more to the third party than perhaps he would be prepared to do when meeting a company for the first time. When the consultant, acting on the client's behalf, is prepared to admit that the job has snags, he is prepared to admit that his knowledge of this is thin, and experience of that is thinner.

Consultants' fees are high because the service provided requires well-educated men with pre-consultancy experience in leading companies, and a substantial investment in training. Given that the fees are high, clients should demand first-class service. Such service requires adequate time spent on the preliminary briefing and full contact maintained over a period of time sufficient to allow the consultant to do an adequate job.

Companies often feel that with a bare telephone conversation, a management recruitment exercise can be launched with hope of success. Give your consultant your confidence and make enough time available to ensure that he can fulfil your needs. You have lived with your company for five, ten, or twenty years and know your real requirements in detail. Make sure that you pass all this valuable background information on to the man who is temporarily acting on your behalf. Do not allow the consultant to terminate by simply supplying the dossiers of his recommended candidates, and allowing you to get on with it. Although it is not common practice among selection consultants, insist that he should attend the short-list interviews with his recommended candidates. There are several very good reasons for this:

(a) He has seen many application letters, interviewed many people, and while he may be discussing only the best of these, all the interviews in question provide valuable information and background to your final choice. He may, for instance, be able to reveal details about your company's image and reputation, previously unknown to you. As an objective outsider, he may be able to sound warnings about individual reputations, the company's products or its services, and the attractiveness or otherwise of employment by your firm.

Few candidates would make such comments face to face—it may be that they would never agree to meet you if there was something drastically wrong.

(b) By far the strongest reason for his attendance at the short-list interviews is that your consultant has already spent several hours with the people he is presenting. During previous discussions he will have established their strengths and weaknesses and can, in a preliminary presentation, outline the type of man you are about to meet. Being already known to the candidate, he can carry out the preliminary warming-up session which so often is necessary before the conversation arrives at a natural level.

Your consultant can save time in covering ground that is perhaps factual and detailed although, nevertheless, important in the final decision. He can prompt you to check on specific areas where you need to be convinced that your candidate has the necessary qualifications, technical or professional experience or knowledge of your products or processes.

Your consultant will have interviewed many more people at this level than you yourself, simply because he is a specialist in selection. Watch his technique of interrogation and you may learn something. Many a client has commented after such a short-list session that he learned some invaluable lessons by watching a specialist at work.

You cannot abdicate the final decision. The choice is yours. Make sure that you are making your choice with as much information as possible.

After the short-list session you will want to meet your preferred candidate alone, and to take adequate steps to ensure that he is not only acceptable but competent to fit successfully into your team. Advantages accruing by the use of consultants in the other areas covered already in this section will be apparent. When dealing with problems of executive pay and motivation, the organization of management teams, the drawing-up of job definitions, the mounting of management development programmes, the qualified outsider who has specialized in these subjects has much to offer. Apart from the broader contact he has had with different situations in a variety of companies covering numerous industries, he can bring to bear knowledge of the problems and their solution. This can save a great deal of time and effort and ensure a greater prospect of success.

Reading list

BOOKS

The Selection Process, M. M. Mandell (American Management Association, 1964)
The Evaluation Interview, Richard A. Fear (McGraw-Hill, 1958)
Organization—the Framework of Management, E. F. L. Brech (Longmans, Green, 1965)
Skills of Interviewing, E. Sidney and M. Brown (Tavistock, 1961)
Personnel Selection and Placement, M. D. Dunette (Tavistock, 1967)
Training Managers, Michael Argyle and Trevor Smith with M. J. Kirton (Acton Society Trust, 1962)
Management Recruitment and Development, National Economic Development Council (H.M.S.O., 1965)
Improving Management Performance, J. W. Humble (British Institute of Management, 1965)
The Making of Managers, Final Report of the B.I.M. Management Development Scheme Committee (British Institute of Management, 1963)
Group Selection Procedures, N.I.I.P. Paper No. 5 (National Institute of Industrial Psychology, 1967)
Developing Effective Managers, T. J. Roberts (Institute of Personnel Management, 1967)

JOURNALS

'Developing Executives: How the Big Companies Go About It' (B.I.M. Management Education Review Conference, London 4–6 January, 1966, *The Manager*, March 1966)
'Following Father in the Family Firm', John Tyzack (*The Director*, May 1967)
'Sizing up Men for Promotion', Dr McMurry (*The Director*, December 1965)
'How to Pick a Winner', A. R. Cooper (*The Director*, January 1962)

'The Losers: Every Company's Personal Problem', Andrew Cooper (*The Director*, September 1967)
'What Kind of Executive', W. J. Reddin (*The Director*, December 1966)

Useful addresses

National Institute of Industrial Psychology, 14 Welbeck Street, London W 1
The Psychological Corporation of America, 304 East 45th Street, New York City, N.Y.
The Tavistock Institute of Human Relations, 3 Devonshire Street, London W 1
Management Consultants Association Limited, 23 Cromwell Road, London SW 7

5.2 The Recruitment of Graduates

C. E. Escritt

In the United Kingdom the term 'graduate' means 'university graduate', which does not necessarily apply abroad. In industry, except in a few particularly well-organized groups, it still means 'man', unless otherwise mini-particularized. In too many firms, graduates either are an unwelcome necessity and, therefore, uneconomically used, with resultant high turnover, or are blithely hired with the needs of the 1960s in mind instead of those of the 1980s, and, therefore, ill-assorted by function and exposed to no programme of development of a costly, because in most areas scarce, asset. In this, as in investment planning, Britain has much to learn. The process begins with a company's internal development forecast over the next five to ten years, moves in detail to categories and numbers of people to be brought in over the next twelve months, then reviews known, and explores new, sources of supply of these people.

For graduates who are taking up their first posts, the main source of supply is the university appointments boards. Timing is determined by graduation in mid-summer, and by the supply-and-demand position. Forecasting should be done in the previous autumn; notification of requirements made. to appointments board secretaries as long before Christmas as possible; initial screening interviews done by early March; in-plant employment interviews completed by the end of April.

In practice, much time and money would be saved if companies insisted on candidates writing to them a proper letter of application for interview, and completing an official application form. Too often, a panel of 'candidates' to be interviewed on campus at a university between mid-January and mid-March is no more than a list of those who have indicated to the appointments secretary that they 'want an interview'. If a positive application is made, the company can make a firm arrangement with each candidate a week or more ahead, and keep the appointments secretary informed. Interviews are held either in the university or in a local hotel.

Appointments board secretaries must receive in good time (between October and December) precise details of the job or jobs to be filled, the qualifications required, where these are specific, the training and early work experience envisaged, some realistic indication of prospects (vague statements such as 'excellent prospects' or 'the sky's the limit' may excite the sort of candidate you don't want, and warn off the sort you do), the salary starting rate or bracket, and instruction on how to apply. This essential detail must be supported by equally essential notes of the company's history and development (e.g., diversification, exploitation of overseas markets, technical innovation), and its current product range and organization structure. The nature and quality of environment are as important as the nature and quality of the job.

Failure by recruiting companies at this stage may be traced, in most cases, to standard errors, failure being defined as failure to attract any interest at all, or as failure to attract the interest of worthwhile candidates. Quality, not quantity of applicants is what really matters. A candidate comes forward as the result of personal recommendation, the known reputation of a company, or (in most cases) the quality of the company's own literature. Individual appointments board secretaries often supplement this literature by giving details of other university graduates in the company, for instance, or by bringing it up to date if the literature had gone to press before a merger, before an important export drive, before an AGM report.

The booklet/brochure mortuary shows up four common symptoms in a fatal syndrome:

1. To save expense, the text is pitched at sixth-form level of perception and appreciation, in literature ostensibly written for undergraduates and graduates.
2. The infant Raleigh gazing raptly at the old salt as he points to the horizon . . . 'Wonderful opportunities await you in this fascinating business', 'a dramatic challenge faces you in this dynamic, forward-looking concern'. The candidate has spent three years or more learning to go to the frontier for data on which to form his own conclusions. He wants data, not conclusions; if he doesn't, he has been wasting his time and is a poor candidate. Infant Raleigh-ism is still common and is usually fatal.
3. Creeping initial-itis, endemic in business literature. Initial capitals are clapped on words like manager, traveller, board, department, cash-flow, industry, chairman, production. In extreme cases the result resembles translation from German into

318

English by a German with little English. The impression is of pomposity; the effect often fatal.

4. Personification of abstractions is another endemic industrial disease, particularly in training and management literature. Things like: 'it is the responsibility of supervision to ensure that'; meaning, in fact: 'supervisors must ensure that'. Combined with creeping initial-itis, this symptom is often fatal. As in medicine, what supervenes kills.

Printed brochures and booklets should not exceed the 12-inch by 8-inch format. Oddly enough, few personnel men realize that the best size is that of the literature you carry away with you, because it slips easily into your jacket pocket.

Companies often fail to realize that at the initial screening interview stage, the interviewer *is* the company. He will see far more people than will eventually be hired. With what impression will they go away? The screening interviewer's job is essentially one of public relations.

Membership of the Careers Research Advisory Centre in Cambridge provides up-to-date knowledge of university courses, of undergraduate attitudes, and of problems generally associated with recruitment. Space taken in the *Directory of Opportunities for Graduates*, published annually in October/November, ensures 100 per cent coverage of all final year undergraduates at British universities. Participation in the Centre for Careers Information (Industrial and Professional Careers Research Organization) opens a window in London on a company's performance and recruitment needs.

University appointments boards deal also with graduate job-changers, but the main traffic in the 'with experience' area runs in the columns of the *Daily Telegraph* and the *Sunday Times*. There are two specialist firms who build up registers of experienced graduates: the Careers Register Ltd, and the Graduate Appointments Register, both in London.

Two government organizations can, for practical purposes, be regarded as providing services for job-changers (not only for graduates), but they also take newly-qualifying graduates on to their registers. The Technical and Scientific Register of the Ministry of Labour (now the Department of Employment and Productivity) provides an employment service for physicists, mathematicians, chemists (other than pharmacists), metallurgists, agriculturalists, biologists, and other scientists, professional engineers, architects, surveyors, town planners, estate agents and valuers. Qualification for enrolment is a degree or diploma in technology, science, or engineering, membership of a recognized professional institution, or higher national diploma or higher national certificate in scientific or engineering subjects, including building construction. Full-time students at universities and colleges of advanced technology may enrol before they graduate. It operates from London and has a Scottish branch office. Fuller details about the service it offers can be obtained from either of these (*see* addresses at the end of this section), or from any office of the Department of Employment and Productivity.

The Professional and Executive Register of the Department helps professionally qualified men and women, other than those catered for by the Technical and Scientific Register, people who have had managerial or executive experience in commerce or industry, and also younger people of good education, particularly newly-qualified arts graduates, to find trainee executive posts. It operates through the larger employment exchanges. Full information about the service it provides may be obtained from any local office of the Department of Employment and Productivity.

Failure to recruit a graduate is less serious than failure to utilize his services intelligently after recruitment. Only three situations exist that justify the hiring of graduates:

1. An immediate need for skills which only degrees in particular subjects can provide, e.g., chemical research, some chemical development, occasionally some chemical testing.
2. The same need, but viewed by the company as required for work out of which senior managers will eventually emerge.
3. Recognition by a forward-looking company that management services and other sophisticated techniques will accelerate in development; that pressures on top managers will build up as a result of these and of the increasing scale of industry; of automated processing (with premium placed on pre-planning and control systems); of computerized information retrieval; of rapid rate of change in the nature of materials and processes; and of the annihilation of space and time as factors delaying competitors' decisions; and that all these things put a premium on intelligence *in addition to* guts, gumption, go, and staying power.

In the first situation, the graduate leaves a company if the work does not need degree standard of knowledge, or if he has business ambitions beyond that of becoming leader of a research team or equivalent sectional responsibility.

In the second situation, he leaves if it becomes clear that his managers have no idea how his experience can be diversified without unnecessary and uneconomic delay, of how his responsibilities can be developed, and his knowledge opened up and deepened.

In the third situation, the only one in which arts men and women can be successfully recruited, he leaves if it is clear that his managers have no idea how to train and develop people to improve existing practices and to cope quickly with such problems as the rapid technological change. Board members and general managers are often timid, or unrealistic, in their conception of time-scales appropriate to business developments, and consequentially of training and executive development. This has nothing to do with showing undue favour to university graduates; it concerns the survival of the fittest.

The shortage of mathematicians, engineering, and other scientists is acute. But industrial and commercial functions are not all technical. It can be argued that in a community of over 60,000 firms (excluding the very small ones) into which about 1,300 arts graduates now enter annually, the shortage of *arts* graduates in the 1960s will have proved by the 1980s to have been at least as acute.

The very factors suggested above, as creating the 'third situation' in which graduates should be recruited, re-focus attention on universities as extra-mural supplements or adjuncts to in-plant training. Graduate business schools, still rare here, will become more important and numerous. Higher business studies at establishments of tertiary education cannot be regarded as appropriate for undergraduate study, except for their basic disciplines of economics, statistics, social studies, psychology, law. Furthermore, postgraduate business studies are best pursued post-experience, rather than end-on to a first degree. Most students at any good university business school will bring one, two, or three years' working experience gained since they took their first degree. It will soon become widespread practice for companies to use the business schools as essential components in executive development programmes. There will, however, always be men and women unsponsored on graduate business courses for diplomas or higher degrees such as an M Sc, so the graduate business schools should also be regarded by companies as a normal source of recruits, *assuming that companies know what a business school graduate is.* This subject is developed elsewhere in this chapter by an expert in the field (*see* section 5.4).

Many sixth-formers, fully up to university entrance standards, fail to gain places at universities. This element in the top 5 per cent of the nation's intelligence can be recruited both locally, by direct contact with schools, and through the Public Schools Appointments Bureau. The PSAB helps careers masters in about 200 member schools, including many leading grammar schools, to provide a good careers advice and information service. The secretaries also advise individual boys, aged sixteen to twenty-three, on career choice, and place many with industrial and commercial firms.

Reading list

BOOKS

University Appointments Boards, Report by Lord Heyworth (H.M.S.O., 1964)
Comment by the Federation of British Industries on the Heyworth Report (Confederation of British Industries, 1965)
Cornmarket Directory of Postgraduate Courses and Opportunities (Cornmarket Press, 1968)
First Employment of University Graduates 1961/2; 1962/3; 1963/4; 1964/5; 1965/6, University Grants Committee (H.M.S.O.)
The Employment of Cambridge Graduates, Christine Craig (Cambridge University Press, 1963)
A Degree Nearer Industry, Kenneth Harris (Imperial Chemical Industries, 1960)
The Arts Graduate in Industry, Audrey Collin, Anthony M. Rees and John Utting (Acton Society Trust, 1962)

JOURNALS

'Is the Board to Blame for the Graduate who Flops?' (two articles in May and June 1963, *The Director*)

'Spotting a Future Chairman at the Hiring Fair' (*The Director*, April 1967)

'Engineering's Twelve Graduate Guinea-pigs', Nigel Farrow (*Business* (now *Business Management*), February 1967)

'The Reluctant Graduate', Gareth Jones (*Personnel Magazine*, June 1966)

'Why Brains Shun Business', A. J. Merrett (*Management Today*, October 1967)

Useful addresses

Confederation of British Industry, 21 Tothill Street, London W 1 (for list of University Appointments Boards)

Graduates Appointments Register, 86–88 Edgware Road, London W 2

Centre for Careers Information, Industrial and Professional Careers Research Organization, Gillow House, Winsley Street, London W 1

Careers Register Ltd, 9 Manchester Square, London W 1

Department of Employment and Productivity Technical and Scientific Register, Almack House, 26–28 King Street, London SW 1

Public Schools Appointments Bureau, 17 Queen Street, Mayfair, London W 1

5.3 Manpower Management

T. G. P. Rogers

A business is an interaction of men, materials, and money. Materials and money appear on the balance sheet and so excite the interest of management and stock-holders, but the critical asset of a business is surely its manpower. What distinguishes the successful company from its neighbours is the quality of management—and this means the quality of managers. In turn, able managers will build competent teams under them so that the mix of skills in a business and the morale and teamwork of employees is the direct product of having able managers.

The task of the board of a company is not only to set and achieve today's objectives; it is also to provide for the growth and stability of the organization in perpetuity. The building of the manpower assets of a business is a long-term task, and today's recruitment and training decisions are the key to the future of the company —materials and money can be found overnight, but it takes years to build and weld an effective team of people.

These are the reasons why there has been growing recognition by chairmen that the most important decisions they have to make are those relating to people— appointments, organization and personnel policies. From this has stemmed the trend that a personnel executive is needed to assist the chairman in these matters and participate in the top level operating and planning decisions of the company. It is no longer tenable that 'personnel' is something that only operates at the foreman level, coping with the consequences of management decisions; today, all directors need to recognize both the critical importance of the personnel decisions they have to make and, therefore, their need for the assistance of personnel specialists.

The 'complete manager' therefore needs personnel skills whether he is a foreman or chairman of the board. So what follows is an attempt to define, first, the personnel skills every director needs, and secondly, the assistance and service members of a board should demand and receive from their personnel specialists.

The title 'director' conveys a supervisory relationship with other people. It indicates that a director achieves his ends through the agency of others. If those he directs resist or resent his instructions, he will fail in large or small measure. Therefore, by definition, no director can afford a negative or unconstructive attitude to the people on whom he depends, particularly since today he exercises his authority 'by consent' rather than by any autocratic right.

His philosophy has to be that if he chooses his subordinates well, provides them with work and an environment that creates satisfaction, and remains alert to his responsibilities to his subordinates, he will be a successful director.

To restate this and put it in perspective, the philosophy is advanced that management is a service occupation with the director or manager acknowledging that it is his role to serve three groups dependent upon him—shareholders, customers, and employees. This attitude is as necessary for the owner/manager as it is for the employee/manager because there is for both an interdependence and a unity of interest between these three groups. Of course, there are conflicts of interest to resolve between and within these groups at the tactical level, but more broadly, shareholders, customers, and employees all have vested interests in the stability, productivity, and growth of the enterprise. If, therefore, the director sees his task in relation to his people as that of servant rather than master, he will be motivated to provide his people with the training, development opportunities, rewards, and recognition they legitimately seek; he will see that if he helps them by removing obstacles and irritations they will perform more effectively; he will see that if he explains and delegates and encourages—all 'giving' activities—instead of demanding and criticizing, the company will benefit from the high productivity that comes from good morale and job satisfaction.

This is amiable theory—the Papal *servitor serventium* or MacGregor's Theory Y —but how does the director apply it in practice? First, he must be sensitive to the views and feelings of the people for whom he is responsible, secondly he must be competent in the skills of human relationships, and thirdly he must make use of personnel advice and service.

One basic skill he needs is that of assessing individuals in relation to a job. This arises in the employment interview, in the appraisal and counselling role, and in everyday dealings with colleagues and subordinates. The skill lies in minimizing subjective impressions and replacing them with factual data and judgements supported by evidence. This involves identifying and analysing the significant variables and

324

considering the relative balance between them. For example, A and B are candididates for a job in which high intelligence is a prerequisite. Intelligence can be measured reasonably in finite terms. A is found to be more intelligent than B, but clearly this does not necessarily mean that A is the superior candidate. Is the difference between A and B's test scores significant? Are both above the standard deemed necessary for the job? How do A and B compare in terms of attainments and motivation? If B is less well endowed with IQ than A is, does he compensate for this by being harder working and more painstaking? Much has been written on this subject, but as a minimum, every director should be familiar with the NIIP's pamphlet, 'The Seven Point Plan''.

A second fundamental skill is competence in the field of communications. This requires both facility in the use of the spoken word and written word and the conviction that conveying understanding between people at work is central to morale and productivity. No director can afford not to be trained in this subject and he should discipline himself to the practice that every decision has its communications consequences which often need more time and consideration than the decision itself.

What is your attitude towards training? Is it something that happens to youths between sixteen and twenty-one? Is it the task of manipulating grant applications to your Industrial Training Board to see that you do not show a loss on your levy/grant account? Or is it the lifeblood of your company's future, enabling you to cope with drastic changes in organization, markets, and technology without damaging the morale and relationships that have taken so long to create? How much of your time this year will be spent in your undergoing formal training? Unless you are consciously seeking and receiving training this year, next year, and every year, you are rapidly approaching the scrap-heap—'poor old so-and-so, nice chap, but he hasn't changed his ideas since the 'fifties'. If you are not learning year by year, you cannot hope to sustain a wide-awake enquiring attitude under you, and that is why you should be on the scrap-heap. The only tenable philosophy of training today is that it is a process that begins at birth and ends at death.

What is it that motivates your staff? The short answer to that question is that the same factors motivate your staff as motivate you. What you are seeking from your work is what you should be aiming to give to your people. Praise and recognition, the satisfaction of a worthwhile job well done, adequacy of rewards in cash or kind, the security provided by continuous training and opportunity for development, and the satisfaction of being a part of a well-led successful team. For a more complete examination of this important subject every director should be familiar with the writings of Douglas MacGregor on motivation in *The Human Side of Enterprise*.

The personnel specialists of your company exist to give you experienced advice and service. To offer guidance on what this should be, these thoughts are offered. The personnel director is concerned with what may be termed the 'social system' of the company, encompassing the profitable employment of the human resources of the business, the human problems associated with resistance to change, the aspirations, motivation and satisfaction of each individual in the social system, and the maintenance of dignity and justice for each individual. While there needs to be differences of method and approach for different levels within the organization, the personnel director should be concerned with maintaining a consistent and integrated community with common purposes and loyalties. He is the enemy of any 'we' and 'they' attitudes. His role is both 'executive' and 'staff': 'executive' in the sense of being a member of the company's top management team and participating in the collective decisions of the boardroom, and also in having executive authority on such matters as the board may delegate to him; 'staff' in that he can be judged successful only if he can persuade managers at all levels to use the philosophy and advice he expounds.

Having stated this philosophy in broad terms, a brief analysis under major subject headings is needed to translate philosophy into practices. These are presented as questions for you to think about—your personnel colleague is there to help with the answers.

The logical starting point is management development because this is basic to the future existence and profitability of the company. What do you have today in terms of management competence? What will you need in two, five, and ten years' time, having regard to growth and steadily rising standards of management? What is the gap between the answers to these two questions? What are you doing about this gap by way of selection, training, job rotation, and promotion policy? What are the reasonable career aspirations of individuals in the company, and can you meet them? These questions are what management development is all about. One aspect deserves special emphasis because of its importance—there is need for urgent national activity in the field of management training. Speak of management training, and the training of the young hopefuls comes to mind. But what about the existing manager who is just coping with his present responsibilities? Unless he is helped to improve his knowledge year by year he will not keep up with rising standards, and it will be management's fault if he is, later, judged inadequate, not his. Take your company's total number of man/weeks spent in the past year in formal classroom management training and divide it into the total number of managers times forty-eight weeks. If the result shows that you are spending less than two weeks per manager, on average, in management training, you are falling behind and heading for disaster. Your personnel man is there to prod and help you in this.

What pay and benefits should each individual under you receive? Can incentives help you? Is money a motivator? The whole field of rewards is a personnel subject of complexity—earnings relationships with other organizations, between jobs in the company, and between individuals in the same job, calls for coherent and logical practice. There are conflicts to resolve between market place competitiveness and profit, between different parts of the company and between different locations. A company with international operations has another dimension of complexity to resolve.

In five years time the kinds and mix of manpower you will need will be different from today. How different? What jobs and skills will you need that do not exist today? What training is needed to meet this need? How well do you know the manpower mix you have today? Is this a country of labour shortage or one where there would be a surplus if we used our human resources more effectively? Is the only way to adjust our overmanning situation to exploit a trade recession so as to create massive redundancy? The whole question of manpower planning is an underdeveloped area, but surely of great importance to the future of every company that uses skilled staff. If you have, say, a toolroom, and in the future this will be unnecessary but in its place you will need an electronic repair and test workshop, how will you cope with the change from a human standpoint? You have two choices; either you can make your toolmakers redundant and then recruit electronic technicians, or you can retrain your toolmakers to be electronic technicians. Please do not dismiss the latter course as impossible; it has to be made possible. Such retraining is essential to the modernizing of British industry. It is a perfectly practical exercise in retraining and need only take about six months of theoretical and practical classroom work.

What does the phrase 'industrial relations' mean to you? Is it the negative and defensive task of 'how to live with unions'? Or is it the constructive and purposeful task of selling better ways of managing staff to achieve higher standards of productivity and job satisfaction? Surely it is high time that management, which is paid to deliver dynamic leadership to its staff, should cease this protective stagnant attitude to employees and set out to change the industrial relations climate by constructive initiative. Or have we abdicated this role to the government?

There are many other subjects on which you and your personnel colleague can constructively devote time and thought together—communications, medical services, recruitment, relationships with the academic world, the behavioural sciences, and organizational planning, to name but a few. All these subjects add up to the basic task you have of seeing that the company has the manpower resources it needs, that these resources are profitably employed, and that each individual in the organization has the dignity, opportunities, and satisfactions essential to his leading a meaningful life.

Reading list

The Human Side of Enterprise, Douglas McGregor (McGraw-Hill, 1960)
The Practice of Management, Peter F. Drucker (Heineman, 1955)
Manpower Planning in a Free Society, R. A. Lester (Princeton University Press, 1966)
The Seven-point Plan for Interviewing (National Institute of Industrial Psychology, 1952)

Selecting and Training the Training Officer, Nancy Taylor (Institute of Personnel Management, 1966)

Personnel Management and Industrial Relations, Dale Yoder (Pitman, 5th Edition, 1963)

People at Work: Essays and Commentaries, John Marsh (The Industrial Society, 1957)

Personnel Management, Scott, Clothier and Spriegel (McGraw-Hill, 6th Edition, 1961)

Personnel Administration: A Point of View and a Method, Pigors and Myers (McGraw-Hill, 5th Edition, 1965)

Human Relations in Management, Huneyager and Heekman (Edward Arnold, Second Edition, 1962)

Case Studies in Human Relations: Productivity and Organization, edited by M. Ivens and F. Broadway (Business Publications, 1966)

Useful addresses

Institute of Personnel Management, 5 Winsley Street, Oxford Circus, London W 1

The Industrial Society, 48 Bryanston Square, London W 1

National Institute of Industrial Psychology, 14 Welbeck Street, London W 1

Tavistock Institute of Human Relations, 3 Devonshire Street, London W 1

British Association for Commercial and Industrial Education, 16 Park Crescent, London W 1

5.4 Education for Managers

Arthur F. Earle

Management education in Britain is a growth industry. Since the publication of the Robbins Report on Higher Education in 1963, there has been a steady expansion both of the facilities available and in the number of students making use of them. Management education has its own sub-committee of the National Economic Development Council and attracts the attention of many business leaders through the governing bodies of the schools and universities concerned, and through the committees of such organizations as the Confederation of British Industry and many other professional and trade associations.

Concern with the shortage of management education, particularly at higher levels, did not begin with the Robbins Report. A number of public-spirited men had been working for decades to prepare a climate of opinion in government and industry which would seize and act upon the principal recommendation of the report, i.e., that two post-graduate business schools of high standard should be established in London and Manchester without delay.

By the second half of 1966, both schools were in full operation within the limits of the capacity of their temporary buildings, and plans were in hand to provide substantially higher capacities in permanent buildings. Side by side with this development, and no doubt catalysed by the publicity attending it, there developed a considerable upsurge of interest in business studies in other British universities.

The idea of graduate level business studies is, of course, not new. The first university business school was established in the United States more than a century ago, nevertheless it is an idea that is still unfamiliar to many businessmen, and it deserves some explanation, if not indeed justification.

Essentially, graduate level business studies reflect a belief that management is a profession in the sense that there is a body of knowledge that will enable the manager to perform his social functions more efficiently, and that it can be taught. Such a belief is analogous to similar beliefs held for longer periods and, therefore, less open to question about, say, engineering or medicine. In medicine, and for some purposes in engineering, society is prepared to say that men who have not demonstrated that they have acquired the requisite body of knowledge should not be allowed to engage in such work, for the consequences of ignorance may be disastrous to life and health.

The consequences of managerial incapacity are much less dramatic. The lack of adequate knowledge may mean that a manager spends his life less productively and with greater anxieties and fewer satisfactions than he ought. It may mean that he has to spend decades gaining knowledge by experience that could be taught to him in a year or two in order to provide him with a much longer period of peak performance. It may mean that, without a conceptual framework in which to generalize the lessons he learns from experience, he will find it difficult to move out of the specialized department or company where the experience is gained.

No one would claim that a course of graduate business studies will provide the only route to senior executive appointments in the future. Nor is such graduation a substitute for those personal qualities that will always be required in positions of leadership. But business school graduation should enable a given man to make more of his potential, and to do so much more quickly than he would otherwise. It is this that makes graduate level business studies a good investment for suitable students, and for the companies who employ them.

The content of business studies falls into two categories. First, we have the underlying disciplines akin to the mathematics and physics of the engineer or the chemistry and microbiology of the doctors. In business studies these disciplines are mathematics and statistics, economics, the behavioural sciences (psychology, social psychology, and sociology), law, and logic. Secondly, we have the applied subjects—accounting, operational research, marketing, finance, production, personnel management, industrial relations, business strategy, and policy. These subjects are taught by a wide variety of methods, depending upon the nature of the subject, the experience of the students, and the particular talents of the teacher. Some of the techniques used such as the 'case method' are novel and attract a good deal of attention. Methods are, however, only means to an end, and it is the end sought that should be the major source of concern.

Material of the kind described is taught in a wide range of courses. The standard two years Master's Degree course typical of the American business schools is being provided in the two British business schools for men within two or three years of taking their first degrees. Such courses should, in this writer's view, be designed to accommodate entrants from any first degree subject, for I believe that business studies should supplement a good education in any field and not be a substitute for such education. In this way, the business schools can provide a channel by which able men of any background can find an opportunity in management. There can be little doubt that this will add to the supply of able men who do so.

Industry has, of course, a serious challenge to face in recruiting and placing these young business school graduates if it is to hold them and to derive the full benefit of their potential. They are not yet managers, but experience in the United States indicates that they can very quickly become so if they are handled boldly.

Work with young first degree men is, of course, only part of the task of British business schools and universities. British industry has an enormous backlog of able executives who have already established their ability as managers but who can benefit enormously from educational experiences of shorter duration yet otherwise comparable to the Master's Degree programmes offered to the younger men. Such 'post-experience' courses come in a bewildering variety of shapes, sizes, and descriptions. The difficulty for most companies lies in making a choice. By building on the experience of the men involved, by making the courses residential, and by making the hours of work long and arduous, it is possible to provide a general course covering the same ground as the Master's Degree course, described above, for experienced executives in their thirties, in about three months. To attempt to reduce this period for a general programme is to reduce the value much more than proportionately. Executive development programmes of this type are offered at the business schools and at a number of universities, ranging in length between three months and a year. They are expensive—mostly in terms of the cost of releasing the employee concerned—but in my judgement there are few investments that show a quicker or better pay-off. We receive a great deal of feed-back in London to support this view, particularly when a company follows our suggested pattern of moving a man to a new job when he has completed the course. What one expects to get from these programmes is a man with new-found confidence and powers, and companies that place him in a new environment and face him with a new challenge help to 'fix' the benefits of the course in ways that are often quite remarkable.

Shorter post-experience programmes are also offered at a wide variety of institutions with more specialized objectives. Both London and Manchester have shorter programmes designed for senior executives, and there is a wider variety of specialized functional courses on marketing, finance, computer usage, and so on.

Many companies have formed a desire to pursue systematic management development activities, and the number of such companies is being increased by the operations of the Industrial Training Boards, and the opportunities these afford of obtaining grants towards the cost of management development. The use of external sources of management education will require choices of the men to be sent and of the institutions to be used. The longer general post-experience programmes are usually designed for promising men in their thirties. Where age is specified, it is usually an important criterion, and companies will find it wise to observe the bracket even if the school is willing to depart from it. The general programmes are not intended to rectify particular deficiencies. Where help of a particular kind is desired, an effort should be made to seek out a suitable specialist programme. Educational qualifications for post-experience programmes are not usually specified by the schools, and considerable reliance is placed on company assessments of a candidate's intelligence and abilities. There is, therefore, a need for considerable care in assessing the suitability of men being considered in the light of the indications, given by the school, of the type of man desired and the difficulty of the work to be covered. Placing a man in programmes beyond his capacity may well do him more harm than good.

Given a supply of suitable men, there is a great deal to be said for concentrating on the use of a particular institution's courses over a period of time, rather than seeking variety. The reason is that there is a considerable advantage to be gained by building up a cadre of men who have undergone a similar experience and whose business studies have taught them the same language and approach. The ease of communication within an organization and the facilitation of the re-entry of students is greatly helped by this practice.

How does one make a choice between the institutions available? There are no absolute standards. Checks with other companies will often be helpful, and so, too, will the advisory service offered in this field by the British Institute of Management. The most important and independent test is to examine the qualifications, size, and continuity of the teaching faculty. By continuity I mean that a distinction should be made between an institution having a high proportion of its faculty who are full-time long-serving members as compared with institutions where a high proportion are short-term visitors or occasional lecturers from other institutions or departments of the university. Quality in institutions of the latter type is inevitably patchy, and there is an unavoidable loss of institutional spirit and drive.

A continuing institutional spirit and drive is important for the reason that participation in a business studies programme should be only the beginning of a continuing process of self education and up-dating. Return to the institution for short study periods, under the auspices of active alumni activities, can offer great benefits to participants.

Reading list

BOOKS

The Education of American Businessmen, Frank C. Pierson (McGraw-Hill, 1959)

Higher Education for Business, R. A. Gordon and J. E. Howell (Columbia University Press, New York, 1959)

A Conspectus of Management Courses, British Institute of Management (Gee and Co., 1968)

Management Recruitment and Development, A Study by the National Economic Development Council (H.M.S.O., 1965)

British Business Schools, Report by the Rt Hon. Lord Franks (British Institute of Management, 1963)

Higher Education, Report of the Committee appointed by the Prime Minister under the chairmanship of Lord Robbins, Command Paper 215 4, 1961–1963 (H.M.S.O.)

European Guide to General Courses in Business Management (O.E.E.C., now the O.E.C.D., Paris, 1960)

Biography in Management Studies, Humphrey Lloyd (Administrative Staff College, Henley, 1964)

Issues in Management Education (O.E.C.D., Paris, 1963)

Enquiry into the Flow of Candidates in Science and Technology into Higher Education, Council for Scientific Policy, Command Paper 3541 (H.M.S.O., 1968)

Management Education and Training Needs of Industry (Confederation of British Industry, 1963)

Education in Transition—The Implications for Industry (Confederation of British Industry, 1965)

Management Education, Report of a Conference at Ditchley Park (The Ditchley Foundation, 1966)

JOURNALS

The Integration of Business Studies at the Conceptual Level, Basil W. Denning (*Journal of Management Studies*, February 1968)

The Business School: A Problem in Organizational Design, Herbert A. Simon (*Journal of Management Studies*, February 1967)

Education and Training Bulletin (Confederation of British Industry, London SW 1)

Technical Education and Industrial Training (monthly) (Evans Brothers Ltd)

Useful addresses

London Graduate School of Business Studies, 28 Northumberland Avenue, London WC 2
Manchester Business School, Hilton House, Hilton Street, Manchester 1

5.5 Industrial Training

Sir John Hunter

Industrial training in the United Kingdom has long been dominated by the apprenticeship system, and largely based on the efforts of individual employers. In the years following the Second World War, the recurrent shortages of workers in skilled occupations made it clear that such a system could not, on its own, succeed either in training enough people or in training them to the high standards technological changes in industry were making increasingly necessary. It was also apparent that the training effort, and its cost, were unfairly spread between different firms. By the early 1960s, there were growing demands for the Government to take a more active part in the overall direction of training, and in March 1964, the Industrial Training Act was passed.

The establishment of industrial training boards

The Act empowers the Department of Employment and Productivity, by means of an Industrial Training Order, to set up industrial training boards for what it calls 'activities of industry and commerce', with the responsibility of ensuring that the quantity and quality of training are adequate to meet the needs of their industries, and that the cost of training is spread as equitably as possible between member firms. The scope of each industry or group of industries for which a Board is established is determined after consultations between the Department and appropriate organizations of employers and employees. Consultations are required by the Act, and the

334

final scope of a board is set out in a Schedule to the Statutory Instrument which establishes the Board. The Order is subject to a negative resolution of either House of Parliament.

By early 1968, twenty-two industrial training boards had been established. Together they account for one million of the eighteen to nineteen million employees to be covered by the Act. The board for the distributive trades (less, fresh foodstuffs) set up during 1968 took in a further $2\frac{1}{2}$ million workpeople, and other boards scheduled to be established at the time of writing will be for the printing and publishing industries; the paper and paper products industries; the food, drink, and tobacco industries; and the footwear, leather, and allied industries.

The organization of the training boards

The Act requires the Department to appoint to a training board a Chairman and an equal number of members appointed after consultation with appropriate organizations of employers and employees in the industry to be covered by a board. Further members are appointed after consultation with the Secretaries of State for Education. The general practice has been to appoint boards initially for a period of three years, after which they are reconstituted. Boards enjoy a large measure of autonomy within certain constitutional safeguards. They recruit their own staff, and are responsible for their own administrative arrangements.

Training recommendations

One of the primary duties of a training board is to consider the different occupations within its industry and to recommend training standards for them. The most important items covered by a board's recommendations are the nature, content, and methods of training, the selection of trainees, and the standards of instruction. The task of preparing, presenting, and administering these recommendations is a particularly demanding and complex one for all boards.

During its first term of office the Central Training Council, on which I shall have more to say later, has made some study of the recommendations so far made by the training boards. It has been able to distinguish two broad types of recommendation—first those which provide detailed guidance to employers in the industry both as regards the syllabus to be followed and the methods of training to be used. This is the sort of recommendation that has been framed, for instance, by the Engineering Industry Training Board for first-year apprentice training in the metal and allied trades, and by the Shipbuilding Industry Training Board for apprentice boat builders.

For some occupations it is more difficult to offer detailed guidance. A second type of recommendation has, therefore, been made by boards to cover, for example, the training of managers, supervisors, or clerks. Here they have acknowledged that the training required can be decided only in the light of a firm's specific requirements and of a careful analysis of the job itself and the needs of the individual concerned. Under this type of recommendation the board proposes the particular steps that should be taken by a firm to establish its own training scheme (including, for example, the preparation of a planned and written programme based on job analysis) but does not attempt to stipulate the particular syllabus that should be followed. This may be the way in which a good many training recommendations will have to be framed.

Some of the recommendations break quite new ground. Among the most interesting that have so far appeared are the Engineering Industry Training Board's recommendations for engineering craft and technician trainees. The Board decided that, for the greater part of the first year, trainees in all the main metal trades should follow a common, broad-based syllabus, and that only in the last three months of this first year should any specialization take place. Furthermore, the Board has announced its intention that, in subsequent years, craft skills should be identified by a process of analysis and taught on the basis of 'modules' of knowledge and skill required to reach specified levels of attainment. Under this system a trainee will, therefore, be given instruction according to modules that will depend both on his own capacities and the requirements of the employer, and this will doubtless create 'trades' and 'levels of skill' rather different from those previously existing. It is also clear that each module will not require the same amount and length of training. Thus, the total period of training of the craftsman or technician of the future will vary according to the skill required.

Another far-reaching proposal has been made by the Committee set up jointly by the Engineering and Iron and Steel Industry Training Boards to determine training policy for foundry occupations. This Committee has proposed that a substantial part of the training of pattern-makers should consist of integrated whole-time courses of training and further education in selected technical colleges. By this means, the Committee is confident that a pattern-maker will be able to reach a high degree of skill in three years as compared with five years at present.

Training recommendations are published by boards, and all employers in the industry are made aware of them. But the matter cannot end there. The Boards must see that, as far as possible, firms put these recommendations into effect. Through the visits paid by their training advisory staff they are able to do a great deal by way of advice and information in persuading firms to adopt the recommended methods. It is also the developing policy of boards to make it a condition of an employer receiving a grant that he conducts his training according to the Board's recommendations.

The levy and grant system

The powers of an industrial training board to impose a levy on employers in its industry and to pay them training grants, subject to the approval of the Department of Employment and Productivity, is an essential feature of the operation of the training boards under the Act. It is, in the first place, the means adopted of sharing the cost of training more evenly between firms. From the proceeds of the levy the board pays grants to those employers who train to a satisfactory standard. But beyond this, the levy/grant system is the principal means whereby the board is able to encourage employers to increase the amount of training being done and to improve its quality.

There are two broad ways in which boards have approached the question of levy and grant. The first is to attempt, from the very outset, to redistribute what the board estimates to be the total cost of all training required in its industry. The alternative is to attempt, as a first step, to redistribute only part of that total. The former course poses the problem of reaching a reasonable assessment for the total cost of training, and the latter requires decisions as to which part of training costs should first be redistributed.

Most boards have adopted the latter course. They begin by laying down broad interim standards of training based on the best existing practice in the industry, and confine payment of grant to training that conforms to these standards. The more ambitious course has been adopted by the Engineering Industry Training Board, and, in the long run, most boards will need to move towards a levy and grants scheme which, like theirs, covers something approaching the full cost of training. In general, under either type of scheme, an employer who is training to the extent and degree regarded as appropriate by his board is able to obtain by way of grant at least as much as he pays in levy. Employers who do not do their fair share of training contribute through their payment of levy to the costs of those who in fact do so.

Further Education

Even before the Act was passed, it was becoming a feature of training arrangements that trainees should be released by their employers to undertake courses of further education. The Act has taken this further by giving to boards the duty of specifying in their recommendations the course of further education that should be associated with the industrial training. This calls for a large measure of co-operation between boards, colleges, and the various examining bodies, since significant alterations in courses of industrial training proposed by boards may well call for corresponding changes in the relevant educational courses and examination syllabuses. Moreover, the Minister of Labour announced, in July 1965, that in future he would approve boards' proposals only if they made it a condition of grant to employers that they should release young people to attend further education classes in all occupations where a substantial amount of training (a year or more) is required. They all, therefore, include this provision in their grant schemes.

12*

Off-the-job training

Quite soon after the Industrial Training Act was passed, the Minister and the Central Training Council recognized the importance of off-the-job training, namely, training given in an area set aside exclusively for this purpose, away from the pressures and demands of the job. There is now a general realization that for most occupations with any skill content it is essential to have a period of full time off-the-job training, even if in some cases the period is quite short. The Department (previously the Ministry) encourages the creation of additional training places in employers' centres or training bays by giving grants towards the running costs associated with them. Boards have followed this lead, and in some instances supplement the Department grant when passing it on to firms that qualify.

A number of boards have themselves set up training centres. The Wool, Jute, and Flax Industry Training Board has its own school for burlers and menders in Bradford; the Construction Board has opened a training centre at Bircham Newton in Norfolk for plant operators and other civil engineering workers; and the Shipbuilding Board has a Centre at Southampton for the first-year training of apprentice boatbuilders. The Engineering Industry Training Board has helped many employers who have got together to undertake training as a group to set up centres for the first-year training of engineering apprentices, and has plans to open a centre of its own for the same purpose.

Central Training Council

Although Training Boards are set up as executive bodies directly responsible to the Department, the Act makes provision for a Central Training Council. It is the Council's responsibility to advise the Department on the exercise of its functions under the Act, and on any other matters relating to industrial training that they may wish to refer to it. The constitution of the Council is laid down in the Act, and its members are taken from employer organizations, trade unions, the nationalized industries, and the chairmen of training boards, together with some educational and independent members.

The Council has made two reports to the Minister of Labour, one in November 1965, and the other in June 1967. It has been principally concerned with matters affecting the general implementation of the Act, and it has published a number of Memoranda, obtainable from the Department, dealing with specific aspects of general interest to all boards, such as those on identification of a board's main tasks, and the co-ordination of industrial training and further education. A large part of the Council's work has, however, been conducted by various specialist committees which it has set up to consider matters of common concern to all boards. These include a Commercial and Clerical Committee, whose first report was published in September 1966. The

338

Committee drew attention to the essential features that should be included in training schemes for young office workers, and made detailed training recommendations for the main categories of office staff. It went on, subsequently, to examine training in office supervision and the training of export staff, and published a further report on the first of these last year. The Council also published, in October 1967, a report from its Management Training and Development Committee, in which it set out what it considers to be the common features of effective schemes of management training, and suggested how the available facilities for management education might best be used. It has advised the training boards how their grant schemes could be framed to encourage firms to introduce comprehensive schemes of management training and development.

The first report of the Council's Committee on the Training of Training Officers was published in May 1966. This recommended a practical six-week sand-wich-type course, followed by a period of systematic training on the job, as the initial training required by these vitally important training specialists. The Committee then went on to look at their training in the longer term, and in a second report published last year recommended the follow-up training needed to supplement the introductory courses, and made proposals for training at graduate and post graduate levels.

The Council has another Committee to deal with research activities. Its purpose is to consider the needs for research into industrial training, how these needs can best be met, and how the results of completed projects can be applied by industry. The Department makes grants to individuals and organizations who undertake research into industrial training, and also to the training boards themselves who are concerned with projects of particular relevance to their own industries. In making grants, the Department takes the advice of the Research Committee which examines applications put forward.

There are also Committees for Scotland and for Wales, these being the only ones of a regional nature the Council has established. They consider the implementation of the Act in their particular regions, and both have devoted a great deal of attention to the special problems that arise in connection with the development of remote areas. On the basis of their findings, the training boards have been able to co-ordinate steps to increase the industrial training required.

The Industrial Training Service

The Industrial Training Service is associated with the Council. It is a non-profit-making body whose Board of Directors is appointed by the Department of Employment and Productivity from among the members of the Council. The Service has a staff of training development officers, based throughout the country, who are engaged in assessing training needs, analysing particular jobs, and developing schemes of training at many different levels. Demands for its services come from training boards, employer organizations, group training associations, as well as from individual firms, both large and small.

Although an increasing proportion of its finance is covered by the fees charged, it is also grant-aided by the Department so that it can undertake training development work.

The Industrial Training Service has done an extremely valuable job—and will, I am sure, continue to do so—in giving practical advice on many of the problems that have arisen in the implementation of the Industrial Training Act.

The future

The Council's second report to the Department is a fair summary of the work of the training boards and the Council so far. It has to be remembered, of course, that all the boards and the Council itself are relatively new creations. The full development of their activities is bound to take time. Such a radically new system of directing and encouraging industrial training is bound, also, to bring some problems in its train. Some of these, and the way they are being tackled, are mentioned in the report. To quote just one example, reference is made to the problems that arise in connection with the small firm. The complaint is heard that the activities of training boards and their recommendations bear heavily, and sometimes, it is said, unjustly on the small firms that cannot afford substantial training facilities and full-time training staff. Some directors genuinely believe that the levy and grant system operates to their disadvantage, either because their training needs are modest or because they are unable to provide a form of training the boards recognize. It is most important that the Council and the boards take these complaints seriously, because most industries include a very great number of small firms who have a significant contribution to make to industry's training effort. The formation of group training schemes and training centres is one of the solutions to their problems that boards have already done a good deal to encourage.

In general, a good start has been made in implementing the Industrial Training Act, but a great deal more remains to be done. It was reasonable that some training boards should have concentrated their early efforts on the training of apprentices and other new entrants to their industries. It was necessary, also, that they should introduce interim schemes of levy and grant in order to make an impact on employers and to make it possible for their own work to proceed. In the future, they will be turning their attention increasingly to the training and retraining of adult workers, and supervisory and managerial staff, and making plans to meet the full volume of training their industries demand. In these immense tasks they will require the co-operation of all employers. This, indeed, was what the Act set out to achieve—the active participation and co-ordination of industry in the vital matter of planning and expanding industrial training.

Reading list

BOOKS

Industrial Training Year Book (Kogan Page Ltd, London)

Training of Training Officers: A Pattern for the Future, Report by the Committee on the training of training officers, Central Training Council (H.M.S.O., 1967)

Books for Training Officers (National Book League and the British Association for Commercial and Industrial Education, London, 1967)

Training Board Guides: Engineering (Kogan Page Ltd, London WC 1, 1967)

Memoranda on Industrial Training (Booklets 1–6) (Central Training Council, Ministry of Labour, London, 1965–1966)

Industrial Training Boards, Progress Reports (No. 1—1966, No. 2—1967, No. 3—1968) (Published by British Association for Commercial and Industrial Education, London)

British Industrial Research Associations: Report of Industrial Training Act Symposium— 16th November 1966. (Published for Committee of Directors of Research Associations (CDRA) by the British Welding Research Association, Abingdon Hall, Cambridge)

Management Education and Training Needs of Industry (Confederation of British Industry, London, 1963)

JOURNALS

The Production Engineer (Special issue on Industrial Training) (Institute of Production Engineers, London, May 1967)

Industrial Training International (monthly) (Pergamon Press, Oxford)

On Course (quarterly) (Department of Education and Science, Curzon Street, London)

Education and Training Bulletin (Confederation of British Industry, London SW 1)

Technical Education and Industrial Training (monthly) (Evans Brothers Ltd)

Useful addresses

British Association for Commercial and Industrial Education, 16 Park Crescent, London W 1

Central Training Council, 168 Regent Street, London W 1 (for up-to-date lists of names and addresses of secretaries of industrial training boards)

Industrial Training Service, 53 Victoria Street, London SW 1

National Institute of Industrial Psychology, 14 Welbeck Street, London W 1

Department of Education and Science, Curzon Street, London W 1

6. Labour Relations

6.1 The Role of the TUC

George Woodcock

The title 'Trades Union Congress' belongs, strictly, to the conference of delegates appointed by affiliated unions that is always held in the first week in September of every year. One of the functions of this Annual Congress is to elect an Executive Committee. The full title of this executive—'General Council of the Trades Union Congress'—is rather a mouthful and is seldom used. References to the 'Trades Union Congress' or 'the TUC' are usually to be taken nowadays as references to the day-to-day activities of the General Council rather than to the Annual Congress itself.

This transference of title has been accompanied by a similar transfer of authority and responsibility from the Annual Congress to the General Council. Indeed, the adoption (in 1920) of the name 'General Council' to describe the executive committee marked both a recognition of and an intention to develop a new relationship between the annual congress of delegates and the body elected 'to transact the business in the periods between each Annual Congress'.

It was not the belief or the intention of those who called the first Congress that the common purposes with which the Congress would deal would ever become as important to the unions as their domestic activities in their own particular trades or industries. Originally, the executive body had been known as the Parliamentary Committee, and the name was a fair description of its purpose and activities. For the most part, its work consisted of bringing to the notice of Ministers (usually by deputation) the motions passed at the preceding Annual Congress. If a congress motion required the introduction of a Bill to Parliament it was the duty of the Parliamentary Committee to find sponsors among Members of Parliament. It reported faithfully back to the next Annual Congress the outcome of its representations and its efforts to advance the decisions of Congress. But it seldom acted on its own initiative, except perhaps in some purely domestic affair.

The scope of the Congress motions up to the outbreak of the First World War was also somewhat limited. The problems of unemployment and demands for the nationalization of land and of particular industries were regular subjects of pre-First World War Congress motions. But, mostly, Congress was concerned with measures to ameliorate social conditions, i.e., to secure straightforward extensions or improvements in the public health and education services, and in legislation concerning industrial safety and welfare, including regulation of the hours and conditions of employment of special classes, national health and unemployment insurance, workmen's compensation, old age pensions, etc.

The First World War brought the old Parliamentary Committee into closer and more extensive contact with the agencies of government on matters of policy and administration. This came about on the initiative of Ministers and Departments of State (grappling with problems of manpower and production and so needing the advice and assistance of a representative trade union body) rather than as a result of pressures exerted by the Parliamentary Committee itself.

Nevertheless, this war-time experience of consultation with Ministers was an important influence on the post-First World War development of a more representative and powerful executive body. An even more important influence was the view taken by some of the far-sighted trade union leaders of those days about Britain's post-war position and prospects. They foresaw tougher times ahead for British trade and industry, with an increasing need, and increasing willingness, on the part of the Government to take a greater interest in industrial and economic affairs. Clearly, these potential developments on the Government's side had to be matched and indeed encouraged by corresponding changes in the scope and structure of the TUC.

The replacement, in 1920, of the Parliamentary Committee of sixteen members by a General Council of thirty-two members was the first of the structural changes. A General Council, able more accurately to reflect the wide range in industrial interests and experience of the trade union movement, was not of itself, however, enough. For the General Council, to be able to carry the responsibility for close consultation with the Government on complex issues of economic policy, needed to be well briefed in those subjects. The creation of specialist committees of the General Council—economic, social insurance, etc—and of specialist departments at headquarters were, therefore, necessary subsequent developments.

Today, the General Council of thirty-six members is slightly larger than the original, there are many more specialist committees, and there is a larger and more professionally qualified staff. But the present structure of the TUC is essentially that which had already been firmly established before the end of the nineteen-twenties.

The effect of these structural changes on the scope and the quality of TUC pronouncements and on the discussions at the Annual Congress become noticeable very quickly. Closer consultation with the departments of government was a much slower development. For example, the decision made by the Government in 1925 to return to a gold standard, and the various steps taken to that end were taken—despite the tremendous repercussions on wages and employment—without any reference to the TUC or, for that matter, to the equivalent employers' organizations.

Right up to the onset of war in 1939, consultation between the General Council and the Government remained entirely *ad hoc*. In other words, though the range of subjects discussed at meetings between Ministers and the General Council was wider than in the days of the old Parliamentary Committee, the method was almost exactly the same, i.e., a request from the General Council to a Minister to receive a deputation leading to an afternoon's discussion. In these discussions, the Minister usually took the view that his policy was already decided and that all he was called upon to do was to explain and, if necessary, to defend the decisions he had already made. In fact, very much the same attitude that he would take in replying to a House of Commons debate.

The Second World War changed all this. Starting with the National Joint Advisory Council to the Minister of Labour, a whole series of committees were established. In form, the more important of these committees consisted of representatives of the Ministry (usually including the Minister himself as Chairman) and the employers (either the British Employers' Confederation or the Federation of British Industries or both) and of the TUC. As a whole, the committees covered pretty well every aspect of the war effort. More important than their scope, however, was the fact that they met regularly and could carry a discussion forward from one meeting to the next. Most important of all was that, in many instances, the object of the discussions was to reach agreement on issues still to be decided.

Not all of the war-time committees survived the war, but tripartite discussions and continuous consultation through committees has remained a feature of post-war consultation between Ministers and the TUC. Even with Ministries for which no formal committees exist, the practice of frequent meetings, with discussion ranging over more than one subject, and carried forward, is the rule. And, of course, there is now the National Economic Development Council, whose discussions can extend to almost every aspect of the work of pretty well every Ministry. The NEDC is unique not only in that it enables the activities of different Ministries to be brought under the review of a single body, but also in that it has its own office and staff working under the direction of the Council.

Members of the TUC were first brought into personal contact with the representatives of employers' associations through the International Labour Organization established by the Peace Treaty of 1919. But there was no formal contact between the TUC and employers' organizations until after the General Strike of 1926. Following the strike, and with the intention of improving relations between the two sides of industry, and also of bringing their joint influence to bear on the Government, there was a series of meetings known as the Mond-Turner Conferences. Neither the Federation of British Industries nor the British Employers' Confederation were officially represented at the Mond-Turner meetings, but the three organizations—TUC, FBI, and the BEC—agreed that for the future they would jointly discuss and try to reach common agreement on industrial questions. Nothing specific, however, came out of this agreement, and it was not until the National Joint Advisory Council was established in 1939 that the TUC and the BEC came together in a tripartite committee. Nowadays, representatives of the TUC and the CBI meet each other regularly on a host of committees of one kind or another. The most recent development in these relationships is the creation of a CBI/TUC committee in which the two sides meet by themselves without the presence of government representatives.

There is, probably, no other country in the world in which the opportunities for joint consultation between the Government, the employers, and the trade unions are as far advanced as in Britain. The idea behind this network of committees is to enable each of the three parties deeply concerned with industry and economic affairs to reach a common understanding about the nature of Britain's economic problems, and agreement as to the best way of tackling them. The machinery is there. What is needed is the will to make the machinery work.

Reading list

BOOKS

Modern Trade Union Law, Cyril Grunfield (Sweet and Maxwell, 1966)
The Trades Union Congress 1868–1921, B. C. Roberts (Allen and Unwin, 1958)
Industrial Relations: Contemporary Problems and Perspectives, Edited by B. C. Roberts (Methuen, 1962)
Trade Union Leadership: Based on a Study of A. Readkin, H. V. Allen (Longmans Green, 1957)
Citrine's Trade Union Law, M. A. Hickling (Sweet and Maxwell, 3rd Edition, 1967)
Trade Union Structure and Government, Research Paper No. 5 of the Royal Commission on Trade Union and Employers' Associations, John Hughes (H.M.S.O., 1967)
Annual Reports of the Trades Union Council to Congress and Proceedings of Congress (Trades Union Congress, London)
The TUC, 1868-1968 (Trades Union Congress, London)

Useful addresses

The Trades Union Congress, Congress House, Great Russell Street, London W 1

6.2 Working with the Trade Unions

Ronald Stevens

Something like 10 million of Britain's working population of 25 million are members of trade unions. By comparison with most other industrial countries, this is a high proportion, especially when it is remembered that $8\frac{1}{2}$ million British workers are women, who are notoriously difficult to recruit. The strength of the unions naturally varies, not so much according to size but rather according to the degree of organization achieved in the workplace. For example, the Transport and General Workers, though the biggest of British unions, probably has less bargaining power, taken as a whole, than the Electrical Trades Union. But on London Transport buses, where membership of the T and GW is a condition of employment, it is clearly a force to be reckoned with. Broadly speaking, unions tend to be stronger in the North than the South, and in the older industries employing large numbers of manual workers than in the newer industries with more 'white collar' employees. Thus, they are firmly established in the coal mines, the railways, heavy engineering, and shipbuilding. The pattern is, however, gradually changing. As the traditional industries contract, displaced trade unionists are moving into areas of the economy where organized labour is less of an institution. At the same time, the exclusively 'white collar' unions are vigorously expanding. As a result, though the total number of union members is fairly stable, their distribution and character is not.

Some businessmen regard dealing with unions as an unavoidable nuisance—one of the penalties of success. Certainly, the unions are not very interested in organizing labour in the smallest companies. The cost of recruiting and representing

349

small and scattered pockets of workers far outweighs their weekly contributions. But once a company starts to expand it can expect to attract the unions' attention. Their first approach can take various forms. Sometimes a local official will write a polite letter to the management asking for permission to address the workers during their lunch hour on the benefits of union membership. Sometimes he will not get in touch with the management until he has already held a recruiting meeting, either outside the factory gates or elsewhere, such as an upstairs room in the nearest pub. Then he will write to ask for 'recognition', on the grounds that a sufficient number of the company's employees have joined the union to justify its claim to be their representative. Whatever the approach, the management will, sooner or later, be faced with the question of whether or not to concede 'recognition'. This is not a token gesture. It means that the company relinquishes the power to determine its workers' terms and conditions of employment unilaterally. It entails a commitment to negotiate on these matters with the union, and usually implies an increase in labour costs, since the union will only keep its new members by demonstrating its ability to obtain benefits that would otherwise remain beyond their reach. Some companies successfully resist the introduction of trade unionism in their factories. Unless, however, they adopt a firm policy of employing only non-unionists, they can do this only by paying higher wages and providing better conditions than the unions could achieve. In other words, it costs more to keep the unions out than to let them in. A formal anti-union policy can also be prohibitively expensive. For one thing, it embroils the company in an endless war of attrition, perhaps with trade unionists employed by its customers or suppliers refusing to handle its goods. For another, it is bad for its public reputation. On the whole, it is wiser to accept the unions as one of the facts of modern industrial life.

What disturbs many employers is not trade unionism in principle, but the presence of so many separate and sometimes competing organizations in a single industry. There are, at present, 161 different unions affiliated to the Trades Union Congress, and several dozen more outside its ranks. Broadly speaking, they can be divided into four different types, though the gradual process of amalgamation is blurring the traditional distinctions. First, there are the craft unions, which tend to be small in numbers and conservative in outlook. Their members, because they have been through formal apprenticeship training schemes, look upon themselves—with some justice—as an élite. They frequently have 'mates' to carry their tools and to perform the rougher and dirtier parts of their work. Above all, because they are skilled men, they can command higher rates of pay than most other workers. It is, however, their scarcity as much as their skill that accounts for their high wages, and this is something the craftsmen themselves bring about. The ratio of apprentices to craftsmen is often controlled strictly by the union, and adult entry to the trade is almost unheard of. Despite the general shortage of skilled labour, these restrictions are still rigidly enforced.

350

The craft unions owe their considerable bargaining power to their control of recruitment and the demand for their skills. Others owe it mainly to the number of members they can enrol in any one place. The second and third types—the so-called 'industrial' and 'general' unions—are, in fact, variations of the same thing. Both accept contributions from anybody who cares to join them. The difference is that the 'industrial' unions confine themselves, in the main, to one industry: the best examples in this country are the National Union of Mineworkers, and the National Union of Railwaymen. The 'general' unions, though representing the same categories of unskilled and semi-skilled labour, acknowledge no industrial boundaries. Thus, the Transport and General Workers has members in practically every major industry, and the General and Municipal Workers, though smaller, is just as widely spread. Finally, there are the 'white collar' unions, which usually call themselves 'associations'. Some, like the Civil Service unions and the National and Local Government Officers' Association, operate only in the field of public administration. But others are active in industry at large: perhaps the best-known are the Association of Supervisory Staffs, Executives and Technicians, and the Draughtsmen's and Allied Technicians' Association. One of the interesting features of these unions is that, although their members, by and large, are relatively affluent, middle-class people, their leaders tend to be militantly left-wing. Moreover, the strikes which, for example, the draughtsmen call quite frequently, rarely collapse for want of rank-and-file support. The truth appears to be that the officials of these unions, though politically unrepresentative of the members, provide the kind of aggressive generalship 'white collar' workers seem to want. There is, after all, a fairly general feeling that for the last twenty years manual workers have had too much of their own way.

The employer is, then, extremely fortunate if he finds that he has to deal with only one trade union. He is much more likely to be confronted by at least three, and perhaps half a dozen or more. Most British factories have several unions representing their unskilled and semi-skilled workers. Their craftsmen, whether employed on production or maintenance work, will be members of the appropriate organization: fitters in the Amalgamated Engineering and Foundry Workers' Union, welders in the Boilermakers' Society, electricians in the Electrical Trades Union, and so on. In addition, staff employees, though unlikely to be completely organized, are joining the 'white collar' associations in steadily increasing numbers. There is little the employer can do to prevent this multiplication of trade unions within his establishments. But he can limit its extent, as far as unskilled and semi-skilled workers are concerned, by reaching a '100 per cent membership' agreement with a particular union. Unlike craftsmen, workers in this category are eligible to join several organizations: they can belong to either of the two general unions, and often to the AEF or the Vehicle Builders as well. As long as he acts before several unions have got a foothold in his factory, it is open to the employer to make membership of a particular organization a condition of employment. Then, at least, he has simplified the position and reduced the danger of inter-union disputes, though only at the price of complete unionization. Agreements on 100 per cent membership are often confused with agreements on a closed shop. They are not, in fact, the same thing. Making trade union membership a condition of employment means that after a probationary period every new recruit to the firm is obliged to join the union: he need not have been a member before. The closed shop means that only existing members of the union are eligible for employment. In other words, the closed shop gives a union effective control over a company's recruiting policy.

Trade unions exist primarily to bargain for better wages and conditions on behalf of their members. In most industries, though not all, they carry out this function at two levels: nationally and locally. The machinery within which national negotiations are conducted varies considerably. In some industries National Joint Industrial Councils, consisting of representatives of the unions and of the appropriate employers' association, have been established and meet at regular intervals. In others, the two sides meet whenever there is an issue one or the other wishes to discuss: the best example of this informal approach is, perhaps, engineering. Finally, there are industries whose pay and conditions are regulated by wages councils. These are bodies set up by the Ministry of Labour (now the Department of Employment and Productivity) where union organization is judged too weak for normal collective bargaining to be possible. Like NJICs, they consist of union and employer representatives, but they also contain a minority of independent members whose votes, when the two sides disagree on a particular issue, are inevitably decisive. When a wages council decides, say, that pay should be increased by a specified amount, or working hours reduced by a specified period, it sends a recommendation to the Department. This, however, is little more than formality. The Department is not at liberty to reject or even to alter a wages council recommendation. The most it can do is delay its implementation, or send it back for further consideration. If the council sticks to its guns, the Department is obliged, sooner or later, to make an Order giving effect to its proposals.

Whatever the form of the national negotiating machinery, the individual employer in the industries where it exists will probably find that the basic wage rates and working conditions of his employees are outside his control. In the Wages Council industries, this is inescapable: once the Department has made an Order it is a legal offence to ignore it. Elsewhere, the employer is free to remain outside the national machinery, and to negotiate directly with the unions; but, under conditions of full employment, most companies that have done this find that they have to apply the terms of national settlements to their own employees, more or less to the letter. In any case, whether a company belongs to an employers' organization or not, it is likely to be engaged in plant negotiations with the unions representing its own workers. If it is not a party to national settlements, factory bargaining will cover everything

352

from minimum rates to the length and frequency of tea-breaks. If it is, only those matters decided on a national basis will be excluded. A firm distinction used to be made between joint consultation and collective bargaining at the factory level. Collective bargaining, it was said, concerned issues on which a conflict of interest might exist between the management and the men. Joint consultation, on the other hand, was supposed to be confined to subjects on which the two sides had a common interest. Thus, productivity, which everyone accepts should be as high as possible, was regarded as a matter for consultation rather than negotiation, while wages and conditions were clearly suitable only for the negotiating machine. In the last few years the artificiality of this distinction has been increasingly recognized. It is now widely accepted that, although unions and employers may share common aims in certain fields, profound differences can exist over how they should be achieved. Because of these differences, common objectives can be as much a matter of bargaining between two sides as pay and conditions. Agreement on measures to improve workers' productivity, for example, has usually been obtained only in return for substantial concessions on wages.

This is not to say that joint consultation in the orthodox sense has no place in the life of a factory. Properly used, it is a valuable part of a company's internal communications, of which a wall newspaper or house magazine may be other manifestations. It enables the management to tell the workpeople of its problems, and to try to enlist their support; and it enables the workpeople to 'let off steam' about their grievances before they have time to fester and erupt into disputes. Perhaps its greatest virtue is that it can give the individual employee a sense of participation in the company's fortunes, instead of being left to regard himself as no more than a hired hand. These desirable aims can, however, be achieved only if joint consultation is effectively organized and taken seriously by the management. Ideally, a works council should be established, with representatives from every department, and should meet at regular intervals—in the company's time. The managerial members should not be junior executives with limited authority to discuss the company's affairs. The works manager should certainly be on the council, and the personnel manager if one exists, together with at least one member of the board (preferably the managing director), who should act as chairman. The composition of the council will be regarded by the company's employees as an indication of the importance it attaches to joint consultation. So will the matters it allows the council to deal with, and the notice that it takes of its decisions. Generally speaking, anything of interest or concern to the labour force should be regarded as a legitimate subject for discussion. A works council whose deliberations are limited to the taste of the canteen tea will soon be discredited. At the same time, although the council will be a purely advisory body, the management should never reject its decisions out of hand—and still less ignore them. The reasons for not adopting a proposal from the council should always be explained.

The joint consultation machinery will be formally separate and distinct from the trade union organization in the factory. But the fact that some of the workers' representatives on the council are likely to be shop stewards as well is one of the reasons why it is unrealistic to try to keep consultation and negotiation apart. Shop stewards, though they have existed for more than half a century in British industry, are still something of an unknown quantity. Even the total number is a matter for speculation, and their functions vary from one union to another. The one generalization that can safely be made about them is that they are the unions' principal recruiting agents. When a non-unionist is taken on it is usually the shop steward who tries to convince him of the benefits of union membership. They are often responsible for collecting the weekly contributions as well, but by no means invariably. Since shop stewards are unpaid servants of the union (except that, if they collect contributions, they may receive a commission), they clearly belong to the active minority of trade unionists. The reasons why workpeople become shop stewards are naturally varied. In some cases, no doubt, they are inspired by a praiseworthy desire to be of service to their fellow-workers. In others, which are perhaps more numerous, the motive is ambition: a shop steward is on the first rung of the ladder to becoming a full-time union official. The simple appeal of power and influence is another explanation, and it is particularly strong for men with an anti-employer bias, such as Communists. It is, however, a mistake to assume that most shop stewards are left-wing agitators dedicated above everything else to disruption. In some companies even Communists are accepted—and deserve to be accepted—as trustworthy and responsible representatives of the men. The main reason why shop stewards as a body are regarded with suspicion lies in the structure of the British trade union movement, rather than in the character of the men concerned.

The lowest unit of trade union organization is the branch, but the branch is almost invariably a geographical rather than an industrial institution. It usually consists of all the union's members within a particular area, regardless of where they work or even whether they are working at all. Only a minority of trade unionists are sufficiently interested in the union's affairs to attend branch meetings. The branch, therefore, seems remote and comparatively unimportant, whereas the shop steward is close at hand every working day on the factory floor. He is elected by the workers, he deals with all their grievances, and he negotiates with the management on pay and conditions. It is scarcely surprising that to many rank-and-file members, the shop steward *is* 'the union'. Nor is it surprising that his power is often resented by officials of the branch. They, too, are elected, though only by the handful of members who attend branch meetings. Their knowledge of the factories in the area is usually limited to those they happen to work in, and elsewhere their knowledge is inevitably less than that of the shop stewards. Above all, they are less well-known to the ordinary members, and lack authority as a result. This situation contains all the ingredients for a contest of wills, which is what frequently develops. The shop stewards come to be looked on, both inside and outside the union, as irresponsible freebooters enjoying too much of their own way. It is fair to say that they sometimes lend weight to this criticism by their activities inside the factory. They have no constitutional power to organize any kind of industrial action, but this does not prevent them calling the occasional strike. They also establish their own organizations—joint committees of shop stewards from different unions within the factory or, in large companies, combine committees of shop stewards from different plants. The main purpose of these committees is the co-ordination of policy, and the policy that emerges is sometimes in direct conflict with that of the unions to which the shop stewards belong. But although the unions are frequently enjoined to control the activities of their shop stewards, there is, in fact, little that they can do. The ultimate sanction of expulsion from the union for indiscipline is, in most cases, an empty threat. The plain truth is that many unions would disintegrate if it were not for the recruiting and contribution-collecting work of the stewards, to say nothing of their efforts to keep rank-and-file interest alive. The unions need their shop stewards at least as much as the shop stewards need the unions.

It is therefore, unrealistic to argue, as managements sometimes do, that the unions should exercise firmer control over errant members. Despite the existence of long and elaborate rule books, the essential point about British unions is that such authority as they possess is of a moral rather than a constitutional character. This is true of all levels of the movement, including the Trades Union Congress. The TUC can expel an individual union for disregarding its policies, just as a union can expel an individual worker. But in most cases, nothing would be gained by doing so. Expulsion from a union is only an effective sanction if it deprives a man of his employment. Similarly, expulsion from the TUC would matter only if it put the union concerned out of business. The fact that it does not is illustrated by the vigorous survival of the National Amalgamated Stevedores and Dockers, expelled in the 1950s for 'poaching' members from the Transport and General Workers. (In the United States the Teamsters' Union, the country's biggest labour organization, has continued to thrive since its expulsion from the American Federation of Labour-Congress of Industrial Organizations, the American equivalent of the TUC.)

The employer's best insurance against industrial indiscipline is a negotiating procedure that is accepted by the workpeople as fair, and that is also capable of dealing with problems quickly. A procedure that takes months to settle a dispute is often worse than none at all. Formal negotiating machinery is fairly common in Britain: sometimes its provisions are laid down in detailed written agreements, and sometimes they rest upon a verbal 'understanding' between the unions and employers. But whatever form it takes, it is customary for the procedure to contain two or more 'stages'. The first stage normally provides for on-the-spot discussions between the shop stewards or local officials of the unions and the junior management of the company. If they fail to find a solution to the difficulty or grievance, the issue is automatically referred to a higher level: as a rule, to district officials of the union and the senior management—possibly directors—of the firm. The advantage of this arrangement is not merely that fresh minds are brought to bear. It also introduces an element of flexibility into the procedure: if intransigence has set in at the first stage, the situation can be eased by a new set of negotiators without any personal loss of face. Sometimes, however, the problem remains unsettled even then. To cover this possibility, some procedures provide for independent arbitration, either at the request of one side or the other, or by agreement between both. It can also be laid down that the arbitrator's verdict will be accepted as binding. Alternatively, arbitratively, arbitration can remain discretionary, with the agreed procedure ending at the second stage. Regardless of these differences, however, the essential point about procedure agreements is that industrial action of any kind is ruled out until their provisions have been exhausted. If this prohibition is ignored, the management is entitled to refuse to participate in negotiations until normal working has been resumed.

A good procedure can do a lot to prevent outbreaks of industrial warfare, but it cannot do everything. In the last analysis, harmony between employers and unions (or between managements and men) depends on the attitudes of the two sides to each other. It is sometimes suggested that it is out-of-date to talk about the 'two sides' of industry, and in the sense that the wellbeing of both is determined by the commercial success of the firm this is true. But it is also true that the area of common interest, though vitally important, is limited. There is ample scope for conflict over how the fruits of commercial success should be shared. Enlightened employers and unions recognize the legitimate interests of the other side, and do their best to satisfy them. Unenlightened employers and unions do not. It is, however, unusual for both to be equally at fault from the outset. As a rule, organizations, like people, react to the treatment they receive. If it is sensible and considerate (though not necessarily indulgent), they are sensible and considerate in return, and vice versa. Which is only another way of saying that employers get the unions, and unions the employers, that they deserve.

Reading list

BOOKS

Three Studies in Collective Bargaining, Research Paper No. 8 of the Royal Commission on Trade Unions and Employers' Associations (H.M.S.O., 1968)

Trade Unions and the Government, V. L. Allen (Longmans Green, 1960)

Essence of Trade Unionism: A Background Book, V. Feather (Bodley Head, 1963)

Systems of Industrial Relations in Great Britain, A. Flanders and H. A. Clegg (Blackwell's, 1954)

The Blackcoated Worker; A Study in Class Consciousness, D. Lockwood (Allen and Unwin, 1966)

What's Wrong with the Unions, E. Wigham (Penguin, 1961)

Report of the Royal Commission on Trade Unions and Employers' Associations (Department of Employment and Productivity, 1968)

Labour Relations and the Law: A Comparative Study, Editor Otto Kahn-Freund (Published under the auspices of the British Institute of International and Comparative Law and the United Kingdom National Committee on Comparative Law by Stevens & Sons, London, 1965)

International Protection of Trade Union Freedom, C. Wilfred Jenks (Published under the auspices of the London Institute of World Affairs, Stevens and Sons, 1957)

The Right to Membership of a Trade Union, R. W. Rideout (University of London, Athlone Press, 1963)

Trade Unions in a Free Society, B. C. Roberts (Published for the Institute of Economic Affairs by Hutchinson, Second Edition, 1962)

Conspiracy, Douglas Rookes (Johnson Publications, London, 1966)

Report of the Chief Registrar of Friendly Societies (H.M.S.O., 1967)

Trades Union Acts 1871 and 1913 (H.M.S.O., 1964 and 1967)

Useful addresses

Chief Registrar of Friendly Societies, 17 North Audley Street, London W 1

Confederation of British Industry, Tothill Street, London SW 1

Department of Employment and Productivity, St James's Square, London W 1

6.3 Positive Labour Relations

John Garnett

A company's labour relations are as important as its relationships with its customers and suppliers. Labour relations depend as much as anything else on the trades unions, and any company that fails to set about taking the initiative to improve these relationships is neglecting a golden opportunity to increase its efficiency.

Few boards of directors are satisfied with their companies' labour relations. Searching for ways of improving them, boards try any number of solutions: they strive to improve their wages structures, they try to get incentive schemes established, they tighten up on discipline, they introduce productivity committees and profit-sharing plans. Few ask themselves what can be the most important question of all: is it within our power to do anything to improve our relationships with the trades unions?

Even those who do ask this question often come up with a negative answer and conclude that nothing short of radical changes in the law, or a complete reform of the trades union movement, from the TUC downwards, will do any good whatever.

Trade union recognition

Most companies give trade unions only grudging recognition. True enough, most companies have a grievance procedure, and agreements about wages and working conditions that have been signed by the unions; but recognition goes little further.

358

The reason is that comparatively few companies are prepared to accept that, if a trades union is functioning properly, as a system of representation it can help managers to do their jobs better and help to make the company more efficient. Trade unions can be

1. an effective way of settling wages and conditions of employment;
2. a useful way for management to sound out employees' views;
3. a help in ensuring that employees' interests are (and are seen to be) taken into account, and in giving employees a sense of involvement.

Of course, the importance of these things depends a lot on size, and in small companies a representative system, however good, cannot be as useful as in a large organization. However, in companies with, say, more than five hundred employees, the purely practical argument for having a representative system is overwhelmingly strong. No one suggests that there is not massive room for improvement in the trade unions, but the point is that a good representative system (which, by definition, must be quite independent and quite separate from management) can help management to do their job better.

Trade union membership

'It's up to the men themselves—we don't try to influence them'. Many companies take this line about trades union membership and, traditions being what they are, employees know all too well what lies behind statements of this sort. Management can no more afford to take a neutral line of this kind about something as important as union membership, than it can about the reactions of its customers or its suppliers. The neutral line will certainly be interpreted as anti-union.

Management gains, if union membership is high, in the following ways:

Officials and shop stewards are more likely to be able to make agreements 'stick' if they have the authority that goes with high membership.

Officials with a high membership behind them are less likely to have to kowtow to extreme elements.

The higher the level of membership the more difficult hotheads and troublemakers will find it. It will be more difficult for them to bring their influence to bear on a large group, than on a small minority.

Inter-union rivalries, with one union trying to outbid another, and splinter groups of employees trying to form their own pressure groups are much less likely, if membership is high.

For these reasons it is very much in the company's interest not to sit on the fence about union membership, but to encourage employees to belong and to take an active part in union affairs. How can this be done without going to the lengths of a closed shop?

A written statement is needed, saying that management wants employees to belong to a union and believes in active membership. Foremen and junior managers need to have this carefully explained to them.

All new starters should have the company's attitude explained to them and be put in touch with their shop steward.

Examples of other steps that can be taken by management are to allow union meetings to be held on company premises outside normal working hours, say in the canteen; the deduction of union dues from wages; certain notice boards can also be set aside for trades union announcements.

If claims for a closed shop are made, and they are less likely to come if management is taking the line of encouraging union membership, the company can prevent the injustices of a closed shop by negotiating an agreement which recognizes that:

new starters should be told that trades union membership is a condition of employment and that they will therefore be expected to join a union if they join the company.

existing employees who are not union members will be encouraged to join the union, but will be allowed to continue as non members if they cannot be persuaded to join.

Genuine conscientious or religious objectors are few, but they cannot be expected to join a union. Unions generally recognize this and accept the man, provided that the equivalent of his dues are paid to charity.

Supervisors and foremen often remain trades union members in name alone when they are promoted. If they are anything more than this, and continue to be members of the same trades union branch and to be represented by the same shop stewards as the men they supervise, they cannot do their jobs as supervisors properly. Some major unions accept as a matter of policy that supervisors should not be members of the same branch as the people they supervise, and that they should not be represented by stewards drawn from the shop floor.

Shop stewards

Shop stewards are concerned in most companies' industrial relations problems. This is not surprising, because so much now depends on local rather than national bargaining. It is primarily this that has made the shop steward's job so important. In the future, it is, if anything, going to be more important for management to have responsible stewards who understand the issues at stake, who can present a case logically and reasonably and report back to their members clearly and persuasively.

No company in its senses wants to have stewards who are 'in the management's pocket' (or who are thought to be) but there is a good deal that management can do to improve the calibre of its stewards, without getting them dubbed as management men. Perhaps the most important single contribution the company can make, both to influence the quality of men who get elected as stewards and to make sure that they are properly equipped to carry out their work, is to recognize that negotiation and the settlement of grievances is only one part of a steward's job. If contact between managers and stewards is confined to the negotiating table, stewards will not do their jobs properly. They must be kept well informed about management's plans and developments, and must be consulted.

Management should take up the question of shop stewards' qualifications with the unions, and a minimum period of service with the company should be agreed. The number of stewards to be elected should also be agreed with the unions. Stewards should have written credentials, preferably issued jointly by their management and their union, which should specify the period of office, the department/section the steward represents, and the agreements and rules the steward undertakes to abide by. The circumstances in which they can leave their normal job in order to carry out their duties as steward should be defined; so should their wages while carrying out trade union business in working hours.

Shop stewards will not do their jobs properly unless they are properly trained. They need to understand:

their role as shop stewards

the company's aims and employment policies and organization

their union's policies and aims

the company/union agreements, particularly those covering negotiating and grievance procedure, wages and other working conditions.

Unless they are given formal training by the company as well as by the unions (and preferably jointly) they will not do an effective job.

Negotiation, consultation, and communication

A formal written negotiating and grievance procedure is essential in all except the very smallest companies, and it is the first steps in procedure that need to be most carefully thought out. The first step of all should be for an employee to see his foreman or supervisor; only if this fails should the shop steward be called in. Friction between supervisors and stewards is almost inevitable if this stage is omitted from the procedure, and relationships at this level are quite crucial.

Labour relations will not run smoothly just on the basis of a sound negotiating procedure. Consultation between management and employee representatives has an important part to play, and in anything other than small organizations a formal advisory committee is needed. This should be made up of shop stewards and one or two members of management, and committees should be encouraged to talk about everything that affects the efficiency of the company. The only thing that should be barred is negotiation. On the whole, joint consultation has earned itself a bad name in the last twenty years, but this is very largely because companies have failed to use it properly and have frequently established committees that have been separate and distinct from the unions and have had terms of reference that put quite unrealistic limitations on the things that can be discussed.

Management and shop floor employees have, broadly speaking, three methods of communicating with one another: through managers and supervisors, through representatives, and by mass methods such as works newspapers and notice boards. The last are effective for conveying facts, but when it comes to getting explanations across they are virtually useless. Companies that rely on their shop stewards as a way of communicating and 'selling' management decisions to the shop floor are asking for trouble. Either the shop steward conscientiously tries to explain what the issues are, and gets labelled as a management man, or else the proper explanation is not put across. In both cases management is the loser. The value of stewards as a means of communication is that they can communicate shop-floor points of view effectively to management.

Full-time trades union officials

All too often full-time trades union officials get called in only when things have already gone wrong. They will not do a constructive job if this is their only contact with management. It is as important for managers to build up something more than a negotiating relationship with full-time officials as it is with stewards. Close informal relationships obviously help, but something more is needed. Regular meetings between managers and officials, say twice yearly, to keep the officials up to date with company and works affairs, can be most valuable.

White collar unions

Staff unions have grown very rapidly in the last few years, and there is every indication that they will continue to grow. In a great many companies it is quite contrary to tradition for staff employees to belong to a union, but the force of this tradition has been weakening. The most difficult decision that directors face is the point at which to recognize staff unions and to set about getting relationships with them right, from the beginning. When the decision to recognize staff unions has been taken, the company must set about making the new arrangements work and must take the initiative in the same way, and for the same reasons, as it should with blue collar unions.

Reading list

BOOKS

Labour Relations in the Motor Industry, Turner, Clark, and Roberts (Allen and Unwin, 1967)
Industrial Relations, Michael Clarke (The Industrial Society, 1966)
Industrial Relations in Engineering, A. Marsh (Pergamon, 1965)
The Fawley Productivity Agreement, Alan Flanders (Faber and Faber, 1964)
Industrial Relations Handbook, Ministry of Labour (H.M.S.O., 1961)
Labour Relations and Conditions of Work in Britain, Central Office of Information, Reference Pamphlet 31 (H.M.S.O., 1967)
Positive Employment Policies (Ministry of Labour, H.M.S.O., 1958)
Status and Benefits in Industry, Produced by the Central Committee of Study Groups based on HRH The Duke of Edinburgh's Commonwealth Study Conferences (The Industrial Society, London, 1966)
Industrial Relations: Contemporary Problems and Perspectives. Edited by B. C. Roberts (Methuen, 1968)

Useful addresses

The Industrial Society, Robert Hyde House, 48 Bryanston Square, London W 1
Department of Employment and Productivity, St James's Square, London SW 1

6.4 Industrial Tribunals

H. Samuels

Industrial Tribunals are administrative tribunals set up originally under the Industrial Training Act, 1964, for the purpose of hearing appeals from employers against levies imposed on them for the financing of industrial training schemes. Since then, they have been given a number of other functions, under the Redundancy Payments Act, 1965, the Contracts of Employment Act, 1963 (as amended), the Selective Employment Tax Act, 1966, as well as twenty-three other enactments under which they have the functions previously exercised by referees and boards of referees.

An industrial tribunal consists of a chairman and two members. The chairman is selected by the President of the Industrial Tribunals (who is appointed by the Lord Chancellor) from a panel of legally qualified persons. The members are also selected by the President, one from a panel of persons representative of employers, and one from a panel of persons representative of employees. The number of such tribunals is determined by the President from time to time, as necessary.

Reports of selected cases heard by the tribunals are published in a series of official reports—ITR—and a useful digest of these is given monthly in *Knight's Industrial Reports*.

The most numerous class of cases are those brought under the Redundancy Payments Act. Where an employee's claim for redundancy payments is disputed, the employee may refer his claim to an industrial tribunal and the employer may contest the entitlement or the amount (or both). Disputes over entitlement cover a wide range (e.g., as to whether there was a contract of employment; as to its terms relevant to the matter in dispute; whether there was a dismissal; whether the dismissal was caused by redundancy; whether alternative employment offered was suitable), and disputes on the amount of payment raise questions of calculation of length of service, contractual rates of pay, and the like. Other matters referable to the tribunal are employers' claims for rebates from the Redundancy Fund, and questions arising under exempted schemes.

Under the Contracts of Employment Act, 1963, an employee is entitled to report to a tribunal his employer's failure to furnish him with a written memorandum of terms of employment under section 4 of the Act, and to refer a question whether a memorandum that was supplied sufficiently complies with the section.

Under the Selective Employment Tax Act an employer who disputes a decision of the Department of Employment and Productivity as to his right to repayment of tax or payment of premium may require the question to be referred to a tribunal. In these cases (as in appeals under the Industrial Training Act) the question usually turns on the point whether the activities or processes carried on by the applicant come within the statutory definition—the kind of questions that in an earlier period would have been decided departmentally.

Appeals

The decision of an industrial tribunal on a point of fact is conclusive, but a party may, on a point of law only, appeal to the High Court (in Scotland, the Court of Session).

Costs

In cases under the Industrial Training Act, a tribunal has the power to award costs against the employer or the Industrial Training Board, and similarly, under the Selective Employment Tax Act, against the employer or the Department of Employment and Productivity. In redundancy payment cases, the parties have to bear their own costs, but the tribunal may award costs against a party whose conduct has been frivolous or vexatious.

In appeals to the High Court against the decisions of tribunals, questions as to costs follow the usual High Court practice, and costs may be awarded against a tribunal for the latter's misbehaviour.

Reading list

BOOKS

Tribunals and Inquiries: A Guide to Procedure, N. D. Vandyk (Oyez Publications, 1965)
The Legal Aspects of Industry and Commerce, W. F. Frank (George Harrap, 4th Edition, 1967)

Labour Relations and the Law: A Comparative Study, O. Kahn-Freund, editor (Stevens and Sons, 1965)

Industrial Relations Handbook, Ministry of Labour (H.M.S.O., 1961)

The Modern Law of Employment, G. D. L. Fridman (Stevens and Sons, 1963, supplement, 1967)

Reports of decisions of the Industrial Tribunals on Appeals and References under the Industrial Training Act 1964, the Redundancy Payments Act 1965, Section 4A of the Contracts of Employment Act 1963, and the Selective Employment Payments Act 1966, Edited by Gerald Angel (H.M.S.O.)

Useful addresses

The Law Society, 113 Chancery Lane, London WC 2

The Industrial Society, 48 Bryanston Square, London W 1

Justice: British Section of the International Commission of Jurists, 1 Mitre Buildings, London EC 4

Central Office of Industrial Tribunals for England and Wales, 93 Ebury Bridge Road, London SW 1

7. Health, Welfare, and Pensions

7.1 Pension Schemes for Directors

John Gaselee

Sole proprietors and controlling directors are not allowed to join any pension scheme their firm may run. They fall into the 'self-employed' category, which, incidentally, includes anyone, from senior executives to the humblest factory-floor worker, who is not eligible to join an occupational pension scheme.

Certainly there is no need to despair about being in this position. There are even a few firms that do not believe in providing pensions, feeling that, if a man is paid an adequate salary, it is up to him to make his own arrangements for his future.

Perhaps the provision of pensions has gone too far. Certainly, for anyone who is ineligible to join an occupational scheme, good alternative arrangements can be made.

As a result of the Finance Act of 1956, it is possible to pay for a pension on terms with similar advantages to pension schemes approved under Section 379 of the Income Tax Act 1952, which favour those with high incomes. Unfortunately, however, not all insurance brokers are keen to suggest this kind of contract; generally, the commission they receive on it is lower than from other types of policy they may advocate.

Before the passing of this Act, anyone who made private provision for a pension could not claim relief of income tax on the premiums. Since then, however, relief of both income tax and surtax has been allowed on all premiums (whether on an annual or a single premium basis) where they are paid towards a special deferred

13*

annuity. When the pension is paid out, it is treated for tax purposes as earned income.

Clearly, therefore, for a comparatively high surtax payer, this is a most useful way of providing for the future from gross income. Added to this is the fact that the funds of the insurance companies for this type of contract carry valuable tax reliefs.

The maximum premium on which relief of income tax and surtax can be claimed is £750 or 10 per cent (whichever is smaller) of net relevant income from non-pensionable employment for anyone born in 1916 or later. For anyone born earlier, the limits are as follows:

Year of Birth	Sum		Percentage
1914 or 1915	£825	or	11
1912 or 1913	£900	or	12
1910 or 1911	£975	or	13
1908 or 1909	£1,050	or	14
1907 or any earlier year	£1,125	or	15

For anyone who is considered to be partly self-employed for these purposes, the position is a little complicated. If he has a pensionable post and also non-pensionable earnings, the maximum premium on which relief of tax will be allowed is 10 per cent (rising to 15 per cent, as above) of non-pensionable earnings. The other limit of £750 (rising to £1,125) is reduced by 10 per cent (rising to 15 per cent) of the pensionable emoluments.

Perhaps the best way of appreciating this is to look at two straightforward examples. If a man has a pensionable salary of £1,000 a year and non-pensionable earnings of £4,000 a year, he can pay a premium of £400 a year to one of these policies. This is a straight 10 per cent of £4,000, since this is less than £750 minus 10 per cent of £1,000. But if his pensionable earnings were £5,000 a year (instead of £1,000), the maximum premium would be £250, i.e., £750, minus 10 per cent of his pensionable salary of £5,000.

There is a wide variety of policies, and it is unfortunate that many people do not choose the contract best suited to their particular needs.

There are policies that operate on a level premium basis (in much the same way as a conventional life assurance policy) and there are others where a single premium can be paid each year. In the latter case, the payment of each premium represents a separate contract and, thus, the benefit it will secure will depend on the terms being offered at the time.

For anybody who cannot be certain that he will be entitled to pay the maximum premium in the years ahead, quite a good arrangement is to effect a level premium policy for a reasonable premium (i.e., below the maximum it is expected will apply) and for this to be 'topped up' each year with a payment towards a single premium policy. In this way, it is possible to make sure that the maximum premium on which relief will be granted is paid each year. Incidentally, relief can be claimed on the premium provided it is paid at any time up to six months *after* earnings for the year have been agreed with the Inspector of Taxes.

Another decision that has to be taken is whether the contract should be arranged on a non-profit or with-profit basis. Although nobody can forecast the future profits of the insurance companies with accuracy, since these depend not only on the yields obtainable on investments, but also on the mortality experience, actuaries are notoriously cautious and seldom declare a rate of bonus unless they are fairly sure in their minds that it should be possible to maintain it in the future. On this basis, provided it is effected with a first-class office with a good bonus record, the with-profit contract is likely to provide the best value for money.

The main drawback to with-profit life assurance is that, in the event of premature death, the benefits received will not be so high as if a non-profit policy had been arranged. This argument does not hold good in the case of a deferred annuity since, in the event of death before reaching pension age, no lump sum is payable. There is simply a return of the premiums paid to date (with or without interest, as agreed), although a few policies make provision for a pension to be provided for a widow.

Nevertheless, the majority of with-profit contracts do not increase the value of the pension once it has begun to be paid. As a result, as the cost of living continues to increase, the purchasing power of the pension is reduced.

There are, however, one or two contracts on the market where the bonus additions are made in the form of increases to the basic pension both *before* and *after* pension age. With one office, if its current rate of bonus is maintained (and, although this cannot be guaranteed, there is a good chance that it will be increased), for every £100 of annual premium paid by a man who first effects a policy at the age of forty, the annual pension at sixty-five will be £518 (of which £338 is the basic guaranteed figure). After the pension has been paid for five years, it is estimated that it will rise to £554, and that it will be £590 after ten years.

As an alternative arrangement, a pension can be based on the market value of equities. Good as this may sound in principle, it should be remembered that the amount paid in benefit will fluctuate from one payment to another (by no means always in an upward direction). There is no basic security, and one is solely at the mercy of Stock Exchange fluctuations. For these reasons it is seldom a good idea to arrange for the whole of a pension to be provided by this means.

In one case, premiums and benefits are linked to Investment-Trust Units. Premiums are paid as a succession of single payments, and the only stipulation is that the minimum that can be accepted at one time is £200, and the maximum £1,125, or the maximum permitted under the Act if this is lower.

Instead of each premium earning a cash annuity, the pension payments are expressed as a cash sum equal to a stated number of Investment-Trust Units. If someone aged exactly forty pays a premium that happens to be equivalent to the current price of 100 of the units, this will earn him a pension, paid quarterly in advance, at the age of sixty, amounting to the price of 3·05 units, whenever the pension is due. If, a year later, another premium equal to 100 units is paid, this will increase the quarterly pension by the equivalent of 2·95 units.

One leading insurance company has a scheme whereby similar 'single premiums' are carried to a special fund. Normally, this is invested almost entirely in ordinary shares.

For simplicity, the benefits from this arrangement are expressed in units, and their value fluctuates with the experience of the fund. Tax advantages are enjoyed by the fund. All commission, stamp duties, and brokerages are paid out of the fund. In addition, to cover the expenses of management, the insurance company retains 4 per cent of the premiums received, 5 per cent of the dividend and interest income, and 2 per cent of the annuities actually paid out.

With all 1956 Act policies there is a good deal of flexibility about when the pension will be payable. Basically, it can be any time between one's sixtieth and seventieth birthdays. Since it is usually impossible to tell in advance exactly when the pension will be needed, quite a good plan is to arrange for the pension to begin at the age of seventy. If it transpires that one will retire earlier, usually an insurance company will pay the pension that would have been purchased had it been arranged for the pension to be payable at the time in the first place. Incidentally, there is nothing to prevent anyone from drawing the pension and continuing to work.

Generally, in the event of death before pension age, the premiums paid to date will be returned, perhaps with the addition of a modest rate of interest. Those who do not have any dependants whom they wish to benefit in this way can arrange for no return of premiums in these circumstances, in which case the company will grant a modest increase in the basic amount of the pension.

Where possible, however, there is much to be said in favour of a married man arranging for the policy to pay a pension to his wife for her lifetime after his death, whether this occurs before or after he reaches pension age. If necessary, subject to the approval of the Inland Revenue, a pension along these lines can be provided for a dependant other than a wife.

This is, of course, particularly useful from the tax point of view. The total cost of providing this joint pension will be eligible for full relief from income tax and surtax (subject to the statutory limit). This, therefore, is a first-class way for anyone eligible for this kind of pension to provide for himself and his wife from gross income. A further advantage is that the value of the widow's pension will not be aggregable with the free estate for the purpose of estate duty.

Nevertheless, despite these advantages, a deferred annuity has a certain rigidity. It is non-commutable and non-assignable. Thus, cash may not be taken in lieu of a pension when retirement age is reached, nor may the policy be sold or be used as security for a loan.

Some people think it an adverse feature that the policy cannot be surrendered for cash. There is, however, much to be said for knowing that a pension is secure and that this particular nest-egg cannot be raided by anybody.

The main alternative arrangement for providing a pension does not have this rigidity, although it is inflexible in certain other ways. This method, by the way, can be used by anyone, including those who wish to supplement the benefits they will receive from an occupational pension scheme.

The plan of campaign in this case should be to effect an endowment life assurance policy, the point being that it will be necessary to arrange for it to mature on a set date. That is part of the inflexibility, and the rest lies in the fact that there is no scope for varying the premium each year—although, of course, at a later date, contributions could be stepped up by arranging a further policy, provided there has been no serious deterioration in health.

When the policy matures, it can be used to purchase an immediate annuity in the open market.

Unlike the deferred annuity, an endowment policy acquires a surrender value, which will be based on the premiums paid to date, although it is likely to be less than their sum total.

As a result, the policy can be used as security for a loan. Incidentally, the majority of insurance companies look upon it as their duty (even when credit is difficult to obtain) to provide loans when required, at a reasonable rate of interest, for up to 90 per cent of the surrender value of the policy.

The tax position so far as this kind of arrangement is concerned is quite different from that applying in the case of a deferred annuity. Only income tax relief is allowed, and this is restricted to a maximum of two-fifths of the premiums. There are two limits so far as this relief is concerned. In the first place, for this maximum amount of relief to be granted, the total payments for life assurance premiums must not exceed one-sixth of the policy holder's income. Second, relief will be given only in respect of the annual premium that is less than £7 per cent of the sum assured. In practice, the premium for a policy taken out at the younger ages should be well within this limit. But, for a with-profit policy for a comparatively short term, this may well be exceeded.

When the policy matures, the capital sum is free of all tax. There is no *need* for it ot be used to purchase an annuity, although this will be the best course if a pension is required.

There is no reason why the annuity should be purchased from the same company as issued the life policy, and it is probable that another company will be more competitive. Nevertheless, as a safeguard, there is much to be said in favour of having an annuity option included in the endowment policy. The yield quoted will be on the low side, as an insurance company will not wish to commit itself to a high yield many years in advance. If, however, there should be a sharp drop in yields in the future, it could act as a useful long-stop, and the company is unlikely to charge for including it.

When, in due course, the annuity is purchased, there is much to be said in favour of securing the same kind of guarantee as will be provided by a pension scheme, i.e., that the benefits will be paid for a minimum period of, say, five years, whether one survives for that period or not.

It is when the annuity is paid that the largest saving in tax will be experienced. For instance, whereas the whole of the pension from a 1956 Act deferred annuity is treated as earned income for tax purposes, when a man aged sixty-five purchases an immediate annuity, about 65 per cent of every payment may be free of tax altogether; the remainder is treated as unearned income.

Irrespective of the actual yield on an annuity, for a man of this age, the Inland Revenue arbitrarily lays down that £7 0s. 11d. per cent of the annuity shall be free of tax. This is considered as being repayment of capital, and is termed the capital element. The remaining part of the annuity is regarded as the interest element, being wholly liable to tax on the basis of its being unearned income.

It is impossible to be specific about the best means of providing for the future since so much depends on personal circumstances. A good firm of life assurance brokers specializing in this field should, however, be able to go into details and show what is likely to be most worth while. Nevertheless, some of the best arrangements are sometimes provided by long-established life companies who do not pay away commission for the introduction of business. Rather naturally, few brokers are likely to be sufficiently altruistic as to recommend them!

Reading list and useful addresses

See p. 380.

7.2 Pensions for Employees

John Gaselee

About 50 per cent of all workers in Britain are currently included in occupational pension schemes, which are either contributory or non-contributory. The proportion of those included for whom it would be practical to make pension provision is much higher, bearing in mind the self-employed, part-time workers, and others for whom the provision of a pension would not be justified. Each year there are about half a million fresh employees to these schemes.

The stage has been reached where the majority of large firms have pension schemes (at least for staff), and in most cases it is obligatory for eligible employees to join them, either on taking up the employment, after reaching a certain minimum age, or after a qualifying period of service.

At the moment, most activity in connection with the larger schemes is centred round the improvement of the benefits and, government restrictions allowing, increases in the benefits of existing pensioners. Although there may be nothing in the rules about such increases, in practice, as surpluses are thrown up by the funds, rather than use them to reduce contributions in the future the vast majority of companies are using them to increase pensions—usually by a flat percentage increase in the case of those already on pension, although this may vary according to the period during which employees have been retired.

Smaller firms, down to those with literally no more than a handful of employees, have felt the competition from large groups that can offer pension schemes (which, often, are non-contributory) and thus have been setting up their own schemes, either for all members of the firm, or on an individual basis for selected employees.

It is generally only among the smaller firms that there is now much scope for the introduction of an occupational pension scheme. There is, however, still considerable scope for the improvement of benefits among the larger firms that already have schemes. The great majority of pension schemes (even taking into account supplementary 'top hat' arrangements) still provide much less than the maximum Revenue limit, which is two-thirds of final salary at retirement, and less for those who have been in the firm's employ for less than twenty years before retiring.

Increasingly, large firms are being tempted to do-it-yourself. Instead of paying premiums to an insurance company, they consider they may be large enough to administer their own pension funds, and obtain a better result than the insurance company. There are many companies that have achieved first-class results in this way. Usually, they have resulted from taking a gamble at one stage—and this has paid off. An obvious example is the 'cult of the equity' which was practised by some self-administered funds extensively before the insurance companies entered this market. Equally, there are plenty of cases of self-administered funds that have been very much less successful than would have been a middle-of-the-road insured scheme. These may have taken gambles that did not come off, and a slightly one-sided picture of self-administration can be given since, rather naturally, very little is ever heard of these funds.

Generally, there is no point in even considering the possibility of a self-administered pension fund if the annual contributions amount to less than £10,000, and in a great many cases there are strong arguments for having an insured scheme where the contributions are considerably in excess of this figure.

Naturally, the insurance companies advocate insured schemes, whereas trust companies and those who are prepared to manage self-administered funds point out the advantages of the latter arrangement. Unbiased advice on the subject is difficult to obtain; in any case it is practically impossible to tell with certainty whether an insured or private scheme will be most satisfactory until it has been running for, probably, thirty years or more.

The main justification for a private fund is to obtain a higher yield, and thus be able to provide higher benefits at the same cost. Advocates of these funds point out that yields can be higher because non-productive overheads are reduced, including the broker's commission. But, in the case of a private fund, the company concerned will have appreciably higher administrative costs. Whether the investment and running of the fund is farmed out or is managed within the company, investment expertise is not cheap. When the management is undertaken by an outside trustee, usually the charges it makes are based on a graduated percentage of the capital value of the fund. In addition, it will be necessary to use the services of a consulting actuary.

376

Leaving aside administrative costs, the question of security needs to be considered. An insured scheme has the advantage that, if yields drop, it has the solidarity of the assets of the life office on which to fall back. This acts as a cushion, and so the drop to the scheme should not be so pronounced.

It is easy to think that having one's own fund is like buying wholesale instead of retail. This does not necessarily follow, especially when the insurance managers of the British life offices are thought by many to be among the most skilful investment men in the country, even though by no means do they all take the same line. Incidentally, even if a self-administered fund is set up, it may be necessary to 'lay-off' certain large risks with an insurance company.

There is no easy way of making this choice. Whereas insured schemes are generally sound and represent good value for money (especially if handled by a first-class firm of brokers) a private fund may do better, or it may do worse.

There is a wide variety of insured pension schemes, most of which participate in the profits of the insurance companies and many of which are geared to the yield obtained by the insurance company on its investments. Schemes are becoming very much more sophisticated, and this is where the advice of a good broker should help a company to take advantage of the latest technical advances. Unfortunately, the insurance companies themselves are not always quick to point them out to their clients. Perhaps one of the main drawbacks to so many of these new arrangements for the provision of pensions is the difficulty in estimating the level of contributions that may be required in the future.

Rather naturally, smaller firms usually have to work on a different principle. Almost certainly it will be impossible to institute a non-contributory scheme with an adequate level of benefits. There is, however, nothing unreasonable about asking employees to contribute towards their pensions. Not only is there a certain advantage in them taking this interest in their future, but also that they should have a reasonable pension is much more important than who meets the cost.

In deciding on the level of pension to be provided, there is no reason why the State pension should not be taken into account, provided it is borne in mind that it is at little more than subsistence level. Furthermore, it will be a long time before the graduated scheme has any effect on a man's total pension.

Some employers, therefore, think of a figure for a total pension and then deduct, say, £200 to £300 to take some account of the State pension. There is, however, no doubt that during the past ten years, employers have been more generous in outlook, so far as benefits are concerned, than in the previous decade.

There are policies on the market that simply provide a lump sum for an employee on his retirement. The point to watch in this case is that, if this is the sole arrangement, usually the pension that could be secured with the capital sum (by purchasing an immediate annuity at retirement) is quite low. It is generally much better for the pension to come straight from the employer's arrangement, and to be payable for life.

377

In practice, most pensions are guaranteed for five years (sometimes ten years) even if the pensioner dies within that period. It is, however, a good plan for every employee, shortly before he retires, to have the option of taking a reduced pension that will continue for the lifetime of his wife, should he predecease her. Sometimes such a pension is level for the whole period, or it may drop when the pensioner himself dies. Incidentally, if the pension counts as earned income in the hands of the pensioner, the same principle applies when it is received by his wife.

There is no doubt that the type of pension arrangement likely to be of most value to employees is one where the benefits are linked in some way to final salary. But this is not cheap. For instance, if considering a company with predominantly young employees, the cost for a reasonably generous final salary scheme could be in the region of 15 per cent of payroll, although this should be taken as no more than a very rough guide.

Small companies, generally, cannot attain to these heights, at least when they first institute a scheme. Thus, it is more usual for them to have a scheme whereby a certain level of earnings in a particular year earns a set amount towards the pension at retirement. Both the length of service and the earnings are reflected in the ultimate pension. With young employees, the total cost of a reasonable scheme along these lines (including life assurance benefits) may be in the region of 8 per cent of payroll, of which the employees can be asked to contribute half.

A basic drawback to this arrangement (and this is why many large firms are converting from this to a 'final salary' basis) is that it is based to some extent on average earnings throughout service, whereas the cost of living (and of earnings), due to inflation, is likely to rise substantially before an employee retires. Thus, what now appears to be a reasonable pension may be quite inadequate by the time it is actually paid.

As a result of this built-in inadequacy, usually a careful revision of this type of scheme needs to be made at periodic intervals so that improvements can be made. They, however, are likely to prove quite expensive.

A point that always has to be faced when a new scheme is set up is the position of employees who have been in service for some years. Usually, arrangements can be made for this past service to qualify for benefit accruing from the employer's contributions. Most employers like to spread this cost into the future. Even so, it may be too expensive to pay at the full rate. In this case, 'past service', as it is known, can earn, say, half or a quarter of the pension applicable after the introduction of the scheme. Unfortunately, an employee cannot help to boost this himself by paying in a lump sum.

Unless pensions are arranged on an individual basis for employees in a small firm, any pension scheme will have the effect of casting all employees in the same mould. Quite often, a company will wish to provide additional pension benefits for selected employees, especially since this is likely to be of much more value to them than a straight increase in salary on which they will have to pay a high rate of tax.

This is where the 'top hat' pension arrangement can be of considerable advantage, although it has suffered a slight fall from favour in the last ten years or so in view of the higher limits at which surtax is applied and the fact that there has been a steady improvement in basic occupational arrangements.

'Top hat' policies are flexible, in that the benefits for employees can be varied; in addition, they have the great advantage that they can be commuted for cash at retirement. Thus, employees can build up a cash sum (which can be claimed at retirement) without bearing tax on any of it.

Even when an employee would prefer a pension rather than cash at retirement, almost certainly it will still pay him to commute the maximum permitted pension for cash and to use this cash to purchase an immediate annuity. Not only is the yield for the annuity likely to be better (although this cannot be forecast in advance), but the capital content of the annuity payments (which may amount to up to two-thirds of the total for a man aged sixty-five) will be completely free from tax; the remainder will be taxed as unearned income.

The point to bear in mind about commutation is that only up to one quarter of an employee's benefits from all retirement schemes to which an employer has contributed (apart from the National Insurance scheme) may be commuted by an employee on retirement. Thus a 'top hat' pension may be commuted in full only if it represents no more than one third of the benefits available from the underlying occupational scheme.

A 'top hat' policy can be particularly useful for an employee joining a firm with fewer than twenty years' service before retirement. Since this is a completely individual arrangement (although not exactly cheap for an employer), it is a first-class way of seeing that such a man obtains a worthwhile pension, subject to the Revenue limits.

Although there is nothing to prevent an employee from contributing towards a 'top hat' pension from his salary, if he does so he will be allowed no more than the normal tax relief for life assurance, which, within limits, is relief of income tax on two-fifths of the premiums. There is, however, a way round this problem. It is simply for the employee to sacrifice part of his salary so that this can be paid direct by the firm to the insurance company. In this case, the employee obtains full relief of tax, for his salary will actually have been reduced by the amount of his contribution. Merely deducting the contribution from an employee's salary will not have the same effect as actually reducing his salary.

A problem connected with pensions as a whole is the increasing cost of living. It is for this reason that many pension schemes are being converted to the 'final salary' basis. Even so, once it begins to be paid, this pension is fixed and can mean a very real drop in purchasing power over the years of retirement.

Most employers are raising pensions, where they can, when surpluses are thrown up following a valuation of the funds. But pensioners cannot depend on such increases as a right. As a result, there is a move towards arranging pensions which provide increasing benefits after retirement. For instance, a pension scheme that has a built-in increase of $2\frac{1}{2}$ per cent per annum (although rises may be effective only, say, every three years) can be arranged. Basically, however, this is likely to cost 15 per cent more than a level pension. Although lower increases are sometimes mentioned, usually they take into account certain assumed bonuses. Actuarially, there is no way of escaping from the fact that this is the extra amount of contribution needed.

Although there are moves on foot to introduce compulsory transferability of pension rights when an employee leaves one employer for another, few employees under the age of forty-five are displaying any interest in taking their pensions with them. Contributory schemes usually allow an employee to take a 'frozen' or 'paid-up' pension with him, which is simply a pension based on contributions made to date that will be paid when normal retirement age is reached. Increasingly, employers are allowing their contributions to help swell the pension, although in some cases this applies only for men who have been in the pension scheme for, say, five or ten years.

Even with this incentive, the majority of employees are still choosing to take a refund of their contributions. This is attractive from the tax angle, since if they have been allowed full relief of tax on the contributions, tax is deducted at only one quarter of the standard rate when the cash refund is made.

Nevertheless, it is right and proper that pensions should be looked upon as deferred pay, and should not be lost or deliberately forfeited on transfer from one employment to another. It has been estimated that the overall cost to employers for all pension rights to be preserved would be in the region of £50 million per annum, or about 0·05 per cent of payroll.

Reading list

BOOKS

The Complete Guide to Pensions and Superannuation, G. D. Gilling-Smith (Penguin Books,– Pelican Book A 844–1967)
Directors' Pensions (Institute of Directors, London, 1962)
New Trends in Pensions, Michael Pilch and Victor Wood (Hutchinson, London, 1964)
Planned Life Assurance, Martin Paterson (Business Publications, 1966)
Insurance, Michael Pix (Arco Publications, 1962)
Occupational Pension Schemes: A New Survey by the Government Actuary (H.M.S.O., 1966)
Your Retirement (Engineering Industries Association, London, 1968)
Pension Schemes and Retirement Benefits, Gordon A. Hosking (Sweet and Maxwell, London, 1968)
Social Security and Pension Practice in Western Europe (The Noble Lowndes Group, 1964)

Pension Schemes, Michael Pilch and Victor Wood (Hutchinson, London, 1960)
Insurance, John Gaselee (Collins (Nutshell Book) 1967)

Useful addresses

Life Offices' Association, Aldermary House, Queen Street, London EC 4
Corporation of Insurance Brokers, 15 St Helen's Place, London EC 3
Chartered Insurance Institute Library, 20 Aldermanbury, London EC 2

7.3 Executive Health: Living with Stress

H. Beric Wright

In medical terms, the problem with executives is not to make them work but to stop them working too hard, and to help them get their work priorities right.

The director is, more or less by definition, a highly motivated individual who wants to excel in a very competitive field. There is little or no place in industry or commerce for a young man unless he has a well developed will to succeed. He is competing both personally, in his own drive, to get to the top, and, as part of a team, in order to expand his firm and improve its profitability. His own rewards and chances of success are linked to those of the organization.

This means that, for better or worse, the executive is 'married' to his firm, and their problems cannot meaningfully be considered in isolation. If the above is true (and considerable experience of dealing with the executive health problems has convinced me that it is) it means that living with stress can be a much more important factor in the lives of directors than in the lives of most others. This is not to say that others are not stressed at all; far from it, because stress is an essential biological feature of life. But it does mean that if executives are to flourish and survive in what is, by definition, a stressful and challenging environment, they are likely to benefit more than others from a knowledge of what stress is all about and how it influences their behaviour and limits their performance.

The term stress has been borrowed from engineering. In its original context, stress has a precise meaning and can indeed be measured. Engineers, architects, and draughtsmen can design into a structure the ability to withstand a defined amount of load or strain. If this load is exceeded, the structure will collapse or the girder will bend. Thus, in engineering terms, the qualities of stress resistance of a given metal or structure imply a capacity to carry a load. 'Pre-stressing', as in concrete or some other tensile materials, actually increases their strength or resistance. The same may be truer of human reactions than is generally realized. Mental breakdown is not far removed from the sudden shattering of a laminated windscreen, when it is suddenly 'de-stressed'.

As far as medicine is concerned, stress has come to be known only by its harmful effects: a stressed man being one who is, by implication, below par or feeling the strain. This ignores the fact that there is a basic need for stress and that it is to this extent good and desirable; indeed, essential. All living things if they are surviving reasonably successfully are in a state of equilibrium with their environment. This means that they are, in fact, overcoming the challenge presented by the environment. The very presence of this challenge is essential to existence. If an individual is placed in a situation or environment that includes everything necessary to sustain life but excludes any contact with, or stimulus from, the outside world, there is fairly rapid disintegration of the personality.

Man needs the constant challenge of the environment to give tone to his existence. Overcoming challenge gives an individual the satisfactions and the motivation to go on, and makes life worth living.

Stress or, in more general terms, anxiety is equally a part of normal everyday life. If the director is to succeed reasonably well, he must have an above-average ability to deal with stress and live with anxiety. One of the attributes of success is thus likely to be a high stress threshold.

If life becomes too much for someone, either emotionally or environmentally, he will opt out by developing symptoms that make it impossible or difficult for him to carry on. The Victorians had this problem well worked out. If mother was presented with a conflict she could not resolve, usually something she did not want to do, she got an attack of the vapours, or a headache, and then everyone was sorry for her.

Illness is mostly painful: pain is, biologically, a call for help. People who do not need help—those who stand robustly on their own feet—seldom feel 'pain', and indeed they are seldom ill.

These are the factors behind stress disease. Illness is basically a need to opt out. It is usually the individual who decides that he is ill (life is too much for him) and his doctor who tells him what is wrong. Later, they jointly decide that all is well, and that he can resume his wage-earning role and get back into the community.

Stress symptoms are perfectly genuine and are produced at a subconscious level. Psychosomatic disease is real disease.

The director or manager is a major part of the environment in which his employees struggle for their existence and look for their satisfactions. The way in which he behaves and the success with which he manipulates the climate is reflected in the morale and success of the organization. This is, of course, why a bloody-minded departmental head or an irascible tycoon is such hell to work with.

Similarly, there must be 'horses for courses'. The man who will relish the tough atmosphere in a high reward, hire-and-fire firm is not the man for a large and rather gentle bureaucracy, where he would go mad from frustration. The bureaucrat or large-firm man would equally feel desperately insecure in a small results-oriented firm. It is the job of the individual himself, his potential employer and, perhaps, the selection consultant, bearing these considerations in mind, to fit people into the right niche.

Stress reactions are individual and personalized. One man's personality environment equation may be upset by the same kind of employer who would inspire someone else. All this is important for the philosophy of medicine and the way in which doctors assess patients. It is easy to relieve the symptoms of an ulcer with an alkali, but to effect a cure requires an analysis of why the symptoms have been caused. Dyspepsia is a very common stress symptom, and ulcers are said to be the business-man's disease (in fact, in Britain, they are not). Other manifestations of stress are far commoner; and coronary thrombosis and high blood pressure are what kill middle-aged men.

Common stress symptoms are insomnia, dyspepsia, skin irritation, irritability, headaches, and so on. Diseases generally agreed to have a large stress element are migraine, asthma, psoriasis, and peptic ulcers.

What we unfortunately do not know much about is why one person reacts in one way with, say, a skin rash, and another with a headache, or a third gets no symptoms at all until his coronary hits him. What we do know is that everyone, sooner or later, has his breaking point; the point beyond which he cannot go on functioning smoothly. Stress thresholds vary enormously; poor fish give up soon, others last much longer. As already suggested, successful businessmen are likely to have high stress thresholds. Happy, well-adjusted people doing what they enjoy are seldom ill. They are beating their challenge and getting a kick out of it.

This last point has two important implications: the first is that if one knows one's stress symptoms, what they mean, and why they have arisen, one knows when the margin is narrowing. The time to let up has arrived. Second, and more important, it suggests the need to set oneself realistic targets. Set them too low, and the challenge and satisfaction are inadequate: too high, and the goal becomes unachievable and frustration sets in. Underemployment is as big a cause of stress as overemployment or overpromotion.

Insight and understanding, and a realistic assessment of one's own aims and abilities, provide the key to health, which may be defined as the successful matching of aspirations to attributes.

There are three useful ways in which stress thresholds can be raised and effectiveness increased.

First, by realizing that stress exists and has its basis in conflict and indecision. It is essential not to get cluttered up with unsolved or nagging problems. This is obviously, in business, a counsel of perfection; but once a problem is recognized and defined it is nearer solution. One must be ready to accept that a problem may not be soluble and that it must be put aside, at least for the time being. In this way, energy is released for less intractable problems. All this sounds so simple, but how seldom is it acted on!

Second, by avoiding fatigue. Fatigue is essentially the physical expression of an emotional state; it is not the same as stress, but clearly the tired man has a lower stress threshold.

Business life is so demanding and so satisfying that businessmen tend to neglect the other side of their lives, their families and their relaxations. Success and satisfaction from outside activities are just as good for morale as success at work.

If all his targets are work-oriented, a man is vulnerable. If all his interests and contacts are at work, he has nothing else to talk about; at best, he becomes, by the age of fifty, a thundering bore who is lost once he leaves the office.

It is legitimate to work hard to build up one's career, but once well up the ladder it is essential to balance one's personality and one's life with outside interests. For the man who has nothing to do when he retires, challenge has gone; and life may end —often rather suddenly.

We must realize in dealing with our stress/personality problems that most of us are average men and we must abide by the rules. Only the outstanding people can break them and survive; they are, in fact, outstanding because they have this ability.

This article is concerned with executive health in general, but as stress is the key to health and disease it has dominated the discussion. It must now be fitted into the general pattern.

Cardiovascular disease, coronary thrombosis, and high blood pressure, are the main killers of middle-aged men. The factors that predispose to coronary thrombosis are as follows:

1. *Genetic* or inherited disposition. Coronary heart disease runs in families and if there is such a history, the other warning signs must be treated with even greater respect.

2. *Lack of exercise.* Coronary heart disease is, at younger ages (below sixty) preeminently a disease of the sedentary. But not only does exercise protect, it has other values in toning up and blowing away cobwebs; often it is pleasurable too. Half an hour a day brisk walking is enough. Stairs are also good exercise.

3. *Smoking cigarettes.* Cigarette smokers have a between two and three times higher coronary rate than non-smokers; they also get chronic bronchitis and lung cancer. Smoking a cigarette puts up blood pressure by 10 to 15 points, and cholesterol levels are higher in smokers. Pipe and cigars are seemingly safe.

4. *Raised Cholesterol*. Cholesterol is blood fat; men with a raised level have roughly the same added risk as cigarette smokers. Raised cholesterol tends to be associated with obesity and stress, as, of course, is smoking. It is now a treatable condition.

5. *Obesity*. Obesity has been called the commonest disease in developed countries. Life insurance experience shows that there is a 13 per cent increase in mortality for every 10 per cent increase in weight. Most of this is due to raised blood pressure. The main cause of obesity is eating too much.

6. *Stress*. Stress causes tension and frustration, which puts up blood pressure and cholesterol, and acts in a number of other ways, such as increasing fatigue and causing delusions of indispensability.

The point about most of these factors is that they are all likely to be present in the life of an ambitious businessman unless he has the sense and insight to deal with them by living sensibly and within his limitations. If health is a vital and precious asset, it is surely worth preserving. If people are valuable, as indeed they are, they are surely worth the same sort of expenditure and effort on maintenance as goes for plant or cars.

The executive health examination is really preventive maintenance on senior people; strictly speaking it should be equally valuable right through the population. A properly done executive health examination is much more than just a life insurance medical. It should aim at two objects.

First, to look at the individual in relation to his environment; to assess the balance of this and discover the reason for any symptoms that may be present. This assessment gives the individual the chance to talk about his problems, and the doctor an opportunity to influence the environment or climate within the firm.

Second, by a series of screening tests, clinical examination, X-rays, cardiograph, blood chemistry, and so on, to pick up the early signs of unsuspected disease and start appropriate treatment. From what has been said, treatment is just as likely to involve the radical altering of a man's way of life as it is to include the prescription of drugs. But both can be valuable. It is astonishing how much better and more effective a man becomes if he can be helped to equate his aspirations with his attributes, and to stop smoking, lose weight, take exercise, and enjoy himself more often.

At the Medical Centre of the Institute of Directors we had, at the time of writing, carried out some eight thousand medical examinations and run schemes for about two hundred companies. We find something wrong with over a third of the people we see, and it is probably more important to pick up an early high blood pressure in a man of forty than it is to find a lung cancer in a man of seventy. Of course, one finds all sorts of conditions, many of them unsuspected; but cardio-vascular disease predominates and much can now be done about it. More important is the legitimate value of the reassurance that can be given to the man who is standing up well to a demanding existence.

386

The businessman can be helped to remain effective and well by two things. The first is to understand what he is trying to do and what are the pitfalls; this is mainly concerned with stress and dealing with people. The second is regular maintenance to keep the machine running smoothly. A balanced interest in health is prudence, not hypochondria. A director owes this interest to himself, his family and his shareholders, as well as to his staff. He should facilitate maintenance on them, too.

How to cut down the stress

Unless the director and his family are prepared to take their place in the NHS queue and accept the uncertainty as to who might treat them in any given hospital, it is wise to provide 'insurance' cover for private treatment. This can be done through schemes such as British United Provident Association, Private Patients Plan, or some similar scheme. Rebates are available for group schemes, which are provided as a benefit of membership by several professional organizations, such as the Institute of Directors. Many firms run groups internally; twelve is the minimum number required to form a group, and these can be subsidized to a varying extent. The AA (Automobile Association) runs a rebate scheme for members joining the Private Patients Plan.

Remember that relationships are based on communication and that communication implies a 'two-way comprehension'. It is thus worth considerable trouble to think out, in advance, the effect that one's actions and statements will have on subordinates and also, of course, on one's family.

Stress arises from unsolved problems and failure to cope with the demands of the environment. Recognition or acceptance of the fact that a problem may for the moment be insoluble is a step towards resolution.

A realistic assessment of priorities prevents that frittering away of valuable time and energy. Recognition that one's early stress symptoms herald the approach of (mild) breakdown helps to keep the margin on which one lives and works reasonably wide.

Giving reasonable vent to one's feelings is better than bottling them up. Directors find this difficult because they are expected to appear calm at all times and, thus, lack many of the normal outlets for their aggression. Driving fast cars fast is not necessarily the best way of doing this, but hard physical activity is a good antidote to anxiety. Alcohol, in moderation, is a legitimate and desirable tranquillizer.

Life is a 'totality', so domestic worries will lessen the energy available for dealing with those arising from business. Similarly, relaxation adds to the morale available for dealing with problems at work. Balance in life is essential, particularly as one gets older, and it is wise to know and plan for retirement long before it occurs.

Wives and families are as important as profits; the businessman's wife, tucked away in the commuter belt, tends to get, and to accept, a fairly raw deal.

Attention to weight, exercise, and moderation in food, alcohol, and cigarettes all help to increase life expectancy. Enough sleep, holidays, and relaxation are essential, especially for the older man. Walk upstairs and eschew the lift. Get regular health maintenance carried out. Most men over fifty require reading glasses, and eyes should be tested every two years.

More time is spent in the office than at home, and it is worth making this pleasant, comfortable, and efficient, for one's staff as well as oneself. Modern office furniture is much better designed than it was even five years ago. Much office lighting remains appallingly bad.

Delegation is the key to growing old gracefully and to being trusted by one's juniors. Learning is a skill that has to be cultivated in high priority time. Endless committees and the ever-open door are dubiously valuable. Delusions of indispensability are a sign of fatigue and wrong priorities; they usually arise from a failure to delegate and to take adequate breaks. Industry and commerce might, with benefit, adopt the academic principle of the sabbatical break. It is no longer possible to govern New South Wales, but Australia can be visited.

Travel is wearying, and it is ludicrous to expect to work a longer week when away than when at home without feeling the effects. Remember that the body has its own circadian rhythm, which is upset by altering its time base, as occurs during East-West and West-East travel. Time to acclimatize on arrival and return is essential. Time off at home on return allows one to 'catch up' with the family. Well-run companies lay down travel rules and see that they are enforced.

Entertaining is work and should come out of working hours.

Sleep is precious and pills can often help this, particularly when one is in a strange place.

Reading list

BOOKS

Tension Control for Businessmen, E. Jacobson (McGraw-Hill, 1963)
Keeping Young in Business, A. Uris (McGraw-Hill, 1968)
The Advantages of a Company Health Service (Confederation of British Industry, 1964)

Useful addresses

British Medical Association, Occupational Health Committee, B.M.A. House, Tavistock Square, London WC 1
Institute of Directors Medical Centre, 9 Belgrave Mews North, London SW 1

7.4 Industrial Health Services

H. Beric Wright

The origins

Even in ancient times, it was realized that certain occupations carried the risk of 'infection' by a disease peculiar to the industry concerned. Thus, the Romans were aware of the effects of silver and mercury on the miners who worked the shallow hillside mines and quarries. 'Hatter's shakes', a nervous trembling caused by mercury poisoning from chemicals used in dressing fur hats, in the eighteenth century was an occupational disease recognized by European doctors. Ramazzini, a Renaissance Italian doctor and Thackrah, a nineteenth-century Yorkshire general practitioner, are generally regarded as being the fathers of industrial medicine. They were the first doctors to draw serious attention to the fact that several diseases or disabilities arose specifically from the conditions under which the individual worked.

The first effective Factory Act in Britain, concerning the employment of children, was passed in 1833. At about the same time, doctors were taken into mines and factories to advise about the prevention of disease and the conditions under which employees might reasonably be expected to work. The Certifying Factory Surgeon was appointed to certify that a child had the physical configuration of the age of nine before he could go down the mines or work in a mill.

Modern legislation

The Factory Acts have been systematically extended and now cover working conditions in all factories. It must, however, be remembered that the Acts cover only minimal working standards, and enlightened employers can reasonably be expected to provide better than minimal conditions. The Factory Acts also 'prescribe' certain diseases such as silicosis, lead and mercury poisoning, byssinosis, and bladder cancer; the possibilities of exposure to these must be controlled and the worker compensated if he is 'infected'. The Factory Acts are administered for the Department of Employment and Productivity by lay factory inspectors who are chiefly concerned with safety and accident prevention.

The Factory Inspectorate has a small medical branch, under a chief medical officer, and the country is covered—albeit superficially—by regionally based medical inspectors of factories whose main function is to advise on the prevention of industrial poisoning. Also under the Department of Employment and Productivity is the appointed factory doctor, who is the descendant of the certifying factory surgeon. The AFD has a statutory duty to examine juveniles entering industry, to carry out monitoring examinations on workers in dangerous trades, those using lead or benzine for example, and to investigate certain accidents such as gassing or electrocution. The AFD is nearly always a part-time local practitioner. It is possible for a works doctor to carry out some of his tasks within his own factory, if special arrangements are made.

The Department of Employment and Productivity currently has plans to reorganize the AFD service into a smaller, highly trained, and less part-time service. It is also proposed to review and consolidate the Factory Acts.

In 1965, shops and offices were brought under closer supervisory control by the Shops and Offices Act, which is administered by local government authorities. This lays down minimal working conditions in terms of heating, lighting, ventilation, sanitation, floor space, and so on.

The Department of Employment and Productivity has pointed out that a high proportion of the shops and offices inspected up to 1968 do not come up to these minimum standards. Many employers, especially where there had been a change of tenancy, had failed to register their premises with the local authorities.

The employer has a statutory obligation to enforce the minimum standards of health and safety of his employees who are protected by law. Factory inspectors also have power (which is, in fact, not nearly enough used) to close unsatisfactory premises or suspend unsafe operations, such as fume hazards, chemical intoxication, or dust contamination.

Although the United Kingdom compares favourably with America with regard to the medical supervision of workplaces, it lags seriously behind most European countries. Russia and other communist countries have pioneered 'environmental monitoring'. Maximum allowable concentrations of potentially poisonous substances in the factory atmosphere are closely defined, and the works doctor is bound by statutory obligation, as he is in France and Holland. Health-at-work provisions in Britain have been well below those required under the Treaty of Rome.

Unlike their American counterparts, the trades unions in Britain have never taken a sustained and profound interest in working conditions, being more concerned with 'dirty money' and compensation for disease or accidents. It is likely, however, that conditions at work, amenities, and fringe medical benefits will soon play a larger part in their negotiating. The TUC has its own full-time medical adviser who is available for consultation by individual unions, several of whom also 'retain' part-time medical experts.

It is likely that the next five to fifteen years will show a greater demand from the shop floor for the overall improvement of working conditions. Directors will have to be equipped to deal with this.

The development of industrial medical services

Ever since the Industrial Revolution, doctors have been employed to advise directors on the specific hazards of their particular industry. It was soon found that, having got into the workplace, the doctor had another useful role, namely to provide 'on-site' treatment for the sick and injured. In this, he was quickly joined by nurses who could easily take care of the minor medicine and help deal with the growing number of women workers.

By the outbreak of the Second World War, most major industries had their own internal medical departments, and industrial medicine was being recognized as a medical speciality. There is now a flourishing Society of Occupational Medicine with 1,300 members, all of whom must have some contact with industry; 400 of them work full time in firms, university, or government departments. The rest are part-time IMOs, many of whom are also AFDs. There is a special qualification in industrial medicine—the Diploma of Industrial Health (DIH). Industrial nursing, too, has become specialized with its own division at the Royal College of Nursing, and the Industrial Nursing Diploma.

This is increasingly important, because industrial medicine or, as it is now called, occupational health, is a real speciality requiring specific skills, training, and motivation. Much that goes for industrial medical services is often no more than a sticking-plaster service or first-aid for the walking wounded, run by a nurse and supervised once a week by the managing director's or the chairman's GP. But the GP seldom has time to set foot in the factory, to know what is going on, and to become trusted by the people involved.

The growing complexity and potential dangers of industrial life, the increasing need for expert advice, particularly in the field of human relations and motivation, and the realization that health is influenced by the total relationship between the individual and his environment, are increasing the demand for specially trained doctors and nurses in industry and commerce. If management is to get the best value

391

for its not inconsiderable expenditure in this field, it should employ only appropriately trained doctors and nurses. The Royal College of Nursing, the Society of Occupational Medicine, the BMA, university departments, and the Institute of Directors' Medical Centre will willingly advise about recruitment.

The growth of small plant services

The size of the working unit has been a serious limiting factor in the development of occupational health services, because in Britain the vast majority of workplaces employ less than 100 people. This means that it is economically impossible for many employers to provide adequate medical coverage. An attempt is now being made to deal with this situation by developing group or area medical services that serve local industry on a *per capita* payment basis. (This approach was pioneered by Dr Austin Eagger with the full backing of the Slough Industrial Training Estate, and centres at Harlow, Smethwick, Dundee, Rotherham, and the Central Middlesex Hospital in London are now going concerns. This development would not have been possible without the help of the Nuffield Foundation.)

The small plant service provides central facilities and a mobile team of doctors and nurses who make daily visits to each factory and are available for emergencies. Most of what they do is concerned with the treatment of the sick and injured, but they also advise about working conditions, safety and industrial toxic hazards. This service costs the employer about £2 per head per year. A recent annual report of the Smethwick centre showed that 98 per cent of the people treated went back to work, and that, among the 27,000 people from 200 companies looked after during the year, the industrial accident rate was lowered by 15 per cent. And this in a year when the national statistics showed a serious rise.

There is general agreement among public bodies such as the BMA, TUC, CBI, and the political parties, that there ought to be a National Occupational Health Service. But it is enlightened self-interest on the part of employers to pay more attention to the problems of health at work; it might be wise for them to 'do it themselves' before they have an outside service wished upon them. There is little doubt that the group service, adapted to meet local needs, could provide a sensible and relatively inexpensive answer.

Cost and responsibility

The start of the NHS in 1948 has probably created a major disincentive to the development of occupational health services in this country. The argument is that, as the NHS is already being paid for out of taxes and employee/employer contributions, there is no need to subsidize an alternative service, particularly as the existing system does set out to cover all forms of sickness and injury. And the medical and lay factory inspectorate will provide, free, technical advice on safety and toxicology.

However, experience has shown in both large and small plants that there are considerable benefits to be gained by providing an internal 'wholly owned' industrial health service.

A precise cost/benefit appraisal of industrial medical services has, so far, proved impossible. The benefits of a health department include goodwill, the improvement of employee relations, and a better 'image' of the organization. On the other hand, doctors' salaries are high, and nurses cost more than secretaries (both in fact have salary scales defined by the BMA and the RCN, which are useful as a guide). Drugs and treatment facilities are expensive, and the surgery, which must be centrally situated, takes up valuable space.

In many ways an industrial health department is an act of faith, but experience shows that it justifies its cost. Existing medical departments seem to expand rather than contract, yet many large, and thousands of smaller firms, get by with no more than the statutory first-aid box. Only their own experience would show how much they would gain from a properly staffed and run medical department.

Functions

Theoretically the main function of a works medical department is to keep the working force, at all levels, fit and productive. This means that its main work lies in the field of prevention and health education. Obviously, if the company has a known toxic hazard or a clearly defined problem, such as the hygiene of food handlers, the task is relatively clear cut. If, on the other hand, one is dealing with the supervision of a run of the mill factory in terms of lighting, ventilation and safety, the task is far more difficult to define. Whatever the nature of the work, even if it is simply administrative in a large office block, a main function of the medical department should be to advise management about the 'optimization' of the working environment. The word 'optimization' is used advisedly because an enthusiastic health team with expert knowledge is always likely to ask for improvements which, although theoretically advisable, are economically unreasonable. The doctor in industry must realize that he is but one of the boardroom's advisers, and not expect to have his way all the time.

He is concerned both with the physical environment in terms of heating, lighting, ventilation, canteens, and workplace layout, and also the psycho-social environment. The doctor should also be concerned with human relations at work and he should, because he is in touch with both sides, be able to influence morale and motivation.

Prevention is the ideal goal of the medical department; treatment is its bread-and-butter function. If a worker has a minor injury or arrives at work with a headache or needs a penicillin injection, it is clearly quicker for him to have this at once than it is to wait in the GP's surgery or the hospital casualty queue. A well-run treatment facility is one obvious time-saving benefit of a medical department. It is also a morale raiser in a large unit, because the workers know that if there is a serious accident, the injured will be in good hands. The MO and his staff will be responsible for training first-aid workers, supervisory facilities, and emergency plans.

A main problem in industry is the rising toll of sickness absenteeism which, in Britain, now amounts to over 300 million man days a year. It is a well-known truism of industrial medicine that about 80 per cent of the time lost is accounted for by about 15 per cent of the population. If, then, those concerned can be identified, this is at least the first step towards dealing with the national problem. Similarly, absenteeism varies from department to department and section to section, reflecting local morale and supervision. The monitoring and mitigation of sickness experience is a joint responsibility of the medical and personnel departments. It is a much neglected activity and one which, if properly done, is likely to show considerable economic benefits.

'Progress chasing' on those who are away ill, constitutes a problem in the same field. The company doctor can get better liaison with local hospitals and practitioners and can also make arrangements for ill people to be specially dealt with or expeditiously handled by hospitals and specialists. In much the same way, staff returning from periods of sickness, and people with a permanent disability, can be helped back to full work or redeployed so as to be as productive as possible.

The transition of young people from school to being full wage earners is another problem that we have, in Britain, failed to solve. The AFD is supposed to examine all 'juveniles' starting work, and many thousands of examinations are carried out every year, but there is too little success in placing and training these youngsters properly in their work. The reports of the Chief Inspector of Factories have drawn attention to the appalling toll of accidents experienced by this group, mostly from sheer bad supervision. This is another major problem with which the medical department can help to deal.

If a company has its own medical department, responsible for the overall health supervision of the staff, it is right and proper that management should be involved in this brief.

Preventive medicine is rapidly moving in the direction of periodic screening examinations to discover disease at an early or presymptomatic stage. To some extent, the executive health examination is a manifestation of this trend, and it is likely that there will be a growing demand for health examinations for a wide range of people in the community. A well-equipped company medical department, working with a relatively captive population, is well placed to facilitate procedures such as cervical cytology and immunization campaigns.

Companies without their own medical departments are increasingly offering their executives the opportunity to have these examinations done by outside doctors. The Institute of Directors' Centre runs schemes for nearly two hundred companies. (The details are discussed in more detail on p. 386.)

Many firms have pre-employment medical examinations carried out either by a visiting doctor or by local arrangement with an outside doctor. Many of these, especially on office staff who may stay only a short time with the firm are, in my view, unnecessary. But there is a definite place within the organization for a pre-employment examination which aims at putting the potential worker in a job to which he is reasonably suited. The fact that he is so examined also helps to make him feel that the organization is doing its best to fit him in and help him adjust.

The main challenge facing doctors and nurses working in industry is the fact that they are often serving two masters. Their professional integrity demands the trust of the doctor/patient relationship, but they are also advisers to management about individual problems and the working environment. This may cause divided loyalty and, sometimes, makes them rather prickly or demanding colleagues. But the need for this loyalty should be respected by management, who must realize that they will not always get all the confidential information they would like out of the medical department. To facilitate his work, the doctor must be given access to the chief executive, but it is up to him to use this privilege wisely.

In conclusion, it must be emphasized that although a medical department within an organization can be seen to do many useful things such as treatment and rehabilitation, much of what it achieves will be intangible. If properly set up and staffed, a medical department will make, in a number of ways, a major contribution to the health of the enterprise. The provision of such facilities by the directors of a company is a tangible demonstration of their concern for the health and welfare of their staff.

Much can be done by specially trained nurses, but they do need the support and supervision of a doctor. Whether the doctor should be full or part-time will depend on the problems and size of the firm. What is clear is that the doctor will not earn his money by sitting in the works surgery, but rather by being part of the organization and mixing with its personnel, and understanding its problems. In this way, he can use his special skills and perceptions to diagnose and prescribe for the ills of the physical and psycho-social working environment of which he is a part.

Reading list

BOOKS

Health in Industry, Dr Donald Hunter (Penguin Books (Pelican) 1959)

The Diseases of Occupations, Second Edition, Dr Donald Hunter (English Universities Press, 1968)

Organization of Industrial Health Services, Second Edition, Ministry of Labour (H.M.S.O., 1966)

The Appointed Factory Doctor Service, Ministry of Labour (H.M.S.O., 1966)

T.U.C. Policy for Health at Work, booklet published by Trades Union Congress

Useful addresses

Society of Occupational Medicine, Royal College of Surgeons, Lincolns Inn Fields, London WC 1

Royal College of Nursing, 1a Henrietta Place, London W 1

Chief Inspector of Factories, Department of Employment and Productivity, St James's Square, London SW 1

7.5 The Employer's Welfare and Safety Obligations

H. Samuels

How far is a director responsible for the welfare and safety of his company's employees? Most directors will feel that the policies of their companies under both heads go well beyond the legal minimum, but even so they may be vague or uncertain as to what exactly the law does say. This can be highly dangerous: not only for the employees—since the laws are framed carefully to reduce accidents and improve standards—but also for the director, since penalties can, in certain circumstances, fall not only on the company but also on him personally.

The statutory code which relates to the welfare and safety of employees in factories is to be found in the Factories Act 1961 and the regulations made under it. The code which applies to office employees is a parallel one, very similar in the matter of welfare, less detailed and stringent in the matter of safety, and is to be found in the Offices, Shops and Railway Premises Act 1963, and regulations made under this Act. Both these codes are penal in character, i.e., they are enforced as part of the criminal law, and offenders are punished by the imposition of fines.

Obligations under Common Law

These ligislative codes do not by any means comprise the sum total of the employer's duties as to welfare and safety. There are duties of much earlier origin, namely those under Common Law. For under Common Law, the employer is bound to provide each and every employee with:

397

1. a safe workplace,
2. a safe plant and appliances,
3. a safe system of work.

If a young person is employed on a dangerous process there is a fourth duty—to give proper instruction and proper supervision until instructed.

The breach of any of these duties resulting in injury to an employee is ground for an action at Common Law for damages. Unlike a prosecution for breach of a statutory duty (see above) such an action does not involve the employer in penalties such as fines, but in liability to pay damages commensurate with the injuries and loss suffered by the employee. The employer has the same liability if the breach is caused by one of his employees or other agent.

The employer's duty in these matters does not extend to guaranteeing the employee's safety, but he has to take all reasonably practicable measures to prevent dangers that can be reasonably foreseen, and this involves the immediate remedying of known defects plus a system of adequate and regular inspection of premises, plant, and appliances. The breach of any of the statutory duties here set out also affords ground for such an action at Common Law.

Statutory duties

A. *Welfare*

The employer has a number of duties of a general nature which affect his employees' welfare. These are:

1. The premises and their contents must be kept clean and floors cleaned weekly. (Dirt and refuse must be removed daily from factory floors, passages and benches, and inside walls of factories must be repainted every seven years, or in other cases distempered—smooth walls washed—every fourteen months.)
2. The rooms must be properly ventilated, and kept free from harmful fumes.
3. To prevent overcrowding, 400 cubic feet space must be allowed per worker.
4. A reasonable temperature must be maintained. The minimum for sedentary work is 60°F.
5. The lighting must be adequate in all parts (in factories it must comply with the standard laid down in the Order (SR and O, 1941, No. 94).)
6. Sanitary conveniences—separate for each sex—must be provided and kept clean, properly lit, and ventilated; their number must be in accordance with SR and O, 1938, No. 611. (Factories) or SI 1964, No. 966 (Offices).

In addition to the above, the employer has to provide the following specific amenities and maintain them in proper condition:

1. an adequate supply of wholesome drinking water renewed daily (unless piped).

Where there is no jet, cups must be provided with rinsing facilities;
2. washing accommodation with clean running hot and cold (or warm) water, soap and clean towels (or their equivalents);
3. accommodation for all clothing not worn at work, and proper means of drying them;
4. sitting facilities sufficient for the opportunities for rest during the work; for sedentary workers seats of suitable design and with proper supports, footrests being required for office workers and, when necessary, in factories;
5. first-aid boxes, one for each group of 150 employees and each in charge of a responsible officer, who in factories with 50 employees, and offices with 150 employees, must have the necessary first-aid qualifications as laid down in SI, 1960, No. 1612 (factories), and SI, 1963, No. 1970 (offices). The contents of each box must be in conformity with the standard laid down in SI, 1959, No. 906 (factories), and SI, 1963, No. 970 (offices).

Lastly, under this heading there are some thirty classes of factory processes that involve working conditions of special discomfort and have therefore been made subject to additional requirements contained in Welfare Regulations. With these, employers in those processes must comply in addition to the above general requirements.

B. *Safety*

We will first enumerate those statutory provisions as to safety which apply to both factories and offices.

Factories and Offices. All floors, passages, and stairs must be sound, properly maintained and free of obstruction and slippery substance. Each staircase must have a handrail; if one side is open, on that side. A staircase with two open sides, or otherwise dangerous, requires a handrail on both sides. The open side must have a lower rail or equivalent protection. Floor openings must be fenced, wherever practicable.

Certain types of machines have been prescribed as dangerous (*see* SI, 1954, No. 921 (factories), SI, 1964, No. 971 (offices).) In those cases no work may be performed on the machine by the worker unless instructed as to the dangers and precautions and until he has had sufficient training at the machine or is under proper supervision.

No young person may clean machinery if exposed to danger from that or adjacent machinery.

No worker must be allowed to lift or move a load so heavy as to be likely to injure him.

The employer must obtain a certificate from the Fire Authority that his premises have proper fire escapes (a) if there are more than twenty employees; (b) if explosives or highly inflammable materials (of a prescribed kind, in offices) are stored; (c) if there are more than ten employees above the ground floor (in offices, elsewhere than on the ground floor). If the premises or the number of employees is extended, the employer must give written notice to the Fire Authority and carry out any alterations thereupon required by the Authority, but he has the right of appeal to a Magistrate's court against the refusal or cancellation of a fire escape certificate or a requirement to make alterations or the period allowed for alterations.

Doors must be capable of being immediately opened (in factories, from the inside) as long as anyone is working or taking meals in the premises. Exits other than the ordinary exit must be marked by a conspicuous notice and each room must allow free passage for escape.

In all premises that require a fire escape certificate, fire alarms must be provided and examined every three months, and all employees must be made familiar with the means of escape and the route to be followed in case of fire.

In all establishments the employer must provide fire-fighting appliances, maintain them properly, and ensure that they are available for immediate use.

If an accident occurs on the premises, causing the death or more than three days' disablement of a person working there, written notice must be sent immediately to the factory inspector (in the case of factories or offices in factories) or the local authority (in the case of other offices). If the employer is not the occupier of the premises he must report the accident to the occupier immediately.

Factories. The safety requirements which follow apply to factories.

Safe access must be provided by the employer to every place of work. Each workplace must be as safe as reasonably practicable; if there is a $6\frac{1}{2}$ feet drop and no secure hold, there must be a fence or equal protection. Ladders must be sound.

The moving parts of prime movers (i.e., the appliances giving mechanical energy), the head and tail race of water wheels and the parts of stock bars projecting beyond the headstocks of lathes, all require fences. Every part of transmission machinery, electric generators, motors, and rotary convertors require fences or equivalent safeguards. Necessary examinations or adjustments to moving machines may be carried out only by certified machine attendants. The employer must maintain means for promptly cutting off power from transmission machinery. Belts not in use may not rest or ride on revolving shafts. Belts must, by proper mechanical appliances, be prevented from creeping back on fast pulleys. Set-screws, bolts, and keys on revolving shafts or wheels must be guarded; toothed or friction gearing not needing adjustment in motion must be encased or made equally safe. Women and young persons may not be allowed to clean prime movers or transmission machinery when in motion. The traversing carriage of a self-acting machine may not run out within 18 inches from a fixed structure if a person might pass over that space.

All lifts, hoists, cranes, and lifting appliances must be sound and properly maintained in an efficient state, working order, and repair. Any breakdown affords conclusive evidence of a breach of this obligation. Hoists, lifts, and chains must be examined every six months, cranes every fourteen months. Hoists and lifts may be capable of being opened only at a landing, and so made that persons or goods cannot be trapped. Lifts for persons must be prevented automatically from overrunning— each cage must have a gate on each side giving exit to a landing and must be movable only when the gate is closed. New lifts must have two separately connected ropes, each capable of carrying the platform and the maximum load. Steps must be taken to ensure that overhead travelling cranes do not approach within 20 feet of persons employed nearby; and warnings of their approach must be given to persons above floor level liable to be struck.

Steam boilers must have proper safety valves, stop valves, steam gauges, and water gauges and be examined every fourteen months. Steam receivers and air receivers must be similarly fitted and be examined every twenty-six months.

Vessels containing corrosive or poisonous liquids must either be covered or ladders, stairs, and gangways above, across or inside must be at least 18 inches wide, have a 3-foot fence, and be fixed securely. If the edge is less than 3 feet above the ground, it must either be covered or fenced to that height. Where there is less than 18 inches space between two vessels without 3-foot fences, passage must be prevented by secure barriers.

Exhaust appliances must, where practicable, be provided against dust and fumes from any process. Stationary internal combustion engines must be partitioned off from workrooms and have means for letting off the exhaust gases into the open air. Any confined space involving risk of fumes must have a manhole 18 inches long and 16 inches wide, and may not be entered by any person unless (a) authorized by a responsible officer specially designated by the employer for the purpose, and (b) wearing breathing apparatus and, where practicable, a belt with a rope held from outside. Explosive dust may not be allowed to accumulate in the factory; vents must be provided, and the plant used must be enclosed.

Goggles or screens must be provided for eye-protection in any of the processes set out in the Order SR and O, 1938, No. 654. Written notice must be sent to the Factory Inspector of all cases of the bursting of any revolving vessel, wheel or grindstone mechanically moved, fire stopping work in any room for twenty-four hours, electrical short circuits causing five hours' stoppage, and explosion of gas containers.

There are special provisions where poisonous substances or lead are used. Further, as in the case of welfare, about sixty processes involving special dangers have been made subject to additional requirements contained in Dangerous Trades Regulations which are incumbent upon employers in those processes.

Penalties. An employer is liable to a penalty for a breach of any of the statutory provisions as to welfare and safety. For a breach likely to cause death or injury, the penalty is £300. For a breach of the fire escape certificate obligation it is £200. For breaches generally it is £60. A director or officer of a limited company who by his conduct contributes to an offence is liable, in addition to the company.

14*

Reading list

BOOKS

Industrial Safety Handbook, William Handley, Editor (McGraw-Hill, London, 1969)

Basic Rules for Safety and Health at Work, New Series No. 35 (H.M.S.O., 1968)

Safety for Industry, F. L. Creber (RoSPA, 1967)

Industrial Law, H. Samuels (Pitman, 7th Edition, 1967)

The Factories Act: A Short Guide, Ministry of Labour (H.M.S.O., 1962)

Offices, Shops and Railway Premises Act 1963 (H.M.S.O.)

Accidents and Ill-health at Work, John L. Williams (Staples Press, 1960)

The Worker and the Law, K. Wedderburn (Penguin, 1965)

Employer's Liability at Common Law, John Munkman (Butterworth, 6th Edition, 1966)

Damages for Personal Injuries and Death, John Munkman (Butterworth, 1956)·

Industrial Accident Prevention: A Scientific Approach, H. W. Heinrich (McGraw-Hill, 4th Edition, 1959)

Modern Safety Practices, Russell DeReaner (John Wiley, 1958)

Health at Work: A Description of Medical Services in Fourteen British Factories (Ministry of Labour, 1960)

The General Principles of Employers Liability at Common Law and Under the Factories Act 1961, M. H. Whincup (IIS, 1963)

Building and Construction Regulations Handbook (RoSPA, 6th Edition, reprinted with amendments 1965)

Encyclopaedia of Factories, Shops and Offices: Law and Practices, Editor P. Allsop (Sweet and Maxwell, 1962—with regular supplements)

The Offices, Shops and Railway Premises Act 1963—with Introduction and Annotation, I. Fife and E. Machin (Butterworth, 1963)

The Offices, Shops and Railway Premises Act, 1963—with Introduction and Notes, H. Samuels and N. Stewart Pearson (Charles Knight, 1963)

Comprehensive Guide to Factory Law: A Classified Guide to the Requirements of the Factories Act and other Legislation affecting factories and allied premises, including offices and building sites, Robert McKown (George Godwin for *The Builder,* 3rd Edition, 1965)

Useful addresses

Royal Society for the Prevention of Accidents, Industrial Safety Section, Terminal House, 52 Grosvenor Gardens, London SW 1

British Safety Council, 163–173 Praed Street, London W 2

Department of Employment and Productivity Industrial Health and Safety Centre, 97 Horseferry Road, London SW 1

Industrial Safety Advisory Council, c/o The Secretary, Safety, Health and Welfare Dept (SHW C3), Baynard's House, 1 Chepstow Place, Westbourne Grove, London W 2

8. Advertising and Public Relations

8.1 The Economics of Advertising

Lord Robens

Recent years have seen a significant change of emphasis in critical attitudes towards advertising. In the past, public attention was concentrated on control of advertising standards, apparently because of an objection to advertising on moral grounds, which may have derived from a belief that 'economic man' should be rational in exercising choice and that, as advertising sometimes appeals to the irrational, it must be bad! While condemning the intellectual arrogance of this attitude, the advertising world has been more successful in silencing criticism by pointing to the effectiveness of its voluntary control system. This is administered by the recently strengthened Advertising Standards Authority within the terms of the Code of Advertising Practice accepted by all sides of the industry twenty years ago.

There are now signs, however, that the critics have changed their point of attack and that the new battleground is going to be the economics of advertising. In 1966 there were strong suspicions that the Government was thinking of restricting advertising by taxation or legislation. The advertising industry tends to be sensitive about these things, especially under a Labour Government, and may have jumped too quickly to conclusions, but there were undoubtedly some straws in the wind such as the Labour Party's Reith Report and the Monopolies Commission's strictures on the advertising of detergents. The fears were partly allayed when a strong deputation of leading advertisers met the President of the Board of Trade, in November 1966, and presented a strong economic case against interference with advertising expenditure. Considerable interest was shown by the Government in the research initiated by the Advertising Association into the economics of advertising and, later, the Government themselves decided to take a hand directly. In April 1967, Mr Douglas Jay, then President of the Board of Trade, told the House of Commons: 'We know too little about the economic effects of advertising in general and its relationship to competition. Accordingly I have decided to institute some independent research into the subject.'

The Board of Trade's studies were expected to take two years; meanwhile the Advertising Association have already commissioned a report from the Economists Advisory Group—published in 1967—and have made funds available to the London Graduate School of Business Studies to sponsor a Visiting Professorship in Marketing. In addition the AA are appointing an economist/statistician to act as a 'nerve-centre' for collecting and collating information, and are maintaining close contact with the Confederation of British Industry, who have set up an *ad hoc* Committee of advertisers to decide upon CBI policy on advertising.

Clearly, the economics of advertising is the latest enthusiasm—something that should be widely welcomed by the advertising industry, not only because, in Douglas Jay's words, 'too little is known about advertising's economic foundation', but because in any event it is bound to be valuable to objectify discussion on the value of advertising. It is an excellent opportunity to silence the critics once and for all and, indeed, to present a case for more advertising in the future. It is still true, as recent experience has shown, that manufacturers tend to regard advertising appropriations as expendable in times of economic difficulties.

What, then, *is* the economic case for advertising? In my view, there is really no independent case; there is only a case for marketing in the wider sense. But once this is accepted, as it must be, the case for advertising follows automatically because advertising is an essential component in the marketing 'mix', along with pricing policy, a field force of sales representatives, direct mail, point of sale display, special inducements, and so on.

Marketing is more important than ever in the modern technological age. Larger and more specialized machinery enables a manufacturer to cut production costs, but only if the machinery is kept fully occupied. Long production runs are essential, so it is vital to plan ahead and achieve a consistent pattern of demand. In Professor Galbraith's words, a firm must 'incorporate the consumer into long-term planning'. This is only another way of saying that modern technology, relying as it does on specialization, needs more intensive marketing. And it is an economic cliché that 'specialization is limited by the extent of the market'.

Marketing is essentially the link between supply and demand, a means of communication. And like all proper means of communication it is two-way—a dialogue between producer and consumer. It is important to distinguish between marketing and selling in this context. Selling implies pushing a product that is already available

—only one aspect of the whole marketing operation. Indeed, if the whole marketing operation is planned and carried out effectively selling is simplified because the 'foot-in-the-door' man has an open door to push at. The true job of marketing is to combine the *identification* of demand through market research with the *stimulation* of demand through advertising and other means.

There is no difference in character between 'consumer' and 'industrial' marketing. The choice of a combination of components in the marketing 'mix' suitable for a particular task is one for management. It will vary according to the size and organization of the consuming body. To reach a mass audience of individual consumers it is usually necessary to make greater use of mass techniques such as advertising in national media, but this would be inappropriate when selling goods or services to an industry that may consist of a dozen or so large firms.

A popular criticism of advertising is that it is wasteful, that it is bound to add to the cost of the product, and that without it the product price would be reduced. This is true only if the distribution of the product could be cheapened by the adoption of means other than advertising. But if management knows its job and has selected the optimum combination of marketing tools, including some expenditure on advertising, then any arbitrary restriction on any one of those tools is bound to lead to the adoption of others which are, by definition, less efficient. Then either the distribution process would be more expensive or it would be less effective, with the result that less goods would be sold and fixed costs would be spread over a lower output. Either way there would eventually be an *increase* in price, not a reduction. If advertising is used ineffectively or uneconomically it does not mean that advertising itself is uneconomic but only that the management decisions which initiated it were bad.

Another common criticism of advertising is that it is conducive to monopoly. This is dealt with by the Economists Advisory Group in their report, which concludes that the argument is inconclusive: advertising could be used to buttress a monopoly position, but equally it could be used to break into a new market. This is the real point. Advertising is in certain circumstances a most efficient tool which can be used for economically useful or damaging purposes. It is not right or fair, however, to blame advertising for the *way* it is used; that raises far wider issues. In effect, the responsibility for using advertising economically lies with the boardroom.

Advertising should not really be a critical issue in itself; criticism is only valid if advertising is misapplied. If the economics of advertising is going to be the new battleground, there can, therefore, be no doubt of the ultimate victor.

The advertising organizations

Institute of Practitioners in Advertising. 44 Belgrave Square, London SW 1.

The Institute is the trade association of British advertising agencies, and its 279 agency members represent over 90 per cent of the total UK agency business. It is also a professional body for people working in agencies, and has more than 2,000 individual members and diploma holders. On behalf of members, the IPA undertakes services such as research, management aids, international, legal, public relations, information, negotiation with government departments, other trade associations and trade unions, etc., and education, training, and appointments.
Director: James O'Connor, FCIS, FCCS, FIPA.

The Advertising Association. 1 Bell Yard, London WC2.
The Association is a non-profit making concern that aims to promote official and public confidence in advertising and to safeguard the common interests of those engaged in, or using, the industry. It seeks to demonstrate the efficiency of the service offered by advertising and to establish its importance in the economic life of the country.
Director-General: J. S. Williams, OBE, BCom.

The Incorporated Society of British Advertisers. 45 Hertford Street, London W1.
The Incorporated Society of British Advertisers was established in 1900 (with the initial name of the 'Advertisers' Protection Society'). The membership of about 520 is collectively responsible for some 75 per cent of the money spent on advertising. The Society accepts a responsibility for most aspects of the marketing carried out by its members and has the overall purpose of assisting them to market as efficiently as possible. The Society operates an extensive information service and publishes a range of booklets and papers.
Director: Cdr D. C. Kinloch, DSO, OBE.

Reading list

BOOKS

The Economics of Advertising, Economists Advisory Group (Hutchinson and Benham, 1967)
Advertising and Competition, Jules Backman (University of London Press and New York University Press, 1967)
Economic Implications of Advertising, O. J. Firestone (Methuen, 1967)
Economic Effects of Advertising, Neil H. Barden (Richard D. Irwin, 1942)
Economics of Advertising, F. P. Bishop (Robert Hale, 1946)
Measuring Advertising Effectiveness, Lucas and Britt (McGraw-Hill, 1963)
Advertising in Action, Harris and Seldon (Hutchinson, 1962)
Advertising and the Public, Harris and Seldon (André Deutsch, 1962)

Useful addresses

Institute of Practitioners in Advertising, 44 Belgrave Square, London SW1

The Advertising Association, 1 Bell Yard, London WC 2
Incorporated Society of British Advertisers, 45 Hertford Street, London SW 1
Society of Advertisement Managers and Representatives, c/o D. Cobb, Odhams Press Ltd,
    96–98 Long Acre, London WC 2

8.2 Advertising Agencies and the Client

John Bittleston

Types of advertising agency

Although 279 agencies have membership of the Institute of Practitioners in Advertising, it is likeiy that only a small number can, would, or should handle any specific account. (Not all agencies belong to the IPA, of course, but over 90 per cent do, accounting for 90 per cent of total expenditure placed through agencies.) Within the term 'advertising agencies' there are specialist categories—industrial, financial, and classified—as well as general consumer product/full service agencies.

Industrial agencies are usually located in the principal industrial areas such as Birmingham, Manchester, Glasgow, and Bristol. They normally handle some consumer advertising, but will specialize in technical accounts. Many of their staff will have science and engineering backgrounds. These agencies have a special knowledge of, and contact with, the technical press. Normally they will handle accounts of any size, although below a certain level of appropriation, where it is difficult for them to operate profitably, they will expect compensation by way of additional fees as well as commission.

Financial agencies are usually situated in the City of London, since their work is closely connected with the Stock Exchange and financial institutions. As with industrial agencies, they may handle some general consumer accounts, but their special skills are concerned with annual reports and company financial reports, for the layout and design of which they are often responsible. The published report of the chairman's statement is a central feature of their work, and they are also particularly suited to handling unit trust, institutional, and new issue advertising.

Classified agencies and the classified or personnel advertising divisions of large agencies specialize in small and *ad hoc* advertisements normally designed to achieve a limited objective within a short time. For this reason, they know more about the results of their work than other agencies, where an advertisement is expected to work over a period long enough to allow other factors to influence the end result.

Agencies may also be categorized in other less well-defined but still meaningful ways. All agencies handling consumer accounts can be placed in a line, with the large full service agency at one end and what is becoming known as the small 'creative' agency at the other. This seems to imply a certain incompatibility of largeness and creativity: a concept that is now somewhat dated in the agency world. Small new agencies offering creative and media buying services only are constantly springing up and often achieve an initial growth record that makes the slower growth of some of the large established agencies look comparatively insignificant. The range of important accounts that can be handled by an agency offering limited service is necessarily itself limited.

Choosing an agency

Probably a small proportion only of all agencies could, or should, handle any particular account, and the first consideration in selecting an agency is to match the class of agency to the services it is required to supply. Outside the field of specialist agencies, already outlined, this broadly means the size of agency.

Will the agency supply simply creative and media buying services, or will sophisticated media planning be required?

What allied marketing services, such as research and merchandising, will the agency be consulted on, and will it be required to supply recommendations or full service in these areas?

Is it necessary to employ an agency that is experienced in, and fully understands the problems of marketing major consumer products?

Will the operation be domestic or international?

This short and incomplete check-list, which must be supplemented by a detailed scrutiny of the prospective client's operations and needs, should serve to show that the size of agency to be considered must depend on the size of the client's operation and the extent to which the agency will be asked to participate in the client's total marketing plans. It should be remembered here, that a large full-service agency may have difficulty in operating a small account profitably without negotiating a supplementary fee, and, in any case, it is often more satisfactory to match the agency's particular strength and experience to the client's needs.

Once the class and size of agency required has been identified, it should be possible to draw up a preliminary list of agencies to be considered. A standard reference book such as the *Advertisers' Annual*, or the advice of the IPA, may be helpful. Other particular requirements, such as experience with a particular product group, can then be applied, and the factor of conflicting accounts may be borne in mind at this stage. Any agency already handling a direct competitor to the potential client's product may be unable to service the new account so long as it retains the old.

By this time, the list of possible agencies should be short enough to be considered in detail. A preliminary visit to the agencies on the list at this stage, in order to meet senior personnel and examine some of the agency's creative work, is essential in deciding which two or three agencies to include on the final short list. Once this final short list has been drawn up, the agencies on it may be asked to present their ideas, in some detail, on how the account should be handled. In order to do this seriously they will, of course, need a very thorough and frank briefing on a specific project. The short-listed agencies are also often asked to introduce to the potential client the members of their staff who will be appointed to work on the account. On the basis of what they have seen of the agency's management and staff, of their recommendations for the way in which the new account should be handled, and of their other current creative work, the potential client must now make a judgement as to which agency is best suited to handling his account.

Trends in advertising media

Total advertising expenditure grows faster than the economy, a corollary of the translation of a major proportion of growing national wealth into increased discretionary purchasing power. Advertising is not the only way of marketing a product, but in most cases it is the most efficient. It is the means by which the manufacturer communicates to the potential consumer, telling him that his product is available, what it is, and why it is suited to his particular needs. To do this job of communication both effectively and efficiently, the advertising must be seen and acted upon by the people for whom the product is designed.

Impact and selectivity are the two important factors underlying the choice of media in which increasing advertising budgets are spent. The enormous power of television as a medium for creative advertising, together with the freedom of advertisers to buy time in any combination of regions, has given this medium a clear advantage and made it the major growth area in advertising media. This is despite the high cost of television airtime, and its lack of selectivity on a socio-economic basis.

The principal appeal of the television medium is naturally to branded consumer products with a high turnover rate and a wide market, and for which the advertising is primarily required to demonstrate product advantage. The strong impact of the medium, however, can make its use worthwhile, even where the audience profile is less closely matched to the market for the product. Quality newspapers and industrial tools are two examples of this approach, and an increasing number of advertisers may be expected to balance an expensive potential consumer return against the effectiveness with which their product may be promoted on the television screen.

At the time of writing, colour television is in its infancy, and the form in which a colour commercial service will be authorized is not known. If commercial colour television is authorized only on 625 lines, the initial colour audience and its rate of growth will be smaller (and command lower rates) than if it is authorized on the existing 405-line channel, when there would be a large black-and-white audience for colour programmes from the start. Experience in the United States has shown that exposure to colour programmes, even when received in black-and-white, is a significant factor in determining the growth of homes equipped to receive colour. Whichever course is chosen, the effect will be to increase television's share of all media advertising expenditure.

A new channel of 625 lines could produce a new audience drawn largely from upper-income brackets, providing a valuable media opportunity. Introducing colour to the existing commercial channel, on the other hand, will cause the colour audience (and airtime rates) to grow more quickly. In either case, the opportunity for more effective advertising will be provided. Research in the United States has supported the theory that, properly used, there is a differential of effectiveness in favour of colour, although there are considerable variations in this differential according to product type.

Television is the largest single medium in the United Kingdom advertising budget, accounting for slightly under one-third of the total. The various categories of printed media carry most of the remainder. National and provincial newspapers together account for a further third of the total, but this share is declining, with the advertising revenue showing little increase. The national press is economic and selective, enabling an advertiser to reach his target market without undue waste. The provincial press is generally more expensive in terms of consumers reached, but offers regional selectivity. Both lack the great strength of presentation that will often give a commanding advantage to television. The one means open to newspapers to improve their impact is the use of colour. Until 1962, colour reproduction in newspapers was inadequate, but, although standards have improved so that pages with a high standard of colour reproduction are now generally available, the cost remains high. The circumstances in which newspaper colour is a useful addition to an advertising schedule are, therefore, limited, and such advertisements account for a small and static proportion of press advertising.

However, newspaper colour is a useful addition to colour magazines, in that it greatly extends the range of selective markets a media planner can reach with the impact of colour. As standards improve further, the colour facility may help newspapers to improve upon their present level of advertising revenue, although their share of the advertising budget will still decline.

The colour supplements of the *Sunday Times, Observer* and *Daily Telegraph* should be considered distinctly from newspaper colour as such, having the character and format of magazines, with circulation matched to their parent newspapers. Since the *Sunday Times* supplement was launched in 1962, with the *Observer* and *Weekend Telegraph* following in 1964, this venture has progressed steadily, although faltering during the recession of 1966. Giving a wide coverage of the upper-income brackets, at a lower cost than newspaper colour, the supplements are firmly established media. Although they will continue to carry some monotone advertising, for some time to come at least, the proportion of colour will continue to increase.

Womens' magazines and trade and technical journals remain the most healthy areas of press media, enjoying, in common, a clear definition of the markets they reach. The four large-circulation weekly women's magazines dominate most large press campaigns aimed at women in general. The circulation trend is virtually static, but the advertising trend is healthy, with a pronounced swing away from black-and-white towards colour. Young women's magazines show a marked swing away from cheaply produced single colour publications towards full colour 'glossy' publications. This volatile and prosperous group reflects its readers and the increasing amount of advertising being directed towards them as the affluence of the younger age groups increases. Monthly women's magazines are predominantly aimed at the upper-income brackets, and as a group show little circulation movement, although mergers have taken place, and new publications have been introduced.

Outdoor poster advertising is the only other major medium. A background reminder to major national campaigns, it accounts for under 10 per cent of total advertising expenditure, a share that is slowly declining.

Summarizing the trends in advertising media, two points stand out: the increasing strength of television, and the swing to colour in all print media.

Advertisers are continually recognizing the advantages television offers for promoting a wide range of products, and this medium is increasing its share of the total advertising budget. When colour comes to commercial television, the effects are likely to be gradual, at least at first, but the trend towards television will inevitably be strengthened.

The common factor across all print media is the ever-increasing adoption of colour, together with greatly increased quality of production. As the best available means of combating the impact of television, the facility to print colour is becoming almost universal across print media.

Point of sale and merchandising expenditure

Point of sale and merchandising expenditure deals with that part of an advertiser's promotional budget that is *not* spent on theme advertising on television, press, posters, and radio. As well as sales promotion and merchandising it includes direct mail, print, exhibitions, and packaging, tactical expenditure, often at the point-of-sale, supporting the overall marketing objectives.

Unlike other advertising expenditure, which is well documented, it is extremely difficult to estimate the total amount of money spent on these activities. It is, however, certain that it is growing, to the extent where it is a significant and even major part of many advertisers' total marketing appropriation.

This growth has largely come about due to changes in retailing. To take the grocery market as an example; in the early 1950s, self service and supermarket retailing did not exist in the UK, but by 1967 there were over 2,620 supermarkets, and about 18,000 self-service stores. These outlets accounted for just over half of the complete grocery trade. To see this in perspective, it is necessary to remember that there are well over 150,000 retail outlets competing for the business. This result was achieved by intelligent planning, sophisticated layout, and merchandising techniques, as well as by the ability to buy very keenly from manufacturers.

Tactical expenditure supports the overall marketing objectives, and to do this with the greatest efficiency it must be integrated with the main media advertising. The agency role, therefore, must be not only to provide a service to its client, offering the best advice on promotional and merchandising techniques and carrying projects into effect, but also to have a complete understanding of the part played by these activities so that they may be integrated with the marketing and advertising plans.

Media research

Media planners' day-to-day work is concerned with taking decisions about where a client's advertisements should appear. The function of media research is to provide as much statistical evidence as possible on which to base those decisions. The type of media information collected is designed to say what each medium, or each combination of media, delivers: the size and nature of the audience and its behaviour in relation to specific media.

The first task for media research is to collect basic information, employing standard market research techniques.

Television audiences are measured under a contract awarded by the advertising industry as a whole. Panels in each television region report continuously on viewing by means of a meter, attached to the set, which records when the set is switched on and to which channel it is tuned, and supply diaries in which each member of the household records his or her viewing. Weekly and monthly reports are issued and, in addition, a range of facilities for analysing the raw data is available. Pilot work is being carried out to establish a satisfactory technique for reporting on the attentiveness with which commercials and programmes are viewed. Previous work on attentiveness has merely shown how the typical television audience is broken down in terms of varying degrees of distraction. This research, though inadequate, does demonstrate that attention to the television set increases as the evening wears on, is greater for commercial breaks appearing within a programme than for breaks appearing between programmes, and reveals, not surprisingly, that men are able to enjoy their viewing with less distraction than are housewives.

The National Readership Survey, administered by the Institute of Practitioners in Advertising, is the principal press media research survey. About 16,000 adults are interviewed each year; besides being asked about their reading habits, respondents are questioned on ownership and usage of certain products, exposure to some other media, and details such as age and household status. The qualification for readership is having 'looked at' any part of a publication; this definition is a long way short of telling us what audience will actually *see* a particular series of advertisements. To eliminate this gap, separate research has been carried out to estimate the percentage of readers of a publication who could recall looking at an average advertisement, and the way in which these percentages vary between different types of respondent and different types and size of advertisement. Supplementing this work on press audiences is a rich collection of surveys carried out by media owners, advertising agencies and advertisers.

Media other than press and television are very much less well researched. A number of surveys that concentrate on providing press and television information also provide some incidental data on cinema, radio, and posters; however, the most important work that has been carried out on the smaller media has been commissioned by the media owners themselves. By and large, this research does not go beyond measuring *opportunities* of seeing advertising (as opposed to actually *seeing* advertisements).

Data processing

Each major survey contains a large volume of information; every respondent may be asked to make several hundred responses, all of which are recorded. Previously the overwhelming majority of processing was carried out by mechanical counter-sorter machines, but in the last few years the emphasis has switched towards computer analysis.

The tabulations carried out on the raw data range from simple standard analyses, such as the calculation of the proportion of diarists viewing a particular quarter-hour, to extremely sophisticated media models, some of which are capable of constructing schedules.

One of the first to announce such a media model was S. H. Benson Ltd. The Benson model is capable of selecting a complete press schedule to reach a given target group (which may involve weighting different segments of the market) from a specified list of candidate publications. The schedule is selected, insertion by insertion, on the basis of a market- and media-weighted cost per thousand; superimposed on these elaborate costs per thousand is a 'response function', which ensures the most efficient distribution (under present assumptions) of opportunities to see across the entire market. Tests have consistently shown that schedules produced with the aid of the computer model are superior, in terms of the standard criteria, to schedules produced without the aid of the computer.

Computer models have now become so sophisticated that they have outstripped the information currently available. Consequently, the next major steps in media research will principally be in the direction of data collection rather than data processing.

New developments

There are a great many new developments in media research at the present time, but two may be singled out for mention here. The first concerns a move towards greater integration of our basic sources of information. At the moment, media statistics are provided by a host of different companies and services that operate separately. Recent proposals have outlined a scheme whereby a National Media Survey would be set up, using 50,000 interviews each year, collecting basic information on media exposure and product usage. A number of satellite samples and panels would be set up, using sub-samples taken from the 50,000, to investigate specific interesting areas, but at the same time being capable of being related back to the main bank of information.

A second major development area concerns what have been called 'response functions'. Media planners have always made assumptions (usually implicitly) about the value of successive impacts (for example, the first exposure on a housewife is worth twice as much as a second exposure); a 'response function' is merely an explicit numerical statement of such assumptions. This seemingly straightforward step has important effects, for it throws our previous information into a new light, and highlights our ignorance of what happens in the consumers' mind once the advertising has been transmitted and received. At the moment, the industry is still at the initial stage of debating basic concepts and evaluating the various means of defining and measuring 'response'.

A very limited number of studies have already reported on what effect advertising achieves, but it is only too clear that very much more research needs to be done before response functions can be specified with any degree of precision, if indeed this will ever be possible. It is clear from these developments that media research is extending progressively into the field of advertising research, and is growing beyond its previous boundaries; it is getting deeply involved in investigating how advertising works.

Advertising research

In major agencies, advertising research is an accepted part of the creation and assessment of many campaigns, though it is accepted that there are no techniques that can tell beyond doubt whether or not an advertising campaign will work.

Research at the stage of creating and selecting campaigns can greatly reduce the uncertainty, however, and research into the effects of campaigns can establish more precise and realistic objectives. The difficulty of setting realistic targets is one reason why sales cannot be a sole index of the 'effectiveness' of advertising. Advertising research, therefore, is mostly concerned with intermediate measures of effectiveness.

The first stage in the creation of a new advertising campaign, after the marketing brief has been agreed, is the testing of rough versions of proposed advertisements. Copywriters and artists usually welcome information at this stage.

If the advertising objectives are expressed in terms of the response hoped for—for example, what it is hoped people would think, feel and believe, and which of these responses is most important—the research findings are that much more easily used by creative people to assess their efforts.

The range of measures currently used includes recall, interest, and change in attitudes or preference for the product after seeing the advertising, and there are many other related measures. The most widely used and trusted technique is simply to test understanding of the intended message. Some techniques try to avoid direct questioning and the confusion that often arises over the meaning of words. Other quite fruitful techniques involve giving people the opportunity to express their reactions in terms of analogies by selecting photographs of popular situations that seem to fit the advertising.

At the stage of selecting the most promising finished advertisement, standard testing procedures are available from research organizations that use different combinations of such measures. One aim of the standard procedures is to provide comparisons by which advertisements can be judged, such as the achievement of competitive advertising or previous advertising for the same brand. However, the problem of finding a standard by which to judge the performance of a given advertisement is not easily solved. Even successive campaigns for the same product or different advertisements within a campaign are likely to vary in their aims. Advertisers who rely on such standard tests have found it more and more difficult to distinguish between the performance of advertisements tested, because, in fact, their whole conception and execution has been influenced by the known criteria of tests, and the creative individuality tends to be lost.

The choice of a testing technique implies some concept of how advertising works. A well-known researcher commented recently, 'I believe I know less now about how advertising works than I thought I did, say five years ago, and I suspect this is a common experience'. Advertising research has removed many misconceptions about advertising. Even recall of an advertisement is known to be an unreliable guide to its effectiveness—researchers are continually becoming more aware of the complex factors underlying such apparently simple measures. In practice, some well-loved campaigns have been replaced by others more relevant in terms of people's subjective reactions to the product and carefully devised marketing plans, and sales have improved. It has been demonstrated that it is not necessary for an advertisement to be believable, if it creates interest and curiosity of a certain kind. Objective realism is not possible in advertising, but subjective realism is essential; because of this ambiguity, research measures with an implicit basis in 'real life' can lead to confusing results. For example, a housewife with a beard drawn on her face may appear more 'realistic' to an audience, than a cool, somewhat idealized housewife.

The fact that there is debate about research technique and uncertainty about the way advertising works should not throw doubt on the need for advertising research. The requirements from advertising today are more subtle than when consumer choice was limited and goods were asked for by name, and it is more than ever necessary to gauge the return from advertising, and to set realistic objectives. Sales are constantly fluctuating, but it is possible to forestall a serious down-trend by checking attitudes to the product and to the advertising at regular intervals and adjusting advertising accordingly. On the other hand, changing advertising too often can lead to confusion and greater expense. These considerations and others make it well worth testing the effect of campaigns, and experimenting in the form of area tests with different media combinations.

In conclusion, it can be said that advertising research offers the advertiser the opportunity of discovering how to spend his advertising appropriations more effectively. Advertisers increasingly realize this and budget in advance for advertising research. Investment in the USA in advertising research was said recently to be at an average level of about 1 per cent of advertising appropriations, but that this concealed a higher level of investment by leading advertisers.

Reading list

BOOKS

Advertisers' Annual (Admark Publishing Company, London)
Modern Advertising Law, P. Langdon Davies (Business Publications, 1963)
British Code of Advertising Practice (I.P.A. booklet, 1967)
Confessions of an Advertising Man, David Ogilvy (Longmans, Green, 1964)
Advertising in Action, Ralph Harris and Arthur Seldon (Hutchinsons, for the Institute of Economic Affairs, 1962)
Advertising and the Public, Ralph Harris and Arthur Seldon (André Deutsch, for the Institute of Economic Affairs, 1962)

Useful addresses

Institute of Practitioners in Advertising, 44 Belgrave Square, London SW 1
Advertising Standards Authority, 5 Clements Inn, London WC 2
Incorporated Advertising Managers Association, 45 Hertford Street, London W 1

8.3 Public Relations

Tim Traverse-Healy

Public relations is not something that a company can decide to do or not to do. Public relations is something that a company has, whether it wants it or not. It follows that it is part of management's job to 'manage' corporate public relations with as much care and professionalism as it brings to, say, production or marketing.

Public relations was evolved by publicists and advertising men working independently, who realized they had to deal, not with some vague 'general public', but with individual men and women, rich and poor, employees and employers, customers, government servants, members of social institutions with distinctly various opinions and diverse needs. These men found out, often the hard way, that favourable publicity alone could not hope to create and keep good will for an organization unless that organization's contribution to the well-being of the community was fully appreciated, and its acts merited public favour.

Over the past twenty years, the number of practitioners in Britain has increased steadily along with the acceptance of public relations generally. More and more companies are undertaking ambitious public relations programmes, more specialists in the varying aspects of the craft are appearing, and more public relations specialists are offering their services as consultants or agencies.

There are directors who look on public relations simply as publicity or as advertising. It is not. Some believe it is just a means of obtaining free editorial mention. It is not. Others look on it as contact work with politicians and senior civil servants, as public speaking, publishing pamphlets, or producing films. Basically, it is none of these things. Most accurately it can be defined as a corporate attitude of mind, which dictates that all the policies and actions of a particular organization are clearly identified with the public interest and achieve public understanding and acceptance.

The Institute of Public Relations in an official definition put it this way: 'Public relations practice is defined as the deliberate, planned, and sustained effort to establish and maintain mutual understanding between an organization and its public'. Another definition is: 'Taking worthwhile action and getting the credit for it'. A Scandinavian colleague of mine puts it this way: 'If a boy is keen on a girl and writes her a letter telling her what a good fellow he is, that's advertising. If he calls on her and tells her personally, that's sales promotion. But if he takes his girl's girl friend out to dinner and convinces *her* that he's a good fellow, that's public relations'.

No matter how many public relations staff an organization employs, or however experienced the consultant it retains, the job in the end must be done by the members of the organization itself at all levels, from the chairman to the gate-keeper. By its very nature, public relations as such is not a task to be delegated to a team of technicians. And, just as on the sales side the representatives, no matter how determined, cannot sell a bad product, so public relations cannot itself remedy an organization's deficiencies. It is useless, for example, to take advertising space or distribute an expensive film to tell the world how good and successful a company is, if its relations with its labour force, the community in which it operates, or its retailers, are poor.

For a typical manufacturing company, the overall objectives of any public relations programme might be: to gain public recognition for its achievements; appreciation of its contribution to the country's good; acceptance of its operational methods; support for its viewpoints and plans; understanding of its problems. A secondary objective would be to publicize the company's products and services.

As has already been stressed, the company's objectives in its public relations cannot be realized unless it properly appreciates and analyses the 'public' with which it is endeavouring to communicate. Before the question of the boardroom responsibility for public relations is discussed, it is worth making a broad classification of two groups of the general public who are important to any business. These are, first, those on whom the company relies for labour, for capital, or for custom:

(a) Staff, employees (their community leaders and their families)
(b) Shareholders (including financial organizations)
(c) Customers (and their staffs).

Second, the people who influence public opinion and, therefore, whose attitude towards the company are of importance. This could be a large group, varying for different companies. It can be narrowed down to politicians, civil servants, newspapermen and broadcasters, trades union officials, officials of political, trade, social and cultural organizations, educationalists, and professional men and women.

It could be said that whereas the majority of people *adopt* an opinion, in the main, the key groups listed above *hold* an opinion; an opinion arrived at on facts as they see them, and which they pass on to others.

I do not want to give the impression that only those directly involved in a company's activities, or only the 'opinion-makers' should be the objects of a public relations exercise. As far as the general public is concerned, sound public relations can ensure that the company builds up a reputation that will stand it in good stead at difficult times. The public will react in accordance with what it knows of the facts. The long-term task of public relations is to make the facts known to as many people as possible. And this is primarily a boardroom responsibility.

Board action

To ensure that the company's public relations are sound, the board can usefully test its performance against the following recommended initiatives:

1. It should see that machinery exists whereby it is kept constantly informed of what the general public, or various groups of the public, are thinking about the company, and what has caused them to think that way.
2. It should ensure that procedures exist for such 'intelligence' to be passed on to the right people within the organization, in time, and in such a form that action can be taken.
3. It should make certain that planned and sustained efforts are made to disseminate corporate information and viewpoints.
4. It should approve a programme of activities aimed at involving board members, senior colleagues, and company officials at varying levels directly with selected members of the public.
5. It should maintain permanent machinery for the constant review of its public, labour, financial, and trade practices in the light of current public, political, financial, industrial, and social thinking.
6. It should initiate a programme for proving and evaluating the effectiveness of its public affairs and communications efforts against the cost involved.

Whatever the size of the company, responsibility at board level should be given to one director for all matters concerning public policy, public 'image', and public communications. Moreover, whenever possible, executive responsibility below board level should similarly be given to one man. It would depend upon the size and nature of the particular organization whether or not this individual should be a trained public relations or communications staff man, or a consultant. The assistance he would need depends, of course, on the size and complexity of the organization and the nature of its operations. Some situations demand the employment of skilled staff

422

in large numbers, deployed functionally at national and regional levels. In other cases a 'gifted amateur' working with part-time or volunteer assistants can produce the right results, if he is working to a sound plan and is given top-level backing.

Only the board can decide and define the company's overall objective; can determine what the company wants to be known *for*, and *by whom*; can agree the overall public relations plan; and can vote the money necessary to mount an effective internal and external communications programme. If the programme is to be successful, individual directors need to play their parts as and when their own areas of responsibility are subject to outside attention, or are selected for public relations treatment.

The structure of the board varies from company to company, of course. But in discussing the responsibilities of individual directors for the company's public relations, it will be helpful to list them under the headings of chairman, chief executive, personnel director, research director, marketing director, and 'international director', which will correspond to the functions of directors in all sizes of board. What, then, are their responsibilities in relation, say, to a public relations programme aimed at highlighting the company's industrial performance, social record, and labour policy, the quality of its goods and services, the ability of its staff, and its sense of responsibility regarding prices, profits, and trade terms?

The chairman

In a great many companies it is the chairman's job to be the spokesman for the business. Many dislike this duty. Some are good at it; some are bad and so pass the task on to another. Many chairmen, however, appreciate that it is a task that one at least of the directors has to perform well in the company interest, and so have very sensibly volunteered for tuition themselves, often with dramatic results.

Public spokesman or no, the chairman has to act as chief host for his company. In many firms launching public relations programmes, luncheons and dinners to which guests representing various sections of the community are invited are routine affairs. The occasion may be used to tell visitors something about the organization, and at the same time to find out the guests' viewpoints on matters that relate to the company.

The chairman is a key figure in any personal contact programme, and, to be effective, such programmes should be carefully planned. Political and social leaders should be included, as should civil servants, educationalists, trade association officials, and union leaders: all at the level most helpful to both parties. Undoubtedly there are selected journalists who should be given the opportunity to enjoy a personal relationship with the company's top men. They usually welcome this, appreciate the background information they can acquire, and invariably respect confidences. Really informed comment concerning a company is always important, especially when trouble strikes. Longstanding relationships pioneered by the company's directors can reap rich rewards. They ensure that inaccuracies are corrected and that, whatever the issue may be, it is seen in perspective.

In the building of such valuable relationships, the chairman should play a key part. Even if not himself keen on social contacts and activities, he should keep a close eye on the company's programme.

Elsewhere (section 8.4, p. 433), Mr James Derriman deals more fully with public relations in the *financial* area. Obviously this is a particular concern of the chairman and, working to him, the financial director and company secretary. Here it is perhaps sufficient to make the point that the search for capital for a developing organization is a permanent fact of commercial life. Public interest, and therefore the interest of press, television, and other media in company financial matters are continually on the increase. For a company to enjoy the regard of the financial institutions is no longer all that matters. The smaller shareholder is being wooed, and the people who influence him are many and widespread. Significantly, the banks in recent years have paid growing attention to the man–in–the–street, not simply to gain customers, but to increase deposits and improve liquidity for application to their industrial and commercial customers.

The company's own shareholders constitute a separate public, which deserves separate attention. In many firms the whole 'public relations year' is based on the timing of the Annual General Meeting, which starts the round of interim reports, shareholders' letters, institutional advertising, investment analysts' briefing, financial press conferences, the Annual Report and Chairman's Statement, leading to the next AGM. From the public relations standpoint the annual programme needs to be planned as a cycle of related events, rather than emerging as a series of isolated and often unrelated 'happenings'. It is the chairman's responsibility to bring shape and form to this vital area of corporate activity.

The chief executive

In many respects the involvement of the chief executive or managing director in the company's public relations programme overlaps or dovetails with the chairman's activities. Additionally, however, it is usually most convenient and effective for the chief executive to carry the personal responsibility and supply the initiative for seeing that the company's internal relations are sound and that internal communications are efficient.

Studies carried out in different kinds of business have established that from 50 per cent to as much as 80 per cent of management's overall task is concerned with communication: upwards, downwards, and sideways. In today's circumstances it is no longer possible to rely on the accepted methods of down-the-line verbal dissemination of information. This tends to reflect, and sometimes exaggerate, the preconceived attitudes, ignorance, and occasionally prejudices of the 'transmitters'. Traditional methods of communication need to be supplemented by programmes to present company information directly to selected groups of managers and workpeople in a controlled, interesting, and even exciting fashion.

In supervising the company's internal communications, the chief executive is likely to work in co-operation with his senior colleague responsible for staff and personnel affairs. His personal responsibilities are likely to include the job of keeping open the lines of communication with appropriate senior civil servants, with educationalists whose work has a bearing on the company's activities, with trades union leaders, and with trade association officials. Where factories dominate the life of a particular community, a single town, or perhaps more than one locality, he should, in the broadest sense, supervise community relations activity.

As a consultant I have talked with many chief executives who insisted that their job was to keep the goods flowing and the customers buying, and that spending time on any fringe activity was to get their priorities wrong, if not entirely a waste of effort. But a chief executive, surely, is like a commander or a general. His ultimate objective is to win the battle, but battles do not rage in consistent fury over long periods of time. To be in a position to win the battles when they occur, he must ensure that his troops are trained and are adequately supplied. He must ensure that all his men at all levels are 'in the picture', and above all he must visit and talk with the troops personally.

In a company, the same applies, with the proviso that many of those who can seriously influence the outcome of the 'battle' are not necessarily on the payroll. Sending a predetermined message to a selected group of individuals is an act of communication. It is doomed to failure as a piece of persuasion unless the content of the message is, in the final analysis, endorsed by others who are often outsiders. It is in this matter of achieving third-party endorsements for company actions, policies, and plans that the chief executive can play a key personal role.

I have talked with many managing directors who genuinely believed that they were carrying out these duties. Probing revealed, however, that although at one time or another they did do so, operational problems loomed so large in their consciousness that nothing really effective was being done on the communications front. The solution is for the chief executive to draft, or have drafted for him and to agree, a practical programme that he can manage, and that is realistic in relation to the other calls on his valuable time. But certainly not to opt out.

Personnel director

'Good people to work for' is one of the standard phrases used by opinion researchers testing a company's comparative public standing. A company's labour relations record is a significant component of its total corporate 'image' formed in the public mind. Whereas stormy events in this area create their own publicity, most of it bad, regrettably a good labour force story rarely achieves the same dramatic treatment. This makes it all the more essential for the personnel director to take the following action:

1. Working to the chief executive and employing whatever public relations and communications specialist is available, ensure that corporate policy is clearly and constantly communicated, and check that it is understood.
2. Without forming a 'spy ring', see that he is constantly aware of what individuals in the labour force at all levels, and key people outside in the local community, are thinking and saying about the company.
3. See that company news and information is distributed quickly and effectively—and interestingly—via employee publications, notice boards, special meetings, and print.
4. Together with the production director, maintain personal contact with local trades union leaders, and ensure that the outcome of joint consultative activities is accurately and widely released.
5. Make certain that all personnel procedures and related company print are of a high standard in the public relations context. This especially applies to recruitment and training programmes.
6. Appreciate and act on the fact that the following activities are important factors within the overall company public relations programme and also, in themselves, most likely to be successful if public relations techniques are employed in their day-to-day operation:
Recruitment programmes
Health and welfare services
Employee development and training
Safety and accident prevention
Suggestion schemes
Leisure activities
Retirement plans.

In a company that does not employ a community relations manager it should usually be the task of the Personnel Chief to administer such a programme.

In point of fact, the above is a general public relations programme in miniature, and to all intents and purposes contains the same elements. The programme should be planned and budgeted for on an annual basis, and estimates should be debated by management alongside a statement of the overall and specific objectives of the campaign, and an up-dating of the problems being, or likely to be, encountered.

Community and civic activity do not constitute simply a cosy form of paternalism. It should be seen and evaluated as an investment in keeping the wheels of business turning with the minimum of friction. Civic and VIP visits, open days, plant tours, and local exhibitions all form part of such a programme, as do the provision of material, lectures and so forth, for schools and local organizations.

Two aspects of this subject need stressing. First, the director concerned should ensure his personal involvement with civic, political, social, educational, and press leaders in such a fashion and atmosphere, that the company story is told and policy explained clearly and convincingly, and that at the same time candid views and contributions are forthcoming. Second, the real civic and social needs of the community should be identified and studied by the company and assessed in relation to its own long-range intentions as far as the local community is concerned. At the point where the civic and corporate targets overlap, there exists an area for the company to involve itself and its employees with the community at all levels, and over a period of time. In this way all benefit and are seen to benefit, and the company achieves recognition. Recognition in itself is worthless. As a step, however, towards achieving public goodwill and support it is priceless.

Production director

Whatever his actual title, this executive has the delicate task of balancing men and machines, and increasingly this requires an exceptional skill in human relationships. It goes without saying that he will require to employ established methods of passing management policy and decisions down the line, and engage fully in joint consultation activity. In all this he will probably be assisted to some extent by his colleague on the personnel side.

Sophisticated internal communications techniques can be applied to good effect in programmes aimed at increasing the awareness of the whole labour force of the company's position in the market and of its targets; in campaigns aimed at reducing absenteeism, improving time-keeping, or quality controls; in longer-range programmes aimed at increasing the ambition and sense of responsibility of the employees generally; in getting employees to appreciate the significance of productivity drives and longer-term productivity agreements; in cost information programmes, the object of which is to make savings, cut costs, increase output, and improve the company's competitive position.

The degree of success of any of the above will be in direct proportion to the time, money, and professional skill put behind the communications effort. When management mounts a series of half-baked internal campaigns, it risks completely losing the respect of the workforce; respect that has probably been hard won and well deserved on the strictly operational front can be frittered away by inadequate attention to information policies and procedures.

According to this director's own terms of reference, there are three groups of individuals with whom he may become involved personally within the public relations context.

427

First, and obviously, trades union officials at branch and even national level. Second, opinion leaders, such as members of parliament or selected sociologists and research workers interested in industrial conditions and problems. Third, suppliers.

Suppliers can, in some situations, prove real allies to a company. If they are to be rallied successfully and quickly, there should have been previously established a form of 'dialogue' alongside their normal form of contact dealing with the company. At the very least, should no crisis ever occur, they can prove effective 'ambassadors'.

Research director

The word 'research' in public relations terms seems sometimes to possess magical qualities. The aura of research consciousness surrounding a company can create emotional responses, often entirely subjective, among many individuals in various walks of life: from stockbrokers to school teachers.

As a group, research chiefs are sometimes reluctant to release or publicize the results of their efforts. Understandably, they are loath to speak until they are sure of perfect results. To some even 'perfection' is illusory, the results of one research pointing the need for further development or even another project.

The opinion of academics and educationalists towards a company matters, since such men influence others in the political and social spheres. Young men in both the Arts and Science streams of education are influenced by a company's research record.

Seeing the need to tell the research story—and from time to time tolerating the 'antics' of the public relations people—is rightly expected of a research director by his communications colleagues, even if it is sometimes the most they can expect. They should both remember that they both share the benefits of the company's long-term success.

The marketing director

Three 'movements' are causing the marketing director to become more intimately involved with the public relations arm than he was, say, ten years ago.

First, there is the emergence of the 'consumer protection' movement.

Second, there is the growing realization that communications is perhaps the most important factor in the overall marketing programme, and that marketing communication needs to be planned as a process (rather than a series of isolated actions), and constructed around the cycle: Publish, Listen, Revise, Publish. . . .

Third, there is the correlation revealed by research between accepted corporate reputation and the company's known capabilities and sales.

Taking these three points in reverse order, correlations have been established between sales and the quality of informational and technical literature; between sales and a company's reputation for enterprise, and for introducing new products;

between sales and personal contact or involvement with the company; between sales and the general level and intensity of awareness of the company; between sales and customers' views on the handling of complaints or requests for information.

This type of research is being carried out at buyer, trader, purchaser, and consumer levels. As might be anticipated, evidence of the link between reputation and sales is strongest in the industrial fields. A research carried out a few years ago among 4,000 industrial product buyers showed that although 98 per cent felt product quality and importance were the most important factors, 87 per cent also said that the seller's integrity and reputation were important.

McGraw-Hill, in a classic advertisement, made the best case for a corporate public relations programme in support of the marketing programme. It shows a grim-faced buyer seated in a chair facing out of the page with the legend:

I don't know who you are
I don't know your company
I don't know your company's product
I don't know what your company stands for
I don't know your company's customers
I don't know your company's record
I don't know your company's reputation

Now—what was it you wanted to sell me?

Summing up a research study for New York University, Dr F. Robert Shoaf, Associate Professor of Marketing, stated:

> 'To the extent that products and services become more obviously alike, the buyer's decision is based more and more on subjective emotional factors. There is no denying the importance of corporate image as a buying stimulation. People feel safer dealing with a company they know. Who the manufacturer is, is sometimes as important—sometimes even more important—than what the product is. The company behind the product is always part of what the customer is buying, and sometimes the best way to sell a product is to sell the company behind the product.'

Just as marketing itself is becoming increasingly codified, so within it, marketing communications are beginning to be systematized. Marketing men have evolved a list of what they sometimes term 'profit inhibitors' in any particular situation. A number concern marketing communications specifically, since weaknesses or failure in the correlation can, and probably will, affect the total plan. They are:

1. Internal communications failure inside the company.
2. Communications budget deficiencies.
3. Failure to dominate in communications media employed.

429

4. Too generic a communications claim or appeal.
5. Information loss along track from management to point of sale.
6. Giving communications jobs it cannot do.
7. Placing responsibility for communications too low in management structure.
8. Failure to define and manage the corporate image.
9. Imbalance between communications media employed.
10. Copying competition in communications activity.
11. Failure to establish extra benefits or quality or product or service.

Obviously the marketing director, in defining the role of communications within the total 'marketing mix' does this in consultation with his advertising agent, as often as not nowadays with a sales promotion specialist, and increasingly with his public relations colleague.

Working as a team, these men can help select attainable communications objectives keyed to the company mission and shaped against the existing or likely strategy of the competition. It is these professionals who are most likely to develop the message media and audience strategies calculated to communicate, compel, and compete.

The isolation or creation of the 'difference that can make a difference' in the promotion of a product or service, whatever the market, is likely to emerge from individuals who are public or consumer-orientated rather than from those who are company-orientated. The wise marketing executive is the man who, grasping this, can involve and then manage such people effectively.

Dame Mary Stocks has described the period we live in as the age of the 'Consumptive Society'. The organized consumer movement is fast developing under the twin influences of improved educational opportunities, and the sharpening of the critical faculties of the public as regards products, possessions, and services by the mass media.

In the United Kingdom, directors must pay attention to the Government-supported Consumer Council with its own journal, called *Focus*, and the independent Consumers Association with its own monthly publication, *Which?*. Each of these bodies has 'eyes, ears, and voices' in the provinces, in the shape of local advisers and groups. Also concerned with consumer protection matters are the Citizens Advice Bureaux with their 483 local offices, each with its 'specialist' in consumer matters. Both in the United Kingdom and on the Continent, consumer legislation presently in force is considerable.

Today, through their journals and by public statements, the Consumer Council and the Consumers Association do speak for the consumer. In their formative period, whether or not they voiced the opinion of all consumers on a particular issue could be questioned, as could some of the methods of test and research employed. In such early days one could also have questioned some of their methods of consultation and promulgation. But the facts of the matter are that today, consumers, through these above organizations or through a variety of consultative groups, can point the spotlight of public attention; can foster and sponsor political action; can provide telling evidence for governmental and public enquiries. Today, what might once-upon-a-time have remained and been dealt with as a customer complaint in an obscure village, can become a national issue in a matter of days or even hours.

It has been said that a complaint is an opportunity to create a satisfied customer. This overlooks those who do not, or will not, complain, and the negative spirit of a 'Complaints Department'. The public relations way would be to transfer this whole area of activity into a 'Consumer Relations Bureau', and charge it with the task of setting-up corporate lines of communication with customers and with leaders of consumer opinion.

The result would be that marketing management could be kept appraised of consumer protection legislation, actual and projected, early enough to initiate changes either in external thinking or internal practices. And that could mean the difference between profit or loss and between failure or survival.

International director

On an international level the complexity of the company's public relations problem is multiplied directly by the number of countries within which it is manufacturing or marketing. The complexity, however, should apply only to the variety of methods needed to be effective within the varying social, political, and media conditions.

World-wide communications are now so complete and so fast, however, that whatever the variations in the techniques used by the company, its overall public relations policy must be consistant. Seeing that all company subsidiaries and branches understand this policy and appreciate the standards expected is the main responsibility of the international director.

The degree of sophistication in public relations matters, and the experience of local practitioners, varies considerably from country to country. Selecting locally the best advisers and staff, and setting-up the right machinery for the task, is a skilled job needing time and care. Just as the parent company or office works to an annual plan, so each component should be required to develop its own programme and submit it for annual discussion and agreement.

In countries or territories where the company is engaged in marketing rather than producing, extra effort is called for in promoting its reputation. It has been proved time and again that export salesmen get better sales results where, before their arrival, the company has been well and truly 'pre-sold' to introduce the product or the range. Well prepared print, selective informational advertising, and a planned and sustained press publicity programme beamed at specific markets can ensure a favourable climate of opinion among potential customers before the salesmen has left home.

431

Often, an intelligently constructed public relations 'drive' in a selected country can test the market opportunities for a product or service far more effectively, speedily, and inexpensively than a more orthodox test programme.

Top brass has been urged to 'get out there and sell' personally. This is not always the strong point of a particular executive, and indeed the particular product or prospect does not always react to treatment. A senior man with a story to tell, and a dramatic way of telling it, will get an audience.

Directors who have studied this article may feel that since so many of their activities touch on or involve public affairs or communications work, there is a case for the additional appointment of a public relations director or adviser at board level. Many leading companies already believe so. The Chairman of Unilever, Lord Cole, in a notable discussion on the responsibilities of directors, stated recently that, for example, if government intervention in business continued to increase, 'we may be faced with a new sort of director, the man who knows his way around the corridors of power in Whitehall . . .' Whether companies decide that a special man for this kind of public relations is needed or not, they will appreciate the significance for their public relations attitudes in Lord Cole's further reminder that in the future, from the community at large 'there will be more and more demands that business should be conducted in a goldfish bowl'. (From a paper given by Lord Cole to the Industrial Educational and Research Foundation on 30th January, 1968.)

Reading list

BOOKS

Handbook of Public Relations, H. Stephenson (McGraw-Hill, 1960)
Plain Talk about Public Relations, L. L. Knolt (McClelland and Stewart, 1961)
The Practice of Industrial Communication, M. Ivens (Business Publications, 1963)
Practical Public Relations, S. Black (Pitman, 2nd Edition, 1966)
Public Relations in Business Management, J. Derriman (University of London Press, 1964)
Teach Yourself Public Relations, H. Lloyd (English Universities Press, 1963)
Corporate Public Relations, J. W. Hill (Harper and Bros., 1958)
Industry and Press Relations: A Guide to the handling of editorial publicity in national and local newspapers for industrial management, employers' federation, trade unions and technical organizations, P. Hayle (Staples Press, 1957)
Industrial Public Relations, Paul I. Slee-Smith (Business Publications, 1968)

JOURNAL

'Sir this Gentlemen is from the Daily——' John Addey (*British Industry Week*, 8th March, 1968)

Useful addresses

Institute of Public Relations, 20–26 Lambs Conduit Street, London WC 1
International Public Relations Association, Secretariat, 4 Syggrou Avenue, Athens 403, Greece

8.4 Financial Public Relations

James Derriman

Planned action to foster the company's reputation among investors and their advisers has been shown to bring important benefits, both long-term and in dealing with specific situations such as an unwanted takeover bid. Carried out with integrity and expertise, the techniques of public relations practice are appreciated by the City—the arbiter of financial etiquette—as a useful link between capital and industry.

Increasingly, every public company whose shares are quoted by the Stock Exchange is likely to find it necessary to give serious attention to this management tool. A private company, or a public company whose shares are not quoted, may be able to gain advantage from some techniques in this field. To interest the investing public, however, there must naturally be some link between the company's activities and purchasable securities, such as an announced intention to go public, or the generation of business which, in turn, affects public companies.

The role of financial public relations is quite simply to improve and speed up understanding of a company's policy, its activities, its problems and successes, its prospects and the quality of its management. There is not, and must not be, any question of promotion, in the sense of boosting. Still less can misfortune or inefficiency be whitewashed or hidden.

Advantages a public, quoted company may expect to gain from planned financial public relations include:

15*

1. Maintenance of a share price that is realistic, avoiding fluctuations caused by rumour and lack of information.
2. Shareholders who are not merely contented but friendly, taking an interest in the company's progress to the extent of becoming ambassadors for it, and perhaps purchasers of its products.
3. Shareholders whose confidence and loyalty will stand the company in good stead in the event of a capital issue, a takeover, or some other occasion when their active goodwill is needed.
4. Credit for the company's achievements, and understanding of its problems and the steps being taken to overcome or offset them, among the investing public at large, who provide a market for the company's shares and a potential source of new capital.
5. Goodwill among potential employees, existing and potential customers, suppliers and others whose impression of the company is influenced by its financial and management reputation.

Responsibility for company financial matters, including contact with shareholders and the City, has always been rightly held at the top of the management pyramid. The chairman, aided by the finance director and the secretary, contribute a great deal to the company's reputation in this field by their day-to-day decisions and attitudes. So it is with them that steps to foster the reputation and improve goodwill must originate. At the same time there are distinct limits to 'do-it-yourself' in financial public relations work. Knowledge of the differing requirements of varying types of investors, of City Editors and of investment analysts, for instance, and the skills of journalism and typography, are normally best sought from an expert. Even more important, perhaps, the professional financial public relations consultant can offer impartial advice and wide experience of methods found to be successful by other companies.

There are all too few consultants with the necessary knowledge and experience of this specialized field, requiring as it does familiarity with company law, the rules of the Stock Exchange, the City Code on bids and mergers, and the practice of the merchant banks in addition to the techniques and flair of public relations. Recommendation from the company's financial advisers or from another company is probably the best way of finding a good consultant. Alternatively, the Institute of Public Relations will supply names of its members who specialize in financial work.

Financial public relations, like any other management operation, benefits from careful planning in advance. Like other branches of public relations, its results are cumulative, and it is essential that it should be regarded as a continuing programme. A consultant's plan for such a programme would cover objectives, approaches, sections of the public, methods and costing.

Of these, the objectives in many cases will correspond broadly to the advantages

434

listed above. The 'approaches' to be used will vary with the company and its circumstances. Each company has its own personality, and whereas some firms, for instance, may wish to illustrate their technological progress others may find it necessary to explain the stable nature of their trade.

The sections of the public whose understanding and goodwill are being sought comprise the company's existing shareholders, the investing public (potential future shareholders), stockbrokers, analysts, City Editors and other investment advisers.

There is much to be said for enlisting the interest and goodwill of a new shareholder from the outset, by sending a welcoming and informative letter signed by the chairman, and enclosing a copy of the last report together with any descriptive booklet published by the company or group. Many investors buy on outside advice or on a newspaper recommendation with very little knowledge of the business in which they are taking an interest.

Nowadays it is the exception to find a really badly-produced company report, and the average standard of presentation is high. Most companies have found that it is quite possible, with a little trouble, to achieve a design that will do them credit without undue cost. The value of the information contained, however, often lags behind the package in which it is presented. Financial public relations is concerned with both aspects, with emphasis, if anything, on the content. Recent company legislation and Stock Exchange rules have called for many changes in the directors' report and in the accounts. In this atmosphere of change the company that seeks goodwill among its shareholders and the investment world generally will want to keep ahead of legal requirements and disclose all information that will help to give an accurate picture of its progress. With the aid of maps, really good illustrations, organization charts, and practical items such as a 'calendar' of dividend and meeting dates, the report can be made a worthwhile public relations document. The distribution list should extend beyond the company's own members to include the Press, the local MP, major libraries, recruiting sources, and so on.

Since the Companies Act 1967, the directors' report may be expected to become fuller and more informative, to some extent covering ground formerly dealt with in the chairman's statement. In any event, both these items are of key importance in public relations. Although the responsibility is that of the chairman and directors, whose opinions are reflected, a public relations adviser may legitimately and usefully offer suggestions for subjects to be included and on the technicalities of style. Many highly literate chairmen, for instance, are apt to draft their statements in a way that makes it almost impossible for a journalist to select a brief passage for quotation, and thus misses valuable opportunities for helpful publicity.

The question of publishing the chairman's statement or directors' report, either complete or in summary form, as an advertisement is a matter on which the public relations adviser and the company's financial advertising agency should work closely together. Modern advertising techniques can be harnessed to create something of

435

far more value than the perfunctory, solid columns inserted as a sort of annual sacrifice to the gods of publicity.

Nearly every company undertaking financial public relations will wish to produce an effective interim report, whether or not it falls within the Stock Exchange rule on this subject. Although the mere fact of producing a half-time report earns a good mark among investors, here, too, thought and skill achieve something much better than the minimum standard.

Far too many companies, instinctively, and rightly, recoiling from the extravagance of making their annual meeting into a beano for the few shareholders who attend, content themselves with rushing through the statutory business in a bare room from which everyone is glad to escape for lunch. Yet for most shareholders this is the one opportunity to meet their directors. Public relations will suggest items such as a display illustrating the company's activities, inclusion of a brief talk on the same lines, and elementary hospitality to those shareholders who attend and appreciate a personal word with their hosts after the meeting.

Whatever efforts are made to improve communication between the company and its members, most investors rely considerably on the published opinion of the City Editors of the daily and Sunday press, and of writers in the financial weeklies. In the financial field, as elsewhere, the public relations policy must be to provide journalists with every possible help to carry out their jobs and to form a correct judgement based on all relevant facts.

As an early step in any financial public relations programme, it is important to see that the Press is in possession of full and up-to-date background information. As to figures, good annual and interim reports plus the Exchange Telegraph and Moodies cards should meet most requirements. What is often less readily accessible to the journalist is a concise account of what the company does, its general history and development, and the qualifications and background of its top management. The public relations man will compile this material and provide it in a form the newspapers are glad to keep on file for ready reference.

Some of the most dramatic improvements in company-Press relations have come about through quite ordinary personal contact. Consultants frequently find that problems solve themselves once the directors can be shown that City journalists are a most responsible (as well as influential) group of people, often graduates in economics. The Press, for their part, welcome an opportunity to hear the views of management at first hand and to put questions even if the answers have temporarily to remain in confidence. Often a series of small luncheon parties given by the chairman can provide the right setting, and careful planning of the guest list and subjects for discussion will help greatly. The professional consultant can do much to ensure the success of these occasions, carrying out his proper function as a link rather than a barrier between his client and the Press, knowing both sides intimately, as he must do.

436

Once liaison with the financial Press has been established, the opportunities for favourable publicity will multiply. Journalists will approach the company for comment, knowing that they will get fair and informative replies to their questions. Openings will occur for articles and interviews.

Another important but less usual side of financial public relations is the provision of the detailed information needed by brokers, jobbers, and investment managers of the institutions. Possible methods here include statistical supplements to the annual report, invitations to visit the company's factory, and an address to the Society of Investment Analysts.

All the activities described above, together with others appropriate in individual cases, are likely to find a place in any continuing programme of financial public relations. Where particular needs or problems exist, such as a new issue of securities, an amalgamation or a takeover bid, a short-term plan can be made accordingly, covering adequate briefing for the Press and a clear policy running through all communications to investors and the market in order to create the maximum goodwill.

Many merchant banks, as well as the Stock Exchange itself, today have public relations consultants, and all are conscious of the contribution that public relations methods, used skilfully and with complete integrity, can make to the success of company finance. Particularly in the case of special operations such as new issues and bids, it is essential that the financial advisers should be consulted at every stage and that all communications to the Press and others concerned should be agreed in advance.

Financial public relations advice and services, as a job for a skilled specialist, understandably command a specialist's fee. An attempt to do things on the cheap by employing a second-rate public relations firm, or one whose only experience is in the promotion of consumer sales, could be worse than taking no action at all. This does not mean that the whole operation need be expensive, for in the case of most companies the professional time involved is not great.

Proof of results—always a conundrum in public relations—is perhaps easier in financial work than elsewhere. The company that sets out to serve the investor, his advisers, and the Press, presenting effectively all the facts and figures, except only those whose disclosure could harm the business, will be in little doubt of its reward. It will receive full credit for its achievements, and much patience and understanding in adversity. These are valuable, though literally priceless, assets, which go far to ease all the company's financial affairs.

Reading list

BOOKS

Repeating Financial Data to Management, Edited by W. D. Falcon (American Management Association, 1966)
How to Read a Balance Sheet (International Labour Office, Geneva, 1966)

Company-Investor Relations, James Derriman (University of London Press, 1969)
Public Relations in Business Management, James Derriman (University of London Press, 1964)
Financial Public Relations, Oscar M. Beveridge (McGraw-Hill, New York, 1963)
Guide to Company Balance Sheets and Profit and Loss Accounts, Frank H. Jones (Heffer, 6th edition, 1964–supplement 1967)

JOURNALS

'Open Letter from a City Editor' (*The Director*, August 1960)
'How to Win Friends and Influence People in the City' (Patrick Sergeant, *The Director*, August 1967)

Useful addresses

Society of Investment Analysts, 21 Godliman Street, London EC 4

8.5 Satisfying the Consumer

Jean and Andrew Robertson

It does not need a profound knowledge of business history to be aware that consumer protection is not new. The old market rules that prevented merchants from intercepting goods in transit and buying them up (forestalling), that insisted upon everything for sale being displayed openly (market overt), and prohibited purchases that were speculative and not for the buyer's own use (regrating), were all aimed at fair trading. Naturally, there were always those who broke the rules, and with the growth of the scale of business it became impossible to show all goods, and sales were made by example (or sample, as it became), the open market disappeared or turned into a wholesale market (like Covent Garden), and the simple common law rules were forgotten.

The present century has seen a different sort of development. The open market has long gone, except for street traders in perishable foods, and the chain of supply from manufacturer, through wholesaler and retailer to the customer has become long and complicated. At the same time, the goods themselves have become infinitely more varied and in many ways mysterious. How many viewers know how a cathode-ray tube works? How many motor-car owners understand the internal combusion engine? Many people not only cannot tell margarine from butter, they confuse plastics with leather, synthetic fibres with cotton or wool, invert sugar with honey, and Algerian wine with Beaujolais. The formidable combination of engineering advance, with chemical synthesis, food processing, and the brisk, persuasive sales techniques of modern business leaves the average purchaser of goods and services

439

in a very weak position. He needs advice, and indeed education, but he also has a right to a measure of protection.

Many governments have tacitly acknowledged this over the past century, bringing in legislation such as the Food and Drink Act of 1860 (in tardy response to a campaign against food adulteration sparked off by the *Lancet*), the Merchandise Marks Act of 1887, and the Sale of Goods Act of 1893. There have been a number of others since, relating to advertising, hire purchase, the misdescription of fabrics, weights and measures, pharmaceutical products and restrictive trade practices, mainly intended to redress the balance between the skilful business operator (with the inevitable inclusion of the unscrupulous and the fraudulent) and the ignorant customer.

The customer, not surprisingly, rarely knew his legal standing *vis à vis* shopkeepers and merchants, or he might have invoked the Sale of Goods Act on occasions when the item he had bought turned out to be in some way defective, misdescribed, not up to sample, or unfit for the purpose for which it had been sold. This Act has recently enjoyed a resurgence of importance in the public eye as a consequence of the disputes stirred up over the wording of guarantees. Some guarantees contain phrases like 'notwithstanding any other condition or warranty, express or implicit, statutory or otherwise', which purport to deprive the signatory of any right to take legal action against the vendor. This issue was first raised by the now defunct Consumer Advisory Council, founded as a subdivision of the British Standards Institution in 1957. And thereby hangs the tale of the last ten years of consumer protection and advice, for CAC's foundation, shortly followed by the independent Consumer Research (later renamed the Consumer's Association), marked the beginning of the organized 'consumer movement'.

A number of the institutions that are now regarded as part of this 'movement' existed before it began, and some of them were set up by manufacturers and traders as safeguards against malpractice in their line of business. One of the most active, even militant, of these is the Retail Trading-Standards Association, which concentrates its effort largely in the field of textiles, soft furnishings, and related products. In its monthly bulletin it regularly records successful prosecutions it has brought against traders who have advertised or labelled rayon as nylon, fur fabric as real fur, plastics briefcases as leather, and names them.

This is probably the only example of a really aggressive consumer watchdog that predates the launching of the so-called movement, but its protection of the ultimate user is really incidental to RT-SA's policy of correcting trading abuses for the sake of the trade itself.

The British Standards Institution as such was established on the firm foundation of an engineering standards association first begun by the Institute of Civil Engineers, in 1931, with a Royal Charter granted two years before being given its present name. Its consumer side developed under the aegis of the Women's Advisory

Committee, doubtless because traditionally it is the women who do the shopping. It was the WAC that encouraged the setting up of a Consumer Advisory Council, with a magazine of its own, *Shopper's Guide*. But another activity was stirring at the same time.

A group of like-minded people set out, in about 1955, to fill a gap in British society—the absence of a Consumer's Union such as exists in the United States and publishes *Consumer Reports* every month, and does comparative testing. After two years deliberations, and with the active help of the CU they launched what soon became known as the Consumers' Association, publishing *Which?* monthly and conducting highly critical comparative tests. *Shopper's Guide* began life as a quarterly, ran articles about goods that had qualified for the Kitemark seal of approval of the BSI by answering to a British Standard Specification, and at first did no comparative testing. It did carry an article about gas cookers in which the results of Gas Council tests were reported.

The two periodicals ran side by side for five years, while their parent organizations developed in rather different ways. CAC, for example, criticized services as well as goods (car repairs, shoe-fitting, bookselling) and ran a complaints service. While *Which?* occasionally tackled services (bank charges, racing tipsters), they never handled complaints. Nevertheless they grew faster than CAC, being bolder because they were not shackled to a semi-official institution, and ramified, founding such bodies as the Advisory Centre for Education (ACE), the Federation of Consumer Groups (in 1968 there were about eighty of these local groups) their Car Test Unit, and the Research Institute for Consumer Affairs, which has now ceased.

The newspapers, especially the serious Sundays, began to run consumer columns (the *Guardian* had one for a time), the *Spectator* began 'Consuming Interest', then came the *New Statesman's* Value Judgement column. The activities of the Press are interesting as an aspect of the gathering interest in consumer advice in the 'sixties. The women's magazine *Good Housekeeping* used to issue a seal of approval before the war, and had continued to do so even after the arrival of the official Kitemark, the Council of Industrial Design's seal of good design, and the advent of the two specialist organizations. Naturally there was some scepticism as to the value of such a seal emanating from a magazine partly dependent for its revenues on commercial advertising. The main purpose of the seal was apparently that the Good Housekeeping Institute would back up a shopper's complaints if anything were found to be wrong with an approved article, most of which were household goods. The use of this seal ceased in 1965, three years after the report of the Molony Committee on Consumer Protection.

In this Report, issued in July 1962, both this seal and that of the British Safety Council (a private enterprise rival to the sem-official Royal Society for the Prevention of Accidents) were subject to strong criticism. But meanwhile the Council dropped its seal.

During the Molony Committee's session, which lasted three years, there were several public outcries about deaths caused by fires started by drip-feed radiant oil-heaters and by flammable children's clothing made of cotton. The oil-heater scandal led to the first Consumer Protection Act of 1961, which was concerned entirely with domestic safety, and to the setting of a British Standard for this type of paraffin heater. This is a telling example of how consumer protection is needed for more than the mere satisfaction of 'value for money'.

Molony was a watershed in the consumer movement. From the day of publication of its report, with the recommendation that an official Consumer Council should be established, the CAC and *Shopper's Guide* were doomed. The pioneering editor, Elizabeth Gundrey, who had first done battle for the consumer in the columns of the *News Chronicle*, carried on editing a new version of the magazine with private backing and a small grant for testing from BSI, but in May 1963 it ceased publication and left the field to *Which?* The Consumer Council was set up under the aegis of the Board of Trade the very year that the Molony Committee reported, but its magazine *Focus* did not begin publication until early in 1966. Its tone is militant, and it attacks abuses such as doorstep selling of dubious encyclopaedias, but it records no comparative testing because the Council does not have the funds to do them. Nor does it handle complaints, leaving this function to the voluntary Citizens' Advice Bureaux, a survival from the war. How adequate the CAB are is not clearly known, but the fact that both Bristol and Newcastle have set up complaints services under local government auspices, and that consumer groups continue to proliferate, suggests that at least they do not meet all needs.

Looking at this flurry of consumer activity from the point of view of a manufacturer, it must seem as if the world and especially his wife are out to be as difficult as possible. And now that successive governments have decided that to take part has its political advantages, the spate of protective legislation must appear alarming. Reconciling the interests of producer and consumer can probably never be fully achieved, just as finding a common and stable area of agreement between employers and unions is likely to produce a continuing interplay of forces. The manufacturer who makes goods under optimum conditions, applying quality control, sound costing methods, and selling honestly, need not concern himself overmuch with the law. The reading list at the end of this article will provide some general sources that will be helpful without being daunting.

Cases like Donoghue *v.* Stevenson, the celebrated 'snail in the bottle of ginger-beer' case, are probably more amusing than alarming—now. But this case does serve to underline the manufacturers' liability in law to take reasonable care that goods leave his factory in acceptable condition. Lord Atkin, who judged this case, went on record with a new view of an old commandment:

'The rule that you are to love your neighbour becomes, in law, you must not injure your neighbour, and the lawyer's question, who is my neighbour? receives a restricted reply. You must take reasonable care to avoid acts or omissions which you can foresee would be likely to injure your neighbour.'

He went on to explain that 'your neighbour' is anyone closely or directly affected by your action and who should have reasonably been borne in mind when the action was being contemplated.

There is an abundance of case law that affects civil actions in law arising out of common law or statutory breaches that might be considered injurious to a consumer. There is also a growing body of statute law relating not only to the quality and conditions of sale of goods, but also to the way in which the prices of goods are set as well as the method of payment, as with the recent Hire Purchase Act 1964, which was devised to bring many more transactions within the scope of legal control, to make such dealings more equitable as between the seller and the buyer (who is generally less well-informed on financial matters) and to give gullible people, who had been persuaded to sign a hire purchase agreement on the doorstep, a few days in which to consult their spouses or to have a change of heart. It constitutes a reasonable legal barrier to fence off the suckers from their predators.

Another attack on the financial flank was the passing of the Restrictive Practices (Inquiry and Control) Act 1948, and the Restrictive Trade Practices Act 1956. Under these Acts the Monopolies Commission and the Restrictive Practices Court have been empowered to investigate and, if necessary, outlaw agreements on prices and trading methods, and particularly resale price maintenance. In doing this, Britain was the last of the western industrial nations to take action against monopolies and agreements in restraint of trade. (The United States series of enactments began with the Sherman anti-trust laws of 1890.) These two statutes were followed by the Resale Prices Act of 1964, which forebade any contractual setting of minimum retail prices and has enabled the Commission and the Court between them to terminate a number of price-fixing arrangements that were considered to be against the public interest. Resale price maintenance has been drastically reduced in Britain by these measures and may well disappear completely.

If it be thought that this record tends to show that the Government today leans backwards to favour the consumer against the supplier of goods and services, it would be salutary to remember that a number of other protective measures failed to reach the Statute Book during the past ten years. There was an attempt to make the registration of estate agents compulsory and to discipline them by this means, and a similar attempt was made to regulate travel agents and house builders. There have emerged, as a result, somewhat stronger voluntary associations which are attempting to exercise discipline over these particular commercial activities. One of them, the National House-Builders Registration Council (founded more than thirty years ago), has received the sanction of the Ministry of Housing and the Building Societies Association that borrowers will be recommended to use NH-BRC members for their new houses if they want a mortgage from a BSA member. There is no such force behind the Association of British Travel Agents, but the Press and the trade have made great play with the use of the ABTA sign on an agent's window and letter paper, and the backing of ABTA members with a fund to recompense holidaymakers who, for some reason or other, do not receive value for money. A similar scheme for garages, the Fidelity Scheme, was launched by the Motor Agents' Association, but so far has not had the desired impact. With all these voluntary schemes there are always the weaknesses that the membership is voluntary and that this undermines the ultimate sanction of expulsion. Unless expulsion means inability to trade, it means little.

In passing it is interesting to note that the National Board for Prices and Incomes, in its report on *Costs and Charges in the Motor Repairing and Servicing Industry* has entered into the field of consumer protection. Price control is rather a special aspect of this, and applies to many goods that do not reach the ultimate consumer. But the existence of the PIB can hardly be overlooked in any catalogue of consumer protection institutions.

With prices go weights and measures, and packaging; with packaging goes description of contents; linked to that is advertising. The existence of Weights and Measures inspectors is common knowledge; they have been in existence in one guise or another for centuries. The Assizes of Bread and Ale were courts that periodically investigated the size and weight of a penny loaf or a pennyworth of ale. By checking on the amount to be had for a unit of money these ancient courts kept control of the price. The current series of Weights and Measures Acts goes back only to 1878, and was reinforced by the Act of 1963, the main provisions of which came into force in 1965. This long delayed Act was not quite as tough as it should have been and failed to close all the loopholes left by preceding statutes. It is now an offence to supply short weight of any goods, not just food, coal, sand, and ballast, as previously. Weights and capacities must be clearly marked on packs in letters defined by law, and in net terms. But it may still be possible to confuse the buyer with misleadingly large packs two-thirds full of cornflakes or soap powder, and the shopper still needs a slide rule to ensure that he is not being over-charged, as the Act failed to insist on the price per pound being printed on packaged foods.

The most far-reaching statute yet passed on behalf of the consumer is the Trade Descriptions Act, 1968, which has the force of law from 1 December 1968. Its significance for the businessman is fully set out by Bowes Egan in a brief booklet (*see* Reading list below), but suffice it to say that everyone in trade should be reconsidering sales and advertising practice, labelling and descriptions, and pricing, in the light of this extension of the criminal law. Under the Act the old Merchandise Marks series is repealed and replaced.

The Cancer Act 1939, the Pharmacy and Medicines Act 1941, the Labelling of Food Order 1953, and the Food and Drugs Act 1955, all closed various gaps in the

444

law relating to the misdescription of patent medicines and foodstuffs and their provisions remain in force. The Advertising Association has an Advertising Standards Authority to supervise the wording of its members' advertisements and to draft codes of practice. These have undoubtedly had a discouraging effect as regards loose wording, exaggeration, and misleading claims, but legal enforcement of accuracy now replaces this, too. In commercial television there is still the Independent Television Authority's Advertising Advisory Committee which considers the content of 'commercials'.

Lastly, while one is looking at legislation, the Shops Act 1950, should be mentioned. It is not a statute designed to protect the consumer so much as the shopkeeper, but it has a distinct effect on the consumers' behaviour patterns, controlling as it does the hours of shop opening and the kind of goods that may be sold on Sundays. While it is not strictly part of the consumer protection apparatus, it belongs in any survey of the field if only because the consumer would probably like to see it abolished or at least heavily amended. In 1967, the Misrepresentation Act amended the Sale of Goods Act with respect to misunderstandings of an 'innocent' nature. Under it a buyer may bring a civil action to have a contract set aside. It is a controversial measure (see Bowes Egan).

There are numerous specialist consumer protection activities that could be added to the list, such as the hallmark system for precious metals and the Assay Offices, the Consultative Councils of the nationalized industries (Coal, Transport, Gas, Electricity), the Guild of Professional Launderers and Cleaners, with its seal of approval, the National Inspection Council for Electrical Installation Contracting, the Heating Centre and numerous others. Some are official, some are private with a touch of public relations and sales promotion about them. All are symptomatic of the sensitivity of modern commerce to the activity of the militant consumer.

John Ruskin said: 'There is hardly anything in the world that some man cannot make a little worse and sell a little cheaper, and the people who consider price only are this man's lawful prey'. The consumer movement would naturally like to see better goods lower priced, but it is realistic, and would settle for honesty.

Reading list

BOOKS

Final Report of the Committee on Consumer Protection, Command Paper 1781 (H.M.S.O., 1962)
Protecting You, Jean and Andrew Robertson (Newman Neame, 1965)
Information for Consumer Education, Consumer Council (H.M.S.O., 1965)
Consumers, Eirlys Roberts (Watts, 1966)
The Consumer, Society and the Law, Gordon Borrie and Aubrey L. Diamond (Pelican Book A 647, Penguin, 1964)

The Law for Consumers (Consumers' Association, 1962)
Your Money's Worth: A Handbook for Consumers, Elizabeth Gundrey (Penguin, 1962)
At Your Service, Elizabeth Gundrey (Penguin, 1964)
A Foot in the Door, Elizabeth Gundrey (Muller, 1965)
The Affluent Sheep: A Profile of the British Consumer, Robert Millar (Longmans, Green, 1963)
Better Buying through Consumer Information, Jean Meynaud (O.E.E.C.—now O.E.C.D.— 1961)
Competition for Consumers, Christina Fulop (Published for the Institute of Economic Affairs by Andre Deutsch, 1964)
The Consumer Interest, J. Martin and G. W. Smith (Pall Mall Press, 1968)
Trade Descriptions—The New Law, Bower Egan (LRS, 1968)

Useful addresses

British Standards Institution, Standards House, 2 Park Street, London W 1
Consumer Council, 3 Cornwall Terrace, Regents Park, London NW 1
Consumers' Association, 14 Buckingham Street, London WC 2
National Federation of Consumer Groups, 13 Buckingham Street, London WC 2
Retail Trading-Standards Association, Avon House, 356–66 Oxford Street, London W 1

9. Marketing Management

9.1 Marketing: New Attitudes and Methods

Michael Carroll

'Marketing . . . particularly of consumer goods, is the most sensitive point of the whole industrial and commercial process because it is at this point that seller and consumer meet. It is at this point of sale where the feedback begins which eventually controls production. It is also at this point where products cease to be units of industrial output and become a part of the environment of our modern civilization.'

H.R.H. Prince Philip (Patron of
The Institute of Marketing)

Not so long ago, selling and marketing were seen to be substantially synonymous. Marketing was widely regarded as just 'a fancy new name for selling'.

Now, nothing can ever replace a company's sales effort or reduce the status of the sales team, but for company selling in today's competitive markets, the practice of manufacturing goods, then simply passing responsibility to the sales department, is changing. Put in black and white terms, mass production still requires a prodigious selling effort to shift goods in sufficient volume to keep unit costs competitive. But to accomplish this consistently and profitably calls for a broader, more sophisticated marketing approach.

A marketing-orientated company, as Professor Ted Levitt of Harvard, once put it, tries to create value-satisfying goods and services that consumers will want to buy. What it offers for sale includes not only the generic product, but also how it is made available to the customer, in what form, when and under what conditions, and at what terms of trade.

The fundamental difference is that what it offers for sale is determined not by the seller, but by the buyer. The seller takes his cue from the buyer in such a way that the product becomes a consequence of the marketing effort—not vice versa.

Where a company's selling effort and planning run along these lines, the question of description matters little. Otherwise there is a gap to be filled. Few managements today can afford to dispense with this deeper, broader, marketing thinking.

What sort of paragon is needed at the centre of the modern marketing maelstrom? What qualities should be looked for in seeking the right man, and how should the scope of his responsibilities be defined? How can the marketing function be organized and integrated to galvanize unspectacular progress into profitable growth?

In a nutshell, the paragon required still has to be capable of heading the sales organization, but beyond this he must understand the importance of high capital investment and fixed overheads, take responsibility for prices and profits, show a clear grasp of the competitive forces at work in the company's markets, demonstrate wide experience in the use of modern marketing tools and techniques, and lead the firm's product development efforts. Above all, he must stimulate imagination all round, create a receptiveness to new ideas and, most important, to the idea that it is markets and customers who keep the company in business.

To be effective—and to some extent this implies being allowed to be effective—today's marketing 'technician' needs at least five qualities, which should be sought in making such an appointment. He must be:

1. *An outstanding sales executive.* Selling will remain the hard, bread and butter part of the job. He should be expected to deal personally with the company's most important customers; shape, lead, and motivate the sales organization, and train it to feed back information on the market; ensure that it is sufficiently flexible to adapt to the swift changes that characterize today's markets.

2. *A good administrator.* Apart from controlling the sales effort, he will have his own team of diverse talents within and outside the company—market researchers, admen, PR and merchandizing executives, sales analysts and forecasters, cost accountants, planners and brand managers—people of specialized skills whose contribution calls for sound administration and careful blending.

3. *An outstanding innovator.* He will have to encourage and stimulate innovation on many fronts to achieve a switch in emphasis from production to marketing orientation, from (possibly) volume to profit considerations. Innovation will be necessary in terms of continually seeking new and better marketing techniques and tools, new distribution outlets, and new products.

4. *A military type strategist.* He has to be a strategist of the first order to formulate

marketing strategy and tactics in the light of overall business and marketing objectives, often on more than one front.

5. *A diplomat (of the old school)*. Even given boardroom status, a marketing man has to be highly skilled at diplomacy to fulfil one of the most important single functions: integrating marketing thinking into all other sections of the business, and co-ordinating their activities, sometimes in face of tradition.

The following four brief case studies illustrate the problems of introducing, or improving the effectiveness, of marketing in several quite different but fairly typical, situations.

A. *Creating a structure for achieving greater marketing orientation in a highly diversified group of companies*

An amorphous group of about 100 assorted companies, which had grown very rapidly through take-overs and amalgamations, appointed to its main board a marketing director, an outstanding executive plucked from one of its latest acquisitions. His first task was to help the Board create an operational structure based largely on marketing considerations.

This was tackled, after the new marketing director had visited each of the companies, by forming natural operating divisions: natural in the sense that all engineering and related companies were linked in one engineering division, under a divisional board that included an outstanding marketing man. Similarly, all consumer goods companies, despite different classifications, could be matched very well in one consumer goods division.

The next step was to make sure that not only each division, but every company in that division, had the expertise to develop marketing thinking, and to inculcate in each the need to think more in terms of the end-user of its products, rather than about resources at its disposal, and to examine means of developing its potential.

At this point each company had to be initiated in the techniques of charting its own future, knowing where it was going, drawing up a master plan, setting out strategic intentions and tactical methods for achieving these objectives. This called for a close study of the particular company's markets, size, value and, most important, profit potential, relative market shares of competitors, their marketing expenditure and profit earnings.

One of the more interesting features of this attempt to improve the marketing orientation of this highly diversified group was that expertise in consumer goods marketing could be substantially applied to the marketing of industrial products, by:

(a) Inculcating the basic point that marketing is broader than selling and does not start with the product but with the user and potential user.
(b) Internal restructuring to achieve a higher degree of co-ordination between designers, engineers, production, selling, and finance departments to produce what the market required.

451

(c) Encouraging the proper use of marketing tools and techniques—market research and analysis, advertising, promotion, and thorough distribution.

The most important process was clearly the equipping of each company with a small, highly-skilled marketing team, with director backing. In some cases this meant new appointments, or an interchange of personnel, or a structural change.

B. *Revamping an existing structure to switch the emphasis from sales to marketing*

This particular company—in the office equipment field—had failed to capture the larger share that it expected in this greatly expanding market. On the retirement of its managing director, a highly experienced marketing executive was appointed in his place. His first task? To make organizational changes in order to raise marketing efficiency and to improve profitability.

Up to this time, the company had been organized horizontally, with a number of regional managers who were expected to act as regional managing directors. Each local organization was handling the company's entire product range, despite the fact that some products were aimed at industrial markets, others at consumer markets.

The new managing director decided to reorganize on a vertical basis, by creating four new marketing divisions, three for industrial and one for consumer products, to concentrate on marketing, by taking out the administrative side. To manage these divisions, executives were selected from the nucleus of good managerial and marketing-oriented sales personnel. Each new divisional manager was given the support of a product manager. Meanwhile, at head office, a senior marketing 'technician', with responsibility to the managing director, was brought in for the marketing divisions, for product development, and for commissioning market research.

The effect of these structural changes on marketing efficiency began to show within a few months. Communications became easier and quicker; feedback—the exchange of ideas and information leading to swifter product development—more efficient. A new vitality became evident throughout the organization. And several of the new divisions began to show volume increases of 15 to 25 per cent.

This is one of many examples demonstrating how restructuring from a de-centralized management or sales control into marketing divisions, based on products and markets, invariably achieves deeper market penetration.

C. *Injecting new marketing thinking into an old-established consumer goods company*

This is an example of a medium-sized company operating in a large but highly fragmented, saturated and, virtually, static market. Its turnover had been increasing steadily, but unprofitably, when it decided to call in consultants to take an objective look at the business.

The consultants' main conclusions were that the company was insufficiently oriented towards marketing, and lacked clear objectives. Its operating sphere was too limited. It had too many products, some with very limited demand. Sales per call were often marginal; production capacity was under-utilized. The company's image was capable of improvement.

As a first step, a new managing director with extensive marketing experience was appointed. He began by asking some critical questions. What markets are we trying to serve? Are we satisfying these markets? Could we do more business with them? Should we expand into new markets? Is our product 'mix' right, and earning sufficient margins? What lines really sell?

This process led to a start being made on reformulating certain lines and weeding out marginal sellers; in fact, swiftly eliminating about 25 per cent. A consultant designer was brought in to redesign the packaging of every line, as part of a wider 'image' improvement campaign. At the same time, everything carrying the company's name was examined and brought into the redesigning programme—sales promotion material, stationery, signs, vans.

A sales engineer was appointed, his first task being to plot every single customer on maps and to reroute delivery journeys more economically. Despite the problem of timed calls, with customers expecting deliveries at a precise time every day, the result of this process was that average turnover per journey was stepped up by about 90 per cent, and this is still being increased.

At the same time an improved system of management accounting was built up to provide accurate costings.

Within two years, the new techniques began to show results. Turnover increased substantially and profits were up.

One of the more striking advances that followed under the next two-year phase was the emphasis on new product development: the addition of products to satisfy needs that were not being met, concurrent with the continuing elimination of poor selling lines and revamping of the remaining range. Over a period of five years, forty lines were taken out of the range, without upsetting turnover, and some ten new lines were added every year.

In consequence, more than 20 per cent of turnover could be attributed to products that did not exist a few years earlier. A stronger overall position was also becoming evident, with a broader geographical base, higher sales per outlet and per line, a substantially improved image and turnover, which still continues to surge ahead, based on a highly skilled marketing approach, extensive use of market research to keep firm track of customers' changing requirements, and a successful ratio of new product development.

D. *Developing an international marketing organization*

Until a few years ago, much of Britain's overseas trade was still conducted on the basis of direct export—to agents, distributors, or customers. If a company established indigenous marketing organizations, it was often done in a haphazard or opportunist fashion. A firm might accidentally find an outstanding man in Holland who succeeded in building up an efficient distributor network that ultimately justified setting up local production facilities; or an executive's visit to Malta or Gibraltar indicated a healthy potential market, and this was exploited. A systematic country by country assault in Europe or state by state in America, or on a global scale, is still rare.

This case study is based on a company in the power component field, equipment used as part of an end product. Many years ago it set out to treat the whole world as its market and now earns a dominant proportion of its profits overseas, very largely by continually improving its marketing and exercising efficient marketing control over its international operations.

Global activities are divided into six operational spheres and controlled from the UK. Four are concerned with important single markets (including the UK) in each of which it has manufacturing and marketing companies. The fifth covers a number of significant regions in the world in which it has major sales companies; the sixth covers markets where operations are conducted through associates and licencees.

The company concerned, however, regards the setting up of a network of appropriate international offshoots as only a part of the battle. Equally important is the attainment of real market penetration, consolidating markets already established, developing new ones, and making sure that customers, widely scattered all over the world, are fully satisfied with the product and the service.

To achieve this, the entire UK organization has been geared to regard itself as part of a worldwide marketing effort, tuned in to what customers think, do and require, based on on-the-spot experience. At any one time, as many as 200 senior executives, marketing and research specialists, design, development and service engineers, technical instructors and advisors, are travelling around the world, not only selling but finding out what users want, bringing back impressions which, in turn, evolve the sort of products that are going to be world beaters.

Keeping close tabs on every market means that executives have to be prepared to fly out anywhere at a moment's notice. An hour's personal contact is regarded as worth a year's correspondence.

Despite the belief of all companies that they are in close touch with their markets, the evidence of many studies by Economic Development Committees tends to show that there is almost always a need for more direct contact between producer and customer.

More effective marketing, as a paper presented at the Prime Minister's Productivity Conference (July 1967) sought to demonstrate, is as central to economic growth and a better use of national resources as higher productivity.

Marketing, the paper pointed out, is a managerial function 'and since it is so vital to any business, all managers should know something about it'. At many levels, this is not so, a factor that focuses greater emphasis on education and training in marketing. The range and variety of marketing courses now available at technical colleges, universities and other educational establishments, has fortunately increased dramatically in recent years. In addition, the National Marketing Council arranged in 1966 to send fifty top executives to Harvard, with the backing of the Board of Trade. The undoubted success of this experiment led to an expansion of this activity in 1967, when sixty places were arranged at Harvard, fifty at the International Marketing Programme course held at Pembroke College, Cambridge, and forty at the European Institute of Business Administration, Fontainbleau.

In Britain we have still not adopted marketing techniques as fast or widely as they have been adopted in the United States, where larger markets of greater complexity, fiercer competition, more abundant rewards and quicksilver changes have forced the pace.

It is a truism that our most market-conscious companies can match the best in the States. Invariably these are thriving concerns; it is worth stressing that these are also the companies that have shown again and again that they are better equipped to weather rising competitive storms, squeezes and freezes, than those that ignore marketing.

Reading list

BOOKS

The Practical Approach to Marketing Management, Stephen Morse (McGraw-Hill, London, 1967)
The Practice of Marketing, Douglas Smallbone (Staples Press, 1965)
International Marketing: Text and Cases, David S. R. Leighton (McGraw-Hill, New York, 1966)
Marketing, Colin McIver (Business Publications, 1964)
Modern Marketing Management: An Integrated Approach, F. F. Mauser (McGraw-Hill, New York, 1961)
Marketing in a Competitive Economy, Leslie W. Rodger (Hutchinson, 1965)
Marketing Management, G. B. Giles (Macdonald & Evans, 1964)
Marketing in the 1970's: The Use of Operational Research, Paul Stewart (Reprint of a paper given to the Marketing and Promotion Association in January 1966. Available from T. B. Browne Ltd., London)

Useful addresses

British Direct Mail Advertising Association, 3 Salisbury Square, London EC 4

Institute of Marketing and Sales Management, Marketing House, Richbell Place, London WC 1
Marketing and Promotion Association, 4b Frederick's Place, London EC 2
National Marketing Council, Vintry House, Queen Street Place, London EC 4

9.2 Market Research

D. A. Brown

'Our company plan all starts with the annual sales forecast' is a statement with which most businessmen would agree. The amount of production capacity in terms of plant and machinery, the labour force requirements, raw materials procurement, the necessary financial support: all these fundamental factors flow from the sales forecast. Given a faulty forecast it will follow that expensive amendments will be forced upon the company, throwing carefully integrated plans into disbalance.

But what of the sales forecast itself? If it is so important, so central to the business activity and profit, just how reliable is the forecast? What risk are we running that we shall suddenly be faced with falling sales, or even with outrunning production capacity, and thereby missing profitable sales opportunities?

It is precisely this need on the part of company management to be as certain as possible about their sales forecast, both currently and in the future, that has provided the principal stimulus to the growth of market research. It is precisely this requirement, that market research should illuminate all the facets of the selling, promotion, and product development programme, that provides market research with its growth opportunities in the future. It is to an examination of these facets, and to their reflection on market research and its organization, that we now turn.

Our starting point is an examination of the principal features that affect the sales forecast, which we may take as being based on existing products (typically more than one), and development products, which may be in any stage between an

16

original concept and the brink of a national launch. The products we shall consider will be branded articles supported by media advertising at various levels ranging from almost zero (in the case of products sold door-to-door) up to 25 to 30 per cent of sales revenue in the case of certain toiletry and cosmetic products; they will be readily available in distribution even though they may be restricted to particular outlet types.

Without aiming at an exhaustive listing of product attributes we shall consider the following major attributes as being those that must influence the sales of our established products and, thereby, our sales forecast, and we shall consider market research's relationship to these attributes. In a subsequent section we shall consider development products. Our examination will first be concerned with:

A. Product price.
B. Product performance.
C. Product distribution and display.
D. Consumers' attitudes to the product.
E. Product promotion support programme.

A. *Product price*

Few products today are price maintained: moreover, the pricing of products is a sales weapon in the hands of particular elements of the distribution chain in their struggle for ascendancy over each other. The pressure on the manufacturer for better terms, more discounts, extra 'deals' is an undiminishing pressure. To equip ourselves to deal with this pressure from distribution we need to know the range of prices at which our product, and competitive products, are being sold so that we can decide whether existing terms are good enough or, if not, by what extent they should be improved. We also need to know selling prices in order to interpret the movements in brand shares, since any competitor who is selling regularly at a lower price must, in the absence of compensating advantages on our part, be expected to improve his position.

Selling price is best measured on a regular, repetitive basis so that short-term fluctuations may be properly evaluated and long-term trends accurately assessed. The chief market research techniques are the shop audit technique, which is based on auditing sales of a sample of shops at monthly or bi-monthly intervals, or the consumer audit which measures the purchases of a regular panel of consumers. Samples of 500–1,200 shops are normally employed; consumer audits employ samples of around 5,000 housewives. Once-off studies can be mounted by special arrangement with many market research agencies should a single 'snapshot' measurement be required.

B. *Product performance*

Shorn of its promotional support, how well does the product perform in use when

458

compared with competitors?

This fundamental question attracts a great deal of market research activity but, at the same time, causes headaches for researchers.

The general method of tackling this problem is the 'blind test' in which two (or three) products are re-packed into anonymous packs, labelled (no—*not* labelled *A* and *B*: we know that respondents' answers will be biased towards the product marked *A* if they are labelled like that) and handed out to respondents to try in their own homes under normal usage conditions. After an interval, interviewers call again to ask about the products—how they performed under certain conditions, which features were liked/disliked, and, of course, which product was preferred.

This widely-used system of testing has been employed by very many companies with considerable success, and most leading companies mount a regular programme of blind tests of this nature.

These tests give rise to problems for researchers because, although apparently simple, the results obtained are not always easy to interpret. To start with, the whole basis of removing the identity of the product and testing it as an anonymous product is a considerable abstraction and one that can lead to the well-established product being rated lower under anonymous conditions than when its identity is known. This is particularly important when testing new products against such established products, and can easily lead to the erroneous conclusion that because a new product has a high score on a blind test it will out-sell an existing product, whereas real-life conditions in the market-place will not bear this out. Hence the validity of tests of this kind is not straightforward, and great care must be taken in deducing what the findings mean.

Secondly there are difficulties in interpreting the results. 'Out of 400 tests the results divide 54:46 per cent. Are we justified in considering this a clear preference, or could it have happened by chance?' is the question posed by the marketing division. The customary statistical test requires a 55:45 per cent split for 'statistical significance' so the statistician is not quite satisfied but agrees it's a near thing. The brand manager says he is delighted because he thought it was more likely to go the other way—though he can't quite explain why he thought that. Has an impasse been reached? Have the researchers once again taken refuge in what their harshest critics claim is their favourite defence: 'The result is not quite conclusive and further research is needed'?

The answer is almost certainly that no impasse has been reached and that a more detailed analysis of the data, using a range of analysis techniques, including discrimination test, sequential testing, and decision theory, will provide management with a statement, in terms of the risk element involved, of what is involved in preferring one product to another.

Market researchers are currently paying considerable attention to developing their techniques in the field of product testing and trialling. The requirement to provide rapid, reliable, and inexpensive tests of development products, now coming forward in increasing volume, is forcing progress in this area.

C. *Product distribution and display*

Although shop audit panels have been measuring product distribution and display for more than thirty years, the changes in distribution over the last decade, arising from the growth of the supermarkets, have given fresh impetus to this area of research activity.

These measurements are normally made available as part of the research package that subscribers to shop audit research receive, but recently services that measure only distribution and display have been introduced. For this restricted service fees are lower since no data on sales volume or brand share is provided and, therefore, the research task is purely an observational one that does not involve detailed shop auditing.

D. *Consumers' attitudes to the product*

There is an increasing tendency for manufacturers to conduct a regular programme of measurement of consumer attitudes to their products. This arises from the realization that from year to year an established product faces new competitors and obtains new buyers. The new competitors may modify consumer expectations in respect of existing products. For example, if new products all make a 'convenient to use' claim it is likely that the established product, which may have stressed an 'economy' claim, will come to be regarded as 'not so convenient to use' if only by comparison with the new entrants. Although the physical properties of the established product remain unchanged, a change in attitude towards it may well emerge, with possible adverse effects on its sales.

Similarly, as time goes by the established product will, by trialling promotions, attract new buyers whose requirements may not be the same as those of the earlier buyers. Their attitudes towards the product may well differ, and unless these are known, the product qualities may not be attuned in the best possible way to the product's market.

Not only is market research helpful in this regular monitoring of consumer attitudes for existing products, but the techniques employed for this purpose can also be employed—by comparing existing products with 'your ideal product'—in suggesting ideas either for a reformulation and re-launch of the product or for a possible successor to it.

Researchers are using techniques derived from psychological tests in this type of work, which is variously described as 'gap analysis', 'market segmentation analysis', or 'attitudinal profile studies'. It represents an important method of keeping the manufacturer in regular and close touch with the views of his market.

460

E. *Product promotion support programme*

By far the most important component in our sales forecast is the regular estimate of consumer off-take and brand share, and this is usually provided from a market research source. So important is this requirement that it is hardly surprising the companies providing this data—normally based on shop audit or consumer audit data—are the largest market research companies in Britain.

It is to these data sources that manufacturers normally look to provide their basis for measuring the effectiveness of their promotion programmes. The efforts of the sales force in sustaining or increasing distribution; the efforts of a merchandising team in improving display—these will naturally be measured by shop audit research. Promotion activity aimed directly at the consumer, such as coupons, samples, competitions, send-in offers etc., fall more specifically to consumer audits for measurement.

Both types of audit provide the regular measurements of consumer off-take and brand share, which are the central core of the sales forecast. The audits yield a series of trend lines over a long period of time and covering a wide range of past conditions, and it is these trends that assist so powerfully in estimating future sales performance.

A very strict requirement of marketing management today is that its promotion budget be no bigger than is essential to achieve the company plan, and that the allocation of that budget into press, television, other media, sales literature, promotional schemes, etc., should be optimized. This means experimentation to see which marketing strategies pay off best, and this experimentation means measurement—research measurement. Again, it is to this class of research techniques, exemplified by the shop and consumer audits, to which manufacturers turn for the measurements they need to assess the results of alternative marketing strategies.

The Development Products

There are few stages in the development of a new product to which market research cannot make a contribution, and indeed it is not too much to say that the development of new products consists of devising, operating, interpreting, and integrating a wide programme of (usually) small-scale market research studies. Concept testing research deals with the fundamental idea of the very product itself; from that point there stretches out the complete programme of blind tests for product performance, pack design tests, copy tests for the advertising, tests of the appeal of TV commercials, test market measurement, etc., etc. A major British company marketing brand leaders in a number of product-categories has enumerated almost a hundred separate research stages, from the initial stage to the national launch of a new product.

Is this then the complete story of new product development? Does one just hand over the whole problem, and a large cheque, to the market research agencies and then sit back and wait for them to do all the work?

No, one does not! And the market research industry is aware that while its contribution to new product development is positive and valuable there are many unsolved problems still around. Two examples quoted by a well-known food manufacturer will illustrate this.

First, the usefulness of the test market as a predictor of national performance of a brand. Test marketing is a *sine qua non* for all new products with substantial aspirations, and one of the most important findings looked for is that of brand share so that it may be employed in budgeting projections of the national launch. Sad to relate, there have been many examples of poor correlation between actual test market performance, predicted national performance, and actual national performance. Such errors are costly, and market research must improve the predictive power of these important test market measurements.

Second, it is true of food products that when these are test-marketed there is a paucity of verbal description, which prevents the manufacturer from understanding what is being said about his product. 'Tastes fresher', 'tastier' 'has more flavour'— these are not helpful comments to a manufacturer who is unable to relate specific product constituents to 'fresher', 'tastier', 'flavoursome', and therefore cannot tell what action to take to improve his product in these respects. However, since the research industry has been able to evolve a 10-point verbal scale to describe the freshness of white fish one does not despair of its ability to evolve unambiguous verbal descriptions for other food products.

To conclude this section it is worth commenting that perhaps the most puzzling aspect of product development research is, so far as researchers are concerned, why manufacturers bother to do so much of it when so very often they completely ignore the results. And not because the results are wrong but because they've made up their minds anyway. Every research agency of note can quote examples of perfectly good research (involving perfectly good shareholders' money!) being brushed aside in favour of a course of action to which someone was already committed. Manufacturers might do well to recognize this, and marketing groups should be required to write down *in advance of the research being commissioned* what alternative strategies they will adopt in the light of the various likely research outcomes.

Deliberately this section of the chapter has been concerned so far with market research from the viewpoint of the company sales forecast. It is now time to turn to other aspects of market research and to the research industry itself.

In the foregoing we have not dealt with a number of important requirements a manufacturer may wish to place on his research department or agency. These may vary from simple questions such as the number of people who recognize his brand name, to a complex study of product usage by the consumer in which all the alternative uses are established, the product quantity measured for each use, the frequency of use, the quality of performance in use—all these are covered in such enquiries. Enquiries of this kind are often once-off (or *ad hoc* in the customary industry terminology) and involve interviews lasting from a few seconds—frequently through being a small part of a survey covering several simple topics—up to $1\frac{1}{2}$ hours.

To this activity on behalf of manufacturers must be added considerable activity —possibly amounting to 25 per cent of all market research activity, although estimates can only be very crude—generated by the advertising industry and to which some reference has already been made. Through consortia formed from media proprietors, manufacturers, and advertising agencies surveys are made to measure the number of readers of newspapers and magazines and the numbers of viewers of television programmes. The larger advertising agencies have their own market research departments, and the remainder commission research agencies to conduct research into opinions towards products and to test the components of their own advertising output with a view to improving its effectiveness.

So far we have mentioned manufacturers, their advertising agencies, and media proprietors, and certainly it is these groups that provide the bulk of the funds for the market research industry. To this may be added research work coming from government departments (not all of which is conducted by the Government Social Survey), local authorities, banks, hotels, airlines, railways, etc. The list is wide, and in view of the increasing scope of the work being handled there is no doubt that the phrase 'market research' is too restricted.

The market research industry is composed of the market research departments in manufacturing companies and in advertising agencies, together with the market research agencies themselves. It is quite customary for the advertising agencies to take on research assignments for 'outside' clients, although it is unusual, though not entirely unknown, for manufacturers with research departments to conduct work for 'outsiders'. The Market Research Society* maintains a list of organizations in Britain providing research services, and this list is readily available. The Society must, however, remain strictly impartial and so cannot recommend a research supplier.

How then is research bought? How can the most efficient supplier be identified? The answer to these questions is not one to baffle the intellect since it is being solved by someone every day. While there are those who decry the procedure of buying by price, i.e., on the basis of competitive quotations, this procedure is by no means inappropriate to the purchasing of research, and many purchasing decisions are taken on this basis.

* The Market Research Society's 2,000 members include all the senior and most of the junior research executives in the country. Its principal activity is an educative one in which, at weekend courses, seminars, evening discussion groups, and lunchtime talks, it helps in the sharing of knowledge and experience. Its Code of Standards is observed carefully and has the complete support of the industry. This code is framed to protect the research buyer, the research supplier, and the public, from whom the information is derived.

463

Buying by price suffers from the obvious defect that competitive quotations are comparable only if the quotations refer to the same *quality* of research, or if the quality variations are made explicit and have a value attached to them. In market research this is rarely possible; frequently the quality variations go unexpressed, and emerge only after the project has been completed, when a piece of inexpensive research proves to be lacking in value.

While the buyers of research must clearly be wary about the quality they are buying, it is also very much up to the research industry to explain its pricing to the buyers. The relatively expensive companies must prove that high overheads are a guarantee of high quality, low risk research, and that their higher fees are not a reflection of inefficiency or big profits. Inexpensive suppliers must explain honestly what they have dispensed with, in the interests of reducing costs. There are signs that these messages are being put across.

If it is not too obvious to say so, then the best piece of advice to be offered to the prospective research buyer is 'Go and look them over'. Look at the offices, the equipment and meet the people—not just the directors but the field manager, the coding supervisor, the data processing manager, and the statistician. If you are concerned about delivery dates ask to see how production is controlled through its various stages. Ask to see what reports and/or chart presentations of findings look like. Ask for the names of some recent clients and contact them for their opinions of the organization and the people in it.

One of the most difficult problems arises when the buyer has to brief the researchers about his requirements. He knows his own products (and thinks he knows his market) intimately, and this frequently causes him to give to the researcher only a distillation of the research task. By not having the complete background the researcher goes off at a slight tangent, and time and money are wasted. The better briefing, the better will be the research.

This difficulty is minimized when a manufacturer employs its own researcher because, by constant day-to-day contact with his colleagues, he becomes familiar with even the faintest considerations that have to be borne in mind in designing the research. This is probably the strongest single argument for the company market research man. Often this is expanded to an argument in favour of a company market research department with its own interviewers, coders, computing staff, etc., but this expansion is usually based on a cost argument—'We can do it cheaper ourselves'.

This latter view is now being exposed to increasing challenge as the advent of the computer into the research agencies enables them to offer economies of data processing not always available to the manufacturer-owned research department. This challenge is further reinforced by the capacity and increasing willingness of the research agencies to act as sub-contractors for parts of the research project. It is now possible for the manufacturer's research executive to sub-contract field work and both coding and data processing, thereby taking advantage of the economies specialist research agencies can offer, and also avoiding having to spend a lot of his time administering a large staff.

It has always seemed somewhat odd to this writer that the company-research-unit versus bought-in research argument is always conducted in terms of cost. The decisions reached must lie in the personality of the research executive concerned and in the propensity he has towards either creating his own complete department, or towards buying in from outside agencies. From even a slight knowledge of the individuals it is easy to tell which new appointees will begin to create a department around them, and which will not, although both face similar cost alternatives within and without their companies.

Nothing of a general nature can usefully be said about research costs because the requirements from one survey to another vary so widely as to defy generalization. It is hoped that what has already been written will guide the prospective research buyer towards an economic purchase.

The market research industry is estimated to turn over £10m annually and its rate of growth is probably between 5 to 10 per cent p.a. As more and more case-history evidence about consumer behaviour, opinion, and attitude is accumulated, the realization is increasing that market research can eliminate in advance the costly errors that can be made in the selling of established products and the development and launching of new products. This realization certainly accounts for the fact that it is the major manufacturers, who are committed to steady, regular, dependable growth in size and profitability, who tend to be the heaviest buyers of market research.

Reading list

BOOKS

Handbook of Consumer Motivation, Ernest Dichter (McGraw-Hill, 1964)
Marketing for Profit: A Study in the Formation of Commercial Policy with the Business Organization, Leonard Hardy, (Longmans, Green, 1962)
Marketing in Competitive Economy, Leslie W. Rodger (Hutchinson, 1965)
Directory of British Market Research Organizations and Services, Max K. Adler (Crosby Lockwood, 2nd edition, 1968)
Marketing and Market Assessment, J. L. Sewell (Routledge and Kegan Paul, 1966)
The Art of Asking Questions, S. L. Payne (Princeton University Press, New Jersey, 1951)
Survey Methods in Social Investigation, C. A. Moser (Heinemann, 1958)
Motivation in Advertising, P. Martineau (McGraw-Hill, 1957)
Readings in Market Research, Edited by F. Edwards (British Market Research Bureau, 1956)

Useful addresses

The Market Research Society, 39 Hertford Street, London W 1
British Market Research Bureau, Saunders House, 53 The Mall, Ealing, London W 5
Institute of Marketing and Sales Management, Marketing House, Richbell Place, London WC 1
Association of Market Survey Organizations, 85 New Cavendish Street, London W 1

9.3 Industrial Market Research

Max K. Adler

In this day and age, it should not be necessary to prove the usefulness of industrial market research to the average businessman, for industrial market research is not a new arrival on the commercial scene. It has grown steadily in importance as a mangement tool for the last fifteen years, while some larger companies have made use of it for twenty years or more. What is new is its rapid expansion, as shown by the many new industrial market research organizations and the steadily increasing number of market research departments within manufacturing industry.

This development is not surprising in view of the immense value of market research for the industrial company. Nevertheless, objections are often raised against its use, especially by executives in medium-sized and smaller establishments. Most of those without experience of industrial market research think, quite wrongly, that it is far too expensive and that overheads would be too heavy. It is true that market research can cost a great deal. The largest expenditure of which the author has personal knowledge is £225,000 over three years for a survey commisioned by the British affiliation of one of the largest international companies. But it is also true that you can obtain very useful information for fifty or a hundred pounds, and that most surveys cost a very reasonable sum of money that is within the reach of every company.

The problem should really be looked at by the board of directors from the opposite point of view. When discussing the need for a survey, they should ask themselves: Can we afford not to afford it? The answer can easily be arrived at. They have only to consider what financial risk they run when making decisions without the information obtained from the market research survey. How much do they stand to lose if the wrong decision is being made? And what are the chances that the decision will be the correct one? If the combined answer to these questions exceeds the sum to be invested in a survey, clearly it is worthwhile to spend the money; if it doesn't, then it isn't worthwhile.

What, then, are the main reasons for undertaking industrial market research? Every director knows only too well that he often has to make decisions, and some-times vital ones, on the basis of insufficient knowledge. Risk taking is the most important part of his work; however, this does not mean that he should not try to reduce the field of uncertainty. The more facts there are on the strength of which he can make his decisions, the more likely he is to come to the correct conclusions. This is exactly where market research can be of great assistance, for it is nothing but a fact-finding procedure using the scientific method in order to investigate the market for an industrial product objectively.

Industrial market research deals with a considerable number of problems, although there are some for which other methods (such as operational research or mathematical models) have to be used. Every business is interested in the total size of the market for its products. Without this knowledge, no forward planning of production, finance, and sales is possible, nor can any forecasts be made as to the development of the market itself. Equally useful is the knowledge of the share of the market of the company's products. Without this information the company may seem to be doing very well while, in fact, it may be losing ground. The investigation of one's own market share and that of the competitors should be repeated at regular, if not too frequent, intervals, because business conditions change with increasing rapidity.

It should be obvious from the facts stated above that the main task of industrial market research is the forecasting of demand; of competitive activities; and of technological changes. This is not as difficult in the industrial field as it may seem at first sight, because most companies—the existing and prospective customers—know pretty well how their own businesses are going to develop, and what products (in what quantities) will be needed. Naturally, forecasting is always to some extent speculative, and sudden changes in the economy and in the political scene can make a forecast invalid. Yet these economic and political developments themselves can be forecast with some accuracy and applied to the forecast of the market for individual products.

In connection with industrial market research, facts are discovered which, although they may be only by-products, can be of the utmost value. When the research is undertaken by skilled interviewers they can elicit from their informants a great deal of information as to the types of products wanted by them, any modifica-tions they would like to have, their attitudes to the company sponsoring the survey

467

and to its competitors, the credit and discount policies of the competitors, the prices they are prepared to pay, and many other facts that can direct the company's thinking into completely new directions or, and this is equally useful, confirm that the present direction in which the company is developing is correct. The objective interviewer whose only aim is to find hard facts is in the ideal position to learn of the activities of a company's competitor, as they appear to the customers.

A survey will more often than not discover new sales opportunities and new potential outlets for the company's products that would never be discovered by the company's own salesmen. However, this is not the end of the story. One of the least explored areas of industrial marketing is the discovery of the most profitable ways in which advertising should be undertaken. In the consumer field a vast amount of knowledge in this respect has been accumulated, although there are still important gaps to be filled even there. Unfortunately, industrial advertising cannot as yet boast of this amount of knowledge, and the individual company more often than not does not really know whether its advertising budget is spent in the most profitable way. This refers to the two questions every advertiser asks himself: Are my advertisements read and understood? And: Am I using the correct medium for my campaign?

Through a research project the answers to these questions can be discovered, if not completely, at least to a certain degree. By asking questions about what journals are read, the impact made by direct mail shots, what the respondent remembers about specific advertisements issued by the company, and so forth, the effectiveness of the company's advertising can be assessed and the structuring of future campaigns improved.

This is by no means an exhaustive list of the ways in which market research can help boardrooms to narrow the field of uncertainty. There are many more problems to the solution of which market research can contribute successfully, provided it is undertaken by experts. Some companies, especially smaller and medium-sized ones, often fail to realize that thorough training and long experience are needed before a market researcher can work effectively without supervision and support.

Here is a view that is especially dangerous when applied to interviewing: 'Since our sales representatives are in any case on the road and since they are supposed to know their customers and the customers' industries generally, they can and should also be used as market research interviewers'. This view seems sensible at first sight, and admittedly time and money can be saved by replacing the professional interviewer by the salesman. However, experience has proved time and again that the findings of research conducted in this way are invariably wrong and, therefore, dangerous. Solid training in the methods of interviewing is essential. The interviewer must be completely objective. In other words, his training is the opposite to that of the salesman who has an axe to grind and obtains the information he wants to hear. His reports are, by necessity, biased and unreliable; and he will put in his reports his own views instead of the views of those whom he interviews.

The basic condition for the success of a market research survey is the closest possible co-operation between the sponsor and the market researcher. They have to work out together the exact terms of reference for the survey, including accurate definitions of the products involved and of the 'target companies' that should be interviewed. Without complete frankness on the part of the sponsor, concerning the purpose of the research in the context of company policy, this vital first step will be faulty. The terms of reference are the framework, and unless they are precise and based on thorough knowledge disappointments are bound to occur.

Once these terms are settled it is the duty of the market researcher to produce proposals for the survey. They usually contain the detailed terms of reference, but more important is a statement of the procedure that will be used for the survey. Every piece of research has its own problems, and the same techniques can very rarely be repeated on another occasion in exactly the same way. Each survey can also be undertaken in several different ways. So the researcher has to choose those techniques that are the most appropriate in each individual case, always bearing in mind that he has to economise as much as possible. Therefore, the proposals have to show also the precise costs of the survey and the time its completion will take. These facts are not easily ascertained beforehand, and only long experience can produce really accurate estimates.

A good market researcher will never undertake expensive field work until he has convinced himself that the information to be collected cannot be obtained in other and cheaper ways. There is a great deal of knowledge available in government publications, trade and scientific journals, trade associations' files, and so forth; perhaps a survey in a similar field has already been published. The market researcher's art is to know where to find this information, to collect and to collate it. This activity is usually called 'desk research' (although it does not necessarily follow that it can be completed in the office). Visits have to be made to libraries and to what have unfortunately been called 'information concentrates', i.e., people and organizations particularly well informed on the subject matter. The real art of desk research is to know when to stop doing it.

In most instances there will be left a residuum of information that is obtainable only by undertaking field research, i.e., by interviewing a selected number of people: the sample. In industrial market research, statistical sampling methods cannot be applied in the same way as in consumer research where they have reached a high degree of sophistication. A complete list of the companies that constitute the market for the product concerned is rarely available. Even if such a list can be drawn up, it is inevitably limited in usefulness, and less orthodox sampling techniques have to be applied.

Consequently, the method of interviewing is of very great importance. These are the standard approaches: you can interview your informants personally; you can ask them to fill in a questionnaire and return it; or you can conduct your interviews over the telephone. Each of these methods has its advantages and disadvantages. Often, a combination of these interviewing techniques can be used. There is little doubt that the personal interview, if conducted correctly, is by far the best method, yielding more, and more correct, information than the others, but it is very expensive, involving as it does highly skilled interviewers who are scarce and expensive, as well as involving time and money-consuming journeys. The greatest drawback of the mail questionnaire technique is, in most cases, the low reply rate; if only a small percentage of the questionnaires are returned, the information is useless because they do not represent properly the whole 'universe' of potential customers. Mail surveys are much more expensive than popularly supposed. Telephone interviewing can be very successful provided the names of the respondents are known, and this is not often the case.

Every questionnaire has to be constructed, or at least the questions have to be enumerated to which the answers should be given. To write a good questionnaire is an art which, again, demands experience. Many points have to be considered, because people have the habit of interpreting words and sentences in a way different from the researcher's thinking. The questionnaire has to be administered by trained interviewers. In industrial market research, the interviewers must also be well versed in the subject matter of the survey, which will often have a technical and scientific content. An interview will be successful only if the respondent feels that he is talking to an expert who knows the technicalities of the product. When this is so, the interviewer will be able to collect all the information needed, and often much more. He will be alert to the slight remark that may be more important than anything else that is said. An interview can last a long time; on the other hand, the number of interviews to be conducted is relatively small.

Once this part of the survey is completed, the analysis of the information contained in the interviews has to be undertaken by a competent researcher who should have an analytical and logical mind. The facts have to be checked and crosschecked, often with facts known from other sources. Only then can the report be written, and this, again, is a skilled procedure. The report contains the results of the survey, and it has to be so produced that the sponsor can easily digest the facts and act on them in a reasonable way.

Industrial market research needs time and money, not to speak of the expertise of the researchers themselves. How does the Board or the managing director decide whether or not to have his own market research department? Several considerations are involved. The first is obvious: if market research is to be used only sporadically it is not a paying proposition to hire highly skilled people who would not be able to contribute continuously to the company's prosperity. It is, therefore, much better to commission research from an outside organization whenever the need arises. When the company can employ the services of a market researcher profitably, he should be chosen carefully. It cannot be stressed too often that industrial market research is a highly sophisticated technique which needs a great deal of experience. It is not, for example, the job for a young newcomer to the company, whether a graduate or not.

Even when there is a company market research department, professional market research organizations have an important contribution to make. For example, when a survey is to be undertaken, which can be successful only if the respondents do not know which company has commissioned it, the outside agency provides an acceptable 'cloak'. The need for secrecy arises very often, not so much in order to prevent competitors knowing about the survey but because the knowledge of the company biases the replies given by the respondents; in many cases it does no harm to name the company after the interview has been concluded.

The other main reason for entrusting a market research agency with conducting a survey is the need for professional interviewers. Market research departments in small and medium-sized companies consist usually of one man, and perhaps an assistant. This is too small a team to handle a large survey, and there is also no point in their training interviewers especially for the survey, since this is expensive both in terms of money and time. A good industrial market research organization has the apparatus, both in human terms and in machines, and can, of course, spread overheads over all surveys it handles.

But what is a good research organization (or agency, as some people prefer to call it)? In the last five or six years the number of these organizations has increased rapidly. Some do excellent work, others are less good, and it is sad to say that a minority is not even up to average performance. In addition, specialization is continually increasing.

How, then, is one to choose the most proficient organization? A sensible way of doing this is to obtain the services of a market research consultant. He has to know the market research organizations intimately, and he will find the most appropriate one. He has no axe to grind, and it is part of his business to give impartial advice. But he can do more. Since he is experienced in calculating market research costs he will be able to negotiate the best possible terms for his client, thus saving him money and disappointment. He will look after the survey from the beginning to the end, and in this way he will see to it that the research is undertaken properly.

Reading list

BOOKS

Marketing and Market Research, Max K. Adler (Crosby, Lockwood, 1967)
Industrial Marketing Research: Management & Technique, N. Stacey and A. Wilson (Hutchinson, 1963)
The Marketing of Industrial Products, edited by Aubrey Wilson (Hutchinson, 1965)
Selling to Industry, J. E. Lonsdale (Business Publications, 1966)
How British Industry Buys: An Enquiry Conducted by Hugh Buckner (Hutchinson, 1967)

Industrial Marketing Research: Report of the Committee on Marketing Research of the I.C.C. (International Chamber of Commerce, 1963)

JOURNALS

'The Expanding World of Industrial Market Research', W. G. Norris (*The Director*, May 1965)

Useful addresses

Industrial Market Research Association, Dunlop House, Chester Road, Birmingham 24 (addresses of all industrial market research organizations can be found in *Directory of British Market Research Organizations and Services*, by Max K. Adler (Crosby, Lockwood, 2nd edition, 1968)

9.4 The Boardroom Challenge of New Products

M. J. Mills

New products are essential to any company that intends to hold its competitive position and increase profits. In the United States it is now common to find, in a wide range of industries, that 40 to 60 per cent of all current sales are made on products that did not exist ten years ago. The latest US Government projections anticipate a 60 per cent increase in consumption over the next decade: three-quarters of this growth in the next three years will come from new products or services. How likely is the current American situation to be reproduced in the UK?

First, I would submit that this situation is already with us in the late 1960s. But do we acknowledge this? Example: Nielsen Research Co. Ltd. indicate that 52 per cent of expenditure on UK detergents is currently on products that did not exist at all in 1950.

Second, I believe that British industry has not yet aligned its policy thinking to the new high level competitive environment of the 1970s. A new competitive pressure mix is likely from a major shift in concept and demand level for new products, from a very much more volatile and affluent consumer universe. Put this within the new trading and industrial society which UK links with the Common Market, for example, would create, and the result is a potent cocktail of tremendous growth and profit opportunity, mixed with higher risks on the security and tenure of existing business.

This highlights one of the cardinal rules of successful new product activity: namely, the danger of looking at new products simply from a company's production and commercial needs. Whether consumer or industrial products, the requirement is the same: isolate an unsatisfied or potential consumer need; match it with a *competitively* priced offering.

What, then, is the boardroom challenge of new products; what action plan? Clearly, there are as many approaches as there are companies, stemming from resources and personalities involved. It could possibly be helpful to consider the policy steps necessary to achieve an increase in the dynamics of new product output.

Policy action steps — New products

1. *Analyse* current company situation
2. *Define* responsibilities and allocate resources
3. *Set up* organization
4. *Initiate* new product policy, goals, and work programme
5. *Control* progress programme
6. *Decide* on new product launches, linked with *planned phasing out* of existing products, as relevant.

Let us examine some of these areas in more depth.

Figure 9.1 is a chart illustrating the life cycle of a hypothetical product. Several basic points emerge. First, the run-up period on new products, which is often around three years. Second, that the investment recovery may well be three to five years after launch. Third, the importance in profit revenue and asset protection of aiming to slow the decline period by *product revitalization* at the maturity/saturation stage.

An analysis of many companies' 'product assets' against this suggested life cycle can often be a traumatic experience.

What then, has the boardroom achieved to date in providing guide-lines as the basis for ensuring the development of future trading? The check-list of responsibilities (Table 9.1) is not complete, but it is useful nonetheless.

Inherent in this check-list is the belief that new product activity is a top management responsibility; further, that top management must be fully involved and accountable for this area. Regardless of the size or nature of the business, it must be the board that gives direction, authorization, and control to the function of seeking out new products and the best methods of marketing them to provide profit to the company and a real improvement in consumer benefits.

One of the main causes of failure in the new product area is traceable to top management's failure to follow through with genuine interest, personal participation, and explicit direction.

If direction is to be given by top management, is this direction specific enough to give a clear brief to middle management charged with implementation? For example, can a clear policy lead be given in the following areas, and, if not, what should be done to assist the board to formulate policy?

474

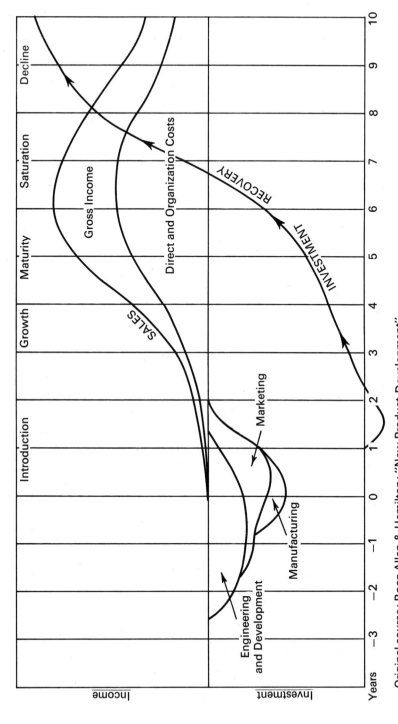

Original source: Booz Allen & Hamilton: "New Product Development"
Reproduced by Permission of Booz Allen & Hamilton Inc.

Fig. 9.1. Life Cycle of a Hypothetical Product

Table 9.1

Area of Responsibility	Have we provisioned?	Action?
Who is responsible in our company for new product development?	?	
How does he do his job and to whom does he report on the board?	Yes/No	
Have we called for and approved an N.P. policy and plan covering both short and long term? Have we provided an authorized framework of company policy, objectives, and profit targets?	Yes/No	
Have we an organization with adequate resources to propose and implement our NP policy? By what criteria do we judge it to be adequate? Size, knowhow, etc.?	?	
Are we capable and do we really need original research or do we need only to apply existing knowledge?	Yes/No	
Have written authority and reporting procedures been assigned to the executive(s) responsible for NPD?	Yes/No	
Is the board able effectively to control the shifting priorities of NPD—is it aware it should?	Yes/No	
Is the acceptance of business risk and the need for an investment period fully understood and accepted by top management?	Yes/No	
To minimize expensive NP failures does our policy call for evidence of consumer acceptance/usage and marketing/selling viability to be presented before authorization is given for manufacture and marketing?	Yes/No	

(Reproduced by kind permission of *The Director*)

Check-list of policy goals

1. What businesses do we want to be in, and when?
2. What are our NP needs in terms of sales and net profits, and can we provide the necessary capital, plant, and personnel from existing resources (i.e., after develop-

ment of our existing business, how much of a gap has to be filled by NPs?)

3. Do we want to be an international business, or a UK manufacturer with some exports?
4. What is the minimum acceptable return on capital employed on new products?
5. What is the maximum period of investment the company is willing to support before initial investment is fully recovered?
6. What resources do we need for expansion, and are we aiming at:
   (a) 'development' or 'acquisition', and/or
   (b) 'diversification' or 'concentration'?
7. Will our management information service be able to deal with the additional calls that will be made on it as a result of NP activity?
8. Are we using to the full our present resources and commercial advantages; have the latter been defined?
9. What broad technological trends are likely in the product field in which the company intends to operate? How will these affect existing products? How will they affect our competitors?
10. What is our NP policy to be if the company fails to expand or if sales start to fall?

Particularly critical to the continuing success of any new product programme is the organization created to operate the policies as directed. Even if a fairly sophisticated operation is currently in hand, it is probably useful to review the organization objectively each year, since in any aggressively expansionist oriented company, the total organization is constantly changing and evolving. The new product organization must be compatible or sympathetic to the line operation, without whose full support its result will be considerably retarded.

There are basically some seven differing organization approaches: these are outlined in the charts, Figs 9.2 to 9.8. A brief commentary is given on each. However, it is sometimes overlooked that the particular new product programme may need two organizations working simultaneously, under central direction, to achieve the required goals in the time available.

The desired approach to the work method, once an organization has been created, may be summed up in one word: *systematic*. Inspiration and good ideas have a role in a successful new product programme, but without a systematic work method, the commercial risks are increased. It is vital for this concept to be grasped by the total organization. Systematic planning is a process of management in action. It is not just a technique or another management 'gimmick'. Richard Beckert, in *Industrial Design* (June 1957) wrote: 'All too much planning is simply scheduling, and in the NP development this will not make the grade. As a process, planning has certain required conditions. One is that the appropriate resources be brought together and allowed to inter-act under conditions which will ensure optimum creative thinking, ... further ... that the involvement of "line management" is apt to produce greater action into the planning process'. Four out of five new products

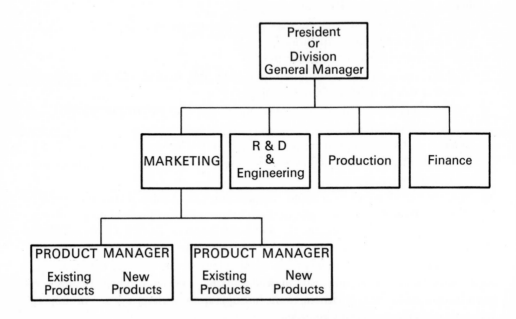

ADVANTAGES : Good for short-term marketing activity. Ensures good marketing/commercial integration and consumer emphasis.

DISADVANTAGES : Difficult to get right mix of pressures between 'day-to-day' and 'long-range thinking'. Harder to achieve full integration of all sections of Company activity.

Fig. 9.2. Product Manager responsible for New Products

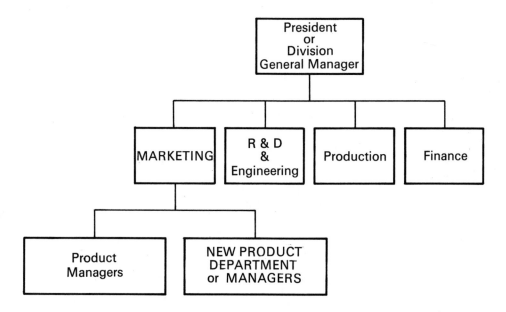

ADVANTAGES : Much to recommend this approach, overcomes disadvantages of product manager orientated new product approach. Assumes 'mass marketing' is important to company, more than, for example, technical selling.
DISADVANTAGES : Places considerable onus on head of marketing to integrate New Product Programme into total company activity.

Fig. 9.3. New Product Department (Marketing Staff) responsible for New Products

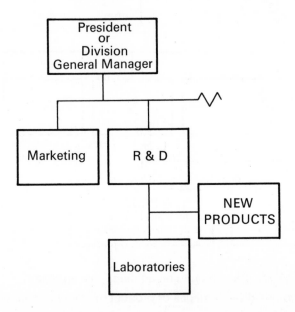

ADVANTAGES: Particularly good where total business has high technical content and technical progress rate is fast, e.g., electronics industry.

DISADVANTAGES: Danger of misalignment to marketing needs, particularly the assessment of shifts in development priorities due to commercial opportunities changing.

Fig. 9.4. New Product Department (Staff of Department other than Marketing, e.g., R. & D.) responsible for New Products

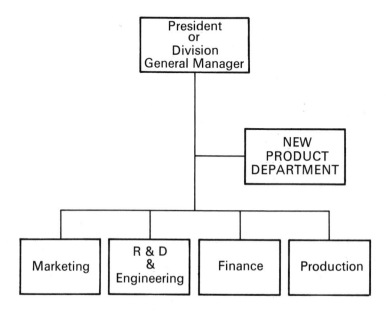

ADVANTAGES: Particularly good for the very large corporation, and where company acquisitions/take-overs are important to the New Product Development programme. DISADVANTAGES: To be really successful, the department must be headed by a senior management member as a full time activity. Thus, management resources will condition this option.

Fig. 9.5. New Product Department (Staff to top echelon management)

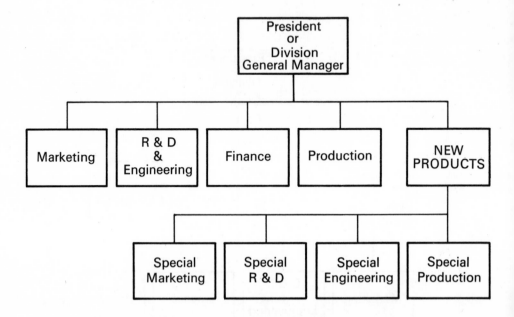

ADVANTAGES: Very measurable on results. Extremely useful where heavy capital plant commitments and production orientation is important.

DISADVANTAGES: Problems of integration with total company, and the difficulty of filling effectively the Head of Department appointment.

Fig. 9.6. Separate department responsible for New Products

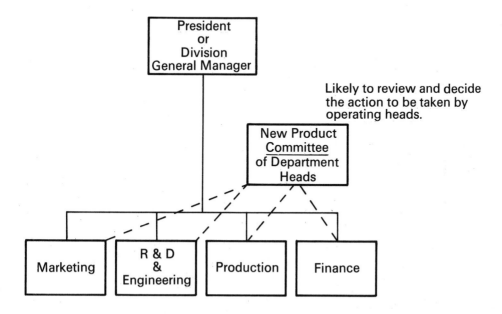

ADVANTAGES: Ensures 'forum' for exchange of all sectional viewpoints, and good backing by departments on any projects undertaken. Can set priorities and allocation of scarce resources.

DISADVANTAGES: Members of committee have other responsibilities, and tend not to remain 'close' to projects. Considerable task for committee to give specific direction without becoming lost in detail.

N.B. Can often be used in conjunction with other organizational forms.

Fig. 9.7. The Role of Committees in New Product Organization

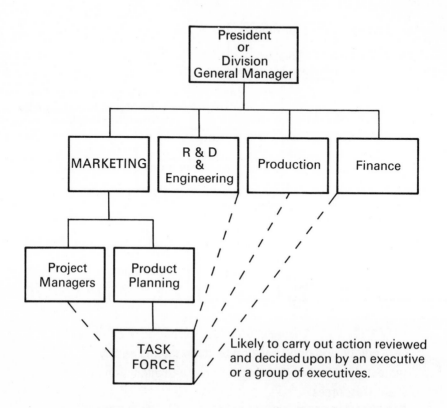

ADVANTAGES: Task force enables management to deploy
special effort without disrupting other new product activity.
DISADVANTAGES: Task force members must be experienced
and well versed in total Company activity—hence this is not
a 'trainee role'. Thus, the problem of manpower availability.
Task force members, if not closely supervised can end up
undertaking projects not directly related to moving the New
Product development goals.

Fig. 9.8. Role of Task Force teams in New Product organization

484

fail in the UK, and a recent survey of the fifty leading consumer goods marketing organizations in the US could turn in a success rate of only 37 per cent of all product launches.

Main steps in systematic NP development

Exploration. The search for products or applications to fulfil new product needs.

Screening. Weighing technological, market, consumer, distributive, and other considerations that will determine whether the idea could fulfil new product needs within the criteria set.

Proposal. Analysing and converting an idea into a concrete recommendation, and determining the advisability of investment in development.

Development. Turning an approved idea into a product the company could manufacture within the set budget.

Testing. Conducting the various product, market, and consumer tests required to confirm earlier judgements, and to assist in the finalization of product specification, manufacturing plans, marketing, pricing, and after–sales service backing. *Commercialization.* Launching the new product on a full-scale plan, within return-on-capital criteria.

Following through the top management task, we turn to the 'loading' and 'decision to launch' of the new product programme. If we assume that most directors are under considerable work pressures, it is imperative that before agreeing the inclusion of a project into the programme, they insist on the following criteria:

1. The project is written up in a concise and quantified form.

2. That this write-up format remains constant for all projects.

3. That the project is fully explained to, and understood by, the Board.

4. That the risks and known losses that could occur are accepted, and standby resources allocated to cover such contingencies should they arise.

Figure 9.9 is an example of a new product proposal evaluation form. There are many variations and adaptations of this. This example is taken from *New Product Decisions: An Analytical Approach.* The form is used in two ways: first, with an outline of data readily available, for authorization of work/study to begin; second, fully completed, as the basis of a decision to 'go', or 'drop the project'.

485

NEW PRODUCT PROPOSAL EVALUATION FORM

SUMMARY—PROPOSAL NO._____

EVALUATED BY _____ DATE _____ PAGE __1__

PRODUCT _____

_____

RATE OF RETURN (1)

Estimated Rate of Return [ ] %

0·01 Probability of Rate of Return Being Larger Than [ ] %

0·01 Probability of Rate of Return Being Less Than [ ] %

CLASS OF PROPOSAL (2)

(circle one)

SPECIAL	REFORMULATION	REPLACEMENT
REMERCHANDISING	IMPROVED PROD.	PROD. LINE EXT.
NEW USES	MARKET EXT.	DIVERSIFICATION

if special, specify _____

_____

PLANNED TIME TABLE (3)

	Start	Complete
Economic Analysis	_____	_____
Development	_____	_____
Test Marketing	_____	_____
Sales Planning	_____	_____
Full-Scale Introduction	_____	_____

QUALITATIVE PRODUCT LINE EFFECTS (6)

1. If the product is added to the existing product line, will it *improve* the company's rate of return more than the marginal new product reviewed this period? Explain. _____
_____
_____
_____

2. If the product is added to the existing product line, will it *decrease* the variability (variance) of the product line's rate of return more than the marginal new product reviewed this period? Explain.
_____
_____
_____
_____
_____

Fig. 9.9. New-product Evaluation Form: Summary Section

3. Will the combined effect on the product line be more desirable than the marginal new product reviewed this period? Explain. _____

_____

_____

_____

_____

| QUANTITATIVE PRODUCT LINE EFFECTS | (7) _____

_____

_____

_____

_____

| RECOMMENDATION | (8)

☐   Unconditional rejection of proposal.

☐   Postpone action. Reconsider after _____ months / years.

Gather the following additional information before reconsidering proposal _____

_____

_____

_____

_____ Research Budget: £ _____

☐   Accept the proposal subject to the following modifications or conditions. _____

_____

_____

_____

_____

_____

_____

_____

☐   Unconditional acceptance

Fig. 9.9. *(continued)*

487

BUDGET (4)

ESTIMATED NEW REVENUE

DESCRIPTION	TOTAL MARKET FACTORY SHIPMENTS	PRODUCT'S FACTORY SHIPMENTS	PRODUCT'S MARKET SHARE	UNIT PRICE	CONTRI-BUTION YIELD*	VARIABLE COST PER UNIT	A.T. PROFIT PER YEAR
Present Year	£						
Year of Intro. ( )	----	£	%	---- £	---- £	£	£
„ 2							
„ 3							
„ 4							
„ 5							
„ 6							
„ 7							
„ 8							
„ 9							
„ 10							
Total	£	£		----	£	----	£
Annual Average	£	£	%	£	£	£	£

If the product will increase the sales of the other company products or reduce the sales of other company products, indicate the nature and extent of the effect. _____

*Contribution

Net Revenue Yield
- ALL DIRECT VARIABLE EXPENSES.

ESTIMATED NEW INVESTMENT

DESCRIPTION	TOTAL	YEAR ENDING	YEAR ENDING	YEAR ENDING	YEAR ENDING	YEAR ENDING
Econ. Analysis	£	£	£	£	£	
R and D						
Test Marketing						
Introduction						
New Capital Expenditures						
Recoverable Capital Required						
Total	£	£	£	£	£	

If the product will require assets which can be used for other purposes or be liquidated, specify their character. _____

Fig 9.9. *(continued)*

488

RISK (5)

	10% PROBABILITY OF LESS THAN	EXPECTED	10% PROBABILITY OF MORE THAN
Economic Life	Yr.	Yr.	Yr.
Average Annual Unit Sales:			
Price *£ _____			
Price **£ _____			
Price ***£ _____			
Average Sales Price per Unit	£ *	£ **	£ ***
Average Variable Cost per Unit	£	£	£
Average Contribution Profit per Sterling Sales	%	%	%
Average After-tax Profit per Sterling Sales	%	%	%
Total New Investment Required	£	£	£
Total After-tax Profits	£	£	£
Payback Period	Yr.	Yr.	Yr.
Average Annual A.T. Profit/Aver. Net Investment = Unadjusted Rate of Return	%	%	%
Probability of Technical Success	——		——
Probability of Marketing Success	*	**	***

Rate company's overall experience with this type of product.

VERY EXTENSIVE			AVERAGE FOR EXISTING PRODUCTS			VERY SLIGHT

Rate company's relative advantage in handling this type of product with respect to

	OVERWHELMING ADVANTAGE			AVERAGE FOR EXISTING PRODUCTS			VERY SERIOUS DISADVANTAGE
R and D							
Production							
Marketing							

Fig. 9.9. *(continued)*

SUMMARY

PAGE 5

Rate the extent that failure might be due to adverse developments with respect to

	VERY IMPORTANT			AVERAGE FOR EXISTING PRODUCTS			VERY UNIMPORTANT
Business cycle							
Competitive action							
General technology							
Market environment							
Socio-political environment							

If the product failed after introduction, what part of the investment could be converted to cash_______________? other uses_______________? cash or other uses_______________?

What would be the cost of postponing the product's scheduled introduction for six months_______________? one year_______________?

Fig 9.9. *(continued)*

Such data collection can form the basis of a New Products Information System, which is essential for effective:

Progress or budget control.
Resource scheduling.
Strategic long range planning of existing and new products.

Considerable progress has been made recently in the development of computerized data banks and new product systems. These offer a new dimension in management decision making and control by:

(a) Providing 'on demand' new product information to *line management*, with continuous updating facilities, through remote computer terminals.
(b) Makes available to the Board, continuous revisions of long range sales and net income projections, allowing for revisions in costs, prices, and launch dates.

While the discipline of new product activity may be daunting, the competitive rewards and the inherent high capital risks are, I submit, reasonable justification. The top management responsibility in new product activity is a never-ending task. If carried out consistently and effectively, the results can be extremely rewarding. Conversely, failure to define and direct the company's new products programme places the company's equity at higher risk. As always, prevention is less expensive than cure.

Reading list

BOOKS

New Product Decisions, E. A. Pessemier (McGraw-Hill, 1966)
Probability and Statistics for Business Decisions, Robert Schlaifer (McGraw-Hill, 1959)
Bradford Exercises in Management: Integrated Brewers Ltd.—a Case of Product Management, Gordon Wills—Editor (Thomas Nelson, 1966)
Planning Tomorrow's New Products: Report of speeches at a one-day conference in London, December 1962 (Institute of Directors)
Product Strategy, H. Underwood Thompson (Business Publications, 1962)
Product Planning: One-day seminar on Product Development, Diversification and Design (Council of Industrial Design, Glasgow, 1962)

JOURNALS

'Reducing New Product Failures', M. John Mills (*Marketing*, June 1964)
'Removing the Chains from Product Strategy', Kenneth Simmonds (*Journal of Management Studies*, February 1968)

9.5 Design and the 'Corporate Image'

James Pilditch

Directors in Britain are now keenly aware of the need for design and, increasingly, they recognize that design influences profit. But the topic is still approached with considerable doubt and caution. It has all changed so rapidly. A few years ago design was thought of as a matter of taste, and designers as people outside the mainstream of commerce—different, vague, extravagant. Thanks partly to the unremitting efforts of the Council of Industrial Design, and largely to the irresistible needs that have arisen, design activity in the UK as in the United States, is now often extremely well organized and purposeful. According to Mr John Davies, director-general of the Confederation of British Industry, 'design, research, and marketing will become the primary functions of management'. Strong words indeed for design—a function that was once thought quite irrelevant to commercial life.

Speaking at a recent international design congress, Dr John Treasure, now the chairman of the J. Walter Thompson Company in London, said: 'Product and package design is now, and will be more so in the future, the single most important variable in the marketing mix'. More strong words.

Why? What has happened to bring about this extraordinary change? Several developments conspire to thrust good design into the centre of commercial life:

1. In the old days if you could make things well you could sell them. Today, many companies in many countries can make things well. Indeed, techniques of mass

production shift the problem from making to selling. Getting rid (profitably) of the vast quantities produced by the modern factory has become a critical problem.

2. Ironically, the strict demands of mass production lead to increasing 'product sameness'. Many product fields are filled with goods that are virtually indistinguishable from their competitors. This sameness is often made worse when market research is carried out to find what people really want, and as the volume of sales required forces manufacturers to seek taste levels acceptable to large numbers of people.

3. As goods grow more alike (often the same products sold through the same shops at the same prices), 'marginal' variations must become more important. Design is such a marginal. It provides the manufacturer with more freedom to manoeuvre. Through design, the manufacturer can create appropriate differences between his and his competitors' products, or can exploit what fractional differences do exist.

4. In many fields goods are becoming far more 'technical'. The 'space-race' has caused an exciting fall-out of technological ideas that can be developed for private use. Here the technical differences that distinguish one product from another may be unintelligible to consumers. The designer may find himself faced with the task of converting these wonders of technology into articles ordinary mortals can understand and like, or of creating differences that shoppers can respond to.

5. As goods become more alike, it is, of course, hard to choose between them on rational grounds. There is no question that, provided the rational requirements are met (performance, price, availability, etc.), people choose emotionally. Evidently, the design of a product can influence the emotional response to that product.

6. Increasingly, marketing success is influenced by the precision with which the manufacturer defines and attacks his particular market. Sometimes what is essentially the same product can be designed in a variety of ways to suit different product concepts and different markets. In this way, design can increase the satisfaction, service, or pleasure that the product provides.

7. In the existing competitive situation, customers have a great deal of choice. They are better-off now than ever before, and so can be more selective. Equally, the shopping public (like industry generally) is better educated, more demanding, and more discriminating. It is no longer enough to believe that performance and price are the only criteria affecting purchase. Design is now a primary factor influencing purchase.

As industry shifts its sights from manufacturing to marketing, it is clear that a need exists for some kind of interpreter: someone who can interpret consumer requirements in production terms, and who appreciates market needs and preferences (including such intangibles as taste and fashion), on the one hand, and production capability, on the other. The designer can fill this role—interpreting factory to consumer, or consumer to factory. This may sound theoretical, until one remembers the number of products in one's own experience that, although functioning well enough, fail to sell because they fail to provide what people want. How many products can one think of that failed because their design was wrong?

Until recently, industry has been preoccupied with designing goods *that could be made easily on machines*. From now on, goods must be designed to *suit the people* who will buy them. Thus, design finds itself plainly and unmistakably a function of marketing.

Up to this point we have been thinking of the design of products. But the influence that design can have on industry spreads beyond that. It may be worth glancing at some of the other areas where design can be a useful tool of industry and commerce, before going deeper into the design process.

If one word could be picked to describe a central preoccupation of business in the years to come, it would almost certainly be *communication*. Already, industry's increased effort in this sphere is evident.

There are at least two strands of thought here. First, as it gets harder for people to choose between competing products, we may expect them to attach more importance to the name of the firm behind the product. The name becomes, rightly, the guarantee of quality and reliability. Second, it is clear to all of us that the success of the modern corporation is dependent on many diverse groups of people. No longer can all our thoughts be devoted to the consumer alone. Obviously, the attitudes of the trade, of employees, of government, banks, local authorities, executive staff, university graduates, and others, have a bearing on profitable performance.

As firms merge, as they grow internationally, and as they diversify, it is harder and harder for people to recognize and trust them. So industry is, quite suddenly, tackling its communications within and without companies, with a new fervour. It is being understood, too, that attitudes to a company are influenced not only by the products and by advertising, but by everything else one sees of the company. To a considerable extent this is a matter of design: of deciding what to say and saying it *consistently*. So, increasingly, designers are being employed in industry to establish consistent and appropriate visual identities. This involves the design of products and packaging, stationery, vehicles, buildings, interiors, flags, badges, annual reports, and all the other visible manifestations of the organization.

To be effective in this role, the designer must take a far-seeing overall look at the company's activities.

At a tactical level, too, industry needs good design. Packaging, for many obvious reasons, has assumed a new importance in marketing and it warrants serious design attention.

Design activity, therefore, runs right through the company. To be really effective, it can no longer be considered in a disjointed, unrelated way, or as a trivial problem for a scattering of junior personnel to arbitrate. Design has become a central function of management, demanding (and getting, nowadays) the serious

494

attention of boardrooms and senior management.

In Britain today, the design profession is extremely active. There are about 2,000 members of the professional body, the Society of Industrial Artists and Designers, acting in industry, or as freelances, or in organized design companies. Apart from these last, designers tend to concentrate on specific design aspects, such as product design, graphic design, or the design of building interiors. In Britain, more than anywhere else in Europe, the design organizations are able to provide industry with really comprehensive design services. While each aspect of design will be handled by a specialist (it is unreasonable to expect one man to be a real master of subjects as diverse as, say, architecture and packaging), the work of the specialists will be co-ordinated in the design organization by overall administrators.

Partially because of the attitude of mind that used to regard designers as un-reliable and extravagant, design organizations, and designers generally, pay great attention to sound budgeting, and time and cost control. The larger design units in Britain, having forty to fifty or more people, are tending to set up client service structures, and to move further into marketing. As time goes by, their experience of working for a wide spectrum of industry will become substantial.

A simple and effective way to find out who's who, and to discover who is best qualified to undertake specific problems, is to approach the Record of Designers, maintained by the Council of Industrial Designers. For a nominal fee they will advise a manufacturer, and furnish him with a list of four or five designers or design organizations selected for their appropriateness. The manufacturer is advised to meet these designers and make his own choice.

In this context it should be pointed out that the designers will be independent consultants, free from ties with any industrial company. There are sound arguments for using such outsiders. They represent a relatively new development, but probably most design work is produced within a client's own company by staff designers.

The arguments in favour of the outside consultant are, briefly:

(a) he is independent and can offer design advice objectively;
(b) his experience is wide; often (though not always) the best designers deliberately stay independent in order to handle a wider range of problems;
(c) the client pays for these specialists only when he needs them; he doesn't commit himself to yearly salaries and pension-schemes every time he hires a designer;
(d) because he is less dominated by the production capacity within a company, the independent is freer to suggest new materials, processes, and ideas than the staff designer.

In favour of the staff designer it can be argued that he knows the company's problems better, and he is available all the time. Good internal design departments undoubtedly exist in many British companies. But it must be said that there are also many bad ones. Few firms appear to be successful in attracting the right designers in the first place, or in creating the environment in which they can do their best work. The problems are by no means insoluble and are often easily traceable to faulty organization or management's outdated view of the role of design.

The tendency in Britain is to bring in outside designers when they are needed, but whether inside or outside designers are used, the principles affecting both are largely the same.

It is very common for a company to bring in a product designer to do the best he can after the products have been developed technically. Often this is too late to be effective. The best the designer can do when presented with a virtual *fait accompli* is to style within limits that are inevitably too narrow. In the radio and TV industry, for example, so-called design is often reduced to the designer's choice of buttons and trim, and even then, within very strict cost limits. Design handled this way can seldom be original, or add in any significant way to a product's success.

The designer is capable of fresh thinking, often of a fundamental nature. To use him as a colourist or stylist after products are developed is to waste his experience and talent. He should be brought in early; in fact, at the very beginning of the development process.

Systems of product planning have been evolved and employed sufficiently (particularly in the United States) for there to be a body of practical knowledge from which any firm can learn. Enormous strides have been made in finding ways of cutting the usual high rate of failure of new products. Methods in use are based on appraisal of market requirements, and incorporate both creative design effort and market research. The modern industrial design organization should be familiar with these concepts and can, indeed, often help companies in a fundamental way by introducing them to new approaches, which grow more and more important as the cost of product development increases.

A clearly thought-out brief is characteristic of all successful design activity. There is no more positive and constructive step an executive can take than to see that his designers have a full and clear statement of the company's aim and the factors influencing it. My own experience is that this is rarely forthcoming. So important do we regard this, however, that it is our invariable practice to create the 'brief' for ourselves, after detailed discussions with clients. This method has a double advantage: the designers get a brief they can work to; the client can see for himself that the designers have grasped the problem properly.

Two other related characteristics of successful design deserve mention. First, it can never be produced by committee; unfortunately, businessmen who joke about the perils of design by committee are often those who, in the end, need the security and lack of risk that committee decisions decide. Second, a really successful design— of a single product or an entire corporate identity—points invariably to the influence of a strong personality in the company concerned. The best design is original and it is extremely difficult to arrive at an outstanding solution if numbers of points of

496

view have to be reconciled.

To ensure good design, a company must use not only good designers, but the *right* designers for the specific task. The choice is wide, but among the criteria for choosing a designer or design organization, the following should be noted:

(a) it must have the knowledge of industry necessary to be able to seek out the real problems;
(b) it should possess the technical knowledge required to produce practical solutions;
(c) it should display the creative ability to arrive at new solutions;
(d) it should command the administrative resources to work within a budget and a time schedule.

It is also worth looking for evidence that the designer is 'in tune' with the company's environment or with the market for which he is aiming. It is not always necessary, or indeed desirable, for him to have direct experience of the company's own field. The designer, like any other mortal, may fall back, unconsciously, on preconceived ideas. It can be salutary to employ designers who need to think problems through from the beginning—drawing on experience gained in other fields, and guided by people within the company—although this approach depends on the complexity of the subject to be acquired.

What we have tried to establish so far is that design is an inescapable and central responsibility of the boardroom, demanding the attention of senior executives; further, that there exists in the UK a large and, at best, highly sophisticated design profession equipped to meet industry's needs. We have looked at a few do's and dont's. One outstanding question remains: cost.

How much does good design cost?

First, the normal methods of charging. There are, generally speaking, five ways of paying for design:

Flat fees. Here, client and designer agree on a flat sum. The amount can be based on anything or nothing—the time involved, the reputation of the designer, the size of the manufacturer, the importance of the job—so long as both parties are happy.

Hourly basis. This is most usual. Here, the designer assesses the time he expects to take and, operating on fixed hourly rates, establishes a budget. As a rule, he does not estimate the cost of any modifications, because it is impossible to calculate what may be called for. Nor does he include the cost of finished art work for reproduction, or out-of-pocket expenses, and for the same reason.

A variation on this is the *acceptance/rejection fee* basis. Sometimes the client is reluctant to commit himself to the full fee, but agrees to pay less if the design is turned down, but over the odds if it is accepted. There is an element of risk on both sides and, if one assumes that a designer isn't chosen unless it is felt that he can do the job, a certain cautious idiocy. But some people like the system. The normal span might be one-third less than the full fee for rejected work and one-third more than the normal fee for accepted work.

In the case of product design, *royalty* arrangements are sometimes made. Difficult to check, they do require a good relationship between client and designer. The advantages to the client are obvious. The normal arrangement is to agree a percentage of the retail selling price or the ex-works price, to be paid either for the life of the product or for a specified number of years. Designers usually receive an advance on royalties or a minimum sum when the design is presented.

For architectural and exhibition design it has been customary to pay a *percentage of the cost* of the job, usually in accordance with the scale of the RIBA or the SIAD. One may perhaps expect this method to be replaced in time by fees arrived at by an assessment of the work involved, and already this is happening.

The Society of Industrial Artists and Designers publishes, for the various kinds of design activity, conditions of contract by which members of the Society are guided. Of course, designers who are not members need not necessarily adhere to these conditions, and in all cases it is desirable to clarify what the designer undertakes for what fee, and to be very clear about copyright, break-off clauses, out-of-pocket expenses, the rights to use the designer's name, and so on.

It is important to have a sense of proportion about design fees. A manufacturer once said to one of my colleagues: 'I can't afford a design fee of £500 because the tools will cost at least £25,000'. An American executive once said to me: 'This design has got to be right. Millions depend on it. I'll pay up to 100 dollars for the design'. In practice, very few design projects cost more than a single advertisement in a newspaper or on television. But all designers have had the experience of seeing a client grow pale at the thought of spending a fraction of his advertising and promotion total on design.

This is putting the cart before the horse. Good design does cost something. Good designers earn proper salaries, carry overheads, need administrative and secretarial support, and are expected to work profitably. Equally, their work takes time. They do not throw off masterpieces in a twinkling. The problems they are given are often extremely complicated, and take time to solve. The fruits of good design, of course, can outweigh a thousandfold the money spent on it. The only extravagance, with industry developing so fast, is to preserve old-fashioned attitudes toward design. It is a luxury few can afford for long.

Reading list

BOOKS

Designing and Programming for World Markets, Dyson and Mayall (British Productivity Council, 1963)

498

Business of Product Design, James Pilditch and Douglas Scott (Business Publications, 1965)
Industrial Design, Harold Van Doren (McGraw-Hill, New York, 1954)
The Silent Salesman, James Pilditch (Business Publications, 1959)
Profit by Design: Some Views on Design Management, Edited by J. Noel White (Published by the *Financial Times* in association with the Council of Industrial Design, 1965)
Designers in Britain, A Review of Graphic and Industrial Design, Edited by David Caplan, compiled by the Society of Industrial Artists and Designers (Andre Deutsch, 1964)
Modern Institutional Advertising, Flanagan (McGraw-Hill, New York, 1968)
Product Strategy, H. Underwood Thompson (Business Publications in association with Batsford, Ltd, 1962)
Design Departments: A Survey of the Role, Organization, and Functioning of Design Departments and Drawing Offices in European Engineering Firms (O.E.C.D., Paris, 1967)
Designing for People, Henry Dreyfuss (Simon and Schuster)
Problems of Product Design and Development, C. Hearn Buck (Pergamon Press)

JOURNALS
Design, monthly (Journal of the Council of Industrial Design)

Useful addresses

Council of Industrial Design, The Design Centre, 28 Haymarket, London SW 1
Society of Industrial Artists and Designers, 12 Carlton House Terrace, London SW 1

9.6 Training for Salesmen

Alfred Tack

A few years ago the view was held by a number of marketing executives that the days of salesmen in many fields were numbered. Heavy advertising, it was claimed, by creating a demand would make person-to-person selling unnecessary. It was subsequently discovered that although advertising motivated the prospective buyers, it did not necessarily make them buy the products advertised, when they were shopping. The advice of an assistant, or impulse buying often led to competitive products being bought.

So the era of merchandising developed. Sales promotion schemes were launched, the battle for shelf space began, and marketing men were back to a belief in salesmanship, merchandising being just as hard to sell as the goods themselves. There is no longer talk of the redundancy of salesmen—only how salesmen can achieve better results.

Better results

How can a company increase its sales? It can introduce new lines, or increase advertising, sales promotion, and public relations expenditure. Eventually, however, it may be faced with the problem of reaching higher sales targets in a competitive market, without increasing the marketing budget.

Two factors must be appreciated. First, in the majority of companies, a small percentage of the sales force usually accounts for the larger part of the turnover. The remaining marginal salesmen—marginal, because it is never certain whether they are paying their way—can be cajoled, threatened, or sacked, but the problem of their lack of effectiveness will remain. Secondly, sales force appraisal carried out on a large scale has proved that few salesmen work to greater than sixty per cent of their capacity. For a company to increase sales, therefore, it must raise the standards of the marginal salesmen, and show the leading men how they can reach their true potential. This can be achieved by sales training.

Why sales training?

Sales training, a distillation of all of the selling experiences of the instructor, the marketing team, and the complete sales force, teaches the best way of influencing people, dealing with difficult customers, handling complaints, opening new accounts, negotiating at top level, obtaining appointments, planning work, preparing quotations, answering objections, and closing orders.

Sales training overcomes positive resistance to selling on the part of some salesmen. The fundamentals of selling never vary, yet every representative believes that he has a problem peculiar to his own work that does not apply in other fields. The industrial salesman, especially if his products are highly technical, often does not consider himself to be a salesman at all. He delights in his technical knowledge, and so loses orders because he does not know how to turn technological advantages into selling benefits.

Sales training reminds the representative selling consumer goods that he is a salesman, and not an 'order taker'. So many of these men are grateful for the retailers' crumbs.

Sales training provides the expert salesman with knowledge that might take him years to acquire (and which sometimes, he never learns), gives confidence to the novice, and teaches negotiating expertise to the representative selling at director level.

Sales training can overcome many of a company's problems, by achieving the following results: Increased overall turnover, increased turnover of more profitable lines, a better service to customers, improved sales force morale, reduction in turnover of salesmen, reduction in sales costs, more new accounts opened, a better company 'image'.

Who?

Few companies can effectively employ the full-time services of a sales training manager. Only ten per cent of British companies each employ over a hundred salesmen. It is usually the sales manager, therefore, who is responsible for sales training. He will succeed only if he has the following attributes:

Enthusiasm for teaching;
A good resonant speaking voice (no-one can learn from a mumbler);

Lack of mannerisms;

Patience and understanding;

The determination never to attempt to inflate his own ego at the expense of a student;

An understanding of human relations.

It is rare to find a sales manager with all these attributes. A potential instructor must, therefore, devote a great deal of his time to self improvement, before beginning to train his salesmen.

What?

Should the emphasis be on classroom training or field training? One should complement the other.

Field training can fail through lack of teaching ability on the part of the field executives. Area managers, regional managers, and supervisors, often expect the men to copy their methods regardless of whether a salesman's personality allows him to duplicate the specialized skills of the field executive.

Classroom training sets a standard that all men can follow, and enhances the value of subsequent field training. Sales training must, therefore, first consist of classroom seminars, and then be followed by instruction in the field. One is of little use without the other.

How long?

The duration of a course must depend on the range and complexity of the products. Sales training is inextricably combined with product training, so that although a complete course might last for several weeks, it will usually be found that the time spent on active sales training is one week.

Visual aids

Visual aids are designed to help the instructor, there being no substitute for good platform teaching. Correctly used, however, they can enhance the value of every session. Among the available aids are the paper board, flannel board, metal board, overhead projector, film strip, slide, film, video tape, charts, demonstration equipment, and closed circuit television. The most effective can be the simple flannel board, and the least effective, an expensive film.

Research

Research is needed to build and maintain the efficiency of a sales training course. There must be research into competition, buyers' attitudes to salesmen, sales presentations, and selling weaknesses. The course must be based on facts. When the facts are accumulated they must be written into a sales manual. Sales training cannot start until this is finalized. The manual must cover a wide area and, in fact, be the 'bible' from which both the instructor and the sales force work.

The training programme

The sales training programme must be all embracing, and will include the following courses:

Product training.
Indoctrination sales training.
Refresher course (sales or product).
Field executive training (leadership).

Product training

Product training does not mean giving the salesmen a handful of leaflets and brochures with instructions to study them. It does not mean sending a salesman to the company's factory to 'look around'. Yet these are the policies of many companies.

Recent research into the reactions of buyers to salesmen show that resistance to buying is often caused by the salesmen's lack of product knowledge. Product training must be complete, and should include planned visits to the factory. Works managers, research directors, even works supervisors, must be briefed. A training schedule must be laid down and fully understood and appreciated by all the personnel involved.

Indoctrination sales training course

The ground covered by the course should be: background of company; company products (unless a separate course is needed); human relations; obtaining interviews; telephone techniques; a complete sales presentation; product analysis; closing sales; answering objections; selling benefits; work planning; reporting; administration; and may also include such subjects as: value of the voice; dealing with customers' complaints; assisting the service engineer; using demonstration models; sales promotion; merchandising; and calling back on customers.

Field executive course

Some companies rely only on field training by area and regional managers, whereas others take the easy way out and allow new recruits to be 'shown around' by a senior representative. In the latter case the results can be poor, because often the more experienced representative may know so little about sales training that he only passes on his own bad habits to the newcomer.

Field executives must all attend indoctrination sales courses so that they can carry out the teachings of the instructor; otherwise there is risk of the field executive greeting the new salesman with the so often used words: 'You can forget all that you have learned at the training course. Now I'll show you how really to tackle the job.'

Field executives must also attend a course specially designed to help them in their work. This course should contain some or all of the following sessions: control of salesmen; how to work with salesmen; reporting on salesmen; how to conduct a meeting; how to review a sales situation; how to analyse a sale; leadership.

503

Other sessions would depend on the product or service being marketed. The field executive is an essential link in the sales training programme, and the importance of his work must be made clear to him at the course.

Sales refresher course

It is the function of the sales manager to control the field executives and salesmen, and if he does not supervise the training himself, to liaise with the sales training manager. It will also be his job to remind salesmen and field executives of selling fundamentals taught at the indoctrination course. He will achieve this by means of sales bulletins, telephone conversations, letters, and meetings.

To be certain that salesmen do not lose enthusiasm or forget the basic principles of their work, he will hold regular refresher courses. Unlike indoctrination courses, in which the new salesman can play little active part, a refresher course must be so designed that those attending have the opportunity of expressing themselves. Discussion groups, therefore, are an essential part of refresher course training.

Whereas indoctrination courses cover a wide range of subjects, the refresher course should deal with only one subject at a time, which must be the theme of the meeting. The following are examples of refresher course themes:

Negotiating at top level;
Opening new accounts;
Making better use of selling time;
Servicing consultants and architects.

Both field executives and salesmen should attend these courses.

Evaluating a programme

The effectiveness of the sales training programme can be judged only by the results achieved.

Are sales increasing?
Have costs been reduced?
Is there improved morale?
Have customer complaints fallen off?
Have new accounts been opened?
Has the turnover of salesmen been reduced?

These are the standards by which the training programme must be evaluated. Whether these results can be achieved will, however, depend a great deal upon the managing director himself. If he is wholeheartedly sales-minded and believes in the sales training programme, then all will be well. If he is lukewarm, it will fail. With the right backing, sales training can achieve results out of all proportion to its cost.

Reading list

BOOKS

Sales Training Manual, Chas. C. Knights (The Gas Council, 1957)
How to Develop Successful Salesmen, K. B. Haas (McGraw-Hill, New York, 1963)
Commercial Salesmanship, Alan Gillam (United Commercial Traveller's Association of Great Britain and Ireland Inc., London, 1965)
Control of the Field Sales Force, Douglas W. Smallbone (Staples Press, 1966)
The Practice of Marketing, Douglas W. Smallbone (Staples Press, 1965)
How to Train Yourself to Succeed in Selling, Alfred Tack (World's Work, Surrey, 1964)
Marketing—The Sales Manager's Role, Alfred Tack (World's Work, Surrey, 1968)

JOURNALS

Marketing, monthly (Institute of Marketing and Sales Management)

Useful addresses

Institute of Marketing and Sales Management, Marketing House, Richbell Place, London WC 1

9.7 Aids to Successful Marketing: Exhibitions

W. G. Norris

There are now so many trade, industrial, and technical exhibitions held in Britain that almost every manufacturer or supplier of goods and services must have been asked to exhibit at one or more of them. Obviously, a great many firms do exhibit, otherwise there would just not be so many exhibitions. Equally obviously, British industry seems to prefer smaller, specialized exhibitions to the vast trade fairs such as Hanover, Milan, Leipzig and Poznan. Britain seems to have said goodbye to huge general exhibitions when the British Industries Fair died. Specialized exhibitions are organized by trade associations and trade journals, often in conjunction with professional exhibition organizers. Sometimes, an exhibition develops the other way: an organizer asks a magazine, journal, or trade association to sponsor it. Almost every exhibition aiming for success requires some form of sponsorship. A contemporary fashion is to hold a conference in conjunction with an exhibition.

At their worst, exhibitions can be an expensive waste of time and money. At their best, they can give a powerful boost to the selling pressure that every boardroom must exert all the time. They are different from other forms of advertising because the product itself takes part: it can be seen, handled, and demonstrated. Then again, the buyer comes to the seller; more personal contacts are made in the course of a few days at an exhibition than are likely to be made in a year of canvassing up and down the country.

With well-established exhibitions, firms can easily find out what they are letting themselves in for, and what they are likely to get out of them. But when considering new exhibitions, directors must insist on receiving a precise definition of the scope and purpose of the show; what is to be exhibited; who will come to see it; what other firms are exhibiting; whether the timing is right (if an industry has a particular selling season); where the exhibition is to be held; what facilities are available in the exhibition hall; whether a conference will be held at the same time; and, most important, who are the organizers and sponsors.

All these factors play important parts in achieving the sole objective of exhibitions: bringing in the right buyers. The quality, not the quantity, of visitors it attracts is almost the only criterion of an exhibition's success. Being conscious of this, many exhibitions refuse admission to the general public and insist that every visitor presents an invitation card from either an exhibitor or the organizers. If a visitor cannot produce an invitation card he is usually asked to identify himself before being admitted.

Some organizers are also following the American practice of requiring visitors to register, to demonstrate their business interest in the exhibition. These methods may cut down numbers, but they do raise the quality of visitors, and lessen the likelihood of exhibitors' time being wasted with casual and irrelevant enquiries.

The length of time an exhibition will run should also be considered and related to the probable number of visitors. There is no point in opening for two weeks if the number of worthwhile visitors can be accommodated in four days.

Having satisfied themselves that participation in an exhibition suits their selling plans, directors should make sure they have the right staff to man their stand. Assuming that the exhibition brings in the buyers, the ball is firmly at the exhibitor's feet, and the way it is played depends on the way he runs his stand. Salesmen are expensive people, and many firms make the mistake of thinking that it is wrong to take them off their territory to serve on the exhibition stand, imagining that it will speak for itself or that, at most, a few attractive girls are enough to make a note of enquiries.

At an exhibition a firm puts its whole organization as well as its goods on show, and its best salesmen should be on the stand. If they don't already know, they should be firmly instructed in the difference between going into a customer's office, and welcoming him on the stand. The techniques are quite different. Everyone manning the stand should actively and positively welcome, and engage the interest of, every visitor. Their job is to talk to visitors, not to each other.

The next problem is what to show. Will it be something new, or a re-vamped product? Is there something new to say about established lines? The number and size of exhibits will determine the size of the stand required, and its design. Engineering and technical products generally do not require elaborate, expensive, 'arty' stands with trick lighting and exotic decoration. Many organizers provide at reasonable cost a 'shell' stand of standard design and colour, with standardized signwriting.

507

The cost of going into an exhibition only begins with the stand rental which, for a London show, can be between 18s. and 32s. a square foot. The higher price usually includes the provision of a 'shell' stand. The total cost of exhibiting can treble or quintuple the stand rental, for the exhibitor must also pay for the design and construction of his stand, fitting out, decoration and lighting, the preparation and transport of his exhibits, hire of furniture and flowers, special services such as gas, water, compressed air, telephones, interpreters, demonstrators, cleaners, etc. His own staff have to be transported and accommodated in hotels. If drinks are served on the stand these have to be bought (usually from the caterer designated by the hall proprietor). So the cost of a modest 350-square-foot stand is nothing like the £400 rental; it would probably come nearer £1,600, though it can be much less if the exhibitor insists on a simple stand, and gets quotations from two or three stand-fitters.

Having spent a thousand pounds or more for his stand and all the other extras, an exhibitor naturally hopes to get orders on the spot. Many do, and many also get serious enquiries that almost certainly end up as orders. Those that get neither should pause before condemning the exhibition as a washout. Were they right in going in at all? Did they give the matter all the consideration it required by asking the questions given above? Did they show their products to the best advantage? (For example, would it not have been better to spend an extra £50 to have the equipment actually working?) Did they have the right people selling on the stand? *After the exhibition did they make sure every enquiry was thoroughly followed up?*

Exhibitions are unique vehicles for selling, but they cannot turn a bad sales organization into a good one.

Reading list

BOOK

Trade Fairs and Exhibitions: A Guide to Cost, Design and Presentation, Hugh A. Auger (Business Publications, 1967)

JOURNALS

Exhibition Bulletin (published monthly by The London Bureau)

Conferences and Exhibitions and The Publicity Manager (published monthly by T.T.G. Publications)

International Business Venues (published annually by T.T.G. Publications)

'Exhibitions: The Price and the Prize' (*The Director*, March 1964)

Useful addresses

Association of Exhibition Organizers, 1–5 New Bond Street, London W 1

Board of Trade, Exhibitions and Fairs Department, 1 Victoria Street, London SW 1

9.8 Aids to Successful Marketing: Industrial Films

Robinson P. Rigg

For more than fifty years, British industrial and commercial enterprises have used films as part of their marketing and publicity campaigns. They believe that the motion picture is a most subtle and powerful instrument of communication. An idea is difficult to re-create with clarity and effectiveness; the spoken or printed word can be misinterpreted; the still photograph is detailed but static. Through technical versatility, the film transcends the limitations of other communications media. Many believe it is the most dynamic medium for mass communication yet devised, with the exception of television. And television is only one of several mechanical means of presenting a film.

These films are not to be confused with TV and cinema advertising 'commercials', but are documentary films in the sense that they portray actual people, events and processes.

It has been estimated that over £3 million a year is spent on sponsored films shown to existing and potential customers and shareholders, as well as to the general public at home and abroad. Compared to printed media, their cost per production unit is high. This is balanced by the increasing availability of film presentation facilities that eliminate waste circulation and produce an amazingly low cost per viewer-impression.

What is a viewer-impression worth to a sales director? If each viewer is a prospect for a contract worth £500,000, the figure is obviously higher than if the product is a pot of jam. If the potential number of prospects is multiplied by the estimated value of each viewer-impression, a broad estimate can be made of what a film is worth to a promotion campaign.

Another factor is the life expectancy of a film: in some cases films are made for short-term campaigns designed for maximum immediate impact, but, on average, a film will be topical for about five years.

Most important is the effect on the viewer created by the combination of movement and 'live' sound projected in colour on a screen, although many of the film's individual characteristics can be provided by other media and at considerably lower cost.

Colour is not confined to films: it can be provided through photographs, transparancies, projected slides, and filmstrips. Sound can be provided on records or magnetic tape with or without accompanying still pictures, and can be most effective. Movement can sometimes be studied and analysed more clearly and effectively through a well-produced series of still pictures.

But the *total* impact of a film is unique in its power to create an emotional involvement in the mind of the viewer and stimulate rapid appreciation of concepts and principles. The man who makes a film with skill and knowledge controls what his audience will see at any given moment, and is able to guide their thoughts in any direction he wishes.

Films have a place in a company's promotional campaign, irrespective of size; but before any film is included, the following points must be considered:

1. Visualization
Is film the most suitable means of putting over a particular message, or would a film-strip, live demonstration, exhibition stand, press advertising, a brochure, or a combination of media be more effective?

Often, films fail because they are not the proper medium for a particular job, or because they are shown in isolation and not as part of an overall communications programme.

2. Audiences
It is essential to identify all audience types in specific terms, and estimate what they already know about the subject. How much can you take for granted in designing the film?

3. What the film should accomplish
What should the audience do after they see the film: think, make further enquiries, change an attitude, buy a product, approve, relax, buy shares, donate to charity, lobby an MP or a local councillor, write a letter to friends or business acquaintances?

4. The producer
Before any producer is chosen, samples of his work should be seen and he should be assessed for these qualities:

(a) Business integrity and reliability.
(b) Experience in producing the type of film needed.
(c) Financial stability.
(d) Availability of creative staff and facilities.
(e) A well-established business.
(f) The ability to understand and interpret clients' policies and needs.

5. Costing
(a) *Production*. A rough guide based on median figures after comparing costs of a wide range of sponsored 35mm and 16mm films (running times from 10 to 30 minutes):

Black and white: £90–£450 per minute (minimum of £1,500 for a 10 min. film)
Colour: £135–£600 per minute

The following factors build up production costs over and above the median figure:

Lighting of large areas, especially with colour film.
Changes of location.
Use of synchronous dialogue.
Cartoon—elaborate animation techniques.

(b) *Distribution*. Many users of film consider that the cost of film prints and distribution should equal the production costs. A rough guide shows distribution cost per viewer-impression-minute, using the three most common distribution methods:

Film library	0.1*d*.
(films borrowed by people with projectors)	
Road Show	½*d*.
(films taken to designated audiences by mobile projection equipment)	

Invited audiences—assess according to normal press and trade reception costs.

Since the advent of commercial television, audiences have become more used to 'actuality' and advertising on the screen, and have become highly critical of the production value of sponsored films. To succeed today, a public relations or sales film needs considerable depth of creative thought directed towards the commercial objective.

There is evidence that the market for sponsored films expands at the rate of 15 to 20 per cent a year. One distribution agency claims an audience of 20 million who saw films on free loan from the library; and 10,000 audiences were assembled in all parts of the country to see films under a road show scheme during 1967. There has also been a marked increase in the number of films shown at exhibitions, conferences, and professional gatherings. Moreover, recent technological developments mean that within the next two or three years members of the public will be able to see sponsored films of their choice on TV sets in their own homes. This could well create an explosion of interest in using sponsored films for mass sales promotion at low cost.

Reading list

BOOKS

Films for Management 1968, An Annual Guide (British Institute of Management)
Motion Picture Production for Industry, Jay Gordon (Macmillan, 1961)
Business Films, Peter Spooner (Business Publications, 1959)
Film and Filmstrip Presentation, A Handbook of Facts and Reminders (Shell-Mex and British Petroleum, 1959)
Industrial and Business Films, Leopold Stork (Phoenix House, 1962)
A Guide to Industrial Film Making, Sam Black (The Whitehorn Press, 1959)
Audiovisual Aids and Techniques, Robinson P. Rigg (Hamish Hamilton, 1968)
Film and Effect, John Chittock (Financial Times, 1967)

JOURNALS

Film User, 69 High Street, Croydon, Surrey
Business Screen International, 139a Bedford Court Mansions, London WC 1
Imagery, Guild House, Upper St Martins Lane, London WC 2

Useful addresses

British Industrial and Scientific Film Association, 193–197 Regent Street, London W 1
Film Producers Guild, Export Services Division, Guild House, Upper St Martins Lane, London WC 2
Federation of Specialized Film Associations, 2 Bouchier Street, London W 1
Films and TV Division, Central Office of Information, Hercules Road, Westminster Bridge Road, London SE 1
Rank Film Library, 1 Aintree Road, Perivale, Greenford, Middlesex
British Film Institute, 81 Dean Street, London W 1
Industrial Film Correspondents' Group, 201 Alexandra Park Road, London N 22

9.9 Aids to Successful Marketing: Premium Promotions

D. J. Ashton-Jones

The phrase 'premium promotion' can be used to refer to the presentation of *any* form of incentive to a potential purchaser, and could thus include trading stamps, 'cigarette' cards, competitions, reduced-price offers, special trade-in terms or, indeed, any encouragement to buy a specific product or range of goods. More commonly, 'premium promotions' are understood to offer the purchaser of a product the opportunity of obtaining something else at a cost considerably lower than that at which it can normally be bought, or at no cost at all.

Marketing history records the first instance of encouraging purchases by the offer of other goods at special terms as having taken place in Great Britain more than a century ago. But it is a technique that has developed most rapidly and attained a degree of sophistication only since the Second World War. Its greatest applicability is in the field of mass-market consumer goods, as is evidenced by the vast number of premium promotions to be found operating in a modern grocery shop at any one time. In modern conditions, the premium promotion has become an integral part of marketing strategy. No longer is it the final desperate expedient in an attempt to revitalize a failing sales effort, or an *ad hoc* measure to effect a temporary uplift in sales.

The essential prerequisites in a successful sales promotion are:

1. Selection of an appropriate premium
The premium offered must be such as to appeal to that sector of the market it has

513

been decided to attack; and the price at which it is offered must be consistent with that sector's spending habits. The ideal premium is the product that is desirable to the consumer but which would normally be considered a 'semi-luxury', e.g., an extra radio for the family, or a kitchen mixer. Obviously, there are certain advantages in offering a premium that has a distinct link with the basic product being sold, so that the premium itself may encourage further purchases.

2. Meticulous costing

The majority of premium promotions are self-liquidating, i.e., the sum paid by the consumer is adequate to cover the cost of the premium to the promotor, plus all outgoings involved in receipt of applications, parcelling, despatch, etc. It may, on occasion, be acceptable to carry out a premium promotion at a loss, but it is vital that this loss be previously budgeted as a contribution from the marketing appropriation.

3. Readily controllable supply of the premium?

It is normal practice for the promoter to estimate a minimum redemption figure for his offer, and to enter into an agreement with the supplier of the premium to make this quantity available according to an agreed programme. Provision is then made for the supply of further quantities of the premium at short notice. The promoter will be anxious not to find himself with a surplus of the premium article on his hands, but it is highly detrimental to goodwill to be unable to meet the demands made by consumer applicants for the premium within a reasonable period—say, two weeks.

4. Setting up an efficient administration

As applications are received from consumers, they must be permanently recorded. The premium must be addressed and despatched with all possible speed. Arrangements must be made for quick responses to enquiries or complaints. Many other similar administrative arrangements can subject a marketing organization to a sudden and severe strain. It is normal practice today to utilize the services of a specialist mailing house to perform these functions, rather than to undertake them internally.

5. Gaining adequate publicity

Most premium offers will be advertised on the pack of the article promoted. This is rarely sufficient publicity, and the aggressive marketing company will design special counter units and other point-of-purchase material to publicize the offer. For a major promotion, advertising in a mass media will also give support. It is essential for the promotion to receive good editorial publicity in trade journals in order to influence wholesalers and retailers.

6. Briefing the sales force

Many a promotional scheme fails to meet its target through inadequate knowledge of the reasons behind it on the part of the sales force who then, undeservedly, incur the blame. A promotion depends, in the end, upon how well it is merchandized at the point of sale. The sales force must be able to explain the objectives of the promotion and the method of its administration to distributors of the product, in order to gain traders' confidence and support.

Marketing companies—even the largest—usually retain firms who specialize in promotion planning and administration to organize their premium promotions, rather than carry out the work within their own organization. Such firms bring their expertise to the selection of an appropriate premium, and negotiate its purchase from the supplier. Applications from consumers are sent direct to the retained firm, who carry out all administration and despatch. This is a highly economic method of mounting a premium promotion, since the retained consultants and agents draw their income entirely from a small mark-up on the premium, and this is written into the redemption price when the offer is costed.

Reading list

BOOKS

Effective Merchandising with Premiums, G. Meredith (McGraw-Hill, 1962)
Marketing in a Competitive Economy, L. W. Rodger (Hutchinson, 1965)
Choosing the Right Sales Promotion, A. Toop (Crosby, Lockwood, 1966)
Sales Promotion, P. Spillard (Business Publications, 1966)
Modern Marketing Strategy, Bursk and Chapman (Editors), (Harvard U.P./Oxford University Press, 1964)

Useful addresses

Incentive Marketing Association, 1 Old Burlington Street, London W 1
Institute of Marketing and Sales Management, Marketing House, Richbell Place, London WC 1

10. Selling Abroad

10.1 Exporting: The First Steps

W. J. Heygate

Every exporting company had to start once, and there is no point in thinking about exporting if it is purely intended to dip in and out, depending on the state of the home market. No company that has not previously exported should try to do so unless there is a real determination to start in a small way in one market, and then build from the success gained in that market.

A firm that markets successfully at home should regard exporting as merely a continuation of this process overseas, but an additional member of staff, preferably someone who has had overseas marketing experience, is the first essential.

Several organizations can give useful help and advice to a potential exporter before there is any need to travel overseas, these include:

1. The manufacturer's own bank,
2. The local chamber of commerce.
3. The relevant trade association.
4. The Export Services branch of the Board of Trade.
5. The British National Export Council.

After obtaining all possible information from the above sources, the potential exporter should then decide on the country that will be his first target. Traditionally, the easiest export markets have been those of the Commonwealth, where there were no language barriers and the buyers understood pounds, shillings, and pence, tons, cwts, lbs, and ounces; it may well be preferable now, however, to consider such markets as Sweden and Holland, both of which are big buyers of British goods and can be visited comparatively cheaply and in a short space of time.

One of the essentials for any market whose national language is not English, is that pamphlets and sales literature be translated into the local language. Another is that quotations should be made c.i.f. or, better still, delivered to the customer in the currency of the country concerned, and in metric weights and measurements where these are applicable.

When this literature is ready, the Export Services branch of the Board of Trade will see that it is forwarded to the Commercial Department of the British embassy of the country, asking them for their comments and advice, and to prepare a list of possible agents whom the manufacturer might see on his first visit to the country. It is usually of importance that a suitable agent is appointed, unless the goods concerned are more easily sold direct to retail outlets.

It is at this stage that the potential exporter should first visit the selected country and give himself sufficient time there to see the agents recommended and also, wherever there is a British Chamber of Commerce, or equivalent body, to discuss with it the product and its potential. The members of the Chamber will usually be experienced British expatriates or nationals of the country concerned, who are interested in the import of British goods.

When an agent has been finally selected, there are many advantages in bringing him to the UK, particularly if the product has technical qualities, so that he can be fully versed in the product, see the factory, and get to know the directors and production personnel.

It cannot be overemphasized how important it is that regular contact between principal and agent should be maintained so that the latter can be kept aware of any new developments, and the former kept closely concerned with the sales progress of his product.

The above is, of course, a very simplified procedure; but it is preferable to keep the operation on a limited scale at the start and then follow success, with the experience obtained, in going into other markets.

There will be important subjects, such as the rate of commission for agents, who pays what for advertising and other promotional activities, which have to be discussed in detail. This is one of the many reasons why new exporters must get advice from embassies, chambers of commerce, and other local bodies, so that they do not run impetuously into problems they do not foresee but which may have particular application in countries overseas. For instance, in some countries, once an agent has been appointed, it is not easy to get rid of him without heavy compensation payments lasting over a period of years; and there are many different rules on matters such as patents, about which it is vital to obtain advice in the country concerned.

Once an export business has become well established abroad, the UK manufacturer may then decide that he should set up a distribution company either on his own or in conjunction with his agent or other locally obtained finance. This will enable him to maintain stocks in the country concerned and extend his business more rapidly.

The third stage (applying particularly where high tariff barriers are in existence) is to set up a manufacturing company. At this point it is possibly advisable to have UK management, at least to begin with, until such time as a national of the country concerned is sufficiently versed in the company's products to take over. It is not possible to be dogmatic about this; companies operate in many different ways, and much depends on the product concerned as well as on individuals and personalities. But one thing is certain, the UK principals must visit their agents' distributing or manufacturing companies regularly. The more the business grows the more frequently these contacts should be maintained.

The establishment of manufacturing companies overseas may reduce direct exports of the manufactured product, but such ventures bring in their wake the export of machinery component parts and, in turn, when they become profitable, they add to the invisible export earnings of the country to an extent that might be better for the balance of payments position than by continuing to export manufactured products direct over high tariff barriers. Alternatively, an increasing number of companies are now going in for overseas licensing arrangements, or the selling of technical know-how; in both a regular income is received, to the benefit of the total invisible export figures.

As far as the new exporter is concerned, another method is frequently preferred: the use of the services of one of the export houses.

These are organizations specializing in selling other people's goods abroad. They have market expertise and a full knowledge of the mechanics of exporting, and can thus act as a ready-made export department for small firms. They also act as buying or confirming houses on behalf of buyers abroad, providing bridging finance and turning an export sale into a home sale as far as the manufacturer is concerned. The costs of using an export house to secure sales in foreign markets may be a useful comparative test for a firm contemplating setting up its own export organization. The British Export Houses Association will provide further details on the services provided by an export house.

Mention will be found elsewhere of the British National Export Council (*see* section 10.5), and although this council is not set up basically to service individual companies, spread over the twelve area committees there is a considerable expertise that can be of considerable benefit to would-be exporters to these individual areas. The committees concerned maintain records of the economic trends in the countries for which they are particularly responsible, and are in close touch with the official and unofficial contacts in the countries concerned.

Apart from this, the British National Export Council plays an increasing role in overseas promotional activities working in close conjunction with the Board of Trade and, in some cases, acting as the agent of the Board of Trade in administrating government funds. As their agents they pay 50 per cent of travel and hotel accommodation for both inward and outward missions, and similarly for market research schemes, in all of which there has to be a non-profit making sponsor such as a trade association, chamber of commerce, or export club.

Other promotional activities with which BNEC are concerned include, for consumer goods, British Weeks, Mini-Weeks, and Store Promotions. On the capital goods side, the Trade Fairs Branch of the Board of Trade is increasingly involved, for the most part directly with trade associations, in joint ventures which now number about 200 a year, and which are increasing at the rate of 10 to 15 per cent each year. These normally take the form of a British section in a specialized fair overseas, and are extremely effective methods of promotion. Although the majority are in capital goods they are also successfully used for consumer goods. There are occasions when an area committee of BNEC undertakes joint venture activities across a range of products not covered by one trade association and where it is necessary to agree a sponsor. In these instances the area committee concerned works closely with the Board of Trade to produce the participants, and may perhaps act also as the sponsor.

The Board of Trade, also under the same Directorate, runs British pavilions in some of the big international fairs, and while it is usual that a central theme dominates the pavilion, it is not entirely necessary. Here, again, the area committee concerned works closely with the Board of Trade to ensure the right participants for the pavilion.

On the special promotional front there are occasions where the market demands a major British demonstration; here, in consultation with the Board of Trade, organizing specialists such as Industrial Trade Fairs International Ltd., may be engaged by the Board of Trade to undertake the complete promotion.

In all these instances the finance is supplied by the Board of Trade in varying degrees, and regular announcements are made in the *Board of Trade Journal* of all these promotional activities.

Reading list

BOOKS
The Exporters: A Study of Organization, Staffing and Training, Douglas Tookey, Eleanor Lea and Camilla McDougall (Ashridge Management College, 1968)
EFTA Trade 1959–1966 (European Free Trade Association, Geneva, 1968).
Open Doors in EFTA (British National Export Council for Europe, 1967)
Export Assistance: Pick-a-back Arrangements (Board of Trade, 1966)
How to Export: A Guide for the Small Businessman, Michael Shanks (Board of Trade, 1966)
Marketing Overseas, Henry Deschampsneufs (Pergamon Press, 1968)

Export Hindrances Survey (Carried out by the Marketing Unit, Urwick, Orr and Partners
    Limited, in 1965/66 (Urwick, Orr and Partners, 1966)
Export: A Handbook of Export Procedure (Engineering Industries Association,
    London, 1963)

JOURNAL
Export Services Bulletin (Board of Trade)

Useful addresses

British National Export Council, 6–14 Dean Farrar Street, London SW 1
British Export Houses Association, 69 Cannon Street, London EC 4
Export Services Branch of the Board of Trade, 35 Old Bailey, London EC 4
Export Marketing Partnerships, Marketing House, Richbell Place, Lamb's Conduit Street,
    London WC 1
Institute of Marketing, Marketing House, Richbell Place, Lamb's Conduit Street,
    London WC 1
Overseas Marketing Corporation, 6 Arlington Street, London W1

10.2 Overseas Market Research

Simon C. Hodgson

Britain's technological lead in many aspects of manufacturing industry has in recent years been narrowed, and in some instances reversed, by the fast developing manufacturing industries overseas. Britain has traditionally been one of the major trading nations of the world and, geographically, is ideally situated to maintain this position. However, in many industries an emphasis on exports to the technologically less developed countries has enabled British manufacturing industry to maintain exports without the need for substantial technical development. With the United States, West Germany, France, and Japan accounting for over 80 per cent of the world growth in manufacturing between 1960–65, these markets for British products have been relatively neglected. They accounted for less than 30 per cent of United Kingdom overseas trade in 1966.

Increasing demands on industry to raise sales and profits are causing manufacturers to consider carefully the export markets open to them. If senior management is to make the most effective use of export departments, then these departments must have a clear knowledge of the key countries that offer them the best potential, and concentrate their efforts on these countries alone. But how can manufacturers isolate these countries? And having done so, how can they obtain the detailed local knowledge necessary to operate a major marketing organization?

Companies that regard exporting as an 'extra' to their home market activities, and that export in small quantities to a large number of countries, have little need for detailed market research. Only the very largest companies can profitably use the wealth of detailed market information available to them in a survey of 'world markets'. However, the company planning a major export exercise can most successfully do this by concentrating its efforts on the market areas most suited to its defined export strategy and objectives. A full-scale study in one or more countries provides the springboard for a major export operation.

By investigating 'piecemeal' in full-scale market research overseas, a firm may be lucky and find a suitable market at the first attempt; but if the country selected does not offer the potential the firm requires, the problem again arises 'which country do we investigate?'

It will not be considered sufficient to regard the findings of the first study as valuable in preventing a costly entry to an overseas market, if subsequent studies reveal similar situations. Market research overseas becomes most effective if it is structured to screen out unlikely areas at an early stage, so that more important countries can be investigated profitably and in greater depth.

The information required for screening out the less attractive market areas is of two sorts. The first is information relating to general industrial activity and climate; the second is specifically relevant to the product or product groups being researched. Thus, a full cross-section of available information is developed, and this enables the export manager to establish an order of priorities for further detailed research.

All this information is of a statistical nature and is obtainable from the Export Services Branch of the Board of Trade, British trade missions abroad, chambers of commerce, foreign embassy commercial libraries, the OECD and a number of other sources.

The screening process—in contrast to the actual research processes—is relatively cheap. It can be done by any firm with a lively market research department, and almost all research agencies will have this facility, since they either retain or can obtain without difficulty the necessary screening information. Countries are screened by considering first their own characteristics (e.g., size and growth of industrial output, state of technological development, tariff barriers, geographical location, political influences, climate limitations) using desk research techniques. A secondary screening phase is based on factors more closely associated with the product to be researched.

Measurable screening criteria are agreed before the research takes place, and quantitative limits are set to each one, above or below which the country becomes an unattractive area, and further market research work is precluded. Consideration of these primary factors alone will usually reduce the opportunities to a fraction of those initially open, and need cost only £300 or less.

Some interesting work has been carried out in presenting in pictorial form the main market areas of the world. Figure 10.1 shows an example of this work in which the area of the respective countries represents their importance in overseas markets. This enables the research to identify important countries on the basis of size of

525

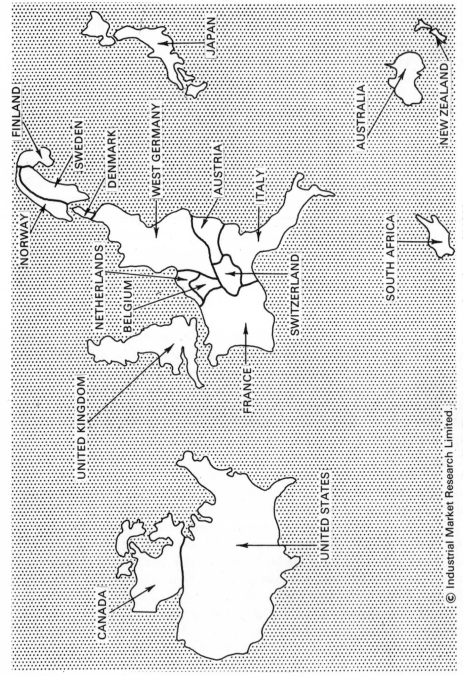

Fig. 10.1. The non-communist manufacturing world 1966
(areas proportional to value of manufacturing)

© Industrial Market Research Limited

overall industrial activity. The map shows the importance of the United States, West Germany, the United Kingdom, and France in relation, for instance, to Canada, Australia, South Africa and other English-speaking countries that have traditionally been Britain's major export destinations.

By using similar information for other primary criteria such as the level of imports, number of domestic producers, sales of the relevant products, the second part of the screening process can be undertaken. This yields information specific to the area of interest and, again, can be generated at relatively low cost. Thus, the second part of the screening process involves factors closely related to the firm's own operation, and will enable a company to reject countries further research shows to be unsuitable.

Such factors as size and growth of market, in broad terms, and climate of competition will be the most obvious ones, although, for instance, the nature of distributive outlets may be particularly relevant for specific products. Further significant market indicators are frequently available with a minimum amount of field-work. For example, world trade in proprietary machinery for colour printing can be obtained through contact with the major machinery manufacturers, of which there are about half a dozen. The destinations of these deliveries give important indications of the demand for colour print in different countries. Selected, cheap-to-research factors such as these are developed for each individual product.

Here, again, the Export Services branch of the Board of Trade can be of help, and many commercial sections of overseas government representatives in the United Kingdom are often well placed to advise on information of this sort. The first and second stages of the screening process thus ensure that, when the detailed studies are carried out, it is unlikely that the markets themselves will be unattractive.

The ease with which market research can be conducted in overseas countries varies considerably. At one end of the scale, in most West European countries and in North America, statistical information on industrial products is readily available, although in varying degrees of usefulness. However, Spain, for example, is an exception, and a good deal of information has to be generated. In communist bloc countries market surveys are almost unknown and virtually impossible to carry out in the accepted sense. Much here depends on establishing the right contacts in the country concerned. The Board of Trade can be of considerable help here, and statistics of import into these countries from Western nations are normally available.

The expenditure necessary for the total screening process varies according to the number of screening factors and the number of countries investigated. However, as an illustration, in a recent study, a total of fifteen countries was reduced to three to be researched in depth at a cost of £750.

The final stage in the project is the depth study of the individual countries selected, in which the detailed information for market entry and expansion is sought.

What alternatives are available for conducting market research overseas? Few but the largest organizations have their own local market research units or a sufficiently versatile unit in the United Kingdom that can work effectively overseas. Most firms have to engage a specialist to carry out the work for them.

The most direct method is for a company to work with a market research agency in the country concerned, especially where the company has previously had satisfactory experience with an agency overseas. However, market research, particularly in the industrial field, is in all countries less advanced than it is in the United Kingdom, and agencies overseas in many areas are sometimes less scrupulous than they might be. This makes the selection of an overseas market research agency a risky business if not backed by previous experience.

Many United Kingdom agencies, however, have affiliates overseas and can offer a 'package deal' in which the UK agency contracts to produce a completed report on the local market concerned. In this way, the report is presented in the correct form and language and in a way that is easily interpreted by the sponsoring firm.

United Kingdom agencies have two alternatives if they undertake market research projects abroad, although variations that embrace a mixture of these two methods are used. They can either sub-contract the project in to a reputable local agency, or they can undertake the study themselves and use locals for interviewing and other processes that involve a language difficulty. In both instances, the UK agency accepts full responsibility for the whole study, but in the first, the agency sub-contracts the survey in its entirety to the relevant overseas affiliate. The study is completed in the name of the UK agency, and very considerable liaison and administration are involved between the two agencies. This is frequently a costly factor.

The advantage of this method is that local agencies are familiar with information sources, and with trading practices generally. For instance, bribery is almost an openly admitted business practice in some countries, and only local market researchers will know the extent to which it is practised. Subtleties of business etiquette may vary considerably from one country to another, and local researchers are more likely to identify these, if they are important, than is a United Kingdom agency. Local agencies are also able to draw upon existing sample frames in the relevant industry sectors and will have established a network of key respondents and contracts that are so necessary for obtaining information often regarded as 'confidential'. However, unless a very detailed and comprehensive briefing takes place between the client and the agencies concerned much of this advantage can be lost, since the researcher will not be able to appreciate the inferences of the prevailing market situations.

In the second alternative, the United Kingdom agency takes complete control of the project itself, but employs local 'leg-men' to do the field work. If the UK has a knowledge of the local industry then they themselves can select, without difficulty, the most suitable respondents for interviewing. In most countries, however, this industrial knowledge can be established from desk research in the UK and does not present a problem. It is important, again, for close liaison to be maintained between the UK agency and the local interviewer, and it can be useful for the researchers themselves to conduct, through an interpreter if necessary, one or two key interviews on the subject in the field. This will help the interviewer to appreciate more fully the reports of his interviews, and to obtain the 'feel' of the market, which is so essential to the interpretation of the information.

Both these methods can be equally successful, provided each party knows clearly the terms of reference from the sponsor and also which agency is to conduct which part of the study.

By using a combination of United Kingdom expertise coupled with local agencies' knowledge of statistical sources, the second method—namely, using a UK agency with overseas affiliates—is probably the most effective way of conducting comprehensive overseas market research.

In the near future, however, agencies in the United Kingdom are expected to be able to offer another possibility. The leading UK agencies are beginning to realize the advantages of employing nationals of a number of important industrial countries on their staff, so that they can offer a better and faster service in overseas market research, especially during the initial stages. Such agencies are not numerous at present, but it is likely that in the next few years this practice will become increasingly widespread in the UK. It will probably provide the best solution to overseas market research for manufacturers considering a profit-oriented export drive.

Given an approach of this nature to market research in foreign countries, manufacturers need have little fear that large investments will be involved in fruitless research. Thus, with clear-cut criteria for screening and a thorough investigation of attractive markets the most profitable use of market research appropriations can be made.

Because the initial screening criteria are based on factors and information normally available only in industrialized countries, the possibility of exploiting, in this method of approach to exporting, hitherto untapped markets in the developing countries has been ignored. Growth in many of these countries is very largely contributed to by inflation. The degree of indigenous skills and experience generally forces the exporting company, from a developed country, to make very substantial product modifications. Further, the wealth of the twenty-four countries officially designated by the United Nations as 'developed' accounts for more than 60 per cent of world gross national product, with only 20 per cent of world population, more than 80 per cent of manufacturing output, and more than 80 per cent of fabricated goods involved in world trade. Only slow changes can be expected to occur in the relative level of prosperity of developed and underdeveloped countries, and it is right that normally the businessman should concentrate his markets research in the developed areas of the world.

Reading list

BOOKS

Short Guide to Market Research in Europe, Max K. Adler (Crosby Lockwood, 1962)
World Marketing—a Multi-national Approach, John K. Ryans Jr. and James C. Baker (John Wiley, 1967)
Plan Your Export Drive, Sydney M. Paulden (Arlington Books, 1965)
The Assessment of Industrial Markets, Aubrey Wilson (Hutchinson, 1968)
The Marketing of Industrial Products, Edited by Aubrey Wilson (Hutchinson, 1967)
Economic Surveys in Under-developed Countries, P. K. Mukerjee (Asia Publishing House, 1962)
Market Research on a European Scale, Report of Paris Conference, July 1959 (O.E.E.C., now O.E.C.D., Paris)
Marketing Advisory Services Provided by Industrial Associations, Report of a meeting in St Gallen, Switzerland (O.E.C.D., Paris, 1961)
New Trends in American Marketing, Arnold Corbin (British Institute of Management, 1965)
Exploration of New Markets by Small and Medium-sized Firms, Report of Conference held in Vienna, October 1961 (O.E.C.D., Paris)
Market Research by Trade Associations (O.E.C.D., Paris, 1964)
Selling in Europe, Henry Deschampsneufs (Business Publications, 1963)
Selling in Africa, Henry Deschampsneufs (Business Publications, 1961)
Selling Overseas: The Principles of Export Marketing, by Henry Deschampsneufs (Business Publications in association with Batsford, 1960)
Marketing and Advertising in Europe (British National Export Council, 1967)
How to Sell Successfully Overseas, Alfred and George Tack (The World's Work, 1963)
A Marketing Plan for the New Europe, J. J. Proudfoot (Hutchinson, 1966)
How British Industry Buys, H. P. Buckner (Hutchinson, 1967)

Useful addresses

British Institute of Management, 80 Fetter Lane, London EC 4
Institute of Marketing, Richbell Place, London WC 1
Confederation of British Industry, 21 Tothill Street, London SW 1

10.3 City and Banking Services for Exporters

J. H. R. Pringle

Financing international trade is the life blood of the City of London. Of all the other activities pursued in the Square Mile, none has deeper roots in the past or retains greater vitality now. The techniques actually employed are, however, continually evolving to meet the changing needs of traders. Some are nearly as old as international trade itself; others have appeared only recently—indeed, the past few years have witnessed a notable extension of the facilities offered. The following is intended to give a brief outline of some of the most useful of them, old and new, but it does not pretend to be comprehensive.

The role of the banks

The City offers an unrivalled range of international banking services. It houses not only the headquarters of Britain's largest domestic banks and merchant banks, but also the world's biggest concentration of foreign banks (about 120 foreign banks are represented there), and the hub of the world's largest overseas branch banking system (British overseas banks operate over 5,000 branches in seventy-three countries). All these banks are involved in international trade. Equally, all traders from time to time use the services they offer. Finance is naturally the first that comes to mind.

Among the various sources of short-term finance, the most convenient and, probably, still the cheapest is the normal bank overdraft. A prime advantage is its flexibility: no separate arrangement is required, so that a company need borrow no more than the amount needed to finance its business operations as a whole from day to day. Interest is charged at a rate varying with the standing of the company from, broadly, half to two per cent over the current level of Bank rate, and is payable on the daily overdrawn balance outstanding in its current account. The amount the bank is willing to advance can be increased if the exporter assigns the proceeds of his ECGD (*see* section 10.6) policy to the bank. The banks normally regard this as acceptable collateral for financing trade in consumer goods (on up to six months' credit) and also for light engineering goods (on somewhat longer credit).

Where customary in the trade or market, further short-term credit can also be raised through bills of exchange—the distinctive instrument of international trade finance. There are four main techniques of providing finance that employ bills of exchange: the negotiation or discounting of documentary collections, acceptance credits, and documentary letters of credit. When a bill is 'negotiated', the exporter, for a small charge, is given additional overdraft or loan facilities to the value of the bill; when it is discounted, it is sold to the bank at a discount. Under the acceptance credit facility, an accepting house (the specialists in this field) or bank undertakes to 'accept' bills drawn on it up to an agreed maximum figure in a given period, and the bills are then readily discountable, the exporter receiving cash immediately.

Under the letter of credit method the overseas buyer requests his local bank to have opened or confirmed, by either its London office or its London correspondent, a documentary acceptance credit in favour of the exporter undertaking to accept bills of exchange accompanied by the specified shipping documents. The seller can then receive his cash immediately by discounting the accepted bill. This is the safest arrangement of all for the seller, who receives his cash at once, and need have no further concern as to whether the overseas customer will pay—that is the worry of the customer's bank. All three methods enable the seller or exporter to obtain cash as soon as possible after the despatch of the goods, while at the same time enabling the buyer or importer to defer payment until the goods reach him, or later. Many variations on these basic methods are practised, and traders should seek further advice from a bank, accepting house, or from a discount house.

Another institution that nowadays plays a prominent role in export finance is the Export Credits Guarantee Department. The ECGD does not provide funds itself, but by insuring or guaranteeing export credits, it increases a bank's willingness to lend against such anticipated receipts. Indeed, thanks to an extension of ECGD policies, a scheme has recently been evolved whereby banks provide short-term finance at Bank rate (with a minimum of $4\frac{1}{2}$ per cent). Broadly, it works like this: customers who have held a normal ECGD policy for more than a year, and who conduct their short-term export sales either on open account or up to six months credit or by drawing bills of exchange with maturities of thirty days to two years, may obtain a comprehensive guarantee of repayment from the ECGD, under which the ECGD guarantees to the bank financing the transaction that the exporter will repay the sum borrowed. The bank, in its turn, being relieved of any risk in respect of such lending, provides finance at Bank rate. A charge of one-eighth per cent per year on the borrowing limit agreed is charged by the ECGD for this facility. It should be remembered, however, that the exporter is still liable for any losses not covered by his ordinary policy.

Co-operation between the ECGD and the banks plays an even more important role in medium-term and long-term export finance—two years and over. Under the pressure of competition, exporters of capital goods are having to concede longer credit terms to their customers, and the rate at which finance is forthcoming can be a crucial factor in winning an order. To help exporters quote a competitive and firm price in respect of these financing charges the banks are willing to provide finance at a fixed rate ($5\frac{1}{2}$ per cent at the time of writing), where a 'Bank Guarantee' from the ECGD is available. This guarantee is applicable to individual contracts for the supply of manufactured goods for a credit period of not less than two years after shipment, with a usual upper limit of seven years. On large capital projects involving even longer credit terms fixed-rate finance at $5\frac{1}{2}$ per cent is also available, the loans in these cases being made direct to the overseas purchaser and, again, being guaranteed by the ECGD (this time under its so-called 'Financial Guarantee' scheme).

All these schemes are basically extensions of existing services, but in recent years all the three main groups of British banks active in international banking—the domestic banks, merchant banks, and overseas banks—as well as foreign banks in London—have developed a range of new facilities for traders based on the Euro-dollar market. This has three main branches: first, there is the Euro-dollar market proper—a short-term, multi-millions dollar market in dollar deposits centred on London; secondly, there is the so-called Euro-bond market, on which large international companies raise long-term finance for European operations; thirdly, intermediate between these two, several new institutions have recently been established to provide medium-term Euro-dollar finance to European companies.

Besides finance, the banks offer many ancillary services. They produce reports on current economic conditions overseas; give information on exchange control and import regulations; arrange interviews with banks and businessmen abroad; supply names of agents; prepare status reports on overseas buyers; advise on methods of payment, and so forth.

The use of insurance

Inevitably, international trade carries greater risks than domestic trade. Insurance, therefore, has a vital role to play. Broadly speaking, the risks in this field can be divided into two main categories, corresponding to the two types of institution that provide insurance against them.

First, there are those that can be insured in the commercial insurance market. These include risks of loss or damage to products in transit (cargo insurance); cover against claims that may arise in overseas countries regarding UK products (products liability insurance); construction insurance, covering risks involved to British building and civil engineering firms when undertaking contract work overseas; and special personal accident cover, for the benefits of executives while visiting markets abroad. These and many other risks facing the trader can be insured in the City's commercial insurance market, which is the largest *international* insurance market in the world.

Secondly, there are risks normally insured by the Export Credits Guarantee Department of the Board of Trade. These include the creditworthiness risks (the buyer's failure to pay), and the political and economic risks (such as the appropriation of goods by a foreign Government, cancellation of a valid import licence, inability to transfer exchange, war, revolution, and so on). ECGD is the only organization in the country that insures exporters and those financing export credits against both types of risk. This is because in export credit insurance the risks cannot be relied upon to 'average out'. In two years, for example, exchange difficulties in a single market involved ECGD in claims payments equivalent to the total premium income received on all markets during the preceding twenty-two years. ECGD's 'Comprehensive Policies' cover up to 90 or 95 per cent (in some circumstances up to 100 per cent) of any loss incurred. As already described, ECGD policies and special guarantees also help to bring forward finance from the banks.

How export houses can help

Export houses probably handle at least 25 per cent of Britain's exports. They may be particularly valuable to the smaller exporter, who cannot maintain a fully-fledged export department of his own. Export houses function in a variety of ways. First, they may act as the manufacturer's export selling agent. Under this arrangement, the manufacturer usually remains throughout as principal in the transaction, while the agent is responsible for promoting sales; looking after the physical, financial and clerical work; stocking goods; following up delivery dates; dealing with formalities; and sometimes providing after-sales service. Secondly, export houses may act for an overseas buyer. This, too, may take a variety of forms: the export house may be granted discretion to find the best sources of supply, or it may simply place orders for goods to be bought from manufacturers specified by the buyer. In either case the export house will arrange shipment and insurance, progress and despatch orders, and finance and confirm contracts on the buyer's behalf. Thirdly, export houses may act as principals, buying goods outright from the manufacturer and selling them on their own account.

Recent developments

The breadth and variety of the City's services to traders need no emphasis. What may tend to be overlooked is the pace at which new facilities are being developed. The last few years have, for instance, witnessed the full establishment of factoring in Britain; this is a method of both providing finance and taking the credit risk off the shoulder of the trader. Several banks, too, have recently set up special export finance subsidiaries, sometimes offering, like factoring, 'non-recourse' finance. Finance houses have also moved into the field of international trade credit, often in association with finance houses or banks overseas; under these arrangements the importer is granted instalment credit terms by an institution in his own country for the purchase of goods overseas. In addition, chambers of commerce, the British National Export Council, and the Board of Trade itself have all extended their services. At the time of writing, the latest addition is the Overseas Marketing Corporation, promoted by the Board of Trade, which is designed to help smaller firms exploit fully the exporting opportunities open to them. In these and many other ways the City has kept abreast of the changing needs of traders.

Reading list

BOOKS

What to Read on Exporting, D. W. Bromley (available from the Library Association, 7 Ridgmount Street, Store Street, London WC 1)
Services for British Exporters (Board of Trade Export Handbook No. 1)
ECGD Credit Insurance and Financial Support Services (Board of Trade Export Handbook No. 2)
Britain's Invisible Earnings: Report of the Committee on Invisible Exports. Director of the Study, William M. Clarke (British National Export Council)
Finance Problems of the Smaller Company (The Institute of Directors, 1967)
The Finance of International Trade (The Institute of Bankers)

Useful addresses

British Export Houses Association, 69 Cannon Street, London EC 4
British National Export Council, 6–14 Dean Farrar Street, London SW 1
Export Services Branch, The Board of Trade, 35 Old Bailey, London EC 4

10.4 The Problems of Taxation

H. B. Jackson

Besides the many factors, commercial and financial, that have to be examined and assessed when considering the economic advisability of entering or expanding in the export field, there is the important matter of taxation both at home and in the countries where markets are to be sought. In the same way as an exporting company must analyse all those items that contribute to its export costs (such as freight and shipping charges, documentation, collection, and the finance of credit periods in order to compare its export prices with those currently obtaining in its overseas markets) it will also need to take into account the overall tax position.

With straightforward sales to overseas buyers, the main concern will be tariffs, revenue duties, surcharges, etc., in the importer's country likely to inflate its sales price, and any tax remissions or exemptions at home that may enable it to reduce that price. Where, however, the exporting company is contemplating investment overseas to manufacture locally, by way of a subsidiary company, or to participate in a local company, or even to set up a sales and distribution office, it will be vitally concerned with the whole framework of company, and income taxation both at home and in the country where it proposes to make the investment.

Let us first take a look at the taxation background at home against which an exporter will operate, and begin with the normal export of goods against orders received from buyers abroad. Such goods will be exempt from any purchase tax that would be applied if they were sold in the home market, and the exporter starts, therefore, with his basic ex-works sales price, to which will be added all the costs entailed in delivering the goods to the buyer, plus any tariffs, revenue duties, surcharges or other taxes levied under the laws of the importing country. There are, however, available at home to the exporter some small direct incentives that may be significant in the calculation of the ultimate export sale price. The most important of these are the export rebates provided under the Finance (No. 2) Act of 1964.*

Who the 'exporter' is may sometimes be open to question, but the Act has taken pains to identify him for the purpose of being an applicant entitled to claim the rebate. Although in every export transaction the manufacturer or producer will ultimately get the major commercial benefit from the transaction, and it is he whom Parliament intended primarily to encourage by the rebate, it does not follow that he should be considered beneficially entitled to the rebate within the meaning of the Act. If the manufacturer or producer is not an actual party to the contract with the buyer (or other party abroad) then he is not beneficially entitled. Nevertheless, the rebate is a payment, made by the Government, which accrues at some point to the benefit of an export transaction and, as such, acts as an incentive to the development of export trade.

The second most important incentive does not come strictly within the context of taxation but it is a Government-inspired scheme and could involve payments from revenue funds. This is the arrangement made between the banks and the Export Credits Guarantee Department (*see* section 10.6) whereby, in approved cases, the banks will provide export finance without recourse to the exporter at rates of interest below those currently in force.

There is also one case of tax remission which directly favours the exporter, i.e., in respect of entertainment expenses. Under Section 15 of the Finance Act 1965, entertainment expenses were disallowed as legitimate expenses for tax purposes, but where reasonable expenses are incurred for the entertainment of overseas visitors then the allowance will be made.

Finally, we come to the controversial Selective Employment Tax, which is payable by the employer in respect of all employees not engaged in actual production, except where the proportion of non-producing workers in the same location is below a certain percentage of the whole work force. As the exemption applies to any employee engaged in the manufacturing process, irrespective of the market in which the company operates, there is no advantage or disadvantage to the exporter as such. On the other hand, the exporter by the very nature of his business has to call upon the services of many outside organizations such as banks, insurance companies, shipping and forwarding agents, merchants, confirming houses, etc. All of these, being non-producers, have to pay the Selective Employment Tax on their employees, although many of them are engaged exclusively in the business of exporting.

* Unfortunately abolished in the 1968 Budget.

The incidence of the tax increases the costs of their operation, hence the charge to the exporter for their services, which automatically adds to the exporter's costs.

We now have to consider the case of the company that decides that the penetration and exploitation of a particular market can best be developed by investment in that market and the establishment of local production, either by way of a wholly owned subsidiary company, or participation in the equity and operations of an existing local manufacturer. Any such investment must first receive the approval of the Bank of England, for, under the Exchange Control Act of 1947, no resident of the United Kingdom may acquire an asset abroad without such approval. Moreover, under the present restrictions on overseas investment, any funds remitted for the purposes of this investment would have to be purchased in the premium market and not in the open foreign exchange market. At the time of writing, the extra cost of foreign exchange in the premium market is 30 per cent and it would, therefore, make such an investment very expensive. It should be mentioned, however, that the Bank of England would not normally object to the necessary funds being raised in the country where the investment is to be made, and the exporter's bankers would be able to put him in touch with a bank overseas for this purpose.

Assuming that the investment is made in one way or the other, and the UK company is operating overseas and in receipt of investment income from non-resident sources, it must now consider what is the position regarding UK tax regulations. The introduction of Corporation Tax in the 1965 Finance Act, to replace income tax and profits tax chargeable on company profits, has done nothing to encourage exporters, and income tax reliefs in the form of double taxation relief are available to any company receiving income from abroad, whether that income is derived from export operations or not.

Before the introduction of Corporation Tax and the associated Schedule F, a company paid income tax and profits tax on its profits, and paid a net dividend out of the net profit after taxation. This net dividend was then grossed at the standard rate of income tax so that the gross equivalent of the net payment became the gross income of the shareholder and was directly related to the profits of the company before taxation. With the substitution of Corporation Tax for Income Tax and Profits Tax chargeable on the company profits and the introduction of Schedule F, the taxation of company profits and the shareholders' liability to income tax have been separated. Under the old system, a company, that received income from abroad and paid foreign taxes thereon, could have its tax bill reduced so that, in effect, UK income tax was paid on the profits at a lower rate than the standard rate; but since 1945, dividends paid by such companies have nevertheless been grossed at the standard rate of income tax although repayment to any individual shareholder has been limited to the 'net United Kingdom rate' (Section 350 of the Income Tax Act 1952 previously Section 52 of the Finance No. 2 Act 1945).

538

The deduction of standard rate income tax from dividends means, as far as the shareholder is concerned, that he has income suffering full standard rate tax which, according to his personal circumstances, might be wholly repayable, and it will be seen that, whereas in the past the dividend income received had suffered only Income Tax and Profits Tax, it now suffers Corporation Tax and, in addition, the full standard rate Income Tax on the distribution. In future, dividend warrant counterfoils will not have to carry the statement regarding the net United Kingdom rate applicable under Section 350 of the Income Tax Act 1952. This new system will, therefore, provide no advantage to a shareholder in a UK company in receipt of overseas income.

A major change introduced by the 1965 Finance Act is the abolition of relief for overseas trading corporations. A company could normally apply for Overseas Trading Corporation status if it carried on a trade outside the United Kingdom, and the trading profits of the company were exempted from UK as long as those profits were retained abroad. In the event of the profits being distributed in the form of dividends, tax was charged under Case VI of Schedule D (subject to double taxation relief) on the gross amount of the distribution. This relief to companies trading abroad now disappears. A company resident in the United Kingdom will still be entitled to claim credit for overseas tax paid on income from any overseas source against the United Kingdom Corporation Tax payable on that income, and it will also be entitled to claim credit for overseas tax paid on capital gains against the United Kingdom Corporation Tax payable on those gains. The relief may be due either under a double tax agreement or under a unilateral relief provision.

Double taxation agreements are already in existence with over fifty countries, and they all follow the same basic pattern. They provide for two distinct measures of relief, the first being for reciprocal exemption, and the second for tax credit. There are no fixed rules for either of these two measures, and it is always necessary to refer to the particular convention; but where reciprocal exemptions are granted, the source of income is fully taxed in one country and exempted in the other. The general principle on which tax credit is allowed is that the country in which the income arises in the first place takes the tax to which it is entitled, leaving the other country to grant the appropriate relief. Where there is no convention, provision is made for unilateral relief to be given in the United Kingdom for overseas taxes paid. The rules governing the limitation of this relief are complicated and it is always sensible to seek professional advice, particularly when the period includes the transitional years covering the change over to Corporation Tax and where the double-tax relief provisions are further complicated.

Besides the overseas income that derives from some form of investment in local production or distribution, there is another source of income where the tax situation has to be specially considered, and this is in respect of royalties and know-how payments. These usually arise when agreements have been made with overseas com-

539

panies for them to manufacture under licence against payment of a fixed sum, and subsequent royalties based on the quantity sold, or for periodic payments in exchange for technical know-how. As far as UK tax is concerned, the Inland Revenue issued a pamphlet in July 1960 to clarify the position. Payments made by residents in overseas countries to a person carrying on a trade in the United Kingdom as consideration for the use in the overseas country of any copyright, patent, design, process, trademark, or formula may be treated for the purpose of credit (whether under double taxation agreement or by way of unilateral relief) as income arising outside the United Kingdom, except to the extent that they represent consideration for services rendered in this country. Traders resident in the United Kingdom will not be entitled to claim credit for any tax levied in the overseas country in respect of payments for services rendered here; but in such cases no objection will be raised if only the net amount of the payments (after deduction of the overseas tax) is included in the computation of profits for UK tax purposes.

It will be apparent from the above that the tax position in the United Kingdom does not provide any financial incentive to the exporter who wishes to develop abroad, nor will the present framework of taxation offer an opportunity to do so. Although tax incentives and other subsidies for exports are forbidden—not only under the General Agreement of Tariffs and Trade (GATT) but, as far as the United Kingdom is concerned, also under the European Free Trade Area Convention— there are two kinds of tax remission on exports permitted under Article XVI of GATT and, also, under the EFTA Convention. They are the remission of charges on relative imports and of indirect taxes levied at one or several stages of production. United Kingdom manufacturers are already able to reclaim import duties on materials directly embodied in exports, but the UK tax system is not geared to take full advantage of large-scale remission of indirect taxes on exports as permitted by the GATT. This could be achieved only with a more broadly based sales tax system on the lines of the Added Value Tax which has been in operation in France since 1954 and is being adopted by the other members of the Common Market as the basis for tax harmonization under Article 99 of the Rome Treaty.

Let us now take a look at the overseas tax arrangements an exporter will have to take into account when assessing the possibilities of gaining entry to a particular market. As with the UK system, let us begin with the normal business of sale to an overseas buyer. In the first place, the goods on entering the country would attract a charge in the shape of tariff or revenue duty, and these would vary according to the type of goods and the country concerned. In some cases there may be special surcharges, import taxes, or anti-dumping duties, and before the goods are sold they may attract a sales tax or equalization tax.

Full details of all tariffs, duties, charges, etc., in any particular market can`be obtained from the Board of Trade or chambers of commerce. Further guidance may be required from the BoT or from the Commercial Branch of the country's embassy in the interpretation of these schedules as some of them are long, detailed, and complicated, for example, that of the United States.

One source of difficulty arises from the definition of the product and the decision as to which category it belongs for tariff and duty purposes. This problem has been eased by the compilation of the 'Brussels Nomenclature', which lists goods under headings and categories agreed internationally. Nevertheless, the description of goods may still give rise to difficulties that can be solved only by reference to the offices mentioned. A typical example of such a problem is the import of carbon paper into Japan. For some time these imports were subject to a 30 per cent charge, when they should in fact have been duty free, and this arose because the Japanese language does not contain a symbol for carbon paper, and they were listed as printing materials. In Canada, the anti-dumping legislation involves very severe control of the prices charged for imported goods relative to the price in the exporter's home market, and any discrepancy attracts a charge. Belgium levies a transmission tax on goods transported by road or rail inside the country, and this has to be taken into account in addition to any import charges. Although the various taxes levied by other countries on imported goods are complicated, full information is available from the three sources already mentioned, and, of course, the shipping and forwarding agents who would be employed to handle the delivery of the goods are usually well informed on these matters.

In this examination of taxation both at home and overseas in its relation to United Kingdom exports, a certain amount of space has been devoted to: (*a*) the tax remissions or benefits an exporter of goods to an overseas buyer may expect to receive at home; (*b*) the import taxes and charges the goods will attract when sold in the overseas market. This is justified in that these factors will play an important part in any consideration the exporter may give to the advisability of investing in the overseas market by way of local production. In other words, the United Kingdom manufacturer must assess the tax advantages and disadvantages at home and overseas as a straight exporter of goods as compared with those applicable to an overseas investor. We have already seen that, as an investor, he will derive little or no benefit from the UK tax system and it remains only to consider the general company taxation background overseas.

Many countries offer important financial incentives to encourage foreign companies to invest and set up production. In some cases, such as Belgium, it is with a view to developing the less industrialized areas; in others, such as the West Indies, it is part of the whole policy of industrial development and economic diversification. These incentives are not necessarily in the form of lower tax rates but may provide for 'tax holidays' in the first year or so of operation. The Statistics and Intelligence Division of the Board of Inland Revenue has published through HM Stationery Office a table setting out the latest known rates of tax chargeable on the income of companies in a large number of countries, including local taxes levied by provinces or municipalities, and also the rates of taxation on non-resident companies where they differ from those for residents.

Generally speaking, where there is any difference, non-resident companies tend to pay at a higher rate than resident companies, a factor that would influence a UK investor in deciding the constitution of a company he wishes to establish in such a country. In this context, it is interesting that France, which has never sought to encourage investment from overseas, levies an additional tax on the net profits of non-resident companies (after French tax) in so far as those profits are distributed and distributed to non-residents of France.

The tax systems and rates of taxation operating in other countries are so varied and complex that it is impossible to generalize, but detailed information on any country can be obtained from the appropriate department of the country's embassy in London. In addition, the Commercial Section of the British Embassy in the centre concerned may be consulted, and a local bank. In fact, if the UK company first approaches its own banker, the latter will put it in touch with a bank abroad which can supply the tax information as well as that on the procedure for the formation of a company, raising finance, and possible locations for operation.

As the most likely areas, at the present time, for investment and local production are the Common Market countries, a brief look at their company tax rates may be a useful conclusion to this survey. Germany levies a corporate tax of 49 per cent on the profits of non-resident companies established in Germany, whether the profits are distributed or not, as against 51 per cent on undistributed profits, and 15 per cent on distributed profits for resident companies. Royalties are subject to a withholding tax of 25 per cent. France has a basic corporation tax on net profits of 50 per cent, and, as mentioned above, levies an additional tax on non-resident companies. Italy still has a schedular system whereby taxes are, in principle, levied on the basis of the source of income, and not on the total income. Turnover tax is the main source of State income and this, together with the schedular and local taxes, is complemented by taxes on the overall income of corporations and individuals. In the Netherlands, a corporation profits tax between 43 and 47 per cent applies to both distributed and undistributed profits. Belgium has a non-resident tax of 35 per cent for corporations against a basic 30 per cent for residents, and this applies whether the profits are distributed or not. Luxembourg levies a corporation tax rising from 20 to 40 per cent.

No attempt has been made to itemize other taxes for which a company may be liable such as Capital Tax, Turnover Tax, local business tax, etc., nor the Social Security contributions the employer has to pay, but the facts given are enough to indicate the need to obtain at the outset full information from the sources mentioned.

Reading list
BOOKS
Selective Employment Payments Act, 1966 (Ministry of Labour)

Corporation Tax Booklet No. 570 (with Supplement), issued by Board of Inland Revenue (Free from H.M. Inspector of Taxes)

Capital Gains Tax Booklet No. 560 (with Supplement), issued by the Board of Inland Revenue (Free from H.M. Inspector of Taxes)

Corporation Tax Synopsis (Chas. H. Tolley & Co., 44a High Street, Croydon, Surrey), published annually.

10.5 National Services to Exporters: The British National Export Council

Peter Tennant

BNEC is a partnership between Government, and industry and commerce, aimed at increasing Britain's foreign currency earnings. It was first formed in the late summer of 1964 and lost no time in playing its role as a prime mover in the British export promotion effort. As the House of Commons Select Committee on Estimates Report on Export Promotion said of BNEC: 'Its independence and freedom of action are clearly of great importance'.

The Select Committee's interest stems from the fact that BNEC, though an industry-based body, receives public money; its routine expenses are met from a Government grant. When the Council was first formed the basis of its finance was a matching Government grant for every pound subscribed by industry, but since then industry's contribution has soared in other ways. Some 250 leading businessmen, drawn from prominent exporting firms, give a portion of their time and the benefit of their experience to BNEC and its area bodies, and often travel abroad at their own companies' expense on work connected with BNEC. In the case of a Committee chairman, this can amount to a very heavy burden.

Now the system is that the Government in effect pays for BNEC's tried and proven activities, while BNEC will draw on its special fund raised from industry to launch new kinds of promotional activity, including market research, and to seize quickly the opportunities which arise.

BNEC's main Council started work in 1964 by gathering under its wing the already existing Export Council for Europe, and Council (renamed Committee) for Middle East Trade. It added to these a series of new regional committees, some of which took over the work formerly done by the Western Hemisphere Exports Council. BNEC area committees were formed for the USA, Canada, Latin America, Caribbean, Africa, Asia, Australia, New Zealand, Southern Africa and Israel. Close relations were established with the existing Sino-British Trade Council, and the autonomous but closely associated East European Trade Council which was formed in January 1967.

The object of each of these bodies is to ensure that, in the markets with which it is concerned, business opportunities are seized by British firms, particularly by those otherwise competitive smaller firms which do not maintain a world-wide marketing organization. The size and industrial sophistication of the American and West European markets is reflected in the fact that both BNEC Export Council for Europe and BNEC United States of America have special sections to promote exports of British-made components for various assembly industries. The European Components Service has been active in seeking opportunities for British firms, particularly in the automotive field, to supply components to the Continent. BNEC United States followed the European experiment with a US Procurement Committee which gives particular attention to supplying the American aerospace, oil, and other advanced technology industries.

Other bodies which, though not part of the BNEC structure, have been launched with the Council's help, include the British Marine Equipment Council, and the Hotel and Public Buildings Equipment Group. The BMEC organizes collective selling of components for ships built in foreign yards, and HOPBEG brings together manufacturers who can quote for—and finance, if necessary—the complete equipping of a hotel, hospital or educational establishment.

Bodies like these, together with the established trade associations and local chambers of commerce and export clubs, are eligible to make use of the trade mission scheme operated by BNEC on behalf of the Board of Trade. BNEC has been backing projects for collective selling and market research tours overseas, and visits to this country by groups of foreign buyers, at a rate of 200 a year, with half the cost of basic travel and accommodation—or three-quarters of the economy-class air fares to Australasian and certain Far Eastern markets.

Apart from the Missions Section, however, the Area Councils and Committees are the main operating arms of the organization. They work in a variety of ways, according to the problems and opportunities to be found in their markets. They are particularly concerned with the detailed preparation of overseas promotions such as British Weeks and store promotions, trade fairs and exhibitions. Day to day work of each committee is conducted by the executive secretary who in some cases has a small staff to assist him.

BNEC supports these area secretariats with a common range of central ser-

545

vices: administrative, research and publicity. A Planning and Promotion Committee co-ordinates the future programmes of the area bodies to ensure that priorities are observed and that every venture will be well supported by industry. The Committee considers suggestions from within the BNEC structure and from outside, for future promotions in a three-year rolling programme. A three-year time scale is necessary because any major overseas fair or British Week needs up to two years of preparation to ensure success.

Research to shed light in dark corners of the British export performance and to determine where the most profitable opportunities lie, has been an increasing BNEC preoccupation and is likely to command more and more of the funds subscribed by industry and commerce. A good example of a major past initiative in this respect was the enquiry into 'Invisible' exports, conducted at BNEC's request by a committee under the late Sir Thomas Bland. This led to the publication in the Autumn of 1967 of *Britain's Invisible Earnings*—the most authoritative source book on the services which contribute over one third of our country's total foreign currency earnings. Then, after further discussions between BNEC and representatives of the City, a permanent Committee on Invisible Exports was formed to carry out a continuous review of performance in this vital field.

The first three years of BNEC's existence were an eventful period in Britain's trading history. The 14·3 per cent devaluation of the pound was a signal for the export drive to be intensified even further. BNEC swung into special activity immediately, with a rapidly-arranged series of meetings entitled 'Action 68' in the main regional centres of the country, at which the opportunities resulting from devaluation were discussed with thousands of key businessmen.

Fortunately, the 1967 sterling devaluation coincided with the beginning of the Kennedy Round world-wide tariff-cutting, which will continue until 1972, and also with moves to bring about an increase in world liquidity. BNEC, therefore, looks forward to the challenge of ever-greater opportunities for British export achievement, and will press on with its work of reinforcing such opportunities through collective promotions and helping more firms to prosper through exports.

Reading list

BOOKS

Britain's Invisible Earnings, (The report of the Committee on Invisible Exports) Director of Studies: William M. Clarke (Published for the Financial Advisory Panel on Exports by the British National Export Council, 1967)
Open Doors in EFTA, report of EFTA Conference in London organized by the British National Export Council for Europe in 1967.
General BNEC publications, available free:
  BNEC in Action
  BNEC Area Councils and Committees

BNEC Pays Half
British Weeks in Action
BNEC News

Useful addresses

British National Export Council, 6–14 Dean Farrar Street, London SW 1
British National Export Council for Middle East Trade, 33 Bury Street, London SW 1
Sino-British Trade Council, 21 Tothill Street, London SW 1

10.6 National Services to Exporters: The Board of Trade and E.C.G.D.

Christopher Fildes

The Board of Trade is the department of state responsible for export. It offers services it classifies as 'information and advice' but which, in fact, go further than this; for example, they include arbitration in business disputes. It stages direct promotions of British business overseas. It offers help with publicity, on its own account and through the Central Office of Information and the BBC. And it acts as a clearing house for all kinds of information useful to the exporter: state agencies, such as H.M. Customs and Excise; private bodies, such as the sources of credit; and hybrids like the British National Export Council (*see* section 10.5).

The information services of the Board are:

1. Market assessments, available on demand, considering possible export markets in relation to your product.
2. Information, in the daily *Export Service Bulletin* and weekly *Board of Trade Journal* (much of the *Bulletin*'s information is summarized in the *Journal*) on specific export prospects. This applies particularly to capital goods, since the papers cover public contracts put out to tender, and possibilities thrown up by the actions of international agencies: development grants and the like.
3. Details of foreign tariff and quota regulations.
4. Samples: the Board will, for a modest charge, obtain (small) samples of foreign products against which you may have to compete.

5. Agents: the Board will send you a short list of suitable overseas agents for your company.
6. Assessments of the commercial standing of foreign firms.
7. Help with business visits: the Board, given fair warning, will supply background information on markets, and letters of introduction to British commercial officers who will, if you want, arrange local publicity for your visit.
8. Joint exporting ventures: the Board will put you in touch with would-be partners.
9. Names of companies that might manufacture your product under licence.
10. An 'honest broker service'—but only where the dispute has not been taken to law.
11. The Board's Statistics and Market Intelligence Library. This is divided into three: economic statistics of every kind about foreign countries; foreign trade and telephone directories; and catalogues published by foreign firms. The library (in London) is open five days a week, or will handle enquiries by telephone, telex, or letter, if they are for details of foreign firms.
12. Protection for your foreign interests: the Board will tell you how you may be affected by a foreign country's regulations, or by international conventions (GATT and the like), or by prospective changes in them.

The Board runs three different kinds of direct promotion abroad: participation in trade fairs, British Weeks (in conjunction with the British National Export Council), and in-store promotions. For *trade fairs*, the Board has a 'joint venture scheme', which means that where a firm is taking part in a group display, sponsored by a trade association, the Board will supply free space and a free stand, and will also subsidize air fairs and the cost of translating sales literature. This applies only to specialist trade fairs, or specialist sections of fairs; and only when a firm repeatedly takes part—five times at an annual fair. The Board also runs British pavilions at some fairs, and will let space at an attractive rate. Although the Board does not stage British trade fairs, it helps to pay for certain services of British and Overseas Fairs Ltd, which does. (You will find details in the *Board of Trade Journal*). *British Weeks* are point-of-sale promotions in foreign cities—two a year—for which a major effort is made, with plenty of publicity and supporting attractions. They are planned long in advance; a British Week office is open on the spot eighteen months before the Week is staged. (Details, again, are available in the *Board of Trade Journal*.) It sometimes happens that a foreign city decides to put on a British Week of its own: the Board will help with display material, supporting events, and so on, according to the merits of the case. Department stores in North America and Europe also put on their own British promotions. These *in-store promotions* are helped in the same way. The Board is experimenting with a scheme for co-operative advertising in support of these three kinds of promotion, with a 50 per cent subsidy for advertisements from groups of firms.

In the general field of publicity, the Board will give you advice on the best ways of promoting products in different markets. It will put you in touch with translators for your sales literature, and can arrange for it to be translated in the country where it will be used. It can also give you names of overseas journalists in London. If you have a newsworthy story, or picture, about your company, the Central Office of Information would like to know. It runs an overseas press service, produces radio and television programmes, and films; publishes booklets and magazines, and runs tours to and around British firms. The BBC external services (write to the Export Liaison Officer) also welcomes information.

To get in touch with the Board of Trade, approach the Export Intelligence Inquiry points in London, Birmingham, Bristol, Cardiff, Cockermouth, Colwyn Bay, Glasgow, Inverness, Leeds, Manchester, and Newcastle-upon-Tyne; or the Ministry of Commerce in Belfast.

The ECGD (Export Credits Guarantee Department) is a governmental agency, run on the lines of a private business and required to pay its own way. It is a responsibility of the Board of Trade's Ministers, but is not part of the Board. It insures credit risks associated with exports. Although it does not itself finance exports, its operations help exporters to find finance elsewhere, often on favourable terms.

The Department's first function is the issuing of *insurance policies*. These do not cover the exporter against the consequences of his own mismanagement, but are otherwise nearly comprehensive. Two main risks are covered:

(i) the customer failing to pay, becoming insolvent, refusing to take the goods up, or simply not paying within six months of the due date.
(ii) the customer being unable, though willing, to pay; for example, because an exchange control regulation is introduced that prevents him.

Various other minor risks, such as the cancellation of an import licence, are included: eleven risks in all. Policies are scarcely ever for the full 100 per cent of the amount at risk.

These policies are useful in obtaining finance, because the exporter can probably borrow from his bank against them, just as one might borrow against a life assurance policy.

From this has grown the Department's second function, now as important as the issuing of policies: the giving of *financial guarantees* direct to banks. What the Department does is to give the bank financing the export a 100 per cent guarantee against default on the bill or note concerned. In effect, the Department is doing the work of an Accepting House (*see* p. 278), endorsing the bill and giving the bank direct recourse to the department. What this means for the exporter is, first, that he can borrow more cheaply (because the Department is pledging the Government's credit on his behalf); and, secondly, that he has made no inroad into his credit limit with his bank.

For loans covered by an ECGD guarantee, British banks have agreed special terms. Where credit is for two years or more, a standard rate of interest is charged, fixed, every few years, by reference to recent levels of Bank rate. Through the years 1965 to 1967, the rate was $5\frac{1}{2}$ per cent, which was singularly favourable to the exporter since Bank rate was never below this level and frequently above it. Where credit is for less than two years it is provided at Bank rate, which again is a finer rate than that normally available.

A financial guarantee is less readily to be had than an insurance policy. An exporter must have had credit insurance with the Department for at least a year before he will be considered for a guarantee. He must also, since his own credit as well as his customer's is involved, be able to show the sort of financial standing appropriate to the sum guaranteed. He is asked to pay a 'facility charge' of 2s. 6d. per £100 p.a. for the amount that he may, during a given year, ask to be guaranteed. This charge, in effect, is his booking fee, and means that there is credit for him when he wants it.

There is a 'Small Exporter Policy' for the manufacturer without export experience, or with an export turnover (in small items) of less than £10,000 p.a. This is intended to make exporting easier for the novice, and is, therefore, a simplified, and less comprehensive, policy offered at a flat rate of 11s. 6d. per £100. With this exception, the Department has no standard tariff of policies. It will consider an individual proposition and, if it accepts the risk, quote a premium. In so doing the Department uses its own records, covering some 130,000 foreign customers, and its means of assessing credit-worthiness by inquiries at home and abroad. It has access to the Government's intelligence, which has special significance since many export risks are political as well as economic.

To deal with the Exports Credits Guarantee Department contact, *not* its head office, but one of the four branch offices in London, or your local office in Belfast, Birmingham, Bradford, Bristol, Cardiff, Edinburgh, Glasgow, Leeds, Liverpool, Manchester, Newcastle-upon-Tyne, Nottingham, or Sheffield. There is also an office in New York.

Reading list

BOOKS

The Board of Trade: A Short Survey (Board of Trade, 1965)
Services for British Exporters, Export Handbook No. 1 (Board of Trade, 1967)
ECGD Credit Insurance and Financial Support Services, Export Handbook No. 2 (Board of Trade, 1967)
Organization for Overseas Marketing, Export Handbook No. 3 (Board of Trade, 1967)
ECGD Services: The British Government's Credit Insurance Facilities for Exporters

JOURNAL

The Board of Trade Journal (weekly)

Useful addresses

Board of Trade, Export Intelligence Department/Statistics and Market Intelligence Library, Hillgate House, 35 Old Bailey, London EC 4

British Broadcasting Corporation, Export Liaison Officer, Bush House, Strand, London EC 2

British and Overseas Fairs Ltd., 1–19 New Oxford Street, London WC 1

Export Credits Guarantee Department, 59 Gresham Street, London EC 2

10.7 National Services to Exporters: The Central Office of Information

Sir Fife Clark

Whether the Central Office of Information (COI) does a first-class job in publicizing Britain's industry overseas depends mainly on the co-operation received from exporting companies.

Advance knowledge of a company's plans, given to the COI in confidence, enables us to concert official publicity measures with those of the firm. We can then assess the best media to use and the most promising angles to exploit, visual, and otherwise; it also enables us to consider translation in up to forty languages, and to get the advice of the Embassy and High Commission officers overseas who will eventually place the material.

The COI's work in support of export promotion is sponsored by the Foreign Office and the Commonwealth Office. On industrial and marketing matters we are advised by the Board of Trade.

A government department, which celebrated its twenty-first birthday in 1967, the COI has a professional staff of 700 men and women skilled in the techniques of the mass media. All publicity outlets are used except direct broadcasting (that is the job of the BBC Overseas Services), and COI material is used in nearly every country in the world. Some 60 per cent of the output gives news of manufacturing industry, technology, or science.

The operation starts with companies and associations making available to COI officers, in London or the Regional Offices, news of new products and processes, major export orders won, the results of research, a technological break-through, news of services rendered by Britain's bankers and insurance companies, participation in trade fairs and British Weeks, and any of the many other facets of Britain's industrial effort. The Government, for its part, provides specialized knowledge of local conditions and contacts as well as the output of skilled publicists. Thus, reports and pictures of what is happening in British factories and research establishments are presented so as to secure maximum impact overseas.

The selection of the right information medium or media is determined by the nature of the story itself and the countries where it is to be publicized. The written word is employed in the form of 'hard' news or feature articles; films are produced, or acquired, for use in cinemas or on television; radio tapes are made for broadcasting on local stations or networks; while photographs are used for poster and display purposes or to illustrate and emphasize the printed word. The COI also has a large Exhibitions Division which organizes a very wide range of projects, from small information stands at specialized fairs to British Weeks, or the national pavilion at a world exhibition such as Expo 67 at Montreal.

Placing the material with overseas countries

In short, the COI can be described as the workshop of the Government Information Services. Journalists, film-makers, designers, photographers, and other experts produce a continuous stream of publicity material in support of the efforts of British firms to sell their goods overseas.

From the COI headquarters in Lambeth, this material is relayed to British embassies, high commissions and consulates in as many as 120 countries, where Information Officers—members of the Diplomatic Service—place it with the local outlets.

The figures COI can quote often surprise our visitors. The Department sends abroad many millions of words a year of Press material, with placings running into hundreds of thousands annually. Some 700,000 photographs and 150,000 printing blocks help in projecting the story of Britain's industrial and technological skill and scientific achievements.

One of the largest Divisions is the Overseas Press Services. It is staffed by about 100 journalists and sixty translators and ancillary staff and is at the service of any firm, big or small, with a worthwhile story to tell overseas. Each year the Division sends out 18,000 stories about British industry, science, and research to find a ready market in the world's newspapers, journals, and the trade and technical press.

Our TV programmes are currently shown by 500 stations throughout the world, which amounts to coverage in almost every country that has a television network, omitting only the Communist bloc. One programme has a regular slot, often at peak viewing hours, on 150 stations in the United States. This output is supple-

554

mented by newsreels in countries where the cinema is still the leading visual medium, and by colour magazine programmes specially edited for the Far East and Latin American countries.

We also select, each year, about 150 films produced by British firms and trade associations and, after editing and dubbing, arrange overseas distribution.

Radio programmes in fifty languages

About 4,000 recorded radio programmes are prepared annually, going out in up to fifty languages to seventy-five countries. Their industrial content is very high.

The biggest task of Exhibitions Division in recent years has been the organization of the successful British Pavilion at Expo 67, which five million people visited. Although this captured the headlines, the bulk of the work of Exhibitions Division is centred on British participation in trade exhibitions and fairs, large and small, throughout the world.

What sort of results does this publicity achieve? Each year we receive about 29,000 cuttings from overseas newspapers and magazines of COI stories and photographs. This is only a sample of total reproduction.

Hundreds of letters from firms are also received. The managing director of a Chichester plastics company wrote about a story placed in two American magazines:

'This release is the most extraordinary I have come across. One would not get a response like it from an ordinary advertisement no matter how large it was. Between June and November we had a total of over 350 enquiries and these were from people like chief engineers and directors. It is an incredible response, and would have cost my firm several thousand pounds to have reached the people COI services have been able to contact. And the remarkable thing is that enquiries are still coming in.'

Other letters from firms, big and small, and from the secretaries of chambers of commerce and trade associations give similar accounts of the ground for selling being prepared by news items, feature articles, films or photographs in the country or countries to be visited by directors, salesmen or trade missions.

How the COI staff will help

The services of the COI and those of the information officers overseas are provided free. There is however, one essential requirement. The story, film, photograph or article must, by its newsworthiness, be thought worth space in a newspaper or magazine, or time on the cinema or television screen. The COI staff will very willingly give advice on possible news angles to firms that may be in doubt whether their products possess a strong enough appeal in information terms.

Industrialists who would like to see more of the COI's operation are invited to spend a day at our office in Lambeth. There we can show them at first hand how the machine works, let them see our news releases, listen to our radio programmes, view the television output—and put as many questions as they like. If any exporter or potential exporter cares to write to me, I will be glad to arrange this. Those who cannot pay a personal visit but would like more information about the export promotion services can get literature from my office at COI Headquarters.

Reading list

BOOKS

Practical Public Relations, Sam Black (Pitman, 2nd Rev. Edition, 1966)

Handbook of Public Relations, N. Ellis and P. Bowman (Harrap, 1963)

The Government Explains, Marjorie Ogilvy-Webb (Allen and Unwin, 1965)

Mass Media and National Development, Wilbur Schramm (Stanford University Press OUP, 1965)

UNESCO Report and Papers on Mass Communications: No. 45 Professional Training for Mass Communications (UNESCO/H.M.S.O., 1965)

Government Information Services, COI Reference Paper 5256 (COI, 1967)

Useful addresses

Central Office of Information, Westminster Bridge Road, London SE 1

10.8 Trade Through Barter

David Galloway

Barter is an ancient system of trading disliked by bankers, who regard money as a more efficient medium for effecting exchanges. It is practised today mainly by communist, primary producing, and chronically insolvent countries, not because they disagree with the financial community on the efficacy of money, but usually because they do not have any that is internationally acceptable.

At the government-to-government level, barter is carried out through bilateral agreements. Typically, such an agreement would be between a primary producing country and a developed country, in which each would agree to take the same value of the other's goods in any one year. To take a theoretical example: Ghana and Czechoslovakia might agree to exchange goods to the value of five million dollars with the intention that Czechoslovakia take cocoa from Ghana and send machine tools and shoes.

Statistics on bilateral trading are sketchy. A gauge of its extent is that its supporters claim that half the world trade is financed on this basis. Certainly the number of these government-to-government agreements is now about 500, and barter in one form or another features increasingly in trade with South America, the Middle East, and the Eastern bloc. German companies, such as Krupps, with large interests in Eastern Europe, have responded by setting up special barter departments.

The origin of bilateral trading, as we know it today, goes back to the last collapse of the international money system, the great depression of the 1930s. At the creditors' meeting of the Creditanstalt in Vienna, in 1931, the then President proposed bilateral agreements as a means whereby two countries could mutually finance imports without either side dipping into its convertible foreign exchange reserves. Nothing came of the proposal at the time, but among the audience was Dr Hjalmar Schacht who took up the idea as a means by which Germany could obtain industrial raw materials without disbursing foreign currency: by the outbreak of war Germany had ten major agreements functioning.

The post-war boom in bilateral trading has its roots in different motives. It is not, as with Hitler Germany, the developed countries seeking to secure their supplies of raw materials. The countries involved are frequently small, economically weak, and usually producers of primary commodities or less sophisticated industrial goods. As such, they usually have inadequate reserves and, consequently, have difficulty in getting their currencies accepted. Furthermore, when it comes to trading with other countries in a similar financial situation, they are not willing to accumulate another weak currency. Accordingly, they prefer to exchange a fixed quantity of goods, denominated in dollars; the trade is regulated solely by book entries made by the respective Central Banks.

Furthermore, bilateral agreements can enable primary producing countries to get rid of embarrassing surpluses, or the producers of less sophisticated industrial goods to find a market. Effectively, it can be the response of these countries to the marketing strength of the advanced industrialized nations, bargaining their purchasing power in an attempt to secure an outlet for their goods. This is particularly vital for some commodity-producing countries, faced in many cases with competition from synthetics, inelasticity of demand, and their own inability to cut production in the face of a fall in demand. If, as frequently happens, a government offers producers a guaranteed price, local embarrassments multiply in the bumper crop years when the Government finds itself saddled with a substantial crop surplus bought at a price probably above the world level. In such circumstances, and given the buyers' market that exists in capital goods, differences between competing tenders for say, a new steel works, will count for much less than a willingness to find a home for an unwanted crop surplus.

The United Kingdom's adherence to multilateralism has ruled out bilateral agreements at government level. Trade agreements the UK Government makes are concerned only with granting quotas, and eschew financing. The Board of Trade and the Treasury have, however, no dogmatic objections to companies undertaking barter transactions on their own account.

Whereas it is certainly possible to make as good a profit on a barter contract as on a cash or credit deal, adding this new dimension can, unless the seller is wise, multiply the risks.

The first rule of wisdom for the novice is: 'On no account attempt to handle the whole deal single-handed'. All that this may do is transfer much of the profit of the deal into the pockets of the commodity merchants, who soon get to hear when there is a forced seller in the market.

For advice on barter, the City admittedly lags behind the European centres, notably Holland and Switzerland. Andre & Cie of Lausanne and the Union Bank of Holland are the acknowledged leaders on the Continent. In Belgium and Germany there are now special Government departments offering advice, and in France the local equivalent of the ECGD can finance barter agreements. In the City of London, where the merchant bankers have long since given up being merchants, bankers' prejudice against barter has inhibited the growth of this business.

In theory, at least, almost any merchant who deals in the commodities on offer ought to be able to help, either directly or by passing on the enquiry. In practice, it is wiser to approach one of the commodity houses that has had experience of barter transactions and knows the hidden pitfalls. Among these are Biddle, Sawyer & Co., Comweld (a Subsidiary of Cocoa Merchants Ltd), M. Golodetz, and Lamet Trading. The assistance offered will range from advice to acting as an agent or principal: this last is probably the easiest for the exporter, as it relieves him of all responsibility for the commodities involved.

For companies constantly coming up against barter and allied propositions, Emerson Associated, a pioneer in this field, offers a specialized consultancy service, based on an annual retainer, confined to one firm in each industry.

Good advice makes it possible to employ barter as a sales aid. If a prospective customer is suffering from a commodity surplus, the capital goods supplier who goes in offering to take payment in that commodity will be sure of a sympathetic hearing. A barter deal is not necessarily for the whole amount of a transaction. In many, the barter part covers the ECGD down-payment, with the balance on conventional credit terms.

An exporter contemplating this positive approach to barter must be prepared to jettison his price list. Any transaction will probably involve him in taking commodities at the world price or above, although they may well have to be sold at less. To maintain his margins and make it worth the commodity merchant's while, the exporter must quote an abnormally high price (the whole stratagem is, after all, in effect a backdoor devaluation). The posture for the exporter to avoid at all costs is to agree a cash price, and then suddenly be presented with a barter proposition.

Although technically not 'barter', the other unorthodox payment frequently offered by the barter-minded countries, settlement in 'clearing', is a development of the barter system. Bilateral agreements sometimes get off-balance: taking the earlier Ghana-Czechoslovakia example—if the Czechs took up their full entitlement of cocoa but the Ghanaians failed to ask for their entitlement of shoes and machine tools, the Ghanaians would have a credit on their clearing account with Czechoslovakia, available for purchasing only in Czechoslovakia. This credit they might offer, at a discount, in payment to a UK exporter. There is now an active market in these credits in Amsterdam, and most of the London houses already named can give further information on this facet of barter, also known as 'switch trading'. Specialists in this field are the London branch of the Moscow Narodny Bank and Bremar International Ltd, a subsidiary of Triumph Investment Trust.

Barter and switch trading can be complex. But the exporter who rules them out from the start is losing markets to more flexible competition.

Reading list

JOURNALS

'Financing Free World Trade with the Sino–Soviet Bloc', Raymond Mikesell and Jack Behrmann (*Princeton Studies in International Finance, No. 8*)

'Mr. Klonarides Barters for Britain', David Galloway (*The Director*, February 1964)

'Finding Your Way Round the Barter Business', Peter Hobday (*The Director*, May 1966)

'How Switch Trading Works' (*The Economist*, January 14, 1967)

'The Sad-eyed Salesmen in Red Europe', Kenneth Ames (*The Director*, April 1967)

10.9 Using the Language of the Country

P. Keith Cameron

In the foreseeable future, growing international trade will demand a much higher degree of proficiency in foreign language communications from British companies, whether in the written or spoken word. Those who are prepared to spend the necessary time, effort and money now, will reap the benefit in the years to come. In a few years time, four-fifths of the British 'home market' may be non English-speaking by birth. This situation will present British industry and commerce with a problem of communication many times more acute than at present. It is the purpose of this section to explore the means of improving our performance in this field, under the two headings of translation* and language training.

Translation

For various reasons, translation is a very undervalued skill. Word-for-word conversion of one language into another is not translation. Translation is really more often a question of rendering the ideas behind the words, as much as the words themselves, into the foreign language, and this requires a highly developed skill. Machine translation has been unsuccessful partly because of the difficulty of translating the nuances contained in many texts. In order to obtain a perfect translation, there are

---

* For advice on the section on Translation, I am greatly indebted to John D. Peck, DCM, FIL, MAIE, Chairman of the Council of the Institute of Linguists.

many qualities the client should seek of the translator, and certain requirements that the translator should reasonably expect from the client.

Translations from English into a foreign language should always be done by a native speaker from English into the translator's mother tongue. If the subject matter is at all technical, a translator should be sought who has knowledge and experience of that particular field. For these reasons one would normally be suspicious of a translator claiming to work in more than two or three different languages, and a wide variety of fields.

Translation requires a high degree of skill, concentration, and knowledge. The translator is a specialist, a professional, and he should be treated and paid accordingly.

A good translation should be the result of close co-operation between the client and the translator. In order to help the translator in his work, the client should ensure that the original document to be translated is clear, unambiguous, and legible. This may seem to be stating the obvious, but it is amazing how many scarcely legible documents are presented to translators. Abbreviations should be given in full and, wherever necessary, the appropriate drawings or plans should be available, so that the translator has as much background information available as possible. The translator will probably want to consult with the client from time to time about the translation, and, therefore, the relevant telephone numbers and addresses should be made available.

A good translation requires time, and cannot be achieved overnight. Although from time to time there is no means of avoiding a rush job, it is often possible to plan ahead for translations for overseas promotions, trade fairs or exhibitions. In these cases, putting translations in hand well in advance will often save money and will certainly contribute to the perfection of the final article.

Once the translation has been completed it should be checked, first of all by another translator, and then by the agent or equivalent in the foreign country, care being taken to ensure that whoever is checking the translation has the necessary technical knowledge. This is a valuable check as well as being a matter of courtesy to the agent concerned. In addition to checking, if printing is involved, the document should be very carefully proof-read. Poor proof-reading can spoil the most perfect piece of translation.

Because of the skills involved, a good translation cannot be done cheaply. Many companies are prepared to spend a great deal of money on all kinds of peripheral activities in promoting a product overseas, but translation costs are frequently overlooked. It is false economy to try to save money by going to an unknown or unqualified translator. As a useful check on what charges can be expected for translations, the Institute of Linguists recommends standard rates, scaled according to the complexity of the work and the language into which it is to be translated.

Provided these points are borne in mind, there is no reason why a good translation should not be obtained, whether it is undertaken by a translation agency, a freelance translator, or a company's own translation department.

Translation agencies

As with other services, the quality of work produced by translation agencies varies enormously. The advantages of such agencies are that they can handle most languages and at short notice, if necessary. Their work is usually neat, copies can be obtained from them easily, and they usually have facilities for duplicating and photocopying, etc. Disadvantages are that prices can be high, there is no guarantee of confidentiality, and it is difficult to consult with the person who is actually doing the translation. Also time may be lost in transmission by post.

The best way of finding a reliable agency is by personal recommendation, or the Institute of Linguists keeps a register of Members of their Translators Guild who run translation agencies.

Freelance translators

A good freelance translator with a knowledge of the field in which the company is involved is often the least expensive way of solving the problem. Because they stand or fall by their own individual work, they usually work carefully and accurately. The disadvantages of freelance translators are that they can seldom undertake urgent work, usually have no facilities other than simple typing, and, of course, there is no guarantee of confidentiality. Again, time is lost in transmission by post, and they have limited resources for objective checking.

The Institute of Linguists gives valuable advice to those seeking freelance translators by keeping a list of members of their Translators' Guild which catalogues their languages and their special subjects.

ASLIB (formerly the Association of Special Libraries and Information Bureaux), also keeps a catalogue of freelance translators that is available to its members, as well as a service for locating reports, journals, pamphlets, etc. that have already been translated into English, together with an index of unpublished translations.

In addition, some of the research associations provide translation services or can give expert advice in their particular field.

The company translation department

The company translation department offers many advantages, provided it is an economical proposition. The time required for transmission by post is saved, close co-operation and communication between the translator and the technical experts is easy and, of course, confidence is guaranteed. In addition, the company translators will be well versed in the company's products and activities. Provided there is a steady flow of work, costs can be considerably reduced.

A bulletin by the CBI on technical translations states that:

A company department of six translators dealing with say 3,000,000 words, half translating from French into English and half from English into French in 200 effective days per year, with three of them typing their own translations into French, and three using dictating machines for English translations from French for audio-typing, in the normal way would cost in salaries, including a chief translator, some £10,000 a year. Their equipment and overheads would add no less than £2,500, making a total of £12,500 a year. Costs will, or course, vary according to the location, overheads in Central London being significantly higher.

The same work done outside the firm at the rates recommended by the Institute of Linguists would total about £22,500 p.a. as an average figure.

Therefore, if there is a steady and abundant flow of translation, a company translation department is more economical. If, of course, a wide range of languages is required, the problem becomes more complex. Each company has to make a careful analysis of past work and estimated future requirements before deciding whether a translation department is an economical proposition.

A small firm with a more restricted requirement would probably send material for translation into foreign languages to outside agencies, while employing one or two English mother-tongue translators to handle the work to be translated from foreign languages into English.

Whatever means are adopted, it is hoped that British commerce and industry will gradually realize what translation involves, and will be prepared to pay for the kind of expertise required by more and more companies in an ever-increasing number of highly complex fields.

Language training

When approaching the problem of language training, it is important to consider the objective of such training before considering the means of attaining it. What in practice does the individual concerned want to be able to achieve upon completion of the training? Unless the objective is carefully thought out, it is unlikely to be attained; 'doing French' is not good enough. It is up to the individual to think out his own objective and then to seek the means of attaining it. The London and Birmingham Chamber of Commerce Oral Tests, mentioned below, describes in some detail the kind of objectives that should be sought. Before examining some of the methods open to the busy executive for attaining these objectives, we should first consider some problems and myths.

The greatest problem facing the businessman who earnestly wishes to acquire some degree of fluency is that of time; this is also the excuse given by those too lazy or too timid to try. Time is inevitably connected with cost. Not only is effective language training fairly expensive, but any time given to it is an indirect cost to the employer. The various methods of language learning will be discussed, bearing these two important factors in mind. Whatever method is selected, it must be made clear that:

(a) To reach even a limited degree of fluency requires hard work.
(b) Such a standard cannot be acquired overnight.
(c) The words 'language laboratory' are not a synonym for instant bi-lingualism.

Any publicity material claiming the contrary is not only being dishonest, but is doing a disservice both to the teaching profession and to those organizations that are conscientiously striving to raise standards in this country.

There are basically five different ways in which language training can be undertaken:

(a) Self-tuition.
(b) Private lessons.
(c) Evening classes.
(d) Intensive or 'crash' courses.
(e) Internal company language training centres.

(a) Self-tuition

This is the most attractive method for the busy executive. He can undertake it in privacy at his home or in his office in any spare moment. In cost it is relatively inexpensive. Unfortunately, for the majority of people, it is relatively ineffective, mainly because few people have the necessary will-power to complete the course. In addition, some of the materials available are out of date both in linguistic content and in pedagogical theory, and speaking to a gramophone or tape-recorder is very different from oral communication with another person.

Suggestions maintaining that one learns a foreign language in the same way, and as easily as a child learns its own language, are, it is considered, misguided. Adults do not learn a foreign language in the same way as their native language. Even if they did, it is impossible to re-create for the adult by means of records, the environment in which they learnt their native language.

Nevertheless, for the talented and conscientious few, self-tuition courses provide a partial answer. They can be of value in accustoming the complete beginner to the sounds and intonation patterns of a foreign language, and they are a convenient and readily available means of revision.

(b) Private lessons

A number of organizations can provide instructors to give private lessons in a client's office or home. Such lessons have the advantage that they can be arranged to cause minimum interference to the student's normal working day. Their effectiveness depends upon the quality of the instructor, but with a good instructor, rapid progress can be made. The disadvantages of such lessons are that they are relatively expensive, and the amount of practice is limited to those hours when the instructor is present.

To overcome this latter problem, one firm of language training consultants provides a tape and language laboratory recorder hire service, so that the student can practise the material covered in the lesson between sessions with the instructor.

(c) Evening Classes

The structure of adult education in this country is extremely complex, and it is not within the scope of this article to describe it. However, the general all-purpose foreign-language Evening Class is of little value to the businessman who wishes to acquire a useful degree of fluency. Experts consulted by the Committee for Research and Development in Modern Languages agreed that with less than four hours per week of tuition, 'no real progress could be expected'. Evening classes are better than nothing as long as too much is not expected of them, and provided they concentrate upon oral fluency. They are, of course, extremely inexpensive.

(d) Intensive or 'crash' courses

Advances in the field of applied linguistics have shortened the time required to acquire a useful degree of fluency. Better descriptions of what language is, have enabled an analysis to be made of those constituents that will be of most immediate use. Intensive courses make use of these advances and teach a carefully selected series of linguistic structures in a short period. Such courses have the advantage that rapid progress is made, and a useful degree of fluency can be quickly acquired. They concentrate upon oral ability, generally have a clearly defined objective in mind, and make use of the most modern aids, such as the language laboratory.

For some time the language-laboratory has been seen as the answer to the linguistically shy Englishman's prayer. How many people demand 'a language laboratory course' without having any idea of its capabilities?

The language laboratory is usually a series of special tape-recorders in individual booths linked to a central console at which the instructor sits.

The advantages of the laboratory are:

(i) The student can work through the material at his own speed, concentrating on those points with which he has most difficulty.
(ii) The student is given concentrated practice in responding to oral stimuli.
(iii) The student is exposed to a wide range of native voices.
(iv) The material is presented to the student in a carefully planned programme.
(v) The teacher can give individual help and instruction to those requiring it, while the rest of the class continue without interruption.

The language laboratory is an electronic device that makes concentrated practice more efficient. It is little more, and depends heavily upon the taped material used in it. However expensive or attractive the equipment, it will only be as good as the material available. Perhaps the greatest problem facing language teachers and language learners in this country is the shortage of suitable material to make the most of the splendid array of hardware produced by enterprising manufacturers.

Intensive courses fall under two headings:

(i) Those run by Local Education Authorities in technical colleges, colleges of commerce, etc. These are usually inexpensive and many of them are now providing excellent courses.

(ii) Those run by commercial or private organizations. Situated particularly in the London area, a number of these schools specialize in courses for the businessman. Such schools depend upon the quality of their instruction for their success, and stand or fall by the results they achieve. These courses usually last from 4–6 hours per day over 3 to 4 weeks and while concentrating upon developing oral fluency, also give a certain amount of background information about the country and its customs, etc. A useful degree of oral fluency can be achieved by the average beginner in about 60–80 hours. Most organizations also run courses for more advanced students. The oldest established of them, the Institute of Directors Language Centre, handled over 3,000 students in the four years 1964–68.

(e) Internal Company Language Training Centre

Some far-sighted and enterprising companies have their own language training centres organized either by their own training department or by outside firms of language consultants who specialize in this field. At present, company language training centres are more common abroad than in this country. Such centres have the advantage that training is available on the premises at virtually any moment of the day. The best possible use is made of both the student and the teacher's time, and no time is wasted in travelling.

Training can also be made available in English for personnel from overseas subsidiaries, in an English environment. Language training is a useful 'perk' to be able to offer out of office hours to staff who wish to learn a language for holidays, etc., and refresher courses can be run whenever necessary to keep the students knowledge up to date.

Shell were the first company in this country to install a language laboratory and, in June 1960, began a series of short intensive courses for staff proceeding overseas. Since then, their need for language training has gathered momentum and become more diffused, and they have continued to pursue a flexible and enlightened programme, covering, in all, about sixteen different languages, to meet the requirements of staff who are either based in this country or taking up assignments abroad. Shell have recently sent two of their personnel on a one-year full-time course in Japanese at Sheffield University.

The Beecham Group have installed a twelve-booth language laboratory at their headquarters at Chiswick, and in it their staff have undergone training in French,

German, Spanish, Italian, Russian, Danish, and Dutch. Language training is an integral part of the Beecham Group's policy for expansion in Europe and other overseas markets.

The Molins Machine Co. of Rotherhithe have a language laboratory where their engineers and sales staff are trained, as many of them are responsible for selling and installing complex machinery overseas. Training has been organized in Japanese and Russian, as well as in the more common European languages.

Several other companies have set up their own language training facilities. Many call in outside specialist organizations to do it for them, as few training officers have the necessary knowledge or experience in a field that is undergoing a revolution in methods, materials and teaching techniques. Provided there is a clear demand for language training, the cost per student hour can be kept low, especially if the facilities are shared with neighbouring companies facing the same problem. Industrial training boards will give favourable consideration to claims for a grant for language training schemes.

Examinations

Until recently, the majority of those interested in foreign languages have had to spend a considerable amount of time studying for examinations that, for most practical purposes, will be of little use to them. Ordinary and Advanced Level, while testifying to the candidate's application, intelligence, and ability to perform mental gymnastics, do not examine or purport to test the kind of skills that industry requires. Fortunately, teaching methods and syllabuses are changing.

The following examinations test practical ability in skills that will be of use in industry.

London and Birmingham Chambers of Commerce Oral Tests. Examinations held twice yearly at three levels of proficiency in many centres throughout the United Kingdom. Full details can be obtained from the London Chamber of Commerce.

The Institute of Linguists holds examinations in languages at five different levels. Successes at the two higher levels give the linguistic qualifications for the Membership and Associateship of the Institute.

The Royal Society of Arts organizes examinations leading to the Certificate for Secretarial Linguists and the Diploma for Bilingual Secretaries.

Reading list

BOOKS

Foreign Language Needs of Industry, Report of a Working Party (Federation of British Industries, 1964)

Guide to Modern Language Teaching Methods, Edited by Brian Dutton (Cassell, 1965)

On Teaching Foreign Languages to Adults, A symposium edited by Margaret Lowe and
John Lowe (The Commonwealth and International Library, 1965)
Technical Translations—Notes for Guidance of Firms, Supplement to the CBI Education
and Training Bulletin (CBI, January 1967)
*The First Report of the Committee on Research and Development in Modern Languages
(Chapter VII)* (Department of Education and Science, 1968)

Useful addresses

ASLIB, 3 Belgrave Square, London SW 1
Centre for Information on Language Teaching, State House, 63 High Holborn, London
WC 1
Institute of Linguists, 91 Newington Causeway, London SE 1
Institute of Directors Languages Centre, 10 Belgrave Square, London SW 1
London Chamber of Commerce, Foreign Language Unit, 69 Cannon Street, London EC 4

11. Physical Distribution and Purchasing

11.1 New Thinking on Distribution

F. R. L. Wentworth

Twenty years from now, physical distribution could be the main preoccupation of industry and by far its largest functional department. To express the revolution that is now taking place in these terms, while no doubt an exaggeration, does contain the seeds of truth.

Physical distribution spans the range of activities from the moment when goods leave the end of the production line right up to the time when they are delivered to the customer. It embraces both their transport and their storage, plus ancillary matters, such as certain aspects of mechanical handling and packaging.

The gradual growth in the importance of distribution begins to show itself if one looks at the main trends taking place in the other principal areas of industrial activity. In manufacturing, automation is growing all the time. In the office, machines and computers are taking over the work of armies of clerks. In marketing, the use of mass media such as television, the trend towards self-service, the concentration of buying power, and the growing use of telephone selling are all bringing about a reduction in the number of people employed in relation to throughput.

In contrast to these, distribution is to a great extent labour-intensive and much less amenable to mechanization or automation, at least in its delivery function: ultimately, virtually every parcel of consumer goods has got to be taken on a road vehicle to its final destination and there lifted or manhandled off. This will continue to be so, and the labour content in distribution costs is bound to continue to get larger.

At the same time, trade is developing more and more along international lines, with industry looking towards ever-wider markets in order to reap the advantages of large-scale production. This is inevitably increasing the cost of distribution.

Already in the United Kingdom distribution costs account, typically, for between 5 and 25 per cent of total turnover, and in the US 40 per cent is not unusual. The figure rises even further if the distribution content of bought-in materials is included.

It is, therefore, almost a matter for surprise to realize that until ten years ago almost no attention had been given to this crucial area of business activity. Until that time, management had, while no doubt realizing that transport and warehousing cost a lot of money, on the whole regarded them as inevitable costs.

Then, a changed attitude towards them began to crystallize in America through the interaction of a number of forces working at the same time. Competition, and its effect on profit-margins, led to searching investigations by business consultants, using the then newly fashionable techniques of operational research. At the same time, air transport, with its fantastic rate of growth in the passenger field beginning to lose impetus, started to look more carefully into the possibilities and uses of air freighting. Various technological advances, the continued rise in the cost of labour, and the upward spiral in property values, all contributed, too.

The result was the fundamental discovery that the transport and storage of goods are interrelated in a particularly close way, and that they need to be regarded as part of a single process, to which the name 'physical distribution' was given.

The term itself is reasonably self-explanatory but a little cumbersome, and it is generally reduced to the one word 'distribution'. This can cause misunderstandings at times, since it is a word that also has other meanings in other contexts. The 'distributive trades', covering wholesaling and retailing, are not in themselves a part of a manufacturer's own physical distribution, since this ends at the point of delivery. They are also, of course, concerned with the marketing of goods just as much as their physical flow into and out of the system. Similarly, marketing people often talk of achieving 'good distribution', by which they mean getting their products into a high high proportion of retail outlets.

This confusion no doubt accounts for the tendency of some marketing people to regard distribution as merely a branch of marketing—itself a relative newcomer in the evolutionary advance of business management. In its broadest sense, marketing is undoubtedly the mainspring of a firm's entire endeavour, but in the narrower sense of specialized and expert function, it cannot really hope to encompass the equally complex expertise of distribution.

Besides, experience has shown that distribution can best perform its task only if it operates on a par with the two other principal functions, marketing and production, both of which exercise a profound influence upon its costs. If it is allowed to be subordinated to either of the other two, its attitude will become slanted in that

574

direction, to the detriment of the business as a whole.

That is not to say that distribution can, or wants to, operate independently of the other two. On the contrary, its *raison d'etre* is to provide a service, on the one hand, to the customers, and, on the other, to production by acting as a buffer between it and the fluctuations of demand. The closest collaboration between all three is, therefore, essential.

At some point, a global view of the company must be taken to see where its best interests lie. It is not enough for the three principal departments to pursue their own separate goals in isolation. It may, for instance, pay the company to increase its distribution costs in order to provide an improved service that will lead to a competitive advantage and increased sales. On the other hand, it may be more advantageous to cut both service and the price. A great deal of work remains to be done on the precise nature of the interaction of customer service and distribution costs.

In the same way, production policy needs to be viewed in conjunction with distribution. For example, flexibility in production output can be traded off against warehousing space for buffer stocks. Some questions of policy involve all three departments, both directly and indirectly, each through the other two, such as whether or not to diversify and extend the product range.

One of the chief factors leading to the present explosion of interest in distribution is, as has been indicated, that it costs so much, and a great deal of the attention being devoted to it is concerned with cost reduction. From what has already been said it will be seen that distribution management has only limited control over its own costs. This is because the requirements placed upon it are determined by marketing and production policies. Within this framework, however, distribution's task—apart from questioning the assumptions underlying these requirements themselves every now and then—is to meet them at the least possible cost.

The first thing is to get the pattern or network of distribution right: assuming that coverage is national, should this be done from a single central warehouse, or from three, or a dozen, or fifty or even a hundred or more? For every industry and for every firm within an industry the answer will be different, depending on all the circumstances surrounding the product itself, its manufacture and its marketing, the volume of sales, and the customers.

Based on existing operations the distribution manager will seek to build up information on how costs would vary with a varying number of distribution points. The main constituent elements of distribution are trunking, storage and handling (including stock financing), and delivery. As the number of depots increases, the delivery costs are likely to fall, the storage costs are likely to rise, and the trunking costs may do either. What matters is that one should find the point at which their combined costs are at a minimum. This process of evaluation is termed the Total Distribution Costs approach.

One of the most striking applications of it can be seen in the rapid development of air freighting in the US, because of the reduction in lead-time and storage costs it has made possible.

In this country, too, even though air freighting is not as relevant (except for traffic to and from Europe), the effects of the new motorways, bigger road vehicles, the new vogue for containers and rail freightliners, are roughly similar. Companies who have re-appraised their distribution networks have often reduced the number of their depots or converted some of them to stockless transshipment depots.

Once the correct number of depots has been determined, and their best location fixed (generally near the main cities and conurbations for consumer goods, following a priority listing which combines the effects of weighting and distance), the boundaries between them can be drawn.

This procedure is in contrast to some of the theoretical and often quoted mathematical techniques which claim to discover the 'ideal' location for a depot within a given area. The point these theories overlook is that they beg the question by requiring the area to be 'given' in the first place.

In order to build up the information needed to do a total costs survey, it is almost certainly necessary to carry out detailed time and work studies of every operation throughout the distribution process, notably on the delivery vehicles. Apart from helping management to discover what is really happening—often different from what it believes is happening—work study provides the only reliable yardsticks by which to measure the efficiency of depots and compare them with each other. Other commonly-used statistics and cost figures can always be invalidated by arguing that circumstances are never the same at any two places.

Work study can also provide a means of improving the effectiveness of that key function, load-planning, by ensuring that every delivery driver and vehicle is given a full day's work to do every day. Mere reliance on experience and general know-how is not enough. Stemming from this, the same information is frequently used as the basis for incentive systems of payment, in substitution for the traditional time-and overtime basis, which encourages time-wasting.

Finally, work-study will highlight areas where better organization or the introduction of mechanical aids can improve productivity, leading perhaps, in some cases, to automatic or semi-automatic warehousing.

To return to total distribution costs, not only does the basic statistical information need to be available; just as important is the need for all the costs to be correct. This may seem self-evident, but in practice it can be a difficult and time-consuming matter to reform the accounting procedures of a company so as to do away with hidden cross-subsidies and to bring under the heading of distribution all the true costs associated with it.

One of the costs often not charged at full value is the cost of property occupation, where the property is owned by the company. Traditional depreciation-oriented accounting is clearly inapplicable in a situation where properties in fact appreciate.

The best answer is to set up a property department as a separate profit centre, charging distribution and other departments an economic rental at current market levels.

Another item often omitted is the cost of financing stocks of full goods. This is not an easy matter to determine because of the question of what rate of interest to apply, and what valuation to place upon the goods. But it is an exercise that must be done if the total distribution costs analysis is to have any real meaning.

There is without question a great deal of room for cost savings in British industry today in the field of distribution. Ignored for decades, it provides one of the last major opportunities for savings. There are clear signs that an increasing number of companies has come to realize this. There are more distribution managers in industry now than ever before, and their number is growing.

Efforts are being made through a number of professional institutes to provide the means for them to meet to exchange experiences and to build up a body of knowledge about problems that are common to many, such as stock control, depot location, the use of computers, work study, the cost of customer service, etc. At the same time, numerous private bodies, sensing the new awareness of distribution, are providing more and more seminars, courses, and conferences on the subject.

Once reorganization of a distribution network is complete, the distribution manager cannot, of course, sit back in the belief that his work is done. Markets, products, and the means of transport are all changing so rapidly nowadays that a continuous reappraisal needs to be made all the time to keep the system operating at peak efficiency.

Nevertheless, the present drive for savings at all costs appears, from American experience, to be only a passing phase. In America, this is being followed by a fresh approach. Having made all the savings that can be made, the fact remains that distribution is a large slice of total costs, and that it is getting larger. This is an inescapable fact of life. The new approach recognizes this in two ways: first, by matching the size of the task with appropriate management resources; and second, by seeking to make the best possible use of distribution as a tool of effective marketing.

It is a fact too little recognized that the act of delivery brings a company into the closest contact with its customers, and that this provides an unrivalled opportunity for creating customer satisfaction. This does not mean just pandering to the whims of customers, but a properly planned programme of research to find out how to serve his interests best, tied in with the whole of the marketing policy.

In Britain we have a long way to go yet, but a good start has been made.

Reading list

BOOKS

Physical Distribution Systems, J. F. Magee (McGraw-Hill, 1967)

Industrial Logistics: Analysis and Management of Physical Supply and Distribution Systems,
   J. F. Magee (McGraw-Hill, 1968)
Transport Finance and Accounting, G. A. Lee (Pitman, 1965)
Integration and Freight Transport, A. A. Walters (Institute of Economic Affairs, 1968)
Total Distribution—Key to Improved Sales Volume and Profit, W. M. Stewart (Industrial
   and Commercial Techniques, 1966)
Freight Transport Planning and Control, M. Turner (Business Publications, 1966)
Decision Rules for Inventory Management, R. G. Brown (Holt, Rinehart and Winston)
A New Approach to Physical Distribution, James Narbury *et al.* (American Management
   Association, 1968)

JOURNALS

'Distribution—Last Frontier of Cost Reduction', F. R. L. Wentworth (*Financial Times*,
   12 June 1967)
'Fleet Management Conference—Efficiency in Goods Transport, The Viewpoint of the
   User', F. R. L. Wentworth (*Commercial Motor*, 22 September 1967)
'Route Planning by Computer', F. R. L. Wentworth (*Data Processing* March/April 1967)
'Distribution Depots', F. R. L. Wentworth (*Freight Management*, February 1967)

Useful addresses

Institute of Transport, 80 Portland Place, London W 1
Road Haulage Association, 22 Upper Woburn Place, London WC 1
Institute of Materials Handling, St Ives House, St Ives Road, Maidenhead, Berkshire
National Joint Council on Materials Handling, 3 Dean Trench Street, Smith Square,
   London SW 1
Traders' Road Transport Association, Sunley House, Bedford Park, Croydon, Surrey

11.2 Cargo Interests and Shipping

Norman J. Freeman

The structure of transport, reflecting the immense technological advances in other industries, is changing rapidly. Economies of scale are being derived from the ever-increasing size of bulk dry cargo carriers and oil tankers. The principles of automation are being applied to the movement of a wide range of cargoes. The roll-on roll-off ships operating in the short sea trades carry significant tonnages of UK manufactured goods for distribution over the road systems of Western Europe. Air cargo is also expanding and is proving the normal method of transport for a wide range of goods. But it is the system of moving cargo in containers that has brought about profound changes in transport.

Containerization is one method of utilizing cargo to obtain reductions in handling costs, and of increasing the speed of ship's turn round time to gain the consequent capital savings. Indeed, the McKinsey Report has estimated that savings in costs of up to 50 per cent will be possible on some major container routes.

The growth of containerization, particularly the groupage system of packing, into one container, goods belonging to several different shippers, will encourage the development of the 'through transport operator' responsible for the routeing and the flow of goods from consignors to consignees by hiring the various transport services best suited to the needs of each particular trade. This overall control of a container's journey is the real revolutionary factor facing transport at the present time, not the use of containers as such.

The increase in labour costs over the last few years has given considerable impetus to the utilization of cargo on pallets or 'Lancashire flats', etc. This allows great savings, for it reduces the amount of cargo handling necessary in the consignment's 'through' transit from consignor to consignee.

An essential feature of container services is the establishment of inland clearance depots at which exports will be grouped and loaded into containers (and, alternatively, imports discharged) under Customs surveillance. The British Shippers' Council took a prominent part in establishing the conditions under which H.M. Customs would co-operate.

These developments have created new problems for shippers, and opened up new opportunities. Distribution costs are a vital calculation in the competitive situation, and exporters have to study virtually a new technology in the physical distribution of goods, and selection of the most efficient mode of transport for their needs. UK exporters now use through transport services, in particular to Western Europe, and are quickly adapting themselves to the concept of regarding Europe as an extension of the UK market. The final delivered price at the customer's premises thus becomes as important to the exporter as it is to the buyer. Traditional terms of sale such as f.o.b., f.a.s., or c.i.f. Port, are being replaced by 'delivered domicile' terms.

The physical distribution of goods is only one of many elements with which a total distribution policy is concerned. Production has to be aligned to the new systems, and stockholding policies in the UK and on the Continent revised in order to take advantage of quicker delivery times offered by the through transport system. An efficient marketing policy must be backed by an effective and sound distribution policy. Major companies engaged in international trades now determine and control these policies at Board level in order to achieve the maximum cost effectiveness. A flexible distribution policy able to adjust quickly to changing transport facilities is now an essential ingredient of transport cost control. An intimate knowledge of the transport market, either by the exporter or his agent is necessary for full exploitation of the cost saving potential.

The individual exporter or importer can do a great deal himself to secure distribution facilities and services adequate enough for his requirements; representation by the British Shippers' Council provides a means of determining a general policy at national level directed to deploying the commercial considerations attaching to international developments in transport.

The British Shippers' Council

The British Shippers' Council was formed in 1955 with the following terms of reference:

To consider, with the object of reaching a united view, all matters of policy on, and any major developments in, the relationship between shippers, shipping, air and other interests, and between shippers, port authorities and the Government so far as they affect the general interests of exporters and importers to and from overseas territories and, where necessary, home trade and coastwise shipping.

To enter into such negotiations, as a united body, may be deemed necessary and, when agreed, to seek the assistance and advice of such other bodies as may be desirable.

The BSC is organized as follows:

The Council
Composed of representatives of Full Members (trade and industrial associations) and Associate Members (individual companies), the Council meets at least twice in the year, and is the forum for the expression of views of Members and for the approval of lines of policy.

The Court
The function of the Court is to give authoritative support to the Council and also to assist in joint summit talks with shipowners and others in matters of major policy.

The Executive
A small elected body, which acts on behalf of the Council between meetings and co-ordinates and organizes the work of the Council. Members of the Executive serve for the contribution they can make in the interests of the Council as a whole and not as representatives of individual members.

Committees
The following specialist committees give detailed consideration to matters appropriate to them. Their members are drawn from the Council and are widely experienced in their particular subject.

Air Transport
Documentation and Procedures
Liner
Maritime Law
Ports
Short Sea Route and Coastal Shipping
Deep Sea Tramp Shipping
Containers

The BSC, although principally concerned with matters of policy at national and international levels, nevertheless carries out and is required to undertake a great deal of practical work in pursuance of its objectives. It is recognized as the national body in the field of the transport of cargo by sea and air by the UK Government, CBI, the Associated British Chambers of Commerce, Chamber of Shipping,

National Ports Council, Dock Authorities as well as, of course, shipping conferences and a number of airlines. In concert with other European Shippers' Councils it is recognized by the International Chamber of Commerce, the International Chamber of Shipping, and the United Nations Organization.

Co-operation with other European Shippers' Councils is carried on through the Documentation Centre, operating under a Secretary General and attached to the Netherlands Shippers' Council. Information concerning the activities of the Shippers' Councils is available on request to the Secretary of the BSC.

In recent years, most providers of transport services have improved their customer relationship services and are now better equipped to tender advice on facilities and services. They have also shown willingness to co-operate with substantial users to develop new practices and equipment. Many shippers find it helpful and economic to employ the services of shipping and forwarding agents to arrange the shipment or clearance of cargo, and these agents, too, are anxious to serve the cargo owner in an advisory capacity. The BSC, for its part, endeavours to keep its members appraised of its activities, and with practical information of use to shipping departments by means of a bulletin published approximately fortnightly.

The activities of the BSC fall roughly into three areas: (*a*) international field, (*b*) the day-to-day relationship between shippers and the providers of services, and (*c*) the encouragement and development of modern techniques in distribution.

In March 1963, the Ministers responsible for transport in ten European countries (and Japan) issued a policy statement of considerable importance. It was the outcome of several meetings covering the general field of the effects of governmental intervention in the commercial operation of international shipping, and more particularly recent US shipping legislation as interpreted by its regulatory agency, the Federal Maritime Commission.

European governments made it clear that they required to be satisfied that effective machinery existed for dealing with shippers' grievances against shipping conferences as well as unfair practices between conference members. The BSC was already directly involved in the USA situation because of its negotiations with the shipping conference serving the North Atlantic trade. United Kingdom shippers objected to signing a form of contract imposed on that conference by the FMC. Apart from the merits of the contract, as such, there was the much more serious objection to the intervention of the USA on shipping contracts made between British nationals.

Shortly after the formation of the BSC, various other West European countries formed shippers' councils, modelled on the same lines as the British, and by 1963 joint consultation between the councils was already well established. Plans for the setting up of consultative machinery with governments and other international bodies were also under discussion. The BSC, following the European governments' 1963 resolution, took the initiative in bringing together European shipowners and shippers to explore ways and means of achieving a better means of co-operation and consultation. On 21 October 1964, in London, European shippers' councils and European shipowners signed a 'Note of Understanding' setting up the machinery for consultation on matters affecting their commercial relationship. It is not practicable in this survey to detail the nature and consequence of this step, but there is no doubt of its importance and it is a good example of the practical work carried on by the BSC.

The need for shippers to ensure they have a voice in the policies adopted by the International Air Transport Association in the sphere of air transport is currently receiving the attention of the BSC.

Although dealing in matters of principle only, matters arising from day-to-day relationships occupy far the greater part of the BSC activities. The work is organized in such a manner that problems are considered, and action taken, by widely experienced persons drawn from the Council's membership. Indications of matters recently considered are:

Air Transport—development and decentralization of air services—structure of air freight rates—IATA procedures—handling and delays at airports—submission of the shippers' viewpoint to NEDO Committees and governmental inquiry.

Documentation and Procedures—simplification of export documentation—revision of H.M. Customs and Excise import procedures—standing deposit system.

Liner Committee—revision of Conference Contracts and agreements—the manifold matters arising from Conference Tariff Conditions including heavy lift surcharges—measurement rules—pallets and containers—port congestion surcharges. The adequacy of services and the general level of freight rates.

Maritime Law—the review of maritime legislation including the Hague Rules—limitation of liability—diversion and other clauses in Bills of Lading—arbitration procedures.

Ports—the reorganization of ports, the constitution of port authorities ensuring cargo user representation—review of the structure of port charges and their levels—availability of modern facilities and the adoption of efficient practices. Local Port Panels provide a means of liaison between the port areas and the Committee.

Deep Sea Tramp Shipping and Short Sea and Coastal—principles involved in Charter Parties generally—the facilities at the smaller ports and the cross-channel services—the availability of specialized ships and the seeking of an open market in unscheduled coastal rates.

Governmental and Private Bill Legislation—a parliamentary panel examines all Bills and advises on action deemed necessary.

Container Committee—the control of the through transport of cargo by one organization will radically change the attitudes of shippers, shipowners, forwarding agencies, insurance companies, etc. Talks between the BSC and potential container operators have already indicated that the new exclusive container services will be both simple and labour saving. Discussions between the Council and Overseas Containers Limited and Associated Containers Limited who intend to operate a container service on the Australia trade have proved particularly useful, as shippers have been able to advise shipowners on the service best suited to their needs and OCL/ACT have, in fact, amended some of their proposed procedures in the light of the BSC suggestions.

The support that BSC will give to such services will, of course, depend upon the costs of shipping containerized cargo. The Council is pressing strongly that the savings anticipated from containerization are passed on to the shipper in the form of lower freight rates, lower insurance costs, simpler documentation, and a speedier and generally more efficient transit.

These are but an indication of a few matters on which it has been found desirable to consider and advance the interest of the cargo user.

Reading list

BOOKS

International Shipping and Shipbuilding Directory (Published annually by Benn Brothers)
Through Transport to Europe, Economic Development Committee for the Movement of Exports (H.M.S.O., 1966)
Future Container Services: What Shippers Require, two reports (The British Shippers' Council, 1967)
Air Freight: Key to Greater Profit, Adrianus D. Gruenewegh and Roderick Hertmeyer (Aerad, Southall, Middlesex, 1964)
Air Cargo, H. Tapner (Cassell, 1967)
Air Freight and Anglo-European Trade (Hawker Siddeley Aviation, 1961)

Useful addresses

International Cargo Handling Co-ordination Association, Abford House, Wilton Road, London SW 1
Lloyd's Register of Shipping, 71 Fenchurch Street, London EC 3
British Shippers' Council, 21 Tothill Street, London SW 1
Association of British Chambers of Commerce, 68 Queen Street, London EC 4
International Chamber of Commerce, British National Committee, High Holborn House, 52–54 High Holborn, London WC 1
International Air Transport Association, Berkeley Square House, 6th Floor, Berkeley Square, London W 1

11.3 The Impact of Containerization

David E. Gibbs

'The present debate in this country is not concerned so much with whether containerization will come at all—it is with us now—as with the rate at which it will take place.'

Some people may think that such an emphatic statement on a revolutionary medium of transport could be made only by an enthusiast with his head in the clouds. In fact, it is an extract from the Government's White Paper on the Ministry decision over the Portbury Harbour project. However, the bald facts reflected in the statement are true. A build up of container services between America and Europe has begun, and the pace is increasing.

No one could possibly welcome the word 'containerization' to the English language, but its practical effects should be welcomed even by those who may find the system a major upheaval to their traditional methods. But, there may still be many who are asking what is it all about, and how will it affect me?

Method of operation

The concept of containers is that it is cheaper, quicker, and more efficient to transport goods in bulk rather than piecemeal. Basically, a ship is a container, transporting a large quantity of individual items in bulk from one port to another. Unfortunately, the conventional method of loading and unloading a ship takes a long time. The

20

process is known as 'breaking bulk', and two to three weeks is not an uncommon period needed to empty and refill a ship with its cargo. The ship is a very expensive 'prime mover', and costs, even excluding fixed charges such as depreciation, can mount to around £750 per day to the shipowner, because of port charges and loss of earnings on a capital asset. The ship is earning money only while she is transporting goods, and as a result of the slowness of the traditional loading process, she is probably earning money for little over half the year only—particularly if she is engaged on relatively short sea routes—and a far quicker method of loading the ship is needed to produce an efficient use of shipping resources.

It was this situation that caused an American truck operator, Malcolm McLean, to become interested in, and to revolutionize, modern shipping trends. He considered shipping to be the same as trucking without the wheels. A form of container had been in use for many years in this country with British Rail, mainly for the Anglo-Irish service. But McLean developed it into a complete service, extending his trucking expertise into shipping. He took the view that if the ship could be loaded with a set of prepacked boxes by a new type of high-speed crane, so that there was a predetermined number of crane cycles, then turn round time could be cut dramatically, and loading and unloading could be carried out simultaneously. There would be no more fiddling around in the ship's hold with numerous packages of varying weights and types requiring different loading processes. The whole operation could now be uniform. Late arrival of small cargo loads, which disrupted loading patterns, could be eliminated, as the ship took only a box, or container, that had been packed at a factory or assembly point.

It was essential that the whole system should be controlled by a computer, and now McLean's company—Sea Land Services—claim that at any time they can tell any customer where his container is anywhere in the world.

This was how container transport was developed in America on local shipping routes. The speed of the development was startling in that, although the operations have been going only for some ten years, American transport is now container orientated. Sea Land Services Inc. itself had a remarkable growth, and in the period 1960–64 saw their revenue from container operations more than trebled from 26·8m to 83·6m dollars.

By 1964 it had become apparent that the system would be extended into world-wide use, and if maximum benefit was to be obtained, uniform standards of equipment must be agreed. An international standard has now been drawn up, and the containers themselves conform to dimensions of 8 feet square by multiples of 10 feet up to 40 feet in length. Ships have no agreed standards, but the hulls of the prospective generation of container-ships will be fairly similar, looking not unlike oil tankers with crews' quarters and funnel at the stern. The rest of the ship is made up of cells, with slides to hold the container in place and enable them to be stowed exactly, one on top of the other, up to six high. The conventional pattern of holds

586

with relatively few hatches is dispensed with, as the containers are stacked in rows down the whole length of the ship and are dropped vertically into their guides. This method of stowage means that, when the ship docks, reloading can take place as soon as one complete stack of containers has been taken off. As the largest twin-lift container crane can cope with unloading thirty containers (and reloading the same number) within an hour, it can be seen how even a large ship carrying up to 1,200 containers can be turned round in a remarkably short time.

Although the major innovations are taking place in the shipping industry, this represents only one stage of a container's journey. The advantages of sending merchandise in a container are that the goods are packed in it as near the point of origin possible, and not unpacked until they are as near their destination as possible; continual handling of the goods is avoided, and the container itself is handled only when it changes from one mode of transport to another; the risk of breakage to the contents, provided the loading of the container has been carried out expertly, is greatly reduced, as is the risk of pilferage; the time taken for the through transit from beginning to end can be cut dramatically.

Not every manufacturer will be able to fill a complete container at any one time, and so assembly areas are being set up in the United Kingdom around some of the main container ports and industrial centres. These are known as 'containerbases'. Here the loading and unloading can be carried out by experts. Customs facilities will be provided, and the area will have road and rail links to the principal ports. By removing the detailed cargo movement and handling operations from the immediate port areas, this will reduce congestion and help the ports to concentrate upon their primary task of speeding the turn-round of the ships. Both road and rail transport are likely to be used between dockside and containerbases, and also between the individual containerbases. For journeys exceeding the 100/150 miles range, rail transport becomes more economical. The attraction of long-distance rail hauls has been underlined recently by the McKinsey report on containerization.

Effect on the user

Probably one of the questions most frequently asked about containers is, what materials or goods are most suitable for containerization? The answer is virtually anything. At the moment, we have bulk carriers for oil, grain, and cargo of this type. These carriers are really outsize containers, for the cargo requires no packaging, and is pumped on and off the ship in a continuous operation. To load this type of cargo into a container would be a retrograde step. But any other type of cargo, which requires a crane to lift it and load it into the ship is suitable for a container. It should be remembered that a container is itself a form of package and, therefore, particularly where a manufacturer can utilize its total space, a saving can be made on individual packaging costs.

A change in export delivery patterns is likely to develop over a period as the technique for container transport becomes more accepted at the manufacturer's end. Where a steady supply of goods is exported to an overseas customer, both sides may find it more convenient, and the manufacturer cheaper, to supply larger quantities at less frequent intervals. This will enable the manufacturer to utilize a whole container himself, and have it delivered straight to his customer, where the goods will be unloaded, having remained sealed and untouched since they left the factory. With the advent of a through Bill of Lading on a door-to-door basis, limited to a single document and a quotation for an overall charge, it will become far easier to quote a 'delivered' cost. Further, for some companies who have overseas subsidiaries, it is already being discovered that certain components can be manufactured far more cheaply in one area than in another. In such situations a regular container service between individual factories and an assembly plant can materially cut the overall cost of the final product.

Other forms of container system

It is around ships that the main interest in container transport is centred at present. However, with the advent of the jumbo jets, air transport of containers is likely to make an impact. Aircraft are also highly expensive 'prime movers' and, therefore, should not be kept waiting on the ground longer than necessary. This new generation of aircraft is likely to accelerate a more sophisticated rail and road interchange at airports. It is essential that the size of air-container conforms to the module of the 8-foot square 10-foot length standards.

A further extension of containers arises, that of inland distribution. Multiple retail chains may well adopt a containerized delivery service from central distribution warehouses. These would be far smaller—perhaps filing cabinet size—but complementary to the standard international container. They could be painted in the company's livery, and even double as display cabinets so that the merchandise could be sold directly out of them. If the loading of the container can originate in the factory the elimination of packing would be an obvious benefit. Goods could come straight from the production line and be stored in the container, perhaps in the open air, and sold direct to the customer without any intermediate handling. The vehicle making the delivery can have an automatic unloading device to enable the operation to be done by one old man or boy, thus cutting transport costs and periods during which the vehicle is halted.

Services available

Container transport services between the United Kingdom and America are already in being, and are increasing steadily. Likewise, more and more of the European trade is turning to containers, which was facilitated when British Rail started their container ship service from Harwich to Zeebrugge and Rotterdam. These ships are fed by Freightliner trains in this country, and link with the international deep-sea container services operating from European ports like Rotterdam.

In 1969, a radical transport revolution is taking place on the trade route between the United Kingdom and Australia. Two consortia of British shipping companies have been formed. Associated Container Transportation, comprising: Ben Line Steamers Ltd, Blue Star Line Ltd, Cunard Steam-Ship Co. Ltd, Ellerman Lines Ltd, Harrison Line, and Overseas Containers Ltd, comprising British and Commonwealth Shipping Co. Ltd, Furness Withy & Co. Ltd, P & O Steam Navigation Co., and Ocean Steamship Co. Ltd. These two consortia offer, from 1969, a regular service with nine containerships from Tilbury to Freemantle, Sydney and Melbourne, with a 'feeder' service connecting Sydney and Melbourne to other Australian ports.

The Australian service may well prove to be the most comprehensive system yet seen in the way of container transport, since it can provide, if required, the carriage of the cargo the whole way from manufacturer to customer. One overall charge would be quoted for the through journey (even perhaps inclusive of insurance), documentation would be reduced to one item, and the date on which the customer is to receive his consignment would be guaranteed.

The entire system will be computer controlled, working like the BOAC booking computer, with inputs at both ends of the service, in order to provide space and containers when and where they are needed. Further, the computer will be controlling the full co-ordination of road, rail, and ship movements, and terminal and container base operations. It may even extend its use into providing all the documentation from manufacturer to consumer.

Cost to the user

The ultimate question that always will arise in the manufacturer's mind when any established systems are changed, is, how much will all this cost? The short answer is, certainly no more than at present.

What should be remembered is that it is the container that is the constant member of the whole transport chain. Therefore, the overall position of transport—road, rail, and sea—must be considered in order to see how cost patterns in the future will be altered.

Introduction of the container is entailing very heavy initial expenditure—the Port of London £20 million, Overseas Containers to the order of £45 million, many others spending similar amounts. In the past, the transport industry has been moderately labour intensive, and it is now turning into a heavily capital intensive industry. It is, therefore, likely that there will, in the future, be a far more stable overall price pattern than has been the experience in the years since the last war, with their continual rises in labour costs. For instance, ships will be turned round in hours instead of days or weeks, and the labour required to do this should be reduced to one tenth of that needed previously. Ships' crews can also be severely reduced, which should mean that rising costs of labour in the future will only marginally affect the total transport cost, whereas the present waste of time and under-utilization of capital equipment all fall expensively on the manufacturer of the goods. A recent Port of London survey of the flow of road traffic around the docks found that 36 per cent of all lorries entering the area were carrying less than ten hundredweight of cargo, and 63 per cent less than two tons. Such wastage of resources, and resulting congestion, shows why transport costs and delays increase. In the container system, the ratio is expected to be one container-carrying vehicle to three or four conventional vehicles, and each container of the 20-foot type will carry, on average, a load of 10 tons.

Container services are intended to be an overall through-transport system on a door-to-door basis. Therefore, although it is possible to join and leave the system at any point up to the final port assembly area, the further back down this chain it is joined, the more advantageous the cost, the speed, and the reliability: both these last affect the cost. To some, costs will materially decrease, to others the cost may appear much the same, but in all cases the customer can expect to receive his order in better condition with more reliability and speed, plus an intangible cost saving through improved goodwill.

The future

What we are seeing now is the birth of worldwide container transport, but how this will develop in the future is difficult to foresee. It originates by taking the most expensive prime mover—the ship—and utilizing it to the maximum. The ultimate ideal is to have the ship continually at sea without even calling at ports, where the dense marine traffic slows speed, and the need to tie up for discharging and loading all consume time. Current container-ship development is taking place only on main world trade routes where there is sufficient two-way trade to justify a regular service, since there is no point in starting an expensive service that is full one way and nearly empty the other.

One might well envisage a fleet of giant 'mother' container-ships circling the globe on a fixed route, whose complement of containers would not be carried as at present in cells, but in fast barges, like the wartime landing craft, which would act as a mobile container for containers. The circling 'mother' ships would form the nucleus of an international transport service, rather like the Inner Circle Underground in London, or a continuous conveyor belt, with strategically sited staging ports round the globe, some of them perhaps islands. When the 'mother' ship passed these staging ports, the predetermined barges would be released with their container cargo, and other barges would join, all under their own power. The released barges would then transfer their containers at the staging ports (where more localized services would operate), thereby providing an efficient interchange system, and a feeder conveyor belt at right angles to the global one. It would mean that if, for example, there was an export trade from Brazil to Great Britain, but Brazil's main imports came from India, then a staging port, in say the West Indies, would operate a two-way container service for Brazil. Likewise, other staging ports would be located near Great Britain and India, providing the local services for these countries. The Brazilian exports would go on the local service to the West Indies, join the global 'mother' ship and be released at the British staging port entering the country on the local service, the same happening with India, but in reverse.

Improbable science fiction? Perhaps! But remember that much of the science fiction written ten or fifteen years ago is already fact, and some is now superseded.

Reading list

Containerisation: The Key to Low-cost Transport A report for the British Transport Docks Board (McKinsey & Co., London, 1967)
Report on Containerisation (National Joint Council on Materials Handling, 1967)
'International Cargoes: a Special Survey', (*Investors Chronicle*, 14 April 1967)
'Containers: *The Times* Special Survey', (*The Times*, September 1967)
'Container Transport', (*The Times* Supplement, 30 November 1966)
'Container Transport' (*Financial Times* Supplement, 8 May 1967)
'The Container Revolution' (Reprint from *Far East Trade and Development*) (Lawrence French Publications, April 1967)
'Cargo Revolutions to Speed Britain's Exports' (*The Illustrated London News*, 7 October 1967)
'The Great Container Gamble' (*The Times*, 13 August 1968)

JOURNALS
Containerisation International (Hulton Publications, monthly)
Ports and Terminals (Maclean-Hunter, monthly)

Useful addresses

National Joint Council on Materials Handling, 3 Dean Trench Street, Smith Square, London SW 1
Institute of Materials Handling, St Ives House, St Ives Road, Maidenhead, Berkshire
Associated Container Transportation, 12 Camomile Street, London EC 3
Overseas Containers Ltd., St Mary Axe House, London EC 3
International Cargo Handling Co-ordination Association, Abford House, Wilton Road, London SW 1

11.4 National Transport Planning

Denys Munby

National planning is inescapable for the transport industries, with implications not only for firms directly concerned with transport, but for all firms, almost without exception. Transport planning can only partially be a matter for government decision by civil servants, economic planners, and local authorities and other public bodies. Most of the day-to-day decisions involving the movement of people and goods are made by individuals and firms. However rigidly the planners set the framework, and however much or little they regard what happens outside, the actual operations are outside their control and have to be taken into account in the formulation of their plans. The users hold the key position, and the more coherently they frame their own demands, the more coherent is likely to be the national framework. Private transport planning is both an aid to national planning and a check on it.

Why is national planning inescapable? The first reason is that major transport infrastructure takes at least five years to complete from the first decision to go ahead, and the assets are then likely to have a technical life of twenty or thirty years or more, and maybe an economic life of much the same length. Much transport infrastructure is everlasting, to all intents and purposes, and has a low rate of obsolescence. One has only to consider the nature of the basic equipment of ports, airports, motorways, or railways. This means that the Government has to plan ahead not merely for five, but for twenty or thirty years.

For some investments, such as the Channel Tunnel, it is possible to make fairly straightforward forecasts of demand, subject to all the errors that are involved in any forecasts for long periods ahead. In such a case the asset is highly specific and the demand for it can be assessed with relation to the present demand for similar services and the likely trends in the future. Another example where these kind of forecasting methods can be used is the third London Airport. Here again, the demand for what is, in effect, a national airport can be directly assessed more or less independently of other decisions. But these investments are rather rarer than those where transport decisions have to be related to all sorts of other decisions.

In more general instances of planning, the decisions about transport infrastructure not only affect such major variables as the location of industry and the distribution of population, but also themselves depend on them. It is, in principle, impossible to make rational transport plans without knowing what the pattern of distribution of the population is going to be twenty, thirty, or forty years hence. This is clearly an enormous problem, as government policy is not yet, in most countries, in a position to make firm decisions about what is likely to happen over this long period.

The publication of strategic plans for the various regions is the first step towards formulating a long-run national policy. But these plans are still very tentative, and it is not certain how far they will form the basis of government policy. Policy makers are rather reluctant to make firm decisions when they do not have to do so immediately. But there is more than their reluctance that is at stake. We know so little about the economic and social factors that would desirably be required before we are able to make a rational decision, that it is natural to hesitate. There are uncertainties about the basic factors determining the level of the population twenty or thirty years hence, though these are among the more certain of the necessary forecasts. Far more important is our ignorance as to the economic costs involved in development of various kinds in various places. Should we, for example, develop a small number of very large modern cities of a million or so in size, and if so, how should we set about developing them within a reasonable time period? Should we concentrate on the accepted pattern of new towns scattered in orbit round the major conurbations or should we concentrate rather on linear towns spread along lines of communication? On the industrial side, how much do we know about the alternative patterns of industrial location? Are there real gains to be obtained from developing around the old conurbations? Are there losses that will inevitably follow a rather more scattered policy for industry throughout the country?

Granted these uncertainties, how are the transport planners to proceed? Admittedly, most of the major decisions about new towns and major industrial locations have much the same time pattern as the planning of transport infrastructure, that is to say, decisions have to be made five years in advance. But historically, in the years since the Second World War, apart from the planning of the first batch of new towns immediately after it, the transport planners have been ahead of the Ministry of Housing and the regional planners. As a result, we have been faced with a situation in which the regional planners have, notably in the 1967 strategic study for the South East, taken it for granted that the new urban developments must be tailored to the transport infrastructure that has been, rather independently, planned by the Ministry of Transport. In principle, this does not make a great deal of sense. Transport facilities should be provided to meet the needs of people and industry rather than people and industry being planned to fit into the transport infrastructure provided by an engineer.

In practice, the matter is rather more complicated. Essentially, the problem arises because the provision of transport infrastructure allows for surplus capacity in the early years of its life. This is true of most large projects such as motorways, airports, or ports. They have to be provided with some relationship to the existing flows of people and goods and, at the same time, to allow for the growth of demand over time. Thus, if it makes sense to provide a link between large centres of population, which is the basis of the motorway network evolved in 1960, and only to be completed by the mid 1970s, then it follows that there is spare capacity which can be used for the needs of new settlements along the line of this network. It can usually be shown that to provide entirely new links to meet the development of a newly-planned centre away from the established pattern of settlement will not bring in such a high return as the establishment of a link between existing settlements. Thus, the whole pattern of settlement becomes rigidly determined. The only escape from this would be if the development of the new centres was much more rapid than the general growth of traffic between established centres. But as, in fact, there are serious practical difficulties in developing new centres at a very fast rate, this may not often occur.

Ideally, what is required is the coordinated planning of the new settlements and the transport links, taking account of all the costs on both sides. By and large, this has tended not to happen. In the past, the new towns have been planned without much relationship to transport links and, vice versa, the new motorways have been planned without regard to new settlements of population. It is to be hoped that in the future these problems will be avoided. The new proposals for the South East allow for the development of new centres of population related to transport links with the old centres, and should enable the planning of a much more coherent structure both by the Ministry of Transport and the Ministry of Housing.

The matter is further bedevilled by the fact that we do not have any very good information about present flows of traffic. It is an astonishing commentary on our ignorance that, on the one hand, British Rail produced no figures of flows of traffic before the Beeching Report of 1963 (and even since 1963 the figures that have been made available are exceedingly limited), and, on the other hand, that nothing was known about the flow of goods from different centres to particular ports until the Martech Study was published in 1966. Information has been available about traffic

594

flows on roads for some time, but only on a scientific basis from 1956. These figures are of overall flows and tell little about the direction of traffic, though this has been the subject of particular origin and destination surveys in relation to particular projects such as the M.1. Only when the regional results of the 1962 Road Goods Transport Survey became available was much known about the flow of goods between different areas, though the Beeching Report did publish a map of road goods flows. Passenger flows between major centres are really not known at all. The information about private motoring is limited to that which has come out of motoring surveys, and tells very little about the detailed way in which people use cars. It is not, therefore, surprising that up to quite recently decisions about major transport infrastructure were made, to all intents and purposes, in the dark. Nor is it surprising that some extraordinary decisions have, as a result, been made, both in terms of the actual location of particular projects and the priorities given to different parts of the system.

It is only recently that the Treasury has adopted the best modern practice in the matter of investment appraisal, as shown in the recent White Paper on the nationalized industries. With the growth of information about flows and the use of more sophisticated investment criteria, it becomes possible in principle to produce more rational transport plans, but it is likely to be a long time before there is a comprehensive framework for rational planning. There are all the inevitable delays in decision-making in the Civil Service, which relies essentially on the cumbersome procedures of inter-departmental committees. The inherent secrecy of British government also makes it very difficult to make the maximum use of information available among outside experts and in the industries that will use the services of the assets the government provides. All too often this information becomes available only after the decision has been made and publicly announced. But, quite apart from all this, there would still remain enormous inherent difficulties in engaging in the kind of planning that would be more or less rational. Even the more sophisticated mathematical models, making optimum use of computers, are not likely to provide answers for the complex analysis that is required in most major decisions. The models are suitable for simple cases, but most of the cases in question are by no means simple. One has only to consider the question of deciding on priorities in the road programme or such a major development as the Portbury liner port project. (This is a very good example of the advantage that can be gained when the government publishes as much information as is available to it of the reasons that led to a decision being made. The decision about Stansted airport is a similar example.)

A further difficulty arises from the fact that these programmes have to be limited by the overall economic and budgetary needs of the country. A specific development such as the Channel Tunnel or the Third London Airport may go ahead once it has satisfied the criterion that it will pay for itself on the basis of an 8 per cent discount rate. But decisions about the motorways programme or the extent of electrification of British Rail can hardly be judged in this way. Not only do we not have a proper pricing system for the roads, so that it is not possible to say how much people would be ready to pay for a given road programme, but it does not necessarily follow that the Government would want to provide such a programme even if it could be assured on this point. It might well claim, as it does in fact, that it cannot allow such a large part of the nation's resources to be so used. It would, indeed, be less able to make this claim if it were possible to devise a rational pricing system for the whole road system, but the claim could still be justified. As the development of such a price system is a good way ahead in our present state of knowledge and the way our affairs are administered, it is quite likely that there will be under-investment or over-investment in such a programme.

But whether the actual programmes are too large or too small, it is not in fact possible in the case of transport infrastructure to arrive at an equilibrium situation immediately. Engineers tend to think of an equilibrium on the roads as being a situation where congestion does not exist at all and roads provide for the smallest peak needs. The same criterion, for example, of the thirtieth busiest hour has been traditionally applied to airport planning, and has been an important factor in the pressure of various interests for a rapid development of a third London Airport. From the economic point of view this does not make sense. Congestion or the temporary overloading of facilities, or even a more or less permanent use of facilities beyond some technical optimum, may make perfect economic sense. Further, in a world that is not in equilibrium, and where it is impossible to provide all the desired assets immediately, we will inevitably be faced with, for example, congestion on some roads and under-utilization of capacity elsewhere. Even in the perfectly simple case of an independent motorway designed solely for traffic between two points, one would expect the rational planning of this asset to result in a situation where for the first half of its life it was under-utilized, and the last part of its life subject to congestion, at least in the limited sense that there would not be a free flow of traffic. The economic level of congestion would depend on the costs of congestion as compared with the costs of building a new asset to reduce these costs earlier rather than later. A full economic calculation would not necessarily result in a second motorway being built as soon as congestion, in the ordinary everyday sense, emerged.

The co-existence in an industry of old high-cost plant and new low-cost plant is nothing strange; similarly, the co-existence, for as long as we can see ahead, of both congested and under-utilized transport assets in different parts of the country has nothing strange about it. However, it does imply that policy decisions affecting the current use of assets, either in the form of physical controls or of prices, should be aimed at making the best use of the newer and cheaper assets and restricting use on the older congested assets. Thus, road pricing for congested areas makes perfect economic sense, whereas tolls on motorways (but not on the substitute older roads) would discourage traffic from using the cheaper modern alternatives.

This leads on to the question of transport planning in the sense of governmental transport policy, as it is more commonly understood. A coherent policy for the construction of new assets over time requires, as its accompaniment, a policy for the rational use of those assets that exist at any given time. This involves all the contentious problems of nationalization; licensing of transport operators, and pricing policy, which have been the stuff of politics for many years. All too often, however, these policies have not been related to the policies for the construction of new assets, or aimed at the exploitation of the most modern technological improvements. Rather, they have tended to be used to bolster up the out-dated forms of transport, such as many railways and bus operations. A few general principles may be laid down on these matters without involving ourselves in too detailed discussion of current policies and their changes.

The first essential point in the field of transport is that the costs to the user, whether a passenger or a consignor of goods, are more than the actual costs of transport incurred by the operator. The user is concerned with all the costs involved in reaching the main transport route and moving from it to his final destination, as well as with all sorts of service elements (frequency of service, safety, certainty, damage, etc.). These cannot all be known either by the providers or by government planners. Thus, an essential part of any rational transport policy must be freedom of choice by would-be users. What the providers have to do is to see that their services are provided at proper costs so that the users' decisions are the best from the national point of view. This is why all forms of cross-subsidization are peculiarly harmful for transport. If services are cross-subsidized, then the user is not faced with the real economic costs involved and is liable to make wrong decisions, which lead to the waste of national resources.

Secondly, similar considerations apply to licensing. The units involved in both road haulage and road passenger services, namely the lorry and the bus, are small in relation to total flows. Capacity can be quickly increased and reduced. There are not, in the view of most economists, any serious reasons why these operations need to be subject to economic controls (as contrasted with controls for safety reasons). These are industries where the market can be expected to work reasonably well, far more than is true of many industries in private hands. The movement away from the rigid licensing control of road haulage operators, initiated in the 1930s, is thus to be heartily welcomed.

Thirdly, on the organizational side, to which governments have directed an inordinate amount of attention in the last thirty years or so, there is scope for organizations of many different kinds in most operational fields. This, however, applies much less to concerns such as the railways, which have inevitable technical advantages from large scale integration, or to airports, and, to a lesser extent, ports. Clearly, however, private industry needs to know what organizational framework the government favours, so that it can make its own adaptation to it. It would also be desirable that this framework should remain both flexible and more or less constant over time. This implies that there can be no rigid form of organization for all the transport industries; nor does one exist at the moment.

Fourthly, a prime consideration in transport policy is the need to provide for flexibility in relation to technical progress. All sorts of changes, occuring both in industry and in distribution as well as within the transport industries, will affect the future pattern of our lives. Innovations in transport in recent years have been very considerable, and transport planning has to take account of the dangers inherent in rigid patterns that can only with difficulty be changed to take account of new facts.

The most important developments in recent years have been, not so much those associated with dramatic technological changes and new inventions, as those involving the better organization of overall transport flows. The container is likely to be more revolutionary in its effect than the mono-rail and the hovercraft. It is, in many ways, surprising how quickly the container idea has spread with the development, on the one hand, of the liner train network and, on the other hand, the acceptance by shipping companies of the need to build new container ships to handle traffic in ways quite different from those they used in the past. The development of new container berths at major ports and the creation of inland clearance depots will affect the whole pattern of goods movements throughout the economy. Transport becomes an integrated operation from consignor to consignee. The growth of the road haulage industry and the use of C licences by firms to deliver their goods to their own outlets or to independent shops was a foretaste of what the container brings about in a bigger way.

Far too much attention in the past has been given to competition between different forms of transport in providing the same services. Now it becomes even clearer than it was that the real problems arise in integrating the overall flow of goods with the use of many different forms of transport. As a model, one may take the integrated transport of oil by the oil industry, where the size of ships, the provision of ports, and the construction of pipe-lines related to local distribution in road tankers is all part of one great industrial operation. The transport of raw materials for the steel industry might be another example. Many more industries need to think in the same way of their transport problems. The growth of the movement by containers gives them the opportunity to do so. Strangely enough, this is a field where the government planners have a great deal to contribute. It does not seem that hitherto they have devoted as much attention to this problem as it deserves.

This section of the chapter has sketched very briefly something of the scope of the present transport planning in this country, and the problems it faces. It has left on one side the enormous complex of issues involved in replanning cities and providing for their traffic needs, which are only beginning to be touched as overall transport surveys are published and new tools of policymaking become available. Important as these issues are for many industrial problems, it is the basic pattern of the inter-urban network and the location of the major port and airport facilities that will determine the main decisions in the manufacturing sector. If directors are to make the best decisions in their own interest and those of the country as a whole, they need to know what the pattern is likely to be. Equally, government planners need to be informed by the most scientific analysis of their own problems by the firms themselves. As indicated above, this analysis has to be much more far-reaching than a mere comparison of rail and road haulage costs, and must involve the optimum location of the various processes of production and of stock-holding depots, as well as a consideration of the overall flow of goods into and out of the factory to their final destinations.

Reading list

Transport and Public Policy, K. M. Gwilliam (Allen & Unwin, 1964)
Traffic in Towns: A Study of the Long Term Problems of Traffic in Urban Areas: Reports of the Steering Group and Working Group appointed by the Minister of Transport (The Buchanan Report) (H.M.S.O., 1963)
Buchanan and After (British Road Federation, 1964)
The Transport Needs of Great Britain in the Next Twenty Years (The Sir Robert Hall Report) (Ministry of Transport, 1963)
I Tried to Run a Railway, Gerard Fiennes (Ian Allan, 1967)
Road Pricing: The Economic and Technical Possibilities (Ministry of Transport, 1964)
The Development of the Major Railway Trunk Routes (British Railways Board, 1965)
Research on Road Traffic, Road Research Laboratory (H.M.S.O., 1965)
The London-Birmingham Motorway: Traffic and Economics, Coburn, Beesley and Reynolds (Road Research Laboratory—H.M.S.O., 1960)
Portbury: Reasons for the Minister's decision not to authorise the construction of a new dock at Portbury, Bristol (Ministry of Transport, 1966)

Useful addresses

Ministry of Transport, St Christopher House, Southwark Street, London SE 1
National Ports Council, 17 North Audley Street, London W 1
Road Research Laboratory, Crowthorne, Berkshire

11.5 Storage and Warehousing

K. Trickett

The function of storage in the industrial context occurs mainly in the chain of movement of goods from raw material source to producer and thence to consumer, and was long regarded as a minor or at least unavoidable cost element in the whole process. With the introduction of more automatic and consequently cheaper processes of manufacture and transportation, however, the cost of storage and warehousing is becoming significant, and increasing attention is being paid to it. The computer is being used for the calculation and control of optimum stock levels and very sophisticated handling devices are being introduced to reduce labour costs. The degree to which these advanced methods will be applicable clearly varies with every case, and my purpose here is to outline the more important factors involved in the problem.

To establish some basic cost dimensions it may be assumed that a store or warehouse will be housed in an industrial type building costing about £4 per sq ft to construct, excluding site cost. In the simplest arrangement where the goods are stacked on the floor to a height of, say, 6 ft the floor area will at best be some 40 per cent utilized, after allowing for access gangways. Given an average density figure of 40 cu ft per ton for the goods, the capital cost of simply housing them is then £66 per ton. The 'cost in use' of the building (that is all the building expenses including amortization) will be of the order 10s. per sq ft, so that the annual cost of accommodation will be some £8 per ton. The labour costs involved in handling the goods in and out of the store will, of course, depend upon their nature and the methods employed, but given largely manual methods and the average run of consumer goods, this would be about £1 to £2 per ton. Labour costs will rise sharply from this basic figure as operations such as goods inward checking and inspection, unpacking, repacking, orderpicking etc. are added. It would be dangerous to generalize further but it will be seen that speaking in terms of goods, the sales value of which might be £300 per ton, the cost of even the simplest storage operation becomes significant in relation to the profit margin.

To minimize accommodation costs, the obvious step is to increase the stacking height in the warehouse. The practical method of doing this is to introduce storage racking, but as this increases in height, accessibility problems arise. These problems become more acute where the 'traffic' through the warehouse is heavy, and quite complex systems of picking towers, stackers, and conveyors are now coming into use to overcome the difficulties. Almost every warehouse is a special case and there can be no universal formula, but the following will describe some of the more advanced ideas and designs being brought into use in the various sections of modern warehouses and stores.

Goods inwards

With the increasing use of palletization, the fork truck is becoming the most common form of transportation in the receiving bay. Dock levellers are therefore becoming a necessity on raised loading banks to allow the trucks to move off the bay on to the transport vehicle decks. At the same time it should be noted that where goods are received mainly on open-deck vehicles, the fork truck can eliminate the need for a raised loading bank altogether. This gives much greater freedom of movement and may reduce building cost.

Mobile conveyor systems are also coming into use on the receiving bay, but the adoption of mechanization generally is limited by the lack of standardization in pallet sizes, carton sizes, or methods of packing. Unfortunately, most organizations have to accept these conditions but there is no doubt that if closer co-operation between receiver and supplier could be established, substantial improvements in receiving bay procedure and methods could be made.

When removed from the delivery vehicle there are often advantages in palletizing all incoming goods on a standard pallet or placing them in a standard container. In this way they are formed into a unit load which offers many opportunities for subsequent mechanized handling.

Storage

In a normal 'manual' warehouse today, the goods will probably be brought in to the storage point from the receiving dock by a fork truck. The height to which the goods can be stacked is limited by the necessity for them to be manually 'picked' for issue. Consequently, the stacking height may be no more than 10 feet and the warehouse/site area ratio is low. If multi-storey, then the building will be expensive.

The manual 'pickers' will circulate in the storage area picking possibly two or three orders on one circuit. The time spent in walking and searching will be a high proportion of the total time, but the efficiency of the operation cannot be improved because experience shows that the 'picker' cannot deal with more than about three orders without making an excessive number of errors. Another limitation may lie in the volume of goods the picker will accumulate on the 'walk'. Even the provision of a truck may not be sufficient to cope with the volume of goods collected and the picker loses efficiency, again, by the need to return frequently to the despatch point.

Improved efficiency in storage can be achieved by stacking high and warehouses are now being built to stack (usually in racks) up to 60 feet. Such heights mean the use of special stacker cranes or floor-mounted high-mast fork truck devices to get the goods into the racks, but the resulting economical use of expensive site area yields overall savings.

With the goods in high racks it is necessary to provide the 'picker' with some means of traversing the high rack face. This can be done by a variety of means, the most sophisticated being a travelling picking tower incorporating a lift. To take away the large volume of goods collected, a system of conveyors from the tower to the despatch point may be provided. In a warehouse with a small number of lines (say, 100 or less) all packed in standard cartons, the automation man's dream may be realized and the goods may be automatically ejected from the racks on to the conveyor system. This dispenses with the order picker, but with the variety of packs and shapes to be dealt with in the average warehouse it is seldom possible to do this.

The kind of equipment installed will vary with the traffic pattern, that is to say the number of lines, the frequency of demand of each, the total throughput, and so on. If the throughput is great enough, it may be better to scrap the conventional conception of storing the goods statically in racks or at fixed points and to store them on some form of moving conveyor, having fixed input and output stations. In such a case the goods are brought to the picker instead of the picker going to the goods. Only very heavy throughput warehouses would justify such a system, but there are organizations in the United Kingdom that deal with distribution traffic of this magnitude.

The advent of the computer will clearly have a major effect on warehousing techniques in general. Not only does it provide a means of keeping stock records and traffic statistics in far greater detail than has been practicable before, but also the random storage principle can be adopted, and substantial space savings obtained because the computer memory can be relied upon to direct the picker to the storage points and work out the optimum route quickly and without difficulty. The computer can even direct the input storage crane or device to the available locations, and can do the same for the output picking tower. In the latter case, and to ensure maximum utilization of the equipment, the computer can summarize a number of branch orders in stock location sequence so that the picker calls at almost every location in a 'round'. If a summary of branch demands is picked in this way, the goods must be sorted into individual branch orders at the despatch point, and this again is possible and can be done automatically under control of the computer.

The degree of sophistication that is economically justified depends upon the nature of the goods and the rate of throughput, and most modern schemes differentiate clearly between the 'slow movers' and the 'fast movers' which will merit most attention in planning a highly mechanized scheme. It is of interest that, with consumer goods, the proportions are so often near to 20 per cent of the lines representing 80 per cent of the traffic, that the 80/20 'law' is often quoted in connection with distribution to retail outlets.

The principle of classifying the lines held by the warehouse and dealing with them in an appropriate manner is probably best exemplified at the new Boots Pure Drug Co. warehouse in Nottingham. This deals with 3,000 lines of toiletries which are divided into 600 small lines, 2,400 general lines, and 500 lines (also in the general section) handled in quantities not less than a 'minimum outer' (i.e. the one dozen or half dozen carton). The small lines are handled in a section of the warehouse that is almost entirely manually operated, the general lines in a more mechanized 'high rack' manner and the 'minimum outer' lines in a most sophisticated on-line computer-controlled section (Fig 11.1).

In all three cases a summary of a number of branch requirements is prepared by a data processing computer and is used by the pickers as a picking list. In the 'small lines' section, the total quantity of any line picked is immediately divided into the individual branch requirements, and placed into the separate compartments of a specially-designed pickers' trolly. In the 'general section' the summary of the requirements is first placed into a mobile sub-rack. This, in effect, is a primary pick, and the individual branch requirements are then picked as a secondary operation from the sub-store thus created. For the 'minimum outer' section, the summary of branch requirements is prepared by the data processing computer in the form of a set of punched cards, which are fed into a control computer that controls and directs a manned picking tower. As the summarized requirements of each line are picked, they are taken away from the picking tower by a parcel conveyor system and are split into individual branch requirements on a special sorting conveyor, the gates of which are operated by the control computer.

Probably the most important single advance in warehouse automation, and certainly the most universally applicable, is represented by the automatic retriever crane (Fig 11.2). This is a development of the stacker crane, and it works in a conventional rack system. It is completely automatically controlled, and from instruc-

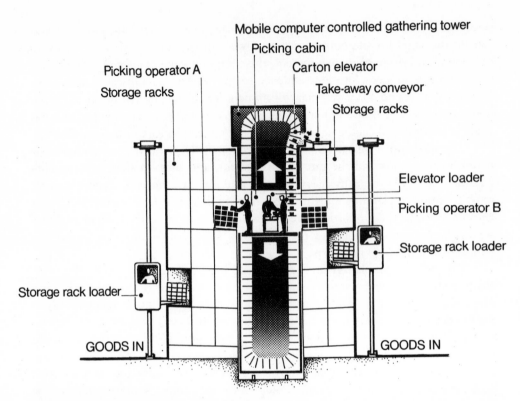

Mobile computer controlled gathering tower

Picking cabin

Picking operator A

Storage racks

Carton elevator

Take-away conveyor

Storage racks

Elevator loader

Picking operator B

Storage rack loader

Storage rack loader

GOODS IN

GOODS IN

Section of gathering tower - racks etc.

Fig. 11.1. A diagrammatic cross-section of the mobile computer controlled gathering tower and
storage racks in the 'minimum outer' section of the Boots distribution warehouse at Nottingham.
System designers: The P-E Consulting Group
Contractors: M.E.L. Equipment Company Ltd.

tions fed into the control unit from a punched card or by manual keying in, the
retriever can be directed to move to a given rack location, to extract a loaded pallet
or standard container, and to bring it to a fixed picking station. It will then return
the pallet or container to the racks. The retriever can be programmed to carry out
more complex cycles, and it is apparent that the control system could be developed
to provide a random storage facility if this were required.

At an installed cost of around £15,000 per unit it will be appreciated that automatic retrievers that permit high racking and, hence, site area conservation, and that
will frequently do the work of two operators with fork trucks, are becoming economic
in an increasing number of situations. Recent installations include the Vauxhall
Motors Ltd's spares depot at Toddington, Bedfordshire, Electrolux Ltd's spares
store at Luton, and the pressed parts store at the Castle Bromwich factory of
Pressed Steel Fisher. The new BEA/BOAC Cargo Handling Depot at Heathrow

Fig. 11.2. Two 30-ft high automatic retriever stacker cranes in operation in a domestic appliance spare-parts store. One operator controls the two retrievers which will handle 64 stillages in or out of the system per hour.

will incorporate thirty-eight automatic retrievers, and the device is being used extensively on the Continent and the USA.

Downstream from the picking operation, and when the goods have been sorted into order groups, considerable economies in labour can be achieved by installing conveyor systems and other devices, as appropriate. If a standard despatch container is in use, much can be done to mechanize subsequent movement and packing operations, and devices such as automatic lidding and strapping machines, automatic column makers, and automatic palletizing machines are commonly used. It will be appreciated that here again, if standardization in despatch containers and pallet sizes can be achieved, much can be done by mechanization to reduce labour cost. If the delivery vehicle fleet comprises standard vehicles, then it is possible to provide removable lorry decks which can be preloaded on the despatch bay, if necessary, in the appropriate sequence of 'drops'. The preloaded decks can then be quickly rolled on to the vehicles, which are thus off the road for an absolute minimum time. At the Courage, Barclay and Simmonds Ltd's bottling store at Southwark this method is in use and a vehicle arriving with a load of empties can be turned round and the fully-loaded vehicle on the road again within ten minutes.

Design

The modern trends in warehouse and stores design and the types of equipment available have been mentioned above. Basic procedure in preparing the optimum design for given conditions comprises a reconciliation between the equipment available, the nature of the goods, and the traffic pattern through the warehouse.

In establishing the traffic pattern, a very thorough factual analysis of the present or required material flow is an essential step. The number of orders per day, their range in volume and weight, and the relative popularity of individual lines are typical of the data that must be derived, often from examination of an existing operation. It is important that the process of data collection takes place over a sufficient period to cover the whole range of traffic conditions, and in this connection it should be noted that a warehouse or store usually fulfils a buffering function in the distribution chain. The traffic will, therefore, often be subject to wide fluctuations in volume, and it is useless to base a design on, say a weekly average throughput when, in fact, there are substantial variations from day to day or even from hour to hour.

Unfortunately, and because of the fundamental buffering function the warehouse or store has to fulfil, a high degree of overall efficiency similar to that achievable on a production operation can seldom be obtained. In a consumer goods warehouse, for example, seasonal variations added to daily fluctuations can result in throughput volume per day varying in the range of 4:1 or more over the year.

In reviewing the traffic data, the techniques of computer simulation can be particulary useful in predicting events at any possible bottleneck and, thus, indicating the design capacity that should be allowed. For example, the optimum number of vehicle bays to be provided on inwards or despatch docks can be determined. Similarly, the maximum queue length that might build up from the random arrival of items at a packing station can also be seen, and appropriate steps taken to limit it. Easy-to-use computer programmes have been developed for purposes of simulation and are available.

In most warehousing operations it is in the order-picking procedure that the greatest opportunity for effecting labour savings lies. In its simplest form, this operation is carried out by a number of stores hands, each of whom is given a branch order and told to go and collect it from the racks and deliver it to a despatch or packing station. The operator may have a trolley or some other form of carrier in which to carry the goods, and time studies on this kind of operation have shown that as much as 95 per cent of the operator's time has been taken up in walking and searching.

Clearly, for a given layout of racks, the distance to be walked and the degree of searching involved can be minimized by a choice of the optimum route, but since this will vary with every order, it may be worth doing only if a computer is available to do the necessary calculations. Another way to improve matters is to arrange that the operator collects more than one order at a time. Thus, one walk is spread over a number of orders, but it is found that errors begin to creep in if the operator is asked to deal with more than about three orders on one walk. To meet this difficulty, the operator could be given a summary of a number of branch orders to pick. This would mean that, having collected the summary, he would then have to take the goods to a sub-sorting station where they would have to be divided into the individual branch orders that made up the summary. Now this system of what might be called the primary and secondary pick has great possibilities if the orders can easily and quickly be summarized, and here again, use can be made of a computer if one is available. If not, the time spent clerically would make the operation uneconomic. There is nothing new in the principle of the primary and secondary pick, and in many manual warehouses where a relatively small number of lines are dealt with, it is usual to bring forward what is called a 'working stock' for picking purposes, the main stock holding being dispersed around the warehouse and often referred to as 'back-up' stock.

Some thought will show that the greatest efficiency will be achieved in the picking operation if the operator works from a summary of orders of such extent that he has to call at every bin location. However, only computer facilities for doing the necessary calculation work, and the kind of mechanization schemes previously mentioned to carry the goods away to the despatch point, will permit this to be achieved. The use of a retriever crane to bring the goods from the racks to a fixed picking location presents a different form of solution, and is likely to be increasingly adopted. At first sight, the use of a fairly complex and substantial piece of machinery to bring a pallet load of goods 100 ft or so, and then to take them back, simply to allow the operator to pick off a few items seems uneconomic. However, calculations deny this, mainly perhaps because electric power at $1 \cdot 75d$. per unit is about a thousand times cheaper than the same energy produced by the human body!

Future development

Now that the cost of operating warehouses and stores is becoming significant, directors will need to examine closely many practices accepted without question in the past. Measures taken to improve efficiency within the warehouse will impose limitations outside it, but these limitations need not necessarily become penalties if all concerned can be persuaded to co-operate. Palletization of goods, incoming and outgoing, is almost standard practice today but, unfortunately, pallet sizes vary widely. Consequently it is not possible to plan simply to place a load of goods on a supplier's pallet straight into the storage racks. Standardization of pallet sizes is being studied, and surely must come very soon.

With pallet standardization there will also need to be attention given to commercial terms of contract. Some manufacturers who have adopted a standard pallet size and proudly declare that their goods are delivered in a standard unit load, offer discounts on quantities which are *not* a multiple of the number of items accommodated on a pallet! On the customers side it will be necessary for purchase orders to specify modes of delivery, nature of packing, number of units per carton, minimum quantity per delivery, etc., in order that their mechanized and computerized warehouses can deal smoothly with the goods received.

Tradition may also be swept aside in the matter of carton sizes. The average despatch carton weighs something between 10 and 40 lb, and has been chosen mainly because it is the most convenient size and weight that a man can handle. However, for purposes of distribution it is often found that the quantities required by the customer vary from one single unit to a carton or a number of cartons. The capacity of automatic handling and conveying equipment is usually fixed by the number of packages per hour to be handled, and on the output side of the warehouse experience indicates that the total number of packages would be very much reduced if the original suppliers carton 'outer' were much smaller in size.

In the main distributive trades, at least, there is likely to be a warehousing 'revolution' in the next decade or so and it will hold lessons for the boardrooms of many companies. With the building of a national network of motorways and the railway liner train service, transport costs and problems will be minimized and an organization will be able to obtain all the advantages of scale and mechanization by discarding the network of warehouses and depots that it now operates and building one warehouse for national distribution. Such a warehouse, computer-controlled and highly mechanized, can reduce warehousing costs by as much as 50 per cent.

Reading list

BOOKS
The Automatic Warehouse, David Foster (editor) (Iliffe, 1968)
Automation in Practice, David Foster (McGraw-Hill, London, 1968)

A Guide to Stock Control, Albert Battersby (Pitman, 1966)

Production Control in Practice, K. G. Lockyer (Pitman, 1966)

More Efficient Warehouses through Modern Handling and System Techniques, Gordon Gale (Industrial & Commercial Techniques, 1966)

Statistical Forecasting for Inventory Control, R. G. Brown (McGraw-Hill, 1959)

Warehousing and Handling Finished Goods, A. B. Waters (Institute of Directors *Better Factories*, 1964)

'HOCUS' (Hand or Computer Universal Simulator) *National Computer Program Index* (National Computing Centre)

PAPERS

'The best location of a warehouse: a mathematical approach'

'The best location of an additional warehouse: a mathematical approach', 1963

'Central warehousing: purchasing procedure and layout', 1961

'Warehouse orders: an investigation into procedures', 1959

all published by DSIR (H.M.S.O.)

JOURNAL

'Computer Controlled 3,000 line store for 1,300 outlets', K. Mumby (*Mechanical Handling*, June 1967)

Useful addresses

Institute of Materials Handling, St Ives House, St Ives Road, Maidenhead, Berks

International Cargo Handling Co-ordination Association, Abford House, Wilton Road, London SW 1

Supermarket Association of Great Britain Ltd, 10 Cork Street, London W 1

National Computing Centre, Quay House, Quay Street, Manchester 3

11.6 Purchasing

C. E. Waller

Purchasing today is closely integrated with many other company functions. It now has a close association, for example, with design and production, an association where give and take permits purchasing costs to be reduced without any reduction in quality or technical performance.

And yet, purchasing remains a difficult function to define shortly. American industry has tended to adopt the word 'procurement', which embraces the whole aspect of buying, controlling, and storing raw materials, components, spare parts, and finished goods that a company may require. 'Purchasing' has been adopted in many British companies, while 'supplies' is a word that recommends itself to others. Those responsible for this broad function have a variety of titles, from purchasing director to stores controller, from manager of supplies to chief buyer, from general manager of merchandise to manager of material control division and, in some cases, simply, buyer.

A management function rather than a technique, the importance of purchasing in recent years has led to the development of techniques such as value engineering (*see* section 3.11) and vendor rating and supplier evaluation. Let me quote Sir Denning Pearson, chairman of Rolls Royce, on the subject:

> The senior purchasing people in a company should be involved in major decisions at a policy-making level. This means both, that the purchasing de-

partment must have a high status in a company, and that its manager should be either a director of the company at divisional or main board level, or have a very close link with the director responsible for the purchasing and supply function. If the purchasing department is to provide the most effective service to a company, the calibre of its staff is as important as the position in the organization held by its senior member.

The importance of the purchasing department, of course, will vary considerably, depending on the nature and size of the enterprise. Buying office supplies for a largely clerical operation does not demand the qualified purchasing staff so vital to a company manufacturing products whose pricing and profitability are crucially related to the cost of the materials brought in. The purchasing methods and decisions of a large international oil company have an economic and political significance to which the main board must give careful consideration. But whether purchasing is done by one man in informal consultation with other managers or a large department directly working with the board through a director, it must be related to the total activities of the company, including production and distribution. Its importance need not depend on the size of the staff: in a small textile firm, for instance, the purchasing policy of, say, the managing director can vitally affect the fortunes of the enterprise. What follows relates mostly to larger organizations, but the director can adapt its message to the requirements of a small business.

To make the policy suggested by Sir Denning Pearson effective, purchasing department staff, with appropriate knowledge, must co-operate in product design, in production, and with every commercial application at all levels. It is obviously important that purchasing staff should be accorded a professional status that will enable them to operate successfully within a company. To obtain trained and professional purchasing men, companies must undertake much of the training themselves. The nature of purchasing demands that a department must possess staff with a very wide range of abilities and experience. The purchasing manager must ensure that his team has a good mix of abilities, ages, and experiences, and that staff changes are planned well in advance so that the continuity of contact with suppliers may be preserved.

The purchasing function should keep top management informed briefly, concisely and regularly. The purchasing executives should keep their colleagues on the sales, finance, and distribution side aware of what is going on within their own sphere.

The subject of negotiation is, of course, immensely wide, important, and intricate. The purchasing man is talking with the full authority of his company, and the skill with which he carries through negotiations can determine the profitability of whole sectors of his company's business. The art of negotiation is a mixture of skill and common sense. Among the very necessary criteria are a carefully worked-out plan of operation, a knowledge of all the arguments for and against a certain course of action, a clearly defined objective to be reached in a negotiation, and a readiness to give a little in order to gain much.

Assuming that the purchasing man is armed with sufficient authority within his firm, he can play an important part in relation to specifications and standards. It goes without saying that precise specifications are needed for the purchase of all plant and equipment, and precise standards for all raw materials and commodities. It is not sufficient, however, for these things to be in existence. The purchasing man must be in a position to challenge these specifications and standards, and he must have a voice in establishing them. He has all sorts of tools at his disposal to help him in this respect, including value engineering and value analysis. He must constantly question and probe whether standards are too high for any particular material, because experience teaches that production executives, technicians, and quality control experts love nothing so much as a quiet life. By specifying one grade higher than is needed they are never operating at marginal efficiency. The purchasing man's job is to stop his colleagues sleeping so quietly at night, and keep them constantly on edge.

Advice from the purchasing department can often lead to the introduction of new techniques or to research and development work by suppliers without any financial involvement by the buyer, to the mutual advantage of both companies.

More and more, a company's purchasing staff is seen by discerning directors as providing an invaluable two-way bridge between itself and the suppliers of services, materials, and equipment. This means that the purchasing officer needs, today, qualities far higher than those of merely a tough bargainer on behalf of the company. Of course, economies will constantly be in his mind, but when he is negotiating shrewdly on behalf of his company, he is also, by his manner and approach, 'selling' his company to the suppliers. In some cases, his knowledge of the supplier's business philosophy and organization—which should rival his insight into the character of his own company—may mean that he must resist pressures from his own company superiors for short cuts to cheaper supplies, knowing as he does that the relationship between a company and its suppliers must be firmly based on long-term understanding and co-operation.

To develop secure relations with his suppliers, the purchasing officer needs, beyond a thorough technical knowledge of supplies and materials, something of the skills of the public relations man. He is in an extremely advantageous position to bring together, on occasions, and as regularly as possible, research and production representatives from his own company and the supplier to discuss joint problems and initiatives, to the benefit of both.

These general recommendations can be adopted to all sizes of company, but a practical illustration of what a reform of purchasing policies can achieve may be more helpful than further generalizations.

The shipbuilding industry has been criticized in the past as being especially slow to develop efficiency in its purchasing methods, and it will be useful to look at the experience of one large yard which decided, a few years ago, to appoint a purchasing director. Buying for a ship is as complex an operation as buying for a town—the same basic services have to be provided, but the buying also encompasses such refinements as games for the ship's crew and pictures for the captain's cabin. When he arrived at the yard, the purchasing director found that each section was doing its own buying on its own terms, and that there was no central control even for such widely used items as tubes, nuts, and bolts. These were being purchased to a variety of specifications, many of which were unnecessary, and usually in quantities far in excess of usage. The first step, therefore, was to centralize as much of this buying as possible, to make accurate estimates of usage, and to reduce stocks across the board. In fifteen months, a reduction in stocks amounting to £55,000 was made.

The stores were also reorganized. Previously, there had been twenty-six stores scattered over the yard, with one manager, on his own, to supervise them all. The stores were resited nearer to the base where the work is being carried out, thus economizing in handling costs and time, and section leaders have been appointed, each with five stores to control. Whereas before there were no mechanical handling aids, containerization or palletization, now there is a model stores layout.

The purchasing director's philosophy is to get as near to stockless buying as possible. With a revised stores system, involving punched cards and computerization, he gains an accurate estimate of monthly usage and movement of stock, which enables him to keep stocks at a minimum, thus releasing more money for production purposes. In the central stock control department there is one set of records, where before there were three, and his constant aim is further reductions in stores by extending his blanket ordering techniques. His aim is the absolute minimum of money tied up in stocks, insurance, handling, and overheads for stores.

Successful purchasing depends a great deal on common sense and even personality. Management skills and techniques, as I have suggested, are increasingly necessary to the efficient buying department, even in smaller companies. For this reason alone it is increasingly important to have access to the pooled knowledge and expertise of a professional organization such as the Institute of Purchasing and Supply, which also provides the services firms now require for adequate training and education.

The professional organization for purchasing, the Institute of Purchasing and Supply, was formed in June 1967, from the merger of two bodies, the Purchasing Officers Association and the Institute of Public Supplies. The Purchasing Officers Association was founded in 1931, its membership consisting of the principal buyers and materials managers of industry and commerce. It also had members in many of the nationalized industries, in hospitals, and in public services. The Institute of Public Supplies was founded in 1949 and drew its members from contract officers and buyers in government service, in local government and hospital service, and from nationalized industries. The new Institute has a membership of more than 10,000, and the combined purchasing power of its members amounts to a sizable proportion of the gross national product.

Training and education play an important part in the work of the Institute of Purchasing and Supply, which has a programme of courses and seminars on various aspects of purchasing and stores control that are open to established purchasing officers and to non-members also.

The Institute is organized on the basis of national headquarters, with a permanent staff, and annually elected officers. There are some fifty branches throughout the country, and others in several overseas countries. The branches arrange meetings which are addressed by experts on their subjects and where an exchange of information and experiences is made. There are also students societies for those young men who have enrolled in the Purchasing Diploma scheme.

In addition, there are specialist sections in which buyers and purchasing people in particular industries meet from time to time to discuss the problems affecting their industry and to agree on common approaches to problems, where this may be appropriate.

The Institute publishes a weekly newspaper dealing with market prices and supply positions of principal commodities, a monthly journal, and a quarterly educational review.

Reading list

BOOKS

Purchasing Handbook, E. W. Aljian (McGraw-Hill, 2nd Edition 1966)
Storage and Control of Stock, A. Morrison (Pitman, 1962)
Terms of Conditions of Contract (Institute of Purchasing and Supply, Revised 1964)
Purchasing and Supply Management, P. J. H. Bailey (Chapman & Hall, 1968)
Purchasing Problems, P. J. H. Bailey and D. Farmer (Institute of Purchasing and Supply, 1967)
Purchasing Principles and Techniques, P. J. H. Bailey and D. Farmer (Pitman, 1968)
Supplies and Materials Management, H. K. Compton (Business Books, 1968)

JOURNAL

Purchasing Journal (Institute of Purchasing and Supply)

Useful address

Institute of Purchasing and Supply, York House, Westminster Bridge Road, London SE 1

12. Location Strategy for Business

12.1 Where to Site Your Business

Richard Bailey

Government regional policy

The most urgent regional problem is the fact that some areas are congested, suffering from a shortage of labour and other resources, while others suffer from high unemployment and a general shortage of industrial opportunities. One of the main reasons for the regional pattern of unemployment is that some industries and services in which big changes have been taking place tend to be grouped for historical and other reasons in particular regions. Much of the early industrial development that took place in the United Kingdom was related to coal, cotton, iron ore, and the existence of adequate water supplies. Employment in these long-established industries has been declining steadily, and in many cases new industries have not been coming in to take their place fast enough to absorb the available labour.

This problem has been the subject of government policy since the 1930s. Measures have been taken either to help the workers to move away from places where there are no jobs available for them, or to take work to the workers in the less prosperous regions. When the Labour Government came to power in October 1964 new machinery for regional planning was set up centred in the Department of Economic Affairs, with Economic Planning Councils and Boards to carry out planning work in the regions. New regional boundaries were worked out that differed in several cases from those formerly in use.

It is important to realize that regional policy is concerned not only with 'depressed areas', with higher than average unemployment, but also with the fact that new and growing industries have tended to concentrate in Greater London, the South East generally, and in the Midlands.

Directors are concerned with regional policy in a broad sense in a number of ways. If they are established in the South East or the Midlands they are well aware of the shortage of labour and its high cost. Furthermore, in the Greater London area in particular, they have all the problems of traffic congestion, staff commuting to work, and the high cost of services, housing shortages, and general overcrowding. If they want to expand their business and build a new factory they may very well find this is not possible in the area of their present operations. Companies operating in a less prosperous part of the country in a situation where there is no scarcity of labour in general, may find that skilled labour of the kind they require is just as scarce as in other regions. They will also have difficulty in attracting managers to live in what are regarded as unattractive parts of the country and will feel themselves to some extent isolated from the main centres of economic and commercial activity.

The problem is made worse by the fact that the less prosperous regions of the nineteenth-century industrial areas tend to have a very large proportion of dreary inadequate housing, and a general lack of social amenities. If people are to be attracted to them from the rest of the country a concerted programme of redevelopment and rehousing is necessary. This clearly has to be carried out with long-term changes in population in mind.

On present forecasts the population of the United Kingdom will grow by twenty million by the end of this century. This increase will make it more important than ever to make the best use of land, to provide adequate communications, and to ensure that certain parts of the country do not become vast built-up areas. While the congestion in the crowded areas of the London region, the Midlands, South Lancashire and Clydeside, must be reduced, it must be done without encroaching unduly on agricultural land or the open spaces needed for recreation, and without increasing the congestion problems of the future.

In order to deal with these problems the Department of Economic Affairs has set up two new kinds of planning body. The first of these are the Regional Economic Planning Councils, the members of which are appointed because of the contribution they can make in the formulation of regional plans and in their implementation. The members are widely representative of different types of experience within their regions. The other new bodies are the Regional Economic Planning Boards, which consist of civil servants representing the main government departments in the regions, sitting under the chairmanship of an official of the Department of Economic Affairs. The boards are responsible for preparing regional plans and co-ordinating the work of the various government departments concerned in its implementation. Co-ordination is necessary because various problems and policies that are each the

618

specialist concern of a separate Ministry interlock at regional level. For example, if a longstanding industry that has been a big employer in the past is contracting, the encouragement of new industry into the area is the responsibility of the Board of Trade. Retraining of redundant workers in new skills is the concern of the Department of Employment and Productivity, while decisions by the Ministry of Transport on the routing of a motorway extension or a proposal to close a branch railway line, may be of considerable importance in the development of the area.

The Regional Economic Planning Councils have three main functions. These are:

(a) To assist in the formulation of regional plans, having regard to the best use of the region's resources;
(b) to advise on the steps necessary for their implementation on the basis of information and assessments provided by the Economic Planning Boards;
(c) to advise on the regional implications of national economic policies.

The Chairmen of the Councils have direct access to Ministers, and there are periodic meetings of chairmen and representatives of management, trade unions, and local government with Ministers to review the work of the Councils. The Councils have undertaken studies of their areas to serve as a basis for broad objectives of policy for the future. These have been published as Regional Studies by HMSO. Directors will find them extremely valuable as a general guide to the development of their regions. They will also find the new Regional Statistics publication helpful, although it is to be hoped that the range of material available will be increased as more experience in compiling regional statistics is obtained.

So far as directors are concerned, the work of the Regional Economic Planning Councils and Boards is of interest in bringing together information not otherwise readily available. The impact of the new organizations on their regions is less easy to assess. This is because their relationship with local government bodies has not been clearly defined and, lacking budgets of their own, they are unable to take policy decisions on what is to be done. No doubt these problems will be receiving attention as the regional planning system develops. So far, at least it can be said that the new arrangements have led to a more detailed and comprehensive study of regional problems than have previously been undertaken.

Location of industry

Responsibility for the location of industry rests with the Board of Trade. In August 1966, large parts of Britain were designated as Development Areas in which industry was to be encouraged to set up new factories. The new areas have replaced the previous smaller Development Districts, and between them they cover Northern England, Merseyside, nearly the whole of Scotland, Wales, Cornwall, and North

Devon. All told, they contain a fifth of Britain's working population. These areas have a higher than average level of unemployment and labour is likely to continue to be available for a number of years because of the presence in them of a number of declining industries.

The Government offers a variety of inducements to new and expanding businesses in the Development Areas. Under the old system, companies received initial and investment allowances as an inducement to set up new plants in the poorer areas. Under the Industrial Development Act 1966, these were replaced by cash grants. The new grants are given irrespective of a firm's profit or tax position, so that it is possible to calculate their effect when investment decisions are being made. The processes eligible for cash grants include, broadly speaking, the manufacture of any article, extraction of minerals, construction and civil engineering, or scientific research related to any of these processes. Grants are not payable on road vehicles nor on such items as office machinery and furniture and canteen equipment. No distinction is made between British and imported plant and machinery, and grants are payable on the instalments of qualifying assets taken on hire purchase. Where assets are let on hire, they are eligible for grants on certain conditions. Individual items costing less than £25 are not eligible for cash grant in any circumstances.

The Development Areas benefit particularly from the new system of investment grants because, whereas the general long-term rate of grant is 20 per cent of the capital cost of eligible plant and machinery, in Development Areas the long-term rate is 40 per cent. For the period between 1 January 1967 and 31 December 1968, the rates were raised to 25 per cent and 45 per cent respectively. Apart from plant and machinery, which qualifies for investment grants because it is used in one of the patent processes, computers, ships, and hovercraft acquired for carrying out business in Britain are also eligible. The rate in this case is 20 per cent.

Directors who wish to know more about the investment grant system, should write to the Board of Trade Investment Grant Office whose address appears at the end of this section, or contact the local Offices in Cardiff, Liverpool, Billingham, or Glasgow.

The Board of Trade can also provide help for projects that will increase employment in the Development Areas, under the Local Employments Acts 1960 to 1966. Under these Acts the Board may:

(a) Provide premises for rent or purchase.
(b) Pay grants of up to 25 per cent of the cost of erecting a new building or extending or adapting an existing one.
(c) Make loans for general purposes of undertaking work in a Development Area whether new to the Area or an expansion of an existing business.
(d) Pay grants towards unusual initial expenditure incurred in setting up business in a developing area or transferring an undertaking to one.

620

The buildings provided by the Board of Trade can be of standard type or designed to suit the applicant's particular requirements. Factories may also be built to rent or for sale, but very large or specialized factories that would be difficult to re-let if vacated, are built for sale only. On the industrial estates, as distinct from individual sites, factories are usually rented. Leases for rented factories are normally for twenty-one years at a rent assessed by the district valuer on the basis of values current for the same sort of property in the district. Firms renting the Board of Trade factory for a new project may qualify for an initial rent-free period of two years in cases where special problems have been involved because of the distance from the firm's existing undertaking.

Other concessions to firms deciding to set up a factory in a Development Area include building grants and loans and grants for general expenditure. Building grants are payable to companies purchasing a new building or who themselves build a new factory or extension or adapt existing premises. The rate of grant is 25 per cent of building costs, including the purchase price of the site, site preparation, the cost of building, the provision of services, and permanent fixtures. Where there are special problems, a higher rate of 35 per cent may be paid at the Board's discretion. The deciding factor is the amount of the grant in relation to the employment to be provided. The Board consults the Board of Trade Advisory Committee (BOTAC), an independent body of professional and business men before reaching a decision on whether a particular project qualifies for a grant.

Applications for building grants should be made to the Board of Trade regional office in the area concerned.

Loans and grants for general expenditure can be made for the purchase of buildings, plant, machinery, equipment (excluding the amount of any investment grant made), and for working capital. Repayment of a loan may be spread over a reasonable period, and interest is fixed at a moderate rate. Grants, apart from investment and building grants, are offered only where an undertaking will incur initial expenses regarded as unusual either in nature or amount because of a project being located in a Development Area. Applications for loans and grants of this kind should be made to the Board of Trade Regional Office in the Development Area concerned. The Board of Trade is able to act only on the advice of BOTAC. Companies have to provide information under a number of heads when asking for assistance. In particular, they must give up-to-date accounts, not more than four months old, and furnish forward estimates in the form of Profit and Loss Accounts for a period of at least three years. In the case of loan assistance, companies are expected to provide a reasonable proportion of the necessary finance themselves and thus take a proper share of the risk.

The Department of Employment and Productivity also provides help for companies moving to the Development Areas. This takes the form of financial assistance under the Employment and Training Act 1948, towards the cost of training the additional labour required by firms moving into or expanding undertakings in Development Areas. If a company sets up a temporary training school or training section in rented accommodation in a Development Area, before its factory is built there, a special grant can be paid for a maximum period of two years. The Department also provides free training in skilled trades for employees in Government Training Centres, and for semi-skilled engineering occupations by the loan of instructors, and for the training of supervisors and operator instructors on assembly lines, processing, packaging, bottling and so on, by special Training Within Industry (TWI) courses. Directors wishing to know more of these services provided by the Department of Employment and Productivity in the Development Areas should contact the nearest local office of the Department in the area concerned.

In any move to a new area, housing is one of the most important considerations. The Ministry of Housing and Local Government in England, the Scottish Development in Scotland, and the Welsh Office in Wales can help in providing houses for key workers in the new locality. Advice on this service can be provided by the Regional Offices of the Board of Trade.

Proposals for building new factories or extending old ones outside the Development Areas are strictly controlled. Before any proposal for building containing over 5,000 sq ft of new industrial space can be considered by a local planning authority in Britain, an Industrial Development Certificate must be granted by the Board of Trade. This control is operated stringently in the Midlands, London, and the South East, where the lower limit is 3,000 sq ft, and the Board of Trade will issue certificates only if projects cannot be sited efficiently in regions with more free manpower. The Board also controls office development over 3,000 sq ft in the Midlands and the South East, and most applications are refused. This means that, at the present time and for the foreseeable future, Industrial Development Certificates are likely to be issued only in special circumstances for projects outside the Development Areas.

Reading list

BOOKS

The Regional Planning Councils have produced surveys of the problems in their regions. Directors should enquire about the reports covering their area from the office of their Regional Economic Planning Board or from H.M.S.O.

In addition the following general references will be found useful:

Abstract of Regional Statistics (Periodical issues beginning in 1965) (H.M.S.O.)
Room to Expand (booklets) (issued free by the Board of Trade)

Economic Planning in the Regions:

The Work of the Regional Economic Planning Councils and Boards, published by the Department of Economic Affairs (free from offices of Regional Economic Councils in England, the Scottish Economic Planning Council, the Welsh Council and the Northern Ireland Economic Council)

622

The Development Areas. A proposal for a Regional Employment Premium, April 1967 (H.M.S.O.)

Papers on Regional Development, edited by Thomas Wilson (Basil Blackwood, 1965)

Useful addresses

Board of Trade Industrial Expansion Office, 1 Victoria Street, London SW 1

Board of Trade Investment Grant Office, Colman House, Victoria Avenue, Southend-on-Sea, Essex

Department of Economic Affairs, Storey's Gate, London SW 1

12.2 The Location of Offices Bureau

E. J. Sturgess

The Location of Offices Bureau was set up as a government commission in April 1963, with the brief 'to encourage the decentralization of office employment from congested central London to suitable centres elsewhere'. Since then it has helped over 700 companies to move more than 50,000 jobs out of central London. The service that LOB provides to directors on all aspects of moving out is free and confidential. It finds places where companies can operate more efficiently, at less cost, and where there is room to expand.

At its London offices, LOB maintains comprehensive information on properties available throughout the country, comparative rents, motorway, rail, and air links, telecommunication and postal facilities, housing, and staffing. Its property register, probably the biggest of its kind in the country, contains details of over nine million square feet of office space available or under construction throughout Great Britain. With this information the Bureau is able to meet the particular needs of individual firms, and pinpoint areas that would be especially appropriate for the firm in question. Preliminary discussion with client firms can be followed up by arranging visits and meetings with local officials. A service that seems to be particularly appreciated by potential movers is the Bureau's map room, which shows where office properties are available; road, rail, and air communication; new and expanding towns; and the location of such facilities as universities, computer bureaux, ports and docks.

When firms consider decentralization, it is usually for one or more of three

624

reasons. The firm is expanding and does not want to pay high central London rents in order to accommodate the new activity; it wants to economize; or its lease is falling in. Many a firm enjoying a low rent based on an early post-war lease has a rude awakening when a renewed lease means a doubling or trebling of its existing rent. Recently, rents for new offices in good positions in central London have ranged from £4 to £5 per square foot compared with typical rents for most major provincial towns varying from between 12s. 6d. to 30s. per square foot (Fig 12.1).

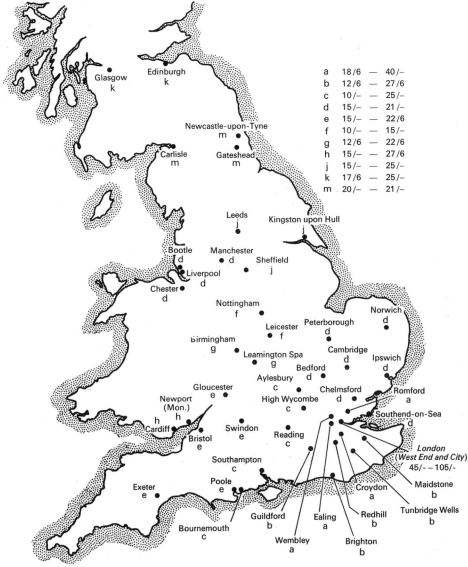

a	18/6	—	40/-
b	12/6	—	27/6
c	10/-	—	25/-
d	15/-	—	21/-
e	15/-	—	22/6
f	10/-	—	15/-
g	12/6	—	22/6
h	15/-	—	27/6
j	15/-	—	25/-
k	17/6	—	25/-
m	20/-	—	21/-

London (West End and City) 45/- – 105/-

Fig. 12.1.

21*

Because of the high ratio of routine office staff they employ, insurance companies lead the way in decentralization, both in terms of jobs and distance moved. In the years 1963–68, LOB helped 44 insurance companies move out 6,271 jobs. Next came the distributive trades with 5,421 jobs moved out by 64 firms, followed by the chemical industry with 4,821 jobs moved out by 36 firms. Other types of industry that make substantial moves are engineering; office machinery and furniture; paper, printing and publishing; the construction industry, and the professional and scientific services. Generally speaking, it is the bigger firms that are able to move the furthest distance. In fact, the 14 per cent of LOB's clients who have moved more than sixty miles accounted for 26 per cent of the jobs. At the same time, the fewer of its existing staff (as opposed to jobs) that the firm wishes to move, the farther it can consider going, as most staff do not like moving long distances.

Larger firms are also giving more thought to the advantages of partial decentralization which, in terms of jobs, accounts for more than half of the moves carried out. Departments being moved out include computer and data processing, staff records and personnel, accounts, property, registrars, securities, and drawing offices. Departmental moves by the larger firms come under one of three broad headings:

1. The company keeps a tightly-knit small head office staff in London, which consists of the directors, group finance, and accompanying 'staff' departments. The rest of the staff is moved out to production divisions or associated companies.
2. The company transfers a major department (notably where a computer is involved). Big insurance companies and brokers provide examples of this type of move.
3. A large head office staff is housed in one building in London, with all future expansion taking place outside. This calls for flexibility in the pattern of growth, which may involve rearranging departments in order to contain the size of the London head office.

Subsequent contact with firms that have left London invariably shows that the moves have been worthwhile and that the advantages more than outweigh the disadvantages. The latter are usually concerned with communication difficulties arising from inadequate postal or telephone services (here LOB is able to forewarn clients of any likely difficulties and, sometimes, help overcome them). Seldom is loss of prestige rated as a disadvantage by companies that have moved out completely. The acid test, of course, is that firms who move hardly ever come back into London.

The main advantage of moving out of London is that it can save a company a substantial amount of money, both directly and indirectly. We have estimated that, on average, the cost of keeping office staff in new offices in central London compared with outside London accounts for at least an extra £465 per head a year in higher rents, service, and salary weightings. For firms who can consider moving longer distances, the development areas have advantages. No office development permits are needed, staffing is easy, and substantial building grants may be available.

On the staffing side, the rate of turnover decreases significantly out of London. Staff morale and efficiency also seem to improve, and I have often heard managers of firms that have decentralized comment on the improved zeal and productivity of staff at all levels. I sometimes suspect that insufficient account is taken of the possible gain in freeing senior executives from the wear and tear of the long commuting distances that many of them have to cover.

Development of offices in and around London is held strictly in check by the Control of Office and Industrial Development Act, 1965. Under this act, which was last modified in July 1967, no office development over 3,000 square feet can be carried out in the Metropolitan Region without an office development permit from the Board of Trade. In the rest of the South East, the Midlands, and East Anglia, new offices of up to 10,000 square feet can now be built without an office development permit. When he announced this restriction on 14 July 1967, the then President of the Board of Trade, Mr Douglas Jay, said that the control would continue to be operated mainly as an instrument of regional planning with the object of encouraging the diversion of office employment throughout the country. At the same time, however, he said that now that the unrestrained development of offices in and around London had been checked, greater weight was to be given to the needs of those office employers who could not move from the South East and who wished to build offices.

A natural consequence of the restriction on office development in central London has been a considerable hardening of rents for large prestige blocks, and it is difficult to see these rents doing anything but climb even higher as supplies diminish.

At the same time, because of the economic 'freeze', demand for smaller offices and older premises in London has fallen considerably. Outside central London, demand for small and medium-sized offices has stayed steady in recent years, and demand for larger areas has increased. The gap between suburban and central London rents has closed rapidly, and rents of 30s. to 35s. per square foot, in the near and more accessible suburbs (notably the boom office centre of Croydon) have been commonplace. Farther out, of course, rents for good new office blocks fall substantially. Bearing in mind the various proposals for regional development, the question of locating the appropriate office activity in the right place becomes increasingly pertinent. A discussion with location executives of the Location of Offices Bureau costs nothing, and may help directors to find the answer to important location problems, and reduce overheads into the bargain.

Reading list

BOOKS

Better Offices, (Institute of Directors, London SW 1, 1964)
The Offices, Shops and Railway Premises Act, 1963 (H.M.S.O.)

Office Decentralization—A Handbook for the Intending Mover (Location of Offices Bureau, 1965)
A Wise Move (Location of Offices Bureau, 1964)
Expanding Towns (Greater London Council Industrial Centre—leaflet—1965)
Room to Expand Series (Board of Trade)

Useful addresses

Location of Offices Bureau, 27 Chancery Lane, London WC 2
Industrial Centre, Greater London Council, The County Hall, London SE 1
Department of Employment and Productivity, 8 St James Square, London SW 1

12.3 Legal Problems: The Land Commission

John Hamway

The intention of the Land Commission Act 1967 is two-fold. In one part, it sets up a system whereby an independent government agency (the Land Commission) can compulsorily acquire land, obtain consents for its development, and deal in it as it considers advisable and necessary in the interests of the community. The expressed intention is that the activities of the Land Commission will give rise to more and cheaper development sites for housing and other requirements.

The second object of the Act (still administered by the Land Commission) is an endeavour to give effect to the politician's dream that increased values resulting from social or political happenings should not accrue solely to those having the good fortune to be the owners of the property affected, but in some measure should return to the community that gave rise to them. This is the object of the Betterment Levy.

Constitution and Financial Provisions

The Land Commission was established by the Land Commission Act on 1 February 1967 and began to function on 6 April 1967 by virtue of the Land Commission (First Appointed Day) Order 1967. It is constituted as a Body Corporate, having a maximum of nine members who are appointed by the Minister of Housing and Local Government, and the Secretary of State for Scotland. Its functions are, however, performed on behalf of the Crown. It is exempt from

629

Stamp Duty and other taxes, but not from building regulations or planning controls.

Just as the Land Commission has two distinct functions, so the monies under its control fall into two distinct sections. Its land dealing and development, and expenses connected therewith, are financed by a Land Acquisition and Management Fund. This fund receives money from the government in the form of advances up to a maximum of £45,000,000. (This can be increased to £75,000,000 by ministerial order.) These advances bear interest at rates the Treasury decides. The proceeds of land dealing, rents, etc., received by the Land Commission go into this fund. The Betterment Levy (q.v.), however, is paid to the Exchequer like any other impost.

The Commission, therefore, has a limited funding for land development when related to the whole of Great Britain and must clearly seek to build up its funds by profitable land dealing on its own account, as by so dealing it retains the betterment element, being itself exempt from taxation. Betterment Levy payable on land sold without involving the Commission is collected by the Commission, but it is then passed to the Exchequer and lost to the Land Acquisition and Management Fund.

Powers

The Commission's powers are wide, and include:

1. *Power to acquire land* if the land is *in the Commission's opinion* suitable for material development. This includes power to acquire adjoining or nearby land required for facilitating the development or use of land.

Land may be acquired either:

(a) By agreement, in which case so long as the above proviso is observed there are no further limitations or conditions restricting what land may be purchased, or

(b) By compulsory purchase, in which case until the second appointed day there are conditions imposed and a limitation of the purposes for which the land can be acquired. After the second appointed day, not yet fixed but to be fixed by ministerial Order confirmed by a resolution of both Houses of Parliament, the Commission can buy land for any purpose whatsoever. However the *conditions* governing purchase remain.

These, apart from the overriding proviso mentioned above, are:

(i) There must be planning permission (outline or detail) in force for material development, and the material development must remain to be carried out wholly or in part. Anyone may, however, apply for planning permission irrespective of the wishes of the landowner, and the Land Commission is no exception; or

(ii) The land must be designated by a current development plan or by regulation as subject to compulsory acquisition or be defined or allocated in the development plan or in any proposals for altering or adding to the plan, or be part of a designated New Town or clearance area.

If one or both of these conditions is complied with, then the land may be acquired but, until after the second appointed day, only for one or more of the following four purposes:

(i) To expedite the development of undeveloped ripe land.
(ii) To ensure or facilitate the development of land as one whole rather than piecemeal.
(iii) On behalf of other bodies or persons having themselves compulsory powers (e.g., a Local Authority) but *only* with their or the appropriate Minister's consent.
(iv) In order to dispose of it by way of Concessionary Crownhold disposition (q.v.). The Commission also has power to repurchase Crownhold land on breach of a Crownhold covenant.

Having regard to the wide powers the Commission will have after the second appointed day, landowners will wish to be able to ascertain the Commission's intentions. The Act accordingly provides that after the second appointed day any person with a material interest in land may, within three months of a planning decision as to that land, serve on the Commission notice requiring the Commission to elect whether or not to acquire such land. Notice must be in a form prescribed by regulations to be made under the Act. It is then the duty of the Commission to indicate within three months whether or not it will acquire the land. If it indicates that it will not, or does nothing, it is then prohibited from acquiring the land for a period of five years. If it indicates a desire to purchase, it must do so within a year, otherwise the effect is as if it had indicated that it would not purchase.

In giving notice that it will *not* acquire land the Commission may attach such conditions as it thinks fit to such notice, and if they are not complied with it is then free to acquire the land.

2. *Power to acquire information as to land*

(a) By compelling the owner of any interest in land to state in writing the nature of his interest in the land and other particulars of its ownership on pain of a fine of up to £50
(b) To enter land at any reasonable time to survey it.
(c) To obtain from the Inland Revenue information contained in documents produced or furnished to the Inland Revenue.

3. *Power to hold and manage land* but limited to ensure that the Commission disposes of the land speedily. It may build on land in its ownership, or carry out works on it, but only if this is necessary to the subsequent disposal of the land. The Commission may *not* carry out building for housing without the Minister's consent. This leaves the question of the Commission's power to carry out housing development very much in the hands of the government.

4. *Power to dispose of land* or rights in or over land in the public interest and at

631

the best market price, but otherwise only as directed by the government. The Commission may, however, sell at less than the best market price in the case of a concessionary crownhold disposition (q.v.). Except where the Commission acquired the land for another person or body, itself possessing powers of compulsory purchase, the Commission may dispose of land for any purpose irrespective of its initial reasons for acquisition. This is in contrast to the present restrictions on the purposes for which land can be compulsorily acquired.

5. *The Commission's powers are controlled* in specific fields as laid down in the Act. Like other public corporations it is not subject to direct parliamentary control. Grievances can, however, be referred to the Parliamentary Commissioner (Ombudsman).

Compulsory purchase

The Land Commission may exercise its powers of compulsory purchase in two ways. By what is called 'The Special Procedure', the Commission is enabled to act very quickly and to avoid the delay that can arise through normal compulsory purchase procedures. This Special Procedure may be invoked only by an order under statutory instrument made by the Minister of Housing and Local Government, or the Secretary of State for Scotland or for Wales, and then only after a draft of such an order has been laid before parliament and approved by a resolution of both houses. Where the land includes a dwelling-house, the dwelling must be excluded if its owner objects. The Special Procedure differs from normal procedure in that the rules for the service of notices are somewhat more lax, and the time for objections, etc., is very much limited, while the Minister, whose authority is required for a compulsory purchase order, need neither hold a public enquiry nor afford to any objectors the opportunity of appearing or being heard. The power is intended to be an emergency one to prevent a land famine, and was scheduled, unless extended by affirmative resolution of both houses of parliament, to expire on 5 April 1972.

The normal procedure for compulsory purchase by the Land Commission is that specified under the Acquisition of Land (Authorization Procedure) Act 1946, with certain modifications. One is that, in the absence of any objection, the Commission may proceed at once to make a compulsory purchase order. If there is an objection then, just as is required for Local Authority acquisitions, any order becomes subject to confirmation by the appropriate Minister with the usual requirements for a public hearing, the consideration of the views of objectors, etc. The Minister in question will in most cases be the Minister of Housing and Local Government, the Secretary of State for Scotland, or the Secretary of State for Wales. If the Land Commission is acquiring the site on behalf of a statutory body, the appropriate Minister could be the one responsible for that body.

Another important modification will apply only after the second appointed day has been fixed. Before that date, the Commission can acquire land for four purposes only (q.v. Powers). After that date it can acquire land for any purpose. However, once it is allowed to acquire land for any purpose, the Commission must, in any notice relating to a compulsory purchase order, specify the reasons for which it proposes to acquire the land.

Whatever compulsory purchase procedures are adopted, compensation will be based on the market value of the land so acquired. Here again, with only minor modifications, the general law applies. However, as any compensation payable is subject to Development Levy the Commission will deduct the Levy in arriving at a compensation figure, and to this extent the Commission obtains the land at a technically cheaper price. Its profit on resale will thus be inflated by reason of its exemption from Levy and, as mentioned above, these profits go into Land Acquisition and Management Fund and not to the Revenue.

Since the Commission has an overriding need to resell any land it buys, its powers under a compulsory purchase order extend not only to allow it into possession but also to make a General Vesting Declaration giving it actual and good title to the land. It is, thus, saved the bother of investigating the Vendor's title, and enabled to dispose of the land quickly with a good title to third parties. The question of compensation can then be dealt with subsequently.

It is not within the scope of this section to set out in detail the general law relating to compulsory purchase and compensation, and those concerned are advised to consult standard textbooks on the subject or to seek the advice of their advisers.

Crownhold

Any land of which the Commission has power to dispose may be disposed of either as freehold or leasehold subject to certain covenants designed to retain for the benefit of the Commission any development value while making the land available for a specified use and/or development. These are called *Crownhold Covenants* and the land will be called Crownhold land.

1. *Concessionary Crownhold* land is Crownhold land sold for use only for the provision of housing for designated persons (no letting or sub-letting permitted without consent) who cannot dispose of the whole or any part of the land without first offering the *whole*, even if they want to dispose of only part, back to the Commission, who may then buy back the whole or only the part under sale at its discretion. For the price payable on repurchase see (3) below.

In disposing of concessionary crownhold land the Commission need not obtain the best market price, but the difference between the actual and the best market price must be stated in the document of sale or Lease and is deducted in computing the price on repurchase by the Commission.

2. A Crownhold Covenant is enforced by notice of breach in statutory form which, if not objected to, then entitles the Commission to make a Vesting Declaration.

633

If objected to, leave of the Court is needed in England and Wales (in Scotland the matter is referred to the Sheriff) before the commission can make a Vesting Declaration. Once a Vesting Declaration is made, the land revests in the Commission.

3.   The compensation payable on the making of a Vesting Declaration, and also the repurchase price of Concessionary Crownhold is based on the value of the land, excluding any value due to any breach of Crownhold Covenants and/or any loss due to disturbance or severance. Compensation or the repurchase price in the case of Concessionary Crownhold is reduced by the value difference stated in the document of sale or lease, as mentioned in (1) above.

The Betterment Levy

1. General

The Act imposes a Betterment Levy, at the moment set at 40 per cent but intended to rise to 45 per cent and then to 50 per cent at reasonably short intervals. Further increases are envisaged. Levy becomes due on the realization of any increased value accruing to land by reason of the prospect of its development. Realization of such increased value is deemed to have taken place on the occurrence of certain events or transactions defined in the Act (called Cases) and for convenience lettered from A to F inclusive. Each Case has its own special circumstances and qualifications, although the whole is intended to be a system based upon common principles. (For a simple outline see the chart (Table 12.1) setting out Cases in detail.)

Levy is payable in every case occurring after, but *not before*, 6 April 1967, and liability to pay cannot be transferred.

2. Exemptions and Special Cases

(a) No levy is payable on acquisitions under compulsory purchase powers where notice to treat was served, or a contract for sale made, before 6 April 1967.

(b) Single family dwelling. The building of a single dwelling-house intended as the only or main residence of the owner or an adult member of the owner's family, built on land owned immediately before 23 September 1965, is exempt from Development Levy under Case C (Table 12.1). Ownership can be freehold or leasehold. However, only one development per person is exempt under this section, and once exemption is granted, whoever is specified as intending to live in the dwelling-house must live there for at least six months or until earlier death. The owner must notify the Commission and claim exemption before starting to build. See also (d) below.

(c) Residential property developers. A developer or builder of residential property who was in business as such before 23 September 1965, may, by giving the appropriate notice to the Land Commission obtain personal exemption under Case C for any freehold or leasehold land he owned or had contracted to purchase before 23 September 1965. A similar concession, limited to established residential builders or developers, covers land for residential housing bought for valuable consideration on or after 1 August 1966, and before 6 April 1967, provided development started before the 6 October 1967. The effect is that the developer may claim the actual cost of the land as previous consideration paid as opposed to the original undeveloped 'current use value' (q.v. Table 12.1, column 3(b)).

(d) As regards 'previous consideration paid' extra-statutory concessions announced since the passing of the Act permit *any* purchaser of land between 22 September 1965 and 6 April 1967 to claim actual cost of land up to a maximum of £2,500. Purchasers of plots for *single* houses between those dates may claim the *full* cost.

Table 12.1

1. CASE	A	B	C
2. Event giving rise to levy.	Sale of freehold or leasehold originally of over seven years or of shorter leases if notified to the Commission.	Grant of lease of over seven years or of shorter leases if notified to the Commission.	Start of project of material development.
3. (a) Levy is payable on:	Total consideration.	Total consideration, which includes capital investment value of rent, any premium, etc., less capital value of any rent paid to a superior Landlord.	Profit rental value of the land in open market capitalized.

(b) after deducting:			

Either'
110 per cent of the 'current use value' applicable to the case
plus: the loss in value resulting to any other of the developer's land by reason of the event.
plus: the proper cost of improvements, easements and/or amenities spent on or after 1 July 1948 in so far as they increased the development value of the land.
or: 'the previous consideration paid' on the last purchase made or contracted to be made between 1 July 1948 and 22 September 1965, or after 5 April 1967 and notified to the Commission provided no event giving rise to Levy has occurred subsequently. But see text: Exemptions and Special Cases.
Whichever is the greater
The 'current use value' or 'the previous consideration paid' applicable to Case B is calculated as follows:

Take Actual current use value of the land *before* the tenancy was granted *or full* previous consideration paid as defined above, as the case may be	Multiply by:	'The Total consideration' as defined above

Divide by: 'The Total consideration' plus the value of the Landlord's right to the undeveloped land after the tenancy ends.

| 4. Who pays the Levy. | Vendor | Grantor | All persons having an interest in the land according to their respective interests. |
| 5. Notification to Land Commission | Compulsory (except leases under seven years) within 30 days of event | | Compulsory. Not less than 6 weeks or more than a year before development |

D	E	F
Receive compensation for revocation or modification of existing planning consent or use rights	Grant of easement or modification or release of easement or restrictive covenant if notified to the Commission.	Cases (not being within Cases A to E inclusive) covering questions of variations in a tenancy, grants of an informal nature, and certain compensation payments and which the Minister may specify by Regulation from time to time.
Amount of compensation plus current use value of land after revocation, etc.	Total consideration plus current use value of land after grant modification, etc.	Regulations have already been made on: (i) The renewal or extension of a tenancy or its variation so as to enable development potential to be realized. Assessment based and payable on Case B principles. (ii) The granting of a Licence to use land (e.g., as for an electricity or telephone cable wayleave) Assessment based and payable on Case E principles. (iii) The right to compensation for loss in value of land not actually acquired (e.g., neighbouring development reduced light amenity, etc.) Assessment based and payable on Case D principles. In each of the above cases Levy will be charged only if notified to the Commission.

Either:
    110 per cent of the current use value of the land before the event.

or:
    the consideration paid on the purchase of the land or the easement, etc., made or contracted to be made between 1 July 1948 and 22 September 1965, or after the 5 April 1967 and notified to the Commission, provided no event giving rise to Levy has occurred subsequently.

Whichever is the greater
plus: in each case the proper cost of necessary improvements, etc. incurred on or after 1 July 1948.

D	E	F
The person entitled to receive the compensation.	The grantor (person granting the concession and receiving the consideration)	*See* above under each category.
Compulsory. By Authority paying within 30 days of payment.	Optional. Within 30 days of date of grant.	Optional. Within 30 days of Event.

Notes:

1. 'Consideration' is generally defined as including price, land given in exchange, rights granted or taken, the release of a debt., etc., etc.; indeed any form of value or consideration whatsoever. In the case of the grant of a tenancy it includes also the capitalized rental value plus any premium.

2. 'Current use' is defined as the actual use of the land at the time when the levy becomes payable, without taking into account any planning consents permitting any material development. Where a project of material development was begun before 6th April 1967, or where notice of intention to carry out the project has been served in the case of a development begun after 6th April 1967 and the development is not complete at the relevant date, then, and only in such case in computing the current use value, may account be taken of the planning consent permitting that development.

3. In Case C, where a Freehold is involved, the capitalized rental value will usually equal the actual market value of the land.

4(a) Valuation costs are deductible from values.
  (b) As a special case, any Capital Gains Tax paid by reason of a disposition of land by way of death, gift or settlement before 6th April 1967 is allowed *as a deduction from any levy* subsequently payable on that land.
  (c) A deduction from Levy is also allowed on the occasion of the first chargeable act or event after 5th April 1967, which is also an occasion for capital gains tax and where base value is calculated by reference to the consideration for a previous transaction.

5. It may pay, in cases where notification is optional (Cases E and F and Leases under seven years), to notify and pay the levy, as the cost involved can then be carried forward and used as a deduction later under column 3(b).

6. Land or rights in land can be sold at a loss. In such a case no levy is payable and the loss can, broadly speaking, be carried forward and offset against any future levy that might arise.

636

(e) Development soon after purchase or lease of land. Any person buying or leasing land on or after 6 April 1967 (seller or lessor pays levy under Case A or B) may upon such purchase or grant of lease or within thirty days afterwards apply to the Commission for a direction in respect of any project of material development he intends to carry out in accordance with planning permission in force at the date of his purchase; and if he intends, and so satisfies the Commission, to start development within two years of purchase on the whole of the land, the Commission may, if it thinks fit, exempt that specific project on that specific land begun within that period (two years) from levy under Case C.

(f) There are special exemptions for charities and housing associations, local authorities, statutory bodies, the Crown, etc.

(g) The Minister also has a general power to grant further exemptions or to extend or add to them.

(h) Where a chargeable event affects only part of the land the value can be divided between the two parts.

(i) Payment of levy in certain cases by persons holding non-immediate interests in land, e.g., freeholder liable under Case C where the leaseholder is actually beginning development, can be deferred at the discretion of the Commission.

3. Other taxes and the Levy

The Development Levy is in every respect a tax. The general law relating to taxation must, therefore, in the absence of any specific statutory provision, be taken to apply to it. In fact, only in respect of long-term capital gains is there a clear cut statutory provision offsetting clearly one tax (Capital Gains Tax) against the other (the Levy). In all other cases, even where provisions are made by statute the levy can be treated only as a deduction, like any other legitimate expense.

(a) *Long-term Capital Gains*. Current use value and development value are separated. The gain, whether chargeable against an individual (Capital Gains Tax) or a company (gain chargeable to Corporation Tax), is computed only on the increase in current use value, leaving any increase in development value to bear the Levy. This applies on or after the 6 April 1967, and there are transitional provisions to cover any possible overlap from 6 April 1965 to this date. This system of separation is also applied to what would have been short-term capital gains were it not for the changes made by the Finance Act 1965.

At any time within two years of the year of assessment the land owner can elect against this separation provision taking effect, in which event both taxes apply together and, further, it is expressly provided that the Development Levy is *not* to be a deduction against Capital Gains Tax; accordingly on a gain, Levy *and* Capital Gains Tax would be payable together! Clearly no one would normally elect for this. However, if there is an established capital gains loss to offset against the capital gain there could then perhaps be some advantage.

(b) *Income Tax* and *Corporation Tax on Profits*. It is submitted that under the general rules for calculating profits, the Levy, like any other expense (e.g., rates), is a simple deduction in computing the final amount chargeable to tax. It should be borne in mind that a *short*-term capital gain (except if altered by the Finance Act 1965) is subject to Income (or Corporation) Tax and that accordingly taxation, as opposed to separation (q.v. (a) above), principles apply to it.

Certain special types of profit-making situations (e.g., premiums on leases granted for less than fifty years) taxable are the subject of special provision in the Finance Act 1967 in order to define the amount of deduction in respect of Levy in computing the sum liable to Income Tax, but the principle is unaltered.

(c) *Estate Duty*. Relief here is given in two situations: (i) Where Levy has been paid *before death* on land the subject of a *gift* (or comprised in a settlement or life interest brought to an end in circumstances by law deemed to be a gift) it can be deducted from the value of the land, thus reducing the principal sum liable to Estate Duty. The rate of estate duty (including reductions allowed according to the number of years between the gift and death) is unaffected.

(2) In reverse, Estate Duty paid on land can be deducted from the value of the land upon which Levy is charged but only if:

(i) the event giving rise to a liability for levy occurs within six years of the date of death;

(ii) it is the first such event since death, and

(iii) the land is owned by a beneficiary of the deceased or some other person who obtained the land without giving value for it.

General information

This section gives only the barest essentials of a very complicated and minutely technical piece of legislation.* Those facing problems should consult their professional advisers or the Land Commission. Addresses of the regional offices of the Land Commission can be obtained from the Land Commission, Government Buildings, Kenton Bar, Newcastle upon Tyne NE1.

Reading list

BOOKS

Housing, Town Planning and the Land Commission, F. G. Pennance (Institute of Economic Affairs, available from H.M.S.O.)

* I must gratefully acknowledge advice and suggestions on my approach to the subject from the Land Commission.

Encyclopedia of Betterment Levy and Land Commission Law and Practice, Desmond Heape
(Sweet and Maxwell, 1967)
A Guide for Estate Agents and Surveyors on Betterment Levy (Ministry of Housing and
Local Government and the C.O.I. 1967 (available from H.M.S.O.)
Betterment Levy and The Land Commission, Harris and Nutley (Butterworths, 1967)
The Land Commission Act, Stewart and Smith (Charles Knight & Co., 1967)

JOURNAL
'The Land Commission in Profile and Perspective', D. R. Denman *(National Provincial
Bank Review*, May 1967)

Useful addresses

Land Commission, Government Buildings, Kenton Bar, Newcastle upon Tyne
The Town Planning Institute, 26 Portland Place, London W 1
The Law Society, 113 Chancery Lane, London WC 2
National Federation of Property Owners, Temple Chambers, Temple Avenue, London EC 4
Country Landowners' Association, 7 Swallow Street, London W 1

639

12.4 Relations with the Town Hall

Elizabeth Burney

Local government is concerned not just with providing schools, council houses, roads, transport, and welfare services. While all these things affect the business man, at least through his employees, and should not be matters of indifference to him, there are many more specific ways in which the powers and actions of local government impinge directly on business activities. Most obvious and important is the system of land-use control. There is also a whole range of detailed supervisory functions, mainly of safety, health or amenity codes, that may affect business decisions in the minutest way.

There are one or two general rules for dealing with local authorities. First, each one has its own way of doing things. The mere existence of a power is no guarantee that it will be used; even a statutory duty may be interpreted in a number of different ways. Local government, by the way, can do nothing without specific authority—the doctrine of *ultra vires*. Some things, such as drainage regulations, still depend on local bye-laws to carry out statutory duties. Building regulations have only recently been codified nationally, and London still has its own code.

In every context the best rule is: know who you are dealing with. The Health Department may seem impersonal, but in the event it is always Inspector X or Y who has to approve your works canteen. He has an office and a telephone, and doubts can often be cleared up by a quick chat when official correspondence too often serves to obscure. It is worth doing a bit of homework to find out which part of which department is responsible for, say, approving the size of your car park, the design of the main road access and the parking regulations outside your door. While such things ought, logically, to be all in one department, they may in fact be scattered among the Borough Surveyor, the Borough Engineer, the Chief Architect, and the Planning Officer (and incidentally two or more of these titles may be combined in one department). This sort of knowledge saves decision time and, therefore, money.

Of all powers of local government, nothing affects directors, and all property owners or occupiers, so much as the real estate tax—the 'rates'—which is, as yet, the only type of tax in Britain levied on a local basis and retained by the local authority. The tax is expressed as a percentage of 'gross value' which, very theoretically, is assessed as the rent a building would fetch for its existing use (which usually has very little to do with market rents). Improvements may result in a higher assessment. Appeal against a rating assessment is, in the first instance, to the local valuation court, subsequently to the Lands Tribunal or (in certain circumstances) to the High Courts. Valuations are revised every five years or more; the rate levied on those valuations is universal throughout the authority and varies, of course, with social demands. Business property is cherished by local councils for its high rateable value compared with domestic property—particularly new business property. At one time 'industrial derating'—charging industry only half its assessment—was used to encourage employment, but this now applies only in Scotland, and even there not to commerce. In England and Wales in April 1967, rateable values totalled £2,255 million, of which £1,178 million was attributable to commercial and industrial property.

Local government, as we know it, came into being through the need to make private enterprise respect public health and safety in the cities of the industrial revolution. Hence, the early building codes, and the whole of the rules aimed to prevent what still is known as 'public nuisance'. Fire regulations and drainage codes are among those that affect all types of buildings and the way they are used—under local authority supervision. Very detailed control, requiring special permission from the town hall in each case, covers the discharge of trade effluent. The Clean Air Act permits local councils to introduce smoke control by stages: some have hardly begun, some have a carefully worked-out programme of phased control, area by area. Where a control order exists it is an offence to emit 'dark smoke' unless this results from government 'authorized fuel'. The top fine for business contravention is £100.

Particular types of business activity may involve licensing or inspection by local government. Anything involving food for sale to the public is an obvious case in point. So is the letting of rooms, where the local authority has a duty to prevent overcrowding, and powers to enforce good management and other codes. The weights and measures legislation is also administered locally, and is a good example of how code enforcement can produce what is also a useful service to business. For public protection, local government has acquired a vast range of licensing powers, from driving licences to liquor sale licences, from street trading

641

to running an employment agency, down to staging a public show of hypnotism.

From the early concern of local government with the health, safety, and convenience of the public, evolved the much more all-embracing powers of town planning as we know them in Britain today. These powers are intended to promote amenity, control urban growth, and facilitate the redevelopment of outworn buildings and badly laid out areas. Many people see town planning as meaning only that a man cannot do what he wants to do with his own land without asking someone's permission, and indeed this is scarcely an exaggeration. As usually administered, the system is too negative and restrictive; at the time of writing, new law was in preparation intended to remedy this, up to a point.

Town planning law and practice is so complex that no serious decision should be taken without expert advice. But here, briefly, are the main points where the director may come in contact with the local planning authority.

Since the 1947 Town and Country Planning Act, local authorities, under the supervision of central government, have had power of promotion or veto of development, in order to achieve patterns of land use judged to be beneficial to the community as a whole. There are two basic tools of this control: the development map prepared by the local authority; and the planning permission, which must be obtained by the private owner who causes any 'change in land use'.* The latter does not just mean building on an empty site or turning a garden into a car-park; it also includes all but very minor additions to buildings and any change of function such as the conversion of a cinema into a factory or even a house into flats. Any sort of public placard or poster will need permission. The granting of an industrial development certificate or office development permit by the Board of Trade does not cancel the need for local planning permission, too, although, obviously, local authorities in areas of unemployment are unlikely to make difficulties. Indeed, experience has shown that, on the whole, provincial authorities are all too ready to give permission for new speculative commercial development without first assessing demand.

Planning permission is granted in two main stages: approval in outline and in detail. The likelihood of outline permission being obtainable is much affected by the development map. This indicates broadly the type of land use—housing, offices, industry, open space, etc.—which the local authority would like to see in that area. Some parts of the map, not yet developed, may have no such indication and are known as 'white land'. Nevertheless, the existence of a particular zoning on a particular piece of land is no guarantee that just any conforming application will be granted. Also, the zoning is constantly being revised, and is never realistic all over the map. Under new legislation it will be limited, in detail, to a few areas the planning authority wishes to redevelop soon. A word of warning: if development is carried out without planning permission, the local authority may demand that the building

*Land whose value has been increased by planning permission or 'material development' now attracts the tax known as Betterment Levy, administered by the Land Commission (see p. 634).

642

be demolished or restored to its original state. But once given, planning permission cannot be withdrawn, except at a price, although under the Town and Country Planning Bill, which became law in October 1968, unused permissions expire after five years.

Development plans are reviewed, at present, every five years. Any consequent changes can be objected to by affected landowners. If the local authority does not meet the objection, it is open to the objector to appeal; this will be heard at a public inquiry held by an inspector from the Ministry of Housing and Local Government. At the appeal, submissions can be made by people with no stake in the particular site; whereas the initial objection must come from an interested party. The inspector's decision is in the form of advice to the Minister, who nearly always takes the advice. (Legislation passed in 1968 will result in the local authority being its own arbiter in smaller planning details; and in the inspector having the final word in all but certain categories of appeal.)

The same machinery of objection, appeal, and inquiry is available when planning permission has been refused (provided steps are taken within a month of the refusal) and when land is being compulsorily acquired by the local authority or one of the 'statutory undertakers' (such as the Gas Board) with powers of compulsory purchase. A businessman who is a landlord or shopowner in a poor district may encounter compulsory purchase under slum clearance schemes (which often embrace adjoining properties not actually classified as slums). Increasingly, urban road schemes and central area redevelopment plans require the negotiated or compulsory purchase of still useful private property by local government. Of course, there is normally the opportunity to buy or lease other premises from the authority, but for smaller businesses in particular, this may prove difficult. Compulsory purchase, incidentally, is at site value only, for slum dwellings (i.e., those classified by the medical officer of health as unfit for human habitation), but at market value, determined by the district valuer, for all other property. There is scope for appeal against the compulsory purchase price, but the authority has power to pull down the building while the price is still being discussed. On the more positive side, redevelopment schemes themselves often provide the opportunity for business to expand in modern buildings and better surroundings: in fact, where shops are concerned the bigger operators can usually obtain very favourable terms from local authorities if they lease premises early on in a redevelopment scheme.

What about compensation to the property owner who is adversely affected by planning activity (such as the construction of a road)? This is rarely available unless part of his own land has been acquired for a public purpose. A road that severed two halves of a works would enable the firm to claim compensation; a road that merely diverted traffic from a petrol station would not be a statutory reason for compensating the proprietor.

One final word. If directors are not satisfied with the policies of local government, they should take their share in running it. At present it is rare to find a business man as a local councillor unless he is a shopkeeper or the proprietor of a hotel in a seaside town. Yet certain things, like transport planning, affect business more than they do the private citizen. Increasingly, local government needs the services of people with management expertise; not just as officials, but to serve on committees and take the lead in modernization. Already even the smaller authorities have budgets far in excess of any save the largest companies; after the royal commission on local government has reported in the autumn of 1968, a new structure is likely to result in large regional authorities and a greater degree of devolution. This will not be effective unless people with experience of the world come forward to make the most of the new opportunities.

Reading list

BOOKS

Royal Commission on Local Government in England Report (Chairman, Lord Redcliffe-Maud) 1968
The Structure of Local Government in England & Wales, W. Eric Jackson (Longmans, Green, 1960, and Penguin Books)
The English Local Government System, J. H. Warren (Allen & Unwin, 1963)
Central Departments and Local Authorities, J. A. G. Griffith (Allen & Unwin, 1966)
The Town Hall and the Property Owner, David Woolley (Methuen, 1967)
An Outline of Planning Law, Desmond Heap (Sweet and Maxwell, 1963)
Municipal Yearbook (published annually by The Municipal Journal Ltd)

Useful addresses

Ministry of Housing and Local Government (and Library), Whitehall, London SW 1
Scottish Office, St Andrews House, Edinburgh
Association of Municipal Corporations, 36 Old Queen Street, London SW 1
County Councils Association, 66a Eaton Square, London SW 1
Institute of Municipal Treasurers and Accountants, 1 Buckingham Place, London SW 1
National Association of Local Government Officers, 8 Harewood Row, London NW 1
Local Government Information Office, 36 Old Queen Street, London SW 1

13. Research and Development

13.1 The £.*s.d.* of R & D

James T. Kendall

The nature of industrial research

Industrial Research may be broadly categorized as:

(a) *Basic Research*. Fundamental scientific investigations designed to discover new knowledge.
(b) *Applied Research*. Development of new processes, new products or new equipment, based on existing scientific knowledge.
(c) *Development*. Continuous improvement of existing processes, products or equipment.

Basic research, except as an incidental by-product of directed applied research, is best carried out in national centres of research, particularly universities. It requires maximum freedom from directive control, it is slow, expensive, and unpredictable, and the rather small percentage of directly useful results obtained will be usable only after a considerable period of time, and will be virtually impossible to keep exclusive. Even the largest companies cannot economically justify the deliberate carrying out of basic research programmes, except possibly for prestige purposes, or if they are funded externally.

However, it is important that the people working in applied research in industry keep in touch with the progress of basic research in their field. Therefore, a firm should seek to secure close liaison with a few carefully chosen university scientists who are working in fields likely to be of importance to the company. This can be accomplished by appointing university scientists as consultants, by temporary secondment of industrial research staff to universities, and by temporary employment of university staff in industry. Additionally, the firm requires a 'technical information' organization, which may be as small as one librarian (*see* p. 785). The total expenditure by an industrial firm on basic research should, therefore, be comparatively small. Some examples relevant to various sizes of company are given below.

Applied research, as defined above, must be a major activity for any size of industrial research laboratory. However, the rules for carrying it out successfully are quite different from those for fundamental research, and failure to appreciate this is all too common. Complete freedom, which is essential for the full flowering of 'pure' research, can very easily, for applied research, become merely an excuse to explore all the interesting side-alleys, instead of following the main road to the planned objective. Detailed planning and continuous control of applied research is essential. No new development should be started unless the following factors are known and assessed beforehand.

1. *The Objective.* A clearly defined technical definition of the new process or product it is planned to achieve.
2. *The Value of the Objective.* Assuming a successful result, how worthwhile is it to the firm concerned? A number of factors need to be considered: the market potential for a new product, the likely profitability, the capacity of the firm to manufacture, the activities of competitive firms, etc.
3. *The Cost of the Research.* Both time and money need to be included, as well as the availability of suitable men and equipment.

On something like the above lines—elaborated to include all the factors relevant to a particular case—a kind of balance sheet can be made out for any proposed new development project. The major unknown factor is the probability of a successful result within a given budget and time, and here reliance must necessarily be placed on the judgement of a research director.

If the preliminary analysis is favourable, Stage 1 of the project should be carried out. This should be strictly limited to preparing reports from the Research Department on all the relevant scientific knowledge available, on the likely feasibility and cost of reaching the objective, and on the time required, together with a report from Marketing or Production Department on the value of the objective. Only after these reports have been carefully considered, should a decision be made. A healthy situation is one in which there are more apparently worthwhile projects to pursue than there are resources to do so, as a choice can then be made of those which are apparently *most* worthwhile. Moreover, many proposed projects may be killed or postponed at

648

the end of Stage 1, before any major expense has been incurred. The survivors will be all the more worth pursuing with enthusiasm.

Once a research project has got over this first Stage 1 hurdle, the most important consideration is *time*, and almost everything else must be subordinated to this. As an example, a buyer who saves £100 at the cost of a week's delay in delivery may be doing his firm a gross disservice. Similarly, it may be foolish not to buy some fairly expensive equipment if by so doing the time taken on the research project is shortened. A corollary of this is that research time must be meticulously accounted for, and progress reviewed frequently and regularly. If the project does not proceed as originally planned, and this will happen much more often than not, then the plan must be reviewed. If this indicates that the project should be dropped, there should be no hesitation in doing so. In research, more money is wasted in 'flogging dead horses' than in almost any other single way.

When a research project has reached an apparently successful conclusion in the laboratory, it is most important the research staff clearly understand that their responsibilities are by no means ended. It is just at this point that the greatest weakness in the process of innovation in industry lies. It is common practice for the research staff to write a polished 'Final Report', often taking several months of valuable time to do so. This is then handed on to 'Production', and the research people proceed to wash their hands of the whole matter. 'Production', of course, simply reinvestigates the whole thing almost *ab initio* from their own point of view. The amount of time unnecessarily wasted, and the number of good projects that fall by the wayside at this stage, is tragic. The point is brought home forcefully when some competing firm successfully brings out a similar new product based on exactly the same initial grain of new basic research that was originally available to all.

The cure for this weakness is close liaison with other departments during the course of the research work, and after it is completed. The first can be achieved if all departments take an active part in the frequent regular reviews of current research. The second is often best achieved by transferring some of the research staff to the production or even marketing departments, either temporarily or permanently. Alternatively, it may be appropriate to start production in the research laboratory itself. Whatever the solution in any particular case, the aim should be to *save time* and to avoid abrupt transfer of responsibility for a new project.

Development, as defined above, is often very difficult to separate from applied research, and except in a large organization it is probably not even advisable to try to do so. Managements should, therefore, not be too dogmatic about how to treat this function organizationally. In some cases it may be obvious that the production department should carry out its own continuous improvements; in others, it may be almost impossible to decide whether one is dealing with a simple improvement or a radically new project. In any case, the principles of initial justification and continuous review and control remain the same as already described.

22

The cost of research programmes

Table 13.1 lists the likely annual expenditure on research and development in industrial firms of various sizes. Since these figures are intended to cover a fairly wide spectrum of British industry, they should be regarded as very approximate. In any individual case there may be all sorts of valid reasons for a quite wide departure from these figures. For example, a firm whose business is based on recent scientific advances, could probably justify a two-fold increase in these figures, while for a firm in a more traditional type of business (with probably a lower percentage profit retention) an expenditure of half these amounts might be more appropriate. However, the national average is quite close to the figures given in Table 13.1, and any radical departure from them, for other than the reasons indicated above, calls for close examination and justification by any individual firm.

Table 13.1

Likely expenditure on research and development in various sized firms

	1,000		10,000		100,000	
Number of employees	1,000		10,000		100,000	
Turnover	£3,000,000		£33,000,000		£360,000,000	
Res. and dev. staff ($=2\frac{1}{2}$% of Employees)	25		250		2,500	
Expenditure on Res. and Dev.	£115,000		£1,100,000		£10,700,000	
−% of Turnover	3·84%		3·33%		3·00%	
Distribution of expenses.	£	%	£	%	£	%
(1) Salaries and wages	43,000	38	425,000	39	4,200,000	39
(2) Other expenses directly related to personnel	5,400	5	53,000	5	525,000	4·9
(3) Materials and equipment expense	20,000	17	200,000	18	2,000,000	18·7
(4) Library and information services	6,600	6	27,000	2	75,000	0·7
(5) General overhead	20,000	17	195,000	18	1,900,000	18
(6) Replacement of fixed assets	20,000	17	200,000	18	2,000,000	18·7
Total expense	115,000	100	1,100,000	100	10,700,000	100

There are a number of explanations required for the items condensed into Table 13.1.

1. Proportion of expenditure applicable to each of the three defined areas of *basic research, applied research*, and *development*.

The expenditure related to *basic research liaison* includes library expenditure on books, scientific and technical journals, patents, abstracting services, scientific consultants, travel and attendance at scientific meetings, exhibitions and conferences, etc., as well as the preparation of reports and the dissemination of technical information throughout the company. Item (4), Library and Information Services, does not fully cover all this (particularly the salaries of the people involved and their travel expenses), and an approximate figure would be obtained by doubling this item. The ratio between *applied research* and *development* is likely to be about 1:4. We thus obtain the breakdown shown in Table 13.2.

Table 13.2

Likely distribution of expenditure
for various sized firms

	Employees=1,000		10,000		100,000	
	£	%	£	%	£	%
Basic research liaison	13,200	11·5	54,000	5·0	150,000	1·4
Applied research	20,200	17·5	209,000	19·0	2,100,000	19·6
Development	81,600	71·0	837,000	76·0	8,450,000	79·0
	115,000	100·0	1,100,000	100·0	10,700,000	100·0

2. Salaries and wages are the largest single expense item, being nearly 40 per cent of the total, and averaging £1,720 per employee. Although this may seem large, it actually represents a considerable advantage for British industrial research as compared to conditions in the United States, where the average wage per research employee is almost exactly double at 10,000 dollars (£3,500). Since there is little difference in the other expense items, the proportion spent on salaries and wages in American research is more like 55 per cent than 40 per cent. This condition has led a number of American firms to establish research centres in the UK, or in other European countries.

For the firm with a research staff of twenty-five, it is of interest to note what kind of people these might be. A typical example in which the ratio of fully qualified professional scientists or engineers to non-professional staff is 11:14, and a ratio significantly less than one is typical for all sizes of firm, is given below:

Research Director	£ 5,500
3 × Senior Scientists or Engineers (@ £3,300)	£ 9,900
3 × Scientists or Engineers (@ £2,200)	£ 6,600
4 × Junior Scientists or Engineers (@ £1,500)	£ 6,000
8 × Technicians (@ approx. £25 per week)	£10,500
4 × Trainees (@ approx. £15 per week)	3,000
2 × Clerical Staff (@ approx. £15 per week)	£ 1,500
	£43,000

651

Table 13.3

Initial investment and depreciation (renewal)

No. of Research Staff	25	250	2,500
Buildings incl. installed Services (@ £10 per sq ft and 200 sq ft per person)	£50,000	£500,000	£5,000,000
Equipment (@ £3,500 per person)	£87,500	£875,000	£8,750,000
Renewal of Buildings (1/20)	£2,500	£25,000	£250,000
Renewal of Equipment (1/5)	£17,500	£175,000	£1,750,000
Total Renewal Expense	£20,000	£200,000	£2,000,000

3. Replacement of fixed assets (which include buildings and capitalized equipment) is calculated on a twenty-year renewal cycle for buildings and a five-year renewal cycle for equipment, as shown in Table 13.3.

The return on research expenditures

Perhaps the most difficult thing for the non-technical director to obtain a feeling for is the *amount* of research work any given level of expenditure can be expected to procure. As an illustrative example we will consider a research department of twenty-five people, as cited in the previous paragraph. Apart from the Research Director, whose time should be fully occupied in overall direction and control, it will be seen that there are only *six* experienced qualified scientists or engineers. Since it is unrealistic to expect that *on average*, these people can look after more than one project at a time, we are limited to a total of *six* projects operating simultaneously. If the quality of the research is not to suffer it is most important that this number should not be exceeded.

Now research and development projects require different times for completion, and we may conveniently consider three types:

(a) Major projects (which may be the development of new products) requiring twelve months, or more, for completion.
(b) Minor projects (which may be improvements of existing products) requiring six months for completion.
(c) Support projects (which may be cost reduction investigations, etc.) requiring three months for completion.

If there are two of each kind of project being carried out simultaneously, i.e., a total of six projects at any one time then we may expect to complete a total of fourteen projects during the year (two major, four minor and eight support).

652

Similar considerations will apply to larger research establishments, although the average number of people assigned to a project (four in the above instance) will probably tend to increase, as some individual projects may become quite large.

The importance of research

Expenditure on research has a long-term effect on the growth and profitability of the business of a manufacturing company. There is a temptation, therefore, during a business recession, to reduce research and development expenditure in order to make an immediate savings on 'overhead' expenses. The Board should clearly realize that this is a dangerous course of action, as it places the company's future in jeopardy. This is even more true now than it has been in the past, since the pace of technological change has become much faster. A company that chronically spends too little on research is doomed to extinction under present-day competitive conditions.

The vital, unanswered question is, 'How much research is enough?' It is impossible to give an unequivocal answer. It will vary from one kind of industry to another; it will depend on the rate of technology innovation in the industry, on competitive pressures to produce new products, and on the capability of the marketing and manufacturing organization to absorb and apply the results of research efforts. This last criterion may be the easiest to use in arriving at an upper limit for useful research expenditure, since it is obviously wrong to carry out more research than can be internally digested by the whole organization. Incidentally, it may also indicate that during a temporary business recession it may be advantageous to *increase* research expenditure, since marketing and manufacturing may be in a better position to use it when it is ready for application.

In any case it is the duty of the Board to decide what is the 'right' level of research expenditure in the company's own particular circumstances, and to stick to this with reasonable consistence, bearing in mind the long-term nature of the 'rewards'.

Reading list

BOOKS

Improving the Effectiveness of Research and Development, R. E. Seiler (McGraw-Hill, New York, 1965)

Managing Industrial Research for Profits, with case studies, D. Chorafas (Cassell and Co., 1967)

Management for Research and Development, H. A. Collinson (Pitmans, 1964)

Improving Effectiveness in Research and Development, Edited by Ralph I. Cole (Thompson Book Co. and Academic Press, 1967)

Management of Research and Development, a symposium by Edward Brech, Clive de Paula and Norman White (British Institute of Management, 1964)

The Organization of Research Establishments, Edited by Sir John Cockroft (Cambridge University Press, 1965)

Co-operation in Scientific and Technical Research, Diana Wilgress (O.E.E.C., now the O.E.C.D., Paris, 1960)

The Overall Level and Structure of Research and Development Efforts in O.E.C.D. Member Countries (O.E.C.D., Paris, 1967)

Pattern of Research in British Industry, report of a Conference at Eastbourne, April, 1962 (Confederation of British Industry)

Statistics of Science and Technology, Department of Education and Science, and the Ministry of Technology (H.M.S.O., 1967)

Research and Development—the Key to Future Profitability, J. Bullock and F. Clive de Paula (The General Educational Trust of the Institute of Chartered Accountants in England and Wales, 1966)

Management and Technology, Joan Woodward (Department of Scientific and Industrial Research—now merged in Science Research Council) 1958.

JOURNALS

'Controlling Research and Development Costs', Jack A. Bump (*Cost and Management*, December 1965)

'Government's Role in Applying Science to Industry', Vol. XXIX No. 474, *Planning* 29 July 1963 (Political and Economic Planning)

Useful addresses

Science Research Council, State House, High Holborn, London WC 1

National Research Development Corporation, Kingsgate House, 66 Victoria Street, London SW 1

Ministry of Technology, Millbank Tower, Millbank, London SW 1

OECD Information and Development Section, 3 rue André-Pascal, Paris 16e, France

13.2 National Centres for R & D

Nigel Hawkes

It is frequently said that Britain makes poor use of her expenditure on research and development. Although the annual bill approaches £1,000 million—2·7 per cent of the GNP—Britain's economic growth is slow. Japan spends less than 1·8 per cent of her GNP on research and development. It would be naïve, of course, to expect a direct relationship between research expenditure and growth, and there are certainly more important factors that affect Britain's performance, but despite the difficulty of defining the relationship, it is probably fair to assume that one exists. In this instance, can a strategy be developed to increase the productivity of R and D? How is research in Britain supported, and what criteria are used in the task of dividing the funds available among the competing interests?

University Grants Committee

Research and development activities in Britain divide very roughly into two groups. As a result of the Science and Technology Act of 1965, responsibility for academic science is vested in the Department of Education and Science, while the Ministry of Technology is responsible for applied science and development. The division is a slightly artificial one, and there is a measure of overlap between the two departments, but for the purposes of this discussion it is sensible to retain it.

Most scientists get their first experience of research within the universities. This work, research of a generally academic kind, is supported from a number of sources, most of them under the control, or at least the kindly eye, of the Department of Education and Science. Money for university salaries, buildings, and equipment is distributed to the universities through the University Grants Committee. Although the UGC is not generally thought of as a supporter of research, it probably provides more for university research than any other body. Its function is to oil the wheels through which the department controls the universities. On the one hand, it must convince the DES that money is being invested sensibly, and that waste is minimized; on the other, it must persuade the universities that their academic freedom is assured. These functions are not entirely compatible, which is perhaps what Lord Robbins meant when he described the UGC as 'the most felicitous constitutional invention of the century'.

The UGC itself consists of a committee of twenty-one (which swells to twenty-three when salary issues are discussed). In 1966–67, the UGC disbursed a total sum of £211 million; of this, perhaps £50 million went towards supporting research in the universities. There is no particular strategy behind the spending of the UGC, which goes out of its way to be scrupulously fair. Its job is to have few vested interests, and no axes to grind. Whether it can retain this lofty ideal as the universities come under pressure to become cost-conscious and administratively efficient remains to be seen.

The Research Councils are rather different. Each is responsible for a different area of research, and there are now five, covering science, medicine, agriculture, social science, and the natural environment. Because they have a good deal of autonomy, the research councils are a flexible instrument for supporting science of a basic kind, often in universities.

Science Research Council

The largest of the five is the Science Research Council, which began life in 1965 with many of the responsibilities of the defunct Department of Scientific and Industrial Research. In 1965–66, for instance, the SRC spent just over £27 million, and by 1966–67 the sum had increased to £33.4 million. The largest part of this budget is spent on high energy physics, which has now become so expensive that it cannot effectively be supported at university level. Instead, the SRC runs two national laboratories, the Rutherford Laboratory and the Daresbury Laboratory, whose facilities are shared between the universities. The Rutherford Laboratory houses Nimrod, a proton synchrotron which can accelerate protons, fundamental particles of matter, to an energy of 7,000,000,000 electron volts (7 GeV). This powerful beam of protons is used to study the structure of the atom. At Daresbury, a slightly smaller electron accelerator called Nina is used in similar work. In addition to these machines, and some smaller ones within universities, the SRC is responsible for paying Britain's contribution to CERN, the European Organization for Nuclear Research in Geneva. Together these activities cost, in 1965–66, no less than 46·1 per cent of the annual budget of the SRC. By 1966–67, however, the proportion had fallen to 43 per cent.

Space research is also expensive, even though Britain makes no attempt to keep up with America or Russia. As well as supporting the Radio and Space Research Station, at Slough, which is principally concerned with studies of radio wave propagation, the SRC is also responsible for paying the British contribution to ESRO, the European Space Research Organization. ESRO is concerned with exclusively scientific space experiments, usually carried in rockets, but sometimes in satellites launched by American help. The SRC also finances a national series of space experiments, launched in small Skylark or Petrel rockets, and supervised the building of the first all-British satellite, Ariel 3, launched by the Americans late in 1966. The total cost of these activities in 1966–67 was £6 million.

The SRC also looks after the oldest form of space research, astronomy. The Royal Greenwich Observatory at Hurstmonceux, and Royal Observatory at Edinburgh are the main centres, and during 1966 the SRC spread its activities to the southern hemisphere by taking over full responsibility for the Radcliffe Observatory in South Africa, and starting to plan a new large telescope for Australia. The rest of the SRC budget is spent in the operation of a computer laboratory, the Atlas Laboratory, for university workers, and in the direct support of work in universities through research grants and postgraduate training awards. About one third of the budget— about £12 million—is distributed directly to universities in this way.

Medical Research Council
The budget of the Medical Research Council is more modest, but if anything more tightly organized. The MRC itself is a council of fourteen, under the chairmanship of Lord Amory, and in 1966–67 it supervised the spending of almost £13 million. Pride of place in the MRC goes to the National Institute of Medical Research at Mill Hill. The institute, under the direction of Sir Peter Medawar, spends £1·5 million annually on a wide variety of medical problems. Principal themes include the mechanism of protein synthesis, the action of viruses on cells, and the nature and control of the immune response. The projects undertaken depend, very often, on the inclinations of the senior staff, so that the institute is in many ways like a university shorn of its teaching function. The other main source of MRC expenditure is through research units attached to universities, medical schools, and hospitals, and there are now more than seventy of these, costing nearly £6 million a year. The council also makes grants to groups working in universities, and to independent institutions carrying out medical research.

The only form of medical research the council has not yet tackled is clinical work, and this omission will be repaired in 1970 when a Clinical Research Centre at a new hospital at Brent in North London opens in 1970. By its policy of backing the man rather than the subject, the MRC has come to dominate medical research in

22*

Britain, and its record is an enviable one. The danger is that research policy may become inflexible, and perhaps unadventurous.

Agricultural Research Council

The Agricultural Research Council spends rather less than the MRC, and most of it goes to institutes rather than research units. The ARC supports twenty-four institutes, from the Institute for Research on Animal Diseases at Compton to the Glasshouse Crops Research Institute. The most expensive is the National Institute for Research in Dairying, which cost £665,000 in 1966. In 1967–68, however, the ARC was spending £12 million, exactly the same as the MRC. With agricultural research, it is often comparatively easy to see immediate financial benefits; the introduction of the barley variety called Proctor, for instance, led to a 14 per cent increase in yields. The development of pesticides, fertilizers, and battery farming methods have also contributed to the very rapid increase in farming productivity since the war, and the ARC has been involved with all of them.

Natural Environment Research Council

The other research councils are more modest in scale. The Natural Environment Research Council looks after the Nature Conservancy, the Institute of Geological Sciences, the National Institute of Oceanography, the Antarctic Survey, and the Marine and Freshwater Biological Associations. The Institute of Geological Sciences (which includes the Geological Survey) is the most expensive, costing just over £1 million.

Social Science Research Council

The Social Research Council will spend £1·2 million in 1967–8 in support of the softest sciences of all—sociology and economics among them. Despite a budget that is increasing very rapidly indeed (by 64 per cent between 1967 and 1968) some university departments have been critical of the scale of support. Perhaps they should take some lessons from the high energy physicists.

Ministry of Technology

The Ministry of Technology claims to have an altogether more hard-headed approach to research and development than this. Projects are supported only if they offer a return on investment within three years, the Ministry says, although it also supports with every sign of enthusiasm projects which, I consider, are unlikely to make money for anyone—the European Airbus, or Concorde, for example. The Ministry's interests include the Atomic Energy Authority, a number of civil and defence research establishments, support for industrial research associations, and the National Research Development Corporation.

658

It is impossible to discuss in detail all the research and development establishments the Ministry runs; a complete list is given in Table 13.4, together with annual costs where these are available. During 1967, the comparatively modest establishments run by the ministry were joined by the much more expensive establishments which, until then, had been part of the Ministry of Aviation. The largest civil research establishment the Ministry runs is the National Physical Laboratory at Teddington. This costs just over £5·5 million a year, and includes sections on physical and chemical standards, materials, aerodynamics, and the design and behaviour of ships. During 1967, the design group responsible for research in hovercraft was transferred to the NPL from Hovercraft Development Limited. The National Engineering Laboratory at Strathclyde (£1·5 million a year) has done a lot of work on the computer control of machine tools. Of the defence establishments, the Royal Aircraft Establishment at Farnborough and the Royal Radar Establishment at Malvern are the best known.

United Kingdom Atomic Energy Authority

The United Kingdom Atomic Energy Authority also comes within the ambit of the Ministry of Technology, although it has a marked individuality of its own. Set up to take advantage of atomic energy, both in weapons and in power reactors, the authority now concentrates on the latter. It runs establishments at Harwell, Aldermaston, Dounreay, Risley, and Winfrith Heath. At Harwell, emphasis is on materials research, and the basic work that lies behind designing nuclear power plant. Recently, Harwell has diversified, controversially, into other fields, and now contains research centres in ceramics and in non-destructive testing, intended for the use of British industry. Aldermaston, notorious as the starting point of the Campaign for Nuclear Disarmament marches to London, has developed the British nuclear weapons. Winfrith is a centre for reactor development, and houses two reactors of possible commercial importance; the steam generating heavy-water reactor and the Dragon high-temperature reactor, which is a collaborative project with the countries of OECD. The steam generating reactor, which is moderated by heavy-water instead of graphite which is more typical of British designs, and is cooled by water instead of gas, went critical in September 1967, and was feeding 100 MW into the National Grid by the end of 1967. At Dounreay, in Scotland, the authority is building the prototype fast reactor, a type that is expected to displace all other power reactors within the next twenty years. It is hopes for the fast reactor that have hurt the authority's other establishment, at Culham. The work here is intended to devise ways of taming the fusion reaction that occurs in the hydrogen bomb—current reactors all use the fission reaction of the crude atomic bomb. Unfortunately, the problems of controlled fusion have proved much more difficult than seemed likely at the time of the Zeta experiment, when for a moment the authority thought it had them beaten. As a result, it has been decided that the expenditure of the Culham laboratory will be reduced from its present level of £4 million a year to some £2 million a year in five years time. The irony of the decision is that, in the United States, expenditure on fusion research has recently been increasing, partly because its supporters pointed to the considerable sums that were being spent at Culham.

The Ministry also supports the industrial research associations, although these find the majority of their support from the industries they represent. There are some forty-seven associations, ranging in size from the British Iron and Steel Research Association with an income of £1.5 million a year, to the Brush Research Association, which gets by on £15,000 a year. The total income of the RAs is £14 million, of which the Ministry supplies about £4 million. The Ministry contributions are strictly geared to the amount of support the associations can get from the component industries they serve.

National Research Development Corporation

Finally, there is the National Research Development Corporation, which exists to exploit inventions made either in government laboratories, universities, or by private inventors. This it does by borrowing money from the Exchequer and investing it in likely inventions. Until 1965, the limit of borrowing was £10 million, but it was then raised to £25 million, and, in August 1967, to £50 million. The total income has recently been running at something about £1 million a year, from the sale of patent rights, development levies, and licences. The biggest project the corporation has been concerned with is the hovercraft, for which it continues to handle licences, despite the translation of the design team to the NPL. Perhaps surprisingly, the highest money-earner the corporation has ever handled was the development of cephalosporin C, an antibiotic discovered by Professor Abraham and Dr Newton at Oxford University. The corporation also handles the development of dracones, in which liquids are carried in flexible towable barges. The corporation has also invested a great deal of money in computer developments.

During 1967, the National Computing Centre in Manchester was opened. The centre is intended to educate management to the qualities of the computer, and hopefully to supply programmes for use in smaller businesses that would be unable to develop their own. The centre, of which Professor Gordon Black is director, cost £300,000 in its first full year.

Research Under Other Ministries

Other ministries also support research on a more modest scale. The Ministry of Transport runs the Road Research Laboratory at Crowthorne, which studies all problems concerned with traffic, road-building, and road safety. The Tropical Products Research Institute is supported by the Ministry of Overseas Development. The Ministry of Public Building and Works supports the Building Research

Station. The Ministry of Health does some research, and the Ministry of Defence spends quite a lot on research (in addition to that spent in defence establishments run by the Ministry of Technology). Of the £260 million defence research budget, most is spent through the Ministry of Technology, £170 million in industry, and £17 million in the defence establishments. The rest goes to support the Royal Navy Scientific Service (£34·6 million), the Meteorological Office (£5 million), and research and development in the Army, which includes the chemical and micro-biological warfare establishments at Porton, and some expenditure on the improvement of ordnance and military ground vehicles.

Nationalized Industries Research

Finally, there is the contribution of the nationalized industries. The Central Electricity Generating Board, for instance, runs laboratories at Marchwood and at Berkeley. British Rail, although much maligned, run a research department that is full of ideas. These include advanced passenger trains using new concepts such as the linear induction motor, but much of the work is devoted to improving the familiar iron wheel on the iron rail; by redesigning the suspension of bogies, it should be possible to get much greater speeds and longer life. The Coal Board research department works, predictably enough, on ways of making better use of coal, while one of the first tasks for the British Steel Corporation was to decide how research and development would be organized after the major companies had been taken into public ownership.

How should businessmen set about using the research work supported on such a splendid scale? This, in a sense, is the crux of the problem I mentioned right at the beginning. University research work can sometimes be useful to industry, and here a direct approach to the university department is probably worth while. The Department of Education and Science publishes annually details of the research in progress in universities. Increasingly, universities are willing to discuss research projects with industry, and even to undertake special projects if asked—the new technological universities are particularly eager to do this.

The Government establishments, of course, are far more directly concerned with industrial problems, and they, too, are trying to get ideas over to industry. Each laboratory publishes annually a report giving details of its work; most of these reports are published by HMSO, or can be had by application to the laboratory concerned. Again, a direct approach to the Director of the laboratory may be helpful, but the Ministry of Technology has also made efforts to put the contact between its establishments and industry on a more formal basis. It has set up more than fifty Industrial Liaison Centres, normally based on Colleges of Advanced Technology or regional and area technical colleges. Each centre has one or more Industrial Liaison Officers, who are members of the college staff responsible for maintaining contact with local firms and encouraging them to make greater use of technical and scientific knowledge. The full list of the Liaison Centres, and the names of the liaison officers are given in a booklet published by the Ministry, called *Technical Services for Industry.* The booklet also contains a full list of the research associations and government establishments for which the Ministry is responsible, and can be had by application to the Ministry.

With this information in hand, industrialists no longer have any excuse for not getting in touch with government laboratories that can help them. The laboratories themselves are aware of the Ministry's determination to help industry, and if not exactly falling over themselves in the rush to help, at least have no excuse for inaction. The trend is an entirely sensible one—all it needs is a growing number of determined businessmen to make sure there is no backsliding by the ministry, or the establishments.

Table 13.4

Establishments of the Ministry of Technology,
with annual costs for 1966–7

Establishment	Total cost (£)
Fire Research Station	262,000
Forest Products Research Station	290,000
Hydraulics Research Station	376,000
Laboratory of the Government Chemist	677,200
National Engineering Laboratory	2,503,000
National Physical Laboratory	3,680,000
Torry Research Station	363,000
Warren Spring Laboratory	811,000
Water Pollution Research Laboratory	318,000
Aeroplane and Armament Experimental Establishment Explosives Research and Development Establishment National Gas Turbine Establishment Rocket Propulsion Establishment Royal Aircraft Establishment Royal Radar Establishment Signals Research and Development Establishment	44,830,000

Table 13.5

Government Laboratories outside the Ministry of Technology

Ministry	Establishment
Agriculture Fisheries and Food	Plant Pathology Laboratory, Harpenden. Infestation Control Laboratory, Tolworth. Field Research Station, Fisheries Laboratory, Lowestoft. Shellfish Laboratory, Burnham on Crouch. Salmon and Freshwater Fisheries Laboratory.

Defence	Army Personnel Research Establishment.
	Fighting Vehicles Research and Development Establishment.
	Military Engineering Experimental Establishment.
	Chemical Defence Experimental Establishment.
	Microbiological Research Establishment.
	Underwater Weapons Establishment, Portland.
Forestry Commission	Research Station, Farnham.
	Scottish Station, Edinburgh.
Health	Biochemical Research and Development Unit.
General Post Office	Post Office Research Station.
Power	Safety in Mines Research Establishment.
Public Building and Works	Building Research Station.
Transport	Road Research Laboratory.
Overseas Development	Locust Research Centre.
	Tropical Products Institute.
	Tropical Pesticides Research Unit.

Table 13.6

Research within nationalized industries

Organization	Establishment
National Coal Board	Mining Research Establishment, Isleworth.
	Central Engineering Establishment, Burton on Trent.
	Coal Research Establishment.
	(Total cost of research £4·5m)
Electricity Council Central Electricity Generating Board	Electricity Council Research Centre, Capenhurst.
	Berkeley Nuclear Laboratories.
	Marchwood Engineering Laboratories.
	(Total cost in 1966–67, £11·8m)
Gas Council	Midlands Research Station.
	London Research Station.
	Engineering Research Station, Killingworth.
	Research, Development and approval testing Centre, Fulham.
British Rail	British Railways Research Department, Highgate.

	Research Association	Location
1	ASLIB	London
2	Flour-Milling & Baking Research Association	Chorleywood and St Albans
3	British Brush Manufacturers' Research Association	Leeds
4	British Cast Iron Research Association	Redditch and Glasgow
5	British Ceramic Research Association	Stoke-on-Trent
6	Construction Industry Research & Information Association	London
7	Coal Tar Research Association	Leeds
8	British Coal Utilization Research Association	Leatherhead
9	British Coke Research Association	Chesterfield
10	Cotton Silk & Man-made Fibres Research Association	Manchester
11	Cutlery & Allied Trades Research Association	Sheffield
12	The Drop Forging Research Association	Sheffield
13	The Electrical Research Association	Leatherhead
14	British Food Manufacturing Industries Research Association	Leatherhead
15	Fruit & Vegetable Preservation Research Association	Reading
16	Furniture Industry Research Association	Stevanage
17	The Gelatine & Glue Research Association	Birmingham
18	British Glass Industry Research Association	Sheffield
19	Heating & Ventilating Research Association	Bracknell
20	Hosiery & Allied Trades Research Association	Nottingham
21	British Hydromechanics Research Association	Cranfield
22	British Industrial Biological Research Association	Carshalton
23	British Iron & Steel Research Association	London, Sheffield, Normanby, Swansea
24	British Jute Trade Research Association	Dundee
25	British Lace Research Association	Nottingham
26	British Launderers' Research Association	London
27	British Leather Manufacturers' Research Association	Egham
28	Linen Industry Research Association	Belfast
29	Local Government Operational Research Unit	Reading
30	Machine Tool Industry Research Association	Macclesfield
31	Motor Industry Research Association	Nuneaton
32	British Non-ferrous Metals Research Association	London
33	Research Association of British Paint, Colour & Varnish Manufacturers	Teddington
34	Research Association for the Paper & Board, Printing & Packaging Industries	Leatherhead, Kenley
35	Production Engineering Research Association	Melton Mowbray
36	Rubber & Plastics Research Association of Great Britain	Shawbury

	Research Association	Location
37	British Scientific Instrument Research Association	Chislehurst
38	British Ship Research Association	London, Wallsend Newcastle on Tyne
39	Shoe & Allied Trades Research Association	Kettering
40	Spring Research Association	Sheffield
41	British Steel Castings Research Association	Sheffield
42	Timber Research & Development Research Association	High Wycombe
43	Water Research Association	Marlow
44	British Welding Research Association	Cambridge, London
45	Wool Industries Research Association	Leeds, Galashiels
46	National Institute of Industrial Psychology	London
47	Welwyn Hall Research Association	Welwyn

Reading list

Technical Services for Industry, (Ministry of Technology, 1967)
An Introduction to the National Research Development Corporation, (N.R.D.C. 1961)
New Technology, broadsheet published monthly—free (Ministry of Technology)
Annual Reports of the Science Research Council (H.M.S.O.)
Annual Reports of the National Research Development Corporation (H.M.S.O.)
Annual Reports of the National Engineering Laboratory (H.M.S.O.)
Annual Reports of the Government Chemist (H.M.S.O.)
Reports of the Council for Scientific Policy (H.M.S.O.)

Useful addresses

Science Research Council, State House, High Holborn, London WC 1
Ministry of Technology, Millbank Tower, Millbank, London SW 1
National Research Development Corporation, Kingsgate House, 66 Victoria Street, London SW 1
Department of Education and Science, Curzon Street, London W 1

13.3 The Research Associations

J. Leicester

The British Industrial Research Associations are autonomous organizations set up on a co-operative basis by various sectors of industry. Some forty-seven Industrial Research Associations are at present active, and they serve over 80 per cent of British Industry. Details of the main laboratories and offices of the Industrial Research Associations can be obtained from the Secretariat of the Committee of Directors of Research Associations in London. A guide to their geographical location is given on the map Fig 13.1. Representation on each Research Association Council from industry, government, and the universities ensures a link whereby the policy needs of government and the economic and technical needs of industry come together at a focal point in the research association.

The majority of the associations are supported by grants from government, but most of the finance is from company membership. This fact obviously opens the doors to the entry of research association staff at all levels to the whole of the particular industry or industries concerned. Over the past few years a new type of special government grant, the 'earmarked' or 'special purpose' grant, is becoming an increasing part of research association finance. Awarded on the basis of urgent need for work on a specified project that may not be capable of prosecution out of the general finances available, it can provide a catalyst for work of importance to the industry as a whole. This method of providing additional government grant has been used to very good effect in connection with the installation of computers in a number

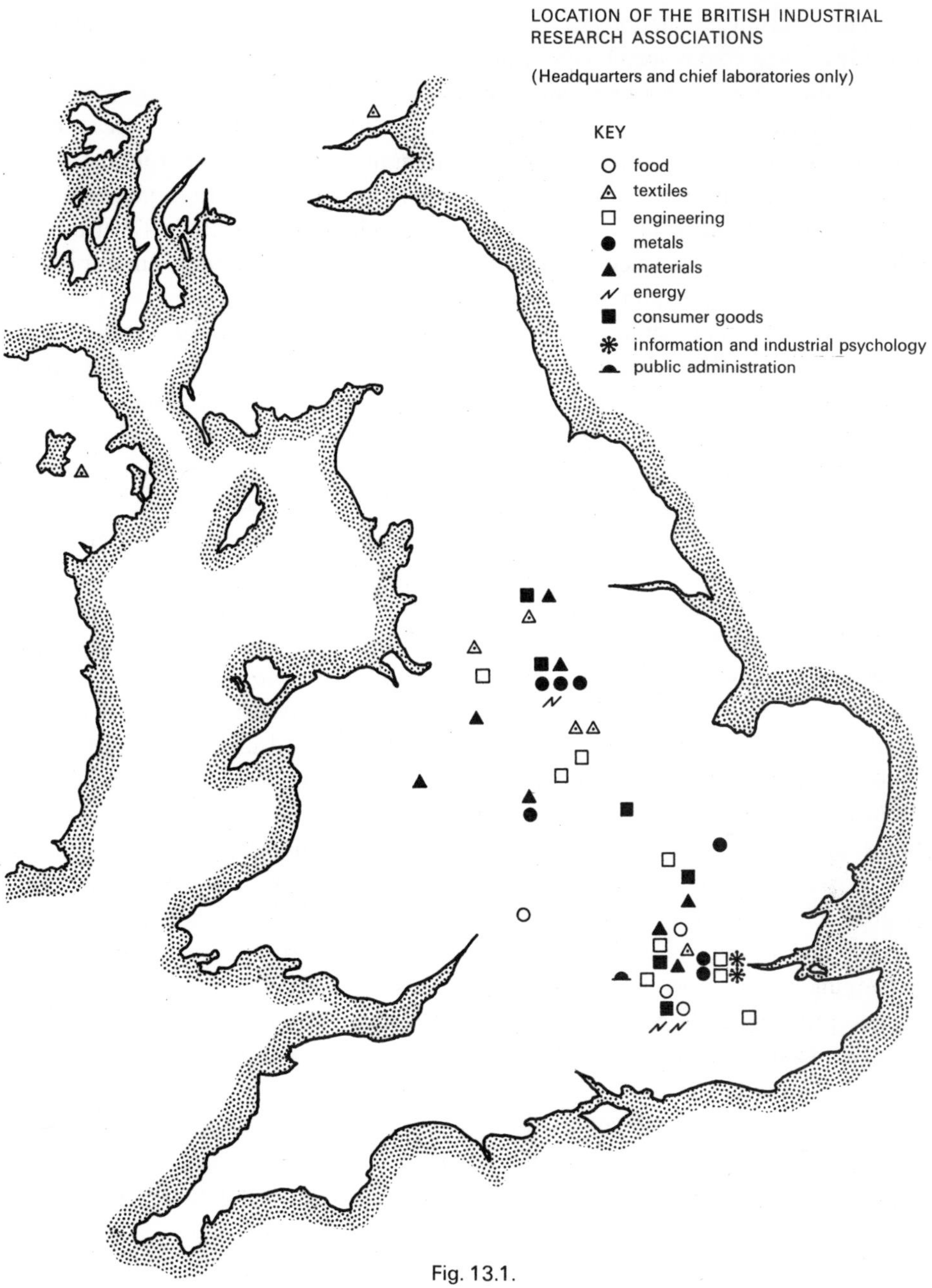

LOCATION OF THE BRITISH INDUSTRIAL
RESEARCH ASSOCIATIONS

(Headquarters and chief laboratories only)

KEY

○ food
△ textiles
□ engineering
● metals
▲ materials
∿ energy
■ consumer goods
✳ information and industrial psychology
⏜ public administration

Fig. 13.1.

of research associations. The result, through the research association, is that industry becomes increasingly aware of the value of computer techniques and their application to industrial control problems.

667

The research associations have, in fact, a special facility that distinguishes them from other industrial research laboratories: the ability to penetrate many companies in the same industry or allied industries, thus providing a pool of very varied expertise. Added to this specialist experience is a carefully planned technical-selling network, manned by qualified scientists and engineers to ensure that industry uses today's research findings at the earliest opportunity. The average percentage of total income allocated by all the research associations to technical liaison and information services to their members amounts to 13·5 per cent, an impressive contribution towards bridging the gap between research and industry.

Over 18,000 companies are linked with the research associations, and their financial support, through subscriptions and other sources, plus the grant from the government, is at the present approximately £14 million. A survey of the 300 largest firms in Britain, carried out in 1966, showed an increase of nearly 30 per cent between 1960 and 1966 (large company membership of forty-two research associations increased from 1,907 in 1960 to 1,315 in 1966). Only thirty-six of the largest firms are not associated with a research association, and most of these are retail or purely commercial organizations.

Many research associations now admit to membership companies operating outside the British Commonwealth, and the present total number of overseas companies in membership of the research associations is over 700. Some of the research associations have developed into international centres of research, with subscribing members all over the world. Income from membership subscriptions and fee-paid sponsored work is already in the region of £435,000 and this is steadily increasing. Of more importance than financial support is the exchange of scientific knowledge that is now moving across national boundaries and linking research workers in this country with their opposite numbers throughout the Eastern and Western hemispheres. The network of industrial research associations has, therefore, a growing international flavour. This has been extended during the past three or four years by exchanging visits between British research association representatives and their opposite numbers in the co-operative research organizations in a number of European countries. Contacts gained and information obtained was of considerable potential value to a future Common Market policy.

Government's investment in the research associations as a national asset is demonstrated in many ways, but Table 13.7 shows the links, through different forms of contract, that exist between nearly all sectors of government as well as the nationalized industries and the Industrial Research Associations.

What then are the advantages to a company seeking membership of one or more research associations? I would give priority to five reasons:
1. To maintain a commanding lead over competitors at home and abroad by actively supporting the research associations and applying the special expertise they can provide.

2. To take advantage of research association findings on the testing and evaluation of new methods of production and, also, types of plant and equipment available to a particular industry. Their job is to assess speculative methods and equipment and by their advice to save businessmen the cost and time of such an exercise.

3. The ability to make full use of expensive research and testing equipment for the many, whereas the few could not afford to acquire such equipment for only occasional use.

4. To help keep companies up-to-date with latest aids to quality control and productivity.

5. Finally, as a result of many of these services to industry, to help companies maintain the level of sales at home and abroad to meet the country's balance of payments demand.

Table 13.7

Government departments, state financed independent authorities, and nationalized industries sponsoring work in research associations 1967-68

Government	Nationalized Bodies	Independent State Authorities
Ministry of Agriculture, Fisheries and Food	Gas Boards	Agricultural Research
Ministry of Defence (Army)	National Coal Board	Council
Ministry of Defence (Navy)	Central Electricity	Medical Research
Ministry of Power	Generating Board	Council
Ministry of Technology	British Railways	Atomic Energy
Post Office		Authority
Foreign Office		National Research
Ministry of Health		Development
Ministry of Overseas Development		Corporation
Ministry of Public Building and Works		
Department of Education and Science		

The research association network provides links across a wide area of industry, government research establishments, the UK Atomic Energy Authority, and university research. These links and personal contacts are invaluable, and often make possible the successful initiation of difficult research investigations. The following are a few of the more recent examples that demonstrate the successful use by industry and Government of the industrial research association network to tackle problems of this nature:

Automation; testing services on building materials; water conservation for the textile industry; studies of problems of cooling-water systems for electrical power stations; operational research studies of refuse disposal in Newcastle; and, very recently, the marine engineering design by the Ship Research Association of a novel vessel for the ship-borne desalination plant commissioned by the UK Atomic Energy Authority.

669

However, the research associations' close and intimate contact with industry is and will always remain their greatest asset. They employ scientists of distinction alongside technologists with extensive practical experience, so that both scientific methods and practical experience can be brought to bear quickly on any industrial problem. Their expertise and information can, therefore, be made available to benefit many firms instead of only one. From the national viewpoint this is the most economic use of the nation's scarcest commodity, qualified scientific manpower.

Industrial boundaries are changing and a wide range of industrial products demand the use of raw materials that once may have been specific to a traditional industry. The trend in modern industry is for the consolidation of numbers of medium-size firms into fewer but more economic larger units. The research associations are alive to this change, and in many cases their work may have been in the van of such altered circumstances. Equally, they recognize the value of the grouping of research associations working in similar fields or on similar raw materials and, in certain cases, even the physical union of what were previously individual research associations, to produce a stronger and better equipped type of organization to deal with new problems as they arise.

What is the future potential of Industrial Research Associations? They are in better shape after nearly fifty years than they have ever been. Industry and government between them hold the key to still greater research association activity and their value to the nation's industrial economy. The research associations are strategically situated as a halfway house between government and industry or between university research and industry. Instead of using that halfway house to its full capacity, diversification of effort elsewhere in fields of industrial work already established in a research association is apparent in many areas. Is this what industry really requires, or, during the next fifty years of research association service to industry, should not the latter become the true focus for government-sponsored industrial research activity? Finance and effort could be channelled by the research association into that outlet where it could best be employed, whether it be in the Government laboratories, within the UK Atomic Energy Authority, the universities, or in the research association itself. The research associations believe they are ready to face the challenge if and when it comes.

Reading list

BOOKS

Industrial Research in Britain, Advisory Editor, A. W. Haslett (Harrap Research Publications, London—4th Edition, 1962)
Structure of Industrial Research Associations, F. N. Woodward (O.E.C.D. Publication, 1965)
Industrial Research Associations in France, Belgium and Germany (O.E.C.D., 1965)
Research Associations in the United Kingdom, Hammond, Attenborough and Ingram, foreword by Miss Arlidge, Secretary, C.D.R.A. (O.E.C.D., 1967)

British Industrial Research Associations: Report of Industrial Training Act Symposium, 16 November 1966 (Published for C.D.R.A. by the British Welding Research Association, Abingdon Hall, Cambridge, 1966)

Useful addresses

Committee of Directors of Research Associations, 24 Buckingham Gate, London SW 1

National Library for Science and Technology, Boston Spa, Yorkshire

Ministry of Technology, Research Association Division, Abell House, John Islip Street, London SW 1

The Science Research Council, State House, High Holborn, London WC 1

13.4 Universities and Industrial Research

J. C. Anderson

Much has been said and written in recent years on the subject of co-operation between the universities and industry, especially in the field of research, and a great deal of it has been uninformed or mistaken. With the modern explosive expansion of scientific and technological research and development, which is the product of work in industry, government establishments and universities, the scientist who shuts himself in an ivory tower will not survive as a scientist for very long. In addition, if a university is to carry out its dual function of education and training effectively, it is important that its graduates should have contact with real problems of practical importance to industry as part of their professional training. Being keenly aware of all this the average academic in any British university can be expected to be most receptive to suggestions involving direct co-operation with industry.

It is the intention of this article to outline the way in which university research is structured and financed and to adduce, from this, acceptable ways in which co-operative ventures can be set up. Finally a few examples of successful schemes will be given.

Financing of university research

The University Grants Committee, which is the main source of funds to the universities, does not finance university research directly. However, the UGC funds do meet the cost of academic salaries, administration, buildings and services and, broadly, may be interpreted as covering all overhead costs of a university research laboratory and providing the senior scientific staff.

Before considering financing of the research itself it is first necessary to describe the framework within which research is conducted.

Structure of research

The principal operatives in any university research group will be the research students. These are men and women who have attained good honours in their first degree and are carrying out research to obtain a Master's degree or a Doctorate. It is worth emphasizing that these students are the university's 'product', and the overriding priority for the academic leading the group must necessarily be the the success of his students. This carries definite implications for the nature of the research projects that are undertaken; they must, in general, be of such a type that a man working alone is able to make an original contribution to knowledge of the subject and, above all, it must be such that the work leads to a written thesis of an acceptable standard. It is this 'product' orientation that is often mistaken for the exercise of that ill-defined and much-abused thing 'academic freedom'. Further-more, it must not be forgotten that an important feature of a PhD programme for a student is that of education and training. In all areas of science and technology it is virtually impossible for a student to reach the frontiers of knowledge in any part of his subject in his first degree course. His postgraduate studies are intended to extend his knowledge to the frontier in his particular field, and his research will necessarily include training in its techniques. The second product of the university research group is the research itself; the results achieved have been traditionally measured in terms of the number and quality of papers published by the group. It is through his publications that the academic achieves a reputation for himself and his group. If that reputation is good, the group will attract good student recruits which, in turn, ensures that the work done is of a high standard. Equally, the progress and promotion of the academic himself depends to a significant extent on the excellence and number of his published papers. Publishing is, thus, a necessary part of the business, and is entirely analogous to the advertising of a product. Insistence on the right to free publication of research results is, therefore, essential to the continued success of a university research group. This is another right often claimed under the heading of 'academic freedom' but has much more to do with survival than with freedom.

As a result of this 'publish or perish' situation, it is often said that all the academic cares for in research is that he will get a 'good' paper out of it. This is an entirely mistaken view; the academic scientist or engineer is just as anxious to see his discoveries and ideas exploited as is his colleague in an industrial or government research laboratory.

Just as there are two main products from university research groups—higher degrees and published papers—there are two main raw materials, postgraduate students and ideas, and it is the responsibility of the academic in charge of the group to ensure supplies. It has been indicated above that a high quality of product is the best way of obtaining an adequate entry of good honours students. To maintain the flow of ideas is equally essential. The good academic will, through familiarity with his subject and with publications in his field, usually generate a number of promising ideas suitable for research in his group. Often these will be of a more speculative nature than would be acceptable in a commercial or government organization, and it is, perhaps, in this area of work that the universities can, and do, make their most significant contribution to science and technology. This is the 'basic' or long-term research with no immediately visible pay-off, without which the technological progress of industry would eventually diminish to vanishing-point. It takes a very determined and far-sighted industrial management to mount and maintain such projects in its own research laboratories, but the universities are uniquely placed to undertake just this sort of work. Geniuses apart, the average academic will be hard put to continue to generate new ideas on a sufficient scale unless he also keeps in close touch with his colleagues in the industries linked with his field of work, through the medium of regular visits to research laboratories, and attendance at conferences. It is this that accounts for that familiar twentieth-century phenomenon the travelling scientist, who is to be found on any train, aeroplane or bus going anywhere at any time.

Sources of finance

The foregoing gives, in broad terms, the framework within which university research is conducted. An academic in charge of a research group, usually a Professor or Reader, carries the responsibility for obtaining sufficient finance to keep his group going, and often the size and success of his group will be a direct reflection of his abilities as a salesman. The Government provides money through various channels, the principal one being the Science Research Council. This provides Research Studentship Awards, normally of three years' duration, to good honours graduates who have been accepted as postgraduate students in a university research group which carries SRC approval. It also provides research grants to support particular research programmes, and such grants will make provision for the purchase of capital equipment, recurrent costs and personnel in the form of technicians, research assistants or fellows. They are usually granted, in the first place, for a three-year term, on the criteria of 'timeliness and promise'. More and more this phrase is having the words 'to industry' tacked on the end. The SRC is uniquely placed to orient university research towards the needs of industry and is, as a matter of policy, using its influence to do this, especially in departments of applied science. As a further means to this end

674

they have introduced a class of studentship award specifically for graduates returning to university to study for a higher degree after a period of between one and five years in industry. These carry higher value than the ordinary award and are based on the supposition that the firm will make up the award to normal salary level. The student is expected to obtain his firm's agreement to a period of study and to remain their employee. This system also applies to students returning to university for one year's formal course leading to the degree of M Sc.

Science Research Council financial support is designed to safeguard the fundamental needs of university research, as outlined above. However, by itself, SRC has not got the resources to provide support on the scale desired or needed. Consequently, the universities are constantly seeking means for supporting both students and research programmes, and much of this additional support, especially in applied science and engineering departments, comes in the form of research grants or contracts from industry, government research establishments or the Ministry of Defence. Basic research is not directly supported by the Ministry of Technology whose policy, so far as it can be discerned, is to select areas of industry in which technological development is needed and to sponsor research and development directly in the appropriate industries. The bases of these additional grants or contracts tend to be much the same whichever body is providing the money, and so they will be dealt with as a whole.

Co-operative schemes

The premise of this section is that a firm, in a science-based industry, wishes to forge links with one or more university research groups. The motives for this must, in the end, be related to company profitability and, in the larger firms, are generally of two types: (1) improved recruitment of better graduates into the company, and (2) procuring research that is relevant to company interests. These are the most direct and visible returns on money invested in supporting university research. There are more intangible rewards to be had, on which it is impossible to put a price tag, in the form of the company image among young graduates. The firm with a reputation for liberal support of university research will tend to get more of the better graduates joining it, other things being equal.

Objectives (1) and (2) can often be realized together by means of a suitable scheme; two possible ones that have been used, are given below.

(a) A new company interest arises in terms of a desirable product that should be added to their range, but falls a little outside their present activities. The R and D department will have to implement a new line of research and to recruit new personnel to carry it through. In its first stages it will possibly be a feasibility study involving a young graduate scientist with technician support and supervision by an experienced researcher, and is, therefore, potentially a Ph D project.

The Research Manager identifies a university group doing work in this field and approaches the academic in charge with a proposal for joint work, offering to provide a student grant to support a suitable postgraduate, and some help on recurrent materials costs. The professor concerned may have a suitable student who has applied to do research in his group, and an agreement can quickly be concluded with the professor or one of his staff supervising the project. A gentleman's agreement is reached with the student by which, on completion of his higher degree, he will join the company's laboratories. (It should be noted that no legally binding agreement of this type can be made.) Alternatively, the student may have been found by the company's university interviewing team in which case the academic concerned would wish to assess the student's suitability himself.

Although schemes of this sort are successfully followed in a number of university departments, it is as well to be aware of the difficulties that arise. The management and direction of the project must be left to the university staff to safeguard the success of the student, and free publication of results must be allowed, as mentioned previously. Very often, students wish to stay on to do research in the university for no better reason than that it defers the day when they have to make up their minds on what career they want and with whom. Thus, many of them are reluctant to tie themselves to working for a given firm after obtaining their higher degree. Because of the normal Ph D period, it is not less than three years before the project is completed and support must be guaranteed for this length of time.

(*b*) A different form of arrangement, achieving the same ends, is open to the company that has a reasonably large research and development activity. Group leaders within the company's laboratories will (or should) invariably be in touch with research groups in the same field in their local university. Applied science and engineering departments in the university often ask the Group Leader to give invited lectures and seminars in his particular field to their students, and generally welcome such contact. The modern trend is that the industrial researcher is invited to become a visiting member of the university staff, making regular visits, say one day a week, to give lectures and to initiate, supervise, and advise on research. This is not without cost to the company, since only the more outstanding of their research staff will be suitable. The dividends, however, can be considerable. Because of the close contact, there is an easy flow of ideas and personnel between the university and the industrial research groups. Projects in the two groups can be complementary, and basic research programmes can be followed jointly. The member of the company staff involved benefits continuously from contact with the academics both within and outside his own field, and the members of academic staff are kept in close touch with industry's needs and interests. The company's graduate recruiting position is considerably improved.

Under such an arrangement, the company can safely sponsor postgraduate students to work in the group. Even if the particular man does not eventually join the

676

company, others from the group will almost certainly do so, and in the meantime the research done will have been relevant to company interests.

Details of such arrangements vary from university to university; some appoint visiting professors while other make *ad hoc* arrangements appropriate to the personnel involved. Some form of honorarium, often as expenses, may be paid to the Visitor, and in some cases the company appoint the principal academic involved as a consultant to the company.

Contract research

University research is cheap since, as indicated earlier, most of the overheads and the supervisory staff are provided from UGC funds. Most universities make a fixed percentage overhead charge on research contracts from non-government sources, to cover additional administrative costs, but these are nowhere near the magnitude of normal industrial overhead charges.

For contract work to be acceptable to a university research group it must obviously be compatible with their normal lines of investigation. If the contract is of such a nature that it will serve as a Ph D project the remarks made above will apply. However, many university research groups welcome contracts in which specific objectives are nominated, and the course of the research is carefully controlled in the interests of the company, provided that the contract includes the provision of a research fellow, research assistant or technician, who will perform the main part of the work. The advantage to the university group is that such a contract may provide items of capital equipment and/or recurrent expendable costs which are of general use to the group, and there may be a 'spin-off' in terms of higher degree projects. The details and terms of the contract will vary, and no general rules can be laid down. The handbook *Research in British Universities and Colleges*, published yearly, will aid identification of universities carrying out research in the desired field.

Miscellaneous

There is a variety of different arrangements by which industry provide support to university research. They are of a semi-charitable nature and provide only indirect advantage to the company. These are greatly valued by the universities, and reflect considerable credit on the company concerned. Some of the possibilities are given below.

1. The Endowed Chair
In the interests of promoting academic teaching and research in their field of work, a company may endow a professorship in a university department, with a supporting secretary and a small sum for materials. The Chair will carry the company's name,

677

and its incumbent will be a distinguished scientist. Financially, the arrangements can be made in the form of a covenant, with the consequent tax advantages, since a university would not, in any case, be happy to accept such an offer for a period of much less than seven years. Alternatively, the arrangement might be made by means of an outright capital sum, in which case something in the region of £120,000 would be required. As a charity, the university would be able to obtain around 7 per cent interest on invested capital.

2. The Postgraduate Bursary

In a similar way a company may provide a bursary, to be allocated by the university to a graduate student, for research in a particular field. Again the bursary may carry the company's name and can be financed under a covenant. The bursary should be for a period of three years for a given student but is a continuing commitment and is awarded to a new student every third year. A capital sum of about £10,000 will provide such a bursary.

3. Equipment Grants

Since most university research groups must obtain their capital equipment via grants for specific research, there are always capital items, essential for running the group, that cannot be justified by one research programme. Some enlightened companies, being aware of this difficulty, offer to buy such equipment for them, yearly or less often, dependent on the cost involved. This earns the undying gratitude of the academic recipient. Financially, the purchase is often placed on the company books, so that it is subject to amortization, and issued to the university on (indefinite) 'loan'.

4. Recurrent Grants

Often a company may come across an on-going project, in a university group, that is of direct interest to it. A small grant of a few hundred pounds per annum for recurrent costs in the group will often 'buy' six-monthly written reports on the project. In this way access to the results well in advance of their publication can be ensured.

5. Consultant Arrangements

A smaller firm which does not have extensive research facilities, wishing to have advice on new product development, may approach an academic to act as consultant to the company. All universities permit such arrangements, which are made personally with the academic concerned. In some there are arrangements whereby the academic may make use of his own laboratories in connection with his consultancy. Often the most effective consultant will be the younger member of academic staff, who is likely to be able to devote more time to the work than is his busy professor.

678

Conclusion

There are many ways in which co-operation between universities and industry can be set up to the profit of both parties. It is emphasized that academics are keenly aware of the advantages, and frequently initiate such arrangements themselves. It is hoped that this section, which is written from the point of view of what the industrialist should do to promote co-operation, will not be taken as academic arrogance. The universities are very willing to meet industry more than half way in the interests of scientific and technological progress, and it is hoped that boards of directors will do all that lies within their power to promote this co-operation.

Reading list

Scientific Research in British Universities and Colleges: Volume 1: Physical Sciences; Volume 2: Biological Sciences; Volume 3: Social Sciences (H.M.S.O. annually)
Higher Education in the United Kingdom, Association of Commonwealth Universities (Longmans, Green, bienially)
Commonwealth Universities Yearbook (Association of Commonwealth Universities, annually)
Report of the Working Party on Liaison Between Universities and Government Research Establishments (Command Paper 3222, H.M.S.O., 1967)

ARTICLE
' "Let's Work Together" Say Industry, Universities', Willem Van der Eyken (*The Financial Times*, 9 August 1967)

Useful addresses

University Grants Committee, 14 Park Crescent, London W 1
Science Research Council, State House, High Holborn, London WC 1
Ministry of Technology, Millbank Tower, Millbank, London SW 1

13.5 Patents and Patent Agents

Herbert W. Grace

The health of an industrial undertaking, as of most living organisms, can be measured by its rate of growth, by its capacity for adaptation to change, and by its own capacity for change. Those industries that can survive by continuing their activities without substantial change in the products they manufacture, or the methods or processes by which they are manufactured, must surely be very few. Innovation, on the other hand, costs money, and if the changes demanded of an industrial organization require not only innovation but invention, the cost is likely to be very high. It is true that inventions sometimes happen in the relaxing steamy atmosphere of a hot bath, but even then, not normally without a substantial background of experience and investigation, which provides the raw material from which the invention grows. More often, invention is the outcome of painstaking, methodical research. Innovation may be founded on invention or it may not, but it is usually expensive.

It would be bad business to embark on a programme of innovation and spend money solving the inevitable problems if, having solved them, the solutions are freely available to one's competitors. If the solutions can be kept secret, at least for a sufficient length of time, then maybe one can deny to one's competitors most of the advantage gained from the research and development on which money has been spent, but so often industrial secrets cannot be kept; either the product itself discloses the invention on which its production is based, or the ordinary hazards of industrial security limit the time during which the secret can be kept. It may not always be the best policy to deny the fruits of research and development to competitors if a new industry is to be built up, but if the results are to be disseminated, at least it is not unreasonable to expect some payment for their use.

Happily, some of the fruits of research and development can be protected by means of patents, and the foregoing introduction should suffice to establish the need and the merits of wise use of the patent system for the protection of one's research and development results.

The patent monopoly

Monopolies, in general, have been the subject of suspicion and misgivings for centuries. Whilst most have been made illegal, one form that survives is that in respect of new 'inventions' for which patents are granted.

Naturally enough, for one specialized form of monopoly to survive, its nature has to be quite precisely defined, and it is interesting that the definition included in the Patents Acts of today, which relates 'inventions' to manners of new manufacture, is in the precise words first used in the Statute of Monopolies of 1623.

Patents for inventions are granted by the Patent Office as though by the Sovereign, and confer upon the patentee the sole privilege 'to make use exercise and vend' the invention, but only subject to the law and to the rights of others. The patent, therefore, does not, in fact, confer upon the patentee the right to use his invention at all, it really only confers upon him the right to prevent other people doing so!

The patent can be regarded as providing the patentee with an instrument constituting a fence surrounding a piece of 'industrial property' which he alone is privileged to use. It can be used in various ways. The patentee can, so to speak, set up a sign 'Trespassers will be Prosecuted, Keep Out' and keep the sole use of his invention to himself. Alternatively, he can grant licences in respect of the whole or any part of the territory protected by his monopoly. The grant of a licence can be in many forms, such as on a non-exclusive basis, leaving the patentee free to use the invention himself, or on an exclusive basis. In this case, the patentee, without vacating his position as patentee, passes on to another the right to use the invention or some part of it while himself refraining from doing so. Such arrangements would normally be restricted as to time or as to the technical field of the invention within which the exclusive right can be exercised, so leaving the patentee a field in which he can himself operate. Moreover, the terms of such an exclusive licence should include some provision such as a minimum annual royalty, which the licensee would inevitably pay, so as to safeguard the patentee from inactivity of the licensee in the field of the licence. Patents, like other forms of property, can be bought and sold, and the rights granted to the original patentee passed on to others.

23

International arrangements

The monopoly granted in respect of an invention by means of a patent obtained in say, the United Kingdom or the USA has effect only in the territory within which it is granted. It follows that, if protection is required over a large part of the globe, many patents have to be obtained in many territories, the laws of which vary considerably.

Most of the major industrial countries of the world, however, are members of the International Convention for the Protection of Industrial Property. The USSR signed in 1965, Argentina even more recently.

This requires the member countries to adhere to certain basic principles in respect of the grant of patents. The most important provision is that the filing of a patent application in any country of the Union provides the applicant with a priority date upon which he can rely in obtaining patents in any other member States, provided that he files an application in that State within twelve months of his originally filed application. Any such application then takes effect as though it had been filed in that State on the same day as his original application.

Patents are expensive to obtain, the cost of filing an application in any country of the world varying according to the length of the specification required (which affects the cost of translation where this is necessary), the number of sheets of drawings, and so on. The cost of filing an application in a single country is often about £100, and thereafter there are, of course, fees to be paid for work to be done in adjusting the wording of the specification to suit the requirements of the various Patent Offices. Moreover, when the examination processes have been gone through, there are fees for sealing or obtaining issue of the patent, fees for publication of the specification, and so on, so that costs of the order of £150 to £200 for these initial stages are common enough. In countries in which the examination is severe, the cost can be much more. Further, when a patent has been granted, most countries require annual renewal fees, usually on a rising scale, to be paid throughout the life of the patent to maintain it in force.

Another factor that has to be taken into account is the variation of patentability from one country to another. That which is validly patentable in one country is not validly patentable in another. For example, in some countries it is possible to protect new substances however they are made. In other countries it is possible to protect them only by reference to the novel process by which they are made. In yet others, it is not possible to protect pharmaceuticals at all. It is important, therefore, to select with some care the territories in which it is intended to obtain patents for the protection of any given invention.

The processes for the granting of patents vary from country to country. There are those countries which grant patents more or less automatically when the application has been filed. These are countries like France, Italy, Belgium, Spain, and many of the smaller territories. In such countries those who may wish to make use of the invention are left wholly in doubt as to what they may or may not do without infringing the inventor's rights. It is necessary for them to make their own investigation to discover what the patent validly covers and whether they will infringe it if they go ahead. Otherwise, or ultimately, this evaluation must be done in the Courts. At the other end of the scale, the examination system in the United States, for example, goes a long way towards resolving the doubt interested parties encounter, by settling with some precision the scope of the monopoly granted by the patent, having regard to the prior art and the various grounds upon which a patent may be invalid. The patent when granted has a reasonably high presumption of validity. In such countries as Germany and Holland the claims (*see* below) that define the scope of the monopoly are also very carefully considered. On the other hand, in those countries, the Courts in interpreting the claims do not regard themselves as so rigidly bound by the wording of the claims as are the Courts in the United States.

In the United Kingdom something between these extremes exists. The claims are quite precisely determined by negotiation between the Patent Office Examiner and the applicant or his agent, and having been so fixed are quite precisely interpreted by the Court if they are ever put to the test. On the other hand, the Examiner, during the prosecution of the application through the Patent Office, is severely restricted as to what objections he can raise against the claims presented by the applicant, so that when the patent is granted the scope of the monopoly claimed is quite well determined but the presumption of validity in the UK is a good deal less than in the USA and Germany.

The term of a patent varies from country to country but is, in most, about eighteen years. In the UK it is sixteen years, while in the USA it is seventeen years, but since the UK term dates from the date of filing of the Complete Specification (*see* below), and the USA patent dates from the date of grant of the patent (which may be as much as ten years after the application was filed) the USA patent is the longer lived.

Because of the diversity of practice between the various countries of the world, two major disadvantages are suffered by the patentee who seeks protection on a world-wide basis, and these same difficulties reflect upon third parties who may be interested in using the invention but are deterred from doing so by patent protection held by another. The first is that, in respect of one and the same invention, patents of differing scope, and therefore different relevance to the industry, are set up in different countries. By the same token, the validity of a patent in any one of the countries is more or less suspect according to the country in which the patent has been granted. The degree of uncertainty tends to bear more heavily upon the industry at large than upon the patentee. The patentee has his patent and can adopt a menacing attitude on the basis of it. He has the initiative, he can 'fight or run'. The intending infringer, on the other hand, must make a choice between fighting and paying.

He must either respond to the patentee's menaces by agreeing to pay him a royalty or by agreeing to desist from infringement, or he must be prepared to fight. Either way he can be put to considerable expense.

The other disadvantage is that the patentee, in obtaining his patents, is put to the expense of having the novelty of his invention examined independently in each of a number of countries. This is a large part of the cost of examination in most countries. This duplication of effort, not to mention the inefficiency involved in having every patent application examined even though it may never be a matter of real concern to anyone, are matters upon which much thought and discussion are taking place at this time. The restricted examination carried out in the UK has enabled the backlog of work in the UK Patent Office to be kept reasonably within bounds. On the other hand, the Opposition proceedings, which are probably a necessary part of any such system, have created their own backlog. In the USA, attempts have been made to streamline the examining procedure, but there is still much anxiety about the ever-mounting backlog of unexamined applications. In Holland and Germany a different system, known as deferred examination, is being tried out. This is a system of putting off until tomorrow something that need not be done today in the hope that it will become unnecessary. Applications are left un-examined for a period of years (seven years at present) unless the applicant or another specifically requests that the examination should take place, and pays the relevant fee. At the end of the twilight period the application must be examined or it dies. The hope is, that many applications will not need to be examined as interest in them fades before the time is up. It is too early to say whether this system will succeed. An impossible overload might develop when the first period of delay since the system started expires.

The Scandinavian countries have already taken some steps towards setting up a system whereby an invention may be protected in all of them on the basis of an application filed in one. The European Economic Community prepared a draft law to enable a single patent, which would cover the whole of the area, to be obtained but this does not seem to have got beyond the draft stage. In the USA, a Bill has been placed before Congress which, if it became law, would introduce some radical changes into the American patent law to align it more closely to the laws of other countries, with a view, ultimately, to making it possible to include the United States in a unified community to enable applicants to obtain one patent on the basis of a single novelty search, which all the territories of the community would accept as 'final'. However, the insularity and conservatism of the legal fraternities in the various countries are such that it will almost certainly be a very long time before these objects are achieved.

Patentability

It has already been said that the criteria for patentability vary from country to

684

country. It is, of course, a fundamental requirement of any system that the invention to be patentable should be new, but the criteria of novelty vary in themselves. In the UK, the invention must be novel in the sense that it has not been published within the United Kingdom. However, in many countries, novelty can be destroyed by publication having taken place anywhere in the world. Again, what constitutes publication is a variable. Printed publication is obviously a form accepted universally, but areas of doubt arise in the context of manuscripts available on a limited basis, for example by being placed in the library of a university and not being made accessible to the public. Publication by word of mouth is effective to destroy novelty in the UK, but if the doctrine of so-called 'absolute novelty' is to be adopted, a measure advocated by some, it is questionable whether verbal disclosure taking place in a remote territory should be regarded as fatal to the grant of a patent at home.

Given novelty, it is still necessary to decide whether or not there is 'inventive merit' in a proposal. The criteria of inventive merit are necessarily subjective. The question is whether the alleged invention amounts to more than what a person 'skilled in the art' might regard as within his own competence.

A person skilled in the art for this purpose is hypothetically someone with the whole stock of prior human knowledge at his command. The invention may, therefore, be new in the sense that its component integers are all known but that they have not been brought together before. It, then, still remains to be decided whether bringing these integers together amounts to an inventive act. For example a British Court once decided that a man who had combined a mincing machine and a sausage-making machine into a single continuous process machine had not made an invention. He had merely aggregated two known machines. In another example, certain engineering principles known for controlling the rise and fall of a marine pontoon were applied to the guidance of the rise and fall of a gas-holder. This was held to be an invention on the ground that the engineer who designs gas-holders is not a marine engineer and could not therefore have been expected to be aware of the principles adopted in the other art. It was, therefore, inventive for him to import from marine engineering principles applicable to his problem in the civil engineering field. On the other hand, the adaptation of a fish-plate known for connecting parts of bridge structures for the purpose of jointing railway lines was held not to constitute invention. One could put it this way; 'A fish-plate is a fish-plate and it has uses in many fields of engineering. To adapt it from one purpose to another, therefore, would not amount to invention'.

Whether or not an invention has been made is a matter sometimes better considered late in the life of the patent. The evidence on which a proper judgement can be made may not exist earlier. The speed and extent to which the invention is adopted and used can well be relevant, and commercial success in a patented invention has often been taken as an indication that the invention had merit. It is for reasons of this kind that the United Kingdom Patent Office Examiners are not empowered to refuse the grant of a patent on the ground that it is not inventive over what has been done before. They can judge only whether the alleged invention is *new*, having regard to what has been done previously. In Opposition proceedings, however, where the grant of a patent is challenged by a third party, it is possible to contend that the invention was 'obvious', having regard to what had been done before. This ground of opposition was introduced for the first time in the Patent Act of 1949, and it has been applied with some reservation by the Comptroller and by the Appeal Tribunal, which is a section of the High Court specially empowered to deal with appeals from Patent Office decisions.

It is in sharp contrast to this that in, for example, the USA, Germany, and Holland, the Examiners have the power to reject applications on the ground that no invention was involved. They commonly cite two or more prior references, then argue that there was no invention in applying the teaching of one reference to that of the other so as to arrive at the combination claimed by the applicant. While these provisions may result in the elimination from the records of a number of patents that would have been of doubtful validity, it is questionable whether the Patent Office Examiners, by the nature of their occupation, have at their command all the information they need to make this judgement, and the British view is that it is better to grant the patent and judge its validity in the Courts, if the need arises, when full opportunity exists, with hindsight, to judge the merits of the invention.

To be patentable the invention must be useful. This means that not only must the invention be applicable to some useful function usually related to manufacture, but that it must work as it is alleged to work. In this country the invention must apply to a 'manner of manufacture'. This definition leads to no difficulty where the invention concerns a manufactured product or a process for its manufacture. At the other end of the scale, the mere discovery of a natural law does not meet the requirement, nor do proposals in the nature of schemes such as systems of navigation or of accounting. However, there is a 'grey' area, between these extremes, which has been investigated over the years in great detail; for example, a method of radio signalling was held to be patentable, the useful product which constituted the 'manufacture' being the electromagnetic signal itself. On the other hand, a method of extinguishing an incendiary bomb was held not to be a manner of manufacture, the end product being no more than an extinguished bomb, which is a singularly unsaleable product. A particular area exercising the minds of many people at this time is that of programmes for electronic computers. On one view of the matter the control a computer programme exercises over the computer can be regarded as setting up, within the computer, a novel interrelation of parts. Indeed, this computer could itself be physically constructed to perform a given programme and, having been so constructed, constitutes in itself a manner of new manufacture. On the other hand, the written programme or the punched paper tape in which it is embodied constitutes a form of product that has not normally come within the field of patentability.

686

In Germany, a special quality of invention is recognized in the so-called 'new technical effect', which it is necessary to be able to find in the proposal before an invention can be said to have been made. In other words, every invention must be regarded as an advance in the art, and the applicant for a patent must make it clear what this advance is in his particular case. Thus, in Germany and in Holland it is necessary in draft claims to start with an introductory passage setting out that which is known and from which the invention springs, followed by a 'characterizing clause' which spells out the advance the invention makes over the prior art thus acknowledged.

Basically, inventions are the solutions to problems. It may be that the concept is new, in which case the problems that have to be solved to carry it into effect need not be very great for the invention to have patentable merit. The merit lies in the basic concept. On the other hand, the problem solved by the invention may have been in existence for a long time, and the merit of the invention may then reside in the fact that the problem has been overcome for the first time or, if it has, in fact, been overcome before, that it has been overcome in a more efficient, more effective or more economical manner. If the invention resides in a combination of known integers, then the combination, to have inventive merit, must provide a result different from or greater than that which was to have been expected from a consideration of the various integers taken separately.

The mechanism

A patent is granted on the basis of a description of the novel process, device, or machine in terms sufficiently detailed and precise to enable an engineer or other person skilled in the art to which the invention relates to carry out the invention. It is also necessary to define the scope of the monopoly claimed. These two functions are performed by the patent specification which consists basically of three component parts. There are the opening passages, which introduce the invention against the appropriate background of prior art, explain it in quite general terms, and go some way towards defining the scope. Then follows the so-called specific description which describes how the invention is to be carried out, quoting examples and, usually, referring to drawings that accompany the specification. The scope of the monopoly is then defined in claiming clauses, so-called 'claims', which are usually set out at the end of the specification and are separate from it in the sense that they are complete in themselves.

In the United Kingdom, as in some other countries that have based their law on British law, it is possible to file with the application a so-called Provisional Specification. Theoretically, and if one is concerned with protection only in the United Kingdom, this Provisional Specification need not contain the full detailed description of the method of carrying out the invention referred to above. It is enough to set out the nature of the invention. On the other hand, since this specification is likely to be used as a priority document for claiming priority in applications later to be filed overseas under the terms of the International Convention, it is desirable that it should be sufficiently full to serve this purpose. It must, in any event, be followed within the year by a Complete Specification. A Provisional Specification lacks the claiming clauses that have been referred to, since at that stage it is not necessary to define the scope of the monopoly. Provisional specifications are not examined.

When a Complete Specification has been filed, the application is referred to an Examiner, who carries out a novelty search to determine whether the alleged invention is new. He also examines it to see that it complies with the other provisions of the law, for example to see that the detailed description is adequate and accurate. If he finds prior art, which robs the invention as claimed of novelty, and defects in the application (and he usually does), these are reported to the Applicant through his Agent who then has an opportunity of amending his claims and his description to meet the objections raised. When all the objections have been met, the application is accepted and the specification is then published. In the United Kingdom, and in many other countries, the initial publication takes place before the patent is granted, and a period of time (three months in the UK) is allotted for third parties to enter Opposition proceedings against the grant of a patent on the application. If there is no Opposition, the patent is then granted subject, of course, to the payment of a sealing fee (there is always a fee!) and the patentee is then in a position to pursue any who infringe his rights. His rights, in effect, extend from the date when the specification was first published, in that he can claim damages for infringement as from that date, but he cannot start proceedings until the Patent has actually been granted. Thereafter the patent has to be maintained in force by the payment of annual renewal fees, which mount on a rising scale over the years. In some countries these fees mount to alarming proportions in the later years of life of the patent so that only those patents that are of real importance are kept alive. In the USA and Canada, however, no renewal fees are payable, and the patent continues in force for the full span of seventeen years.

If Opposition is entered in this country, the Opponent and the Applicants are each entitled to bring evidence in support of their respective cases and they have an opportunity to be heard. It is in the nature of a Court action and, indeed, either party can appeal to the Patents Appeal Tribunal, which is a High Court Judge specially appointed for the purpose. These proceedings are sometimes criticized on account of their cost but they are, of course, very much cheaper to sustain than a full-scale patent infringement suit. Perhaps their main disadvantage is the delay they impose upon the grant of a patent, having regard particularly at the present time to the large back-log of unheard Oppositions.

In other countries the Opponent submits a case, which is considered by the

688

Examiner, and while each party, i.e., the Opponent and the Applicant, can present a case the parties never meet and there is no joint Hearing. There is, of course, usually some provision for the case to be referred to an Appeal Court if the Examiner's ruling is not satisfactory to either party.

The future

The patents system exists to serve the requirements of industry for protection of its investment in research and development. These requirements are subject to change in a changing world and from time to time, therefore, the patent system has to be examined to see whether it is serving the purpose for which it is intended and whether its functioning can be improved.

At the time of writing, such an investigation is taking place in this country. A committee known as the Banks Committee, under the chairmanship of Mr M. A. L. Banks (erstwhile Managing Director of British Petroleum Ltd), is collecting evidence from which it will determine whether any changes are needed in the patent law of the United Kingdom in order to improve the service the patent system provides to industry.

Patent agents

Enough has been said to make it clear that the business of obtaining patents at home and abroad is a skilled matter. It is highly important, therefore, that the work should be carried out by properly qualified practitioners. It is well-established practice with many of the larger industrial organizations to employ their own patent agent staff rather than send their work to firms of patent agents. Whichever way it is done, it is highly important that the patent agent doing the work should be properly instructed and adequately informed. It is important that the patent agent should be consulted at an early stage and given, not only the opportunity but also positive encouragement to examine the invention in depth, discover the background which led up to it, and form his own view as to the nature and size of the invention that has actually been made. It is not enough for him to be fed with information pre-digested by some member of the company's staff not skilled in these matters, so that his appraisal of the invention is circumscribed or he is even misled.

In drafting a patent specification and, perhaps at a later stage, drafting the claims, it is most important that the invention should be presented in its true light and with a proper appreciation of its true scope. The good patent agent, by requiring answers to the appropriate questions, and by bringing his own ingenuity to play, should extrapolate from the particular example given to him by the inventor towards a more generalized concept. Necessity is the mother of invention, and inventions are therefore the solutions of problems. The inventor has set out to solve his own

23*

problem and may have done so quite elegantly so far as his own field of activity is concerned, but in doing so he may very well have solved a much bigger problem than that which confronted him. He does not always realize this, and it is for the patent agent to point it out to him and present the invention in its broadest light. It may, of course, be necessary to curb the exuberance of the patent agent if it turns out that he is presenting the invention too broadly and tending to trespass into fields where the invention is either not applicable or is already old. If he does so, there is normally little lost, because the invention will be cut down to size when the patent application is examined by the Patent Office.

The patent agent has a basic technical qualification with the legal qualification superimposed upon it. He probably has a university degree in science or engineering but is likely to rely more upon his experience in practice as a patent agent than upon his academic training for his technical awareness, which, in general, needs to range over a wide field. However, he cannot be expected to deal equally competently with all subject matter fields and it is usual, therefore, for a patent agent to specialize to some extent. This means only that, if he is basically a chemist, he will work in the chemical field; if he is an engineer he will work in the mechanical engineering field or the electrical engineering field or within particular areas within these fields. In choosing a patent agent, therefore, it is important to see that he has the appropriate technical background for one's own particular work. While the larger firms of patent agents include within their staff people skilled in all the various scientific and engineering disciplines, the smaller practices will tend to be selective in their acceptance of clients.

A difficulty that arises from this specialization within fields comprising different subject matter is that the patent agent sometimes finds himself handling work from clients in closely related parts of an industry. It is usual, then, for the patent agent to make this conflict of interest known to his clients, and he may find it necessary to decline to work for one of them. In the larger firms, however, it is usually possible to arrange for clients whose interests conflict to be served by different people within the same firm. Normal standards of professional behaviour make such an arrangement quite acceptable.

Qualification of a patent agent is by way of examinations organized by the Chartered Institute of Patent Agents, which is the body responsible for keeping the Register of Patent Agents. There are two examinations, the Intermediate Examination, which can be taken after three years' work under a Chartered Patent Agent, or one year if the candidate already has a university degree, and the Final Examination which is taken after a further two years' work. The minimum time for qualification, therefore, is three years after having taken a university degree. The Intermediate Examination is based largely on factual knowledge of the patent law both UK and foreign, with some tests of practical ability. The Final Examination, however, is primarily concerned with productive work, i.e., the drafting of patent specifications and claims, and with the interpretation of patent specifications with a view to assessing the validity and scope of the patent claims, having regard to the prior art. That these examinations are searching is clear from the fact that the pass rate for the Final Examination is usually no more than about one third of those who sit, and sometimes less than that. It is possible to satisfy the Examiners in respect of part of the examination, and sit again for the other half. Nevertheless, there are those who sit the examination time and again and fail to qualify.

Reading list

BOOKS

How to find out about Patents, General Editor, G. Chandler (Pergamon Press, 1967)
The Sources of Invention, Jewkes, Sawers and Stillerman (Macmillan and Co, 1960)
Terrell on the Law of Patents, Aldous, Falconer and Aldous (Sweet and Maxwell, eleventh Edition, 1965)
Patents for Inventions, T. A. Blanco-White (Stevens and Sons, 1962)
Agreement for the Sale of Know-How, T. A. Blanco-White (Sweet and Maxwell, 1962)
Amendment of British Patent Law 1964, Amendment of British Patent Law II 1965, (The Chartered Institute of Patent Agents, London)
Patents for Engineers, Lawrence H. A. Carr and J. C. Wood (Chapman and Hall, 1959)
Practical Trade Mark Protectors, W. C. Duncan (Jordan and Sons, 1961)
Patent Protectors: The Inventor and his Patent, Clifford Lees (Business Publications 1965)
Manufacturing Under Licence, Edited by Clive Bingley (Kenneth Mason, 1963)
Patents, Design and Trade Marks, Annual Report of the Comptroller-General of Patents, Designs and Trade Marks (H.M.S.O.)
The Register of Patent Agents (The Chartered Institute of Patent Agents, London)

JOURNALS

'Industrial Protection: Patents', Engineering Outline 71 (*Engineering*, 12 May 1967)
'How the Countries of the World Treat Trademark Rights', Joseph Lightman (*International Commerce*, 23 May 1966, Bureau of International Commerce, US Department of Commerce, Washington D.C.)
'The Unchartered Seas of Licensing Agreements' (*The Director*, July 1963)

Useful addresses

Chartered Institute of Patent Agents, Staple Inn Buildings, High Holborn, London WC 1
The Patent Office and Library, 25 Southampton Buildings, Chancery Lane, London WC 2
United International Bureaux for Protection of Intellectual Property, Geneva, Switzerland

13.6 Technical Organizations

Elizabeth Mack

Technical organizations include trade, development, research, professional and learned associations and societies. The professional association is a society whose members are engaged in employment requiring the exercise of knowledge and skill gained by study and experience; the members may be shown to have reached a specific standard by their acceptance in membership, and this gives them the privilege of using letters after their names. They have an attitude to their work, their colleagues, and those whom they serve, which involves more than the mere selling of their ability during set hours for a set price; they are usually interested in furthering the body of knowledge of their special study for its own sake; they are concerned to pass on this knowledge to the next generation of practitioners.

Even within the professional associations, however, objectives vary considerably. At one end, the association may be to all intents a trade union, the National Union of Teachers for example. At the other, is the study association which resembles the learned society, and which may admit into membership any individual sufficiently interested to find a more or less nominal sponsor, and pay the subscription; the Geological Society and the Chemical Society fall into this class. In between come the numerous and important associations of specialists, which include those known as the qualifying associations.

In some cases, registration as a competent professional by the society is essential in order to follow the occupation at all: pharmacists, medical practitioners (of all kinds, including medical auxiliaries, veterinary surgeons and dentists), patent agents and architects are among the professions in which only registered members may practice.

The natural sciences are mainly represented by study associations. It is in the applied sciences that the qualifying associations are strong, and in engineering they are most numerous of all. Many study associations are open to the interested amateur, but most of the qualifying associations demand a period of approved service in addition to some kind of diploma. While there are professions in which there is still no recognized qualifying association, such as agriculture and horticulture, or information work, there are some occupations in which there are several. Accountants may be qualified by nearly a dozen associations, and membership of either one of the two largest, the Institute of Chartered Accountants or the Association of Certified and Corporate Accountants, is necessary to permit an accountant to act as auditor to a public company. The ICA will only accept five years' articled service with a member of the Institute, as a preliminary to qualification, but the ACCA will accept as an alternative, approved employment in a company or local government office. There are over one hundred qualifying societies that hold their own examinations, but the majority of these grant whole or partial exemption to applicants with approved alternative academic qualifications. In some cases, time spent on study courses may be accepted in lieu of some part of the period that must be served in employment gaining practical experience.

Besides the societies holding their own examinations, there are some that accept other qualifications, and will award recognition after a period of approved service; a suitable university degree, or Higher National Certificate, or the examination of an allied, perhaps more general, institution may be acceptable. The Institute of Petroleum, for example, accepts a university degree; the Institution of Locomotive Engineers requires the Associateship examinations of the Institutions of Civil, Electrical or Mechanical Engineers; the Corporation of Insurances Brokers uses the Chartered Insurance Institute's examinations. It is common for the qualifying institutions to offer different grades of membership requiring increasing age, years of service, responsibility, and advanced knowledge.

While new professional associations are formed as new occupations arise, there are also amalgamations. The Institute of Physics and the Physical Society merged in 1960; the Institute of Chartered Accountants incorporated the Society of Incorporated Accountants in 1957; the Institution of Mechanical Engineers incorporated the Institution of Automobile Engineers in 1945. A more comprehensive consolidation has been started in the field of engineering by the formation, in 1962, of the Council of Engineering Institutions, on which are represented thirteen chartered engineering institutions. An examination has been arranged through which qualified members of these institutions will become 'Chartered Engineers'.

The majority of associations are incorporated under the Companies Act, usually with a Board of Trade licence to omit the word 'Limited' from their titles.

693

Only a few organizations hold a Royal Charter; and this form of incorporation brings some restrictions on their government, but a Royal Charter is accepted as a mark of distinction in recognition of the disinterested public service performed by the association and its members. In general, the professional association is governed by a voluntary council, elected by and from the membership, which delegates to paid officials the job of running the association. The main income is derived from members' subscriptions. In qualifying associations, the membership normally includes some grade or grades of studentship, sometimes basic and senior grades (Associate and Fellow) of full membership, and honorary or life membership, awarded as a mark of esteem to distinguished men in the field. While the qualifying function is of importance, these associations are also active in many other ways. Despite the increasing opportunities for specialized education, some classes and correspondence courses are still held, and textbooks and student journals are published. The professional associations are usually represented on the committees, and sometimes on the governing bodies, of technical colleges, universities and examining boards.

Besides the publications intended for students, most professional associations publish the papers and discussions at their meetings and conferences. These are often of a high standard, embodying the results of original research. Nearly all the larger professional associations have a library, and many have valuable historical collections including the published work of their members. Some of the associations lend to members, or provide photocopying services, but in many the archive/ museum attitude to the collection takes precedence over the members' current requirements. It is rare to find any kind of information service offered by a qualifying institution, but there are some attempts in existence; for example, the Institution of Electrical Engineers, with a long and admirable publication record in *Science Abstracts*, has developed a more contemporary type of current awareness service in its *Current Papers* series, and the Royal Institution of Chartered Surveyors has an abstracting publication, *RICS Abstracts and Reviews*.

Some of the qualifying associations will discipline members who break the code of professional behaviour, which may cover such practical subjects as scales of charges, forms of contract, and regulations for competition with other professionals. It may also include ethical considerations such as the confidentiality of the client-professional relationship, the solidarity of the profession, responsibility of the senior for his junior partners or assistants. While the statutory registered professions usually receive publicity in their disciplinary actions, where suspension from the Register must prevent the professional from further practice, the associations for the un-registered professions have less power in general, and there are wide variations in their customs. Some, like the RIBA and the Institution of Civil Engineers, have formal codes; others, like the Institute of Practitioners in Advertising, have none, but will take disciplinary action. Many of the engineering institutions, like the

Royal Aeronautical Society, have power to act if necessary, although they have neither formal code nor disciplinary procedure.

Although there are some small, inactive, aimless professional associations in Great Britain, many are important in encouraging the growth of knowledge and application in their fields of activity. The qualifying associations, in particular, hold an important balance between the professional and the public, consolidating and enhancing the status of their members, yet ensuring that selfish ends do not outweigh the general good of the country and of the profession.

Reading list

BOOKS

The Qualifying Associations: A Study in Professionalization, G. Millerson (Routledge and Kegan Paul, 1964)

British Qualifications: A Comprehensive Guide to Educational, Technical, Professional, and Academic Qualifications in Britain (Deutsch, 1966)

The Yearbook of Technical Education and Careers in Industry, Edited by H. C. Dent (Published annually by Adam and Charles Black.)

14. Computers and the Boardroom

14.1 Computers and Company Strategy

Basil de Ferranti

'The electronic computer is probably the most important result of applied scientific effort, not only in the USA, but in the world.' In saying this, Professor Edward Teller made it clear that he was deliberately putting the computer in front of the development of nuclear energy and the exploration of space.

The computer clearly cannot be considered to be just another machine. It is the first device that can automatically manipulate information at immense speed and in large volume. It adds a new dimension to human brainpower. The service a computer can provide for management is virtually all-embracing; therefore, the decision by the management of a company to use a computer marks the end of one era and the beginning of the next. Once the decision is taken, the company can never be the same again.

The computer offers management two major advantages. It enables administrative procedures to be integrated, and alters what may be termed the 'time basis' of management. Both these advantages enable management to establish closer and more effective control over its own organization; and both improve the chances of management achieving its short-term and long-term aims, whether they are to maximize profits, to sell more goods, or to increase output. These are fine words, but although computers are now installed in considerable numbers, for industry as a whole these aims have yet to be achieved. Why should this be? The answer is, of course, that the computer has been with us for less than twenty years. We are still learning to apply it.

Computers were first used to perform repetitive clerical tasks. In the early days, some computers installed for this purpose were complete failures, usually because of lack of proper planning and objectives. In contrast, other computer installations employed on the same work have done well, although in some instances savings were only marginal. This does not imply that this phase of computer development was ineffective. It did enable many companies to expand and handle an increased volume of clerical work without increasing costs, a fact of some significance where skilled staff is in short supply and rents are high. The speeding up of routine accountancy procedures also usefully improved companies' cash flow. Most important of all, however, use of computers on apparently mundane jobs provided the basic data processing with the experience it needed.

Staff and management have been educated in the running of computer installations; methods of capturing and feeding data into the machines have been developed; procedures for creating and handling computer files have been devised: in other words, the 'data base' has been established, together with a wide awareness of what is needed for successful computer operation.

Once this 'data base' had been created, the next step was to introduce computer-controlled management systems that would enable the computer to earn money for its organization. The integration of clerical procedures is often the first indication that a management has appreciated the essence of electronic computing.

Because people can co-ordinate only a limited range of events, the action required of a company in response to, say, a sale, has traditionally subdivided into several discrete activities. Integration of diverse company activities, which in the past were necessarily undertaken singly, is now possible. A set, or suite, of interlinked computer programs, where each program passes on to the subsequent one the data it requires, can be prepared for individual company procedures which can be modified smoothly as the system grows.

Time as a function of management control

The incorporation of discrete administrative activities into an integrated system represents an early phase in the commercial application of computers. Because of the computer's ability to process masses of data rapidly, one immediate consequence of this phase is that the time basis of management decision-making is altered. Previously, management arrived at its decisions by using historical performance data, which was often inherently inaccurate. Now. accurate information about what has actually happened can be made available a matter of hours after the event. The next step, therefore, is to use a computer to project events forward into the future, and to assess what effect specific decisions, made now, would have on the commercial future of the company. Such projections, in the majority of companies, depend largely upon *entrepreneurial* hunch, but computer simulation techniques on computers can remove a considerable amount of guesswork from forward planning.

A computer cannot make decisions, but it can provide facts that will simplify decision making. For example, it can provide answers to such questions as:

'If we initiate development and manufacture of product *A*, what are the capital requirements throughout the life of the project? What is the cash flow? What is the likely outturn?

Although these projections will be estimates only, and only be as accurate as the initial information provided, nevertheless they will facilitate a rational choice between competing projects. Such information will help directors and managers to make the most profitable use of a company's resources. For instance, where many projects are running in parallel, it will enable them to phase development so that embarrassing peaks in the demand for capital, sales effort, or manufacturing facilities, are avoided.

Having helped the boardroom formulate a plan, the computer can be supplied with data enabling it to indicate any significant deviations from the plan. In this way, more exact knowledge is acquired of the performance of the company, and improved control is effected.

To operate simulation techniques, the computer is provided with a model of the project in which the relationships between the various activities are defined. As experience is gained of actual performance achieved, compared with that predicted, the mathematical model can be altered to obtain closer conformity and more accurate forecasts. Many different types of model can be created for this purpose: an overall economic model of the company, a production model, a sales model, and so on. These models can be interlinked and can use common data.

As management tools, in addition to their more conventional role as giant calculating machines for scientists, engineers, and accountants, computers are causing fundamental alterations in companies' structures and modes of operation. Clearly then, before deciding to use a computer, directors must ask searching questions about every detail of their company's organization, its aims, and the policies for achieving them. Furthermore, once the decision to instal a computer has been taken, top management cannot retreat from the scene. It has the responsibility for specifying the goals the information system is to achieve, reviewing the goals continuously, and ensuring that the system produces the data required, when required.

Management at all levels must make itself conversant with computers and computing. The detail can be delegated, but the overall strategy of employing computers is a top management responsibility, and if this responsibility is shirked, failure is almost certain. Management must also keep abreast of current technological trends in computing, because new facilities can have a profound effect on the way work can be tackled. For example, multiprogramming computers are now capable of handling many different jobs simultaneously. More versatile and efficient procedures controlling computer operations have been developed along with equipment such as interrogating visual display units. So it is now economical to answer random queries when they arise. A sales manager, for example, can enter, on a keyboard, questions about the current stock level of a particular project and how much of that stock has already been allocated, and receive the answer on the screen of a cathode-ray tube of his visual display unit. The unit can be located in the sales office, many miles from the computer providing the answers. The use of these techniques not only shortens the response time and, therefore, the efficiency of any sales organization, but it also reduces the volume of internal paper work.

The successful implementation of computer techniques is not merely a matter of overcoming the technical problems. Staff of a different calibre and different outlook are required to operate a computer. This means that the kind of manager employed will change. Many members of a company's existing staff and management will adapt themselves, but others may not. Provision must be made for retraining those who are not adaptable, and re-deploying the rest.

The nature of the individual manager's work will alter. Managers in the middle strata of a company, freed from their heavy load of paperwork, will find new functions as financial planners, provided they are prepared to broaden their knowledge of the company's activities, and their own knowledge. More engineers, for example, will have to learn costing procedures and, as repetitive clerical operations are simplified, office and warehouse managers will face new functions. The lines of communication between middle management and top management will become less cluttered, and every manager's performance will be more exposed to examination. With information reaching top management more efficiently, failures will be more rapidly identified.

Social changes will occur as the result of the need to keep the cost of operating a computer to a minimum. The computer, like any other item of expensive capital equipment, must be intensively utilized. One consequence will be the growth of shift and weekend working.

Today, the decision facing the directors of companies that do not yet use computers is not 'shall we use a computer?' but rather 'when shall we introduce computer techniques?' The timing of this decision and the way it is implemented are critical. Despite every precaution, despite scrupulously performed feasibility studies, a particular machine may not prove ideal for the work undertaken; progress may be slower than anticipated, or costs higher than expected, and so the investment may not pay off as soon as planned. But risk is surely what managers and directors are paid to accept and evaluate. The hazards are there, but the rewards of successfully introducing a computer into an organization are great.

As business grows increasingly international and competitive, it becomes more scientific. In the computer, management has a tool of unique power. Its use is limited solely by the collective intellectual capacity of the people in charge. Companies that know where they are going and why, can control their activities with precision and will prosper where others fail. Computers provide the accuracy of control needed for success in modern commerce.

Reading list

BOOKS

Automation: its Impact on Business and People, W. Buckingham (Harper and Row, New York, 1961)

Living with a Computer, E. Mumford (Institute of Personnel Management, 1964)

The Computer and the Clerk, E. Mumford (Routledge and Keegan Paul, 1967)

The Computer in Society, B. M. Murphy (Anthony Blond, 1967)

Business Systems, T. Radamaker (Systems and Procedures Association, Cleveland, Ohio, 1963)

Management Uses of the Computer, I. Soloman and L. Weingart (Harper and Row, 1966)

Electronic Computers and their Business Applications, A. J. Burton and R. G. Mills (Benn, 1960)

Automation in Practice, David Foster (McGraw-Hill, London, 1968)

Useful addresses

The British Computer Society, 23 Dorset Square, London NW 1

International Federation for Information Processing, 23 Dorset Square, London NW 1

The National Computing Centre, Quay House, Quay Street, Manchester 3

14.2 How to Use Computers

Ronald Clark

Two illusions about electronic computers have more currency than they deserve. One is that these products of the last two decades, conceived and built in an environment that can be fully comprehended only by the specialist, are of use only to a small handful of large companies, and to scientists whose work takes them into the mathematical stratosphere. The other illusion implies, contrariwise, that while computers do sums more quickly than humans, they merely speed up a process that had already been speeded once before, when the abacus took over from fingers and thumbs, and then again when mechanical computers began to take over in the office.

The truth is more difficult to grasp, but it is no overstatement to claim that the electronic computer provides a large sector of industry, of business, and of many other occupations, with a new tool as significant as the first X-ray machines were to medicine and as radioactive isotopes have already become to biology and agriculture, among other sciences.

Electronic computers are basically of two kinds: the analogue computer, which is comparable to the slide-rule and which produces its results in physical quantities or analogues; and the digital computer, which can be compared to the abacus and which provides its answers as a selection of digits. In very general terms, analogue computers have been developed more for scientific than for business use, whereas the reverse is true of digital computers. Thus, it was once held that a digital computer could be developed primarily for clerical and accounting work or for scientific calculations but hardly along lines that would enable it to be used with equal ease in both spheres. However, with increasing sophistication this 'either/or' choice is steadily becoming less important. One typical example is an ICT 1900 machine, which is used for much share registration work and the production of dividend warrants, yet also carries out complicated calculations for the control of a major building project.

It is not only, or perhaps even mainly, the barely comprehensible speed at which computers can carry out operations that makes them as much a part of the modern office as was the typewriter half a century ago. The fact that a week's accounts work can be done in a few minutes is useful—as long as the time saved is properly employed and as long as the cost is not prohibitive; ability to make sales forecasts on figures that go up to last night rather than to the end of last month—a common enough experience when a computer has been integrated into a firm—provides an undeniable benefit. Yet these advantages, sacriligious though the suggestion may sound to the electronics industry, are merely refinements of existing routines. The significant benefits to be gained from the proper use of a computer go much further and far deeper, and they can be summed up under three heads. The wealth of statistical information that can be drawn upon with their help enables tasks to be tackled that could not have been tackled two decades ago by the best-equipped organization in the world. This wealth of available information does, as it has been crudely put, enable the 'gu' to be removed from 'guestimates'. And, on a slightly more esoteric plane, the provision of information on which decisions can be made does clear the decks for what might be called creative decision-making.

This last point has rarely been better made than in a paper by J. H. H. Merriman and D. W. G. Wass presented to a Symposium on the Mechanization of Thought Processes held at the National Physical Laboratory at the end of the 1950s. Automatic data processing, said the authors, could provide administration with some most powerful aids to judgement. 'A good deal of the subjective judgement to which an administrator is driven by defects in his present equipment could be made objective if the means to processing were available', they went on. 'For example, decisions based on purely economic considerations are likely to be made more soundly and with greater realization of their consequences as the theories of econometrics are developed and the formulation of accurate numerical equations in economics and their solution by ADP becomes possible.'

Since this was written, the increased size and sophistication of computers has enabled the process to be taken one more important step forward. Today, the computer can do more than enable management to decide. With the necessary information, adequately presented in assimilable form, it can enable management to decide which of a number of decisions should be taken. By simulation techniques it enables these decisions to be implemented, so that each of them can, as it were, be played over to demonstrate what would happen were it adopted. Too great a claim should not, perhaps, be made for such methods. Such projections, usually made with the help of mathematical models, will still only be estimates, and they will only be as accurate as the data fed into the machine. Nevertheless, they will greatly aid the making of a rational choice—and it must be remembered that such methods are constantly being improved and refined. No one is suggesting that the machine can forecast the future; what it can do, is work out the future interrelationships of results flowing directly from a number of discrete non-related events.

Such work is merely one example of the many ways in which the use of computers has been developed during their relatively short history. The whole science of data processing is still in a state of flux, and it must not be forgotten that development of the 'electronic brain' for practical business purposes has been almost entirely a post-war affair. Its genesis goes back more than a century, however, and if any one man can claim to be 'the father of the computer' it is Charles Babbage, part of whose 'Difference Engine', built in the early part of the nineteenth century, now stands in the Science Museum in London. The use of punched cards to present information to mechanical, and then electric, calculators was developed in the United States by Dr Hollerith, whose activities helped to found both the huge American IBM and the British ICT firms. Then, in the 1930s, an American pointed out the similarities between the on-off states of an electric circuit and the basic twin alternatives of logic. During the war, university scientists on both sides of the Atlantic began to explore the possibilities opened up by expanding wartime technologies, and by the later 1940s prototypes of the first electronic computers were operating in both countries.

Development of the computer, and its language

Like many new inventions, the computer was at first accompanied by certain disadvantages which appeared to be inherent, and the memory of these lived on long after progress had removed them. Thus, the American machine ENIAC, completed soon after the war, weighed thirty tons, used 130 kW, occupied 1,500 square feet of floor space, and was packed with thousands of valves whose heat seemed at times to be equalled only by their unreliability. Most of these inconveniences have now been eliminated by the substitution of transistors for valves. Miniaturization and micro-miniaturization are still reducing the size of computers, output for output, and for most practical purposes the answer to 'Do we want a computer?' is no longer affected by major problems of space, cooling, and air-conditioning.

The increasing frequency with which this question is being asked in so many business and industrial fields, might be said to stem from the basic fact that the channel of communication inside an electronic computer is not, as in an abacus, the human hand; not, as in a mechanical computer, a physical mechanism; but is, instead, an electric current travelling at a speed that allows the information it contains to be transmitted from place to place in a minute fraction of a second. Millions of such currents, travelling along the complex electric systems of a computer, enable the information put into it to be processed, and to be ejected in the form of 'answers', at a rate which, for many practical purposes, can almost be described as instantaneous (although in the language of computers, which often measures time in nano-seconds, or thousand-millionths of a second, it is nothing of the sort).

Incidentally, such words as nano-second are among the many with which the computer-user can be advised to become familiar. In the early days, the language used in this field tended towards gobbledegook. This has now been largely dropped, but there is still a fair number of words that can be thrown at businessmen by the computer experts, and which it is useful to understand. There are two excellent guides. One is *Speaking of Computers* by James Allan, which in the process of providing a glossary gives a first-class account for the layman of what computers are all about. The second, a more technical affair, but quite invaluable to any director whose company has recently acquired a computer and who wishes to understand at least a little of the technology, is the British Standards Institution's *Glossary of Terms Used in Automatic Data Processing*.

In both of these booklets, reference is made to the binary system, a system of representing numbers by the use of only two digits, i.e., 0 or 1. The significance of this to computer operation becomes apparent when it is realized that a basic method of computer-communication is by means of an electrical circuit that is either on or off. These two simple states are, with the help of the binary system, thus able to communicate any number, and it is therefore natural that the system has been utilized from the earliest days of the computer. In the decimal system, the successive digit positions are successive integral powers of ten, whereas in the binary system the same is true of the power of two, the digits representing, from right to left, 1-2-4-8-16 and so on; the number 19 thus being represented in the binary system as 10011— 1 plus 2 plus 16.

The digital computer, using the binary system to make the multitudinous calculations into which it breaks down the most complex problems, and then producing the 'answer' in a language the layman can understand, has sometimes been credited with the ability to 'think', a semantic side-issue on which much argument has been expended. However, there are definite comparisons to be drawn between processes involved in a computer and various human activities; and it is justifiable to compare the handling of a problem by a computer with its handling by a human operator.

In the latter case, information in the form of data is presented to the human brain which already commands its own store of information in the form of learning and experience; the processes of the brain are put into operation and the output is produced by pen or pencil and paper. In the electronic computer, the data, or input as it is called, may be in the form of punched cards, paper or magnetic tape, characters in magnetic type (such as are now seen on the bottom of many cheques), or, in very few cases, ordinary written or typed material which is 'scanned' and read electronically before passing into the vitals of the machine. While the human being calls upon his experience before handling the data he or she receives, the computer calls upon the store of programs (this spelling is now more favoured than 'programmes') which 'tell' it how to handle the input material. These programs, which may consist of instructions stored in magnetic cores or magnetic drums, form part of what might be called the computer's central nervous system and enable it to process the input material as required and to produce the answers to the problems it has been given. These answers, the output, can be recorded on punched cards, on magnetic or paper tape; they can be printed; or they can, if necessary, be presented visually on cathode-ray tubes.

It is not necessary for the director to understand, in detail, how the computer carries out such tasks; in fact, if he wishes to keep time for his own work he will be wise not to attempt the operation. But it will enable him to grasp the essentials of the matter if he realizes that the computer does its task by breaking down even the most complex of mathematical problems into a very large number of very simple problems; that the circuits inside the computer enable these problems to be solved 'with the speed of light'; and that the elegance with which the initial complex problems are broken down and dealt with depends largely on the ability of the 'programmer', the expert, that is, who prepares the set of instructions that control the computer when it starts on its task.

Uses of computers

What sort of problems can really be solved by this new 'tool of management' as it is often called? What can it be used for? And in what sort of businesses?

It is difficult to exaggerate the variety of the answers that can truly be given to such questions. Computers are used to handle the week-by-week 'accounts' work of hundreds of companies. They are used by local authorities to produce rates demands, and by the chemical industry to control the flow of raw materials through plant. There has, in fact, been an immense proliferation of computer-uses since the Morgan Crucible Company installed a computer in its Battersea headquarters about a decade ago—one of the first commercial organizations in this country to do so—and there has been an even greater development since the late 1940s when J. Lyons & Co. forged a link between office and computer laboratory and worked out the details of Britain's first electronic office.

Two instances of fairly general application will serve to illustrate how computers can help. At one level is the firm whose goods are made in many thousands of varying colour/style/length combinations, these being sold both direct to manufacturers and to a large number of retail shops. In Britain alone, nearly 40,000 separate items of stock are involved and, before efficient sales forecasting can be carried out, a vast mass of figures has to be collated and cross-checked. This task is now done in four hours by a computer which, almost as a by-product, also produces a full-capacity weekly production programme.

There is also the specialist chain store with 1,300 branches which stocks some 60,000 'lines'. These 'lines' are today ordered by the branch assistant making a series of pencil strokes on special cards, each of which can be used for ordering up to eight gross of as many as forty-five items. At the organization's headquarters, the cards are converted to punched cards by a marksensing machine, and these are then fed into a computer at the rate of 400 a minute. The information from the computer goes into a special printer, and from this there come invoices listing ordered items in bin-order; out-of-stock advices; and a mass of other paper-ware. And, as is so frequently the case with computer-operation, the machine also turns out, virtually as a free extra, a mass of statistical information. An essential point to be grasped is that in the pre-computer age it would not have been economic to gather such information on the purely speculative supposition that it might be useful.

Such clerical uses are now general—although, perhaps, not as general as they should be—across the whole spectrum of British industry. They are used by at least one rose-grower, they are used by one of the great university presses, and they are used by scores of organizations producing goods as varied as nuts and bolts, and costume jewellery. In fact it is difficult not to claim that the benefits of computer-operation can be utilized in the offices of virtually any company that is concerned with making a large number of different items and that disposes of them through a large variety of outlets.

But the use of the computer in clerical work is only the most obvious use. Many very different commercial and business applications will be suggested by its use in weather forecasting. The Meteorological Office have been operating a computer since 1958, and have more recently been preparing their long-range forecasting by comparing the current monthly average weather charts—for temperatures, air pressures, and rainfall—with charts for the same month back to the 1880s. For each forecast, the computer selects from the earlier charts those which, translated into numerical form, most closely resemble the current month. Next, it picks the corresponding charts for the following month in the previous years concerned, and from them strikes a balance from which the forecast can be made. For the daily forecasting, the computer performs calculations, based on hydrodynamic principles, which consist of the numerical solution of sets of partial differential equations. And in Sweden, the State Power Board has used a computer to work out a plan for the country's entire power production, which takes into account not only such factors as winter ice, water levels in the reservoirs, needs of industry and power-exports to Denmark, but, also, even the amount of water needed by the salmon in Sweden's rivers.

The use of computers as an aid to medical diagnosis is already far advanced, and it has also been proposed that it could help in arriving at legal decisions. In these two fields, the use of the machine is simpler and more obvious than at first appears. What it does is give a 'yes' or 'no' answer to specific questions whose number would be too great for the human brain to handle in the necessary time. It is in such apparently esoteric applications that the word 'judgement' is sometimes used. In general, the computer specialists are unhappy about the use of such words—as they are about 'thinking' and 'intelligence' when applied to non-biological machines. However, an example from British Rail well illustrates how the gloss can creep in. At Paddington, the payroll for some 14,000 workers is handled by a computer. In each case a path has to be picked through a maze of pay-formulae, schedules and mileages; but at the end of each specific case it may still be necessary to ask whether a specific man is entitled to certain specific allowances. It is here that the machine follows the program that has been prepared for it with a greater accuracy than the human mind would be capable of. It produces an answer which is, quite literally, according to the rulebook; but it is still showing accuracy rather than 'judgement'.

Another growing use of computers is in network analysis, which may roughly be described as a method of carrying out complicated, dovetailed operations so that the minimum amount of delay is involved. Thus, the construction and fitting of the main engines of the *Queen Elizabeth II* was aided by a network containing more than 2,500 operations, which was handled on John Brown's ICT 1903 computer; a second operation, dealing with the hull and its fittings, involved more than 11,000 operations and ensured, among other things, that the best use was made of skilled craftsmen. The extent of the material handled by the computer in these operations can be judged from the fact that even the time required to lock cabin doors after all work had been completed on them was incorporated in the analysis.

A further use of the computer, on the same ship, and one that may well extend quickly in the near future, was for production control. The ship was divided into sixty-four blocks, and each was progressed as if it were a separate ship. By using a series of targets, the percentage of completion of each block was calculated and the cost to date compared with that of the tenders. Some idea of the scope of this form of computer control can be gauged from one item alone—the ship's plumbing. More than 100,000 pipes were involved, each having to be sketched, made, taken to the ship, joined up, and tested. The computer produced weekly situation reports, and analysed bore measurements and sizes to ensure that pipes of correct type and size were available as wanted.

These are, of course, only random items chosen from the multiplicity of new uses for computers that are opening up in the building and engineering industry, ranging from those involving design and technology to those allowing more efficient control of site operations.

There can be no doubt of the speed with which the computer has, during the past decade, become an essential part of business and industry; and there are estimated to be more than 2,500 computers now working in Britain, while the number is expected to have quadrupled by the late 1970s.

Problems in installing computers

Even so, many directors who are personally convinced that the computer is, in principle, a necessary tool of the modern world, are yet remarkably cautious in utilizing the tool in their own organization. They are possibly very wise. While there is little doubt that British reluctance to invest in modernity is a national danger, there is a good deal to be said for approaching the 'computerization' of a business with a great deal of care. The reason is not so much any doubt of the long-term advantages as that some implications of the development can easily be overlooked.

If there is one lesson to be learned from the experience of the past decade, it is that no company should think of buying a computer in the same terms as it buys other equipment. With very few exceptions, such a machine is not added to an organization; a computer is bought and the organization is built round it. This probably means that the upheaval will be greater than was initially anticipated, and it certainly means that the changeover to computerized working will have to be spread over a considerable period; of many months, if not of years.

For most firms, the wisest step, once it has been decided to consider the acquisition of a computer, will be to set up a small committee to consider what reorganization will be required to utilize the machine's capabilities to the full. And it is at this stage that the full impact of 'computerization' may well be realized for the first time. Most departments will be affected, and it will be quickly appreciated that if there is one word that is the key to success it is probably 'integration'. A good and typical illustration of the 'rethinking' that will almost certainly be necessary was provided by one firm which turned to computers years ago. Here, as in many other firms, it was appreciated that a man on piece-work could easily handle 150 jobs in a single week; under the methods existing when the firm decided to instal a computer, this meant that 150 cards would be needed for this one man in a single week. The system was, therefore, reorganized into one on which men on piece-work had one card for each day, while time-workers had one card each week; in practice, this meant that about three-quarters of the cards were unnecessary. In any company 'going over to computers' there may well be dozens of such points to be dealt with, and it is only when their scope is fully appreciated that the implications will be fully realized.

When it comes to cost, two points should perhaps be stressed. One is that the range of computers has widened immensely since the early days, and it would not be unfair to say that cost of the central equipment itself can be anything from £20,000 to £2,000,000. It is, therefore, true to claim that, above a certain minimum of requirements, almost any demand can be catered for. However, the phrase 'central equipment' is not used above without reason. To this equipment there must be

711

added the cost of the ancillary devices, and this cost can more than double the cash involved. In a computer marketed for £100,000 for instance, magnetic tape can cost another £80,000, while another £50,000 or so could easily be spent on punched card input and output equipment and on-line printing. A high-speed tape punch allowing 150 lines a minute to be produced might account for a mere additional £6,000 or so. But in total, such figures are enough to underline that it is wise to keep clear in one's head exactly what is covered by any figure being considered.

Any business considering the use of a computer is likely to be overwhelmed by statements concerning the speed at which individual machines can carry out specific operations. Nowadays, manufacturers are sensible enough to admit that speed is only one of the factors to be considered in studying any particular range. Nevertheless, one or two points should perhaps still be underlined. One that can easily be overlooked is that actual computer-speed is in practice slowed down to the pace of its slowest elements—which in most cases will be the input and output ancillaries. This limitation is being steadily diminished by ever-faster print-out machines and by the regular improvement and extension of visual recognition machines, but it does still exist.

Another point is that, with certain specific exceptions, the cost of a computer increases with the speed at which it is able to do its work; the obvious corollary is that a firm will be unwise to buy a machine that will do the required job so quickly that it then stands idle for a sizeable portion of each week or month. However, there is another aspect of this: when a business turns over to computer-operation, new uses for the machine begin to sprout up as unexpectedly as mushrooms in a field.

When, for instance, Boots installed their computer system in their Nottingham headquarters a few years ago, they not only had its immediate tasks lined up but were, as they put it, already considering possibilities for the not-so-distant future. Where orders from the branches fell into a noticeable pattern, it might be possible to make the regular re-ordering of many classes of goods completely automatic, and the control of production and its scheduling to meet fluctuations in demand could be worked out by computer. Any business problem capable of being expressed in mathematical terms could be analysed by the computer, and data could be clearly drawn up to form a basis for decisions. A link could be established between automated paperwork and automated order assembly in the warehouse. The processing of a branch order in the computer could be linked either directly, or indirectly, with the dropping of the goods representing the order from gravity chutes on to a conveyor belt. These were only the first of the multiple possibilities that began to be considered once the value of the new tool began to be appreciated. This is a feature common to many computer installations, and it means that in the planning stage it is wise to allow for a good deal of slack which, later, will be taken up as fresh jobs appear for which staff will be demanding computer-time.

More important than mere speed is the working effectiveness of a computer. Thus, the massive Ferranti Atlas was a great step forward, not so much because it could carry out a million mathematical operations a second, nor only because it could store up to twenty million units of information. Just as important as either of these, was the fact that it could select from a number of different programs with which it had been primed and then operate on a selection of them simultaneously.

However, even when effectiveness and cash cost have been satisfactorily equated, it must be remembered that this cost is only one of the items that must be entered into the profit and loss account. The days when a computer consisted of massed batteries of burningly hot valves are over; the modern machines demand neither the space nor the air conditions of their predecessors. All the same, space will be taken up by an installation, and the office alterations that may well be necessary will also have to be taken into consideration. Training of existing staff in the new procedures, as well as training of staff for operating the installation itself, is another item. These factors are not mentioned as deterrents; but they can be underestimated, and a company that tends to gloss them over may set off on the wrong foot along the computer path.

Any director considering the introduction of a computer will naturally have as his first concern the long-term efficiency of his organization. He will be concerned with the basic economics of the operation. But he will, also, unless he is very lucky or very exceptional, be concerned about all that is summed up in the one word 'redundancy'.

When, some years ago, the Royal Army Pay Corps brought in a computer to handle the pay of the whole Army, it was estimated that the Corps would, as a result, be able to reduce its staff by about 600, and that the savings involved would wipe out the £700,000 cost of the computer in a few years. Contrarywise, there is the fact that a large number of firms have gone on record as stating that the computerization of their businesses has caused no redundancy. 'We have had to sack no-one' has become almost a litany in such cases, and while quite true it does tend to tell only part of the story. Another part lies in the fact that in many cases computers have enabled business to expand and to deal with a greatly increased volume of clerical work without any increase of staff or—of importance in these days of high rents— any extension of offices.

The introduction of a computer into any organization will certainly produce no problem as far as the intellectually high-grade members of the staff are concerned. The demand for first-class men who genuinely understand computer-operation and management is great, and is likely to become greater; if there is any staff problem, it is likely to arise from the difficulty of finding men for the top jobs that will be created. Neither need there be problems at the next level down; re-training can today take care of a whole range of middle-layer staff whose tasks will be vastly changed by the introduction of a computer. It is at lower levels still that planning may well be needed, since in any organization there is almost inevitably a nucleus of staff whom it will be difficult to utilize in the changed conditions. Normal

24

wastage will alleviate the problem, but careful thought may be necessary if it is to be completely solved.

So far, the staff problems inherent in the change to electronic computers have been relatively small—no doubt partly due to the comparatively slow pace at which Britain has moved into the computer age. They may well loom larger in the future; but this is a reason for considering them in advance, and for dealing with them, rather than trying to ignore them.

The 'computer-laundry'

The actual buying of a computer is, however, only the first of the possible paths to computerization of a business. Another is the use of what is sometimes called a 'computer-laundry'. The first of these—centres to which a firm can, as it were, take its clerical washing—was set up more than a decade ago, and there are now many scores of them throughout the country. Their size, and their services, vary very considerably, but there can be no doubt that for some firms they have undoubted attractions. In addition, they are frequently used, with mutual satisfaction, by fully-computerized firms who occasionally find that a flood of work is more than they themselves can satisfactorily handle on their existing machine or machines.

A company may utilize such computer-centres in one of two general ways. In the first, the company concerned goes through most of the preliminary motions it would make were it buying its own computer. Its office routine is reorganized as necessary. Its invoices, delivery bills, together with its other paper-ware, are adapted to one particular mode of computer-operation. Its staff themselves devise the programs necessary for handling the company's work. The company then buys time on the computer of its choice at the centre concerned, staff take their work to it, spend an hour or so operating the machine—with the ancillary services provided by the centre—and then return with the results, much as a housewife returns from the launderette. Charges for such services vary according to the machine hired, ranging from £30 an hour upwards. This method is, of course, particularly useful where regular weekly or monthly jobs, such as payroll work, have to be done.

The second method is for a firm to contract out to a computer-centre, either specific problems as they occur, or the whole of the clerical work. In such cases the operation will be carried out from start to finish by the centre's staff who will, of course, have to be given access to the company's detailed day-to-day records. Such a method is naturally well adapted to *ad hoc* jobs, one of which arose some few years ago when the Hammersmith fly-over was being built. A number of computations had to be made in a hurry, but it was estimated that they would take a fortnight if made by the usual methods. A computer centre was brought in, a program was prepared within a few days, and the computations carried out within a few minutes.

Computer bureaux or centres today offer services almost as varied as computers

714

themselves. Thus, it is possible to utilize, on a time basis, a giant Atlas computer in Manchester, which has already handled such tasks as traffic analysis, flood prediction, large-scale matrix algebra problems, design of a sewage system, market research analyses, and linear programming. But a modern computer can also be hired with its attendant library of complete programs, which make it ideal for many semi-routine jobs, or a smaller machine can be utilized by scientists and technologists on which they can virtually handle their own 'one-off' jobs.

With the increased sophistication of computers, and the growing range of possibilities they offer, the simple concept of computer-bureaux has been greatly expanded. Users may now have in their offices transmitters which are connected by telephone to a central bureau. When a problem on paper tape is fed into such a transmitter, duplicate paper tape is produced at the central bureau, where it can be fed into the computer and processed at the earliest available moment, after which a tape carrying the solution can be produced in the user's own office by the same process carried out in reverse. A more recent development is the continual 'on-line' availability of such services. Somewhat similar is the extension of computer services such as Centre-file, in which a service is available to a large number of stockbrokers any of whom can, in effect, 'plug in' to the service as and when required.

In many cases experience at a computer centre will be followed by installation of a machine on a company's own premises. But this is not the only possibility. An increasing number of computers are today being operated on what can only be called a co-operative basis. Thus, the London Boroughs' Joint Computer Committee first hired time on a computer for six boroughs. But they followed this by buying a computer to work for all six—on a 24-hour day, five-day-week basis—thus giving each borough the use of a powerful computer it could not individually justify.

The future of the large computer

No discussion of the computer in industry would be complete without at least a reference to the wider implications of the larger machines now coming into more general use. It is true that such immensely powerful machines as the Ferranti Atlas— about a hundred times more effective than its predecessor—are more normally linked with scientific than with industrial or business work; and the first three Atlas machines did, in fact, go to Manchester and London Universities, and the National Institute for Research in Nuclear Science at Harwell. Yet there are two ways in which such machines may well affect the business world. One is in national or quasi-national planning. The entire statistical and computational work of the Greater London Council could well be handled by one of the new machines; this work would, moreover, include not only the routine production of payroll and accounting slips, but the production of long-term plans. Thus, it would be possible to estimate with some accuracy the number of two-roomed flats required in a certain area in the mid-1970s, the extent of the traffic-diversions they would necessitate, and the rents that could be paid for them by whom.

Extrapolating such work into a different sphere, it would appear possible to produce a national power plan for Britain which would take account not only of the problems posed by coal's declining importance, the vulnerability of imported supplies, and the North Sea gas potential, but of a vast number of other factors. Of perhaps even greater interest to industry, and to individual industrialists, is the possibility of such computers being used to handle the work of an entire private industry, handling the accounting work on what would be a more economical basis than at present, and helping to plan outright in such a way that the on-off operations which help to bedevil labour relations could be at least partially eliminated. Certain major problems would have to be overcome, but the result might well be a startling increase in efficiency.

Reading list

BOOKS

Glossary of Terms used in Automatic Data Processing (British Standards Institution, 1962)
Speaking of Computers, James Allen (The Accountants Publishing Co. 1965)
Computers, K. N. Dodd (Pan Books, 1966)
Business Data Processing and Programming, R. H. Gregory and Van Horn (Chatto and Windus, 1965)
Basic Digital Computer Concepts, D. Whitworth (Published on behalf of International Computers and Tabulators Ltd. by Heinemann Educational Books, 1965)
Electronic Computers, S. H. Hollingdale and G. C. Tootill (Penguin, 1965)
Introducing Computers, F. J. M. Laver (H.M.S.O., 1965)
An Introduction to Digital Computers, F. H. George (Pergamon Press, 1966)
Why, When and How to Use (or Not to Use) a Computer, Hans R. Scheider (Industrial and and Commercial Techniques, 1967)
Choosing a Computer, David Shirley (Business Publications, 1966)
A Computer ABC, P. D. Reynolds (published by *Accountancy*—the Journal of the Institute of Chartered Accountants in England and Wales, 1965)
Computers for Management, G. J. Morris and H. S. Woodgate (British Broadcasting Corporation, London, 1967)
Computer Applications: A Select Bibliography, compiled by Colin I. Barnes (Hatfield College of Technology, Hatfield, Hertfordshire)

JOURNAL

'Digital Computer Service Bureaux 1968', *Computer Survey*, January 1968 (United Trade Press, 1968)

Useful addresses

Computer Board for Universities and Research Council, 13 Cornwall Terrace, London NW 1
The National Computing Centre, Quay House, Quay Street, Manchester 3

15. Business and Government

15.1 Relations with Government

Roy Hodson

Development of British business on the free enterprise system meant that, until quite recently, successive generations of businessmen and public servants saw their respective roles in simple, straightforward terms. If you were a businessman you would identify your activity in terms of being good for Britain, of course. But you would quite definitely see governments and business in terms of 'them' and 'us'. Civil servants and politicians looked out from the corridors of power and found it satisfactory to have an equally simple window on the world.

It is not like that any more in Britain: nor is it likely to be so again in the future. There are two basic reasons why change has come about. First, Britain has developed a mixed economy system since the end of the Second World War. It has reached a point where there is a mixture of public and private enterprise with neither activity assuming absolute and unchallengeable dominance over the other. Gone is the classically simple concept of governments governing while businessmen carry on the nation's business. Secondly, the state has become by far the biggest customer of British business. Thus, the state has a powerful lever to shift, prod, and stir business affairs without even having to resort to such crudities as direct legislation.

Since 1945, spending by the public sector has tended to run at between 40 and 45 per cent of all the nation's spending. It has not dropped below 40 per cent. Until 1967, it had not climbed above the magical 50 per cent. But nationalization of nine-tenths of the British iron and steel industry in 1967 made it certain that, in

1968, spending by the public sector would rise to new high levels. In fact, the state take-over of steel was an act that made it certain that the public sector spending of Britain would, for the first time, outweigh all the private sector activity.

Government statisticians calculate that Britain's total capital investment by 1966 was shared thus:

Personal sector	20·3 ('000 million £s)
Companies	27·9
Public Corporations	13
Central Government	3
Local Authorities	18·3

It can be seen from this rather crude break-down that the overall private sector accrued investment by 1966 was as follows: £27,900 million, to which must be added the unknown proportion of the £20,300 million personal sector investment representing private businesses. We can estimate safely that the total private sector investment by 1966 comfortably exceeded £30,000 million. Public sector investment by public corporations, government, and local authorities meanwhile amounts to the same order of value—actually £34,300 million. Since then, the public sector has been swollen by inclusion of iron and steel.

Clearly the nation's economy has reached a significant milestone in its progress. These brief examinations in terms of accrued capital and of current spending reinforce a single conclusion. *The public and private sectors are in fine balance with the other.*

Until 1964, the economy had been working towards this state of balance for some years under a Conservative Government. Conservative policy was to keep control of business life to a minimum. As a result, involvement between Government and business was at few, but definite, points. Mr Edward Heath led the Conservative Government forward, against opposition from his colleagues, to involvement with the business world at one of these points, when he carried through the abolition of resale price maintenance. A great deal of what the Labour Government had done in the areas of price supervision, and the minimizing of monopolies and restrictive practices stems from Mr Heath's pioneer work.

Under the Conservatives, there was help available for the industrialist who wished to build his factory in certain areas of abnormally high unemployment. To that extent business growth was being directly influenced. Mr Selwyn Lloyd, when Chancellor of the Exchequer, devised the National Economic Development Council (*see* section 15.4, p.746). The Conservative conception of 'Neddy' was a forum for industry completely outside the Government machine but sufficiently senior to command respect for its views at highest level. It was to carry on a long-range economic planning exercise continuously with government representatives, industrialists, trade-union leaders, and independent specialists sitting as equals round a table with the Chancellor of the Exchequer in the chair. Before Labour came to power in October 1964, it is remarkable how few the other points of contact were between industry and government. There were established channels such as the Board of Trade, with the regional industrial councils safely tucked under its wing. There were other ministries with traditional responsibilities for sponsoring certain industries. There was not much else.

From the day Labour took office, Government policy was based upon the view that there must be a much closer degree of management of the industrial economy than anything seen in Britain before, apart from those muddled years of licences and shortages in the late 1940s when the post-war Labour Government tried and failed to apply its ideas of close management to an economy swinging from a war-time to a peace-time footing. The Labour Government's methods after October 1964 were varied: they included innovation, irritation, flattery, interference, restriction, persuasion, incentives, cajolery, false promises, misdirection, argument, and downright bullying.

Labour Government has produced radical changes in the Whitehall machine. They look like being permanent—give or take a department here and there—and they all have the effect of involving business with government and government with business. They are, indeed, changes which go some way towards acknowledging that an economy in such delicate balance between private and public sectors, as is Britain's today, needs special administrative machinery if it is to run at all.

Two new ministries—both major ones—have been established under the Labour Government.

The Department of Economic Affairs is responsible for strategic economic planning. It is closely involved, naturally, with the imbalances between prosperity and industrial and social decline which are to be found about Britain today despite the island's being geographically so small. Every region now has an economic planning board of the senior government officials in that region. There is, also, a parallel chain of regional economic planning councils composed of senior industrialists, economists, and public regional figures of the active rather than the passive variety. They, and the boards, are supposed to be the initiators, as well as the DEA's channels, of communication with the heartlands of Britain. Unfortunately, two-way conversations appear to be difficult with this system. The men in the regions find that the instructions from Whitehall come bellowing down the line. But proposals thought up in the regions, in conjunction with continuous study of local conditions, all too often do not arrive at the centre of government with sufficient weight to be able to strike sparks of action.

Tight government economic restrictions sent unemployment soaring in the North of England in 1966–67. Matters had deteriorated to the point of threats of resignations from regional councils before Mr Harold Wilson himself took over control of the DEA in mid-1967.

Labour's other new ministry, the *Ministry of Technology*, had a slow start but

24*

is gaining strength. Its long-range responsibility is to ensure that British industry is basing itself upon the technology that will be most useful, most fitted, and most profitable, for the future, rather than clinging to the outmoded. Innovation is the overriding concern of this ministry. It should be anxious to listen to any businessman who believes he has an original idea. Clearly, the more rumbustious innovations of the Ministry of Technology will always conflict with other areas of the Government machine.

The National Economic Development Council, started by the Conservatives, was changed by Labour into a different animal. Mr H. F. R. (Fred) Catherwood left the direction of British Aluminium to become wholly employed with the Labour Government's industrial reform programme. After a spell with the DEA he was appointed director-general of Neddy, now run as a semi-autonomous projection of government.

Just as the DEA has its regional links through the regional planning boards and the councils, so Neddy has its 'hot lines' to most sectors of industry through the economic development committees that represent specific industries. Better known as the 'little neddies', these committees are a pure invention of the Labour Government. They certainly played no part in the Selwyn Lloyd conception of Neddy. A little neddy was even set up for the motor industry by the summer of 1967, after this most autocratic of industries had held out longer than the rest against any government involvement.

The entire Neddy and little neddy system had, by 1969, reached a point where pressures being generated upon Britain's industrial habits were in certain cases causing radical changes. But there are few published reports, criticisms, and counter-criticisms of the process.

Quiet preparation before the curtain rises is also the way in which the Industrial Reorganisation Corporation (see section 15.6 p.757) likes to perform its con-juring tricks. This body was established by the Government in 1966 and did not become a going concern until 1967. Thus, it is a recent arrival to the ranks of government-industry points of contact. IRC has been provided with capital to lubricate the process of industrial rationalization. Reasonable fears of industrialists that this system is simply nationalization by the 'back-door' have been somewhat allayed by the provision that the IRC has to revolve its capital if it is to keep up the lubrication process. Money provided by IRC to aid a merger must be withdrawn at an appropriate time in the future so that the money can be used again for another project. The first venture on these lines was in January 1967 when, oddly enough, IRC cash was used to help a United States company—Chrysler—take over the British car-makers Rootes. The Government was reluctant to ease the way for greater US participation in British car-making but concluded that there was no other acceptable way to keep Rootes in business. Later in 1967, the IRC interest and support for the General Electric Company's bid for Associated Electrical

Industries was frankly explained as IRC's way to get the electrical industry of Britain moving forward towards a more efficient structure. IRC argued that, whatever happened to the two companies concerned, the log-jam checking industrial progress in this sector of British industry would be decisively broken by the bid.

The great rival to Neddy among the quasi-Governmental bodies now interesting themselves in industrial matters has become the National Board for Prices and Incomes (*see* section 15.5, p.750). Boldly led by one-time Conservative Minister of Power Mr Aubrey Jones, the PIB eschews undercover work. Instead, the board uses the weapon of strong publicity to get its message across to industry and to government alike.

Almost any Government reference of a price change or an earnings hike to the Jones Board has been the signal for Mr Jones to report, in swashbuckling fashion, on the shortcomings of the industry concerned, on the prospects for putting things right, and on the reforms that he believes should be introduced. There probably never has been such an uninhibited college devoted to industrial reform as the PIB. Even a body of opinion within the Government that put Mr Jones in business has accused him of going beyond his briefs in his full flow of reports. He is unrepentant, and argues that the prices and earnings he examines cannot be considered in isolation without study and comment about the industries concerned 'in the round'. Probably the greatest incentive to the car-makers to form their little neddy, after stoutly arguing the irrelevancy of such a body for a long time, was the prospect that, otherwise, the prices of cars would certainly have been referred to Mr Jones.

When the Labour Government came to office, it found British labour well represented at national level by a powerful and articulate Trades Union Congress (*see* section 6.1, p.345)—by no means a perfect or a fast-moving machine but one the Government accepted and could understand. But there was no single coherent voice for management. The Government at once made it clear that it wanted to be able to address its discussions with business with a single umbrella organization. The concept of a single management organization happened to be in the planning stage already, so the businessmen played ball with the Government and the creation of the Confederation of British Industry (*see* section 15.7, p.761) was hurriedly completed. Since then, the relationship between Government and industry has undoubtedly become closer and less formal—whether it has become happier and more constructive is much less certain.

The 1964–65 period of grandiose economic planning saw the marriage of the CBI and the Government. Then the planning went wrong and, abruptly, the honeymoon was over. CBI leaders commanded the respect of Government ministers and their departments, and these industrial leaders, together with top men in the Government's organizations for linking up economic affairs, represent a new breed. Loosely, they might be called 'industrial statesmen'. Many politicians, indeed, suspect them because they cannot understand them. It is significant that

Mr Wilson, on the other hand, is known to have considerable personal liking and respect for several of the industrial statesmen, who for their own part, playing themselves into new roles, have quickly learned that what the government says today is not necessarily what will be done tomorrow.

The sheer impossibility of a small number of men being able accurately to represent the diverse views of British businessmen on almost anything in one handy capsule has become steadily more apparent. Autumn 1967 saw industrialists jibbing against the tight harness provided by the CBI.

Twenty-four of Britain's top business leaders formed a so-called 'Industrial Policy group'. The idea was that it should be an unofficial inner cabinet of the CBI and that it should stand for the views and the needs of the really *big* British companies in all negotiations with government. Men such as Sir Paul Chambers, then chairman of Imperial Chemical Industries, Henry Lazell, then chairman of Beechams, David Barran, chief executive of Shell, and Lord Cole, chairman of Unilever, enlisted the support of Davies and the CBI senior echelon in the view that the CBI has indeed been inhibited by its need to reflect the views of a wide cross-section of its members. So much for Mr Wilson's wish for a single voice to speak for all business.

The focus of big business as a loose group parallel with the CBI can be expected to be a new and vigorous force for getting the true views of big business through to the Government.

Other chapters in this *Handbook* deal in detail with the work of business organizations and trade associations, the main Government departments, the joint industry-Government bodies, and the local authority organizations as they affect the business life of Britain. I have been concerned to provide a framework for this information and a sketch of the recent influences upon relations between business and Government.

The most reasonable conclusion I can arrive at is that interaction between business and Government is going to be of necessity a permanent feature of the British mixed economy: but these are early days in an evolving relationship. Little has been done, so far, towards ensuring that the involvement will be constructive. The Government has too often acted wrongly or clumsily. As a result, businessmen are showing themselves suspicious of Government intentions, and nervous about Government capabilities. By and large, the business world is now discarding its traditional secretiveness—an essential reform, most would agree, if a finely-balanced mixed economy is to work. But business can have no confidence yet that the Government will play fair. There must be a vigorous programme of educating government in business affairs before a harmonious business-government relationship results.

Reading List

BOOKS

Management is Responsible—Report of National Conference of the British Junior Chamber of Commerce under the Patronage of H.R.H. Prince Philip, The Duke of Edinburgh, Leeds, 19–21 October, 1962 (British Junior Chamber of Commerce, 75 Cannon Street London EC 4)

The Limits of Business Administration and Responsibility, G. Prys Williams (Pall Mall Press for Christian Economic and Social Research Foundation, 1962)

Management and Society, Sir William Robson Brown, M.P. (Pitman, 1961)

Society and Management, Stanley Hyman (Business Publications 1964)

Business and Society, Joseph W. McGuire (McGraw-Hill 1963)

Business and the National Interest, The General Electric Forum—Vol X, No. 2, April–June, 1967 (Robert L. Fegley, Manager, Public Issues Analysis, 570 Lexington Avenue, New York City)

The Managerial Revolution, James Burnham (Penguin 1962)

Industry and Government, Inaugural Sir George Earle Memorial Lecture by John Davies. December, 1966—Industrial Educational and Research Foundation, 3 Clements Inn, London WC 2 (Second Sir George Earle Memorial Lecture by Lord Carron, December, 1967)

Responsibility of the Industrialist in Modern Society, The Tavistock Lecture, November 1965, by Sir Maurice Laing at University College London (Tavistock Publications)

Private Enterprise in a Changing World, 21st Congress of International Chamber of Commerce, Montreal, Canada 1967

Wider Business Objectives: American Thinking and Experience, Political and Economic Planning, Vol. XXXII No. 495, May 1966 (Research Publications)

The Innovators, Michael Shanks (Penguin, 1967)

JOURNALS

'Government and Industry: The Real Dangers of the Next Five Years', Sir Paul Chambers (*The Director*, May 1966)

'What Business wants from Government', Ronald Grierson (*Observer*, 12 November 1967)

'Capitalist Spokesmen and Socialist Government', Enoch Powell, M.P., Sir William (now (Lord) McFadzean, and Sir Maurice Laing (*The Director*, February 1965)

'Getting the Politicians to see Business Sense' (Editorial *The Director*, January 1968)

15.2 Ministries and Departments

Richard Bailey

Government and industry

For the most part, manufacturing industry and commerce in Britain are carried on in the private sector. However, their operation is influenced by the Government's general economic policy, for example, on taxation, and by specific directives affecting particular industries. The Government element in the economy is extremely important because of the very large share public spending takes of total expenditure. Governments raise large sums of money in taxation, a large part of the basic industry of the country is under public ownership, and the Government is able to exercise authority in many other fields affecting the background in which industry operates. In recent years, the setting up of an economic planning organization, first in the National Economic Development Council and, later, in the Department of Economic Affairs, has served further to increase the economic power and influence of government.

The Departments that most closely concern the businessman in his day-to-day activities are the Treasury, the Board of Trade, the Department of Economic Affairs, and the Ministry of Technology. Each of these, in one way or another, exerts considerable influence on the way in which companies operate. In addition, the Department of Employment and Productivity (formerly the Ministry of Labour) and the Ministry of Transport have considerable influence on the resources available

to the company and the way in which they are used. A number of other departments—
the Ministry of Defence, the Ministry of Housing, the Ministry of Agriculture—
affect particular industries either as purchasers of their products or through controlling the scale of their remuneration. In what follows, the operation of the principal
departments involved in economic policy will be described, as far as possible from
the point of view of how their operations affect the boardroom and the company
rather than the functioning of the economy as a whole.

The Treasury

Most companies are affected by the financial and economic work of the Treasury,
either directly through taxation or exchange control policy, or indirectly through
its control of public expenditure and general short-term regulation of the economy.
For the most part, the Treasury does not have as much direct contact with the
individual companies as some other departments. Exchange control questions are
normally dealt with by the Bank of England, while taxation matters are the concern
of the Inland Revenue and Customs and Excise. The Capital Issues Committee,
which has a considerable influence on investment, is a part of the Treasury.

Formerly, the Chancellor of the Exchequer was in charge of both long- and
short-term economic policy. However, his position has changed since the reorganization carried out as a result of the work of the Plowden Committee in 1962. The
result of this reorganization was to recast the entire structure of the Treasury.
Previously, one Permanent Secretary had been in charge of the Treasury with two
Joint Permanent Secretaries, one responsible for the co-ordination of economic
policy and control of public expenditure, and the other for the management of the
civil service and of some other parts of the public services. In addition, the holder
of this post was also Secretary of the Cabinet. The Plowden Committee decided
that the management functions of the Treasury had been expanding and would
develop further. It was decided, therefore, that the Joint Permanent Secretary in
charge of the civil service should be freed of other major responsibilities outside
the Treasury, and the post of Secretary of the Treasury was detached from this work.

Under the new system, the Treasury was organized on a more functional basis
that lent itself more readily to broader methods of financial control based on long-
term forecasts of resources and expenditure that were being increasingly used in
the Department. The new arrangement was also much more in line with modern
concepts of management.

Functionally, the Treasury is now divided into four groups: the Pay Group,
which deals with pay and working conditions of the various classes of civil servants
and with questions on the pay of staffs in other parts of the public services; the
Management Group responsible for developing management services, whose
activities include organization and methods work, inquiries into and comparisons

727

of management practices over a wide field, and the work on recruitment, training, manning and grading in the civil service; the Finance Group, which brings together all questions affecting home and overseas finance; and the fourth Group, concerned with balancing public expenditure against national resources and organizing the control of this expenditure under such broad headings as Defence, Social Services, Agriculture and Transport.*

So far as companies are concerned, the impact of the work of the Treasury is most noticeable in its dealings with the balance of payments, the strength of sterling, and problems of inflation. Periodic balance of payments crises have occurred when payments both visible and invisible have exceeded receipts. In these cases, the Treasury has acted to check the level of activity in the economy by introducing what has been called a 'squeeze'. This operates through checks on hire purchase sales, principally on consumer durables. Restrictions imposed usually affect the down payment and the period of repayment of the sums involved. The Treasury also has power to use what is called the regulator, which enables a surcharge of 10 per cent to be imposed on the duties on beer, wines and spirits, on hydro-carbon oils, petrol substitutes and methylated spirit, and on purchase tax without any special legislation being necessary.

The main control of the Treasury over expenditure is, of course, exercised through the Annual Budget, which is normally the main occasion of the year for reviewing the Exchequer finances and the economic state of the nation. In his Budget speech, the Chancellor estimates the yield of the Revenue on the basis of existing taxation, and proposes the changes that he considers desirable on economic grounds in order to meet the estimates of expenditure for the coming year. These proposals are later embodied in detail in a Finance Bill.

The raising of taxation is much more than a purely financial operation. It affects the distribution of income and property and the level of expenditure on particular kinds of goods and services. The general level of taxation also affects the degree of activity of the economy as a whole, a matter of considerable importance to industry. Over the last twenty years, Budgets have been consciously designed to bring the total demand for goods and services into balance with the supplies it is estimated could be made available. The main instrument available to the Chancellor is the taxation of income and capital at varying rates through income tax and surtax, and through Company taxation. Taxes on expenditure such as those on drink and tobacco do not affect the distribution of income, and their main purpose has always been the raising of revenue. However, by discouraging or encouraging consumption of particular goods, taxation can be used to influence the allocation of resources and the pattern of trade. For the businessman, the operations of the Treasury at this level mean that money is scarce, so that people have less to spend on his products, or that demand is likely to rise because

* The Management Group has since been detached from the Treasury.

the Chancellor begins to get worried about the number of people unemployed.

A lot depends, however, on the Government's own expenditure. If public spending on the social services, education, defence, goes up without any increase in taxation, then there is more money to spend and the total demand for goods and services rises. This can also mean, of course, that employment goes up. If, however, taxation is increased without any rise in Government spending, then the total demand for goods and services will fall. The businessman may therefore find that the Chancellor, by varying the amount of money available, is having a considerable effect on the demand for his products. In recent years, the aim of the 1961 Budget was to counter inflation and to encourage exports, this was done by higher taxation. The following year it was decided that the process of cutting back had gone far enough and taxation was eased. In 1963 and 1964, the Government had adopted the objective of a 4 per cent growth rate, hence expansionary Budgets were introduced. In the next three years, the main problem was the Balance of Payments deficit, so the Budgets of 1965, 1966 and 1967 had been aimed at reducing the net outflow of long-term capital, through the regulation of overseas investment, changes in company taxation, and cutting down the level of activity in the economy in order to check imports. The 1966 Budget also attempted a new type of regulation of the economy by introducing the Selective Employment Tax, which was aimed at encouraging long-term structural changes in the economy. The 1968 Budget was intended to reinforce the effect of the devaluation of the pound of November 1967, and introduced the heaviest increases in taxation so far known.

Taxes levied in the United Kingdom fall into three main categories. These are taxes on income, including income tax, surtax and Corporation Tax; taxes on capital, including Estate Duty, Capital Gains tax, and the tax on short-term gains; and taxes on expenditure, including Customs and Excise duties, Purchase Tax, Selective Employment Tax, (on services), local rates, stamp duties, licence duties on motor vehicles, etc. The Board of Inland Revenue collects taxes on income and capital while the Board of Customs and Excise collects those on expenditure, including purchase tax.

There are a number of other authorities responsible for the collection of the remainder, including the Ministry of Social Security, which collects the Selective Employment Tax. This tax, which has been widely criticized, was intended to discourage the use of labour in the service industries. It became operative in September 1966. It is paid by all employers throughout the United Kingdom at a rate (revised in 1968) per week of 37s. 6d. for men, 18s. 9d. for women and boys, and 12s. for girls. Employers are affected by the tax in various ways. Those in manufacturing industry and employers in transport, public services, including the nationalized industries, agriculture, extractive industries, and charities have the tax refunded while employers in the service industries and in construction pay the tax without any refund whatsoever. The Selective Employment Tax is the most obvious example, in recent years, of an attempt to influence the policies of business-men through tax system.

Another way in which businessmen are made aware of the work of the Treasury is through changes in the Bank Rate. This is the rate at which the Bank of England will discount approved Bills of Exchange, and it is a key factor in deciding the general pattern of interest rates. The raising or lowering of the Bank Rate is the main instrument in the Government's monetary policy. If the Chancellor believes that industry is embarking on too many new schemes and that too much money is being borrowed from the Banks, he will raise the rate to make this more difficult. If, on the other hand, he wants to stimulate investment the Bank Rate will come down. This means that a businessman may find himself in a position where his company needs to raise money for expansion at the very moment when, because of the balance of payments position or for some other reason affecting the working of the economy as a whole, the Chancellor increases the Bank Rate and puts a check on all borrowing, whatever its motives.

The other way in which the Bank of England most closely affects the activities of businessmen is through its activities as the Government's agent for the admini-stration of exchange controls, determining the movement of money in and out of the country.

The Department of Economic Affairs

The Department of Economic Affairs was set up in October 1964 by the Labour Government and was headed by the First Secretary of State and Secretary of State for Economic Affairs. The Ministry does not have detailed executive functions, its principal concern being with the planning and co-ordination of economic policy, including the efficient use of physical resources over the longer term. Short-term measures to regulate the economy and the balance of payments are dealt with by the Treasury, but as short-term measures can affect long-term plans, and long-term policy may have short-term implications, the DEA and the Treasury neces-sarily have to work in close co-operation. The Department was originally organized in four interrelated groups.

The General Planning Group is responsible for forecasts and projections of the course of the economy over all but the short-term period, and carries out detailed work on particular industries. In this connection, as on the occasion of the pre-paration of the National Plan, businessmen may be asked to provide information on their future investment plans, export prospects, and so on. This Group under-takes and commissions a considerable amount of research into key economic prob-lems as well as being closely concerned with development of techniques of economic projection for the purpose of forecasting the growth and changing pattern of the economy.

The Industrial Prices and Incomes Group is responsible for industrial policy and for prices and incomes policy. This Group has a number of industrial advisers, who are senior industrialists seconded to the DEA for a period. They represent the DEA on the Economic Development Committees (little Neddies) for individual industries. Responsibility for prices and incomes policy was transferred to the Department of Employment and Productivity in 1968.

The Regional Planning Group is responsible for regional aspects of national policies on industry, employment, land use, and transport, and for interdepartmental co-ordination in this field. Here, again, businessmen may find themselves called upon to supply information to the Economic Planning Board in their region.

The External Policies Group is responsible for co-ordinating the views of different government departments on international economic issues. In particular, this group has examined the economic implications of membership of the European Economic Community. It advises on international trade, defence, and other overseas expenditure, aid to the developing countries, export credit, and similar matters concerning the long-term development of the economy.

The principal contacts of the DEA with industry come through the Economic Development Committees set up by the National Economic Development Council. This body, generally known as Neddy, was created in 1962 by the Conservative Government. Its Council was formerly under the Chairmanship of the Secretary of State for Economic Affairs, but the Prime Minister has presided since he took over responsibility for economic policy in August 1967. Its members include the Chancellor of the Exchequer, President of the Board of Trade, the Minister of Technology, the Minister of Employment and Productivity, representatives of Management and of the Trade Unions. The Council has set up a number of Economic Development Committees, each responsible for surveying the affairs of a particular industry. Those so far appointed cover about two-thirds of private industry, with the Post Office the first to be covered in the public sector. The EDCs examine problems in their industries such as the need for rationalization, the slow rate of growth of exports, the inefficient use of labour, and so on. As many of the EDCs have set up Working Parties and sub-committees, the number of businessmen involved in their activities is very considerable. The EDCs played a considerable part in the preparation of the National Plan, and will no doubt do so again in any similar exercise in the future.

As part of the Government changes that took place on 28 August 1967, the Prime Minister assumed responsibility for the Department of Economic Affairs, with the Secretary of State for Economic Affairs and other Ministers in the Department working under his general direction.

The Ministry of Technology (Mintech) was created in October 1964, when the Labour Government came to power. Its task was defined as being to, 'guide and stimulate a major national effort to bring advanced technology and new processes into British industry'. It became the sponsoring department for four industries: computers, machine tools, electronics, and telecommunications, all chosen because of their special relevance to the objectives of the Ministry. Since then, its sponsorship has been extended until it now covers virtually the whole of the electrical, electronic, and mechanical engineering industries, including electrical and mechanical engineering products generally, motor vehicles, electrical and process plant, aircraft and aero engines, and shipbuilding. It has also acquired responsibility for engineering standards, weights and measures, and for the British Standards Institution. Other duties and responsibilities the Ministry has taken over include most of the functions of the Department of Scientific and Industrial Research, including the National Physical Laboratory and the National Engineering Laboratory and, also, responsibility for the National Research Development Corporation and for the United Kingdom Atomic Energy Authority.

The question of sponsorship by a government department is one of considerable importance. It means that it is the main point of contact for the industry with the Government machine. It is a contact that is distinct from the miscellaneous transactions with individual government departments in which companies directly, or through their trade associations, find themselves involved.

The relationship is of a positive nature, involving examination of the problems of particular industries in order to identify measures Government can take in collaboration with industry to help solve these problems. As part of its function, the Ministry of Technology has taken over the responsibilities of the former Ministry of Aviation with regard to meeting the Defence Ministry's requirements for aircraft and airborne weapons and equipment, guided missiles and nuclear weapons, and the greater part of the military requirements for radio, radar, and other electronic equipment. The Ministry is also involved in carrying out and encouraging measures for the design, development, and production of civil aircraft, and of the electronic equipment required for civil aircraft and air traffic control. The research and development resources of the Royal Aircraft Establishment and the Royal Radar Establishment, formerly with the Ministry of Aviation, and also the former DSIA stations are now under Mintech control.

The impact of Mintech on industry is felt in a variety of ways. The industries it sponsors have a direct relationship with it through its work of research and development, for example, in machine tools, or the schemes for rationalization to be carried out by the Shipbuilding Industry Board. Other industries can make use of various facilities that are now available through the Ministry. The National Computing Centre, set up in July 1966 to standardize and simplify the programming of computers and to advise on the training of systems analysts and programmers, is used by firms from a wide range of industries. Companies using machine tools may take advantage of the scheme introduced to shorten the gap between development of advanced machine tools and their adoption by users. For this purpose the

Ministry has instituted a 'pre-production order' scheme in which the Ministry is prepared to buy advanced models and place them out on free loan for initial valuation and trial by potential purchasers. The advantage of this scheme to the purchaser is that he is able to try out a new machine without having to bear an undue risk.

In some cases, as for example electronics, the Ministry is itself a major purchaser of the products of the industry, and a pace-setter in the use of the most technologically advanced products. In the capital goods sector, some 40 per cent of the electronics industry's output is for defence requirements, and the bulk of the research and development financed by the government now takes place in the Ministry's own research establishments and through its contacts with industry and the universities. In this connection, the Ministry has important opportunities for exploiting the fall-out from military research work for civil applications.

Outside the range of its sponsored industries, the main activity of the Ministry lies in the mobilization and deployment of its research and development resources. In its various establishments it has a total qualified manpower of about 9,000 persons. Although a substantial volume of the work is on behalf of other government departments, the research establishments are increasingly emphasizing the importance of their work for the needs of industry. Apart from the major research establishments and research stations, there are some forty-seven Research Associations (*see* section 13.3), which are autonomous cooperative industrial organizations controlled by their members but grant-aided and operating under the aegis of the Ministry. These cater for about 55 per cent of British industry on a turnover basis, and their total income is about £40 million.

The total membership of the Research Associations is about 19,000, which includes multi-memberships for certain large firms of varied interests. Five research establishments obtain the bulk of their industrial income by statutory levy, these are cotton, wool, cast iron, furniture, and cutlery. Outstanding examples of recent achievements by such establishments are the spray steel process developed by the British Iron and Steel Research Association, and now taken up by a number of firms. Another is the baking process for synthetic yarns by the Linen Research Association, and a quick bread-making process by the Flour Milling and Baking Research Association.

The role of technology in improving productivity generally is one with which businessmen are familiar. The Ministry is working in this field through its Industrial Operations Unit, which demonstrates the effectiveness of modern management methods and techniques by investigating problems of interest to a wide cross-section of industry. Regional offices drawing on the resources of the Ministry, the universities, and the research associations, all help local industry directly. The Ministry also provides a Production Engineering Advisory Service, which is organized regionally. This offers technical advice, training and assistance in all aspects of production engineering, mainly through regionally based mobile demonstration units. Visits by these units are free of charge to all firms in the engineering and allied industries.

The Board of Trade

The Board of Trade under its President has a general responsibility in respect of the United Kingdom's commerce, industry and overseas trade, including commercial relations with other countries, imports and trade, the protective tariff, industrial development and consumer protection. In addition, it is responsible for: (1) the promotion of exports, (2) statistics of trade and industry both home and abroad, including the censuses of production and distribution, and (3) administration of certain legislation, for example in relation to patents, registered designs, copyright, trade marks, weights and measures, merchandise marks, companies, bankruptcy, insurance, shipping, distribution of industry, films, and enemy property.

Not all the activities of the Board of Trade will be of equal interest to directors. The weekly *Board of Trade Journal* gives an account of commercial agreements and other developments within the Board's field, together with statistics for trade, feature articles on individual overseas markets, and items of topical interest regarding trade fairs and other events. Directors wishing to know more about particular aspects of the work of the Board should begin by contacting the Information Division in London.

The Board has a public reference library of material on overseas markets of the world, located at Hillgate House, 35 Old Bailey, London, EC4. (Tel: 01-248 5757, Telex 25977). This Library provides a valuable source of information on foreign trade, including a large collection of catalogues of foreign manufacturers and overseas telephone directories.

Particular sections of the Board of Trade of specific interest to directors include:
Overseas Trade Fairs Directorate (Broadway Buildings, 54 Broadway, London, SW1)
British Week and Store Promotions Directorate (Kingsway House, London, SW1)
Export Services Branch (Hillgate House, 35 Old Bailey, London, EC4)
(The Branch provides information about overseas markets and advises on opportunities and methods of exporting British goods. It also gives information on Customs duties, tariff and import regulations in overseas countries, and the commercial status of overseas firms, and helps British manufacturers in finding agents abroad and in making visits abroad. It publishes a daily *Export Services Bulletin* containing information on opportunities for British firms engaged in overseas trade.)
Distribution of Industries Division (1 Victoria Street, London, SW1)
(Deals with the general distribution of industry policy. Liaison on regional development. Administration of local employment acts, including the provisions

734

of loans and grants. Control of office development. The building and leasing of factories and the management of industrial estates through the agency of the Industrial Estates Corporation. Industrialization policy. The issue of industrial development certificates under the Town and Country Planning Acts. General responsibility for Board of Trade Regional organization.)

Registrar of Companies (Companies House, 55–71 City Road, London, EC1)

Registrar of Business Names (Companies House, 55–71 City Road, London, EC1)

Statistics Division (1 Victoria Street, London, SW1)

Exports Credits Guarantee Department (Barrington House, 59–67 Gresham Street, P.O. Box 272, London, EC2, and regional offices in the principal cities.)

Board of Trade Investment Grant Office (Colman House, Victoria Avenue, Southend on Sea, Essex.

The Board of Trade has seven Regional Offices in England as well as offices in Wales, Scotland, and Northern Ireland. These are able to deal with the subjects falling within the Board's responsibility. They are particularly helpful in connection with questions arising regarding the location of industry. There is a number of independent corporate bodies and other organizations whose work is related to the Board of Trade which directors will find extremely useful in certain directions. These are:

British National Export Council (6 Dean Farrar Street, London, SW1)
(This was formed by Government and industry in 1964 to guide and inspire the export efforts of industry. It has a number of area organizations responsible for developing British exports in particular markets.)

British Productivity Council (Vintry House, Queen Street Place, London, EC4.)
(Is concerned with the promotion of industrial efficiency and productivity by films, specialized publications, conferences and seminars and the work of over 100 local productivity committees and associations throughout the United Kingdom.)

British Standards Institution (British Standards House, 2 Park Street, London, W1)
(Is the national body responsible for the preparation and publication of industrial standards and codes of practice in the United Kingdom.)

Consumer Council (3 Cornwall Terrace, London, NW1)
(Examines consumer problems to consider and promote action to resolve them.)

Council of Industrial Design (The Design Centre, 28 Haymarket, London, SW1)
(Promotes the improvement of design of British products by means of various information services and the Design Centre with its permanent but changing exhibition of well-designed British goods and production—The Centre provides a comprehensive reference library and other services.)

The Monopolies Commission (8 Cornwall Terrace, Regents Park, London, NW1)
(Investigates and reports on matters referred to it by the Board of Trade under the Restrictive Trade Practices Act.)

The above account of the work of the Board of Trade has necessarily been selective. As a general rule directors will find that the best course is to get in touch, in the first instance, with the nearest Board of Trade Regional Office.

The four Ministries described above between them cover the whole range of economic policy and industrial development. A number of other Ministries affect the operation of companies in more limited ways. These are described below.

The Department of Employment and Productivity

This department was created as part of the reorganization of the Cabinet in April 1968, to assume responsibility for the productivity, prices and incomes policy set out in the White Paper (Cmnd 3590) published on 3 April. The object of the policy stated in the White Paper was to make certain that rising costs did not cancel out the price advantages accruing to exports as the result of devaluation. The new department was given the task of ensuring that proposed increases in prices and incomes met certain conditions, including a $3\frac{1}{2}$ per cent ceiling on wages, salary and dividend increases. The voluntary operation of the policy was supplemented by reserve powers to enable the Government to delay price and pay increases by up to 12 months in the context of references to the National Board for Prices and Incomes.

The DEP took over existing functions of the Ministry of Labour. These included the provision of a national system of employment exchanges, which includes a professional and executive register at thirty-nine of the larger exchanges, and the operation of government schemes for vocational training and industrial rehabilitation, and the central administration of the Youth Employment Service, and provides the Disablement Resettlement Service, which helps disabled persons find work.

Other functions of the Department include the resettlement in civilian employment of men released from the Armed Forces, the supervision through the Factory Inspectorate, of safety, health, and welfare measures for workers in industry and commerce, the provision of services for conciliation, arbitration and investigation in industrial disputes, responsibility for questions arising from the administration of the Wages Council Act of 1959, and the collection and publication of labour statistics of all kinds.

Of particular interest to directors is the administration of the Industrial Training Act carried out by the Department. Under this Act, provision was made for setting up Industrial Training Boards for individual industries, each consisting of a Chairman from industry, with an equal number of employer and trade union members and a number of educational members. The Act covers all activities of industry and commerce, and the intention is that every industry will eventually come within the scope of the Training Board. Employers are bound to pay a levy at a scale determined by the Board for their industry, and will receive grants in respect of approved training they carry out. It is not possible for employers to challenge the rate of levy the Board has proposed, but they can challenge the assessment, for example, on the grounds that a company is not liable to pay a levy to that particular Board or that the assessment has not been accurately calculated.

The Ministry of Housing and Local Government

Although this Ministry is mainly concerned with housing, and the national housing programme, some of its powers affect industry. In particular, the development of land, sewerage, and other services come within its sphere. Directors concerned over the development of land they may own or be about to acquire may be in contact with the Ministry over questions of planning permission. The designation of new towns and their Development Corporations is also the responsibility of the Ministry.

The Ministry of Power

The business of producing and distributing gas, electricity, and the production of coal is operated by the Boards of the three nationalized industries responsible to the Minister on policy issues. Government relations with the petroleum industry are also within the sphere of his Department. Companies owning or proposing to construct pipelines come under the regulations imposed by the Ministry of Power, which is also specifically responsible for the use of atomic energy as a source of industrial power and for the safety of nuclear installations other than those operated by the UK Atomic Energy Authority. The Ministry is responsible for legislation governing the safety and health of workers in coal mines, metalliferous mines, and quarries.

The Home Office

The Home Office is responsible for certain technical and legal regulations applying to industry. Broadly speaking, the Home Office is entrusted with all the responsibilities of national administration that have not been specially assigned by law or convention to another Minister. Among these are the regulation of the employment of children and young persons, immigration control and naturalization of aliens, granting licences for scientific experiments on animals, supervising the control of explosives, firearms, and dangerous drugs, and responsibility for Civil Defence and the Fire Service.

The Home Office is in manufacturing in a small way, as it is responsible for the administration of the State Management Scheme for control of the liquor trade in the Carlisle district, which places a brewery and 175 licenced premises under its charge.

The Ministry of Agriculture, Fisheries, and Food

Directors are most affected by the regulations affecting food manufacture and processing. These include a number of technical regulations concerning labelling and advertising of food products, questions relating to the supply and manufacture of food, its consumption, composition, preservation and nutritional qualities. The Ministry maintains a comprehensive information service and gives free technical advice.

Directors and government

In recent years, the contacts between government departments and industry have increased considerably. Departments are the main instruments for giving effect to Government policy, when Parliament has passed the necessary legislation. The way in which they do this varies according to what is involved. In some cases they act through local authorities, in others through Statutory Boards, or government sponsored organizations. The contacts between directors and government departments, either directly or through membership of trade association committees, productivity councils, training boards, economic development committees, or any one of the host of working parties and committees that have been set up as a means of discussing, implementing and, in some cases, formulating economic policy.

A change of government does not necessarily affect the number or general functions of government departments although, as happened in 1964, organizational changes may take place on the entry into power of a new government. Some departments operate throughout the United Kingdom as a whole. Others cover Great Britain but not Northern Ireland, and in others the internal organization of departments varies according to the volume, type, and complexity of their work. It is now usual for departments to have information and publicity sections so that directors requiring detailed information about the work of a particular department can usually obtain this without difficulty.

When a particular problem affecting a company has to be raised, the first approach should be through the regional office of the Ministry, where this is appropriate. If it is necessary to take up a question with a department direct, this should be done in the first instance by a letter to a Minister. Much of the subsequent correspondence will usually be with the civil servant who replies on the Minister's behalf. Where an additional approach appears to be advisable, a letter to the member of parliament for the constituency concerned may prove helpful.

Reading list

Vacher's Parliamentary Companion (Vacher & Sons: quarterly)
Anatomy of Britain Today, Anthony Sampson (Hodder & Stoughton, 1965)
Managing the British Economy. A guide to economic planning in Britain since 1962, Richard Bailey (Hutchinson, 1968)

Britain: An Official Handbook, by the Central Office of Information (H.M.S.O., 1969)

Her Majesty's Ministers and Heads of Public Departments (H.M.S.O., 5 issues a year)

The New Whitehall Series on Government Departments. A volume devoted to each Department, prepared under the auspices of the Royal Institute of Public Administration, edited by Sir Robert Fraser (Allen & Unwin)

15.3 'A Businessman's Guide to Whitehall'

Andreas Whittam Smith

Ignorance leads to irritation more quickly in Whitehall than almost anywhere else. If you do not know which department you want, the chances are that you will be further misdirected by clerical staff.

What compounds the original mistake is the dispiritingly poor quality of the lower reaches of the Civil Service. In any case it is no use trying to guess which Ministry is the relevant one in a given situation. For instance, Cunard and John Brown financed the Queen Elizabeth II through the Board of Trade, whereas the Ministry of Technology involves itself with the forward planning for the rest of the shipping and shipbuilding industry, though the Board of Trade still administers the Merchant Navy Acts.

Taxation is no longer an Inland Revenue monopoly. Trouble over selective employment tax takes you straight to the Department of Employment and Productivity; investment grants are a Board of Trade responsibility. The Industrial Reorganization Corporation (IRC) acted marriage broker to English Electric and Elliott-Automation (even providing a temporary dowry) but had absolutely nothing to do with ICT's merger, which was in the hands of the Ministry of Technology. And if the Industrial Expansion Bill becomes law, there will be another support agency to add to a list which also includes the National Research and Development Corporation.

How trade associations help

The first place to turn to if you get stuck in Whitehall—or if you are confused before you start—is your trade association. These have several advantages over the company proceeding alone. Trade organizations not only know where to go, but whom to speak to.

This is a highly sophisticated technique. The more important the subject, the lower down the organization one goes. This puzzling rule is based on the idea that the key figure is the man who is actually doing the donkey work. If he can be persuaded to accept a specific proposal, then he, rather than an outside body, can most effectively persuade his chief, the Permanent Secretary, to agree.

Backing from your trade organization also adds weight to requests or proposals. Letters signed by, say, the president of BEAMA (British Electrical and Allied Manufacturers Association) obviously carry heavier guns than those signed by a company taxation officer. In any case, trade associations first try to obtain support from their 'sponsoring' Ministry before approaching the department concerned over a particular problem.

The habit of using trade organizations as guides through Whitehall varies from industry to industry. One of the most conspicuously successful, the Society of Motor Manufacturers and Traders (SMMT), finds that its members virtually always use its services.

As far as recent legislation goes, most of the business traffic in Whitehall is caused by three measures: investment grants, selective employment tax, and development areas.

How investment grants work

The astonishing fact about the administration of investment grants is that by 1 December 1967, eleven months after the start of the scheme, only 65,500 companies out of the 200,000 or so to whom the scheme is applicable had applied for grants. The switch from investment allowances to investment grants means a radical change in business practice. Instead of one entry on your tax form, horse deals with your local Inspector of Taxes, and the right of appeal to the Special Commissioners, then the High Court and, ultimately, to the House of Lords, there are a whole series of new forms to fill in, certificates from auditors to obtain, and in any case the prospect of getting less (investment grants involve higher returns over a narrower band of assets than investment allowances did), and no right of appeal past the Board of Trade.

The relevant Act provides the Board of Trade with a wide measure of discretion. It is as well to be clear what 'discretion' means in this context. It is largely the discretion to say 'no' rather than to say 'yes'. There is no possibility of persuading the Board of Trade that a particular asset is eligible for a grant if the legislation suggests otherwise; the Board of Trade uses its discretionary powers to make sure that the objectives of the Act are achieved and not whittled away as successive Court judgments distorted the investment allowance scheme (corsets for models and silver for directors' dining rooms were finally treated as capital expenditure). That is also why there is no right of appeal.

Selective Employment Tax problems have now been mostly solved. Unlike investment grants, where the initiative lies with industry to claim what is its due, all firms have been assessed for SET—and premium where appropriate—and now know where they stand. In some cases, High Court decisions have been necessary.

How to build in development areas

As anybody outside a development area who wants to extend his factory by 5,000 ft or more—or by 3,000 ft in the Midlands, London, and South-East—is likely to be refused permission, refused in fact an Industrial Development Certificate (IDC), it is essential to know how the Board of Trade operates the alternative, which is to put the extension into a development area.

Not everybody who goes to a development area has done so because he has been refused an IDC. If you are experiencing severe difficulties in getting the labour you need, you may not contemplate a local extension. You may have already decided to go north (or north-west to Merseyside, west to Wales, south-west to Cornwall). Whatever the background, Board of Trade procedure is the same—and indeed, as those who have successfully cleared the hurdles will acknowledge—highly efficient and sensible.

To start with, you must be able to answer some simple questions: by what date do you want a roof over your head, what size of factory, what size of labour force, what skills, what waste disposal facilities do you require.

You will sometimes get the typically 'civil service' reply that no straight answer can be provided immediately. This reluctance has two causes. In the first place, considerable sums of public money are involved. The Board of Trade has to be satisfied that the schemes it supports have sufficient finance and a reasonable chance of succeeding. To put somebody into a Board of Trade factory and then see him collapse is a disaster. Secondly, each man's needs and problems are surprisingly different.

It must also be realized that from the Government's point of view, public expenditure in the development areas is essentially an exercise in buying jobs.

How long does it take to get a decision in principle out of the Board of Trade? Provided that you are not asking for a building grant (which takes a little longer), or a general purpose loan (which takes much longer), provided that forms are filled up immediately, provided that your scheme is obviously sound, then only two to three weeks negotiations may be necessary.

Businessmen come to Whitehall for help with and advice on exports, though, once again, an approach to the relevant trade organization is a useful preliminary, indeed so far as obtaining backing for inward and outward missions, for market research, and exhibitions are concerned, it is an essential. The basic rule here is that these facilities are made available only to trade associations, chambers of commerce, and similar non-trading organizations—that is, not to individual companies—by the British National Exports Council on behalf of the Board of Trade.

Specific opportunities to sell British goods abroad, often first noticed by embassy commercial staff, are publisised through:

1. *Export Service Bulletin* (daily)
2. *The Board of Trade Journal* (weekly).

And so far as the whole field goes, required reading consists of two excellent handbooks, Board of Trade export handbook numbers 1 and 2.

Finally, there are those who come up to Whitehall in response to the idea that if you are producing something that is in the national interest, say with export or import-substitution potential, then financial help may be available. This boils down to knocking on the doors of three institutions, the National Research Development Corporation (NRDC), the Ministry of Technology, and the Industrial Reorganization Corporation (which chiefly expects to help with structural changes, though it is prepared to support individual projects).

To see which one is relevant to a particular situation, it is best to consider first the NRDC and the IRC. The overlap between these two organizations is relatively small, and both are reasonably sure what their role is. The NRDC states quite openly that it would welcome new proposals from industrial companies. One of its major responsibilities is to assist, financially, development work in industry, provided it is of a novel technological character and likely to be of some value to the national economy. It is as well to be clear what 'development' means in this context. It includes, for example, the construction and testing of prototype and pilot plants, the provision of special equipment, including the first batch of some new product for customer acceptance trials. For this type of scheme, substantial sums are available. What strings are attached?

Sharing the cost of development

The money is usually injected by means of investment in the project in question and not by direct grant. It can take the form of a joint venture in which the company and NRDC share the development costs. If the project fails, the NRDC recognizes that it will lose its money: if it succeeds, then the NRDC takes a fair share of the resulting returns until it has recouped its outgoings with a reasonable profit.

The NRDC also has to be sure that normal sources of finance are, for some reason, unavailable.

Acceptable reasons include:

1. High risk, perhaps some major technical or commercial uncertainty.

743

2. The cost of the project is substantial in relation to the rest of the company's business.
3. The project would normally have been regarded as long-term but international competition means that the timescale has to be concertinaed.

The IRC, on the other hand, is mainly concerned with structural changes, which must be fairly significant in a significant industry. This rules out a large number of small-scale proposals. The IRC is at pains to stress that it is always happy to discuss projects however tentative.

The point about these two agencies is that, strict though their criteria are, help is provided over a wide front. The Ministry of Technology has tended to channel its help to specialized sectors of the economy: computers, machine tools, electronics and ship-building. All the same, the Ministry of Technology overlaps considerably with NRDC and IRC—a needless source of confusion.

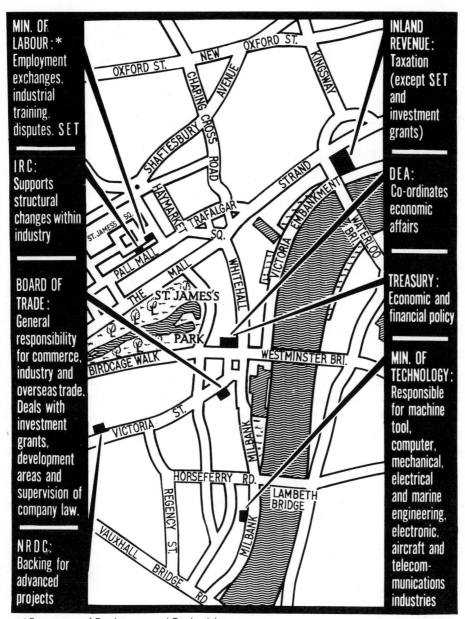

MIN. OF LABOUR : *
Employment exchanges, industrial training, disputes. **SET**

IRC:
Supports structural changes within industry

BOARD OF TRADE :
General responsibility for commerce, industry and overseas trade. Deals with investment grants, development areas and supervision of company law.

NRDC:
Backing for advanced projects

INLAND REVENUE:
Taxation (except **SET** and investment grants)

DEA:
Co-ordinates economic affairs

TREASURY :
Economic and financial policy

MIN. OF TECHNOLOGY:
Responsible for machine tool, computer, mechanical, electrical and marine engineering, electronic, aircraft and telecommunications industries

OXFORD ST.
NEW OXFORD ST.
KINGSWAY
SHAFTESBURY AVENUE
CHARING CROSS ROAD
HAYMARKET
STRAND
VICTORIA EMBANKMENT
WATERLOO BRI.
ST. JAMES'S SQ.
TRAFALGAR SQ.
PALL MALL
THE MALL
ST. JAMES'S PARK
WHITEHALL
BIRDCAGE WALK
WESTMINSTER BRI.
VICTORIA ST.
MILBANK
HORSEFERRY RD.
LAMBETH BRIDGE
REGENCY ST.
VAUXHALL BRIDGE RD.
MILBANK

* Department of Employment and Productivity

25

15.4 National Economic Development Council

H. F. R. Catherwood

The National Economic Development Council was set up in 1961. Its purpose is to bring together government, management, and unions, with independent members, to examine the economic performance of the country, to identify the obstacles to economic growth, to seek agreement in respect of improving our efficiency and competitive power, and to seek further economic growth. The chairman is the Prime Minister. It also enables industry to be consulted about proposed lines of government action and, hence, to participate in the setting of objectives and the moulding of government economic policies at the formative stage.

The secretariat for the Council is provided by the National Economic Development Office which is responsible to the Council through me. It undertakes research, prepares papers and publishes reports as called for by the Council, and through the network of the twenty-one economic development committees maintain closer contact with industry.

As its first task, the Council undertook the preparation of a national growth plan, followed by a second report indicating the major policy decisions required to obtain the growth objective. A subsequent report surveyed the progress made during the first year since publication of the plan. After the 1964 election, the Government assumed responsibility for planning, and the newly-created Department of Economic Affairs prepared the 1964–1970 plan, although it consulted the NEDC throughout its preparation and also drew on the National Economic Development Office's industrial structure for assistance.

Despite the difficulties previous planning efforts have encountered, industry has made it clear that the concept of planning has not been brought into disrepute and that it endorses the objective of improving economic performance and efficiency by making the best use of our national resources. As a result, the NEDC began, in 1967, to make a thorough examination of the methods, aims, and presentation of a future plan. It is clear, however, that forecasts about the economy go hand in hand with a strategy that makes the objectives of the plan obtainable. It is also obviously necessary to relate the intentions of individual industries to overall macro-economic policies. We are in contact with industry through the economic development committees to discuss the work that will need to be done at the industry level on a plan that will be discussed in detail with industry and government before publication.

In addition to planning, the Office has studied specific aspects of the economy. Recently (in July 1967) for instance, a booklet, *Opportunities in the EFTA market*, drew the attention of British manufacturers to the fact that they were not taking full advantage of this wealthy export market to which they have tariff-free access. Other work carried out by the Office resulted in the publication of a booklet, *Investment Appraisal*, explaining modern methods of assessing potential returns from alternative planned investment projects. *Productivity—a handbook of advisory services*, for the first time detailed the assistance provided by some 200 organizations such as trade associations, government bodies, nationalized undertakings, employers' organizations, etc. This has been enlarged and revised, and in October 1968 it was published under the title, *Business Efficiency—An ABC of Advisory Services*.

NEDO was also responsible for organizing the two national productivity conferences in 1966 and 1967 and for carrying out the work arising from the discussions at them. We have also looked at the proliferating facilities for management and education, and the implications of a value added tax in this country.

The Economic Development Committees

In 1963, the Council decided to form economic development committees to look at the prospects, plans, and performance of particular industries, and to consider ways of improving their efficiency and competitive power. Like the Council, EDC members are drawn from management, unions, the sponsoring government departments, with two or three independents, and a chairman from outside the industry.

There are now twenty-one EDCs (often called 'little Neddies') covering over two-thirds of those employed in the private sector and dealing with most of the major industries for which there is no equivalent body already in existence. These committees fill a unique role in enabling the parties interested in a particular industry to meet and thrash out their common problems. NEDO's independence of all sectional interests ensures that the committees are independent bodies, where there can

	EDC	Date of first meeting
1	Agriculture	22.12.66
2	Building	21. 6.65
3	Chemicals	20. 4.64
4	Civil Engineering	21. 6.65
5	Clothing	3. 5.66
6	Distributive Trades	15. 7.64
7	Electrical Engineering	26. 5.64
8	Electronics	23. 4.64
9	Food Manufacturing	5.10.67
10	Hosiery and Knitwear	26. 5.66
11	Hotel and Catering	20. 6.66
12	Machine Tools	15. 4.64
13	Mechanical Engineering	21. 5.64
14	Motor Manufacturing	31. 7.67
15	Motor Vehicle Distribution and Repair	13.10.66
16	Movement of Exports	21. 7.65
17	Paper and Board	20. 5.64
18	Post Office	14. 3.66
19	Printing and Publishing	24. 1.66
20	Rubber	15. 7.65
21	Wool Textiles	25. 5.64

Working Groups/Parties (not EDCs)	Date of first meeting
Construction Materials Group	8.10.65
Process Plant Working Party	11. 8.66
Paper and Board Products Group	29. 3.68
Large Industrial Construction Sites Working Party	9. 7.68

be a meeting of minds with a view to reaching agreement on common objectives. The tripartite membership of the EDCs means that findings and recommendations carry great weight with government and industry. Most committees start their work by identifying obstacles to improved performance, and then they seek the causes. Sometimes these are obvious, and then the problem is to stimulate action, but often the EDC has to set up a specialist group or sponsor research by consultants or similar organizations. Their findings are reported to the EDC, which then decides what action is necessary. The EDC will usually circulate its reports to the industry and, where suitable, publish them.

Remedies are as varied as the problems encountered. They may be concerned with improved statistics from government to enable manufacturers to see the trading position more clearly; or be a matter of bringing together the makers and users of the product to discuss future needs and specifications; or the EDC may think its

748

industry requires a different method of accounting and so it circulates its suggestions to all the members of that industry.

The aim is to improve performance of the industry, and as the EDCs have no executive power, the methods used are education, information, and persuasion. Concerned in a continuing way with their industry's performance they are, in fact, proving extremely effective.

Reading list

The Growth of the Economy (H.M.S.O., 1964)
Growth of the U.K. Economy to 1966 (H.M.S.O., 1963)
Conditions Favourable to Faster Growth (H.M.S.O., 1963)

JOURNALS

'Economic Development Committees: a new dimension in Government and Industrial Relations', T. C. Fraser (*Journal of Management Studies*, May 1967)

National Economic Development Office publications
A full list of publications by the NEDO and the Economic Development Committees is available free of charge from the NEDO
A bi-annual booklet: *Activity Report* summarizes the work being done by the EDCs and the Office.

Useful addresses

National Economic Development Office, Millbank Tower, 21–41 Millbank, London SW 1
Department of Economic Affairs, Storey's Gate, London SW 1

15.5 National Board for Prices and Incomes

Aubrey Jones

In reviewing, for directors, the work of the National Board for Prices and Incomes and the operation of the productivity, prices, and incomes policy as a whole, it is necessary, to my mind, to return to first principles.

First, it is clear that the UK is not alone in trying to combat inflation. Most Western industrialized countries are confronted with the same problem in varying degrees, and most of them, like us, are groping for a solution.

What we all face, in fact, is a residual problem of the Keynesian revolution. Keynes solved for us the chronic problem of unemployment. But what he did not solve—and what is up to our generation to solve—are the problems associated with the relatively full employment our post-war society has enjoyed, apart from a few short-lived interruptions. These problems can be summarized in one question: how can we achieve overall price stability, and, therefore, steadier and more orderly economic growth, without having repeatedly to slam on the brakes, thereby administering successive shocks to boardroom confidence and generating for a period socially and economically wasteful unemployment?

All post-war governments have wrestled with this problem. All of them have contributed, in one way or another, to the advance that I believe was made in 1964 when, to our credit as a nation, we began to demonstrate that in this context at least we had begun to learn from the mistakes of the past.

When the Labour Government came to power in 1964 it sought to build on the

750

valuable experience of the past by evolving a policy covering both prices and incomes in extensive discussion with industry and unions. The ultimate agreement was enshrined in the declaration of aims and objectives—the Statement of Intent—of December 1964. From then on, industry, and unions shared a commitment with Government to pursue the objectives of the declaration.

This agreement was followed by another, published in the form of a White Paper in February 1965, on the types of independent machinery—for example the Board—that would help to direct the policy. Then, in April 1965, when the Board was established initially as a Royal Commission, came the third agreement on the criteria designed to guide movements in prices and incomes. This was also published as a White Paper. The central objective of the policy evolved by this process of consultation is greater price stability and, therefore, steadier and more orderly economic growth.

The Board was established to examine specific movements in prices and wages against the criteria agreed between Government, industry and unions. In discharging this duty, its conscious objective throughout has been to contribute to price stability and continuous economic growth by laying great emphasis on the need to improve productivity. But the Board has never deluded itself into thinking that its task was simple or that success was lurking just around the corner.

In the foreword to its first report, the Board sought first, to define the tasks of Government and itself in the light of two possible causes of inflation: (a) the level of demand in the economy; and (b) the continued existence of old habits, inherited attitudes, and institutional arrangements. The Board saw the Government's duty as being to treat the former cause and its own task as being to deal with the latter while emphasizing how much more difficult it would be for the Board to carry out its job if the Government failed to fulfil its task, and vice-versa. The foreword added:

'We recognize that we have been entrusted with a highly difficult and delicate mission. Experience has shown that attitudes are not changed by the use of fiscal and monetary weapons at the disposal of Government. Nor are they susceptible to legislation—habits are not changed by law. We see ourselves as promoting change by conducting a continuing dialogue with managements, unions and indeed Government.'

There are three basic elements to this continuing dialogue: one educative, another consultancy, and the third judicial.

The Board's educative function extends far beyond a mere attempt to cultivate the arid statistical deserts of modern industry. It is also concerned with bringing into sharper focus the implications of the actions of an individual group for the rest of the community with the objective of securing a wider understanding of the operation of the economy as a whole and, most important, of stimulating a positive and constructive response from that greater appreciation of the country's problems.

The consultancy function is implicit in the application of an independent 'outside' mind to the problems of a particular industry, firm, or plant. The Board's competence as a management consultant is founded on a continuous period of wide-ranging and intensive inquiry into industrial, commercial, and professional efficiency, which now extends over more than eighty reports.

The Board is required by law to operate within certain rules as set out in the various White Papers on prices and incomes policy. Hence, the judicial element in the dialogue. But the Board has never conceived it to be its duty simply to adjudicate on a reference in the light of these criteria. Simply to say 'Yes' or 'No' would be a barren and unhelpful role.

The Board's consistent approach to specific references is not simply whether certain proposals are in line with the rules but more whether, granted the necessary changes are forthcoming, the proposals can be improved consistent with the rules and, therefore, the national, or community's, interest. In short, the Board, with its overall view of the economy, sees its role to be that of a positive administrator and a constructive critic.

The sterling crisis of 1966 led to the imposition by the Government of a stand-still on wages, prices and dividends, subject to certain very limited exceptions. These measures meant that the Board could reach its conclusions only on the basis of exceptions laid down solely by Government. What is more, the Government was in a position to enforce the Board's findings under powers conferred by the Prices and Incomes Act, 1966, although it did not find it necessary to use them.

In July 1967 we returned to an essentially voluntary system. The Board again had to observe criteria that were substantially agreed between the Government, industry, and unions in 1964. But there were two important differences. First, no one was then entitled to anything: the norm was nil, whereas up to July 1966 the standard for judging exceptional pay increases was 3 to $3\frac{1}{2}$ per cent. Second, new legislation gave the Government the power to delay price or wage increases for up to seven months, subject to reference to the Board.

At the beginning of April 1968 the policy entered a further phase with the publication of a new White Paper. Its provisions were expected to operate from 20 March 1968—the day after the presentation of a Budget which was designed to buttress a devaluation of 14·3 per cent on 18 November 1967. The new feature of the policy was an overall annual 'ceiling' of $3\frac{1}{2}$ per cent for wage, salary, and dividend increases whether derived, in the case of wages and salaries, from plant, local, or national bargaining, or a combination of those levels. At the same time the government provided the opportunity for pay increases above the $3\frac{1}{2}$ per cent annual 'ceiling' where they could be justified by higher productivity or efficiency, or where reorganization of wage or salary structures led to greater efficiency and higher productivity.

It also acquired the reserve power lengthening the maximum period of delay for pay and price increases from seven to twelve months, subject to a reference to the Board and an adverse report from it.

Initially, the Government has a month in which to decide whether to refer a particular case to us. If it decides that a reference is necessary, the parties are required to hold up their proposals for three months, or until the Board reports, whichever is earlier. Then, if the Board finds against the proposals, the Government can delay them for a further three months. But there is no power of control after that, and nothing, apart from public opinion, to prevent the retrospective payment of a wage increase, or indeed, an attempt by a manufacturer to recover what he had lost during the standstill by way of a slightly higher price increase than he had originally proposed.

There is now no longer any serious argument about the need for, or desirability of, some kind of productivity, prices, and incomes policy. To complement this, there is some evidence from academic research of a greater understanding of the relationship between productivity, prices, and incomes. It is on the firmer foundation provided by this broad acceptance of the need for the policy, greater public understanding of the economy, and a major development in attitude to productivity bargaining that the Board has been constructing its work.

The Board is evolving to meet the heavier demands that are already being placed upon it. In the first place, it is no longer a Royal Commission. Under the Prices and Incomes Act 1966, the Board became a Statutory Body with power to require evidence and call witnesses. So far these powers have not been used because, on the whole, the Board has had the willing co-operation of the parties involved in its investigations. Second, the 1966 Act gave the Government the power to instruct the Board to keep certain specified prices and incomes questions under continuous review. The first of these standing references were on the pay of university teachers and the Armed Forces. Third, the Government announced, in September 1967, its intention in future to refer all major price increases proposed by nationalized industries to the Board for independent examination. This task has necessitated the establishment of a special unit within the Board to conduct the efficiency audits required by Government.

The Board was strengthened in 1967 and again in 1968, and there is now a Board of fourteen (five full-time and nine part-time) drawn from both sides of industry, the professions, and political and academic life. The Board members are supported currently by a staff of 240 administrators, accountants, statisticians, economists, industrial relations experts, and supporting staff. The Board can also draw on experts from two panels appointed by the Government in consultation with the Confederation of British Industry and the Trades Union Congress.

The Board's functions and powers are often misunderstood. It is, for example, believed that the Board can undertake an inquiry on its own initiative. This is not

753

so. The power of reference lies with the Government, although it is fair to say that, the Government has increasingly encouraged the Board to suggest subjects for investigation and has often taken up its ideas. Similarly, the Board has no power to enforce its findings. It has merely the power of recommendation.

When the Board receives a reference, the chairman generally delegates its study. Board members are supported by a staff working party led by a senior Civil Servant who has the services of a report secretary—he is occupied full time on the report—and such specialist help as he requires.

In its very early days, the Board usually saw the parties to a reference early in the inquiry. Now it concentrates first on fact-finding, and secondly on an analysis of the problem in the light of evidence from all the interested parties, including the consumer. Only when the problem has been analysed are the parties formally seen.

Roughly, two-thirds of the time spent on an inquiry is devoted to fact finding. The remainder is spent on evaluation and the drafting, approval by the Board, and publication of a report. On average, an inquiry takes about four to five months.

Most of the work is done by the Board's own staff, but from time to time it is necessary to engage management consultants or outside specialists. Undoubtedly many directors have misgivings about the use of outside help because of the confidential nature of the Board's inquiries. The Board's experience does not support these fears. Consultants are not only bound by their own code of ethics and the Official Secrets Act, but the Board also refuses to disclose the names of the consultants it employs or their terms of reference. Moreover, outsiders take no part in determining the shape of a report. This is the sole responsibility of Board members.

The Board intends, however, wherever possible to use its own staff, and has built up its own inquiry team to this end.

I now turn to examine how the Board has approached—and is likely to approach—prices and incomes questions.

There may well be an endemic tendency for the public to exaggerate price increases. If this is so—and, if, as experience clearly indicates, price increases promote wage claims—then there are clearly important implications for public policy. The Government, in 1967, comprehensively took up the Board's point about the need for price increases in the public sector to be subjected to independent scrutiny since, by their very nature, they can have a greater impact on the public mind than price increases in the private sector.

Taxes apart, the Board has been preoccupied with the effect on prices of a decline in demand. Because the proportion of capital intensive industries is rising, classical economics are being turned on their head. Instead of prices falling with falling demand we have seen a recession, accompanied by rising costs and prices because capital intensive industries whose fixed costs are large in relation to their labour costs cannot easily adjust their outgoings to their income. In these circumstances, the Board's policy has been to mitigate price increases stemming from rising

754

unit costs so as to avoid their being followed up by inflationary wage increases. It has made only one exception: where the funds available for future investment would have been reduced. This exception was made because a curtailment of investment would have meant even more sharply rising costs and prices, in the long run.

On prices, the Board has always argued the case for its being allowed to examine industries whose prices are stable, especially where there is a *prima facia* case that rising productivity is cutting costs. It is axiomatic that if there is to be price stability, some prices will have to come down to offset price increases that are inescapable.

The Board's general approach to pay questions has been to try to lessen the relationship between pay within a factory or industry and the pay *thought* to be paid outside, and to substitute for this supposition a closer relationship between pay and performance within that factory or industry. At the same time, it consistently tries to ensure that the consumer's interest is represented in the pay settlement.

The Board is as anxious as the next man to raise productivity, because the faster it rises the easier it will be to contain the growth in incomes within the limits of the growth in productivity. But if the economy is to remain stable, pay increases in general should not precede increases in output per head. There is, for one thing, no assurance that an increase in output would follow. And if it did not, the inflationary consequences would have adverse implications for the balance of payments and bring the prospect of a further 'squeeze', a further slowing down of badly needed investment, and further unemployment.

Reading list

BOOKS

Progress Report, The Prices and Incomes Board (Department of Economic Affairs, September, 1967)
Prices and Incomes Policy, Aubrey Jones, The Sydney Ball Lecture, 1st December 1965
N.B.P.I. General Reports, Report No. 19, Command Paper 3087; Report No. 40, Command Paper 3394; Report No. 77, Command Paper, 3715
Prices and Wages Freeze: A narrative guide to the Prices and Incomes Act 1966 together with the text of the Act, Winsley Sergeant. Annotations to the Act by E. Roydhouse (Butterworth: 1966)

JOURNALS

'Report on the P.I.B.', J. Barr, 1. 'Wages' 2. 'Prices' (*New Society* 30th November and 14th December 1967)
'Inside the Jones Board', E. Jacobs (*Management Today*, December, 1967)
'N.B.P.I. Evidence Given to the Royal Commission on Trade Unions and Employers' Associations' (*Minutes of Evidence*, No. 51, 4th October, 1966)

'The British Board for Prices and Incomes', R. B. McKersie (*Industrial Relations* (University of California) Vol. 6, No. 3, May 1967)
'What Price the P.I.B?', Anthony Lejeune (*The Director*, June 1967)
'Mr. Jones on the Tightrope', Michael Shanks (*The Times*, September 4, 1967)

Useful addresses

National Board for Prices and Incomes, Kingsgate House, 66–74 Victoria Street, London
    SW 1

15.6 Industrial Reorganisation Corporation

C. R. E. Brooke

The Industrial Reorganisation Corporation was created by Act of Parliament in December 1966, 'to promote or assist the reorganisation of any industry . . . for the purpose of promoting industrial efficiency and profitability and assisting the economy of the United Kingdom'. The Government's primary concern in establishing the IRC was the need for more concentration and rationalization in British industry. Despite the many mergers that have taken place in recent years, some sectors of industry are too fragmented to compete effectively in world markets. In these sectors, the typical company is often too small to achieve long production runs, or to undertake research and development on an adequate scale, or to match the worldwide marketing efforts of its principal overseas rivals.

This is a problem other countries, notably in Western Europe and Japan, have recognized, and their governments are trying in a variety of ways to stimulate and encourage structural change in their industries. The British Government felt that a new institution, charged with the specific task of seeking out rationalization schemes and equipped with the financial resources necessary to support them, would have a useful role to play in improving the competitiveness of industry.

On the face of it, the creation of the IRC seemed to conflict with the country's anti-monopoly policies, which, indeed, had been strengthened by the Government in the previous year. But the Government had always made it clear that it was not their purpose to hold back mergers that would make a positive contribution to

757

efficiency. Certainly the IRC has to take careful account of the impact on competition of any rationalization proposal; each case has to be judged on its merits. Competition has to be seen in international terms.

Reorganization is the primary task of the IRC, but it also has a 'development' role that could become important. This was defined very broadly in the Act, but in certain circumstances the IRC can support development projects that are of long-term importance to the economy (notably by increasing exports or reducing imports), but where the initial costs are beyond the resources of the company or companies concerned.

Although it was created by the Government, the IRC is not a government department. It is run by an independent board of directors which contains no government representative. The Board is free to reach its own decisions, and is not subject to Ministerial veto.

The IRC is a small body, possessing influence but no compulsory powers. It has no wish to force industries into some predetermined mould. It can persuade, and it can back its persuasion with financial support. It has the right to draw up to £150 million from the Government to support rationalization and development schemes. These funds are not used to subsidize unprofitable ventures or to prop up declining industries. The Corporation aims to earn a commercial return on its investments. But it can offer funds on flexible terms. Many reorganization projects do not get off the ground because the initial burdens on the participants are too heavy; factories may have to be closed down, new plants constructed, and other heavy expenses have to be incurred, perhaps over a period of several years, before the reorganization starts to yield substantial profits.

The IRC can provide financial support in a way that makes the service and repayment burden as light as possible in the early period of reorganization. For example, in the merger between English Electric and Elliott-Automation, announced in June 1967, the IRC provided £15 million on terms that reflect both the initial costs of integrating the two businesses and the higher profits the combined enterprise will eventually achieve. The assistance takes the form of subordinated unsecured loan stock, so that the Company's ability to borrow money from other sources, such as the banks, is not impaired. The loan is interest free for the first two years and carries an 8 per cent rate thereafter. This is equivalent to a flat rate of $5\frac{1}{2}$ per cent during the period while the loan is outstanding. There are also certain rights of conversion into Ordinary shares of English Electric that will enable the IRC to raise its total return on the investment to a normal commercial level.

As part of its financial support, the IRC may become a shareholder in individual companies. But the IRC has no wish to acquire equity securities for their own sake. If it ends up by owning part of the equity of a company, it will regard itself as a temporary trustee for the public and will normally re-offer them to the public as soon as conditions permit. During the Committee Stage in Parliament the Govern-

758

ment gave assurances that the IRC would never buy shares in companies without the knowledge of their Boards. It is no part of the IRC's policy to become a government holding company, with a permanent equity in a number of enterprises.

What kind of projects qualify for IRC support? In evaluating rationalization proposals, the IRC has to satisfy itself both that there are significant gains to be achieved by bringing together the two businesses, and that the management is strong enough to achieve them. This latter point is of paramount importance. A decision has to be taken before the merger as to who will be responsible for the enlarged enterprise. The IRC is not interested in the creation of large holding companies in which there is no clear definition of management responsibility.

Secondly, the IRC will not normally provide financial support if the funds can be raised from market sources. The IRC has no intention of supplanting or competing against existing financial institutions, such as the merchant banks. Many problems have been brought to the IRC by merchant banks, and are worked on in close co-operation with them. Any schemes the IRC initiates are put into effect through the normal machinery of the market or in close collaboration with the market.

Thirdly, the IRC is primarily interested in projects likely to have a significant impact on an industry and on the economy. This does not mean that IRC is not concerned with the problems of smaller companies and smaller industries; often a small project can break the ice in an industry where there is a need for rationalization and can lead to a number of other moves. But in deciding its priorities, especially in the early years of its existence, the IRC looks for projects where the potential gains, in reducing costs, in increasing exports or in other ways, are substantial. Projects involving the very smallest companies are often more suitable for other institutions.

How do IRC projects originate? Any company or institution is free to approach the IRC to discuss rationalization or development schemes, however tentative they may be. The basis of the IRC's existence is a constructive dialogue with industry, and this has already been established. Information given to the IRC is always treated in strict confidence; it is not passed on to government departments without the companies' consent. Similarly, there is a clearly established procedure to ensure that any Board member who has a direct or indirect interest in a project under discussion does not have access to the relevant information.

Some IRC projects result directly from informal approaches of this kind. The project is discussed in detail with the companies concerned and their financial advisers. If the IRC Board considers that the project is sound and that there is a need for IRC assistance, appropriate terms will be worked out. In some cases, of course, the funds can be raised from the market in the normal way, and the IRC's role may simply be to act as a catalyst in speeding up the negotiations. The IRC's neutral position is particularly important in these situations; it provides a framework in which two companies can enter into an agreement without one appearing to be the victor and the other the vanquished.

In other cases, the IRC itself, prompted by suggestions from people inside or outside an industry, may undertake an informal inquiry of its own into a particular sector. The aim is not to produce an elaborate blueprint of how the industry ought to be organized, but simply to take soundings among the leading companies and to investigate the prospects for rationalization and the form it might take. Above all, the IRC tries to help those who want to help themselves, and it takes the view that a move in the right direction, provided it is based on good management and sound finance, is better than no move at all.

The IRC is essentially an experiment in government-industry relationships, and it will take time to prove itself. Experince so far suggests that there is a need for a body of this kind to stimulate initiatives in the field of industrial reorganization. Where there is a need for rationalization in a particular sector, most people in the industry are aware of it, but progress tends to be slow. The IRC can provide an extra push to start the process moving.

Reading list

BOOKS
Industrial Reorganisation, Command Paper 2889 (H.M.S.O., January 1966)
Industrial Reorganisation Act, 1966 (H.M.S.O., 1966)
Industrial Reorganisation Bill 1966, Second reading, Dehale, Hansard, Wednesday, 19th October, 1966 (H.M.S.O.)

JOURNALS
'I.R.C.: Friend or Foe?' Anthony Lejeune (*The Director*, October, 1967)
'The Industrial Reorganisation Corporation' (*Accounting*, March, 1967)
'What Kind of Intervention?' (*The Economist*, 1st July, 1967)

Useful addresses

Industrial Reorganisation Corporation, 46 Pall Mall, London SW 1

15.7 The Confederation of British Industry

John Davies

The Confederation of British Industry was founded in 1965 when the British Employers Confederation, the Federation of British Industries, and the National Association of British Manufacturers agreed to merge their activities into a single unit to produce a central representative organization for the management side of British industry. This important step was taken to enable the resources, that had previously been spread over several organizations, to be concentrated into one body, giving it the expertise and industrial support necessary for it to play a full part in the industrial affairs of the nation.

The strength of the CBI is derived from its membership which includes some 12,500 manufacturing firms, over 230 trade associations and employers' organizations, 200 commercial associates and 10 industrial associates. This last category of membership is a special one devised to enable the nationalized industries to participate in the work of the CBI without being committed to parts of CBI policy that might conflict with their position as state-owned enterprises.

The governing body of the CBI is the Council, which meets monthly in London and has the final authority over CBI policy. There are over 400 members of Council, representing employers' and trade associations, CBI Regional Councils, and individual firms. Meetings are chaired by the President, who normally serves a two-year term of office, assisted by a Deputy President and two Vice Presidents. Although ultimate approval for CBI policy must come from the Council, it would be impractical for so large a body to attempt the analysis of problems in depth, which is necessary in so much of the CBI's work. The formulation of CBI policy is, therefore, delegated to thirty standing committees, composed of specialists drawn from all parts of industry, and covering a wide variety of subjects ranging from the problems of small firms to overseas investment. In addition to these permanently constituted committees, the Council can also receive recommendations from working parties specially set up to study particular problems or aspects of government legislation.

As well as its central organization, the CBI also has a Regional Council and office in each of the administrative regions of the UK, including Northern Ireland. This regional network enables members to debate problems within the local context and is also a valuable way of keeping in touch with the day-to-day problems of individual firms.

Although much of the CBI's work is carried out in the terms of the general industrial environment, CBI head and regional office staff are able to advise individual members on a wide range of problems that may occur in particular circumstances not covered by the type of information generally available. The CBI is frequently asked for advice on noise abatement, fuel economy, and other technical subjects where its experience of many firms in different industries is often put to good use in finding a workable solution. On other matters, such as the recent legislation concerning prices and incomes, the CBI can add to the knowledge derived from government negotiations the experience gained from explaining the intricacies of the various acts as they affect individual associations and companies.

Another activity of particular interest is the four-monthly Industrial Trends Survey in which the CBI asks a sample of some 1,700 firms a series of questions covering past and future trends in the economy. The results of the survey provide an up-to-date picture of the latest trends in output, orders, prices, export orders, export deliveries, the factors limiting output, and the factors limiting new export orders.

The Overseas Directorate of the CBI undertakes a wide variety of work to help the overseas activities of British firms. Apart from giving day-to-day advice on such matters as tariffs, trade openings, overseas markets and export intelligence they are also concerned with long-term projects such as the 'Europe Study', which was published in 1967. The complete study sets out the changes needed in industry and the economy to prepare Britain for entry into the Common Market.

Inevitably, a large part of the CBI's work results from industry's need for a national spokesman. As the Government has followed policies that have led to its becoming very much more closely involved in the affairs of industry, so also has the representative role of the CBI become increasingly important. The CBI must operate from a position of strict political neutrality if it is to enjoy official confidence and have influence on the shaping and interpretation of national policy. CBI opposition to some government measures is not based on allegiance to any particular group or doctrine but on its own assessment of what is in the best interests of industry and the country.

Much of the CBI's dialgoue with the government is conducted by the President and Director General, who have frequent meetings with the various ministers. At a lower level, CBI staff maintain a close liaison with their counterparts in the civil service and they are, therefore, in a position to advise on the formulation and implementation of government policy. On occasions, the CBI has felt that a particular policy or measure has been introduced without adequate consideration being given to the industrial implications. Similarly, the CBI is sometimes not in a position to make as positive a contribution as it would like because the background information behind a particular proposal is not made generally available. Studies such as that commissioned by the CBI into the effects of overseas investment on the balance of payments can assist in creating a more balanced appraisal.

Looking ahead, the trend towards closer involvement between government and industry will place greater responsibility on the CBI. The existing network of consultation will need to be simplified and streamlined if industrial opinion is to be adequately expressed. At the same time, both government and industry must seek to break down the barriers that still exist and that so often place even the most constructive proposals in jeopardy.

Reading list

BOOKS

Effects of U.K. Direct Investment Overseas, W. B. Reddaway (Cambridge University Press, 1967)
Report of the formation of a National Industrial Organisation, Sir Henry Benson, CBE, and Sir Sam Brown (CBI)
Britain and Europe—Volume 1: An Industrial Appraisal (CBI)
Britain and Europe—Volume 3: A Programme for Action (CBI)
Overseas Investment—Why and How (CBI)
Manufacturing Powers of the Nationalised Industries (CBI, 1966)
Industrial Management and the Next Two Years (CBI, 1968)
Annual Reports of the Confederation of British Industry (CBI)

JOURNALS

Industrial Trends Survey (3 times a year) (CBI)

Useful addresses

Confederation of British Industry, 21 Tothill Street, London SW 1

15.8 The Institute of Directors

Sir Richard Powell

At the beginning of 1969, membership of the Institute of Directors was 44,000, and at the present rate of growth, by the early 1970s the Institute will represent at least 50,000 directors. This rate of growth has been steadily maintained since the end of the Second World War and is, I think, impressive evidence of the appeal of the Institute's aims and services to the British business community.

The growth in numbers has been matched by the strengthening of the Institute's influence on the business life of the country: all the more remarkable when one remembers that, although the Institute was founded as long ago as 1903 and granted its Royal Charter three years later, it claimed only 420 members in 1948. In that year, responding to the twin challenge of the need for higher business standards and the encroachment of the State on free enterprise, the Institute was virtually 'reborn'. Distinguished businessmen were recruited to the Council, and the Institute's services steadily expanded. Today its influence is felt in both the national and the international business scene.

The Institute is governed by a Council under the chairmanship of Lord Renwick, to which what may be described as the permanent executive, with its headquarters at Belgrave Square, is responsible. In the United Kingdom it has eighteen very active regional branches (including the Channel Isles) and overseas there are nine flourishing branches, as well as an Australian division and several thousand individual members. Any director of a public or private company or

764

body corporate not incorporated by statute may qualify for membership. But membership is far from being automatic. It is by election, and the Council scrutinizes each application, making its decision not only on the size of the applicant's company but on his general fitness for membership. Applicants must be nominated and vouched for by an existing member. There is no entry fee, and the annual subscription of £8 a year is an allowable expense for Schedule E tax purposes, since the Institute is recognized as a non-profit-making body with activities chiefly directed to the spreading of knowledge.

The 'politics' of the institute

The Institute of Directors is sometimes accused of interfering in politics. This is true, not in the sense that the Institute supports any one political party against another or is in any way allied to any political movement, but in the sense that it is the foremost defender of the principles of free enterprise by which its members earn their bread and butter and on which, it is convinced, the prosperity and freedom of the country alike depend.

Clearly, in a 'mixed economy' the Institute is not concerned to accept the role of being always 'agin the Government'. But it is concerned to resist by argument and persuasion acts of government that unduly extend the powers of the State and in so doing inhibit the vital growth of free enterprise companies, large or small. In this context, the Institute is never afraid to speak out in criticizing any government when it threatens the prosperity or freedom of action of private enterprise; and indeed, the warnings it has uttered during recent years on the dangers of State encroachment have proved only too prophetic.

The Institute's work is not, of course, confined to general policy issues. On a day-to-day basis, it works, often in friendly collaboration with government, to guard and strengthen the interests of its members. For example, top-level liaison is maintained with the Board of Inland Revenue and other government departments on matters of interest to directors and, where a principle of general application to directors arises, a member's action may be given legal support; the Institute has made successful representations to the Government about the effects of death duties on family businesses; it has made recommendations and representations on the Companies Acts; and since 1954 (with a notable success in the 1961 Finance Act) it has pressed energetically for a reduction in the graded surtax rates on higher incomes. Through its Parliamentary Panel, it maintains an invaluable two-way communication system with the country's political leaders.

Boardroom standards

From its own unrivalled experience, the Institute knows that the professional and

765

ethical standards of British directors are as high, if not higher, than anywhere in the world. This is not simply a question of observing the law (although as business legislation has grown more complex, the Institute's advice and guidance has proved increasingly valuable to directors in their company and personal capacities). It is as much a question of giving guidance to directors on the whole range of their responsibilities—primarily to the company but also to the shareholders, the employees, the consumers, and the nation itself. The Institute's dedication to a high standard of behaviour by directors is clearly spelled out in the book, *Standard Boardroom Practice*, which in its successive editions has won acceptance as a classic guide to the conduct found in the leading company boardrooms of the country.

As directors have increasingly needed to improve their professional standards and executive skills, while retaining their clear responsibilities for direction rather than management, the Institute has kept well abreast of the advances being made in management education, both through its conferences and publications and through the financial support given to higher management studies at Oxford, Henley, Warwick, and elsewhere. Practical, down-to-earth conferences and courses at regular intervals, with expert industrial and university speakers—backed by a series of publications aimed at extending boardroom knowledge and efficiency—have proved an extremely successful feature of the Institute's work.

Educational activities

Education, indeed, is the basis of the Institute's activities in publishing, notably through the pages of its monthly journal, *The Director*, which is supplied free to members but also enjoys an international readership that recognizes its unrivalled contribution to business literature. *The Director* is supplemented in its role as a higher management journal by a series of Institute publications, but it also reflects the Institute's aim of meeting, imaginatively and flexibly, the personal needs of the director as well as assisting him (or her) directly in company matters.

Like any sound organization, the Institute is geared to a planned programme of diversification and is constantly searching for new products. Just how wide its services are may be seen in the accompanying list.

Its *raison d'être* remains the defence and promulgation of free enterprise principles, the raising of standards among directors, and the supply of services of all kinds to the director in both his boardroom and his personal capacity. Surprisingly rarely does the Institute, with its real independence of government or any kind of vested interest, duplicate the work of other national business organizations. It has a unique role to play.

For the future, the Institute recognizes that society and the State are placing ever more onerous demands on the director, who will require continually more extensive guidance and services. Directors in the 1970s will be better educated, and younger men than their predecessors (if not invariably more successful). They will be working close with the professions, in turn being transformed to serve the heavy demands of a dynamic society. They and their businesses will still thrive only if enterprise stays unfettered. And they will expect an increasingly effective Institute to keep its roots in this creed.

Some of the Institute services to members

Medical Research Unit, which has developed a special executive health or 'check up' examination for directors and senior executives. The Unit runs the Medical Centre, staffed by eleven visiting doctors.

Languages Centre, where the modern language laboratory technique is used for courses varying from one to six weeks. Quick Reading courses and courses on Effective Speaking are also organized.

The Number Ten Club (in Belgrave Square), which all members may join and whose amenities include dining room, grill room, bar, library, writing rooms, interviewing rooms, and secretarial services, etc.

The Arts Advisory Council which puts at the disposal of members unrivalled experience in the fields of art, music, theatre, and historic objects, and organizes occasional exhibitions and tours abroad.

The Retirement Advisory Bureau, which puts members in touch with voluntary organization in need of senior administrative assistance.

General Advisory Service, which exists simply to answer any reasonable question put to it.

Annual Conference: the 'highlight' of the Institute's year, which attracts an audience of 5,000 and speakers of the highest calibre.

Reading list

BOOKS
Standard Boardroom Practice (Institute of Directors, 1968)
What Does the Institute Do? (Institute of Directors)
The Assault on Free Enterprise (Institute of Directors, 1965)
Reports of proceedings of Annual Conferences (Institute of Directors)

JOURNAL
The Director (monthly), Institute of Directors

Useful address

The Institute of Directors, 10 Belgrave Square, London SW 1

15.9 British Institute of Management

John Marsh

It is now widely recognized that Britain's prosperity depends largely on the calibre of its managers, and of top management in particular. Government and private enterprise alike are aware of the need for more 'professional' standards in management, and all manner of developments are taking place to meet it. Much, however, remains to be done.

It is within this context that the aims and activities of the British Institute of Management—which celebrated its 21st anniversary in 1968—are shaped and implemented. Since its establishment in 1947, following the recommendations of a special Board of Trade committee, the role of the Institute has steadily grown in scope and importance. It has become the national clearing house for information on management policies, practices, and techniques, in particular from the point of view of general management at senior levels. In addition, it provides a number of advisory services and is taking an important part in the expansion of management education and training in the United Kingdom.

As befits an organization offering services of this kind, the Institute is self-supporting, non-political, and independent, and the largest body of its kind outside the USA. Its policy is determined by a National Council, which is assisted by a number of advisory committees; it is also helped by seven Regional Councils in developing activities on a country-wide basis. Completing this national framework are fifty BIM branches extending from Scotland and Northern Ireland to the South of England; branch members meet on a voluntary basis for a varied programme of activities suited to local needs.

Responsibility for carrying out the Institute's policies at headquarters and in the regions is vested in the permanent staff which is headed by the Director-General who has the authority of a chief executive. Total staff now numbers more than 230, many of whom have specialist qualifications and wide industrial and commercial experience.

BIM membership, which has grown steadily year by year, covers two categories: collective subscribers and individual members. Collective subscribers who now total more than 10,000, include all manner of private and public companies, nationalized industries, banks, finance houses, government departments, trades and employers associations, trades unions, management consultants, professional bodies, educational institutions, and so on. More than 300 of the 400 largest companies in Britain are collective subscribers of the Institute.

BIM individual members, of whom there are now more than 20,000, are members in their own right. There are three corporate grades; namely, Fellow (FBIM), Member (MBIM) and Associate Member (AMBIM). Admission to Fellowship is by invitation and is restricted to people with eminent achievement in the practice of management, while appropriate qualifications based on education and experience are required for the other two grades. BIM membership also includes a grade known as 'Management Student', which is open to younger men studying at post-graduate level at universities and technical colleges.

The services provided by the Institute to its members are many and varied. Direct and practical benefits to collective subscribers include:

1. Information and advice on management policies, practices and techniques in practically all areas of management.
2. Information notes and summaries based on surveys and special studies carried out by BIM staff.
3. Direct exchange of information through study groups, top management meetings and general management presentations.
4. Liaison and exchange of facilities with management organizations overseas.
5. Priority access at preferential fees to BIM conferences, courses, and seminars.
6. The opportunity of taking part in special surveys in which the findings are confidential to participants, and in valuable interfirm comparison projects.
7. The monthly magazine *Management Today*, the leading publication of its type in Britain. Started in April 1966, the magazine has a circulation of 47,000.
8. Collective subscribers also receive the quarterly *Management Abstracts*, which contains digests of important management articles, lectures and books, and the bi-monthly *Notes for Collective Subscribers*.
9. The use of the BIM Library which, with 40,000 volumes on management and related subjects, is the largest of its kind in Europe.

769

Service to individual members include branch activities, overseas facilities and introductions, reduced fees for BIM courses, seminars and conferences, advice on careers and management education, and special arrangements for private treatment during illness. Individual members also receive *Management Today, Management Abstracts*, and a quarterly *Bulletin for Individual Members* containing news of BIM activities and services of special interest to this category of membership.

Mention should also be made of four BIM specialist units which provide information and advice on selected areas of management. These are the Management Education Information Unit (MEIU), the Management Consulting Services Information Bureau (MCSIB), the Executive Remuneration Unit and the BIM Secretariat for Overseas Countries (BIMSOC).

The function of the MEIU is to advise individual and company members (and non-members as well) on the selection of management education and training courses; the staff of the Unit will also advise on individual career and educational needs. On its files are details of courses available at 600 education centres in the United Kingdom and at 130 leading centres in Europe and the USA: altogether, it has details of more than 5,000 courses. The Unit, which was recently given a Government grant to extend its work, is currently dealing with some 600 enquiries per month.

The Management Consulting Services Information Bureau (which is sponsored jointly by the Institute and the Confederation of British Industry) helps companies select the right consultants for specific assignments. During 1967 the Bureau dealt with some 1,400 enquiries. For its part, the Executive Remuneration Unit conducts surveys into salary rates for all echelons of management. Its work, though confidential to the companies taking part, is of special value as a means of providing information on which companies can build fair and realistic salary structures. The fourth unit, BIMSOC, acts as an adviser to the Ministry of Overseas Development on management education and training for students from developing countries. It also advises on the establishment of sound management practices in such countries.

To maintain a balanced perspective, the numerous seminars, forums, courses, conferences, top managerial discussion meetings and other events staged by the Institute in the course of any year must be mentioned. In 1967–68, for example, we held more than 550 seminars up and down the country, to mention only one type of event. These various types of event provide not only a valuable cross-flow of ideas and information but also enable BIM members to meet and keep in touch with each other.

The BIM's first duty is, of course, to its members, but no organization such as ours could afford to ignore developments beyond its own immediate horizons. A managerial revolution is taking place in Britain, involving all areas of the economy. For this reason, the Institute's links with government departments and with other professional bodies have steadily widened and strengthened.

At government level we have close working ties with a number of Ministries and departments with home and overseas responsibilities. In particular, we keep in constant touch with NEDC and many of the little Neddies on a wide range of management subjects. This area of liaison and cooperation is growing in importance, as also are our links with the Central Training Council and the Industrial Training Boards.

The Institute also collaborates on a day-to-day basis with: the Confederation of British Industry, British National Export Council, British Productivity Council, Foundation for Management Education, and many professional, research, and trade associations. It is also a founder member of the Consultative Council of Professional Management Organizations (CCPMO) set up in 1966. Abroad, too, the BIM has special links with management and productivity organizations in the five continents.

Reading list

BOOKS

Board of Trade: A Central Institute of Management, The report of a Committee appointed by the President of the Board of Trade in November, 1945, to formulate detailed proposals for setting up a Central Institute for all questions connected with Management, British Institute of Management (H.M.S.O., 1946)

British business schools: the cost. report of a working party under the Rt. Hon. Lord Normanbrook (BIM, 1964)

British Business Schools, O. S. Baron Franks (BIM, 1963)

Education for Management: management subjects in technical and commercial colleges, Report of a special committee (The Urwick Report) (H.M.S.O., 1947)

A Memorandum on Diploma of Management Studies, by the Committee for the Diploma in Management Studies (Department of Education and Science *and* Northern Ireland Ministry of Education, 1965)

Annual Reports of the British Institute of Management (BIM, 1948–)

JOURNAL

Management Today (monthly), (Published by Haymarket Press on behalf of Management Publications Ltd., owned by the British Institute of Management, *The Financial Times, The Economist,* and the Haymarket Press)

Useful addresses

British Institute of Management, Management House, Parker Street, Kingsway, London WC 2

15.10 The Trade Associations

David Boyd

'Business, you know, may bring money, but friendship hardly ever does.' On this the 1,750 Presidents and the member companies of Britain's trade associations would have to take issue with Jane Austen. The basis of a trade association is not only a kind of qualified friendship but the profit-promoting services it can offer its members.

Typically, a trade association's structure consists of a Council, sub-committees whose subjects will include education, technology, exports and publicity, and a permanent staff whose size can vary enormously. The British Mechanical Engineering Federation's 49-man council and eight 15-man committees, representing nine associations whose members sell 70 per cent of Britain's engineering exports, are backed by a highly qualified staff of five officers and their assistants. In contrast, the Cement and Concrete Association's roll totals some 400.

Basically, the association's tasks are to collect and disseminate information about its particular sector of business or industry. Members are provided with marketing statistics extending from import levels to interfirm comparisons. Government departments are informed of output and export figures, for instance, and are given large amounts of help on specific projects, including in the past the National Plan, the Monopolies Commission Report on the Brewery Industry, and the work of Economic Development Committees (known, not always affectionately, as 'Little Neddies' in their position as diminutives of the National Economic Development

772

Council). Associations may organize conferences, publish bulletins and reports on trends and statistics (often making these available to non-members), issue standard specifications, publish trade directories, administrate cooperative advertising campaigns, stimulate and organize research and technical education, supervise exhibitions in Britain and abroad, and run press or public relations offices.

But among the many roles played by the associations, one of the most urgent is to crystallize members' points of view and to act as channels conveying these to the Government. This role is based on the sponsorship of every branch of industry, however small, by a government office, often within the Board of Trade or Ministry of Technology. It means that the association has formal access to the Minister or his civil servants and can speak with a collective and authoritative voice on actual or proposed legislation regarding taxation or import tariffs, or, indeed, any national issue affecting members.

Ideally, the association is primarily a species of superior and benevolent computer. Its input will be as many statistics, trends, and opinions as can be got from its members, combined with government and public opinion. Its output will tell the world at large, and Westminster in particular, what its members need, think, and can contribute in any relevant political, industrial, or financial situation. While Resale Price Maintenance on confectionery was being discussed, for instance, The Cocoa, Chocolate and Confectionery Alliance swung into action to represent the manufacturers' viewpoint.

The association seeks out the theme and interests common to its members and leaves the details on which they differ—and which otherwise might debar them from achieving their common aim.

Because of the many types of association serving both the commercial and industrial sectors, and their varying scope and breadth, as shown on Fig. 15.2, it is difficult to describe them collectively in detail. Their interests range from a single product, as in the National Federation of Umbrella Manufacturers or the Society of Snuff Grinders, Blenders and Purveyors, to a whole industry such as the Machine Tools Association or even a group of industries such as the British Electrical and Allied Manufacturers' Association. Income correspondingly runs the gamut from a bare three figures to the Society of Motor Manufacturers and Traders' £600,000, a substantial part of which goes directly to support the Motor Industry Research Association. The only important source of income is generally members' subscriptions, which usually vary according to the firm's size, although a few associations have arrangements for supplements by special levies, and some derive revenue from exhibitions, publications, and other publicity activities.

Links need not be simply across the board of British industry. The International Cargo Handling Co-ordination Association, as its name suggests, represents companies in many countries. The Rubber and Plastic, Cotton, Silk and Man-Made Fibre Associations are all primarily concerned with research. In horizontally

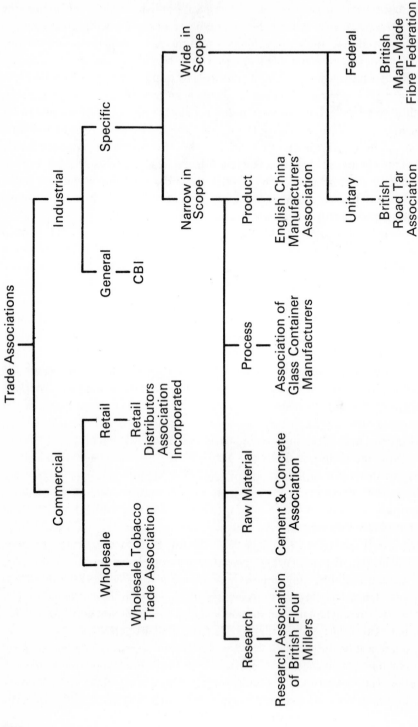

Fig. 15.2. Trade Associations: Structure and Examples

774

organized industries, associations are typically concerned with a single process, while at the other extreme the Society of Motor Manufacturers and Traders embraces importers and wholesalers as well as makers and distributors. Federations have been formed to emphasize the common interests among product associations, working mainly through the individual associations and having few direct contacts with firms.

In addition to formal federal links, joint committees, such as those formed by BEAMA, SMMT, SBAC, and BMEF, are often set up to consider those problems common to all their members. Increasingly, too, international links are being created such as the one between SBAC and the French Aero-Space Organization, or Orgalime (Organisme de Liaison des Industries Métalliques Européennes) which is a means of liaison between twenty-five of the principal mechanical engineering, electrical engineering and metalworking federations of thirteen countries, including all those of the EEC and EFTA.

Until 1965, the triumvirate that could speak and act for British industry as a whole consisted of the Federation of British Industries, the National Association of British Manufacturers (previously the National Union of Manufacturers) and the Association of British Chambers of Commerce. In that year, however, the FBI which already included the British Employers' Federation, became one with the NABM, and the Confederation of British Industry was born.

Britain's hundred chambers of commerce—unrelated to the locality-based trading organizations of the same name—are grouped round geographical centres of trade, business, and commerce and include manufacturers and merchants as well as ancillary traders. In order to belong to the Association they must be incorporated under the Companies Act, and each is an independent body financed by its members who may be as many as 14,000 firms or as few as thirty. The Association's total membership, including twenty affiliated British chambers overseas, is some 60,000 firms of every type and size. Either directly or through the medium of the Association, every chamber takes part in a constant current of information and communication, which is intensified by their joint membership of the Federation of Commonwealth Chambers of Commerce and the International Chamber of Commerce. The Federation holds a well-attended triennial conference in a Commonwealth country; the International Chamber was granted consultative status when the United Nations Organization was set up, and links fifty-five countries. Britain is represented on it both by individual chambers and the National Committee.

The Association acts as a co-ordinating body, and the chambers' individual, local, and national services are similar to those carried out by trade associations. In addition, their certificate as to bona fides is accepted abroad as proof on many important matters, such as the origin of a consignment of goods. Their many commercial and industrial interests give them an influence on affairs at a local level similar to the trade associations' at national level on such matters as town planning, public transport, and technical education. Their nature differs from the trade association's in that their members' common interest is one of region rather than business although, of course, in some areas such as Lancashire, these two interests will largely overlap.

Among the current problems facing associations, the need to increase their strength and usefulness through wider membership looms large, but their original aims were primarily defensive. Until about 1914 these were to control competition, usually through restrictive practices, negotiate with labour, and to deal with international trading problems. The British Engineer's Association, for instance, was founded in 1912 on the initiative of some twenty prominent companies, and the first move was to set up an office in Peking to protect British interests. Postwar depression killed some associations, but government encouragement of closer industrial organization after the 1932 Tariff Act revived their steady growth. During the Second World War this reached a second peak. Despite the Restrictive Trading Practices Act (which, in 1956, outlawed collective enforcement of resale price maintenance and required that wide ranges of agreements should be registered with the Registrar of Restrictive Trading Agreements, to be brought in due course before the Restrictive Practices Court) the associations have maintained their strength and authority by shifting the emphasis of their role to the two areas previously discussed, collecting and disseminating information.

The farthest-reaching development has been the closer governmental relationships as, on the one hand, Ministries have needed more trading statistics in greater detail, and, on the other, they have become a more accessible and more vital target for industry's view-point.

Indirectly, of course, an association's functions are, in fact, carried out by its member companies. It is from their records and trading statistics that facts and opinions must be gleaned, often painstakingly, to provide each industry with a corporate profile and direction. Their trust in their associations is demonstrated by the willingness of directors of companies that may be virtually at war in industrial terms to send these vital facts to the same office.

Legally, a trade association may be a company, an unincorporated body, or a trade union; in fact about 180 are registered as companies and most are unincorporated, non-profit-making associations. These have no corporate legal existence and, in theory, every member must consent to its actions or to changes in the rules.

One of the most important pieces of legislation affecting all associations has been the Restrictive Trading Practices Act. One of the earliest was a House of Lords decision in 1892, which became known as the 'trade associations Charter'. This distinguished between trading combinations that interfered with the trade of others with a direct intention to inflict an injury, and those that were intended solely to protect the combination's own interests. This position began to change only in 1948 when in certain circumstances trade associations were investigated by the

Monopolies and Restrictive Practices Commissions, and the Government was empowered to combat practices found to be against the public interest. Investigation by the Monopolies Commission and, now, trial before the Restrictive Practices Court, have been introduced because it is recognized that a collective agreement need not be a conspiracy against the public; firms may co-operate either informally or in trade associations for common services, and their combined strength may not amount to monopoly or may merely offset the weight of suppliers or customers. One result of the Monopolies Commission's investigations has been evidence that the dangers of trade associations, where they exist, lie less in price-fixing than in protection of established firms and, therefore, opposition against new-comers and innovators. The arrangements that tend towards this state are, un-fortunately, often the easiest for firms to agree upon.

The strength of the association lies in the services it can provide which its individual members cannot. Its weaknesses vary according to whether its members are drawn from a wide or narrow sector of industry. Companies with a wide spread of interests may be apathetic until a common problem turns up, and this means that the wider the association's interests the greater responsibility must be placed upon its permanent officials. On the other hand, if the association covers a narrow range of activities its members may be in close competition with one another. Each firm will be more concerned with its own progress than with that of the industry, and any cost saving will be equally shared. The net result is that associations are most important in those fields where contractual relations between suppliers and buyers of a service are hardly feasible, especially where the purpose of union is to marshal influence and authority. Collective organizations are less important in the field of ordinary commercial services, though they can play a large part in the initiation of services involving high risks or heavy resources.

Rival associations tend to divide on size of firm—one motive for non-membership often given by small firms is fear of being tied to policies designed for much larger ones, and there is, therefore, an inherent tension within the associa-tion when its members vary widely in size. At the same time, much of the voluntary work, which of course benefits the entire industry, is done by the larger firms, since only they have the necessary expertise and finances.

The trade association movement has travelled a long way in fifty years. From being an inward-looking, protective, and even negative organization, it has become the voice of its industry to the public and to government, speaking with authority based on hard facts. Its future role can be an even more positive one, combining its democratic structure with the enormous need and potential for leadership in indus-trial efficiency. It is essential that pressure in this direction should come from members rather than from outside; the day may come when businessmen regard the efficiency of their Association as just as vital a matter as the efficiency of their own firms.

Reading list

BOOKS

Trade Associations and Professional Bodies of the United Kingdom, Patricia Millard (Pergamon, 1966)
Directory of British Associations, 2nd Edition (CBD Research, Beckenham, Kent, 1967–68)
Trade Associations in the Distributive Trades (Distributive Trades Economic Development Committee, May, 1967)
Industrial Trade Associations (Political and Economic Planning, 1955)
British Mechanical Engineering Federation: a background survey (condensation of the P.E.P. report mentioned above), 1966.
The Role of Trade Associations in the Study of Markets (Organization for Economic Co-operation and Development, 1961)
Productivity: a Handbook of advisory services (National Economic Development Office, 1967)
Review of the Mechanical Engineering Trade Associations (Confederation of British Industry, 1966)

JOURNAL
'Ideas of Association' (*The Director*, November 1962)

Useful addresses

Guildhall Library, Guildhall, London EC 2
Secretaries' Club, 125 High Holborn, London WC 1
Association of British Chambers of Commerce, 68 Queen Street, London EC 4

778

16. Keeping the Boardroom Informed

Keeping the Boardroom Informed

Elizabeth Mack

The director, to remain on top of his job, ought to keep abreast of new developments in many fields: in new materials and processes; in new outlets for manufactured products; in national and international political and economic changes, and the resulting alterations in regulations, restrictions and tariffs; in personnel and financial management techniques; and in the reactions of his company's competitors to these and other influences. Not only must the facts of new developments be sought, but also comments on their implications from theorists and practical experts. Current trends and their effects on business can be followed by attending meetings, conferences, and seminars; talking and listening to business associates; and by wide reading of newspapers, periodicals, and books.

There can be few businessmen who do not take the *Financial Times*, and to read this newpaper daily is a good start to being well-informed. Other dailies such as *The Times* or *Daily Telegraph*, with their extended business coverage, will, of course, be read from personal preference, as well as a local weekly newspaper. General and specialist weekly and monthly newspapers and journals, related to the company's activities or the individual's professional interests, should be read or scanned. General periodicals of this kind include Government publications such as the *Board of Trade Journal* and the *Ministry of Labour Gazette*; the Confederation of British Industry's *British Industry Week*; the British Institute of Management's *Management Today*; The Institute of Directors' *The Director*; the *Economist*; the *New Scientist*.

Within more specific subject areas there are weekly specialist publications such as *Engineering, Rubber and Plastics Age, Electrical Times, Building, European Chemical News, Taxation, Stock Exchange Gazette, Advertiser's Weekly*. In weekly journals like these, the general editorial columns and news items contain useful topical information.

The monthly trade journals are more numerous, and are extremely important. They cover all fields of activity and interest, and include specialities such as *Steam and Heating Engineer, Shipbuilding International, Iron and Steel, Tobacco, Stores and Shops,* and even *Perambulator Gazette.* Many of the professional and other associations publish their own monthly journals: *Chartered Mechanical Engineer, Chemistry in Britain, Production Engineer, Accountancy, Town and Country Planning.* You will find all these technical and professional periodicals listed in the annual *Newspaper Press Directory*, which also includes a section on foreign publications.

At another level, the professional and learned societies publish papers and discussions from their meetings, in the form of Transactions or Proceedings. There are also many commercial journals covering scientific, technical, and professional subjects in depth: examples are the *Journal of Scientific Business, Programmed Learning, Chemical Engineering Science, Filtration and Separation, Journal of Fluid Mechanics,* and *Tropical Agriculture.*

Another kind of periodical publication is the 'house journal', produced by a company to convey news of its activities. Contents vary from simple reports of social activities like staff weddings and inter-firm football matches, to prestige reports and commentaries on achievements, to be found in such publications as Unilever's *Progress* and ICI's *Endeavour*. The British Association of Industrial Editors publishes a list of these *British House Journals*.

Since specialized information can be published in so many different sources, some periodicals are indexes to articles from other journals. By scanning these indexes regularly, articles can be selected for further reading. Many of these indexes are restricted to technical fields, but there is one general technical index, the monthly *British Technology Index*, which covers about 400 British journals. For a moderate subscription this is well worth taking, although the arrangement makes searching slow.

More specialized indexes are compiled by organizations with libraries in which the literature on the particular subject is received from all over the world. The indexes cover new books, pamphlets, patents, and standards, as well as articles in journals. Many provide 'abstracts' (summaries) of the items indexed, to give a closer guide to the exact content.

The industrial research associations, receiving grants from the Ministry of Technology, prepare valuable abstract bulletins of this kind; most may be purchased by non-members, and some (such as *Packaging Abstracts*, and *Instrument Abstracts*) are of interest to a range of industries. Several government departments produce technical abstracts: the Ministry of Public Building and Works, for example, issues a fortnightly *Library Bulletin* listing new books, pamphlets, and articles in newly-received journals. The Ministry of Technology (Aviation), and the Ministry of Agriculture, prepare similar publications. The Building Research Station's *Building Science Abstracts*, and the Overseas Geological Surveys' *Overseas Geology and Mineral Resources* are examples of abstracts published by HMSO. The Commonwealth Agricultural Bureaux all issue excellent abstract publications, such as *Nutrition Abstracts and Reviews*, *Dairy Science Abstracts*, and *Index Veterinarius*.

Some of the learned and professional associations issue abstracts; for example, the Society of Analytical Chemistry (*Analytical Abstracts*), and the Institution of Electrical Engineers (*Electrical and Electronics Abstracts*). Trade and professional journals also include abstract sections; for instance, the *Iron and Steel Institute Journal*, and *Glass Technology*. Similar, and sometimes even more useful, services are published abroad. The American *Chemical Abstracts* and *Engineering Index* are outstanding; *Excerpta Medica* with numerous sections, is published in the Netherlands; from Russia come a large number of abstracts bearing the main title *Referativnyi Zhurnal*. Not unnaturally, most of these publications show a preference for the literature of their own countries and some, *Hungarian Technical Abstracts*, for example, are deliberately restricted to the national periodicals. The National Federation of Science Abstracting and Indexing Services has issued a list of scientific abstracts and indexes called *Abstracting and Indexing Services in Science and Technology*.

Locating the journals and other publications referred to in the abstracts can be a problem. Only the larger public libraries take a wide selection of specialist journals, and those are almost entirely British. Technical college and university collections go further in the provision of technical periodicals, and alumni can usually obtain access to their libraries. The National Lending Library of Science and Technology in Boston Spa, Yorkshire, will enrol any firm as a borrower, and offers reference facilities to visitors.

In London, the National Reference Library, at the Patent Office, is open to the public, and it has an extensive collection of technical journals, abstracts and indexes, besides sets of patent specifications from foreign countries. Many professional, research association, and government libraries, will permit reference to, or even lend, periodicals. Fortunately, British copyright law includes a fair dealing clause which permits copying of periodical articles, for study and research use, by individuals and non-profit libraries. Only limited copying is permitted from books: the position has been clarified by the Society of Authors and the Publishers Association in *Photo-copying and the Law*. Many of the libraries producing abstracts and indexes, and most college and association libraries, can offer an inexpensive photocopying service, usually to members.

There are fewer indexes or abstracts covering the non-scientific fields, and many companies make their own arrangements for keeping track of important subjects like marketing and market research. Advertisements, publicity announcements, and reports from other companies must be collected and added to internal sales records. Government action at home and abroad must be followed closely. News columns of trade journals must be sifted for facts or conjectures to add to the information needed to forecast trends. On a day-to-day basis this is not difficult, but to search retrospectively is time-consuming. One general index that is proving useful because it covers daily and Sunday newspapers as well as a cross-section of trade weeklies and monthlies, is the *Research Index*. This is intended to provide trade, commodity, and company information for investors, but it is the only British indexing publication attempting to provide current-awareness for businessmen. The British Institute of Management's *Management Abstracts* includes very few articles; *Anbar Abstracts* is useful on office management; *Market Research Abstracts* deals with methodology. The American *Business Periodicals Index*, although almost entirely restricted to American journals, and the broader *Public Affairs Information Service*, are often more useful. *Economics Abstracts*, produced in the Netherlands, is rather theoretical.

Sources other than periodicals must also be covered, and a careful watch kept on book reviews, announcements, and advertisements in trade and professional subject journals. Specialized books and pamphlets may be found in this way, or through the weekly issue of the *British National Bibliography*, based on the copyright intake at the British Museum. The larger booksellers and some publishers will send new books for inspection. New government publications are included in the *British National Bibliography* or are listed in the daily and monthly lists issued by HMSO. These include new legislation and regulations. New standard specifications are in the *BNB* or in the British Standards Institution's own news-sheet. Many trade journals and abstracts list new British patents, and a full list is published weekly in the *Official Journal* (*Patents*). Derwent Publications publish *British Patent Abstracts* and also offer abstracts of foreign patents. Government and other research institutions issue highly specialized reports of their investigations, many of which are available to the public. The National Lending Library of Science and Technology lists some of these in *British Research and Development Reports*.

Information on quoted companies is found in financial journals, the *Financial Times*, and indexed in *Research Index*, which has a separate alphabetical section for companies; or may be obtained on subscription through Moodies Services. Trade literature is listed in, and offered through, many trade journals, and there are several services offering current files of trade catalogues in certain fields; for example, the *Barbour Index*, *Chemical Engineering Index*, and *Indata*.

Statistical information is not so well organized in Great Britain as, for example, in the United States or the Common Market, and often the only sources are government departments. The Board of Trade's *Business Monitor* series supplements the

Monthly Digest of Statistics, and it is sometimes possible to find useful British market information in the US Department of Commerce *Overseas Business Report*. Among the few trade associations who collect and issue figures for their own commodities are the British Non-Ferrous Metals Federation, and the British Iron and Steel Federation. The Society of Motor Manufacturers and Traders also issues a *Monthly Statistical Review*. The Board of Trade maintains a separate Statistics and Market Intelligence Library, with a comprehensive collection of foreign statistical publications.

Most directors accumulate a basic quick-reference library which includes a dictionary, an encyclopedia, local and trade directories like *Kelly's* and *Kompass*, *Who's Who*, the *Directory of Directors*, the *Stock Exchange Year Book*, an atlas, a gazetteer, a railway time-table, a list of hotels, a book of quotations, a list of abbreviations, a ready-reckoner, and Whitaker's *Almanack*. There will also be directories and standard reference works on the particular trade, technology, or profession of the company or of the individual; and catalogues and brochures of the company, its competitors, its suppliers, and its customers.

When the reference shelf fails to provide the answer to a specific problem, enquiries must be made outside, first, usually, to the company's or the director's professional associations. If these fail, the services of other organizations must be sought. As a start, a check should be made to the *Aslib Directory* and the *Directory of British Associations*, both of which provide useful classified addresses. Many trade and research associations will give occasional help to a non-member; colleges teaching a subject can usually produce a knowledgeable lecturer to discuss a problem; editorial offices of some journals are well-informed; government offices are organized to receive telephone enquiries, usually through their press or public relations departments.

For anyone anxious to make a serious attempt to find information in any field, there are available a number of guides to sources; these include Pergamon's *How to Find Out* series, particularly K. Bakewell's *Management and Productivity*, and F. Newby's *How to Find Out About Patents*.

The information department

No director would attempt to carry out personally the duties of the accountant, sales manager, company secretary, purchasing officer, works manager, or personnel officer. By the same token, he should allow information to be handled by an expert information officer, skilled in the collection, organization, and dissemination of information. Whether small or large, general or specialized, technical or commercial, an Information Service is invaluable. Properly operated it becomes the centre of obtaining and disseminating information, whether held inside or outside the company. It will have its own indexes, shelves, and files, but it will also be fully aware of other collections of similar material throughout the company, and be competent to exploit many outside corporate and personal contacts.

The proper responsibility of an information officer is selection. First, he must inspect possible material and decide what should be acquired. All incoming publications must be scanned, and summaries or the full publications, circulated to appropriate individuals within the company. Much of this circulated material is recorded for future retrieval, together with material which, while not of immediate news-value, is of permanent usefulness. In this way the busy executive is spared the time-consuming search through irrelevant material to find what he wants. On demand, a good information officer can produce any amount of reading, at any depth, on any topic, by retrieval from his organized files, by retrospective searching in abstracts, and by knowing where to make outside enquiries.

The profession of information officer is still evolving, and no accepted qualifications are yet fixed, although three first degree courses have now been planned, an MSc in Information Science is offered at the City University, and several post-graduate librarianship diplomas are available. The Library Association's examinations are taken by assistants in some special libraries. A good information officer must have sufficient knowledge to understand the material he handles so that he can analyse it for indexing, and summarize it for the executives he serves. Linguistic aptitude, with at least reading ability in several foreign languages, is important.

Information centres within companies vary enormously; there is no basic minimum in scope or stock, and each centre evolves the services its company demands. Most provide library facilities to some extent, with a collection of reference books, a display of current periodicals, a limited space for reading and research, and files of back-number periodicals, indexes, and abstracts. In some companies the centre also files and controls standards, technical data sheets, drawings, and correspondence.

In technical fields, the sheer quantity of information is leading to the development of mechanical retrieval systems. Research in this is being conducted largely in the United States, but even there much of the work is still experimental, and by no means all of it is suitable for immediate use in Britain. Ultimately, the actual information content of a document may be coded into a computer, from which it can be retrieved automatically in a printed form. At a lower degree of automation, topics within documents are indexed in a computer, which lists on demand all the documents on the desired specific combination of topics. At a practical stage, now, is the use of computers for indexing. A number of abstracting publications are issued with machine-generated indexes, frequently the 'key word in context' (KWIC) type. Machines will eventually be brought into use to handle information; but a mechanical index, like a manual one, can only retrieve what has been inserted. A computer will not correct inefficient information indexing systems.

Since 1944, the Government has shown its recognition of the importance of information in industry by making an annual grant to Aslib (formerly the Association of Special Libraries and Information Bureaux) to aid and encourage the development of information services. Subscribing member firms can obtain advice on the best methods of organizing their information departments, and assistance in answering enquiries, in locating publications, and in obtaining translations. Courses are held on general and specific procedures in information work, and members exchange views at meetings and conferences. A research department is investigating the development of mechanized methods of information retrieval, and analysing the requirements of information users. Among Aslib's publications are two periodicals dealing with developments in information handling, *Aslib Proceedings* and the *Journal of Documentation*. There have been several editions of the *Aslib Directory* (to sources of information) and of the *Aslib Handbook* (a manual of procedure for information centres).

Although some of the best information services in the country are in the larger manufacturing companies, there are many big concerns in which information is sadly uncoordinated. By comparison, there are many small, highly specialized companies with efficient technical or economic intelligence departments providing management with background material, news of current developments, translations of foreign papers, and factual reports for decision making. It has been possible here only to outline the types of sources of information that are available, to mention a selection of them, and to sketch the possible activities of an information service and the qualities of an information officer. The real essential of an efficient information department is that the right person runs it. Here, as everywhere, the department's efficiency depends on its head but, given an intelligent, energetic expert, no company can fail to benefit from the centralized collection and interpretation of information.

Reading list

Newspaper Press Directory (Benn Bros, annually)
British House Journals, 2nd Edition (The British Association of Industrial Editors, 1962)
A Guide to the World's Abstracting and Indexing Services in Science & Technology (Science and Technology Division, Library of Congress, 1963)
Aslib Directory, Vol. 1: Science, Technology and Commerce (Aslib, 1968)
Directory of British Associations, 2nd Edition (C.B.D. Research Ltd, 1967)
Current British Directories (C.B.D. Research Ltd: 5th Edition, 1967)
Photocopying and the Law (The Society of Authors and The Publishers Association)
How to Find Out: Management and Productivity, A Guide to Sources of Information arranged according to the Universal Decimal Classification, K. G. B. Bakewell (Pergamon Press, 1966)

Useful addresses

Aslib, 3 Belgrave Square, London SW 1
The Library Association, 7 Ridgmount Street, London WC 1
H.M.S.O. (Headquarters), Atlantic House, Holborn Viaduct, London EC 1
National Lending Library for Science & Technology, Boston Spa, Yorkshire
National Reference Library for Science & Invention, Southampton Buildings, Chancery Lane, London, WC 2 (The Patents Office)

Index

Agricultural Research Council, 658
Air-containers, 588
Air freighting, 576
Aldermaston atomic energy establishment, 659
Allan, James, 707
Amalgamated Engineering and Foundry Workers' Union, 351
American Federation of Labour—Congress of Industrial Organizations, 355
Amory, Lord, 657
Analogue computer, 704
Analysis—
    financial, 234
    new project, 181–5
    value, 240
    variance, 152
Analytical Abstracts, 783
Analytical solution, 172
Anbar Abstracts, 784
Annual General Meeting, public relations and the, 424
Annual plans, forecasting for, 195
Annuities, 372–4
Antarctic Survey, 658
Appeals, against development plans, 643
Applied research, 647, 648–9
Appraised cost, 188–9
Apprenticeships, 334
    trade unions and, 350
Architect, Chief, 641
Articles of Association, 8, 9–10
Arts Advisory Council, 767
ASLIB, 563, 786, 787
Aslib Directory, 785, 787
Aslib Handbook, 787
Aslib Proceedings, 787
Assay Offices, 445
Assizes of Bread and Ale, 44
Associated Bristol Chambers of Commerce, 581
Associated Container Transportation, 589
Associated Containers Limited, 584
Associated Electrical Industries, 722–3
Association of British Chambers of Commerce, 775
Association of British Travel Agents, 444
Association of Certified and Corporate Accountants, 102, 693
Association of Supervisory Staffs, Executives and Technicians Union, 351
Astronomy, 657
Atkin, Lord, 442
Atlas computer, 712, 715
Atlas Laboratory (computer), 657

Atomic Energy Authority, 658
Attitudinal profile studies, 460
Audiences, film and TV, 511–12
Auditors, company, 102–4
Austen, Jane, 772
Australia, containerization service with, 589
Automatic data processing, 705
Automation, warehouse, 603–4
Automobile Association, 387
Aviation insurance, 264, 266

Babbage, Charles, 706
Bakewell, K., 785
Balance of Payments, 729
Balance sheet, 98–9
    content of, 99–101
Bank Charter Act (1844), 254
Bank credit, 69–70
Bank for International Settlements, 255
Bank of England, 4, 246, 250, 253–6, 538, 727, 730
    directors of, 254–5
Bank of England Act (1946), 254
Bank of Scotland, 256
Bank Rate, 70, 256, 257, 532, 730
Banks—
    ancillary exporting services, 533
    and short-term finance, 160–1
    financing trade, 246
    services to exporters, 531–3
Banks, M.A.L., 689
Banks Committee, 689
Barbour Index, 784
Barges, container, 590, 591
Barran, David, 724
Barter, trade through, 557–60
Basic research, 647–8
Basic research liaison, cost of, 650, 651
BEA/BOAC Cargo Handling Depot, 604
Beckert, Richard, 477
Beecham Group language laboratory, 567–8
Beeching Report (1963), 594, 595
Belgium, taxes on exporters to, 542
Benson Ltd, S.H., 416
Berkeley laboratories, 661
Betterment levy, 93–4, 629, 630, 634–8
Bilateral trading, 557–60
Bill finance, 70
Bill of Exchange, 70, 161, 532, 730
Binary system, 707
Bid and board, 33–4
Bid auction, 33
Biddle, Sawyer & Co., 559
Black, Professor Gordon, 660

English Electric Company, 740, 758
Environment, influence on executive appointments, 303
Equipment leasing, 71
Equity capital, 74
Estate agents, registration of, 443
Estate Duties Investment Trust, 72
Estate duty, betterment levy and, 638
Euro-bond market, 533
Euro-dollar market, 533
Europe Study, 762
European Airbus, 658
European Chemical News, 782
European Components Service, 545
European Economic Community, 731, 775 (*see also* Common Market)
European Free Trade Association, 775
European Free Trade Area Convention (EFTA), 540
European Organization for Nuclear Research, 656
European Space Research Organization, 657
Evening class, for languages, 566
Excerpta Medica (Netherlands), 783
Exchange Control Act (1947), 538
Exchange Control Office, 255
Exchange Equalization Account, 255
Exchange Telegraph, 436
Executive Remuneration Unit (BIM), 770
Executives—
    health and, 382–8
    recruiting and training, 289–315
    (*see also* Management)
Exempt private company, 5, 11
Exercise, necessity for, 385
Exhibitions, marketing, 506–8
Expectation criterion, 165–6
Expo 1967, 555
Exponential smoothing, 197
Export Council for Europe, 545
Export houses, 534
Export Services Branch (BOT), 734
Export Service Bulletin, 743, 548
Exporters—
    Corporation Tax and, 538
    financial services for, 531–5
    investment abroad and, 538
    overseas investment and, 541, 542
Exporting, 519–68
    available advice on, 519
    insuring risks, 533–4
    market research for, 524–9
Exports Credits Guarantee Department (ECGD), 160, 259, 532, 533, 534, 537, 735

as accepting house, 550–1
External Policies Group, DEA, 731

Factoring, 283–6, 535
    of book debts, 161
Factory Act (1833), 389
Factory bargaining, 352–3
Factory building, in development areas, 742–3
Factory inspectorate, 390
Federation of British Industries, 347, 348, 761, 775
Federation of Commonwealth Chambers of Commerce, 775
Federation of Consumer Groups, 441
Feed-back control, 236
Feed-forward control, 236
Ferranti Atlas computer, 712, 715
Field executive sales course, 503–4
Field Work—
    marketing research, 469
    overseas, 528–9
Films—
    industrial, 509–12
    marketing, producers of, 511
Filtration and Separation, 782
Finance—
    choice of, as function of management, 130–1
    IRC for rationalization of industry, 758
    medium-term, 70–2
    methods of, 154–62
    obtaining outside for private company, 11
    short-term, 69–70
Finance Act (1956), 369
Finance Act (1961), 765
Finance (No. 2) Act (1964), 537
Finance Act (1965), 4, 5, 537, 539
    eighteenth schedule of, 5
Finance Bill, 70
Finance Corporation for Industry, 72–3
Finance Houses Association, 276–8, 281
Finance, Problems of the Smaller Company, 11
Financial accounts, integration with cost, 144
Financial advertising agencies, 410
Financial analysis, 234
Financial guarantee system, 533
Financial planning, 154–62
Financial public relations, 433–7
Financial Times, 781, 784
Financing Your Business, 161
Fire Service, 737
Fit, in relation to new projects, 183
Fixed interest issues, 74–5
Flax Industry Training Board, 328

Hire purchase, 281–2
  effects of 'squeeze' on, 728
  finance, 70–1, 246
Historic costs, 140–1
Holding company, 100
Hollerith, Dr, 706
Home Office, and industry, 737
Hotel and Public Buildings Equipment Group, 545
House journals, 782
Hovercraft, 598, 659, 660
Hovercraft Development Limited, 659
How to Find Out, 785
Hudson's Bay Company, 4, 249
Human Side of Enterprise, The, 325
Hungarian Technical Abstracts, 783
Hyman, J., 289

ICT 1900 computer, 705
ICT 1903 computer, 710
Implementation, of OR findings, 173
Income Tax, 538, 539
Income Tax Act (1952), 369, 538
Income Tax reliefs, 369
Incentives, for executives, 306–7
Incorporated Society of British Advertisers, 408
Incorporation documents, 8
Indata, 784
Index Veterinarius, 783
Indexing, by computer, 786
Indexes, technical, 782
Indoctrination sales training course, 503
Industrial advertising agencies, 410
Industrial and Commercial Finance Corporation, 72
Industrial and Finance Corporation, 246, 248
Industrial and Professional Careers Research Organization, 319
Industrial Bankers Association, 276
Industrial Design, 477
Industrial Development Act (1966), 620
Industrial Development Certificate, 622
  how obtained, 742
Industrial Educational and Research Foundation, 432
Industrial Estates Corporation, 735
Industrial Expansion Bill, 740
Industrial Fairs International Ltd., 522
Industrial films, 509–12
Industrial health services, 389–95
Industrial liaison centres, 661, 662
Industrial market research, 466–71
Industrial Nursing Diploma, 391

Industrial Operations Unit, Mintech, 733
Industrial Policy Group, of CBI, 724
Industrial Prices and Incomes Group, DEA, 731
Industrial relations, 327
Industrial Reorganisation Corporation, 72, 113, 261, 722, 740, 743, 744, 757–60
Industrial research, 647–79
  and universities, 672–9
  cost of, 674–53
Industrial Revolution, 391
Industrial sites, rented premises, 621
Industrial Training Act (1964), 334, 338, 364, 365, 736
Industrial Training Board, levy and grant system, 336–7
Industrial training boards, 325, 331, 334–5
Industrial Training Order, 334
Industrial Training Service, 339
Industrial Trends Survey, 762
Industrial tribunals, 364–5
Industrial unions, 351
Industrial Welfare Society, 23
Industry—
  and design of products, 494
  and government ministries, 726
  and research opportunities, 661–2
  and trade unions, 349–65
  CBI and overseas activities of, 762
  graduates in, 317–27
  rationalization, 757–60
  relations with government, 719–24
  siting of, 617–22
  the community and, 59
  training for, 334–40
Information department, company, 785–7
Information officer, 785, 786
Information science degree, 786
Information services, Central Office of Information, 554
Information sources, 781–7
Information systems, 41–2, 238
Ingham, H., 219n
Inland Revenue department, 727
Instalment credit industry, 280–2
Institute for Research on Animal Diseases, 658
Institute of Chartered Accountants, 102, 693
Institute of Directors—
  aims and services of, 764–7
  Medical Centre, 386, 392, 394
Institute of Directors Language Centre, 567
Institute of Geological Sciences, 658
Institute of Linguists, 561n, 562, 563, 568
Institute of Petroleum, 693

799

Management (*contd*)
  planning, 132–3
  production, 128–9
  public relations and, 420–32
  recruitment and training programmes, 289–315
  research and development, 134–5
  sales, 129–30
  summary of techniques for good, 231–40
  value of quality of in public relations, 433, 434
Management Abstracts, 769, 770, 784
Management accounting, 235–6
Management and Productivity, 785
Management by objectives, 236
Management by exception, 152
Management consultants, and selection of executives, 311–15
Management Consulting Services Information Bureau (BIM), 770
Management control, 236–7
  time as function of, 700
Management Education Information Unit (BIM), 770
Management organization, maintaining, 40–1
Management personnel, motivation of, 302–7
Management ratios, 219–23
Management studies, higher, 766
Management systems, computer-controlled, 700
Management Today, 769, 770, 781
Management Training and Development Committee, 339
Managerial functions of directors, 37–42
  defining corporate policies, 39–40
  maintaining effective planning, information, and control systems, 41–2
  maintaining management organization, 40–1
  making major decisions, 42
  setting corporate objectives and strategies, 38–9
Managers—
  education for, 329–32
  development of, 307–10
  recruitment of, 291–310
  relations with directors, 44–5
Managing director—
  functions of, 26–7
  public relations and the, 424–5
  (*see also* Management)
Manchester University computer, 715
Manpower management, 323–7
Marchwood laboratories, 661
Marginal costing, 142–3

Marine and Freshwater Biological Associations, 658
Marine insurance, 264, 265
Market, elasticity of, 187–8
Market areas, world, 525, 526, 527
Market research, 237, 457–65
  industrial, 466–71
  industry, 462–5
  overseas, 524–9
Market Research Abstracts, 784
Market research agency, overseas, 528
Market Research Society, The, 463
Market segmentation analysis, 460
Marketing, 449–55
  advertising a component of, 406
  as function of management, 131–2
  case studies, 451–5
  defined, 406, 407
  design and, 492–8
  exhibitions, 506–8
  exports, 519–68
  industrial films and, 509–12
  international, 454–5
  premium promotions, 513–5
  public relations in, 428–31
  relationship with distribution, 574–5
Marketing director, qualities required in, 450–1
Markets—
  futures, 270–2
  physical, 269–70
Marksensing machine, 709
Marples, E., 264
Martech Study (1966), 594
Materials and components, value engineering and, 208
Mathematical programming, 204
Maudling, R., 264
Mechanical retriever systems, information, 786
Medawar, Sir Peter, 657
Medical diagnosis by computer, 709
Medical Examinations, pre-employment, 394–5
Medical Research Council, 657–8
Medical Research Unit, Institute of Directors, 767
Medical services, industrial, 391–2
Medium-term capital, 159–60
Meetings, conduct of, 25–6
Memorandum of Association, 8
Merchandise Marks Act (1887), 440
Merchandising expenditure, 414–5
Merchant bankers, 75, 245, 258–62
  and public relations, 437
Merger broker, role of the, 120–2

806